企业应用架构设计——
Struts 2+Hibernate 3+Spring 2

希赛 IT 教育研发中心　组织编写

谢星星　主编

中国水利水电出版社
www.waterpub.com.cn

内 容 提 要

本书由希赛 IT 教育研发中心组织编写，是关于当前流行的开源框架技术 Struts 2、Hibernate 3 和 Spring 2 的整合书籍。本书详尽分析了这 3 种技术，并通过实例讲解这 3 种技术的整合。

本书分为 5 篇共 21 章，包括环境准备篇、Struts 2 篇、Hibernate 3 篇、Spring 2 篇和实战篇。本书实例丰富、内容知识全面，浅显易懂，能够帮助读者尽快掌握这 3 种框架技术的使用。

本书适合作为 Java/Java EE 开发的初、中级读者的参考书，也可作为需要掌握 Struts、Hibernate 和 Spring 开源框架技术或学习其整合的读者使用，也非常适合高校相关专业的学生、社会 Java 技术培训班作教材使用。对于缺乏项目实战经验的程序员来说，通过本书的学习，可快速积累项目开发经验。

本书免费提供实例源程序，读者可以到中国水利水电出版社网站（http://www.waterpub.com.cn/softdown）和希赛教育网下载中心（http://www.educity.cn/data）下载。

图书在版编目（CIP）数据

企业应用架构设计：Struts2+Hibernate3+Spring2
／谢星星主编；希赛IT教育研发中心组织编写. -- 北京
：中国水利水电出版社，2010.5
　ISBN 978-7-5084-7371-0

　Ⅰ．①企… Ⅱ．①谢… ②希… Ⅲ．①软件工具—程序设计　Ⅳ．①TP311.56

中国版本图书馆CIP数据核字(2010)第050370号

书　　名	企业应用架构设计——Struts 2 + Hibernate 3 + Spring 2
作　　者	希赛IT教育研发中心　组织编写　谢星星　主编
出版发行	中国水利水电出版社 （北京市海淀区玉渊潭南路1号D座　100038） 网址：www.waterpub.com.cn E-mail：sales@waterpub.com.cn 电话：(010) 68367658（发行部）
经　　售	北京科水图书销售中心（零售） 电话：(010) 88383994、63202643、68545874 全国各地新华书店和相关出版物销售网点
排　　版	北京英宇世纪信息技术有限责任公司
印　　刷	北京瑞斯通印务发展有限公司
规　　格	184mm×260mm　16 开本　34.5 印张　905 千字
版　　次	2010 年 5 月第 1 版　2013 年 1 月第 4 次印刷
印　　数	6501—8500 册
定　　价	68.00 元

凡购买我社图书，如有缺页、倒页、脱页的，本社发行部负责调换

版权所有·侵权必究

前　　言

　　Struts 2 整合了两个优秀的 MVC 框架：大名鼎鼎的 Struts1.x 和成熟的 WebWork，因此它既具有 Struts1.x 的简单易用性，又具有 WebWork 的高扩展性，使其成为了一个高扩展性的成熟框架，因此也成为了时下 Java EE 项目 MVC 框架的理想选择。

　　关系数据库使用广泛，它存储的是非面向对象的关系数据，JDBC 是访问关系数据库的最原始和最直接的方法，该方法虽然运行效率高，但是会使项目难以维护。现在，越来越多的 Java 开发人员将 Hibernate 作为关系数据库与企业应用之间的中间件，它减少了开发人员的开发工作量。它使用方便，具有高扩展性，是一种流行的持久化中间件。

　　Spring 2 为各种 Java EE API 的使用提供了一致的抽象和集成工作，从而使开发者对许多与业务无关的技术细节不用再去打理，而专注于业务应用。Spring 提供控制反转容器（IoC）和面向切面编程技术（AOP），为 Java EE 项目提供了 DAO 层、Web 层，以及各种服务的支持。

1. 知识体系

　　本书的知识体系结构如下图所示，笔者采用实例的方式讲解，遵循循序渐近的原则，逐步引领读者从基础到各知识点的学习，而后开发出完整的基于 Struts 2+Hibernate 3+Spring 2 的 Web 系统。

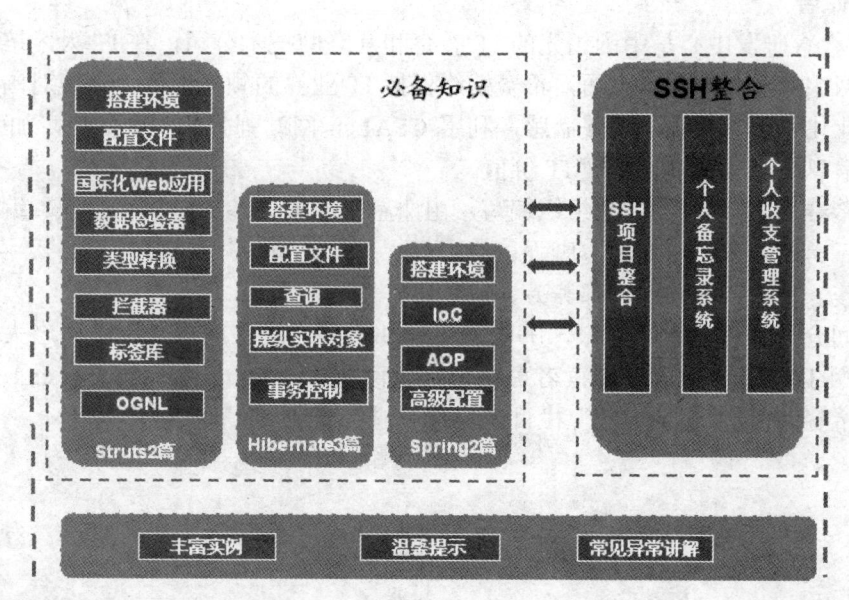

2. 章节内容

　　全书共分为 5 篇。

　　第 1 篇为环境准备篇。讲述如何搭建本书实例开发的环境：JDK1.6+Tomcat 6+Java EE Eclipse+MySQL 5.0，以及相关环境的配置。

　　第 2 篇为 Struts 2 篇，共分为 8 章。讲述 Struts 2 这个 MVC 开源框架方方面面的知识点，例如配置文件（web.xml、struts.xml、struts.properties 和 default.properties）、如何国际化 Web 应用、如何使用 Struts 2 中的数据校验器来完成客户端或服务端的校验。

在 Struts 2 中可以通过继承 DefaultTypeConverter 类或 StrutsTypeConverter 类进行类型转换，本篇对这些内容进行了讲解。拦截器是 Struts 2 中常用的一个组件，本篇对拦截器的使用、内建拦截器、以及如何自定义拦截器都进行了详细讲述。Struts 2 为开发者提供了强大的标签库，方便了 Java EE 开发人员的开发工作，本篇对其各种标签进行了详细说明。

第 3 篇为 Hibernate 3 篇，共分为 5 章。主要讲述持久化中间件技术：Hibernate 3，重点讲述 Hibernate 的配置文件的配置，以及如何使用 Hibernate 进行数据查询、新增、修改和删除操作。还讲述了数据库事务，以及如何在 Hibernate 中使用事务。

第 4 篇为 Spring 2 篇，共分为 4 章。讲述 Spring 2 技术中强大的 IoC 容器和面向切面编程技术（AOP），以及 Spring 2 的高级配置（配置定时任务、邮件服务等）。

第 5 篇为实战篇，共分为 3 章。首先通过一个整合实例讲解如何进行 Struts 2、Hibernate 3 和 Spring 2 技术的整合，接着通过两个项目实例"个人备忘录系统"和"个人收支管理系统"深化了 3 种技术的整合。

本书内容由浅入深，并辅以大量的实例说明，可供有一定 Java Web 编程基础的程序员作为参考用书，也可供社会 Java 技术培训班作为教材使用。对于缺乏项目实战经验的程序员来说，本书内容可用于快速积累项目开发经验。

本书提供所有实例的源代码，以及项目案例的源代码，供读者学习参考使用，所有程序均经过了作者精心的调试。读者可以到中国水利水电出版社网站（http://www.waterpub.com.cn/softdown/）下载，也可以在希赛教育网下载中心（http://www.educity.cn/data/）下载。

3. 关于作者

希赛 IT 教育研发中心是中国领先的 IT 教育和互联网技术公司，在 IT 人才培养、行业信息化、互联网服务及其他技术方面，希赛始终保持 IT 业界的领先地位。希赛对国家信息化建设和软件产业化发展具有强烈的使命感，利用 CSAI.cn 网站强大的平台优势，加强与促进 IT 人士之间的信息交流和共享，实现 IT 价值。

本书由希赛 IT 教育研发中心组织编写，由谢星星主编。参加审稿和组织、编辑工作的还有邓子云、王勇、施游、胡钊源、唐强、何玉云、王冀、黄少年、谢顺、周玲、黄燕、符春、陈倩、李双霞、杨花、王欣欣、郑美芳、何东彬、唐科萍等。

由于时间仓促和作者水平有限，书中的错误和不妥之处在所难免，敬请广大读者批评指正。有关本书的意见反馈和咨询，读者可在希赛教育网社区（http://bbs.educity.cn）"书评在线"版块中的"希赛 IT 教育研发中心"栏目中与作者进行交流。

作者
2010 年 1 月

目 录

前言

第1篇 环境准备篇

第1章 搭建开发环境 ··· 1
【例1-1】下载和安装JDK ·· 1
【例1-2】安装Tomcat ··· 8
【例1-3】下载和安装JavaEE Eclipse ·· 14
【例1-4】下载和安装MySQL ··· 22
小结 ·· 28

第2篇 Struts 2篇

第2章 步入Struts 2框架开发的殿堂 ·· 29
【例2-1】下载Struts 2 ··· 29
【例2-2】搭建Struts 2的开发环境 ·· 31
【例2-3】用Struts 2实现用户登录 ·· 35
小结 ·· 42

第3章 配置文件 ·· 43
【例3-1】配置web.xml ·· 43
【例3-2】配置struts.xml ·· 46
【例3-3】配置struts.properties ··· 50
【例3-4】struts的默认配置文件default.properties ·· 52
小结 ·· 57

第4章 国际化Web应用 ··· 59
【例4-1】常见中文乱码问题的解决方案 ··· 59
【例4-2】使用资源文件 ··· 63
【例4-3】参数化字符串 ··· 67
小结 ·· 75

第5章 数据校验器 ·· 77
【例5-1】使用重写validate()方法进行手动校验 ··· 77
【例5-2】使用重写validateXxx()方法进行手动校验 ······································· 84
【例5-3】使用Struts 2的验证框架完成服务端校验 ··· 88
【例5-4】使用Struts2的验证框架完成客户端校验 ·· 91
【例5-5】国际化校验的提示信息 ·· 92

【例 5-6】非字段校验器规则 ··· 94
　　【例 5-7】常用内建的校验器 ··· 96
　　小结 ·· 101

第 6 章　类型转换 ··· 106
　　【例 6-1】不使用 Struts 2 的类型转换器进行类型转换 ······················· 106
　　【例 6-2】继承 DefaultTypeConverter 类进行类型转换 ······················· 112
　　【例 6-3】继承 StrutsTypeConverter 类进行类型转换 ························ 115
　　【例 6-4】数组的类型转换 ··· 117
　　【例 6-5】集合的类型转换 ··· 120
　　【例 6-6】Struts 2 中内置的类型转换 ··· 122
　　【例 6-7】类型转换的错误处理 ··· 127
　　小结 ·· 131

第 7 章　拦截器 ·· 133
　　【例 7-1】理解拦截器 ·· 133
　　【例 7-2】拦截器的配置 ·· 138
　　【例 7-3】内建拦截器 ·· 141
　　【例 7-4】自定义拦截器 ·· 147
　　小结 ·· 150

第 8 章　Struts 2 标签库 ··· 152
　　【例 8-1】控制标签 ··· 152
　　【例 8-2】数据标签 ··· 164
　　【例 8-3】UI 标签 ··· 180
　　小结 ·· 197

第 9 章　OGNL ··· 202
　　【例 9-1】OGNL 的使用 ·· 202
　　【例 9-2】EL 表达式 ··· 208
　　【例 9-3】Lambda 表达式 ·· 213
　　小结 ·· 215

第 3 篇　Hibernate 3 篇

第 10 章　Hibernate 入门 ·· 217
　　【例 10-1】Java 对象持久化技术 ··· 217
　　【例 10-2】搭建 Hibernate 3 开发环境 ·· 221
　　【例 10-3】用 Hibernate 实现用户信息查询 ····································· 225
　　小结 ·· 233

第 11 章　Hibernate 配置文件 ·· 234
　　【例 11-1】配置 Hibernate.cfg.xml ··· 234
　　【例 11-2】.hbm.xml 文件基本配置 ·· 241
　　【例 11-3】配置一对多关联 ·· 249

【例 11-4】配置一对一关联 ··· 254
【例 11-5】配置多对多关联 ··· 260
小结 ··· 265

第 12 章 Hibernate 查询 ··· 267
【例 12-1】Hibernate 查询语言：HQL ································· 267
【例 12-2】条件查询（Criteria Queries）······························ 280
【例 12-3】SQL 查询 ··· 283
【例 12-4】连接查询 ··· 286
小结 ··· 289

第 13 章 操纵实体对象 ·· 292
【例 13-1】解说 Hibernate 对象的 3 种状态 ·························· 292
【例 13-2】保存实体对象 ··· 295
【例 13-3】更新实体对象 ··· 299
【例 13-4】删除实体对象 ··· 303
【例 13-5】绕过 Hibernate API 对数据进行操作 ····················· 305
【例 13-6】使用 Hibernate 调用存储过程 ····························· 307
小结 ··· 311

第 14 章 Hibernate 的事务控制 ······································ 314
【例 14-1】解说数据库事务 ·· 314
【例 14-2】在 Hibernate 中进行事务控制 ····························· 318
小结 ··· 321

第 4 篇　Spring 2 篇

第 15 章 Spring 入门 ··· 324
【例 15-1】Spring 2.0 简介 ·· 324
【例 15-2】下载 Spring 2.0 ·· 326
【例 15-3】搭建 Spring 2 开发环境 ···································· 327
【例 15-4】使用 Spring 2 开发 HelloWorld ··························· 331
小结 ··· 333

第 16 章 核心机制——IoC ··· 334
【例 16-1】解说 IoC 的相关概念 ······································· 334
【例 16-2】XML 格式配置元数据 ······································ 338
【例 16-3】实例化容器的几种方式 ···································· 340
【例 16-4】实例化 bean 的 3 种方式 ··································· 344
【例 16-5】注入方式——构造子注入 ································· 348
【例 16-6】注入方式——setter 方法注入 ····························· 352
【例 16-7】注入方式——接口注入 ···································· 354
【例 16-8】bean 属性及构造器参数 ···································· 357
小结 ··· 366

第 17 章 Spring 的 AOP ... 370
【例 17-1】解说 AOP 的概念 ... 370
【例 17-2】AOP 实现原理 ... 371
【例 17-3】@AspectJ 支持 ... 378
【例 17-4】使用 Spring AOP 实现异常拦截 ... 387
小结 ... 390

第 18 章 Spring 的高级配置 ... 393
【例 18-1】数据源配置 ... 393
【例 18-2】Hibernate 事务配置 ... 402
【例 18-3】邮件服务配置 ... 408
【例 18-4】定时任务配置 ... 412
小结 ... 415

第 5 篇　实战篇

第 19 章 Struts、Hibernate 和 Spring 整合 ... 421
【例 19-1】使用 Struts 实现用户注册 ... 421
【例 19-2】在 Struts 项目中整合 Hibernate ... 427
【例 19-3】Struts+Hibernate 中整合 Spring ... 435
小结 ... 444

第 20 章 SSH 实例——个人备忘录系统 ... 448
20.1　系统需求分析 ... 448
20.2　系统架构设计 ... 449
20.3　数据库设计 ... 450
20.4　系统详细设计 ... 452
20.5　系统实现设计 ... 457
小结 ... 495

第 21 章 SSH 实例——个人收支管理系统 ... 497
21.1　系统需求分析 ... 497
21.2　系统架构设计 ... 498
21.3　数据库设计 ... 498
21.4　系统详细设计 ... 499
21.5　系统实现设计 ... 504
小结 ... 541

第 1 篇　环境准备篇

第 1 章　搭建开发环境

【本章导读语】

本章讲述如何搭建开发环境。在本章中，笔者将与读者一起搭建起全书所有实例使用的开发环境：JDK 1.6 + Tomcat 6.0 + Eclipse + MySQL5.0，这有助于后阶段的理论知识学习以及开发实例的学习。

其中 JDK（Java Development Kit）是 Sun 公司针对 Java 开发的产品。自从 Java 推出以来，JDK 已经成为使用最广泛的 Java SDK（Software Development Kit）。

Tomcat 是一个免费开源的 Servlet 容器，它是 Apache 基金会的一个核心项目，是 Java Web 开发时常用的一款轻量级 Web 服务中间件软件。

Eclipse 是一个广受 Java 开发人员欢迎的集成开发环境（Integrated Development Environment，IDE），它由 IBM 公司于 2001 年首次推出，是一个功能完整且成熟的软件。

MySQL 是一个小型关系型数据库管理系统，目前 MySQL 被广泛地应用在 Internet 上的中小型网站中。其体积小、速度快、总体拥有成本低，并且开放源代码，许多中小型网站为了降低网站总体成本而选择了 MySQL 作为数据库。

这四者从不同方面满足了 Java EE 项目开发的需要，笔者相信这种组合能给读者的开发工作带来事半功倍的效果。

【例 1-1】下载和安装 JDK

〖实例需求〗

JDK 是开发 Java 应用程序和 Web 程序的基础环境，它为 Tomcat 运行提供了环境支持。本实例讲解如何下载和安装 JDK，以及 JDK 的相关配置。

〖开发过程〗

第一步：下载 JDK

（1）进入 JDK 下载页面。

JDK 的下载地址为：http://java.sun.com/javase/downloads/index.jsp

下载页面如图 1-1 所示。

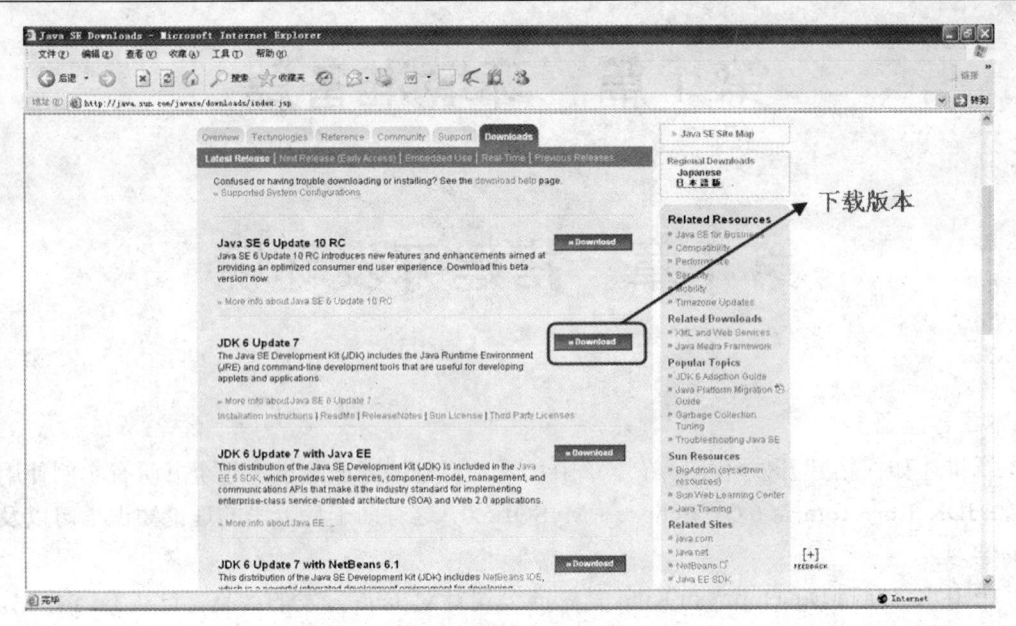

图 1-1 Sun 公司网站上 JDK 的下载页面

【提示】至本书成稿之日，JDK 的最新版本为 JDK 6 Update 7，读者可以下载更新的版本。

JDK 6 Update 7 中包含了 JRE（Java Runtime Environment，Java 运行时环境）和用于开发 Java Applet 与 Java 应用程序的命令行开发工具。

（2）下载 JDK。

在图 1-1 中单击 JDK 6 Update 7 后的 Download 按钮，进入如图 1-2 所示的 JDK 6 Update 7 的下载页面。

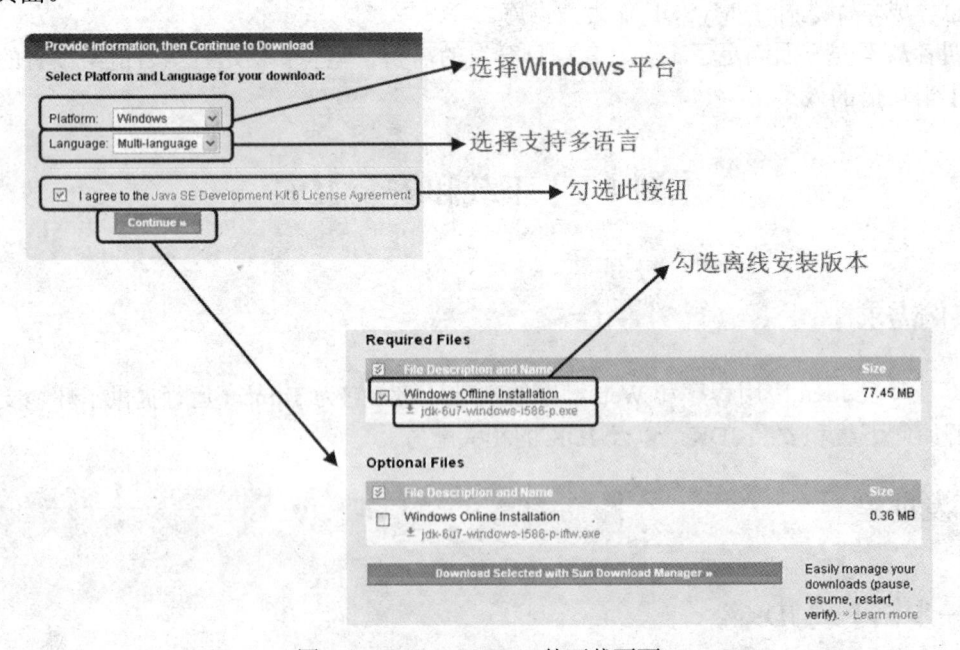

图 1-2 JDK 6 Update 7 的下载页面

在出现的第一个界面中，在 Platform 的下拉列表中选择 Windows，并勾选"I agree to the Java SE Development Kit 6 License Agreement"同意 JDK 6 的许可协议。接着单击 Continue 按钮进入

下一个界面，在之后的界面中点击 jdk-6u7-windows-i586-p.exe 链接开始下载。

【提示】下载得到的 jdk-6u7-windows-i586-p.exe 安装文件是专用于 Windows 平台的 JDK 6 安装包，如果需要其他平台（如 Linux、Solaris SPARC 等）的 JDK 6 安装包，请读者自行选择相应的下载链接。

第二步：安装 JDK

（1）安装向导界面。

双击 jdk-6u7-windows-i586-p.exe 安装文件，弹出如图 1-3 所示的安装向导对话框。

图 1-3　安装向导对话框

（2）许可证协议窗口。

在图 1-3 所示的向导框中等候片刻，将会弹出"许可证协议"窗口，如图 1-4 所示。

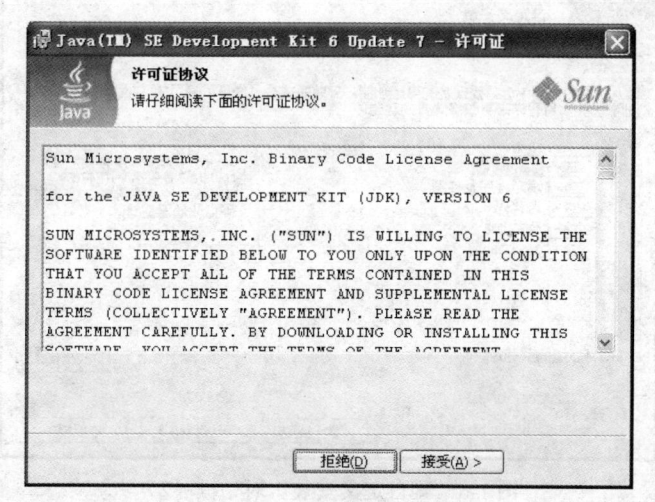

图 1-4　"许可证协议"窗口

（3）自定义安装窗口。

在图 1-4 中单击"接受"按钮接受 Sun 公司的许可证协议，进入"自定义安装"对话框，如图 1-5 所示。

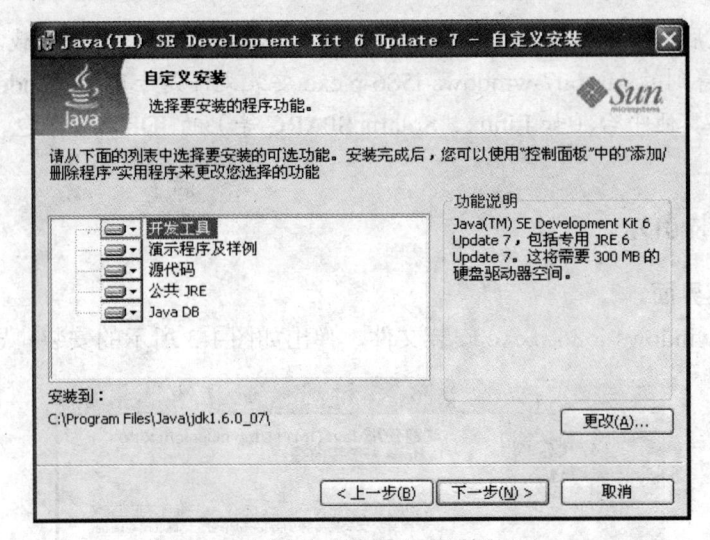

图1-5 "自定义安装"对话框（1）

在"自定义安装"对话框中可以选择需要安装的组件以及安装路径。

可选的组件中，开发工具为 JDK 6 Update 7，约需 300M 空间。演示程序及样例中包含一些小程序和应用程序的示例。源代码是构成 Java 公共 API 的类的源代码。公共 JRE 是独立的，任何应用程序都可以使用，安装时还会向浏览器和系统注册 Java 插件和 Java Web Start。Java DB 是 Sun 支持的纯 Java 技术实现的一种数据库。

单击"更改"按钮可以更改组件的安装位置。

读者可以修改 JDK 的安装路径，例如修改为 E:\jdk1.6.0u7\jdk1.6.0，如图 1-6 所示。单击"下一步"按钮，开始安装。

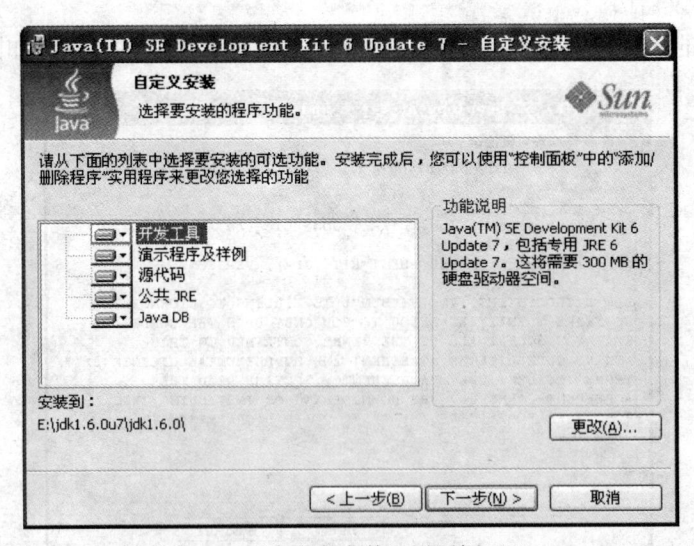

图1-6 "自定义安装"对话框（2）

【提示】JDK 和 JRE 的安装目录读者可根据需要更改。

（4）安装进度。

安装进度界面如图 1-7 所示。

第1章 搭建开发环境 5

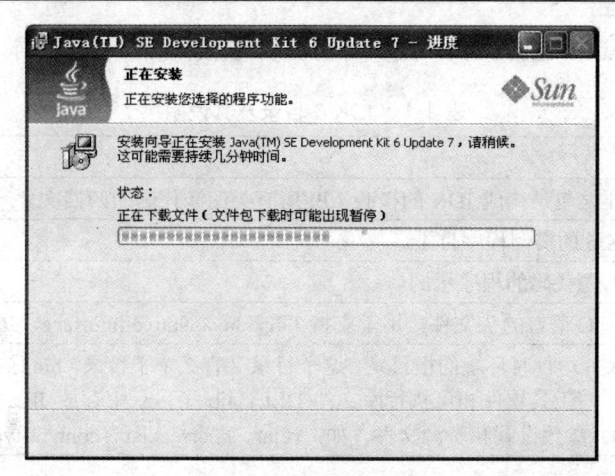

图 1-7 安装进度界面

（5）安装完成界面。

在安装的过程中，会出现 JRE 安装界面，读者在该界面中可以更改路径，也可以使用默认设置，单击"下一步"按钮继续进行安装，安装完成后界面如图 1-8 所示。

图 1-8 安装完成界面

单击上图中的"完成"按钮完成安装。

（6）JDK 目录结构。

JDK 6 Update 7 安装完毕后，进入安装路径，其目录结构如图 1-9 所示。

图 1-9 JDK 6 安装后的目录

JDK 6 的安装根目录下包含版权声明、许可文件等，各种文件和目录的说明如表 1-1 所示。

表 1-1 JDK 6 目录及其说明

文件或目录	说明
src.zip	该压缩包是构成 JDK 的核心 API 所有类的源代码的归档文件
sample	JDK 6 的实例程序目录
demo	含有源代码的程序示例
include	一些 C 语言的头文件，用于支持 JNI（Java Native Interface，Java 本地接口）
jre	JDK 6 运行时环境的根目录，这个目录又有 2 个子目录，bin 子目录中存放 JRE 要用到的一些工具软件和可执行库文件 DLL；lib 子目录中存放 JRE 要用到的一些类库（jar 包）、参数设置和资源文件，如：rt.jar、charsets.jar、content-types.properties 等

第三步：设置环境变量

JDK 安装成功后，为了保证 Tomcat 等的正常运行，还需要设置 Path 和 JAVA_HOME 这两个系统环境变量。两者的详细设置如下所示：

（1）设置 Path 系统环境变量。

在 Windows 系统环境变量 Path 中应当添加一个指示 JDK 6 的 bin 目录的项。

在系统变量中修改 Path 系统环境变量的操作步骤图如图 1-10 所示。

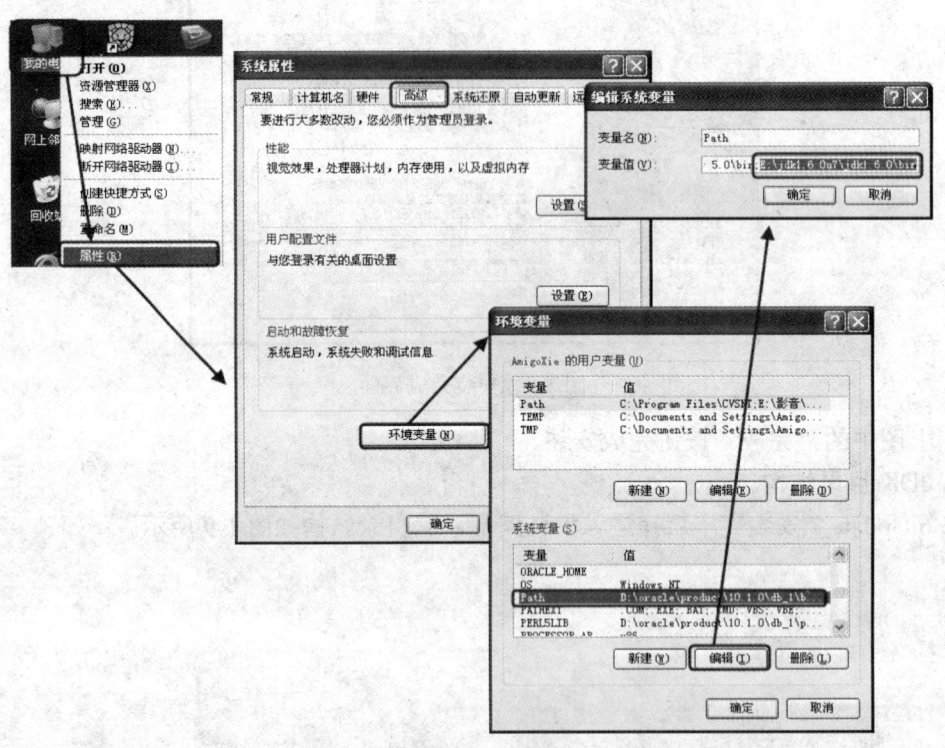

图 1-10 修改 Path 系统环境变量

读者可按图 1-10 所示的操作步骤编辑名为 Path 的系统环境变量，如果没有 Path 系统变量，则需要添加系统变量。

在 Path 系统变量中添加的信息如下所示：

E:\jdk1.6.0u7\jdk1.6.0\bin

其中 E:\jdk1.6.0u7\jdk1.6.0 是指 JDK 6 的安装目录，若 Path 不是新增的系统变量，则还需要在 E:\jdk1.6.0\jdk1.6.0\bin 前加 ";"，表示区分 Path 的各个值。

测试 JDK 是否正确安装需要在命令窗口中输入如下命令：

java -version

操作步骤如图 1-11 所示。

图 1-11　测试 JDK 是否正确安装

（2）添加 JAVA_HOME 系统环境变量。

JDK 6 安装目录中的 lib 目录是开发类库存放的目录。这些文件包括 tools.jar，它包含支持 JDK 的工具和实用程序的非核心类；还包括 dt.jar，它是 BeanInfo 文件的 DesignTime 归档，BeanInfo 文件用来告诉 IDE（Integrated Development Enviroment，集成开发环境）如何显示 Java 组件以及如何让开发人员根据应用程序自定义它们。

为了 Tomcat 等的正常运行，读者还需要设置名为 JAVA_HOME 的环境变量，添加 JAVA_HOME 系统环境变量的步骤如图 1-12 所示。

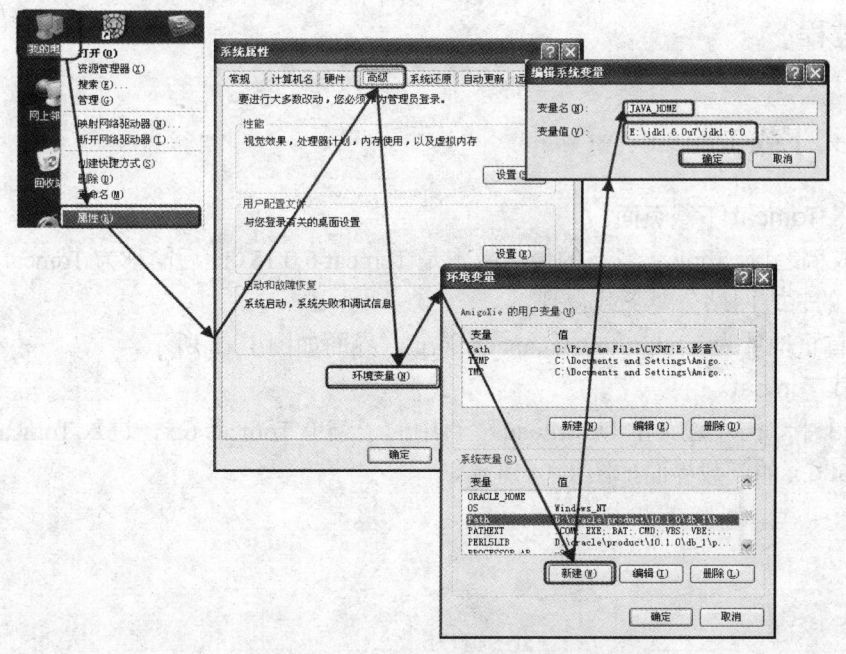

图 1-12　添加环境变量步骤图

添加的系统变量的名称为：JAVA_HOME，其值为 JDK 的安装目录，例如：E:\jdk1.6.0u7\jdk1.6.0。

【例 1-2】安装 Tomcat

〖实例需求〗

Tomcat 作为一款轻量级的 Java Web 应用中间件，备受 Java 开发人员的青睐。

它所占用、消耗的系统资源相对 Weblogic、Websphere 等重量级的商业 Web 中间件少得多。另外，从成本上来考虑，Tomcat 免费开源，成本很低；其次，Tomcat 的版本升级快，功能也在不断地完善。因此，Tomcat 已成为 Java Web 开发人员的首选开发工具。

Tomcat 是一个实现了 Java Servlet 和 JSP（Java Server Pages）的容器，不同版本的 Tomcat 容器实现了不同的 Servlet/JSP 规范，比较典型的情况如表 1-2 所示。

表 1-2 典型的 Tomcat 容器实现的 Servlet/JSP 规范情况

Tomcat 版本	实现的 Servlet/JSP 规范
Tomcat 6.0.18	Servlet 2.5/JSP 2.1
Tomcat 5.5.27	Servlet 2.4/JSP 2.0
Tomcat 4.1.37	Servlet 2.3/JSP 1.2
Tomcat 3.3.2	Servlet 2.2/JSP 1.1

本实例讲解如何下载和安装 Tomcat，并将讲解 Tomcat 的常用配置，为后续的 Java EE 项目开发打下基础。

〖开发过程〗

第一步：下载 Tomcat

（1）进入 Tomcat 下载页面。

至本书成稿之日，Tomcat 发布的最新版本是 Tomcat 6.0.18（此后简称为 Tomcat 6）。Tomcat6 可从 Apache 的官方网站免费下载得到。

Tomcat 首页地址为：http://tomcat.apache.org/，界面如图 1-13 所示。

（2）下载 Tomcat。

在图 1-13 中单击左边菜单 Download 栏目中的子菜单 Tomcat 6.x，进入 Tomcat 6.x 的下载页面，Tomcat 6.x 的下载界面如图 1-14 所示。

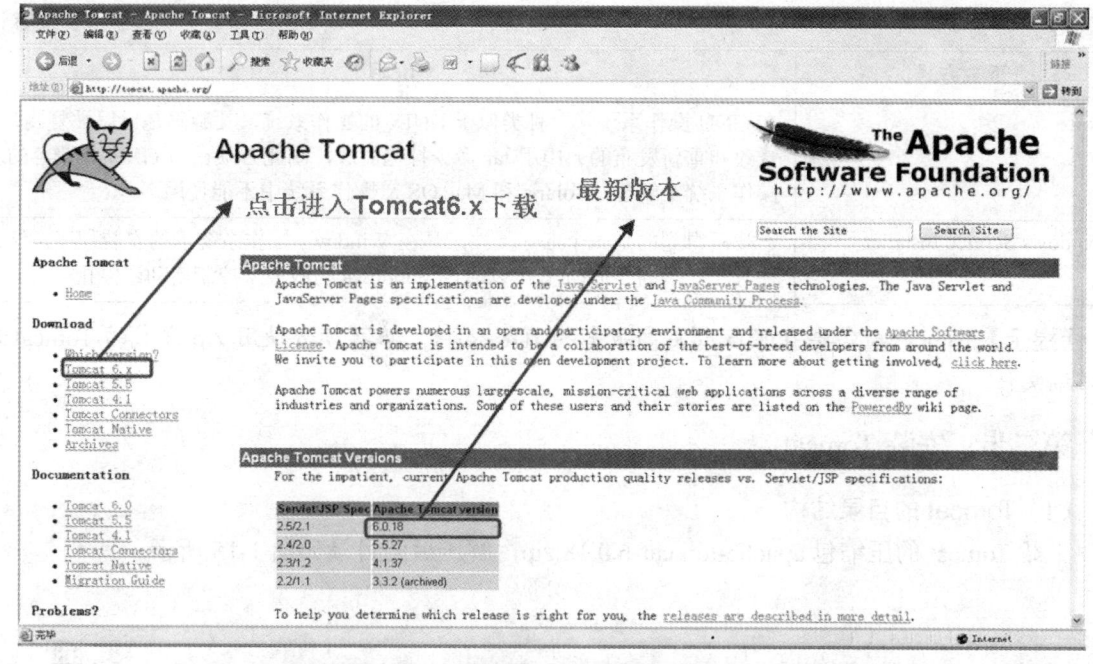

图 1-13　Apache 网站上的 Tomcat 子网站

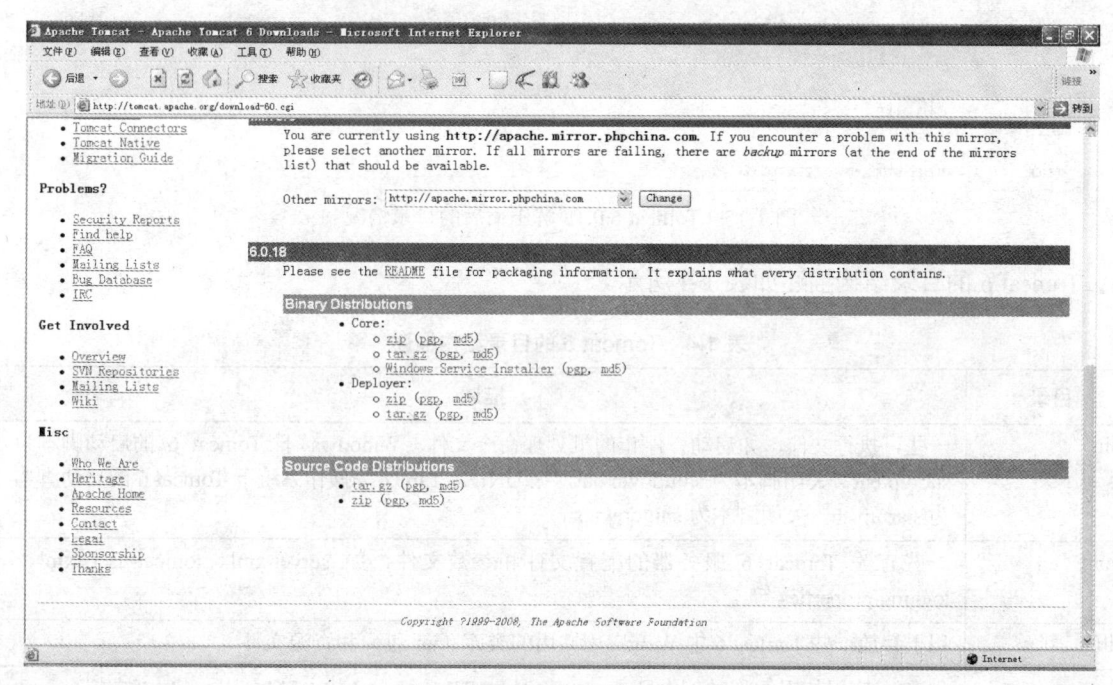

图 1-14　Tomcat 6.x 的下载界面

在 6.0.18 栏目下的子栏目 Binary Distributions 的 Core 下提供了 3 种 Tomcat 6.0.18 的下载方式：zip、tar.gz 和 Windows Service Installer，这 3 种方式的说明如表 1-3 所示。

表 1-3　Tomcat 6.0.18 的 3 种下载方式

下载方式	说明
zip	无需安装，解压缩后即可使用

下载方式	说明
tar.gz	在 GNU 操作系统（一种类似于 UNIX 的操作系统，其源码是可以被复制、修改和重新发布的）中用 tar 命令打包而成，因此必须在与 GNU 相兼容的操作系统中解包，Solaris 和 Mac OS X 操作系统中不能使用
Windows Service Installer	下载后得到的是一个 exe 文件，是在 Windows 操作系统下的安装程序，这种方式安装的 Tomcat 6 可以通过 Windows 的服务来控制启动、停止

【提示】Tomcat 6 需要 JDK 5 或更高版本的 JDK 支持。推荐读者使用 zip 方式的 Tomcat 6 解压缩文件。

第二步：安装 Tomcat

（1）Tomcat 的目录结构。

下载 Tomcat 的压缩包 apache-tomcat-6.0.18.zip，解压后的目录如图 1-15 所示。

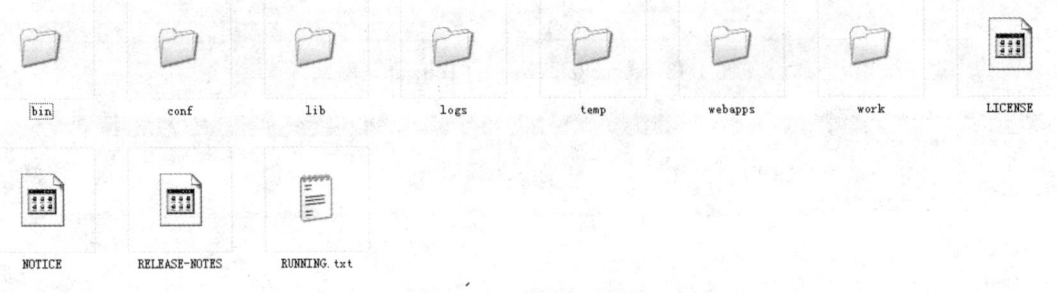

图 1-15 Tomcat 6.0.18 解压缩后的目录情况

Tomcat 6 的目录结构描述如表 1-4 所示。

表 1-4 Tomcat 6 的目录结构描述

目录	描述
bin	一些可执行文件，如启动、停止的批处理命令文件。Winodws 下 Tomcat 6 的启动脚本为 startup.bat，关闭脚本为 shutdown.bat，在 UNIX、Linux 等操作系统下 Tomcat 6 的启动脚本为 startup.sh，关闭脚本为 shutdown.sh
conf	一些有关 Tomcat 6 服务器的配置文件和参数文件，如 server.xml、tomcat-users.xml、logging.properties 等
lib	用于存放一些 Tomcat 6 中 Web 应用共用的类库（jar 包）和资源文件
work	供 Web 应用使用的临时工作目录。temp 是供 JVM（Java Virtual Machine，Java 虚拟机）使用的存放临时文件的目录
webapps	用于存放一些 Tomcat 6 自动装载的 Web 应用，可以是 Web 应用的整个目录。这个目录中已自带了一些 Web 应用，其中 ROOT 应用是默认的根 Web 应用

【提示】可以简单地把 Web 应用理解成 Web 服务器中一个独立的、完成一定业务和功能逻辑的应用系统所处的目录，客户端访问这个目录中的文件时需要在 URL（Uniform Resource Locator，统一资源定位器）中输入目录名。如果服务器地址为 localhost，Web 服务端口号为 8080，要访问 ssh 应用中的 login.jsp 页面，访问的 URL 为：

http://localhost:8080/ssh/login.jsp

但如果 login.jsp 页面位于 ROOT 应用中，则输入访问该页面时，不必再输入应用名 ROOT，只需要输入 URL：

http://localhost:8080/login.jsp

（2）启动 Tomcat。

安装好 Tomcat 6 后，双击安装目录的 bin 子目录下的 startup.bat，启动 Tomcat 6，如图 1-16 所示。

图 1-16　成功启动 Tomcat 6 的界面

【提示】若启动 startup.bat 时界面一闪而过，读者可以通过 UltraEdit 等软件打开 startup.bat 批处理文件，在文末新增一行，内容为：

pause

保存后，重新启动 startup.bat，可看到完整的出错信息。例如若 JAVA_HOME 环境变量未进行设置，可能出现这种一闪而过的现象，加入 pause 后，重新启动可看到如图 1-17 所示的错误信息。

图 1-17　未设置 JAVA_HOME 环境变量时的错误信息

此时请读者自行设置 JAVA_HOME 环境变量。

【提示】Tomcat 默认占用的端口为 8080，若该端口被占用，例如安装了 Oracle 等时该端口会被占用，则启动 startup.bat 时出现的错误信息如图 1-18 所示。

图 1-18　Tomcat 的端口被占用时的错误信息

此时读者需要停止其他占用了 Tomcat 端口的程序，或者对 Tomcat 的端口进行修改。

接下来测试 Tomcat 6 是否启动成功。在浏览器中输入地址：http://localhost:8080，将出现如图 1-19 所示的界面，该页面显示的是 Tomcat 6 根目录\webapps\ROOT 应用中的 index.jsp 页面的信息。

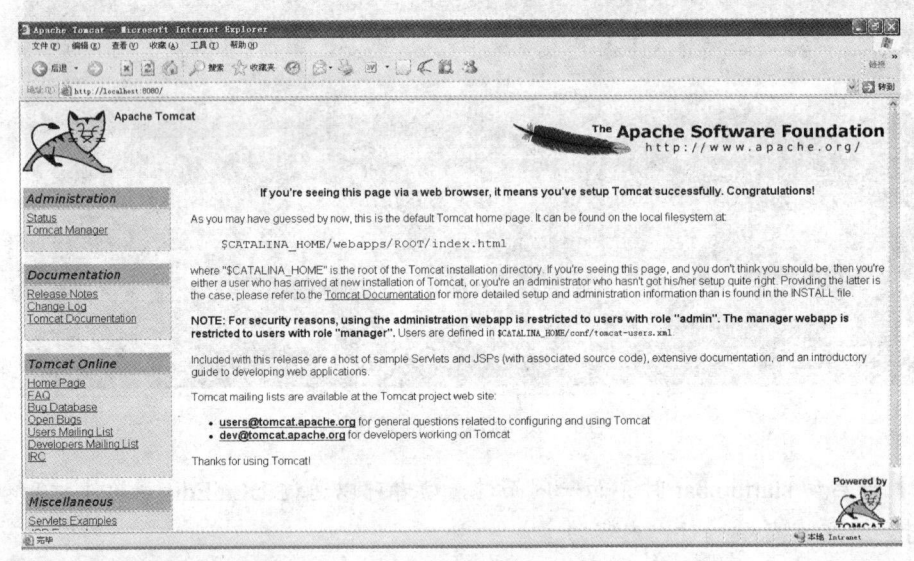

图 1-19　访问 Tomcat

【提示】访问 Tomcat 的 URL 中，localhost 也可以改为机器名、IP 地址，如果是在 Internet 中，还可以使用域名。localhost 与 127.0.0.1 均表示本机。

第三步：配置 Tomcat

（1）配置端口。

在图 1-19 所示访问 Tomcat 6 的 URL 中，带了 Web 服务的服务端口号 8080。8080 是 Tomcat 的默认端口，读者可以通过修改 Tomcat 的配置文件对端口进行重新设置。

修改文件：Tomcat6 安装目录\conf\server.xml，打开后搜索 8080，对应文字为：

```
<Connector port="8080" protocol="HTTP/1.1"
          connectionTimeout="20000"
          redirectPort="8443" />
```

将其中的 port 属性值修改为需要的端口（例如 8899）即可。

【提示】在读者看到的很多 URL 地址中，并不带有端口信息，这是因为 HTTP 协议访问默认的端口号为 80，当 Web 服务器的端口号正好设为 80 时，访问时可不必输入端口号。

【提示】在一些 Windows 操作系统中，请读者注意操作系统可能自带了 IIS（Internet Information Services，Internet 信息服务）Web 服务器软件，用于支持 ASP 或 ASP.NET 技术，它使用的默认端口号是 80，可能会产生冲突。

（2）设置管理界面用户信息。

Tomcat 提供了一个管理界面，用于进行 Web 应用的部署、启动和停止等操作。点击图 1-19 所示的图形左上方的链接 Tomcat Manager，出现如图 1-20 所示的对话框。

Tomcat 中 Web 管理后台用户的设置文件为：Tomcat 安装目录\conf\tomcat-users.xml，默认情况下，没有设置用户，读者可在该文件中添加登录管理界面的用户。例如为管理界面添加用户名和密码都为 tomcat 的用户，修改后的文件内容如下：

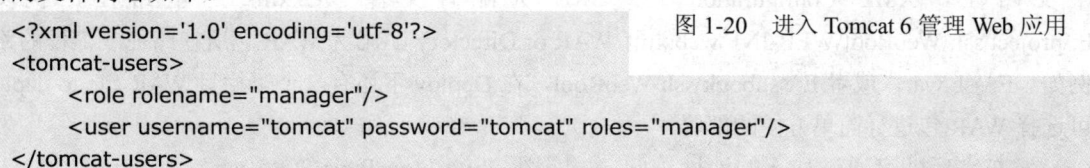

```
<?xml version='1.0' encoding='utf-8'?>
<tomcat-users>
    <role rolename="manager"/>
    <user username="tomcat" password="tomcat" roles="manager"/>
</tomcat-users>
```

图 1-20　进入 Tomcat 6 管理 Web 应用

其中 <role rolename="manager"/> 表示增加一个名为 manager 的角色，而 <user username="tomcat" password="tomcat" roles="manager"/> 表示新增一个用户名和密码都为 tomcat 的用户，并设置其所属角色为 manager。

设置完成后重启 Tomcat，访问 Tomcat Manager 界面，输入用户名和密码信息，可进入如图 1-21 所示的 Web 管理后台首页。

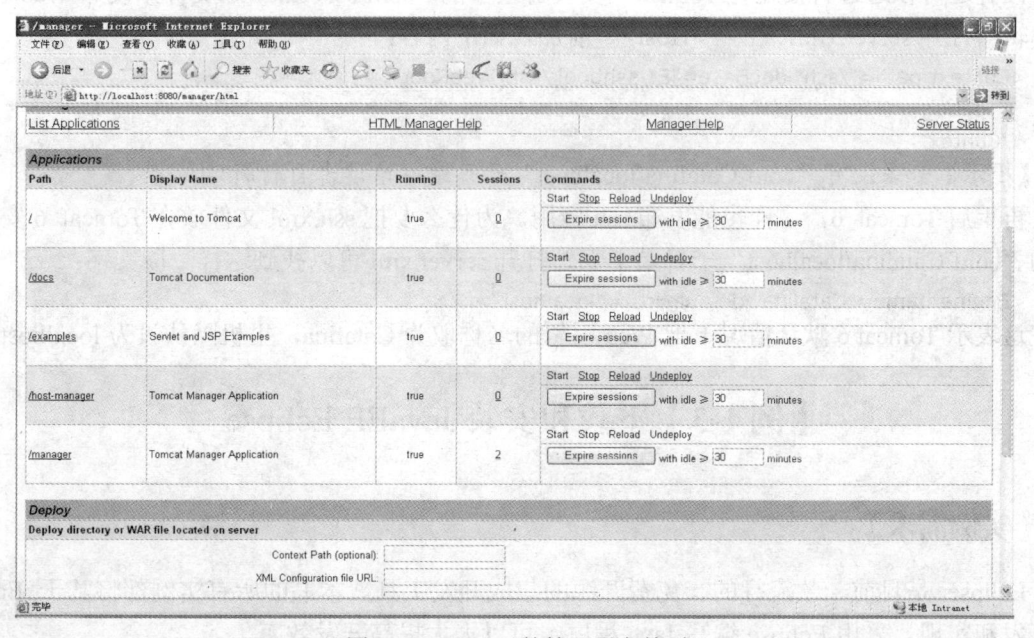

图 1-21　Tomcat 的管理后台首页

在 Applications 下显示的是 Tomcat 中当前的 Web 应用列表。列表中的每行如图 1-22 所示。

| /host-manager | Tomcat Manager Application | true | 0 | Start Stop Reload Undeploy
Expire sessions with idle ≥ 30 minutes |

图 1-22　Tomcat 的 Web 管理后台中的 Web 应用

表格的 Commands 列对每个 Web 应用都有一些集中管理的命令，命令用途如下：
Start：启动 Web 应用。
Stop：停止 Web 应用。
Reload：重新装载 Web 应用。
Undeploy：用于撤消 Web 应用。
Expire sessions 按钮后的文本框用于填入此 Web 应用的会话超时时间，默认为 30 分钟，设置后单击 Expire sessions 按钮即会生效。

在下方的 Deploy 栏下读者可以新部署一个 Web 应用程序，其中 Context Path (optional)为上下文路径，XML Configuration file URL 为配置文件 web.xml 的全路径，例如：E:\project\ssh\WebRoot\WEB-INF\web.xml，WAR or Directory URL 为 WAR 包所在路径或工程的路径，例如：E:\ssh.war，或者 E:\sshbook\ssh\WebRoot，在 Deploy 下还有一个子栏目 WAR file to deploy，可选择 WAR 包进行简单方便的部署。

发布完后即可通过如下的地址访问 ssh 应用：http://localhost:8080/ssh

【提示】可以结合一些自动化的发布 Web 应用工具来执行一连串的指令，如 Ant。本书中不必用到 Ant，因为编译程序的工作由 Eclipse 完成了，只要将 Web 应用指向 Eclipse 工作区的对应目录中，就不必做文件复制了，发布动作则使用 Tomcat 6 的 Web 管理方式或命令方式进行即可。如果是多人的团队式开发，还是提倡使用 Ant 这样的发布工具。

读者还可以通过直接配置 Tomcat 6 安装目录中的"conf\server.xml"文件来发布 Web 应用。用编辑器打开 server.xml，在"</Host>"前加入如下内容：

```
<Context path="/ssh" docBase="E:/sshbook/ssh/WebRoot"
    debug="0">
</Context>
```

【提示】如果没有"conf/Catalina/localhost"子目录，请读者自行新建。

再重启 Tomcat 6，这样也能发布 ssh 应用。为什么要把 ssh.xml 文件放在 Tomcat 6 安装目录的"conf/Catalina/localhost"子目录下呢？打开 server.xml 可以找到这样一段文字：

```
<Engine name="Catalina" defaultHost="localhost">
```

这表示 Tomcat 6 默认情况下把 Web 引擎的名称取为 Catalina，主机默认设为 localhost。

【例 1-3】下载和安装 JavaEE Eclipse

〖实例需求〗

Eclipse 是目前一款流行的、免费开源的集成开发工具。本书的所有实例都将基于 Eclipse 来开发和实现。采用 Eclipse 编写 Java 程序，可以大大提高开发效率。

本实例讲解在何处下载 Eclipse，并将讲述如何安装和启动 Eclipse，最后，为了后续项目的开发，笔者将详细讲解在 Eclipse 中如何新建工程、包、类、JSP，以及如何进行 Web 工程的调试等知识。

〖开发过程〗

第一步：下载 Eclipse

首先进入 Eclipse 首页，地址为：http://www.eclipse.org。
Eclipse 首页界面如图 1-23 所示。

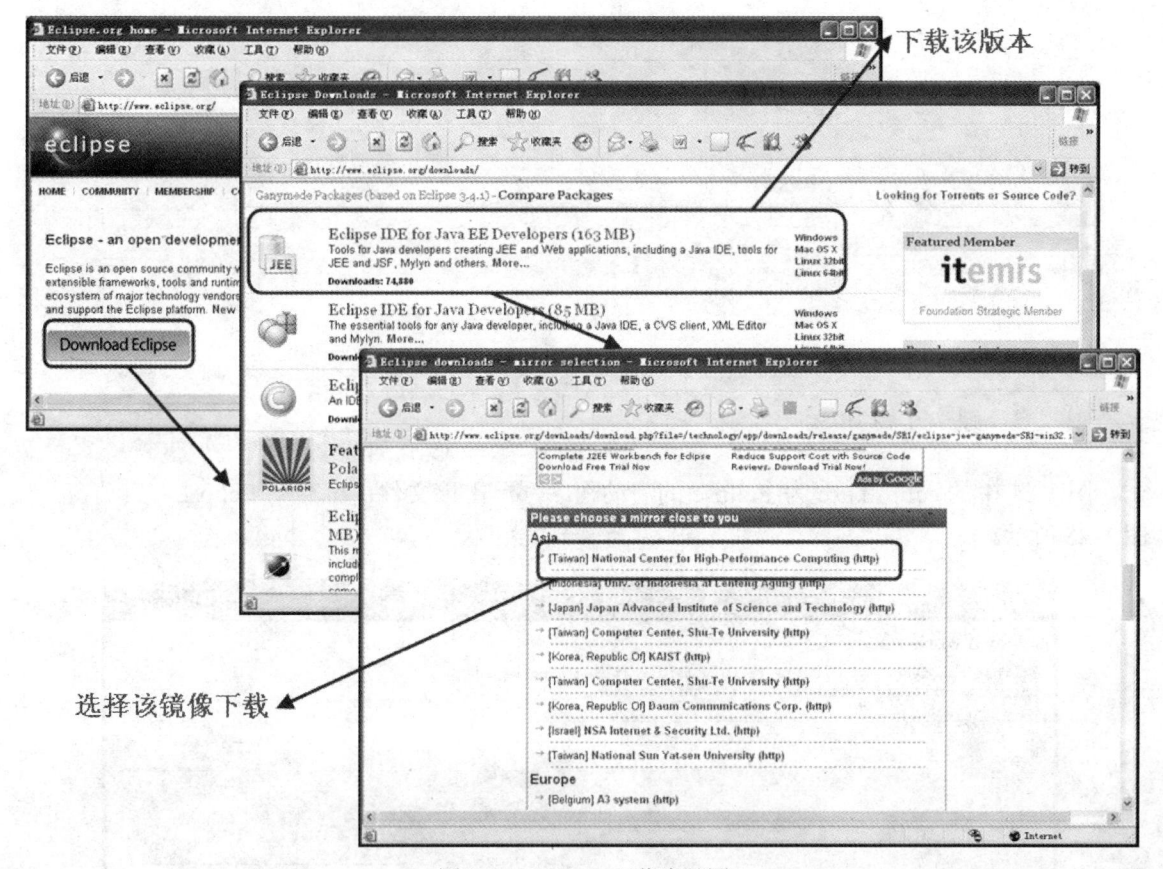

图 1-23　Eclipse 下载步骤图

单击上图的 Download Eclipse 按钮，可进入 Eclipse 的下载主页面。读者也可以直接通过下载地址进行下载：http://www.eclipse.org/downloads/。

从图 1-23 中可以看出，Eclipse 开发工具有很多种，如下所示：
- Eclipse IDE for Java Developers：专用于 Java 应用程序的开发，带有 Java IDE、CVS 客户端、XML 编辑器等工具，但对 Java Web 应用系统的开发支持不够，需要另外加装插件。
- Eclipse IDE for Java EE Developers：适合进行 Java 企业级应用系统开发，特别是 Java Web 应用系统的开发，但此工具软件需要 JDK1.5 或更高版本的 JDK 支持。
- Eclipse IDE for C/C++ Developers：C/C++的开发包。
- Eclipse for RCP/Plug-in Developers：专门做插件和 RCP（Rich Client Platform，富客户端平台）开发的开发包。

- Eclipse Classic-3.3.1.1 -Windows：是传统的 Eclipse 下载包，包括 Eclipse 平台，Java 开发工具和插件开发。

为方便开发 Web 程序，这里下载的是 Eclipse IDE for Java EE Developers。在图 1-23 所示的界面中，单击 "Eclipse IDE for Java EE Developers" 即可下载得到。解压缩到某个目录（如 E:\）后就算安装完毕了。解压后的目录结构如图 1-24 所示。

图 1-24 Eclipse 的目录结构

第二步：启动 Eclipse

图 1-24 中的 eclipse.exe 为 Eclipse 的启动程序，单击该文件，可启动 Eclipse，启动窗口如图 1-25 所示。

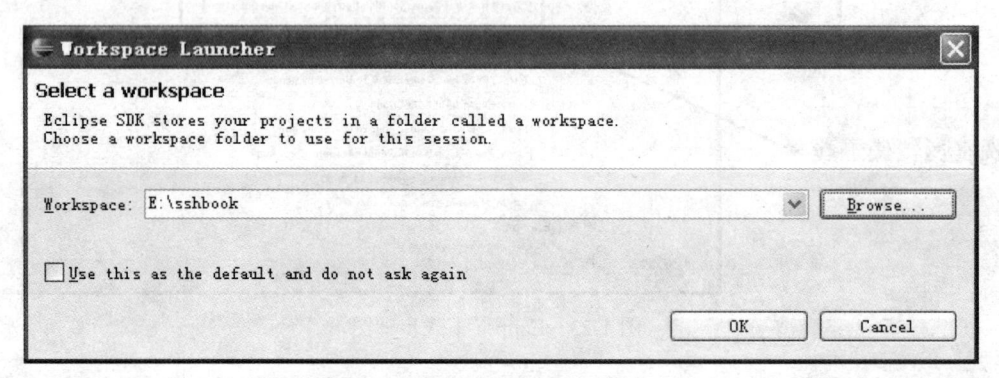

图 1-25 Eclipse 的启动窗口

在图 1-25 中，读者可以指定工作空间（即 Workspace），例如可指定为 E:\sshbook。选中 "Use this as the default and do not ask again" 复选框，可将选中的工作空间作为默认的工作空间，之后不会再有工作空间选择的窗口出现。

第三步：使用 Eclipse

（1）Eclipse 工作窗口。

单击图 1-25 中的 OK 按钮后，将出现 Eclipse 的欢迎界面，单击欢迎界面的关闭窗口后，将出现 Eclipse 的工作主界面，如图 1-26 所示。

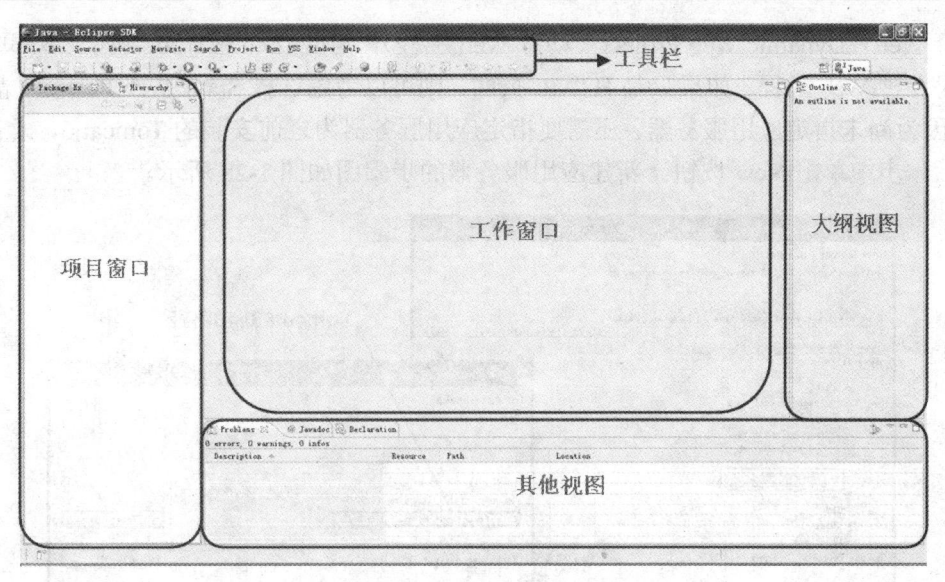

图 1-26 Eclipse 的主界面

（2）新建工程。

新建一个 Web 应用的方法有两种，一种是在工具栏中通过选择菜单命令 File→New→Project，另一种方法是在项目窗口中单击鼠标右键，然后选择 File→New→Project 菜单命令。第一种方式的操作步骤图如图 1-27 所示。

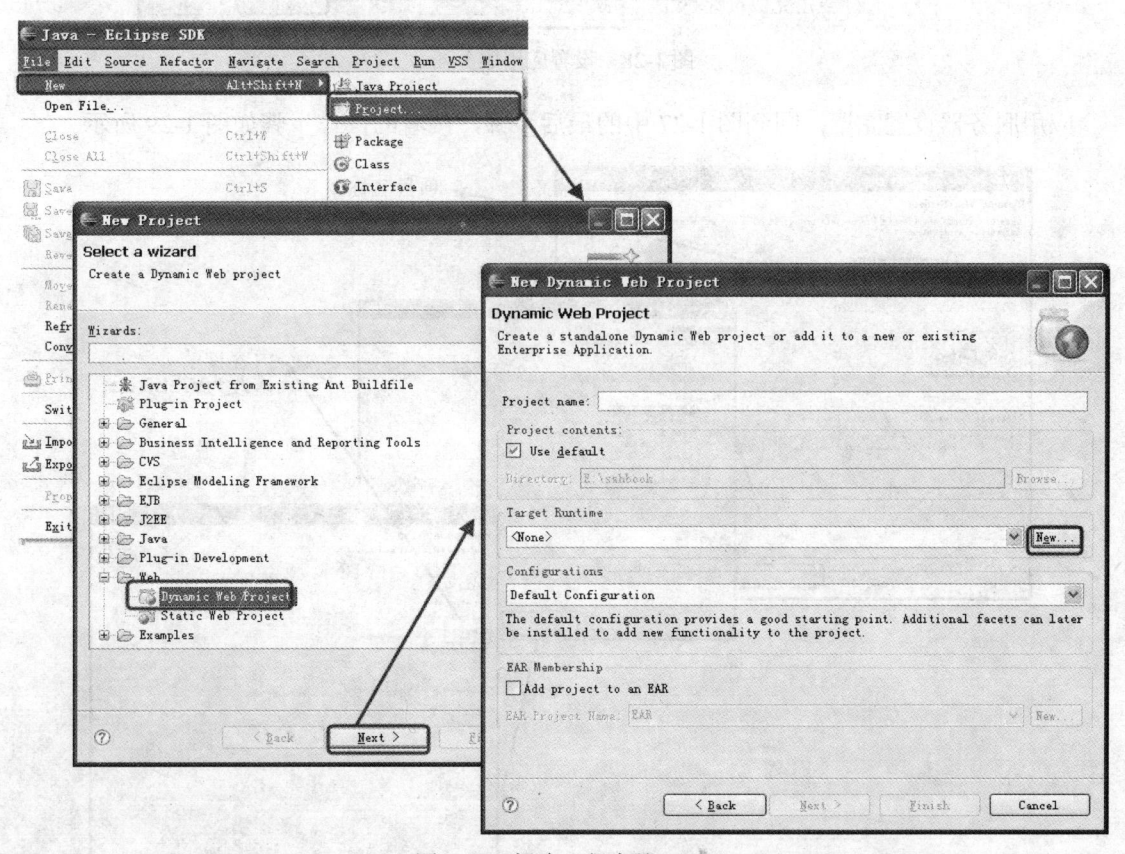

图 1-27 新建工程步骤（1）

选择 Web→Dynamic Web Project（动态 Web 工程），可建立动态 Web 工程。本书中要建立的大都是此种 Web 工程，如果只是 HTML 页面，则可以考虑选择 Static Web Project（静态 Web 工程）。因为尚未指定应用服务器，还需要指定应用服务器为之前安装的 Tomcat 6，读者可在上图的最后一步中单击 New 按钮。新建应用服务器的步骤图如图 1-28 所示。

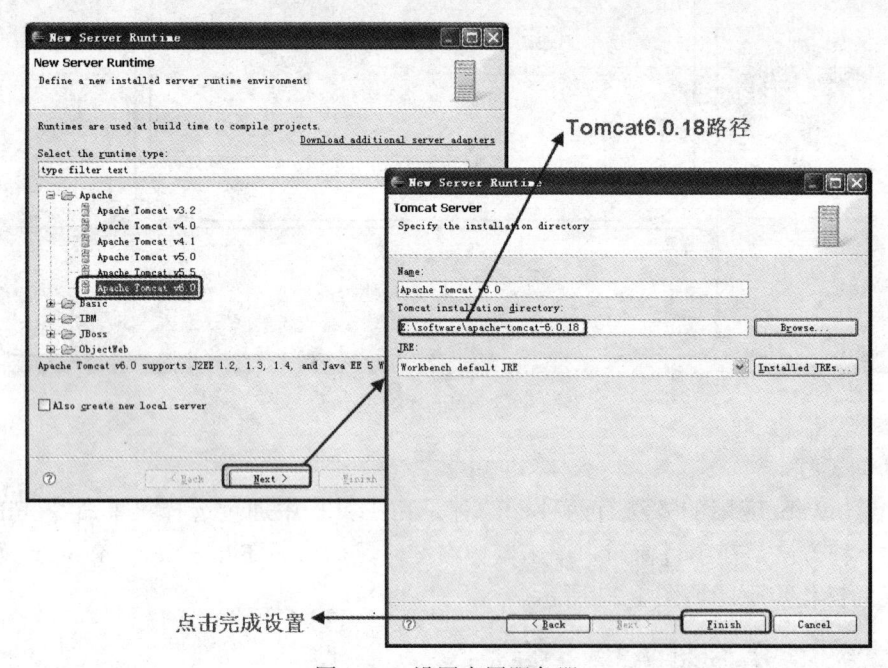

图 1-28　设置应用服务器

应用服务器设置完毕，回到图 1-27 中的最后步骤，接着的操作步骤如图 1-29 所示。

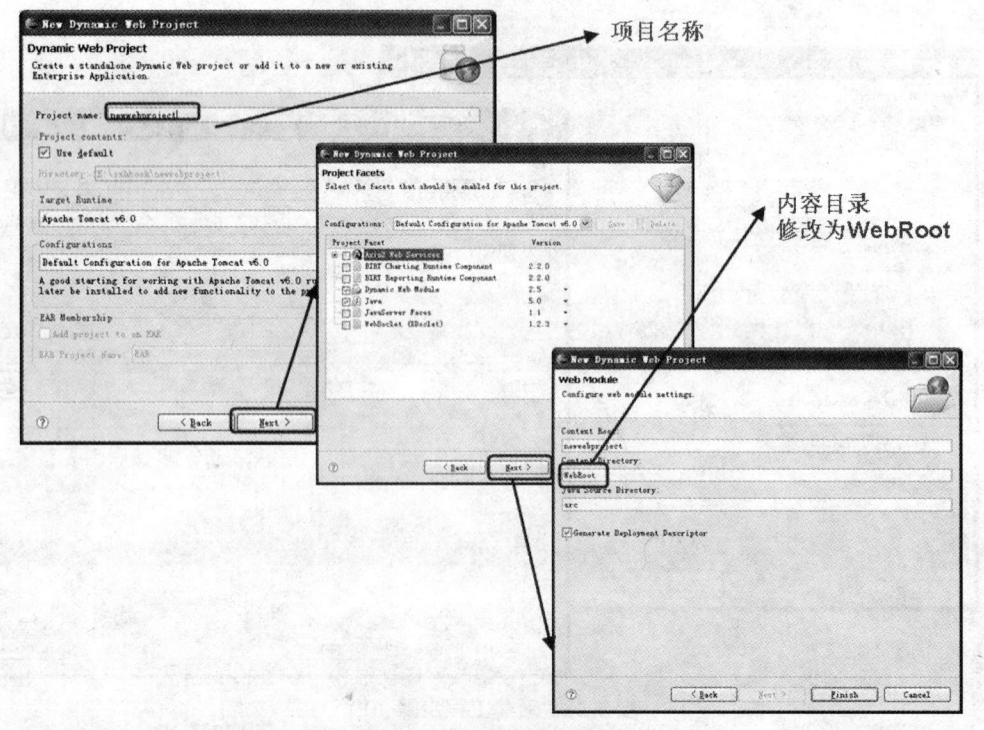

图 1-29　新建工程步骤（2）

在 Project name 后输入工程的名称（例如：newwebproject）。默认情况下新建工程的所有文件都会存放在工作区内。如果想存放到别的目录，不选中 Use default 前的复选框即可。通过下面的路径浏览按钮 Browse 来设置存放工程文件的目录。

在上图中的第二步使用默认设置，在最后一步中，Context Root 设置工程根目录的名称；Content Directory 设置此工程中 Web 应用目录的名称（例如：WebRoot）；Java Source Directory 设置 Java 源码的放置路径。设置完后，单击 Finish 按钮完成新建工程 newwebproject 的创建。创建完的 newwebproject 工程在 Eclipse 的 Project Explorer 中的树形结构图如图 1-30 所示。

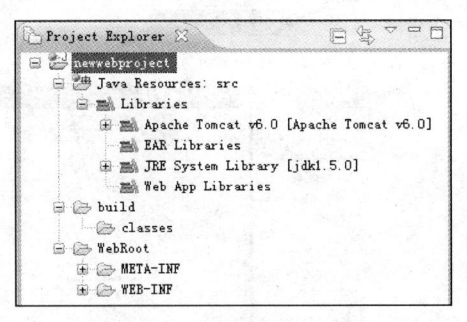

图 1-30　工程的树形结构图

新建的 Java 类或接口的源码将放在 src 目录中，编译后的字节码放在 build/classes 目录中，WebRoot 是 Web 应用的根目录。

（3）新建包。

若要在 src 源码目录下新建 amigo.eclipseuse.test 包，可选择"Java Resources：src"节点后，单击鼠标右键选择 New→Package 命令，在弹出的新建包窗口的 Name 输入框中输入包的名称，操作步骤如图 1-31 所示。

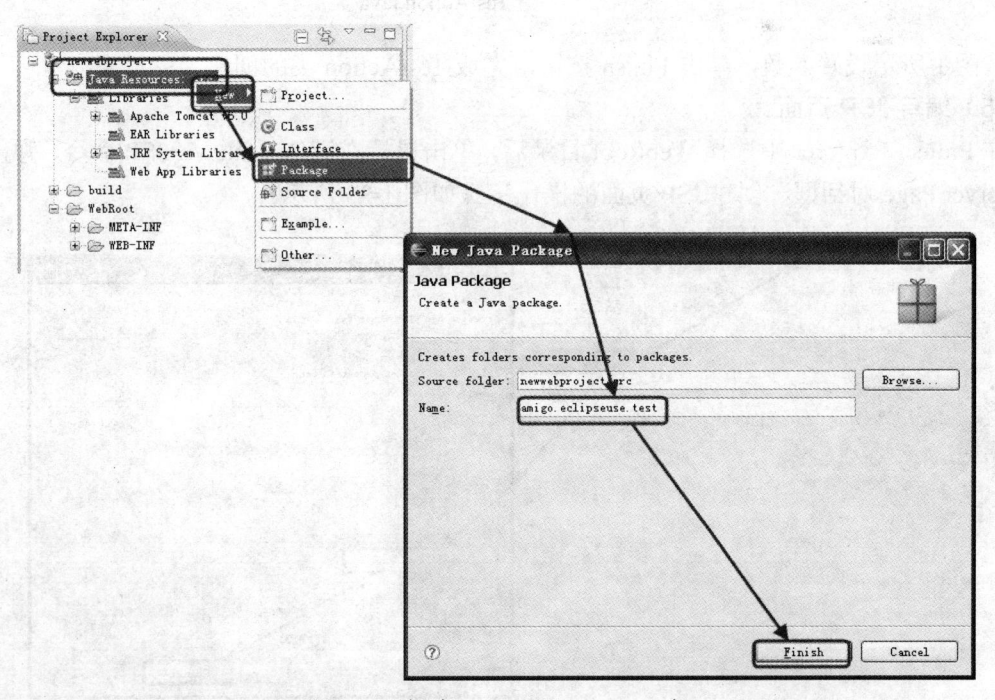

图 1-31　新建 amigo.eclipseuse.test 包

Name 后的文本框中用于输入包的名称，请注意要使用英文标点的"."。
(4) 新建类。

在 Eclipse 的 Project Explorer 子窗口中选中树形菜单的 amigo.eclipseuse.test 包这个节点，单击鼠标右键，在弹出的快捷菜单中选择 New→Class 命令。操作步骤如图 1-32 所示。

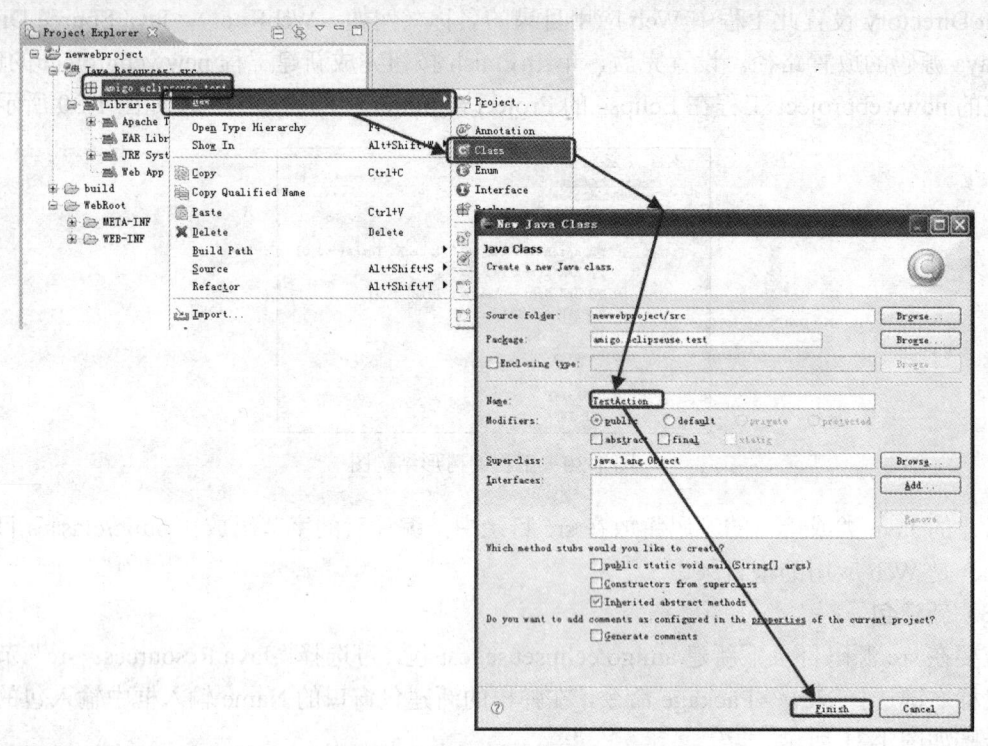

图 1-32　新建 TestAction.java 类

按图中所示设置参数，单击 Finish 按钮，完成 TestAction 类的创建。
(5) 编写 JSP 页面。

在 Project Explorer 中选择 WebRoot 目录后，单击鼠标右键选择 New→JSP 命令，弹出 New JavaServer Page 对话框，创建 JSP 页面的操作步骤如图 1-33 所示。

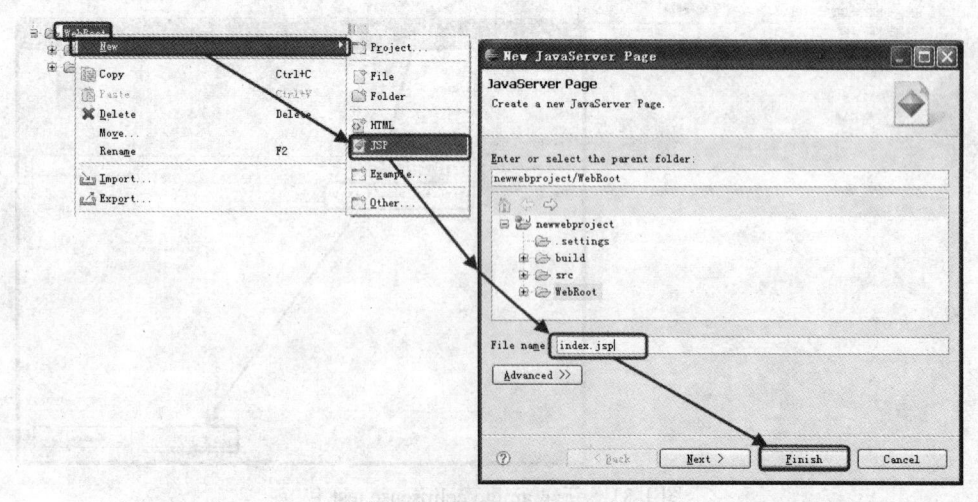

图 1-33　新建 index.jsp 页面

打开新建的 index.jsp 文件,修改其内容如下:

```jsp
<%@ page language="java" contentType="text/html; charset=UTF-8"
    pageEncoding="UTF-8"%>
<!DOCTYPE html PUBLIC "-//W3C//DTD HTML 4.01 Transitional//EN" "http://www.w3.org/TR/html4/loose.dtd">
<html>
<head>
<meta http-equiv="Content-Type" content="text/html; charset=UTF-8">
<title>首页</title>
</head>
<body>
    Hello,阿蜜果
</body>
</html>
```

(6) 调试 Web 工程。

在 Project Explorer 中选中 Web 工程,在常用按钮栏中单击 后向下的小黑箭头,弹出菜单如图 1-34 所示。

图 1-34 Run As 菜单图

选择 Run As→Run on Server 命令,弹出 Run on Server 对话框。在 Run on Server 对话框中选中 Tomcat V6.0 Server at localhost,单击 Next 按钮。在弹出的对话框中选择要调试的 Web 应用,单击 Finish 按钮,即可在 Eclipse 环境中调试运行程序。

在浏览器中输入地址:http://localhost:8899/newwebproject/,界面如图 1-35 所示。

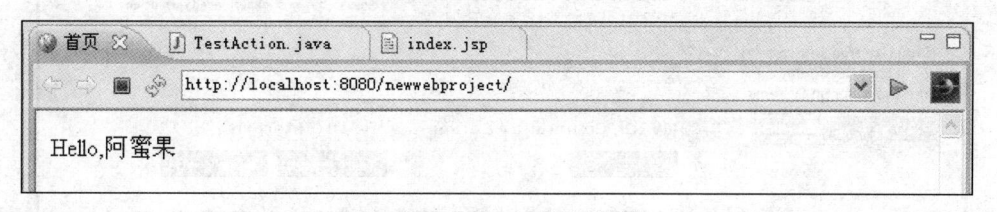

图 1-35 index.jsp 运行效果

Servers 窗口如图 1-36 所示(该窗口可以直接控制 Tomcat 6 的启动、停止,并在 Console 选项卡中报告 Tomcat 6 的控制台输出)。

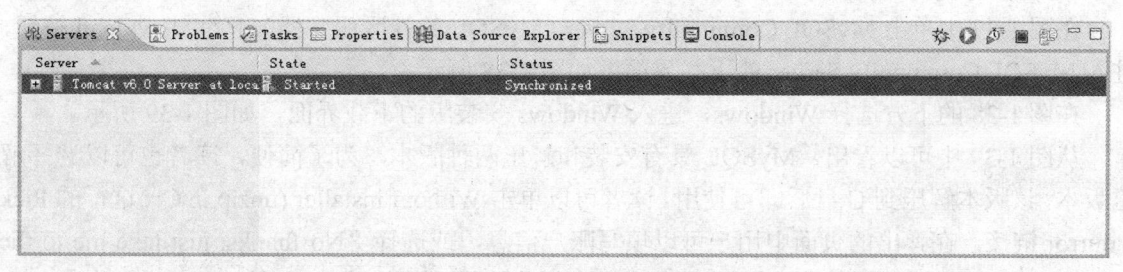

图 1-36 Servers 窗口

【例 1-4】下载和安装 MySQL

〖实例需求〗

MySQL 是一个真正的多用户、多线程的 SQL 数据库服务器，它是一个客户机/服务器（C/S）结构的实现。MySQL 是现在流行的关系数据库中的一种，相比其他的数据库管理系统（DBMS）来说，它具有小巧、功能齐全、查询迅捷等优点，对于一般中小型，甚至大型应用，它都能够胜任。

在本书的各开发实例中，采用的数据库为 MySQL，本实例讲解如何下载和安装 MySQL，并将对使用 MySQL 的控制台窗口进行简单的数据库操作进行讲解。

〖开发过程〗

第一步：下载 MySQL

（1）进入 MySQL 下载主页。

下载首页为：http://dev.mysql.com/downloads/，界面如图 1-37 所示。

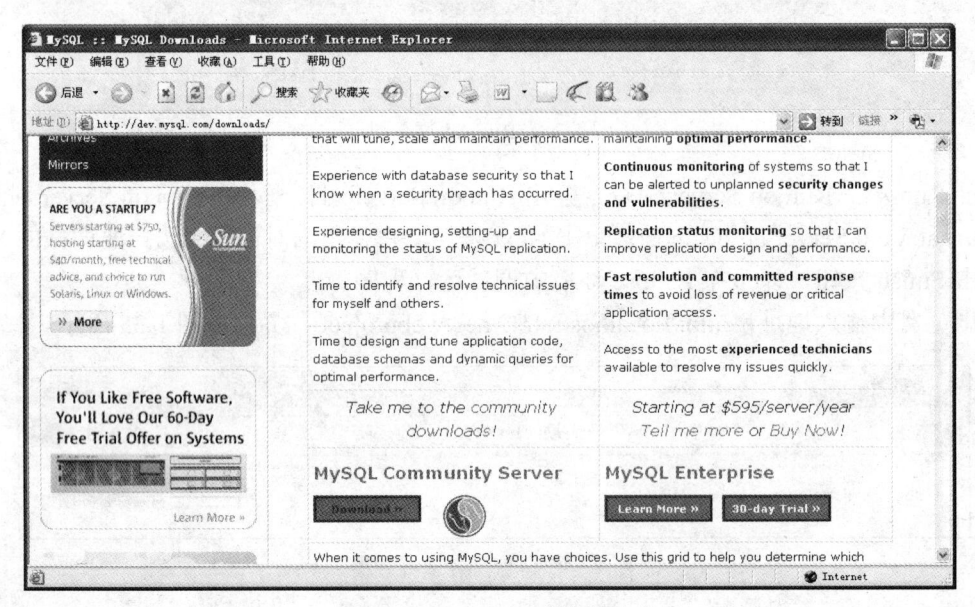

图 1-37　MySQL 下载首页

（2）进入 MySQL Community Server 的 Windows 版本下载界面。

在图 1-37 中单击 MySQL Community Server（MySQL 的社区服务器）下的 Download 按钮，进入 MySQL Community Server 的下载界面，如图 1-38 所示。

在图 1-38 的下方选择 Windows，进入 Windows 安装版的下载界面，如图 1-39 所示。

从图 1-39 中可以看出，MySQL 具有安装和解压两种版本，为了简便，读者也可以选择解压版本，该版本解压到 C 盘后即可使用。读者可以单击 Without installer (unzip in C:\)这行的 Pick a mirror 链接，在弹出的页面中用户可以填写账户信息，或选择"No_thanks, just take me to the downloads!"链接跳过该步骤直接下载，弹出的下载镜像页面如图 1-40 所示。

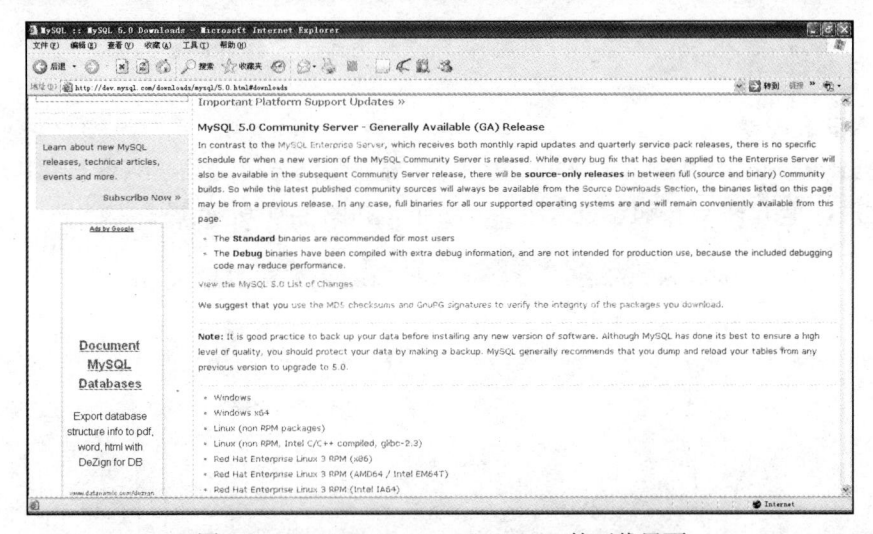

图 1-38　MySQL Community Server 的下载界面

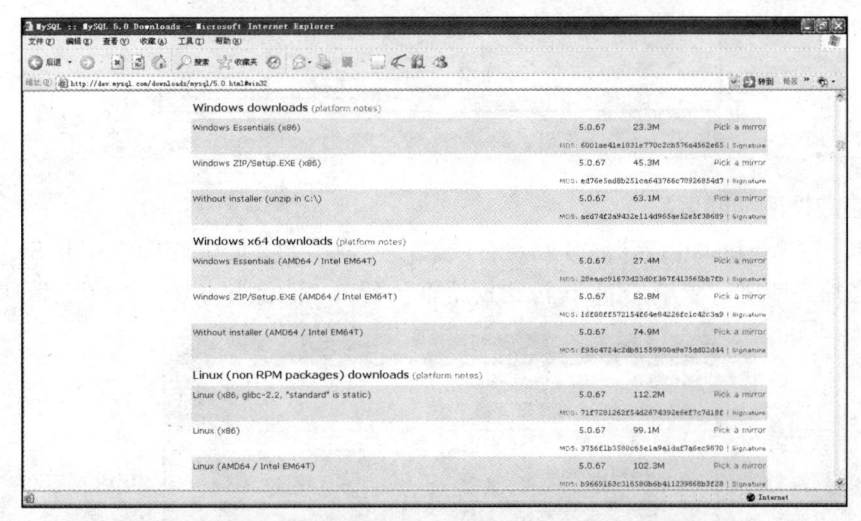

图 1-39　MySQL Community Server 的 Windows 安装下载列表页

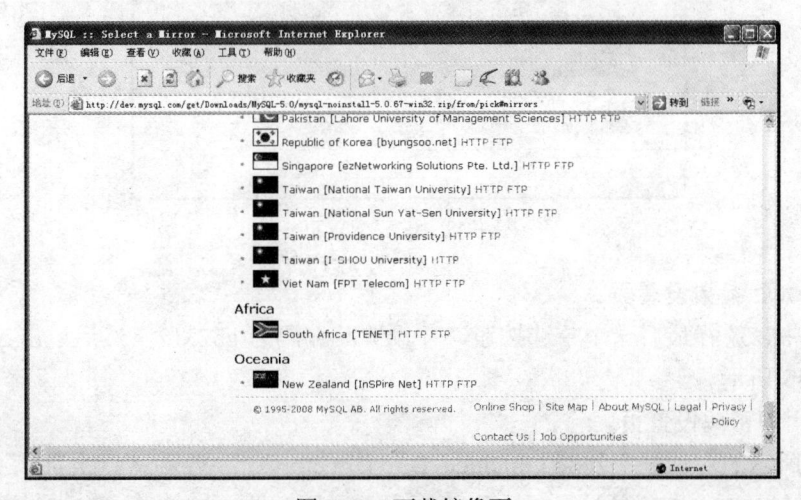

图 1-40　下载镜像页

在图 1-40 中，读者可以选择一个镜像点下载。

第二步：安装 MySQL

（1）进入安装向导。

双击 mysql-essential-5.0.67-win32.msi 文件，弹出安装向导页，单击 Next 按钮，选择安装类型为 Typical 后，单击 Next 按钮，进入准备安装页，如图 1-41 所示。

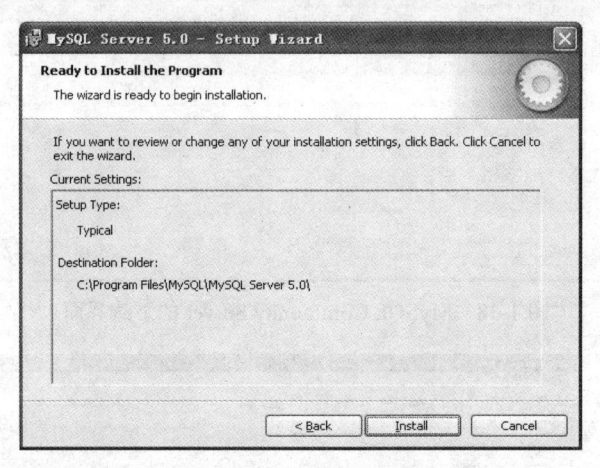

图 1-41　开始安装窗口

（2）设置数据库编码页。

在图 1-41 中单击 Install 按钮后开始进行安装，在弹出的界面中选择"Skip Sigh_up"跳过填写信息，之后各步骤一直单击 Next 按钮使用默认配置，直到显示图 1-42 所示的界面。

图 1-42　编码配置页

（3）Windows 参数设置页。

在图 1-42 中，选择最后一个单选按钮，并设置其编码为 gb2312，然后单击 Next 按钮，弹出界面如图 1-43 所示。

（4）root 用户密码设置页。

在图 1-43 所示的对话框中勾选"Include Bin Directory in Windows PATH"复选框，使得 MySQL 的路径包含在 PATH 环境变量中，而不用再进行配置。接着单击 Next 按钮，弹出的对话框如图 1-44 所示。

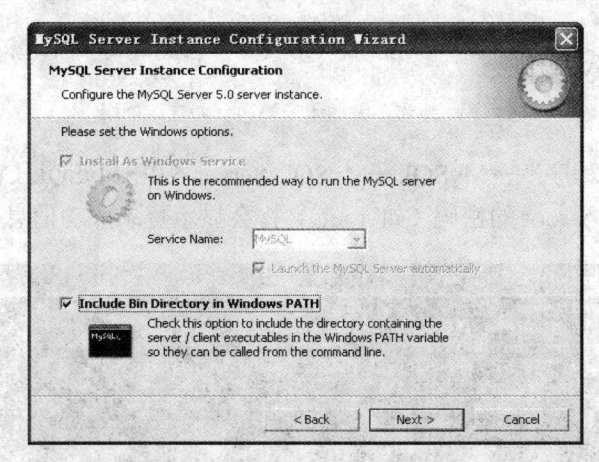

图 1-43 Windows 参数设置页

图 1-44 root 用户密码设置

图 1-44 所示为 MySQL 数据库 root 用户的密码设置，默认的密码为空，在这里笔者设置的 root 用户的密码为 root，接着勾选 "Enable root access from remote machines" 复选框，使得能通过远程主机进行 root 用户的登录，填写完毕后，单击图 1-44 中的 Next 按钮，弹出的界面如图 1-45 所示。

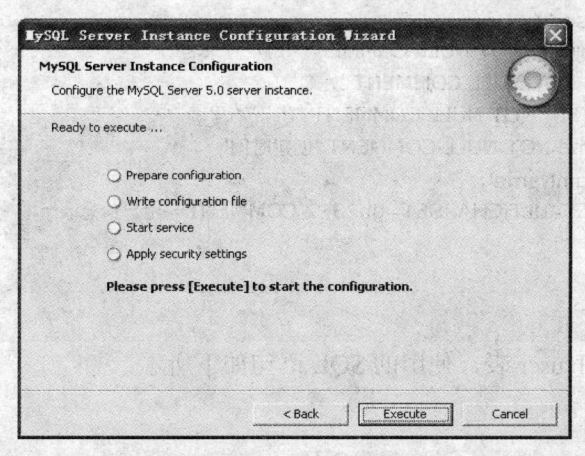

图 1-45 准备执行界面

在图 1-45 中单击 Execute 按钮后，当单选按钮都出现蓝色对勾时安装成功。

第三步：使用 MySQL

（1）登录 MySQL。

选择"开始"→"程序"→MySQL→MySQL Server 5.0→MySQL Command Line Client 命令，在弹出的界面中输入 root 的密码（如 root），将会显示登录成功信息，界面如图 1-46 所示。

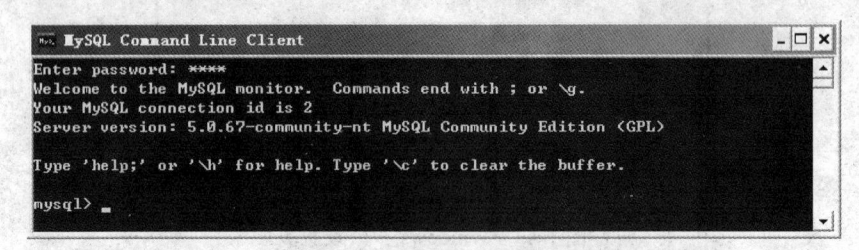

图 1-46　登录 MySQL Server

（2）MySQL 操作数据库。

显示当前 MySQL 所有数据库的命令为：

```
SHOW DATABASES;
```

删除数据库的命令为：

```
DROP DATABASE 数据库名称;
```

创建数据库的命令为：

```
CREATE DATABASE 数据库名称;
```

使用数据库的命令为：

```
USE 数据库名称;
```

（3）MySQL 操作表。

- 创建表

创建表的命令为：CREATE TABLE …，例如想要在 testsql 数据库中创建一个用户信息表 tbl_user，tbl_user 表包括 loginName（用户登录名）、name（姓名）、password（密码）和 createTime（创建时间）字段，对应的 SQL 语句为：

```
USE testsql;

CREATE TABLE 'tbl_user' (
  'loginName' varchar(50) NOT NULL COMMENT '用户登录名',
  'name' varchar(50) NOT NULL COMMENT '姓名',
  'password' varchar(50) NOT NULL COMMENT '登录密码',
  'createTime' datetime NOT NULL COMMENT '创建时间',
  PRIMARY KEY  ('loginName')
) ENGINE=InnoDB DEFAULT CHARSET=gb2312 COMMENT='用户信息表';
```

- 删除表。

删除表的语句为：

```
DROP TABLE 表名称;
```

例如若需要删除 tbl_user 表，使用的 SQL 语句如下所示：

```
DROP TABLE tbl_user;
```

- 修改表名称。

若需要修改表的名称，可以使用 ALTER TABLE 命令，SQL 语句格式为：

```
ALTER TABLE 原表名称 RENAME TO 更改后的表名称;
```

例如需要将 tbl_user 表的名称修改为 t_user，使用的语句如下所示：
ALTER TABLE tbl_user RENAME TO t_user;
- 添加列。

有的时候，需要为某表添加列，使用的 SQL 语句为：
ALTER TABLE 表名称 ADD COLUMN 列名 类型;
例如需要为 tbl_user 表添加 address 字段，对应的语句为：
ALTER TABLE tbl_user ADD COLUMN address VARCHAR(255);
- 改变列的名称。

若需要修改列的名称，使用的 SQL 语句也是 ALTER TABLE…语句，SQL 语句格式为：
ALTER TABLE 表名称 RENAME COLUMN 列的原名称 TO 修改后的列名称;
例如若需要将 tbl_user 表中的 name 字段修改为 username，对应的语句为：
ALTER TABLE tbl_user RENAME COLUMN name TO username;
- 删除列。

当某个表的某字段被弃置不使用时，需要删除该字段，可使用如下语句删除列：
ALTER TABLE 表名 DROP COLUMN 需删除的列;
例如需要删除 tbl_user 表中的 address 字段，对应的 SQL 语句为：
ALTER TABLE tbl_user DROP COLUMN address;
- 创建索引。

有的时候，需要为表的某个字段创建唯一索引，或其他的索引，使用的语句为：
CREATE [UNIQUE] INDEX 索引名称 on 表名称(列1, 列2…) ;
创建索引也可以使用 ALTER TABLE 语句，例如可使用如下语句：
 ALTER TABLE 表名称 ADD [UNIQUE] INDEX 索引名称 (列1, 列2);
UNIQUE 用于指示索引是否为唯一索引。
- 删除索引。

若不再需要某索引时，可使用如下语句将索引删除：
drop index 索引名称;
删除索引也可以使用 ALTER TABLE 命令，SQL 语句为：
alter table 表名称 drop index 索引名称;

【说明】索引是不可更改的，想更改必须删除重新创建。

（4）MySQL 操作表记录。

常用的表记录操作包括查询、添加、修改和删除表记录。下面来看看其各自的用法。
- 查询记录。

查询记录使用 SELECT 语句，基本格式为：
SELECT [字段] FROM 表名称 [WHERE where 条件] [ORDER BY …] [GROUP BY group 条件];
下面来看几个查询记录的实例：

例 1 查询 tbl_user 表中 loginName 包含 amigo 的记录：
SELECT * FROM tbl_user WHERE loginName LIKE '%amigo%';
例 2 按照 tbl_user 表中的 createTime（创建日期）进行升序排序查询记录：
SELECT * FROM tbl_user ORDER BY createTime asc;
例 3 查询 tbl_user 表中的总记录数：
select count (*) as totalcount from table1;
- 添加记录。

添加记录使用 INSERT INTO 命令，格式为：
INSERT INTO 表名称 (字段1, 字段2,…) VALUES (字段1 的值, 字段2 的值，…);

例如需要在用户信息表 tbl_user 中插入一条记录，可使用如下 SQL 语句：
INSET INTO tbl_user (loginName, name, password, createTime) VALUES ('amigo', '谢星星', '123', sysdate());

如果是按照表字段的顺序进行插入，可省掉前面字段的书写，例如前面的 SQL 语句是按照表字段的自然顺序，所以可使用如下简便的 SQL 语句来代替：
INSET INTO tbl_user VALUES ('amigo', '谢星星', '123', sysdate());

- 修改记录。

修改记录的 SQL 语句为 UPDATE 语句，格式如下所示：
UPDATE 表名称 SET 字段1=字段1的值，字段2=字段2的值,…WHERE where 条件

【说明】UPDATE 语句后的 WHERE 条件是可有可无的，当没带 WHERE 条件时，将对所有记录进行更新，若加上 WHERE 条件，将通过条件过滤记录，只有满足条件的记录才会被修改。

例如若要将 tbl_user 表中 loginName 为 amigo 的记录的 name 修改为：阿蜜果，密码修改为：12345678，使用的 SQL 语句如下所示：
UPDATE tbl_user SET name='阿蜜果', password='12345678' WHERE loginName='amigo';

- 删除记录。

删除表记录的语句为 DELETE FROM 语句，SQL 语句格式为：
DELETE FROM 表名称 WHERE where 条件;

【说明】DELETE 语句后的 WHERE 条件是可有可无的，若没带 WHERE 条件时，表示删除表的所有记录，若加上 WHERE 条件，将通过条件过滤记录，只删除满足条件的记录。

例如若要将 tbl_user 表中 loginName 为 amigo 的记录删除，使用的 SQL 语句如下所示：
DELETE FROM tbl_user WHERE loginName='amigo';

小结

本章详细讲解了全书实例的开发与运行环境的安装与配置，以及其使用的相关知识。本书实例采用 JDK1.6+Tomcat 6.0+Eclipse3.3+MySQL5.0 组合，这些软件都是免费开源的版本，并且本章下载的都是本书成稿之日的最新版本，读者可以根据教程一步步学习使用。

Tomcat 和 Eclipse 都需要 JDK 作为基础支持环境。Tomcat 6 实现了 Servlet 2.5/JSP 2.1 规范，Eclipse 适合用于 Java 企业级应用系统的开发，且免费开源，是进行 Java EE 项目开发的首选 IDE。

MySQL 是现在流行的关系数据库，相比其他的数据库管理系统（DBMS）来说，MySQL 具有小巧、功能齐全、查询迅捷等优点，读者可在 MySQL 的官方网站上下载免费的官方版本。在安装时，为了避免中文问题，可以将编码设置为 gb2312 或 UTF-8。还可以在安装时修改 root 用户的密码。常用的针对 MySQL 的操作包括三类，分别为对数据库、对表、对记录的操作，实例【1-4】对这几种常用操作进行了详细讲解。

第 2 篇　Struts 篇

第 2 章　步入 Struts 2 框架开发的殿堂

【本章导读语】

Struts 框架是一种流行的 MVC 框架，掌握这个框架将给 Java EE 项目开发带来诸多方便，从而能成倍地提高开发效率。

例如采用 Struts 框架的 Web 应用能够自动保留表单中的输入数据、能够自动进行常见的数据校验工作、能够通过 OGNL 表达式简化 JSP 页面的代码，另外该框架实现了 MVC 模式，从而使系统具有更好的可维护性，并能适应更大的应用场合等。

要运用 Struts 框架进行 Web 应用开发，第一步就是要搭建 Struts 2 开发环境，本章将采用 Struts 的最新版本 Struts 2，并通过实例详细讲解搭建环境的步骤，和读者一起来开发第一个使用 Struts 2 框架技术的应用：用户登录实例。

【例 2-1】下载 Struts 2

〖实例需求〗

本实例讲解如何下载 Struts 2，并将对 Struts 2 解压后的目录结构进行详细讲解。

〖开发过程〗

第一步：下载 Struts 2

Struts 的下载首页为：http://struts.apache.org/download.cgi，下载列表界面如图 2-1 所示。

从图 2-1 中可以看出，Struts 的最新版本为 2.0.11.2，为方便得到 Struts 的相关资料，建议读者单击"struts-2.0.11.2-all.zip"链接下载"Full Distribution"版本。单击后即可开始下载，完整的下载地址为：http://apache.seekmeup.com/struts/binaries/struts-2.0.11.2-all.zip。

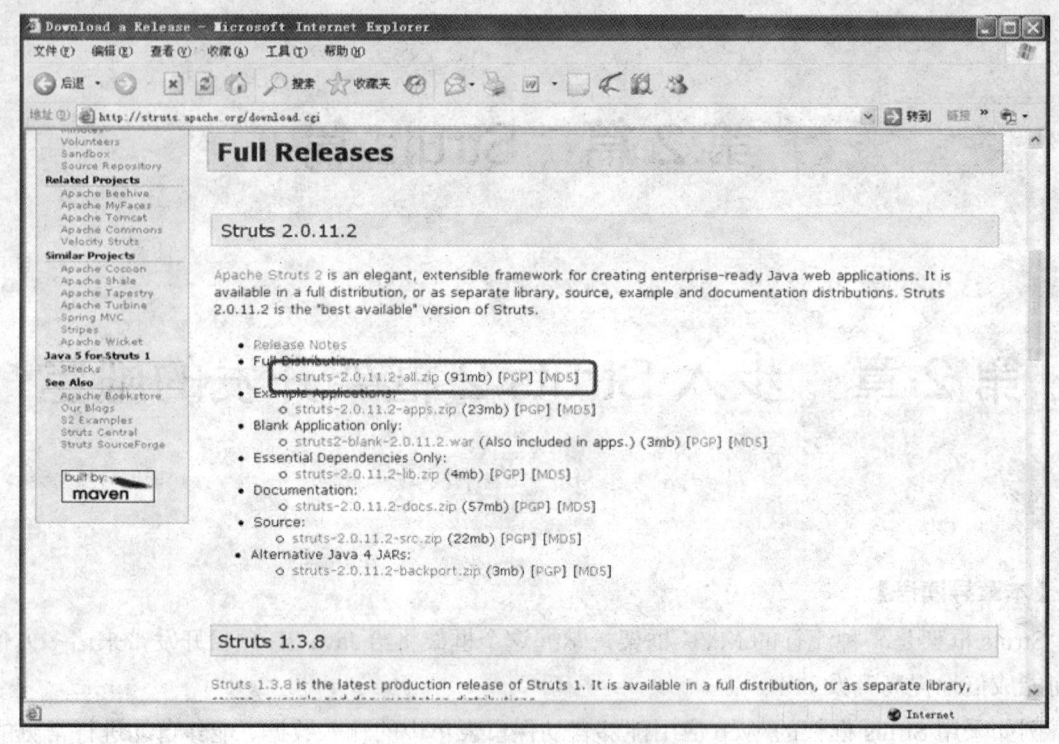

图 2-1 Struts 的下载列表页

【提示】至本书成稿之日，Struts 的最新版本为 2.0.11，读者可自行下载最新的版本。

第二步：Struts 2 目录结构

下载完毕后得到一个 ZIP 压缩文件，解压缩即可得到 Struts 的所有相关资料、源码和 jar 包等。解压后的目录结构如图 2-2 所示。

图 2-2 Struts2 的目录结构

Struts 2 软件包中包括 jar 组件包、API 手册、示例代码等。从图 2-2 中可以看出，文件包中有 5 个文件夹，各文件夹的内容如表 2-1 所示。

表 2-1 Struts 2 压缩包中各文件夹的内容

文件夹名称	文件夹内容
apps	4 个 war 包示例应用，附带有源码，可供读者阅读源码学习
backport	用于 JDK 1.4 版本下的核心类库以及转换工具
docs	javadoc 和在线文档的离线版本，可以双击 index.html 开始阅读
lib	Struts 2 的全部核心类库和依赖包
src	源代码

【例 2-2】搭建 Struts 2 的开发环境

〖实例需求〗

本实例需要搭建起利用 Struts 2 框架开发的工程环境，在 Eclipse 中新建一个工程，以方便本章实例可以开发、运行在这个环境中。在该步骤中需要新建一个名为 strutslogin 的工程，并将所需的 Struts 2 的 jar 包及其依赖包加入到 WEB-INF/lib 目录下，最后还需要在 web.xml 中进行 Struts 2 的相关配置。

〖开发过程〗

第一步：建立工程

按照第 1 章新建工程的方式新建一个名为 strutslogin 的动态 Web 工程，将 WebRoot 设置为工程的根目录。

动态 Web 工程默认的 classes 文件的存放路径为 build/classes 目录，读者可以进行修改，在这里笔者将展示如何将其 classes 目录修改为 WebRoot/WEB-INF/classes 目录。

首先在 WebRoot/WEB-INF 目录下建立 classes 目录，而后选择 strutslogin 工程，单击鼠标右键，选择 Properties 命令，显示属性对话框，操作步骤如图 2-3 所示。

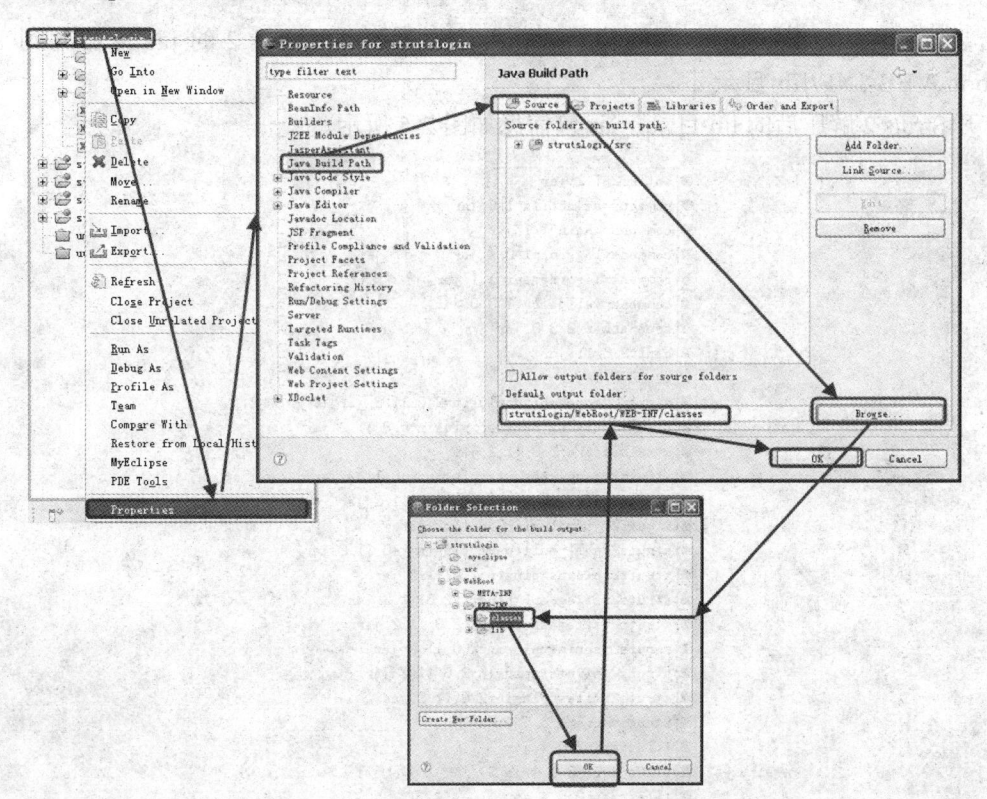

图 2-3　设置编译后 class 文件的存放路径

在图 2-3 的左菜单中选择 Java Build Path，并在右边选择 Source 标签，在默认的输出路径

（Default output folder）下单击 Browse 按钮，选择工程的 WebRoot/WEB-INF/classes 目录。因为此时 build/classes 目录已经没有用处，读者可将该目录删除。

完成配置后的工程结构如图 2-4 所示。

```
strutslogin
    src
    JRE System Library [jdk1.5.0]
    Apache Tomcat v6.0 [Apache Tomcat v6.0]
    WebRoot
        META-INF
            MANIFEST.MF
        WEB-INF
            lib
            web.xml
```

图 2-4　strutslogin 工程的目录结构

其中：

src 目录：存放 Web 应用的所有源代码。
WebRoot 目录：当前 Web 应用所在的目录，可存放各 JSP 页面等。
WebRoot/WEB-INF 目录：存放工程的配置文件等。
WebRoot/WEB-INF/classes 目录：存放 src 目录编译后的 class 文件和配置文件等。
WebRoot/WEB-INF/lib 目录：存放 Web 应用类库的 jar 组件包。

第二步：添加 Struts 2 的 jar 包

若要在工程中加入 Struts 2 的支持，读者首先需要将 Struts 2 的 jar 包加入到工程的 WebRoot/WEB-INF/lib 目录下。

打开 Struts 2 解压后的 lib 目录，jar 包信息如图 2-5 所示。

```
antlr-2.7.2.jar
commons-beanutils-1.6.jar
commons-chain-1.1.jar
commons-logging-1.0.4.jar
commons-logging-api-1.1.jar
commons-validator-1.3.0.jar
freemarker-2.3.8.jar
ognl-2.6.11.jar
oro-2.0.8.jar
struts2-codebehind-plugin-2.0.11.2.jar
struts2-config-browser-plugin-2.0.11.2.jar
struts2-core-2.0.11.2.jar
struts2-jasperreports-plugin-2.0.11.2.jar
struts2-jfreechart-plugin-2.0.11.2.jar
struts2-jsf-plugin-2.0.11.2.jar
struts2-pell-multipart-plugin-2.0.11.2.jar
struts2-plexus-plugin-2.0.11.2.jar
struts2-sitegraph-plugin-2.0.11.2.jar
struts2-sitemesh-plugin-2.0.11.2.jar
struts2-spring-plugin-2.0.11.2.jar
struts2-struts1-plugin-2.0.11.2.jar
struts2-tiles-plugin-2.0.11.2.jar
struts-core-1.3.5.jar
tiles-api-2.0.4.jar
tiles-core-2.0.4.jar
tiles-jsp-2.0.4.jar
xwork-2.0.5.jar
```

图 2-5　struts-2.0.11.2\lib 目录下的 jar 包列表

需要添加到工程中的 jar 包及其说明如表 2-2 所示。

表 2-2 Struts 2 的 5 个重要 jar 包的说明

jar 包	说明
struts2-core-2.0.11.2.jar	Struts 2 的核心包
xwork-2.0.5.jar	XWork 2 库，Struts 2 核心包将其作为底层库存在
ognl-2.6.11.jar	Object Graph Navigation Language（OGNL）的 jar 包，OGNL 是一种类似 EL 的功能强大的表达式语言
freemarker-2.3.8.jar	Struts 2 所有的 ui 标记的模板均使用 freemarker 编写，可通过修改或重写模板使 Struts 2 的 ui 标记按用户的需要进行显示
commons-logging-1.0.4.jar	Apache 的 Commons Logging 包，封装了通用的日志接口，可自动调用 Log4J 或者 JDK 1.4 或者更高版本的 util.logging 日志包

【提示】不同版本的 Struts 的 lib 子目录中的各种 jar 组件包版本可能会有所差异。不要将 Struts 2 软件包 lib 子目录中的所有 jar 组件包放入 WebRoot/WEB-INF/lib 目录中，否则会根本无法发布 Web 应用。因为 Struts 2 发布包中 lib 目录下面的 jar 文件中很多都是插件，并不是构建 Struts 应用所必须的，而这些插件还需要相关的其他组件作支持。

第三步：配置 web.xml

web.xml 位于 WebRoot/WEB-INF 目录下，用于配置 Web 应用，需要 Struts 2 起作用，还需要配置 Struts 2 的过滤器 org.apache.struts2.dispatcher.FilterDispatcher，配置完成后 web.xml 文件的内容如下所示：

```xml
<?xml version="1.0" encoding="UTF-8"?>
<web-app version="2.4"
    xmlns="http://java.sun.com/xml/ns/j2ee"
    xmlns:xsi="http://www.w3.org/2001/XMLSchema-instance"
    xsi:schemaLocation="http://java.sun.com/xml/ns/j2ee
    http://java.sun.com/xml/ns/j2ee/web-app_2_4.xsd">
    <filter>
        <filter-name>struts2</filter-name>
        <filter-class>org.apache.struts2.dispatcher.FilterDispatcher</filter-class>
    </filter>

    <filter-mapping>
        <filter-name>struts2</filter-name>
        <url-pattern>/*</url-pattern>
    </filter-mapping>

    <welcome-file-list>
        <welcome-file>index.jsp</welcome-file>
    </welcome-file-list>
</web-app>
```

第四步：创建 struts 配置文件：struts.xml

Struts 2 的核心配置文件是 struts.xml，它负责管理 Struts 2 框架的 Action，在本实例中详细讲解 Struts 2 的常用配置和需要注意的若干问题。读者需要在工程的源码目录 src 下建立 struts.xml 文件，创建的方法如下：

选择 strutslogin 工程的 src 目录后，单击鼠标右键，弹出快捷菜单，选择 New→Other 命令，弹出新建向导对话框，在弹出的新建窗口中选择 XML→XML，单击 Next 按钮后输入 XML 文件的名称：struts.xml，最后单击 Finish 按钮完成新建。创建 struts.xml 配置文件的操作步骤如图 2-6 所示。

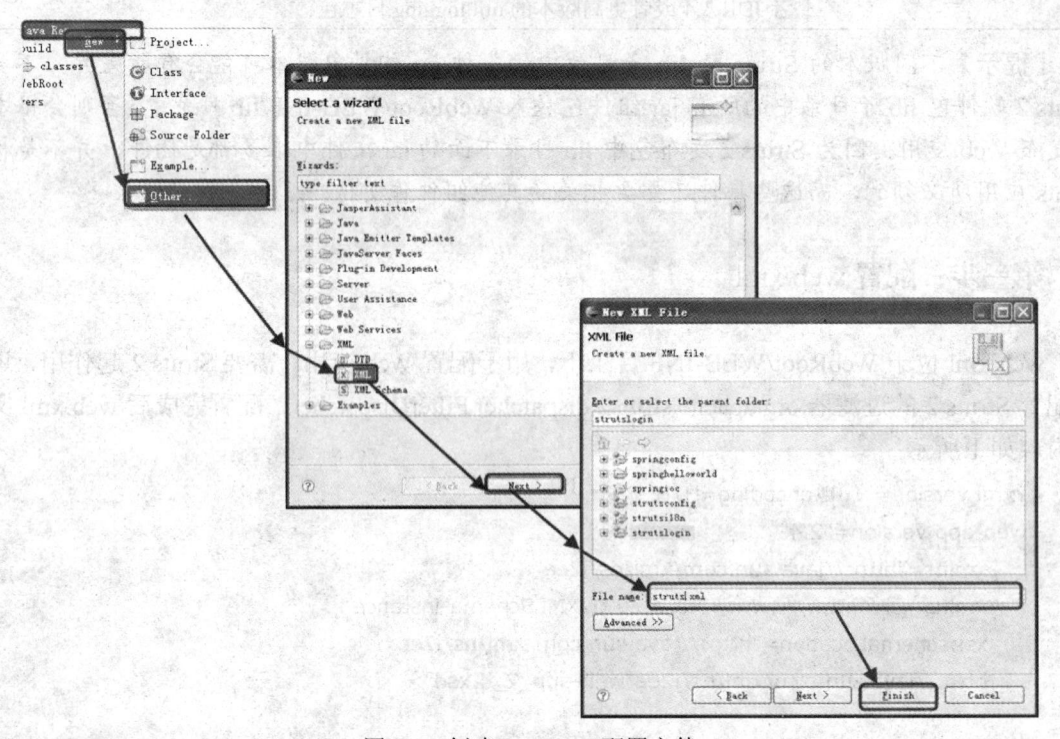

图 2-6 创建 struts.xml 配置文件

（1）修改 struts.xml 文件。

struts.xml 文件创建成功后，还需要修改其内容，该文件的内容如下所示：

```xml
<!DOCTYPE struts PUBLIC
    "-//Apache Software Foundation//DTD Struts Configuration 2.0//EN"
    "http://struts.apache.org/dtds/struts-2.0.dtd">

<struts>
    <include file="struts-default.xml"/>
    <package name="amigo" extends="struts-default">
    </package>
</struts>
```

（2）工程的目录结构。

Struts 2 所需的文件添加完毕之后，工程的目录结构如图 2-7 所示。

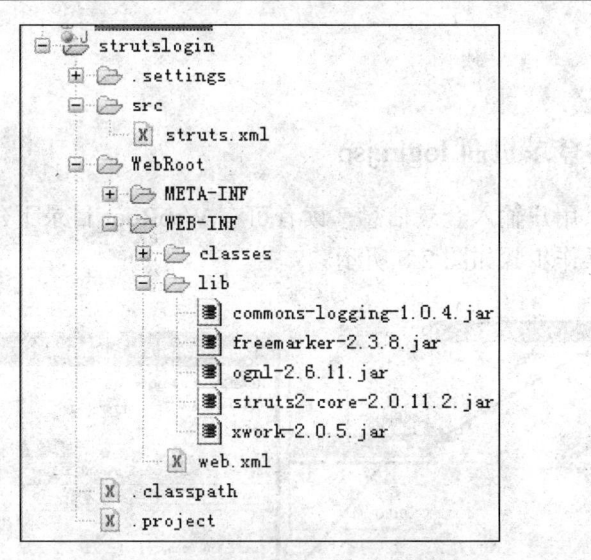

```
strutslogin
├── .settings
├── src
│   └── struts.xml
├── WebRoot
│   ├── META-INF
│   ├── WEB-INF
│   │   ├── classes
│   │   └── lib
│   │       ├── commons-logging-1.0.4.jar
│   │       ├── freemarker-2.3.8.jar
│   │       ├── ognl-2.6.11.jar
│   │       ├── struts2-core-2.0.11.2.jar
│   │       └── xwork-2.0.5.jar
│   └── web.xml
├── .classpath
└── .project
```

图 2-7 添加 Struts 2 工程的目录结构

〖实例剖析〗

在第三步的 web.xml 文件中配置了 FilterDispatcher。
<filter>中的<filter-name>指出了过滤器的名称。
<filter-class>指出过滤器对应的类。
<filter-mapping>中的<url-pattern>指出过滤匹配的 URL 模式，设为/*表示均匹配，这样所有的请求都会过滤，从而通过 FilterDispatcher 查找 actionMapper 的设置来决定请求对应的是哪个 Action。
<welcome-file-list>的<welcome-file>指出进入 Web 应用访问的默认的文件。

【提示】这里的 web.xml 中的配置是相对通用的，读者在工程实践中可以复制这个文件中的内容，再根据需要适当修改即可。

【例 2-3】用 Struts 2 实现用户登录

〖实例需求〗

本实例用于实现用户登录的功能。
当用户名和密码输入正确（都为 amigo）时，跳转到登录成功界面；而当登录失败时，继续跳转到登录界面，提示用户继续输入。
本实例需要提供两个页面，分别为 login.jsp 和 success.jsp，其中 login.jsp 为登录界面，而 success.jsp 为登录成功界面。
另外还需要提供一个登录的 Action 类 LoginAction，该类对登录页面传入的 username 和 password 进行验证，当验证成功时，跳转到登录成功页面 success.jsp，而当登录失败时，跳转到登录页面，并给出输入失败的提示信息。

〖开发过程〗

第一步：编写登录页面 login.jsp

登录页面用于供用户输入登录信息，读者可在 WebRoot 目录下建立登录页面 login.jsp。新建 login.jsp 页面的操作步骤如图 2-8 所示。

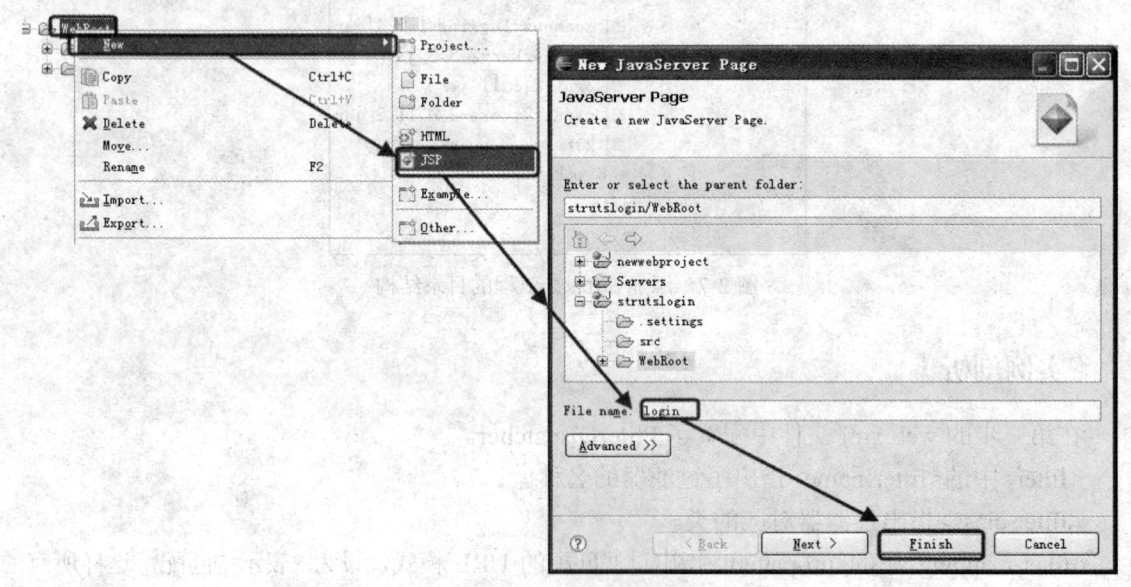

图 2-8 创建 login.jsp 页面

按照图 2-8 所示的步骤创建 login.jsp 页面后，还需要对 login.jsp 文件的代码进行修改，修改后该文件的代码如下所示：

```jsp
<%@ page contentType="text/html; charset=UTF-8" %>
<%@ taglib prefix="s" uri="/struts-tags" %>

<html>
    <head>
        <title>登录系统</title>
    </head>
    <body>
        <div align="center">
            ${requestScope.message}
            <s:form action="Login" method="POST">
                <s:textfield name="loginName" size="20" label="用户名"/>
                <s:password name="password" size="20" label="密码"/>
                <s:submit value="提 交"/>
            </s:form>
        </div>
    </body>
</html>
```

第二步：编写登录成功界面 success.jsp

接着还需要在 WebRoot 目录下创建 success.jsp 页面，操作步骤图如图 2-9 所示。

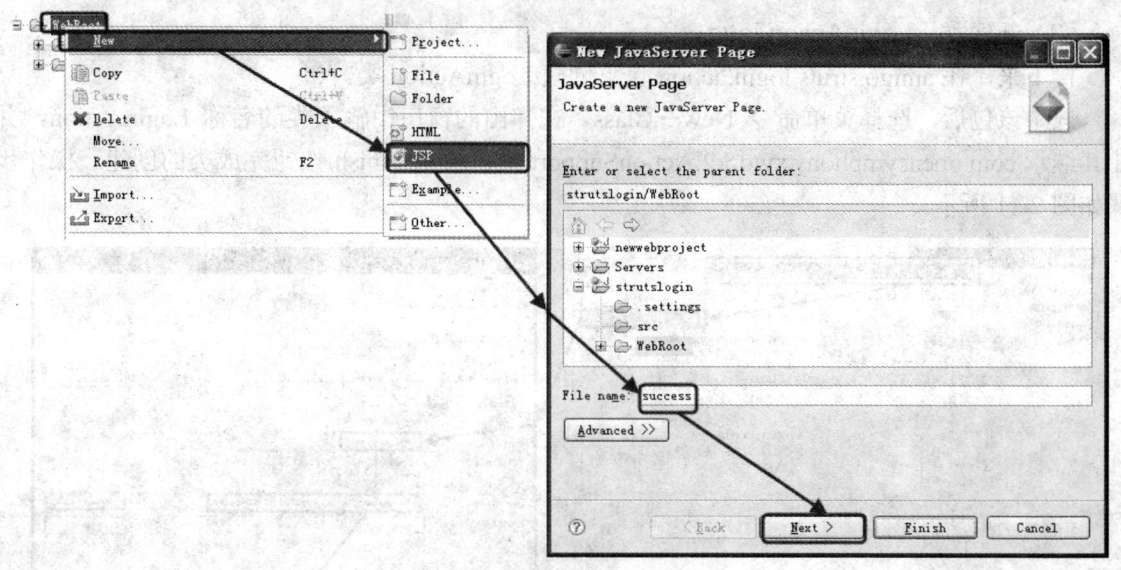

图 2-9　创建 success.jsp 页面

success.jsp 页面的内容很简单，只是简单地输出登录成功的信息，代码如下所示：

```jsp
<%@ page contentType="text/html;charset=UTF-8" %>
<html>
    <head>
        <title>登录成功界面</title>
    </head>
    <body>
        登录成功!
    </body>
</html>
```

第三步：编写登录 Action LoginAction

（1）新建包 amigo.struts.login.action。

在 src 目录中新建包：amigo.struts.login.action，操作步骤如图 2-10 所示。

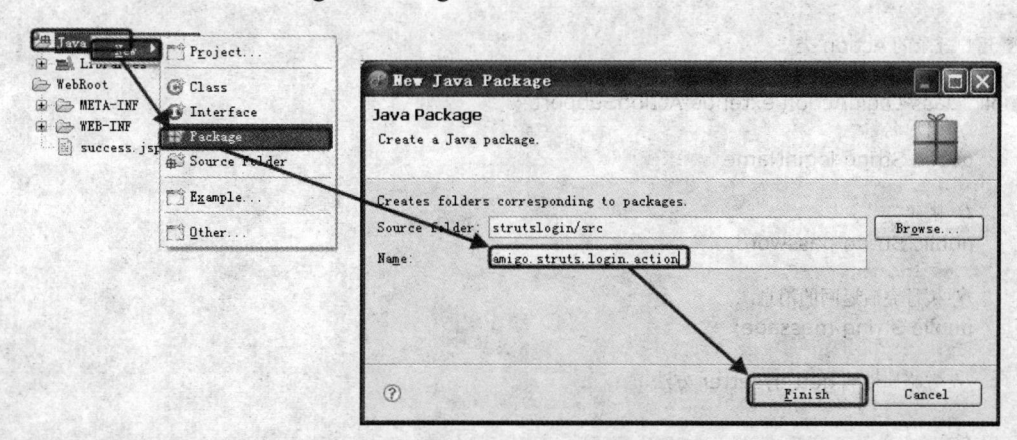

图 2-10　创建 amigo.struts.login.action 包

在 Name 输入框中输入包的名称：amigo.struts.login.action，单击 Finish 按钮，完成包的创建。

（2）新建类：LoginAction.java。

接下来，在 amigo.struts.login.action 包下创建 LoginAction 类。

选中该包后，选择菜单命令 New→Class，在弹出的窗口中输入类的名称 LoginAction，并让其继承 com.opensymphony.xwork2.ActionSupport 类，单击 Finish 按钮完成类的创建。操作步骤如图 2-11 所示。

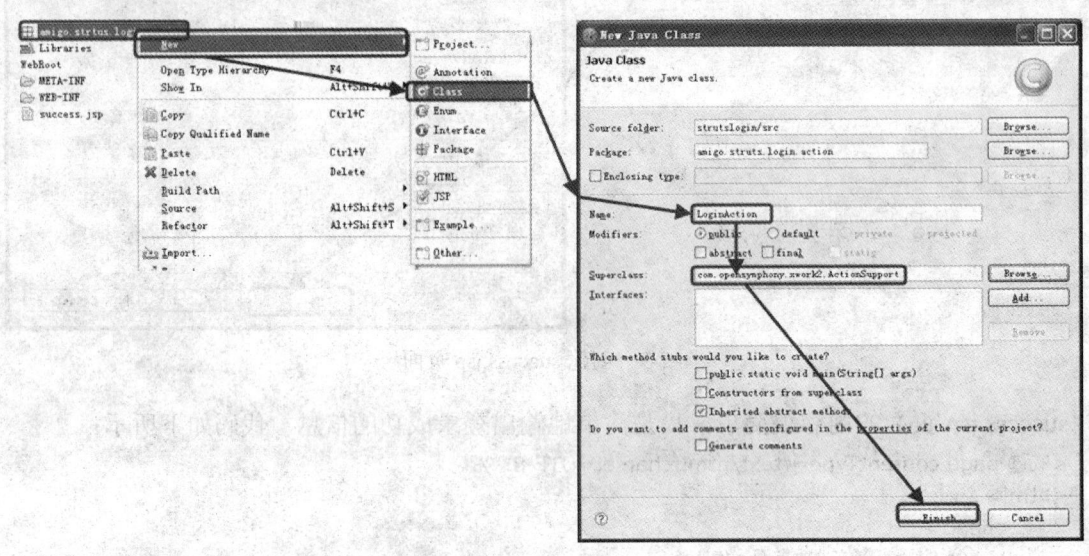

图 2-11　创建 LoginAction 类

（3）修改类：LoginAction.java。

接着修改 LoginAction 类的代码，在该类中包含 loginName、password 和 message 三个属性，其 execute()方法验证用户名和密码是否都为 amigo，若输入正确，message 被赋值为登录成功的信息，否则被置为错误信息。修改后的 LoginAction.java 的代码如下所示：

```java
package amigo.struts.login.action;

import com.opensymphony.xwork2.ActionSupport;

/**
 * 用户登录的 Action 类
 */
public class LoginAction extends ActionSupport {
    // 用户名
    public String loginName;

    // 密码
    public String password;

    // 执行完后返回的消息
    public String message;

    // 省略属性的 getter/setter 方法

    /**
     * 执行用户验证的方法
     */
    public String execute() throws Exception {
        if ("amigo".equals(loginName)
                && "amigo".equals(password))
```

```
                message = loginName + "登录成功！";
            else {
                message = loginName + "登录失败！";
                return INPUT;
            }
            return SUCCESS;
        }
}
```

第四步：修改 Struts 配置文件：struts.xml

最后还需要在配置文件 struts.xml 中配置 LoginAction，并配置跳转成功和失败的页面，修改后的 struts.xml 文件的内容如下所示：

```xml
<!DOCTYPE struts PUBLIC
    "-//Apache Software Foundation//DTD Struts Configuration 2.0//EN"
    "http://struts.apache.org/dtds/struts-2.0.dtd">
<struts>
    <include file="struts-default.xml"/>
<package name="amigo" extends="struts-default">
        <!-- 配置登录的 Action -->
        <action name="Login"   class="amigo.struts.login.action.LoginAction">
            <result>/success.jsp</result>
            <result name="input">/login.jsp</result>
        </action>
    </package>
</struts>
```

第五步：程序完成后工程的目录结构

程序开发完毕后工程的目录结构如图 2-12 所示。

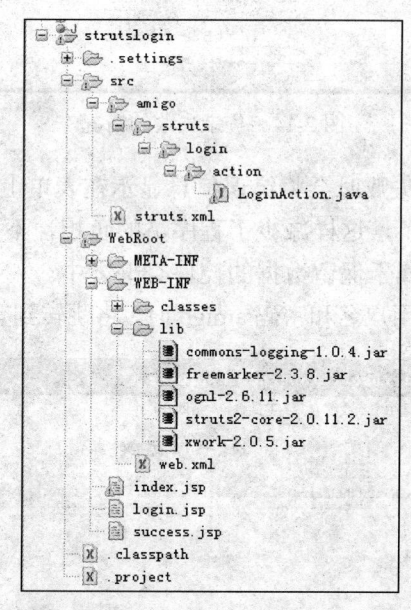

```
strutslogin
├── .settings
├── src
│   ├── amigo
│   │   └── struts
│   │       └── login
│   │           └── action
│   │               └── LoginAction.java
│   └── struts.xml
├── WebRoot
│   ├── META-INF
│   ├── WEB-INF
│   │   ├── classes
│   │   └── lib
│   │       ├── commons-logging-1.0.4.jar
│   │       ├── freemarker-2.3.8.jar
│   │       ├── ognl-2.6.11.jar
│   │       ├── struts2-core-2.0.11.2.jar
│   │       └── xwork-2.0.5.jar
│   ├── web.xml
│   ├── index.jsp
│   ├── login.jsp
│   └── success.jsp
├── .classpath
└── .project
```

图 2-12 开发完毕后工程的目录结构

第六步：运行结果

启动 Tomcat 后，访问 login.jsp 页面，执行结果如图 2-13 所示。

图 2-13　登录页面

输入如图 2-13 所示的错误登录信息后，输入验证将通不过，失败后又会跳转回 login.jsp，显示结果如图 2-14 所示。

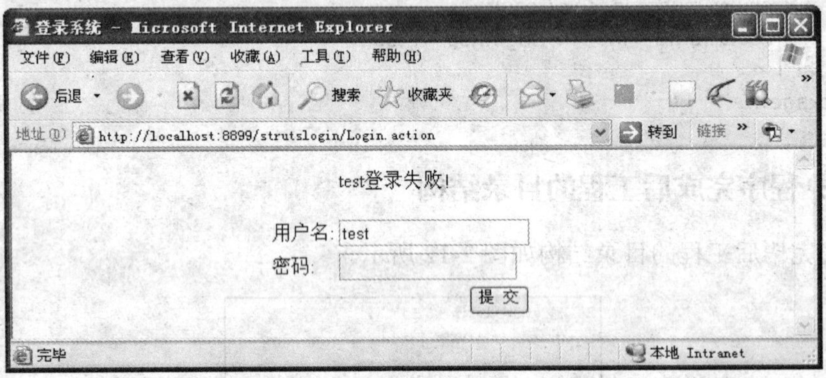

图 2-14　登录失败的情况

从图 2-14 可以看出，登录失败时会将错误信息显示在表单上方。前面输入的用户名在失败后导向的目的页面中仍然保留了，这样减少了程序员的负担，不必再编程实现保留之前已经输入过的数据，但密码输入框不属于保留数据的控件类型之中。

当在图 2-13 中输入正确的用户名和密码 amigo 时，将跳转到登录成功页面，如图 2-15 所示。

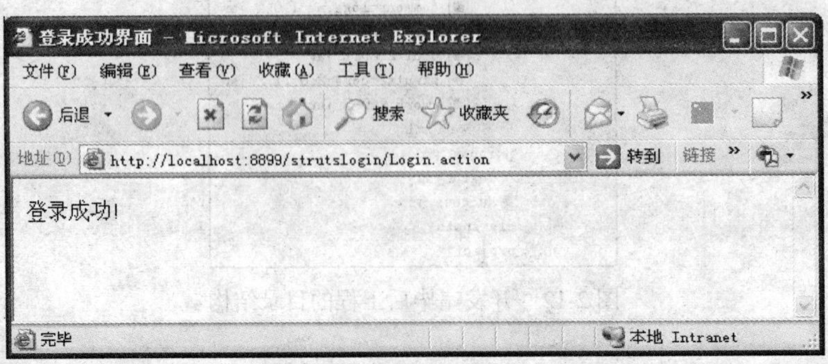

图 2-15　登录成功页面

〖**实例剖析**〗

在编写 login.jsp 时，在文件首部加了如下语句：

```
<%@ taglib prefix="s" uri="/struts-tags" %>
```

该语句用于将 Struts2 的标签引入，并将标签的引用名称设置为 "s"，这样，在使用 Struts 2 的标签时就需要在标签名称前加入 "s:"。

"${requestScope.message}" 是一个 EL 表达式，表示 request 范围内的变量 message 的值。这里的 message 是指在 LoginAction 中用户登录校验失败返回的报错信息，在 Action 中将 message 设为一个属性，用户登录校验失败后，设置 message 属性的值，系统即可将 message 属性的值保存在 request 范围中。

声明一个表单使用<s:form>标签，action 属性值为 Login，Login 是 struts 配置文件中指出的 action 配置的名称。

<s:textfield>标签表示文件输入框，<s:password>标签表示密码输入框；<s:submit>标签表示提交按钮。

在 Struts 2 中，<s:form>、<s:textfield>、<s:password>、<s:submit>这些表单标签会自动生成<table>、<tr>、<td>，login.jsp 最终回传给用户浏览器的代码如下：

```html
<html>
    <head>
        <title>登录系统</title>
    </head>
    <body>
    <div align="center">

    <form id="Login" name="Login" onsubmit="return true;" action="/strutslogin/Login.action" method= "POST"><table class="wwFormTable">
    <tr>
    <td class="tdLabel"><label for="Login_loginName" class="label">用户名:</label></td>
    <td
    ><input type="text" name="loginName" size="20" value="" id="Login_loginName"/></td>
    </tr>
    <tr>
    <td class="tdLabel"><label for="Login_password" class="label">密码:</label></td>
    <td
    <input type="password" name="password" size="20" id="Login_password"/></td>
    </tr>
    <tr>
    <td colspan="2"><div align="right"><input type="submit" id="Login_0" value="提 交"/>
    </div></td>
    </tr>
    </table></form>

    </div>
    </body>
</html>
```

从上面的代码中可以看出，系统自动生成了<form>的 id、name 属性值，值为目标 Action 的名称；<form>的 action 属性值为 "/strutslogin/Login.action"，代码中<s:form>的 action 属性为 "Login"，系统自动作了转换，为表单中的输入控件自动生成了 id 属性值，如果控件有 name 属性值则自动生成的 id 属性值的生成规律为"表单 id 属性值_控件 name 属性值",如果没有 name 属性值则自动生成的 id 属性值的生成规律为"表单 id 属性值_数字 n",数据 n 的值从 0 开始。

在第四步中,<struts>与</struts>之间的内容是 actionMapper 相关的配置。一个 Web 应用系统可能会有相当多的配置,因此需要使用<package>分门别类地进行整理,这种组织方式就好像是 Java 类开发时使用的包。

<action>的 class 属性指出了 Action 对应的类,<result>指出 Action 执行完毕后要导向的目标页面。<result>的 name 表示 Action 的 execute()方法返回的相应字符串。如果没有指出 name 属性值,则默认为"success"。

execute()方法有两种返回值:INPUT 或 SUCCESS。SUCCESS 和 INPUT 都在 com.opensymphony.xwork2.Action 接口中进行了定义,类型为 String,分别用来表示输入("input")和成功("success")。com.opensymphony.xwork2.ActionSupport 类实现了该接口,而 LoginAction 类继承 ActionSupport 类,故此可以直接使用这两个变量。

小结

搭建 Struts 2 开发环境主要有 4 个步骤:第一步是建立工程,第二步是要在工程中加入所要用到的 jar 包,其中 5 个 Struts 2 的核心 jar 包如下所示:

- struts2-core-2.0.11.jar
- xwork-2.0.4.jar
- ognl-2.6.11.jar
- freemarker-2.3.8.jar
- commons-logging-1.0.4.jar

第三步是配置 web.xml,将 Struts 2 的过滤器加入到其中,以便在请求时,能经过该过滤器进行过滤。Struts 2 的核心配置文件为 struts.xml,它负责管理 Struts 2 框架的 Action。

第四步是配置 struts 的配置文件 struts.xml,它是 Struts 2 的核心配置文件,负责管理 Struts 2 框架的 Action。

要实现用户登录功能,需要 4 个步骤,包括编写登录界面 login.jsp、编写登录成功界面 success.jsp、编写登录的 Action 类 LoginAction、修改 Struts 2 的配置文件 struts.xml。Struts 2 实现了 MVC 设计模式,基于 Struts 2 编写出来的系统具有良好的可重用性和可维护性,Struts 2 框架也给程序员的开发带来了许多帮助,可降低程序员的劳动强度。

第 3 章　配置文件

【本章导读语】

为了在 Web 应用中加入 Struts 2，需要在 web.xml 中进行 Struts 2 过滤器的设置。本章将讲述 web.xml 的配置，包括 Struts 2 过滤器的配置、标签库的设置、欢迎页面和错误页面的设置。

struts.xml 是 Struts 2 的核心配置文件，它用于管理 Web 应用中的 Action 配置。本章将讲述其常用的配置，例如<include>元素、<package>元素、<action>元素等的配置。

struts.properties 为 Struts 2 的另一个核心配置文件，它用于配置 Struts 2 框架的各个属性。本章将讲解其常用属性，例如编码（struts.i18n.encoding）、本地化（struts.locale）等常量的设置。

struts.properties 的各配置项都来自 default.properties，Struts 2 为这些配置项设置了默认值。本章最后的实例对常用配置项的默认值进行了详细说明，从而使读者在配置 struts.properties 时有一个参考。

【例 3-1】配置 web.xml

〖实例需求〗

任何 MVC 框架在与 Web 应用进行整合时，都是借助于 web.xml 的配置，例如 Struts 1.x 等。Struts 2 也不例外，它需要在 web.xml 中配置 FilterDispatcher，本实例讲解在加入 Struts2 作为 MVC 框架的 Web 项目中如何配置 web.xml 文件。

〖开发过程〗

第一步：建立工程：strutsconfig

按照第 1 章新建工程的方式新建一个名为 strutsconfig 的动态 Web 工程，将 WebRoot 设置为工程的根目录，并设置 classes 文件的存放路径为：WebRoot/WEB-INF/classes。

第二步：导入包

读者还需要将上一章所需的如下 jar 包加入到工程的 WEB-INF/lib 目录中：
- struts2-core-2.0.11.2.jar
- xwork-2.0.5.jar
- ognl-2.6.11.jar
- freemarker-2.3.8.jar
- commons-logging-1.0.4.jar

加入 jar 包后，工程结构如图 3-1 所示。

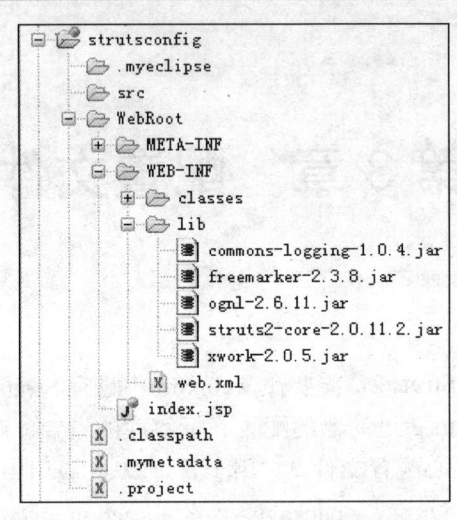

图 3-1 strutsconfig 工程的目录结构

第三步：配置 web.xml 文件

一般的 MVC 框架都需要与 Web 应用整合，需要在 web.xml 文件中加入一些配置，例如 Struts 1.2、JSF 等，Struts 2 也不例外，不过它与 Struts 1.2 又有些不同。Struts 1.2 需要在 web.xml 中配置 org.apache.struts.action.ActionServlet 才能被应用加载。而对于 Struts 2，web.xml 中需要负责加载 FilterDispatcher。修改后的 web.xml 文件如下所示：

```xml
<?xml version="1.0" encoding="UTF-8"?>
<web-app version="2.4"
    xmlns="http://java.sun.com/xml/ns/j2ee"
    xmlns:xsi="http://www.w3.org/2001/XMLSchema-instance"
    xsi:schemaLocation="http://java.sun.com/xml/ns/j2ee
    http://java.sun.com/xml/ns/j2ee/web-app_2_4.xsd">
    <filter>
        <filter-name>struts2</filter-name>
        <filter-class>org.apache.struts2.dispatcher.FilterDispatcher</filter-class>
    </filter>

    <filter-mapping>
        <filter-name>struts2</filter-name>
        <url-pattern>/*</url-pattern>
    </filter-mapping>

    <welcome-file-list>
        <welcome-file>index.jsp</welcome-file>
    </welcome-file-list>
</web-app>
```

在配置 FilterDispatcher 时，可以通过<init-param/>标签为 Filter 配置初始化参数。例如可通过如下方式配置 configProviders 参数：

```xml
<filter>
    <filter-name>struts2</filter-name>
    <filter-class>org.apache.struts2.dispatcher.FilterDispatcher</filter-class>

    <!-- 配置 Struts 2 框架的配置提供者类-->
```

```xml
        <init-param>
            <param-name>configProviders</param-name>
            <param-value>amigo.struts.config.MyConfigurationProvider</param-value>
        </init-param>

        <!-- 配置 Struts 2 默认加载的 Action 包结构-->
        <init-param>
            <param-name>actionPackages</param-name>
            <param-value>org.apache.struts2.showcase.person</param-value>
        </init-param>
    </filter>
```

比较重要的几个参数如下所示：

config：该参数用于指定 Struts 2 的系统配置文件，多个文件时，以英文逗号（,）隔开。

configProviders：Struts 2 框架的配置提供者类，如果开发人员需要指定自己的配置提供者类时，可以使用这个参数，该参数的值为类名。

actionPackages：该参数用于设置默认加载的 Action 的包结构。Struts 框架将会扫描这些包结构下的 Action 类，当有多个包结构需要设置时，以英文逗号（,）隔开。

<filter-mapping>用于配置拦截器所拦截的 URL，在本实例中，使用如下配置将拦截所有的 URL：

```xml
<filter-mapping>
    <filter-name>struts2</filter-name>
    <url-pattern>/*</url-pattern>
</filter-mapping>
```

<url-pattern>设置为"/*"表示拦截所有的用户请求。

【说明】对于 Servlet 2.4 及其后续的版本，会自动加载 Struts 2 的标签文件，因此不需要在 web.xml 文件中配置加载 Struts 2 标签库。而对于之前的版本，需要在 web.xml 文件中进行配置。Struts 2 的标签库文件 struts-tags.tld 位于 struts2-core-2.0.11.2\META-INF 目录下，该文件前面的内容如下所示：

```xml
<?xml version="1.0" encoding="UTF-8" standalone="no"?>
<!DOCTYPE taglib PUBLIC "-//Sun Microsystems, Inc.//DTD JSP Tag Library 1.2//EN"
"http://java.sun.com/dtd/web-jsptaglibrary_1_2.dtd">
<taglib>
    <tlib-version>2.2.3</tlib-version>
    <jsp-version>1.2</jsp-version>
    <short-name>s</short-name>
    <uri>/struts-tags</uri>
    ……
</taglib>
```

从上面可以看出，uri 被指定为：/struts-tags，因此读者可以在 Servlet 2.4 及其后续版本的 JSP 页面中直接使用此默认的 uri，而不需要另外配置。

对于前续版本，读者可将标签库文件 struts-tags.tld 复制到 WebRoot/WEB-INF 目录中，接着需要在 web.xml 中配置如下内容：

```xml
<!--Servlet 2.4 以前的版本，需要手动配置 Struts 2 的标签库_>
<taglib>
    <taglib-uri>/s</taglib-uri>
    <taglib-location>/WEB-INF/struts-tags.tld</taglib-location>
</taglib>
```

使用<welcome-file-list>元素来配置欢迎界面，例如在 web.xml 中配置如下信息：

```
<welcome-file-list>
    <welcome-file>index.jsp</welcome-file>
    <welcome-file>index.html</welcome-file>
    <welcome-file>welcome.html</welcome-file>
</welcome-file-list>
```

这样配置时，当用户没有带上访问页面信息访问根目录时，将自动去找根目录下的 index.jsp 页面，若 index.jsp 页面也不存在，则继续根据配置信息寻找 index.html 页面。找到了配置的页面时，将内容显示给用户。

error-page 用于配置错误界面，可以通过错误码来配置 error-page，其内容如下所示：

```
<error-page>
    <error-code>500</error-code>
    <location>/error.jsp</location>
</error-page>
```

上面配置了当系统发生 500 错误（即服务器内部错误）时，跳转到错误处理页面 error.jsp。还可以通过异常类型来配置 error-page，其内容如下所示：

```
<error-page>
    <exception-type>java.lang.NullException</exception-type>
    <location>/error.jsp</location>
</error-page>
```

上面配置了当系统发生 java.lang.NullException（即空指针异常）时，跳转到错误处理页面 error.jsp。

【例 3-2】配置 struts.xml

【实例需求】

Struts 2 的核心配置文件是 struts.xml，它负责管理 Struts 2 框架的 Action。在本实例中详细讲解 Struts 2 的常用配置和需要注意的若干问题。

【开发过程】

第一步：创建 struts.xml 文件

struts.xml 一般在工程的 src 目录中创建，运行时，该文件将被自动加载到 WebRoot/WEB-INF/classes 目录中，该 xml 文件的根元素为<struts>元素，初始时该文件的内容如下所示：

```
<!DOCTYPE struts PUBLIC
    "-//Apache Software Foundation//DTD Struts Configuration 2.0//EN"
    "http://struts.apache.org/dtds/struts-2.0.dtd">

<struts>
</struts>
```

第二步：struts.xml 的常用配置

（1）<include>标签的使用。

当工程比较大时，会使struts.xml的配置过多，文件过于臃肿，此时为了增强可读性和更容易地维护配置信息，读者可将配置分模块或分功能放在不同的struts配置文件中，同时，使用struts.xml中的<include>标签来将其余的配置文件包括进来。

下面的实例中，struts.xml文件使用<include>标签引入了一个struts配置文件struts-web.xml和一个后台管理的struts配置文件struts-backend.xml。

其中struts-web.xml文件的内容如下所示：

```xml
<!DOCTYPE struts PUBLIC
    "-//Apache Software Foundation//DTD Struts Configuration 2.0//EN"
    "http://struts.apache.org/dtds/struts-2.0.dtd">

<struts>
    <package name="web" extends="struts-default">
     <action name="userLogin" class="amigo.struts.config.UserAction">
        <result>main.jsp</result>
     </action>
    </package>
</struts>
```

struts-backend.xml文件的内容如下所示：

```xml
<!DOCTYPE struts PUBLIC
    "-//Apache Software Foundation//DTD Struts Configuration 2.0//EN"
    "http://struts.apache.org/dtds/struts-2.0.dtd">

<struts>
    <package name="backend" extends="struts-default">
     <action name="userManage" class="amigo.struts. config. UserAction">
        <result>userList.jsp</result>
     </action>
    </package>
</struts>
```

struts.xml中使用了<include>标签，完整内容如下所示：

```xml
<!DOCTYPE struts PUBLIC
    "-//Apache Software Foundation//DTD Struts Configuration 2.0//EN"
    "http://struts.apache.org/dtds/struts-2.0.dtd">

<struts>
    <include file="struts-backend.xml"/>
    <include file="struts-web.xml"/>
    <package name="totalConfig" extends="struts-default">
    </package>
</struts>
```

（2）<package>标签的使用。

在（1）的例子中读者可以看到，它使用了<package>标签，它类似于 Java 中的包。它与 Java 中的对象一样可以包含多个文件，不过 Java 中的包是不可继承的，而 Struts 中的包是可继承的。

在使用 Sturts 2 的过程中，读者可将 Action 分类到不同的 package 中，当某个包需要使用到另一个包的拦截器和 action 时，可以使用<package>标签继承另一个包。

在（1）的例子中读者可以看到 extends="struts-default"，说明 struts.xml、struts-backend.xml 和 struts-web.xml 文件都继承了 struts-default 这个包。事实上，struts-default 这个包是由 struts 2 自带的，它位于 struts2-core-2.0.8.jar 包，解开该 jar 包后，目录结构如图 3-2 所示。

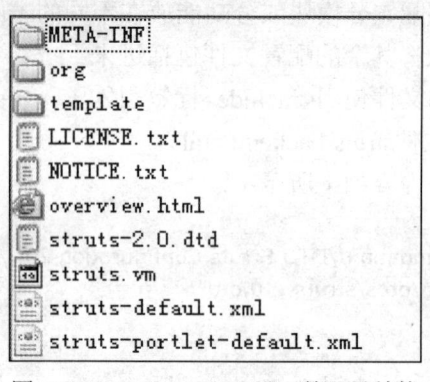

图 3-2　struts2-core-2.0.8.jar 的目录结构

从图3-2中，读者可以看到它包含了一个struts-default.xml文件，打开该文件后，可看到第51行及后续的各行有如下内容：

```
<package name="struts-default">
    <result-types>
        <result-type name="chain" class="com.opensymphony.xwork2.ActionChainResult"/>
        <result-type name="dispatcher" class="org.apache.struts2.dispatcher.ServletDispatcherResult" default="true"/>
        ……
    </result-types>
    ……
</package>
```

在此处定义了一个名为 struts-default 的包，它为应用程序提供了大量默认的配置，所以一般读者在定义包时，都需要继承 struts-default 这个包。Struts 2 框架会自动加载 struts-default.xml 文件。

<package>标签的属性如表 3-1 所示。

表 3-1　<package>标签的属性

属性	是否必须	说明
name	Yes	package 的名称，用于供其他 package 引用
extends	No	表示该包从哪个包继承
namespace	No	命名空间，使用 namespace 可避免 action 重名的冲突
abstract	No	定义这个包是否为抽象的，值可为 true 和 false，默认为 false，为 true 时表示该 package 不需要定义 action

（3）<action>标签的使用。

<action>标签用于将一个请求对应到一个Action处理上去，每当一个Action类匹配一个请求的时候，这个Action类就会被Struts 2框架调用。

<action>标签的常用属性如表3-2所示。

表 3-2 <action>标签的常用属性

属性	是否必须	说明
name	Yes	action 的动作别名，其值与其 package 的 namespace 来唯一区分 Action
class	Yes	对应的 Action 类
method	No	动作指向的 Action 类的对应方法

例：配置名为userLogin：

```
<action name="userLogin" class="amigo.struts.config.UserAction">
    <result>main.jsp</result>
</action>
```

这个动作将名为userLogin的动作与amigo.struts.config.UserAction的相应方法对应。可以为一个Action类配置多个<action>动作，例如在（1）中的struts-backend.xml和struts-web.xml两个文件中都配置了对应amigo.struts.config.UserAction这个类的动作，不同的是<action>的name属性值不同。

有些时候对Action类中方法的调用满足一定的规律，例如add动作对应Action类的add方法，delete动作对应Action类的delete方法，这时读者可以使用方法通配符，例如：

```
<action name="*User" class=" amigo.struts. config.UserAction" method="{1}">
```

这时，addUser这个动作将会调用amigo.struts. config.UserAction类的add方法，同理，deleteUser这个动作将调用amigo.struts. config.UserAction类的delete方法。

（4）<result>标签的使用。

<result>标签既可以为<global-results>标签的子标签，用于定义全局的结果信息；也可以为<action>标签的子标签。<result>标签的常用属性如表3-3所示。

表 3-3 <result>标签的常用属性

属性	是否必须	说明
name	No	与 Action 中返回的字符串对应
type	No	类型，其默认值为 dispatcher（即转发）。值的设置在后面将会详细介绍

使用举例如下：

例1：全局<result>标签配置如下：

```
<struts>
<package name="amigo" extends="struts-default">
<global-results>
<result name="success">/success.jsp</result>
<result name="error">/error.jsp</result>
</global-results>
</package>
</struts>
```

在上例中，配置了一个名为success和error的结果，分别指向success.jsp和error.jsp。

例2：在下例中，配置<result>标签的type的redirect值，即重定向，配置如下：

```
<result name="result" type="redirect">/result.jsp</result>
```

<result>标签的type的值读者可以在图3-2的struts-default.xml文件的51~66行中看到，内容如下：

```
<result-types>
<result-type name="chain" class="com.opensymphony.xwork2.ActionChainResult"/>
<result-type name="dispatcher" class="org.apache.struts2.dispatcher.ServletDispatcherResult
" default="true"/>
```

```xml
<result-type name="freemarker" class="org.apache.struts2.views.freemarker.FreemarkerResult"/>
<result-type name="httpheader" class="org.apache.struts2.dispatcher.HttpHeaderResult"/>
<result-type name="redirect" class="org.apache.struts2.dispatcher.ServletRedirectResult"/>
<result-type name="redirectAction" class="org.apache.struts2.dispatcher.ServletActionRedirectResult"/>
<result-type name="stream" class="org.apache.struts2.dispatcher.StreamResult"/>
<result-type name="velocity" class="org.apache.struts2.dispatcher.VelocityResult"/>
<result-type name="xslt" class="org.apache.struts2.views.xslt.XSLTResult"/>
<result-type name="plainText" class="org.apache.struts2.dispatcher.PlainTextResult" />
<!-- Deprecated name form scheduled for removal in Struts 2.1.0. The camelCase versions are preferred. See ww-1707 -->
<result-type name="redirect-action" class="org.apache.struts2.dispatcher.ServletActionRedirectResult"/>
<result-type name="plaintext" class="org.apache.struts2.dispatcher.PlainTextResult" />
</result-types>
```

（5）<param>标签的使用。

<param>标签为<action>标签的子标签，它用于为action设置参数。在struts 2中，可以通过<param>标签指定任意多个参数。使用举例如下：

```xml
<!DOCTYPE struts PUBLIC
    "-//Apache Software Foundation//DTD Struts Configuration 2.0//EN"
    "http://struts.apache.org/dtds/struts-2.0.dtd">

<struts>
    <package name="amigo" extends="struts-default">
<action name="userLogin" class="amigo.struts. config.UserAction">
<param name="username">amigo </param>
<param name="password">198211</param>
<result name="loginSuccess">/main.jsp</result>
</action>
</struts>
```

在上例中，为名为userLogin的动作指定了两个参数：username和password。

【例 3-3】配置 struts.properties

〖实例需求〗

struts.xml 和 struts.properties 为 Struts 2 的两个核心配置文件，其中【例 3-2】所讲解的 struts.xml 文件用于管理 Web 应用中的 Action 配置，而 struts.properties 用于配置 Struts 2 框架的属性。

struts.properties 文件通常放在 src 目录下，编译后将会放在工程的 classes 目录中（在本例中位于 build\asses 目录）。本实例详细讲解 struts.properties 中常用的属性，例如 struts.locale、struts.i18n.encoding 和 struts.configuration 等。

〖开发过程〗

第一步：创建 struts.properties 文件

struts.properties 文件通常放在 src 目录中，编译后将会放在工程的 classes 目录中（在本例中位于 build/classes 目录），struts.properties 文件可在 struts 2 的下载包中找到，读者可将 struts-2.0.8-all\struts-2.0.8\src\core\src\test\resources 目录中的 struts.properties 文件复制到 strutsconfig 工程的 src 目录中。

该文件的默认配置如下所示：

```
struts.i18n.encoding=ISO-8859-1
struts.locale=de_DE
struts.multipart.saveDir=\temp
struts.multipart.maxSize=12345

### Load custom property files (does not override struts.properties!)
struts.custom.properties=test,org/apache/struts2/othertest

# added the MockTag to the path of Tags that the TagDirective will search through
struts.velocity.tag.path = org.apache.struts2.views.velocity.ui, org.displaytag.tags

struts.ui.templateDir = template

### Load custom default resource bundles
struts.custom.i18n.resources=testmessages,testmessages2

### XSLT Cache
struts.xslt.nocache = true
```

在后面的讲解中还需要对这些属性进行修改。

第二步：struts.properties 的常用配置

struts.properties中可配置的属性都可以在struts的default.properties中找到。

常用的属性如下所示：

（1）struts.i18n.encoding。

该属性用于设置 Web 应用的默认编码集，该属性对于处理中文请求参数很有用，在中文系统中，可设置为 UTF-8、GBK 和 GB2312，笔者建议在工程中统一使用 UTF-8。具体设置如下：

```
struts.i18n.encoding=UTF-8
```

（2）struts.locale。

该属性用于指定Web应用的默认Locale，即默认的国际化地区信息。对于中文系统，可将其设置修改为：

```
struts.locale= zh_CN
```

（3）struts.multipart.saveDir。

该属性用于指定上传文件的临时保存路径。在本例中设置的值为\temp目录。

（4）struts.multipart.maxSize。

该属性用于指定Struts 2上传文件时请求内容允许的最大字节数，在本例中设置的值为12345。

（5）struts.custom.properties。

该属性用于指定应用加载的用户自定义的属性文件，当为多个文件时，可以用逗号（,）隔开。在本例中不需要设置自定义的属性文件，因此可以删除该属性。

（6）struts.ui.templateDir。

该属性用于指定视图主题所需要的模板文件存放的路径，默认为template，即默认加载template路径下的模板文件。

（7）struts.custom.i18n.resources。

该属性用于指定工程的国际化资源文件，当为多个文件时，可以用逗号（,）隔开，例如，可设置其值为：

```
struts.custom.i18n.resources= ApplicationResources
```

（8）**struts.xslt.nocache**。

该属性用于指定XSLT Result是否使用样式表缓存，可设置其值为true或false。在开发阶段，设置为true，在产品阶段，设置其值为false。

第三步：修改后的 struts.properties

在第二步中对struts.properties进行修改后，修改后的文件内容如下所示：

```
struts.i18n.encoding=UTF-8
struts.locale=zh_CN
struts.multipart.saveDir=\temp
struts.multipart.maxSize=12345

# added the MockTag to the path of Tags that the TagDirective will search through
struts.velocity.tag.path = org.apache.struts2.views.velocity.ui, org.displaytag.tags

struts.ui.templateDir = template

### Load custom default resource bundles
struts.custom.i18n.resources= ApplicationResources

### XSLT Cache
struts.xslt.nocache = true
```

当然，开发人员也可以不编写struts.properties文件，Strtus 2中也提供了其他的方案来实现同样的功能，Struts 2允许在struts.xml文件中配置constant元素来达到同样的目的。例如开发人员想将"struts.ui.templateDir"设置为"template2"，可在struts.xml中加入如下配置：

```xml
<!DOCTYPE struts PUBLIC
    "-//Apache Software Foundation//DTD Struts Configuration 2.0//EN"
    "http://struts.apache.org/dtds/struts-2.0.dtd">

<struts>
<constant name="struts.ui.templateDir" value="template2" />
    <package name="web" extends="struts-default">
    ……
    </package>
</struts>
```

【例 3-4】struts 的默认配置文件 default.properties

〖实例需求〗

struts.properties 的各配置项都来自 default.properties，Struts 2 为这些配置项设置了默认值。本实例对常用属性的一些默认值进行详细讲解。

〖开发过程〗

第一步：default.properties 文件内容

default.properties 这个文件读者可在 struts2-core-2.0.8.jar 解压目录 struts2-core-2.0.8\org\pache\struts2 中找到，该文件的具体内容如下：

```
## START SNIPPET: complete_file

### Struts default properties
###(can be overridden by a struts.properties file in the root of the classpath)
###

### Specifies the Configuration used to configure Struts
### one could extend org.apache.struts2.config.Configuration
### to build one's customize way of getting the configurations parameters into Struts
# struts.configuration=org.apache.struts2.config.DefaultConfiguration

### This can be used to set your default locale and encoding scheme
# struts.locale=en_US
struts.i18n.encoding=UTF-8

### if specified, the default object factory can be overridden here
### Note: short-hand notation is supported in some cases, such as "spring"
###       Alternatively, you can provide a com.opensymphony.xwork2.ObjectFactory subclass name here
# struts.objectFactory = spring

### specifies the autoWiring logic when using the SpringObjectFactory.
### valid values are: name, type, auto, and constructor (name is the default)
struts.objectFactory.spring.autoWire = name

### indicates to the struts-spring integration if Class instances should be cached
### this should, until a future Spring release makes it possible, be left as true
### unless you know exactly what you are doing!
### valid values are: true, false (true is the default)
struts.objectFactory.spring.useClassCache = true

### if specified, the default object type determiner can be overridden here
### Note: short-hand notation is supported in some cases, such as "tiger" or "notiger"
###       Alternatively, you can provide a com.opensymphony.xwork2.util.ObjectTypeDeterminer implementation name here
### Note: if you have the xwork-tiger.jar within your classpath, GenericsObjectTypeDeterminer is used by default
###       To disable tiger support use the "notiger" property value here.
#struts.objectTypeDeterminer = tiger
#struts.objectTypeDeterminer = notiger

### Parser to handle HTTP POST requests, encoded using the MIME-type multipart/form-data
```

```
# struts.multipart.parser=cos
# struts.multipart.parser=pell
struts.multipart.parser=jakarta
# uses javax.servlet.context.tempdir by default
struts.multipart.saveDir=
struts.multipart.maxSize=2097152

### Load custom property files (does not override struts.properties!)
# struts.custom.properties=application,org/apache/struts2/extension/custom

### How request URLs are mapped to and from actions
#struts.mapper.class=org.apache.struts2.dispatcher.mapper.DefaultActionMapper

### Used by the DefaultActionMapper
### You may provide a comma separated list, e.g. struts.action.extension=action,jnlp,do
struts.action.extension=action

### Used by FilterDispatcher
### If true then Struts serves static content from inside its jar.
### If false then the static content must be available at <context_path>/struts
struts.serve.static=true

### Used by FilterDispatcher
### This is good for development where one wants changes to the static content be
### fetch on each request.
### NOTE: This will only have effect if struts.serve.static=true
### If true -> Struts will write out header for static contents such that they will
###           be cached by web browsers (using Date, Cache-Content, Pragma, Expires)
###           headers).
### If false -> Struts will write out header for static contents such that they are
###           NOT to be cached by web browser (using Cache-Content, Pragma, Expires
###           headers)
struts.serve.static.browserCache=true

### Set this to false if you wish to disable implicit dynamic method invocation
### via the URL request. This includes URLs like foo!bar.action, as well as params
### like method:bar (but not action:foo).
### An alternative to implicit dynamic method invocation is to use wildcard
### mappings, such as <action name="*/*" method="{2}" class="actions.{1}">
struts.enable.DynamicMethodInvocation = true

### Set this to true if you wish to allow slashes in your action names.  If false,
### Actions names cannot have slashes, and will be accessible via any directory
### prefix.  This is the traditional behavior expected of WebWork applications.
### Setting to true is useful when you want to use wildcards and store values
### in the URL, to be extracted by wildcard patterns, such as
### <action name="*/*" method="{2}" class="actions.{1}"> to match "/foo/edit" or
### "/foo/save".
struts.enable.SlashesInActionNames = false
```

```
### use alternative syntax that requires %{} in most places
### to evaluate expressions for String attributes for tags
struts.tag.altSyntax=true

### when set to true, Struts will act much more friendly for developers. This
### includes:
### - struts.i18n.reload = true
### - struts.configuration.xml.reload = true
### - raising various debug or ignorable problems to errors
###     For example: normally a request to foo.action?someUnknownField=true should
###                  be ignored (given that any value can come from the web and it
###                  should not be trusted). However, during development, it may be
###                  useful to know when these errors are happening and be told of
###                  them right away.
struts.devMode = false

### when set to true, resource bundles will be reloaded on _every_ request.
### this is good during development, but should never be used in production
struts.i18n.reload=false

### Standard UI theme
### Change this to reflect which path should be used for JSP control tag templates by default
struts.ui.theme=xhtml
struts.ui.templateDir=template
#sets the default template type. Either ftl, vm, or jsp
struts.ui.templateSuffix=ftl

### Configuration reloading
### This will cause the configuration to reload struts.xml when it is changed
struts.configuration.xml.reload=false

### Location of velocity.properties file.   defaults to velocity.properties
struts.velocity.configfile = velocity.properties

### Comma separated list of VelocityContext classnames to chain to the StrutsVelocityContext
struts.velocity.contexts =

### Location of the velocity toolbox
struts.velocity.toolboxlocation=

### used to build URLs, such as the UrlTag
struts.url.http.port = 80
struts.url.https.port = 443
### possible values are: none, get or all
struts.url.includeParams = get

### Load custom default resource bundles
# struts.custom.i18n.resources=testmessages,testmessages2
```

```
### workaround for some app servers that don't handle HttpServletRequest.getParameterMap()
### often used for WebLogic, Orion, and OC4J
struts.dispatcher.parametersWorkaround = false

### configure the Freemarker Manager class to be used
### Allows user to plug-in customised Freemarker Manager if necessary
### MUST extends off org.apache.struts2.views.freemarker.FreemarkerManager
#struts.freemarker.manager.classname=org.apache.struts2.views.freemarker.FreemarkerManager

### See the StrutsBeanWrapper javadocs for more information
struts.freemarker.wrapper.altMap=true

### configure the XSLTResult class to use stylesheet caching.
### Set to true for developers and false for production.
struts.xslt.nocache=false

### A list of configuration files automatically loaded by Struts
struts.configuration.files=struts-default.xml,struts-plugin.xml,struts.xml

### Whether to always select the namespace to be everything before the last slash or not
struts.mapper.alwaysSelectFullNamespace=false

### END SNIPPET: complete_file
```

第二步：常用属性的默认配置

（1）struts.i18n.encoding。

该属性值的用途在【例3-3】中已进行了详细说明，其默认值为UTF-8。

（2）struts.locale。

默认值为en_US。

（3）struts.objectFactory。

该属性用于指定默认的ObjectFactory Bean，默认值SPRING。

（4）struts.objectFactory.spring.autoWire。

该属性用于指定Spring的自动装配方式，默认为name，即采用按照name方式自动装配，与在Spring中设置为byName的功能类似。

（5）struts.multipart.parser。

该属性用于指定处理multipart/form-data的MIME类型的HTTP POST请求，可设置为cos、pell和jakarta。默认值为jakarta。设置为cos表示使用cos的文件上传框架，设置为pell时表示采用pell上传，设置为jakarta时表示采用common-fileupload文件上传框架。

（6）struts.multipart.saveDir。

该属性值的用途在【例3-3】中已进行了详细说明，默认值为空字符串。

（7）struts.action.extension。

该属性用于指定需要Strut 2框架进行处理的请求后缀，默认值为action。

小结

Web 工程若加入 Struts 2 的 MVC 框架的支持，需要在 web.xml 中配置 FilterDispatcher 过滤器，添加的配置信息如下所示：

```xml
<filter>
    <filter-name>struts2</filter-name>
    <filter-class>org.apache.struts2.dispatcher.FilterDispatcher</filter-class>
</filter>

<filter-mapping>
    <filter-name>struts2</filter-name>
    <url-pattern>/*</url-pattern>
</filter-mapping>
```

若需要为过滤器配置初始化参数，可在<filter/>元素中使用配置<init-param/>子元素，配置格式如下所示：

```xml
<init-param>
    <param-name>参数名</param-name>
    <param-value>参数值</param-value>
</init-param>
```

本章还讲述了在 web.xml 中如何进行标签库的配置、欢迎页和错误页的设置等。

Struts 2 的核心配置文件是 struts.xml，它负责管理 Struts 2 框架的 Action，struts.xml 的格式如下所示：

```xml
<!DOCTYPE struts PUBLIC
    "-//Apache Software Foundation//DTD Struts Configuration 2.0//EN"
    "http://struts.apache.org/dtds/struts-2.0.dtd">

<struts>
</struts>
```

本章讲述了其子元素<include>的配置，<include>标签将其余的配置文件包括进来。例如，将 struts-backend.xml 包含进来，需要在<struts/>元素下使用<include/>子元素：

```xml
<include file="struts-backend.xml"/>
```

子元素<package/>与 Java 中包的概念类似，将某些配置放在一个包中，别的包可以继承该包，例如定义一个 amigo 包，它继承 struts-default 包，配置如下所示：

```xml
<package name="amigo" extends="struts-default">
    ……
</package>
```

<action>标签用于将一个请求对应到一个 Action 处理上去，例如指定 amigo.struts.config.UserAction 类的访问路径为 user.action，其在 struts.xml 文件中的配置如下所示：

```xml
<action name="user" class="amigo.struts.config.UserAction">
    ……
</action>
```

<result>标签既可以为<global-results>标签的子标签，用于定义全局的结果信息；也可以是<action>标签的子标签，用于确定走向。例如指定 UserAction 的 success 跳转页面为 loginSuccess.jsp，指定其 input 跳转页面为 login.jsp，使用的配置如下所示：

```xml
<action name="user" class="amigo.struts.config.UserAction">
    <result>loginSuccesss.jsp</result>
```

```
            <result name="input">login.jsp</result>
    </action>
```
<param>标签为<action>标签的子标签,它用于为 ACTION 设置参数。例如为 UserAction 指定 username 和 password 参数,值都为 amigo,配置信息如下:
```
<action name="user" class="amigo.struts.config.UserAction">
<param name="username">amigo</param>
<param name="password">amigo</param>
......
</action>
```
struts.properties 文件是 Struts 2 的另一个核心配置文件,它主要用于配置 Struts 2 框架的各属性。在该文件中使用键值对的方式配置各项的值,常用的配置项有 struts.i18n.encoding 和 struts.locale 等。例如配置 struts.i18n.encoding 配置项的值为 UTF-8,使用的配置如下所示:
```
struts.i18n.encoding=UTF-8
```
各配置项及其默认值都可在 default.properties 中找到,default.properties 设置了各属性的默认值。例如 struts.locale 的默认值为:en_US,struts.i18n.encoding 的默认值为:UTF-8,struts.action.extension 用于表示请求后缀,默认为 ACTION。

本章通过对配置文件各项配置的学习,使得开发人员可以对 Struts 2 的配置有一个全面的了解,为后续使用 Struts 2 进行 Web 项目的开发打下坚实的基础。

第 4 章　国际化 Web 应用

【本章导读语】

国际化（Internationalization，简称 I18N）指的是在软件的设计阶段，已经设计了针对不同的语言和地区显示不同页面的功能。当系统需要支持另一个不同的语言和地区时，只需要添加另一个资源文件，例如中文使用中文资源文件，英文使用英文资源文件，而不需要修改程序代码。

本章讲解在 Struts 2 中如何实现 Web 应用程序的国际化。在进行项目开发时，大部分人都遭遇过中文乱码问题，本章将对这些常见的乱码问题提供解决方案，而后将讲述如何在 Struts 2 中通过使用资源文件和本地化字符串来实现 Struts 2 应用程序的国际化。

【例 4-1】常见中文乱码问题的解决方案

〖实例需求〗

中文乱码问题经常以不同的形式困扰着 Java Web 应用程序开发人员，本实例从引起乱码的根本原因讲起，并提供了一些常见的中文乱码问题的解决方案。

〖开发过程〗

第一步：建立工程：strutsi18n

按照第 1 章新建工程的方式新建一个名为 strutsi18n 的动态 Web 工程，将 WebRoot 设置为工程的根目录，并设置 classes 文件的存放路径为：WebRoot/WEB-INF/classes。

第二步：常见乱码问题解决方案

中文编码问题的最根本的解决方法是指定整个应用系统的统一编码集，建议统一使用编码集：UTF-8。

当然读者也可以统一设置为 ISO8859_1，因为目前大多数软件系统都是西方人编制的，他们的默认编码集都是 ISO8859_1，例如 MySQL、Linux。

Eclipse 中默认的文件编码方式也是 ISO8859_1。但是它要求操作系统的默认编码是 ISO8859_1。若读者统一设置编码集为 GBK，它只能运行在默认编码集为 GBK 的操作系统，例如中文 Windows。所以考虑到这些问题，将编码集统一设置为 UTF-8 最合适不过。

（1）将代码文件的字符集统一设置为 UTF-8。

将 Web 工程的所有文件的编码设置为 UTF-8，例如 Java、JavaScript 和 JSP 等文件。

在 Eclipse 可以设置单个文件的字符集，还提供了统一设置某个工程字符集的方法，另外还可以对某种确定类型的文件的字符集进行设置。

设置单个文件的字符集的方法如下所示：

在 strutsi18n 的 src 源码目录中建立 Test.java 文件，选择该文件后，单击鼠标右键，在弹出的菜单中选择 Properties 命令，在弹出的对话框中设置编码为 UTF-8。操作步骤如图 4-1 所示。

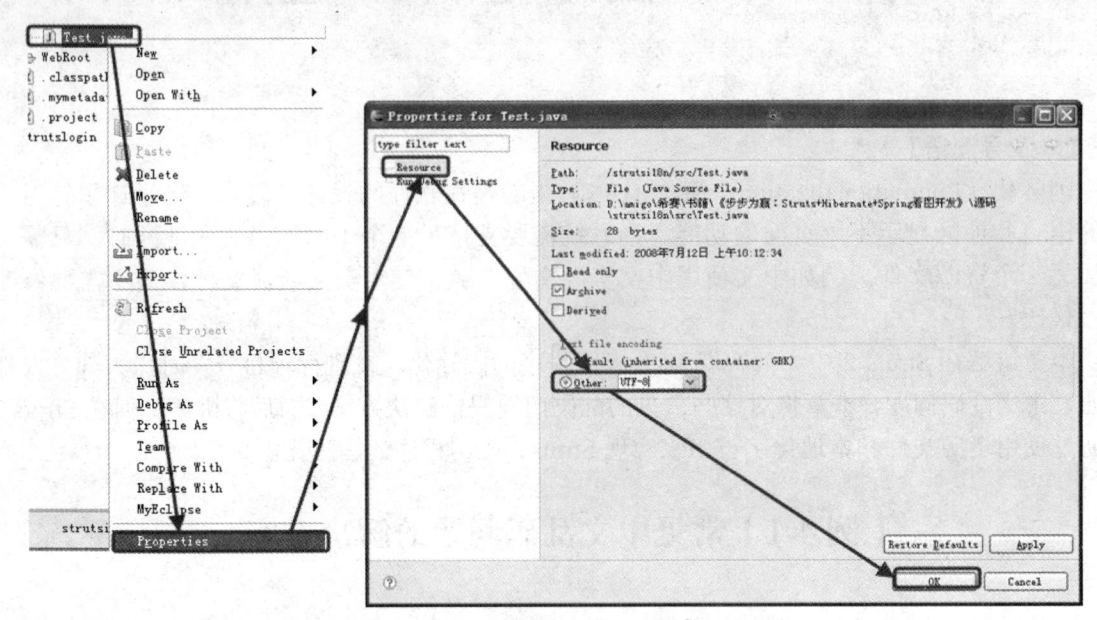

图 4-1　将单个文件的字符集设置为 UTF-8

在图 4-1 中，单击 OK 按钮完成单个文件字符集的设置。

若为每个类文件设置编码比较麻烦，较好的习惯是在工程开始前统一对编码进行设置，例如将编码设置为 UTF-8。设置的方法是选中需要设置编码的工程后，单击鼠标右键，在弹出的菜单中选择 Properties 命令，在弹出的窗口中设置编码为 UTF-8，操作步骤如图 4-2 所示。

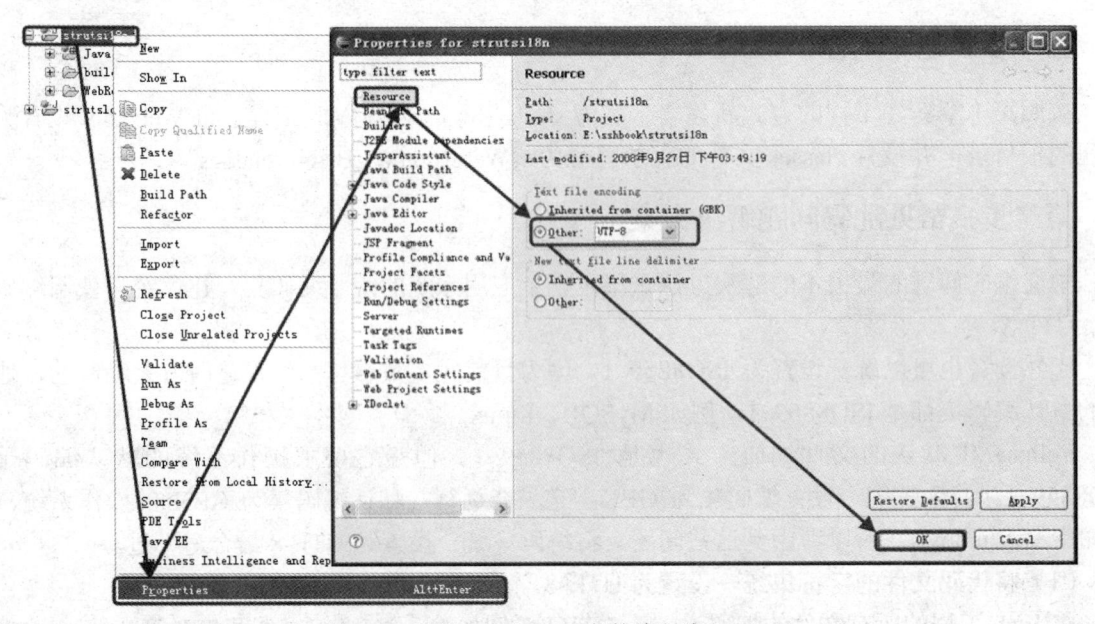

图 4-2　设置 strutsi18n 工程的编码为 UTF-8

若只需要为某种文件（例如类文件）进行统一编码设置，可选择菜单栏上的 Windows→Preferences→General→Content Types，在弹出的对话框的 Default encoding 处可设置默认编码集，操作步骤如图 4-3 所示。

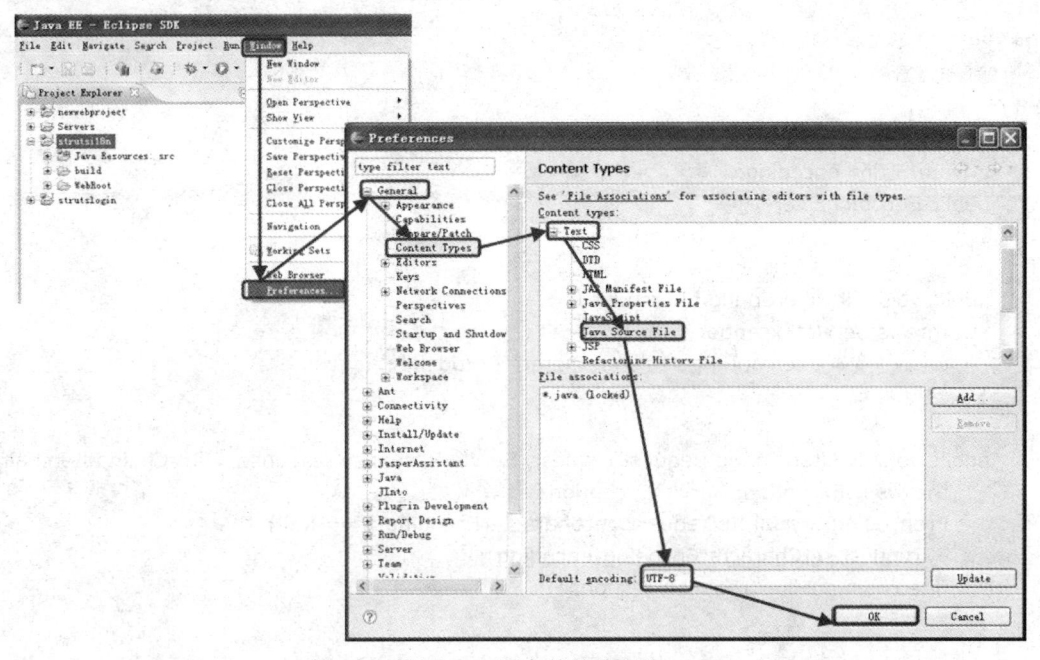

图 4-3　设置 Java 源文件的编码为 UTF-8

通过图 4-3 所示的方式，读者还可以设置 CSS 文件、JavaScript 等文件的编码。这样修改之后，新建的工程的对应种类文件都会使用设置的默认编码。

（2）在 web.xml 文件中配置编码过滤器编码为 UTF-8。

读者可以通过一个过滤器来对来自浏览器的所有请求的编码统一设置为 UTF-8，设置请求的编码的语句如下：

```
request.setCharacterEncoding(encoding);
```

有一些容器（例如 Spring）中提供了编码过滤器，只需要在 web.xml 中设置该过滤器即可，下面来看看过滤器类是如何实现的。读者可在 strutsi18n 的源码目录下建立 amigo.struts.i18n 包，建立该包的操作步骤如图 4-4 所示。

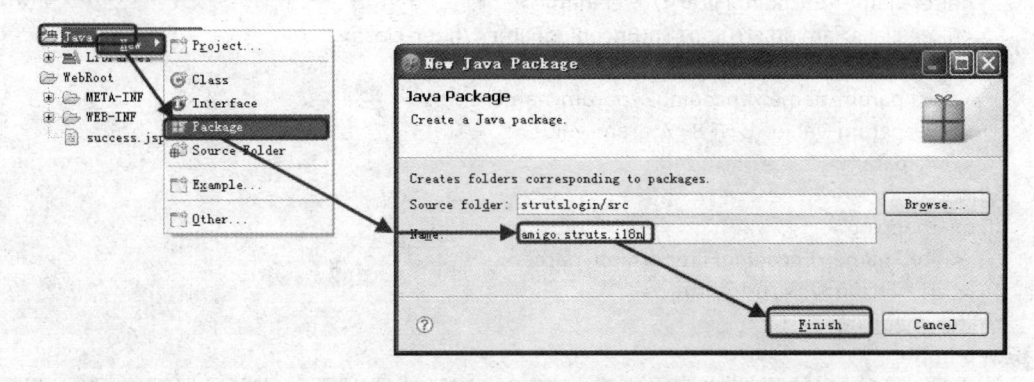

图 4-4　创建 amigo.struts.i18n 包

编码过滤器 EncodingFilter.java 类的代码如下所示：

```java
package amigo.struts.i18n;

import java.io.IOException;
import javax.servlet.*;

/**
 * 编码过滤器
 */
public class EncodingFilter   implements Filter {
    private String encoding;
    public EncodingFilter(){
    }

    public void init(FilterConfig filterconfig)
        throws ServletException{
        encoding = filterconfig.getInitParameter("encoding");
    }

    public void doFilter(ServletRequest request, ServletResponse response, FilterChain filterchain)
        throws IOException, ServletException{
        if(encoding != null && request.getCharacterEncoding() == null)
            request.setCharacterEncoding(encoding);
        filterchain.doFilter(request, response);
    }

    public void destroy(){
    }
}
```

从该过滤器中可以看出，该类的编码来自初始化参数，该过滤器还需要在 web.xml 中进行设置才能生效，修改后的 web.xml 文件的内容如下所示：

```xml
<?xml version="1.0" encoding="UTF-8"?>
<web-app xmlns:xsi="http://www.w3.org/2001/XMLSchema-instance" xmlns="http://java.sun.com/xml/ns/javaee" xmlns:web="http://java.sun.com/xml/ns/javaee/web-app_2_5.xsd" xsi:schemaLocation="http://java.sun.com/xml/ns/javaee    http://java.sun.com/xml/ns/javaee/web-app_2_5.xsd"    id="WebApp_ID" version="2.5">
    <display-name>strutsi18n</display-name>
    <filter>
        <filter-name>EncodingFilter</filter-name>
        <filter-class>amigo.struts.i18n.EncodingFilter</filter-class>
        <init-param>
            <param-name>encoding</param-name>
            <param-value>UTF-8</param-value>
        </init-param>
    </filter>
    <filter-mapping>
        <filter-name>EncodingFilter</filter-name>
        <url-pattern>/*</url-pattern>
    </filter-mapping>
</web-app>
```

从该设置中可以看出设置的编码集为 UTF-8，该过滤器对所有的浏览器请求进行过滤。设置完成后，所有的浏览器请求将会通过 UTF-8 编码进行过滤。

（3）将 JSP 和 HTML 文件页面编码设置为 UTF-8。

在 strutsi18n 工程 WebContent 目录下建立 test.jsp 文件，新建成功后，使用的是默认的编码 ISO8859_1，该文件的代码如下所示：

```
<%@ page language="java" contentType="text/html; charset=ISO-8859_1"
    pageEncoding="ISO-8859_1"%>
<!DOCTYPE html PUBLIC "-//W3C//DTD HTML 4.01 Transitional//EN" "http://www.w3.org/TR/html4/loose.dtd">
<html>
<head>
<meta http-equiv="Content-Type" content="text/html; charset=ISO-8859-1">
<title>Insert title here</title>
</head>
<body>

</body>
</html>
```

读者可以将该文件中的 ISO-8859-1 全部替换为编码 UTF-8，在此需要修改两处，一是修改头部声明：

```
<%@ page language="java" contentType="text/html; charset=ISO-8859-1"
pageEncoding="ISO-8859-1"%>
```

为：

```
<%@ page language="java" contentType="text/html; charset=UTF-8"
pageEncoding="UTF-8"%>
```

二是将 JSP 中的 HTML 代码的编码修改为 UTF-8，即将代码：

```
<meta http-equiv="Content-Type" content="text/html; charset=ISO-8859-1">
```

修改为：

```
<meta http-equiv="Content-Type" content="text/html; charset=UTF-8">
```

（4）设置数据库编码为 UTF-8。

一般数据库都可以将数据库的编码设置为 UTF-8，读者也可以在连接数据库时指定 UTF-8 编码，例如在进行 MySQL 数据库连接时，在其连接字符串后加上 characterEncoding 参数，例如：

```
jdbc:mysql://localhost:3306/testencode?useUnicode=true&characterEncoding=UTF-8
```

（5）URL 传递中文参数时进行 ISO8859_1 到 GBK 的转码。

笔者不建议在 URL 串中直接传递中文，建议在进行传递前先进行编码，或将中文参数放在表单的隐含字段中进行传输。对于不得不进行中文参数传递的情况，读者可将接收到的参数进行 ISO8859_1 到 GBK 的转码，例如：

```
String param = new String(request.getParameter("param").getBytes("ISO8859-1"), "GBK");
```

【例 4-2】使用资源文件

〖实例需求〗

若要实现国际化，则需要借助于资源文件，不同国别的配置信息采用不同的资源文件表示。

本实例将讲述资源文件的创建和配置，并讲述如何通过配置 struts.xml 文件或 struts.properties 文件实现资源文件的加载。

〖开发过程〗

第一步：导入包

因为读者需要在本实例中使用 Struts 2，所以还需要将 Struts 2 的 jar 包以及相关的 jar 包都复制到 strutsi18n 工程的 lib 目录中。方法同第 3 章，在此不再赘述。

第二步：配置 web.xml 文件

在 web.xml 中需要配置 Struts 2 的 FilterDispatcher，添加的配置信息读者可参考第 3 章的相应内容。

第三步：建立资源文件

资源文件一般建立在 src 目录中，资源文件是一个文件系，这些文件的前缀和后缀是相同的，不过其国家和语言字符串不一样，例如一个资源文件的基本名称为 messages，对于中文，其资源文件的名称为：

messages_zh_CN.properties

而对于英文，其资源文件的名称为：

messages_en.properties

在本实例中，在 src 目录中建立 messages.properties、messages_zh_CN.properties 和 messages_en.properties 三个资源文件。

创建 messages.properties 资源文件的操作步骤如图 4-5 所示。

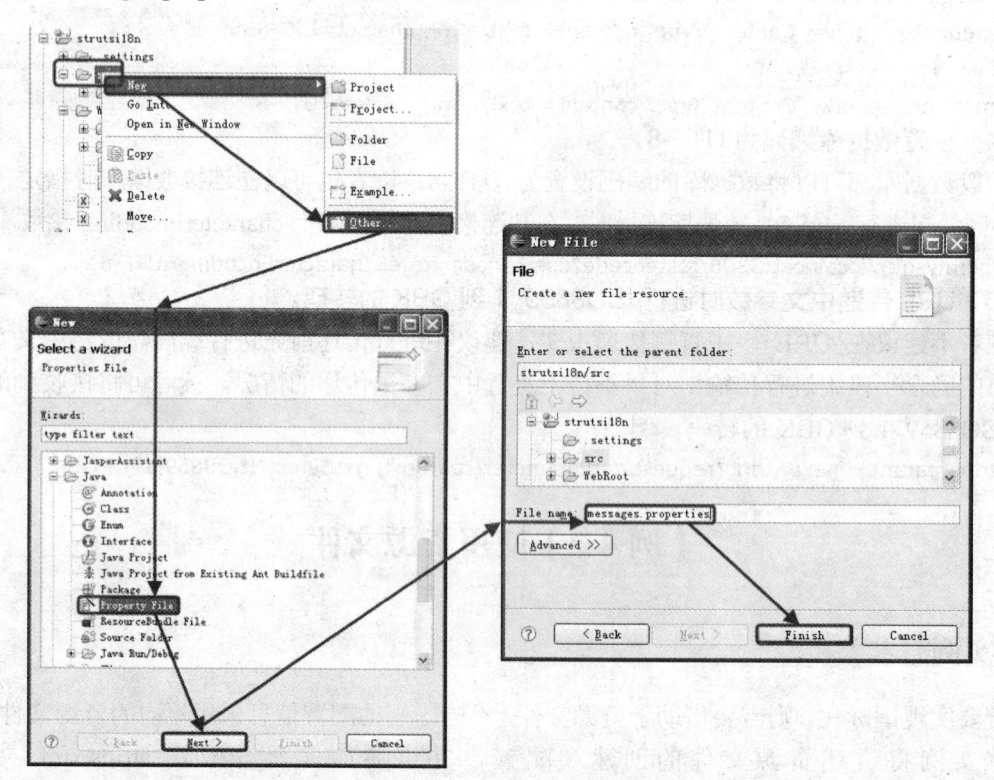

图 4-5　创建 messages.properties 资源文件

选择 messages.properties 后，单击鼠标右键，选择 Open With→Text Editor 命令，将以文本方式打开资源文件，操作步骤如图 4-6 所示。

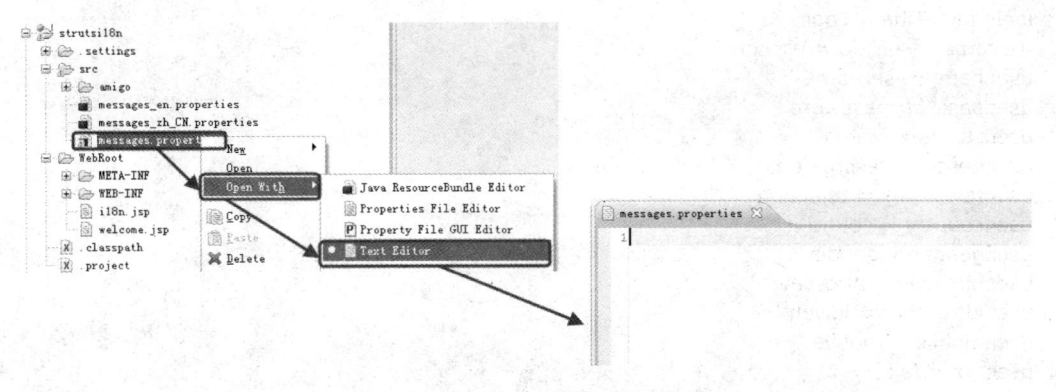

图 4-6　以文本方式打开资源文件

messages.properties 文件存放原始的中文参数信息，内容如下所示：

```
# -- direct output message --
message={0}

login.pageTitle = 登录界面
welcome.pageTitle = 欢迎界面
user.name = 用户名
user.passwd = 密码
user.status = 状态
user.descn = 描述
user.telephone = 电话
user.country = 国家
user.gender = 性别
user.birthday = 生日
user.idNumber = 身份证号
user.mobile = 手机号
user.fax = 传真
user.language = 语言
submitButton = 提交
```

【提示】若修改 messages.properties 文件后，保存时出现如图 4-7 所示的提示框。

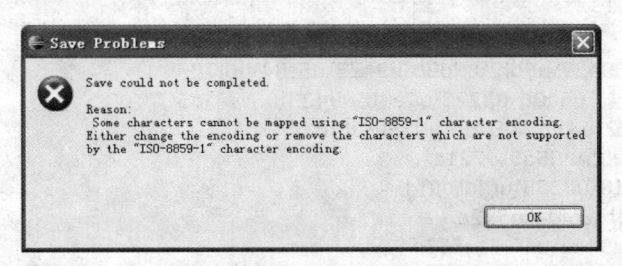

图 4-7　资源文件编码错误提示框

该提示表明该资源文件设置的编码集是 ISO8859_1，而文件中带有 ISO8859_1 不支持的中文字符，此时可选择该文件后，单击鼠标右键，在弹出的菜单中选择 Properties 命令，在出现的对话框中将 Text file encoding 中的编码由 ISO-8859-1 修改为 UTF-8，修改完成后再重新打开文件，此时输入中文字符不会再出现该错误提示框。

messages_en.properties 文件存放英文的参数信息，内容如下所示：

```
# -- direct output message --
message={0}

login.pageTitle = Login
welcome.pageTitle = Welcome
user.name=username
user.passwd=password
user.status = status
user.descn = description
user.telephone = telephone
user.country = country
user.gender = gender
user.birthday = birthday
user.idNumber = idNumber
user.mobile = mobile
user.fax = fax
user.language = language
submitButton = submit
```

messages_zh_CN.properties 存放中文编码后的参数信息，中文参数信息需要通过 Java 的 native2ascii 命令进行编码才能进行正常显示，读者可以在命令行中用该命令将 messages.properties 编码后再将内容复制到 messages_zh_CN.properties 文件中，但为了减少麻烦，笔者建议在 src 目录中建立一个名为 code.bat 的批处理文件来进行该操作。

code.bat 文件的内容如下所示：

```
// 删除 messages_zh_CN.properties 文件
del messages_zh_CN.properties
// 拷贝 messages.properties 到 messages_zh_CN.properties.gbk 文件
copy messages.properties messages_zh_CN.properties.gbk
// 将 messages_zh_CN.properties.gbk 文件进行 GBK 编码后将内容拷贝到 messages_zh_CN.properties 中
native2ascii -encoding GBK messages_zh_CN.properties.gbk messages_zh_CN.properties
// 删除 messages_zh_CN.properties.gbk 文件
del messages_zh_CN.properties.gbk
// 删除所有后缀为.bak 的文件
del *.bak
```

运行该批处理文件后，可自动生成经过编码后的中文资源文件 messages_zh_CN.properties，生成的文件内容如下所示：

```
# -- direct output message --
message={0}

login.pageTitle = \u9427\u8bf2\u7d8d\u9423\u5c84\u6f70
welcome.pageTitle = \u5a06\u3223\u7e4b\u9423\u5c84\u6f70
user.name = \u9422\u3126\u57db\u935a\ufffd
user.passwd = \u7035\u55d9\u721c
user.status = \u9418\u8235\ufffd\ufffd
user.descn = \u93bb\u5fda\u582a
user.telephone = \u9422\u4f43\u763d
user.country = \u9365\u85c9\ue18d
user.gender = \u93ac\u0443\u57c5
user.birthday = \u9422\u71b8\u68e9
user.idNumber = \u97ec\ue0a1\u5524\u7487\u4f78\u5f7f
user.mobile = \u93b5\u5b2b\u6e80\u9359\ufffd
user.fax = \u6d7c\u72b5\u6e61
user.language = \u7487\ue161\u2588
submitButton = \u93bb\u612a\u6c26
```

对于简体中文的 Locale，各个资源文件的优先顺序为：

1）messages_zh_CN.properties
2）messages.properties

若这两个文件都找不到时，系统将出现异常。当系统使用的是英文的 Locale，且 messages_en.properties 资源文件不存在时，将去取默认的资源文件 messages.properties，若 messages.properties 文件为中文，则会显示乱码。

第四步：在 struts.properties 或 struts.xml 文件中加载资源文件

读者可选择在 struts.properties 或 struts.xml 文件中加载资源文件，例如资源文件的基本名称为 messages（文件后缀：.properties），则可在 struts.properties 文件中添加如下配置：

```
struts.custom.i18n.resources = messages
```

当然读者也可以在 struts.xml 文件中添加如下内容来达到同样的作用：

```
<constant name="struts.custom.i18n.resources" value="messages" />
```

当有多个资源文件时，例如 ApplicationResources 和 messages 时，可以使用英文逗号（","）隔开。

【例 4-3】参数化字符串

〖实例需求〗

在 Struts 2 中，既可以在 JSP 页面中通过标签输出国际化信息，又可以在 Action 中获得国际化的信息。

本例通过一个用户注册的实例，在 JSP 页面展示了如何通过标签输出国际化的文本信息，在 Action 中获得经过国际化的提示信息，在操作结果页进行显示。

〖开发过程〗

第一步：创建 JSP 文件：i18n.jsp

在工程的 WebRoot 目录中创建输出国际化信息的展示页面 i18n.jsp。操作步骤如图 4-8 所示。

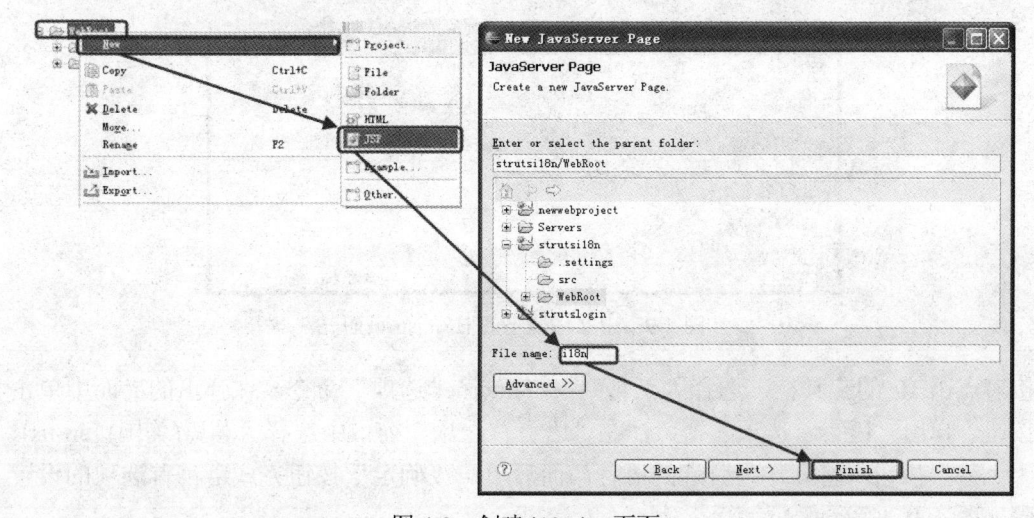

图 4-8　创建 i18n.jsp 页面

第二步：在 JSP 页面中输出国际化信息

（1）<s:i18n.../>标签。

<s:i18n.../>标签用于指定从某个特定的资源文件中取数据，使用举例如下：

```
<s:i18n name="messages">
<s:text name="user.name"></s:text>
</s:i18n>
```

上面的语句指定从messages资源文件中获得user.name这个资源名称。

（2）<s:text.../>标签。

<s:text.../>标签可以用来输出国际化信息，i18n.jsp页面的代码如下所示：

```
<%@ page contentType="text/html; charset=UTF-8" %>
<%@ taglib prefix="s" uri="/struts-tags" %>
<!DOCTYPE HTML PUBLIC "-//W3C//DTD HTML 4.01 Transitional//EN">
<html>
    <head>
        <!-- 使用 s:text 标签输出国际化的标题信息 -->
        <title><s:text name="login.pageTitle"/></title>
    </head>
    <body>
        <h3>
            <s:i18n name="messages">
                <s:text name="user.name"></s:text>
            </s:i18n>
        </h3>
    </body>
</html>
```

在上述代码中，通过<s:text.../>标签输出经过国际化的标题信息，在简体中文环境下的界面如图4-9所示。

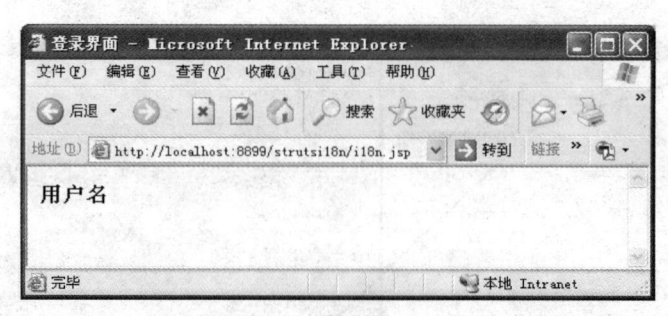

图4-9 中文环境下的 i18n.jsp 页面

接着点击 IE 的工具栏，选择"工具"→"Internet 选项"命令，在弹出的界面中单击"语言"按钮，弹出"语言首选项"窗口，在"语言首选项"窗口中选择"英语(美国) [en-us]"后，单击"上移"按钮，将其作为首选的语言，而后单击"确定"按钮完成语言首选项的设置。操作步骤如图 4-10 所示。

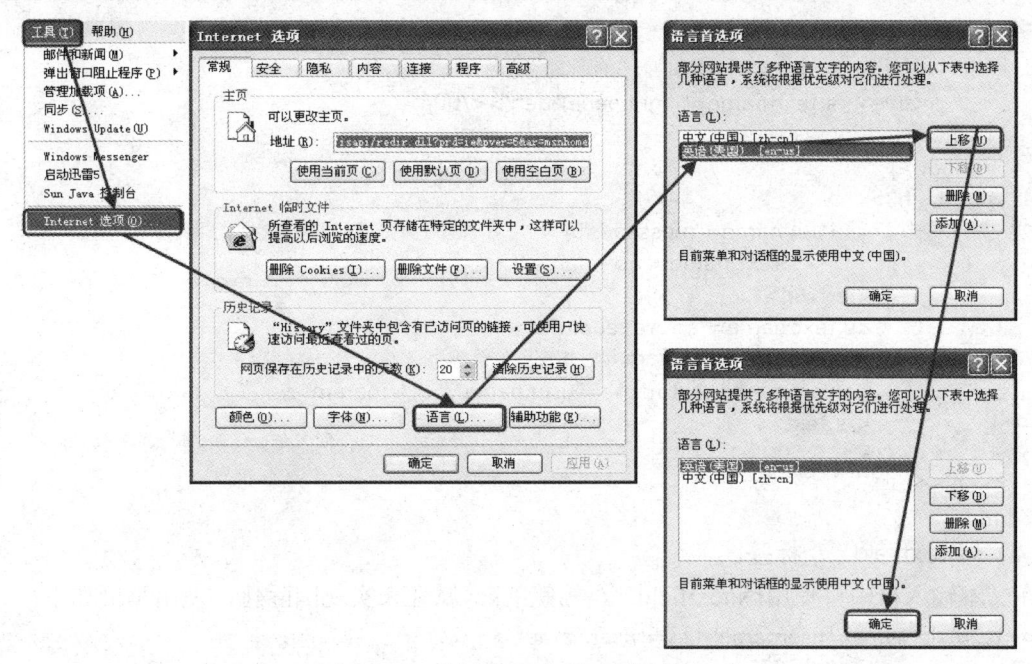

图 4-10　设置 IE 语言首选项为英语

将"英语(美国) [en-us]"设置为语言首选项后,读者可以再次访问 i18n.jsp 页面,此时界面如图 4-11 所示。

图 4-11　英文环境下的 i18n.jsp 页面

从图4-11中可以看出,当处于英文环境下时,将输出英文的配置信息。

（3）<s:param…/>标签。

使用<s:param…/>标签来填充带有占位符的国际化信息,在资源文件messages.properties中添加如下信息:

```
errors.required={0}不能为空.
```

在messages_en.properties中添加如下英文资源信息:

```
errors.required={0} is required.
```

在经过code.bat处理得到的中文资源文件messages_zh_CN.properties中添加如下信息:

```
errors.required = {0}\u6d93\u5d88\u5158\u6d93\u8679\u2516.
```

接下来笔者将向读者演示如何通过<s:param…/>标签填充资源文件中的{0}这个占位符。修改i18n.jsp页面,修改后的代码如下:

```
<%@ page contentType="text/html; charset=UTF-8" %>
<%@ taglib prefix="s" uri="/struts-tags" %>
<!DOCTYPE HTML PUBLIC "-//W3C//DTD HTML 4.01 Transitional//EN">
<html>
```

```
        <head>
            <!-- 使用 s:text 标签输出国际化的标题信息 -->
            <title><s:text name="login.pageTitle"/></title>
        </head>
        <body>
            <h3>
                <s:i18n name="messages">
                    <s:text name="user.name"/>
                </s:i18n>
                <s:text name="errors.required">
                    <!-- 使用 s:param 标签填充占位符 -->
                    <s:param><s:text name="user.name"/></s:param>
                </s:text>
            </h3>
        </body>
</html>
```

（4）<s:textfield.../>标签。

在文本输入框中可使用<s:textfield.../>标签的key属性来实现国际化，使用举例如下：

`<s:textfield name="username" key="user.name"/>`

（5）<s:submit.../>标签。

在Struts 2中也可以通过<s:submit.../>的key属性实现提交按钮的国际化，举例如下：

`<s:submit key="submitButton"/>`

上述代码指定提交按钮的名称自资源文件中取得，在中文环境下将显示：提交，在英文环境下将显示：submit。

第三步：在 Action 中获得国际化信息

（1）getText(...)方法。

ActionSupport类提供了 getText(String str)方法来获得资源文件中的国际化信息，使用举例如下：

`String errorMessage = this.getText("loginError");`

若需要填充资源文件中占位符的信息，可以使用 ActionSupport 类提供的 getText(String str, String[] params)方法来将信息传入进去，例如若资源文件中包括如下资源信息：

`loginSuccess = welcome ,{0}`

在 Action 中可以通过类似如下的语句获得完成的登录成功信息：

`String successInfo = getText("loginSuccess", new String[]{this.getUsername()});`

（2）在资源文件中添加登录成功和失败的信息。

在资源文件messages.properties中添加登录成功和失败的信息，添加信息如下：

`errors.loginErrorMessage = 登录失败,用户名或密码错误!.`
`errors.loginSuccessMessage = 欢迎您, {0}！`

在英文的资源文件messages_zh_en.properties中添加的信息如下：

`errors.loginErrorMessage = Login error:error username or password!.`
`errors.loginSuccessMessage = welcome, {0}`

在经过code.bat批处理文件处理的中文资源文件中添加的信息如下：

`errors.loginErrorMessage = \u9427\u8bf2\u7d8d\u6fb6\u8fab\u89e6\u951b\u5c80\u6564\u93b4\u5cf0\u6095\u93b4\u6827\u7611\u942e\u4f80\u654a\u7487\ufffd!.`

`errors.loginSuccessMessage = \u5a06\u3223\u7e4b\u93ae\ue7d2\u7d1d{0}\u951b\ufffd`

第 4 章 国际化 Web 应用

（3）创建包：amigo.struts.i18n。

在src源码目录中创建名为amigo.struts.i18n的包，用于存放本实例的Java源文件，操作步骤如图4-12所示。

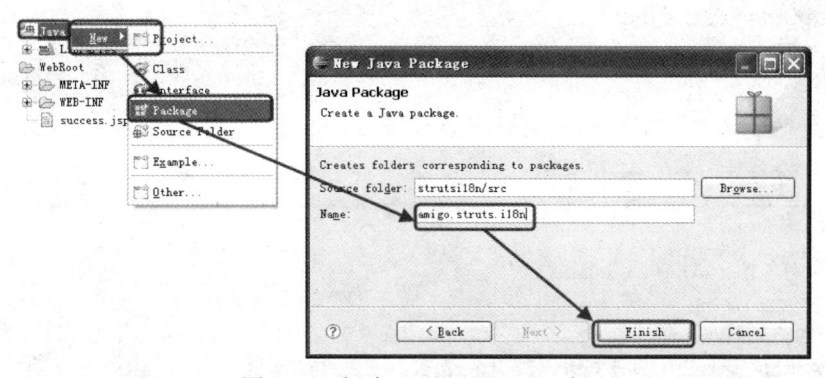

图 4-12　创建 amigo.struts.i18n 包

（4）创建类：I18nAction.java。

接着需要在 amigo.struts.i18n 包中创建本例的 Action 类 I18nAction.java，创建步骤如图 4-13 所示。

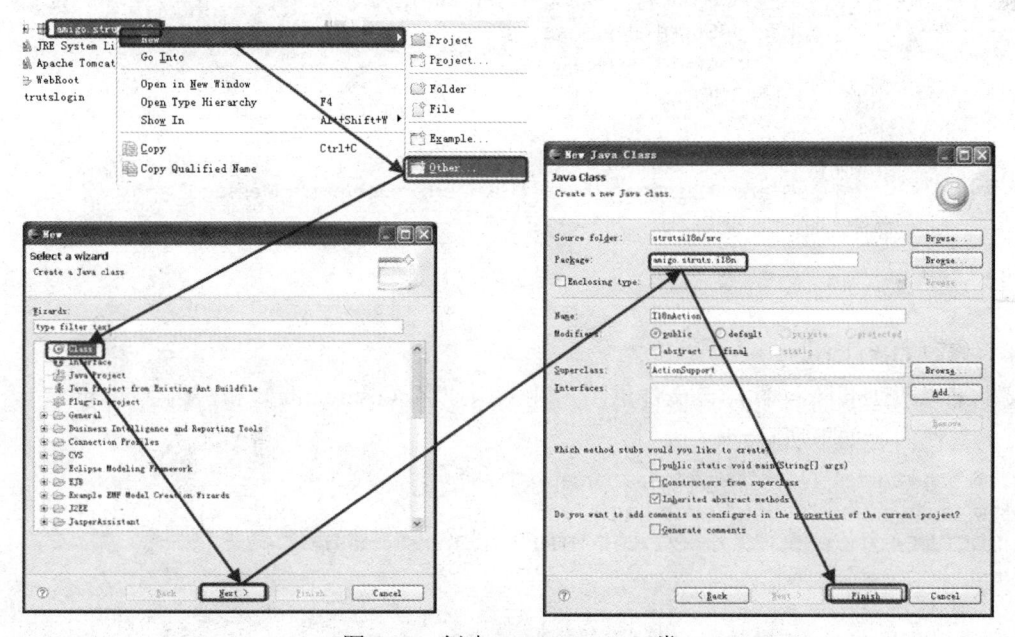

图 4-13　创建 I18nAction.java 类

（5）修改 Action 类：I18nAction.java。

I18nAction.java类演示如何在Action中实现国际化，该类的代码如下所示：

```
package amigo.struts.i18n;

import com.opensymphony.xwork2.ActionContext;
import com.opensymphony.xwork2.ActionSupport;

/**
 * 国际化的 Action 演示.
```

```java
 */
public class I18nAction extends ActionSupport {
    private static final long serialVersionUID = 6820659617470261780L;
    /** 用户名. */
    private String username;

    /** 密码. */
    private String passwd;

    // 省略属性的 getter/setter 方法

    /**
     * 定义处理登录请求的 execute 方法.
     */
    public String execute() {
        ActionContext ctx = ActionContext.getContext();
        if ("amigo".equals(this.getUsername())
                && "amigo".equals(this.getPasswd())) {
            // 登录成功，将用户名放入 session 中
            ctx.getSession().put("username", this.getUsername());
            String loginSuccessMessage = this.getText("errors.loginSuccessMessage",
                    new String[]{this.getUsername()});
            ctx.put("loginSuccessMessage",
                    loginSuccessMessage);
            return this.SUCCESS;
        } else {
            //登录失败，取得国际化的错误信息，放入到 request 中
            ctx.put("errorMessage", this.getText("errors.loginErrorMessage"));
            return this.ERROR;
        }
    }
}
```

（6）修改 i18n.jsp。

接下来修改i18n.jsp文件，该文件供用户输入用户名（username）和密码（passwd）信息，修改后的文件内容如下所示：

```jsp
<%@ page contentType="text/html; charset=UTF-8" %>
<%@ taglib prefix="s" uri="/struts-tags" %>
<!DOCTYPE HTML PUBLIC "-//W3C//DTD HTML 4.01 Transitional//EN">
<html>
    <head>
        <!-- 使用 s:text 标签输出国际化的标题信息 -->
        <title><s:text name="login.pageTitle"/></title>
    </head>
    <body>
        <s:form action="I18nAction" />
            <s:textfield name="username" key="user.name"/>
            <br>
            <s:textfield name="passwd" key="user.passwd"/>
            <s:submit key="submitButton"/>
        </s:form>
    </body>
</html>
```

（7）在 struts.xml 中配置 I18nAction。

若想能访问Action，需要在struts.xml这个配置文件中进行配置，修改后的struts.xml文件的内容如下所示：

```xml
<!DOCTYPE struts PUBLIC
    "-//Apache Software Foundation//DTD Struts Configuration 2.0//EN"
    "http://struts.apache.org/dtds/struts-2.0.dtd">

<struts>
    <include file="struts-default.xml"/>
    <constant name="ruts.custom.i18n.resources" value="messages" />
    <package name="amigo" extends="struts-default">
      <action name="Login"   class="amigo.struts.chapter4.I18nAction">
            <result name="success">/welcome.jsp</result>
            <result name="error">/ i18n.jsp</result>
        </action>
    </package>
</struts>
```

从上面的配置中可以看出，当登录成功时，跳转到welcome.jsp页面，显示欢迎信息，当登录失败时，将在输入界面显示对应的错误信息。

（8）创建欢迎界面：welcome.jsp。

在strutsi18n的WebRoot目录中创建登录成功后的欢迎界面welcome.jsp，操作步骤如图4-14所示。

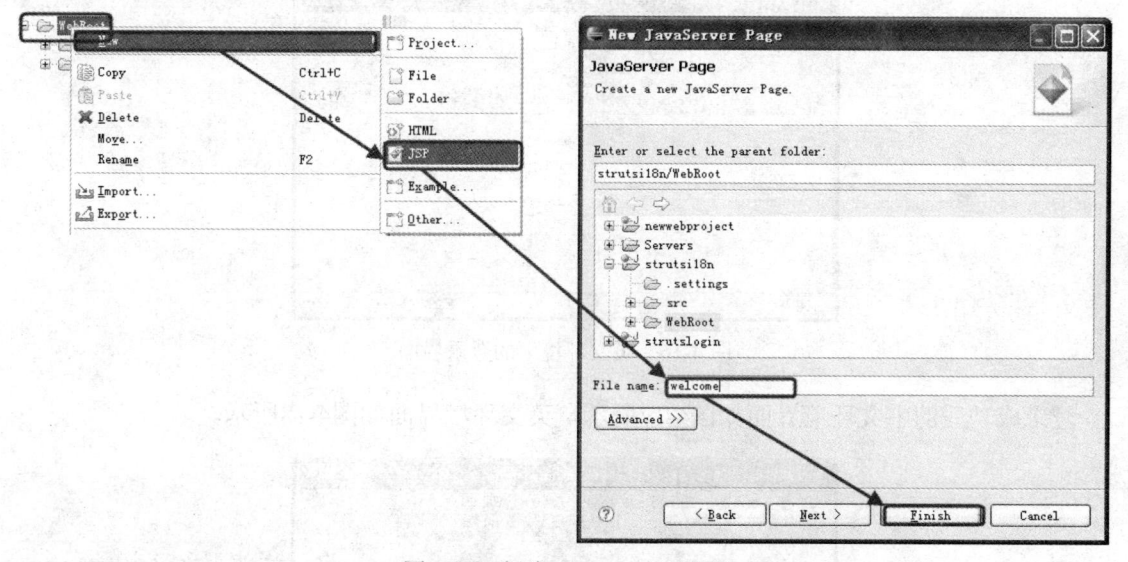

图 4-14 创建 welcome.jsp 页面

（9）编写欢迎界面 welcome.jsp。

该页的内容如下所示：

```jsp
<%@ page contentType="text/html; charset=UTF-8" %>
<%@ taglib prefix="s" uri="/struts-tags" %>
<html>
<head>
    <title><s:text name="welcome.pageTitle"/></title>
</head>
```

```
<body>
    <!-- 输出国际化的欢迎信息 -->
    ${requestScope.loginSuccessMessage}
</body>
</html>
```

(10) 运行结果。

部署工程后,在浏览器中输入地址:http://localhost:8899/strutsi18n/i18n.jsp,在中文环境下的界面如图4-15所示,英文环境下的界面如图4-16所示。

图 4-15 中文环境下的登录界面

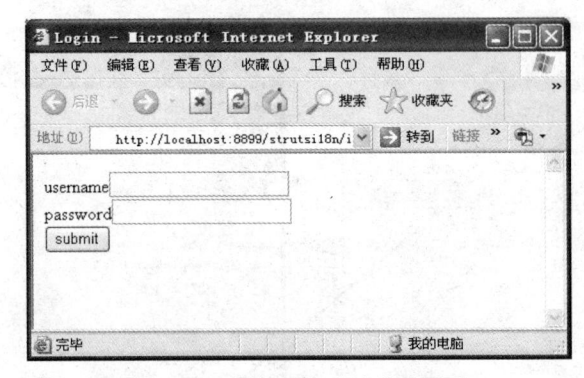

图 4-16 英文环境下的登录界面

登录成功后的中文环境界面如图4-17所示,英文环境界面如图4-18所示。

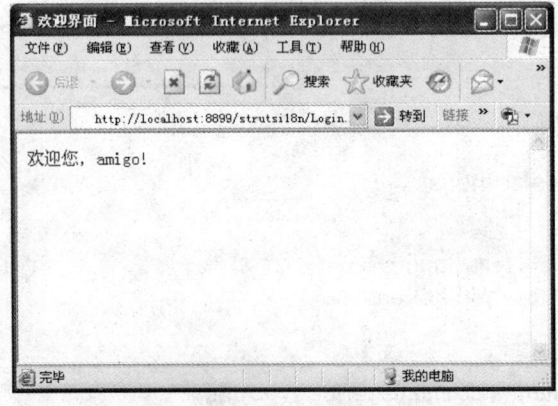

图 4-17 中文环境下的登录成功界面

图 4-18　英文环境下的登录成功界面

小结

中文乱码问题经常困扰着使用中文进行程序开发的 Java Web 应用程序开发人员，为了避免产生中文乱码问题，需要注意如下问题：
- 将代码文件的字符集统一设置为：UTF-8。
- 在 web.xml 中配置编码过滤器，并设置编码为：UTF-8。
- 将 JSP 和 HTML 文件的页面编码设置为：UTF-8。
- 设置数据库编码为：UTF-8。
- URL 传递中文参数时进行 ISO8859-1 到 GBK 的转码。

在涉及需要国际化的 Web 项目中需要编写资源文件，在 Struts 2 的 Web 项目中，可以通过配置 struts.properties 或 struts.xml 来将资源文件加载进来。

在 struts.properties 中的配置格式如下所示：

```
struts.custom.i18n.resources = messages
```

在 struts.xml 文件中配置时，可使用如下类似语句：

```
<constant name="struts.custom.i18n.resources" value="messages" />
```

当有多个资源文件（例如ApplicationResources和messages）时，可以以逗号（,）隔开。

为了支持国际化，在 Struts 2 中提供了如下标签：
- <s:i18n.../>标签：用于指定从某个特定的资源文件中取数据，使用格式如下所示：

```
<s:i18n name="messages">
<s:text name="user.name"></s:text>
</s:i18n>
```

- <s:text.../>标签：用来输出国际化信息。
- <s:param.../>标签：用来填充带有占位符的国际化信息，使用格式如下所示：

```
<s:text name="errors.required">
    <!-- 使用 s:param 标签填充占位符 -->
    <s:param><s:text name="user.name"/></s:param>
</s:text>
```

- <s:textfield.../>标签：在文本输入框中可使用<s:textfield.../>标签的 key 属性来实现国际化，例如：

```
<s:textfield name="username" key="user.name"/>
```

- `<s:submit.../>`标签：其 key 属性用来实现提交按钮的国际化，例如：

`<s:submit key="submitButton"/>`

在开发过程中，读者也可能会遇到需要在 Action 获取国际化信息的情况，ActionSupport 类提供了 getText(String str)方法来获得资源文件中的国际化信息，使用举例如下：

`String errorMessage = this.getText("loginError");`

国际化对于那种需要支持多种语言或可能有支持多种语言需求的 Java EE 应用程序是很重要的内容。

第 5 章 数据校验器

【本章导读语】

为了防止正常用户的非正确输入，以及恶意用户的恶意输入，Web 系统必须将这些输入阻止在应用之外，形成一面"防火墙"。

输入校验分为客户端校验和服务端校验，这两者对系统来说缺一不可。其中客户端校验主要通过 JavaScript 实现，阻止非法数据进入系统。而服务端校验是阻止非法输入进入系统的最后一道关卡，通过 Java 代码编程实现。

Struts 2 提供了强大的校验客户端和服务端数据的校验体系，它自身提供了绝大部分的校验，而且还提供了良好的扩展性，允许开发人员重写 validate 方法来自定义验证规则。本章讲解在 Struts 2 中如何进行客户端校验和服务端校验，以及详细讲解验证时需要注意的问题。

检验分为几种：一种是手动进行服务端校验，可以通过重写 Action 的 validate()方法或 validateXxx()来完成；第二种是通过 Struts 2 的验证框架完成服务端校验；第三种是使用 Struts 2 的验证框架进行客服端的验证，客户端通过 Struts 2 的验证框架自动生成 JavaScript 代码来实现。

为了对校验的提示信息进行国际化，本章通过实例讲解了国际化的方法。校验器可通过两种方式来编写：第一种是编写字段校验器，另一种是配置非字段校验器。这些知识都将在本章的实例中深入讲述。本章最后讲述了常用的内建校验器，例如必填字符串校验器、整数范围校验器和正则表达式校验器等。

【例 5-1】使用重写 validate()方法进行手动校验

〖实例需求〗

各种 MVC 框架都提供了数据验证的框架，Struts 2 中可通过在 Action 中重写 ActionSupport 类的 validate()方法来完成 Action 中各方法的验证。本例通过对注册信息验证来讲解在 Struts 2 中如何重写 validate()方法。

〖开发过程〗

第一步：建立工程

读者可以参考前几章建立工程的方法在 Eclipse 中新建一个名为 strutsValidation 的动态 Web 工程，并将所需的 jar 包导入到 WEB-INF/lib 目录中，接着在 src 目录中建立 amigo.struts.validation 包、在 WebRoot 目录中建立 validation 子目录来存放本实例的 JSP 页面。最后在 web.xml 中配置 Struts 2 的 FilterDispatcher。

操作完成后工程的结构如图 5-1 所示。

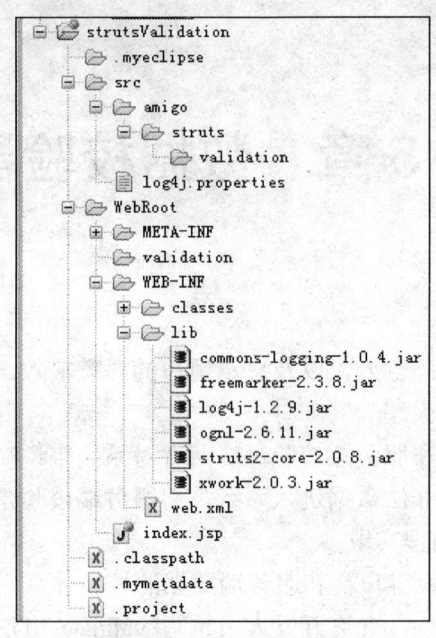

图 5-1　工程的目录结构

第二步：编写用户信息的 POJO 类：User.java

在 amigo.struts.validation 包中建立用户信息的 POJO 类，该类包括 username（用户名）、password（密码）、birthDate（生日）等属性。操作步骤如图5-2所示。

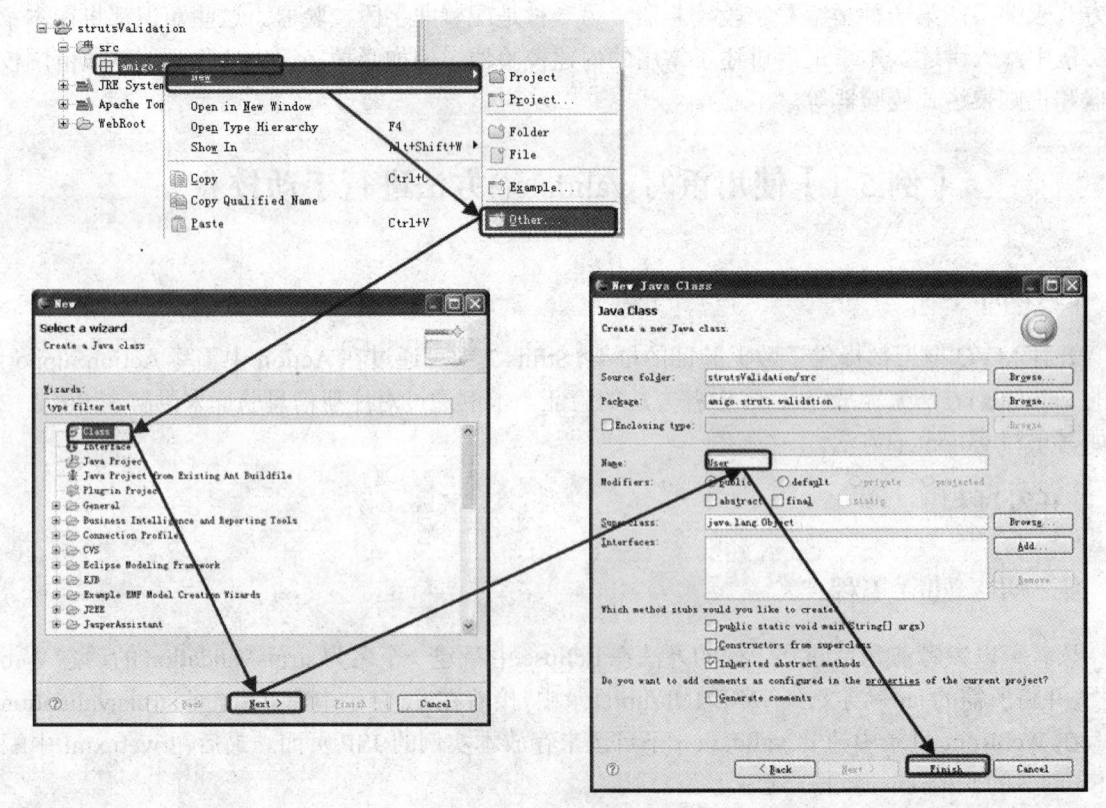

图 5-2　创建 User 类

该类的代码如下所示：

```java
package amigo.struts.validation;

import java.util.Date;

/**
 * 用户信息的POJO类.
 */
public class User {
    /** 用户名. */
    private String username;

    /** 密码. */
    private String password;

    /** 性别. */
    private int gender;

    /** 年龄. */
    private int age;

    /** 出生日期. */
    private Date birthDate;

    /** 联系电话. */
    private String tel;

    /** Email. */
    private String email;

    /** 个人首页. */
    private String url;
    // 省略各属性的getter/setter方法
}
```

第三步：编写注册的Action：RegAction.java

在amigo.struts.validation包中建立RegAction.java类，该类继承ActionSupport类，并重写了ActionSupport类的validate()方法，对用户名和密码信息进行验证。当然还需要对birthDate（出生日期）、age（年龄）和email等进行验证，为了简便起见，本实例并没有实现，在后面的各实例讲解中读者将陆续接触到这些知识。创建RegAction类的操作步骤如图5-3所示。

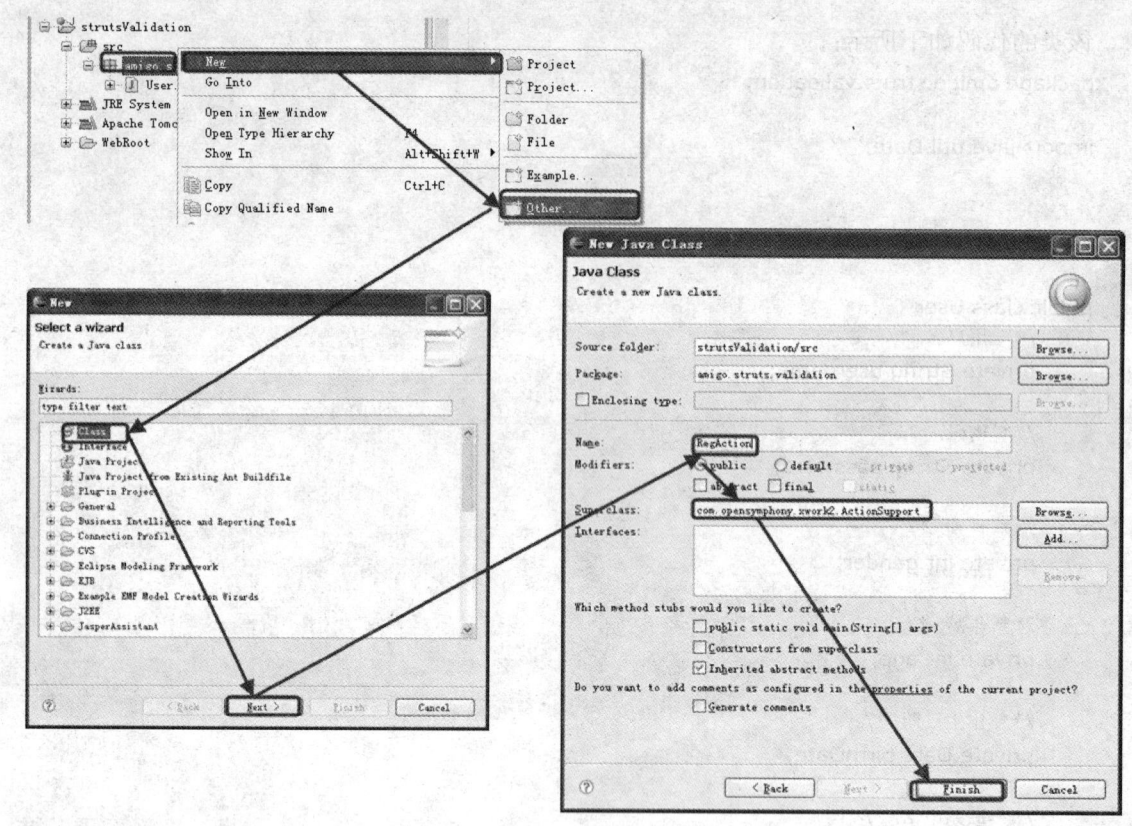

图 5-3 创建 RegAction 类

该类的代码如下所示：

```java
package amigo.struts.validation;

import java.util.regex.Pattern;

import javax.servlet.http.HttpServletRequest;

import org.apache.struts2.interceptor.ServletRequestAware;

import com.opensymphony.xwork2.ActionSupport;

/**
 * 使用 validate()方法完成注册验证.
 */
public class RegAction extends ActionSupport
            implements ServletRequestAware {
    private User user;

    private HttpServletRequest request;

    // 省略 request 、user 的 getter/setter 方法

    public void validate() {
        // 非空验证和输入合法性验证
        if (user.getUsername() == null
```

```
            || "".equals(user.getUsername().trim())) {
        this.addFieldError("user.username",
                "用户名不能为空");
    } else if(user.getUsername() != null
            && !Pattern.matches("\\w{5,50}", user.getUsername().trim())) {
        this.addFieldError("user.username",
                "用户名输入不合法,必须为长度为 5~50 之间的字母或数字");
    }
    if (user.getPassword() == null
            || "".equals(user.getPassword().trim())) {
        this.addFieldError("user.password",
                "密码不能为空");
    } else if(user.getPassword() != null
            && !Pattern.matches("\\w{5,50}", user.getPassword().trim())) {
        this.addFieldError("user.password",
                "密码输入不合法,必须为长度为 5~50 之间的字母或数字");
    }
    if (user.getAge() < 0 || user.getAge() > 130) {
        this.addFieldError("user.age",
                "年龄输入不合法");
    }
}
public String execute() {
    return null;
}
}
```

第四步:编写注册页面:reg.jsp

在WebRoot/validation目录中建立注册页面reg.jsp,该页面用于填写注册信息,当校验失败时将在该页面输出错误信息。创建reg.jsp文件的操作步骤如图5-4所示。

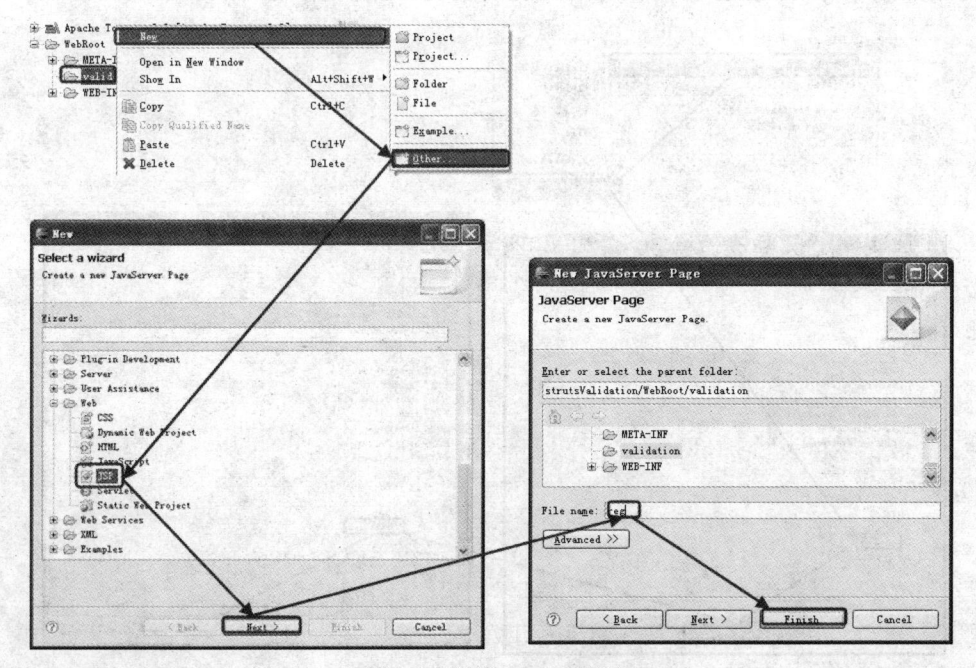

图 5-4 创建 reg.jsp 页面

该页面的代码如下所示：

```jsp
<%@ page contentType="text/html; charset=UTF-8" %>
<%@ taglib prefix="s" uri="/struts-tags" %>

<html>
 <head>
    <title>注册用户</title>
    <meta http-equiv="Content-Type" content="text/html; charset=UTF-8"/>
 </head>
 <body>
    <s:form action="reg">
        <s:textfield name="user.username" label="用户名"></s:textfield>
        <s:password name="user.password" label="密码"></s:password>
        <s:select label="性别" name="user.gender"
            list="#{'1' : '男', '0' : '女'}"
            listKey="key"
            listValue="value" value="0"/>
        <s:textfield name="user.age" label="年龄"></s:textfield>
        <s:textfield name="user.birthDate" label="出生日期"></s:textfield>
        <s:textfield name="user.tel" label="联系电话"></s:textfield>
        <s:textfield name="user.email" label="Email"></s:textfield>
        <s:textfield name="user.url" label="个人首页"></s:textfield>
        <s:submit></s:submit>
    </s:form>
 </body>
</html>
```

第五步：配置 struts.xml

在src目录中创建配置文件struts.xml，在该文件中配置RegAction，并配置其校验失败时的跳转页面为本页面reg.jsp。创建struts.xml文件的操作步骤如图5-5所示。

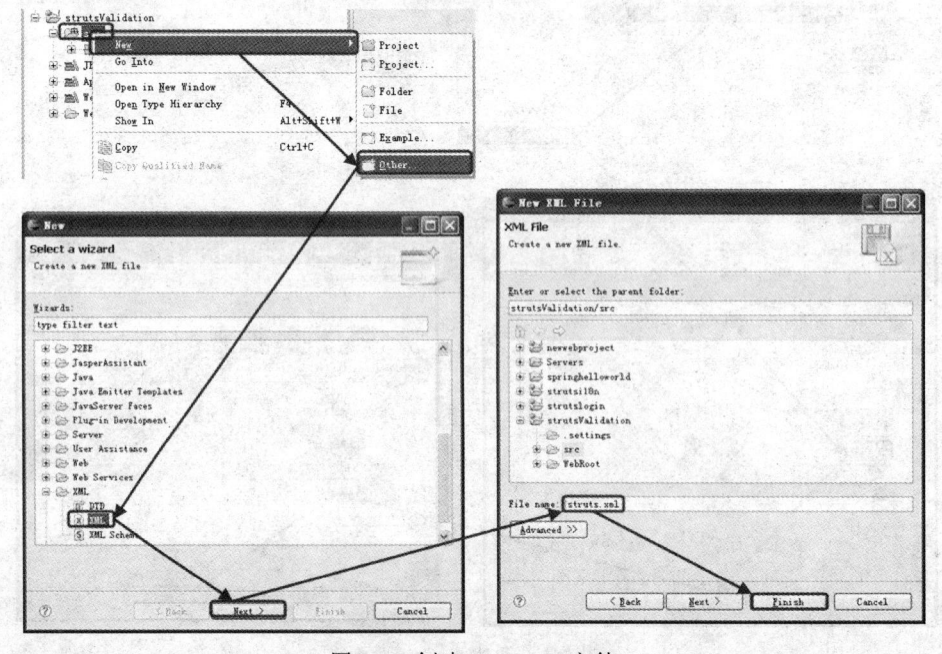

图 5-5 创建 struts.xml 文件

该文件的配置信息如下所示：

```
<!DOCTYPE struts PUBLIC
    "-//Apache Software Foundation//DTD Struts Configuration 2.0//EN"
    "http://struts.apache.org/dtds/struts-2.0.dtd">

<struts>
    <include file="struts-default.xml"/>
    <package name="amigo" extends="struts-default">
      <!-- 在 Action 中使用 validate 方法来完成数据校验 -->
      <action name="reg"   class="amigo.struts.validation.RegAction">
            <result name="input">/validation/reg.jsp</result>
      </action>
    </package>
</struts>
```

第六步：运行结果

在浏览器中输入reg.jsp的地址，输入用户信息后界面如图5-6所示。

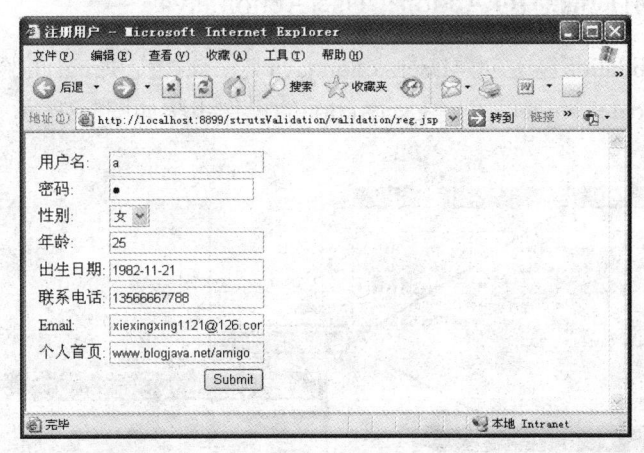

图 5-6 注册界面

在图5-6中，输入的用户名和密码信息长度太短，此时单击Submit按钮后提交表单将输出失败信息，界面如图5-7所示。

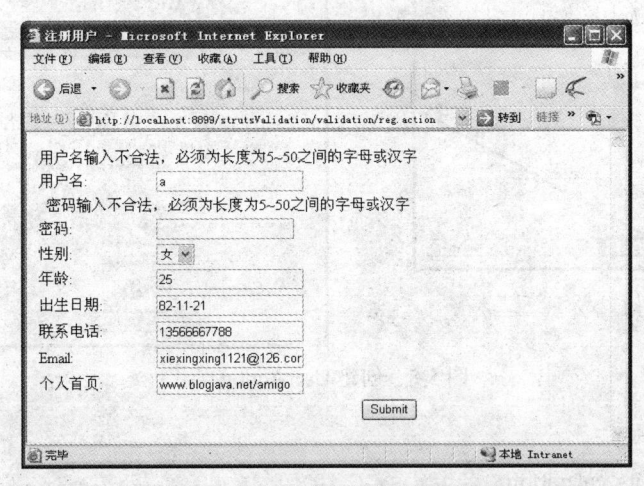

图 5-7 注册信息校验失败界面

【例 5-2】使用重写 validateXxx()方法进行手动校验

〖实例需求〗

Struts 的 Action 类包含多个方法，例如若 UserAction 类包含 reg（注册）和 login（登录）方法，此时若使用重写 validate()方法进行输入验证，所有的方法将进行同样的输入验证。但在日常的开发过程中，通常各方法的验证并不相同。例如注册时需要验证用户名、密码、年龄、出生日期等信息，而登录时只需要对用户名和密码进行输入验证。此时可使用 validateXxx()方法进行输入验证，本实例讲解如何在 Struts 2 中通过 validateXxx()方法对各 Action 的指定方法进行输入验证。

〖开发过程〗

第一步：编写用户信息的 Action：UserAction.java

在amigo.struts.validation包中创建UserAction.java类，该类提供reg()的验证方法validateReg()、login()的验证方法validateLogin()。创建UserAction的操作步骤如图5-8所示。

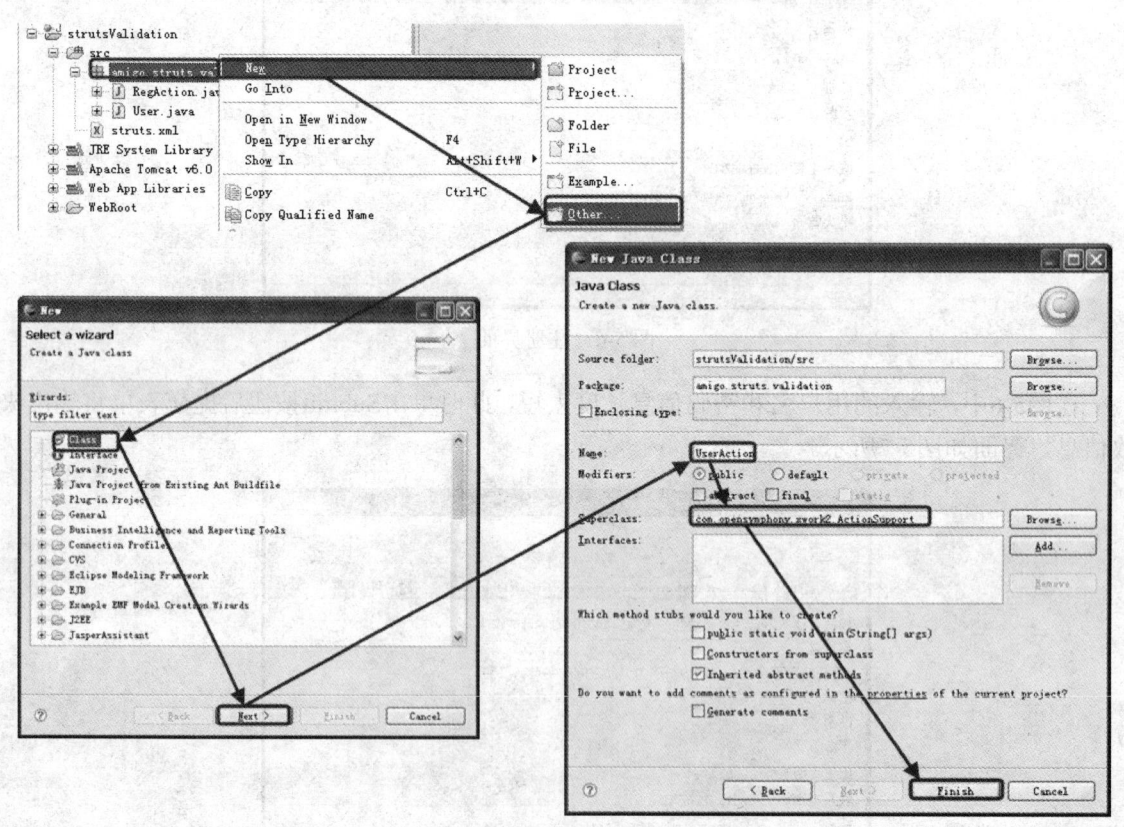

图 5-8　创建 UserAction 类

该类的代码如下所示：

```
package amigo.struts.validation;
```

```java
import java.util.regex.Pattern;

import com.opensymphony.xwork2.ActionSupport;

/**
 * 使用 validateXxx()方法完成注册验证.
 */
public class UserAction extends ActionSupport {
    private User user;
    // 省略 user 的 getter/setter 方法

    /**
     * 验证用户信息注册表单
     */
    public void validateReg() {
        // 该方法同上实例的 validate()方法
    }

    /**
     * 完成用户登录表单
     */
    public void validateLogin() {
        // 非空验证和输入合法性验证
        if (user.getUsername() == null
                || "".equals(user.getUsername().trim())) {
            this.addFieldError("user.username",
                    "用户名不能为空");
        }

        if (user.getPassword() == null
                || "".equals(user.getPassword().trim())) {
            this.addFieldError("user.password",
                    "密码不能为空");
        }
    }

    /**
     * 完成用户注册.
     */
    public String reg() {
        // 实现代码省略
        return null;
    }

    /**
     * 完成用户登录
     */
    public String login() {
        // 实现代码省略
        return null;
    }
```

```
public String execute() {
    return null;
}
}
```

第二步：编写注册页面：validateXxxReg.jsp

在WebRoot\validation目录中创建注册页面validateXxxReg.jsp，该页面与上例的reg.jsp页面类似，不过action的指向为userReg，该页面的代码省略。

第三步：编写登录页面：validateXxxLogin.jsp

在WebRoot\validation目录中创建登录页validateXxxLogin.jsp，操作步骤如图5-9所示。

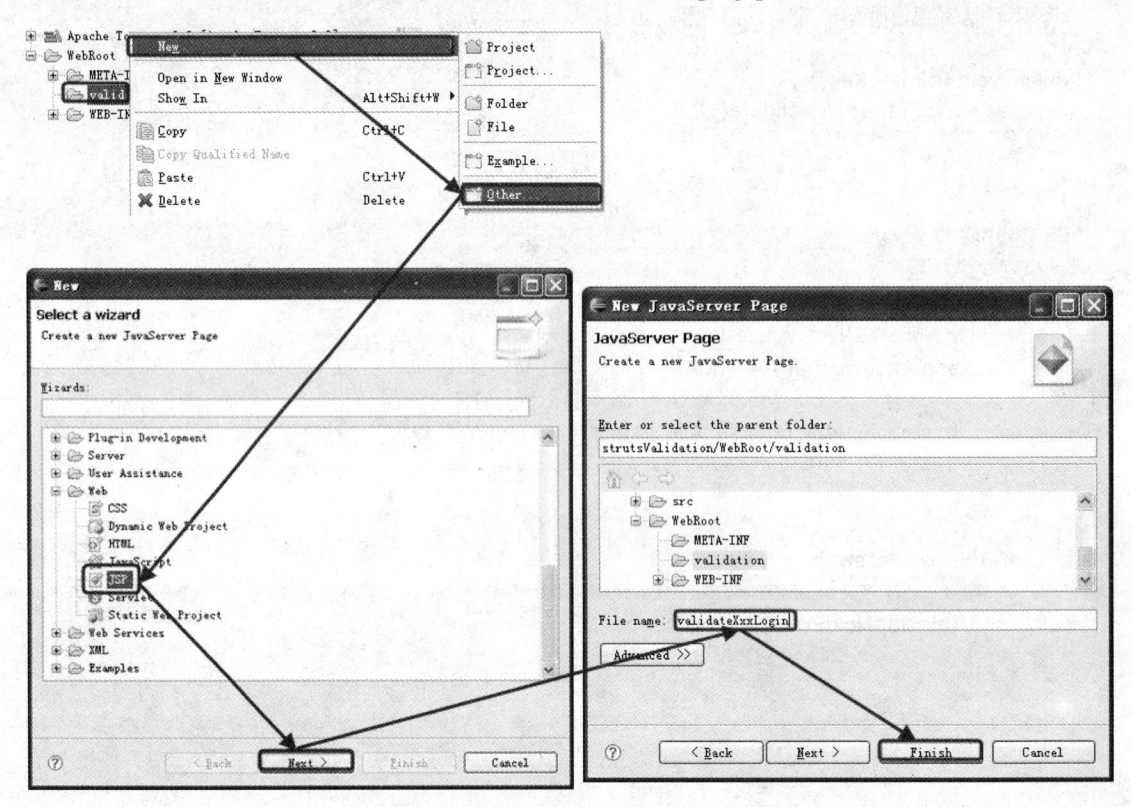

图 5-9 创建 validateXxxLogin.jsp 页面

该页面的代码如下所示：

```
<%@ page contentType="text/html; charset=UTF-8" %>
<%@ taglib prefix="s" uri="/struts-tags" %>
<html>
 <head>
     <title>用户登录</title>
     <meta http-equiv="Content-Type" content="text/html; charset=UTF-8"/>
 </head>
 <body>
     <s:form action="userLogin">
         <s:textfield name="user.username" label="用户名"></s:textfield>
         <s:password name="user.password" label="密码"></s:password>
```

```
            <s:submit></s:submit>
        </s:form>
    </body>
</html>
```

第四步：配置 struts.xml

最后在UserAction类的两个方法中配置两个不同的请求路径，添加的配置信息如下所示：

```xml
<!-- 在 Action 中使用 validateXxx 方法来完成数据校验 -->
<action name="userReg"   class="amigo.struts.validation.UserAction" method="reg">
    <result name="input">/validation/validateXxxReg.jsp</result>
</action>

<action name="userLogin"   class="amigo.struts.validation.UserAction" method="login">
    <result name="input">/validation/validateXxxLogin.jsp</result>
</action>
```

第五步：运行结果

在浏览器中输入validateXxxLogin.jsp页面的地址，界面如图5-10所示。

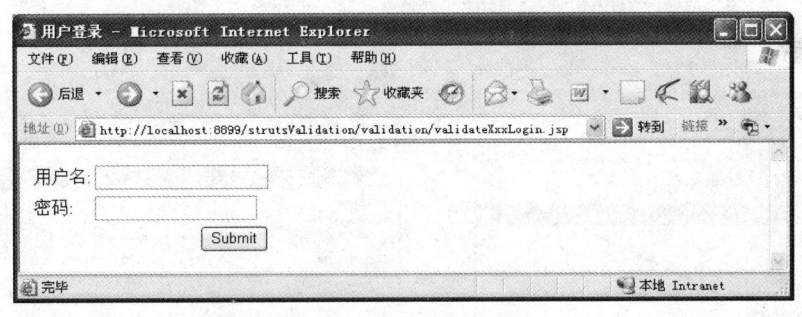

图 5-10　用户登录界面

不输入"用户名"和"密码"信息，单击Submit按钮，将弹出校验错误信息，界面如图5-11所示。

图 5-11　登录信息校验失败界面

在浏览器中输入validateXxxReg.jsp的地址，页面请求的效果与【例5-1】一样，不再赘述。

从运行结果中可以看出，在调用UserAction的不同方法时，执行了不同的数据校验方法。若Action中重写了validate()方法，又为reg方法编写了特定的验证方法validateReg()方法时，将首先执行validateReg()方法，然后执行validate()方法。

【例 5-3】使用 Struts 2 的验证框架完成服务端校验

〖实例需求〗

在上面的两个实例中，都是通过编写大量的 Java 代码来完成服务端的验证，这种验证重用性低，而且不利于管理。Struts 2 提供了一套验证框架来进行服务端和客户端的数据校验，本实例讲解如何利用配置文件来完成服务端的数据验证。

〖开发过程〗

第一步：编写 Action 类：ValFrameworkRegAction.java

在 amigo.struts.validation 包中创建 ValFrameworkRegAction 类，该类与 RegAction 类代码类似，不过它去除了 RegAction 类中带有繁琐的验证代码的 validate() 方法。操作步骤如图 5-12 所示。

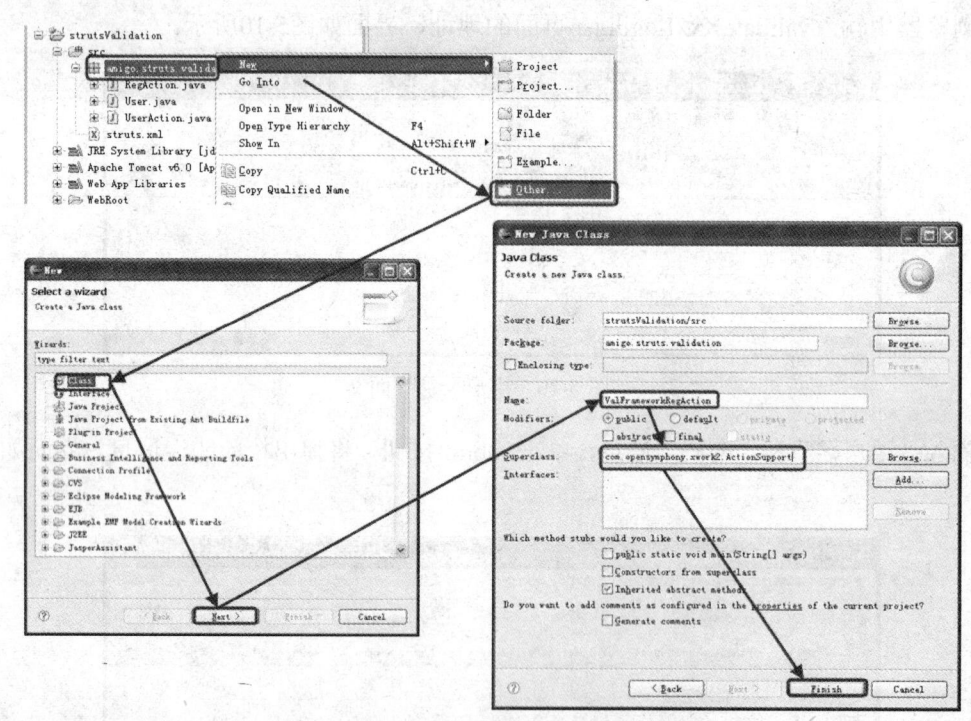

图 5-12 创建 ValFrameworkRegAction 类

该类的代码如下所示：

```
package amigo.struts.validation;
import com.opensymphony.xwork2.ActionSupport;

/**
 * 使用 Struts 2 的验证框架完成数据校验.
 */
public class ValFrameworkRegAction extends ActionSupport {
  private User user;
  // 省略 user 的 getter/setter 方法
```

```
public String execute() {
    return null;
}
}
```

第二步：编写验证文件：ValFrameworkRegAction-validation.xml

Struts 2 中的每个 Action 都可以有一个验证文件，该验证文件与 Action 处于同目录中，命名格式为：

Action 的名称-validation.xml

其中"-validation.xml"是确定的，而"Action 的名称"会根据不同的 Action 而有所不同，本实例的验证文件的名称为：ValFrameworkRegAction-validation.xml。

该验证文件对 username（用户名）、password（密码）进行了非空和合法性的验证，对 age（年龄）进行了非空的验证。创建 ValFrameworkRegAction-validation.xml 文件的操作步骤如图 5-13 所示。

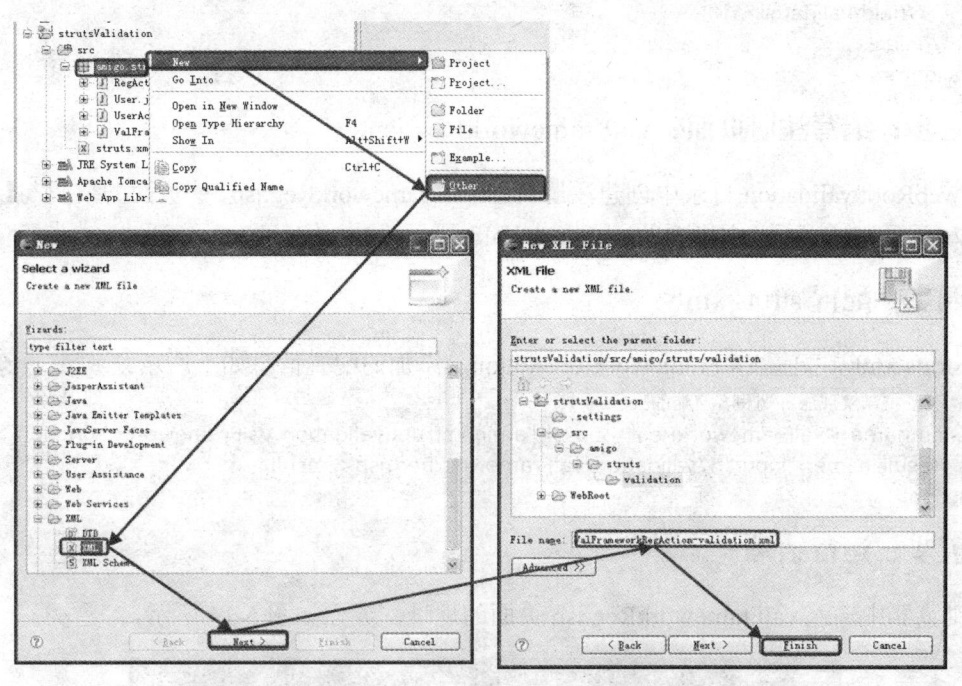

图 5-13　创建 ValFrameworkRegAction-validation.xml 文件

该文件的完整内容如下所示：

```xml
<?xml version="1.0" encoding="GBK"?>
<!DOCTYPE validators PUBLIC "-//OpenSymphony Group//XWork Validator 1.0.2//EN"
 "http://www.opensymphony.com/xwork/xwork-validator-1.0.2.dtd">
<validators>
  <field name="user.username">
      <field-validator type="requiredstring">
          <param name="trim">true</param>
          <message>用户名不能为空</message>
      </field-validator>
      <field-validator type="regex">
          <param name="expression"><![CDATA[(\w{5,50})]]></param>
          <message>用户名输入不合法，必须为长度为 5~50 之间的字母或数字</message>
      </field-validator>
```

```xml
        </field>
        <field name="user.password">
            <field-validator type="requiredstring">
                <param name="trim">true</param>
                <message>密码不能为空</message>
            </field-validator>
            <field-validator type="regex">
                <param name="expression"><![CDATA[(\w{5,50})]]></param>
                <message>密码输入不合法，必须为长度为 5~50 之间的字母或数字</message>
            </field-validator>
        </field>
        <field name="user.age">
            <field-validator type="int">
                <param name="min">1</param>
                <param name="max">130</param>
                <message>年龄输入不合法</message>
            </field-validator>
        </field>
</validators>
```

第三步：编写注册页面：valFrameworkReg.jsp

在 WebRoot\validation 目录中创建注册页面 valFrameworkReg.jsp，该页面的代码与【例 5-1】的 reg.jsp 页面类似，不过它指向的 action 为 valFrameworkReg。

第四步：配置 struts.xml

在 struts.xml 中配置 ValFrameworkRegAction，添加的配置信息如下所示：

```xml
<!-- 验证框架实现服务端和客户端的校验 -->
<action name="valFrameworkReg" class="amigo.struts.validation.ValFrameworkRegAction">
    <result name="input">/validation/valFrameworkReg.jsp</result>
</action>
```

第五步：运行结果

在浏览器中输入 valFrameworkReg.jsp 页面的地址，界面如图 5-14 所示。

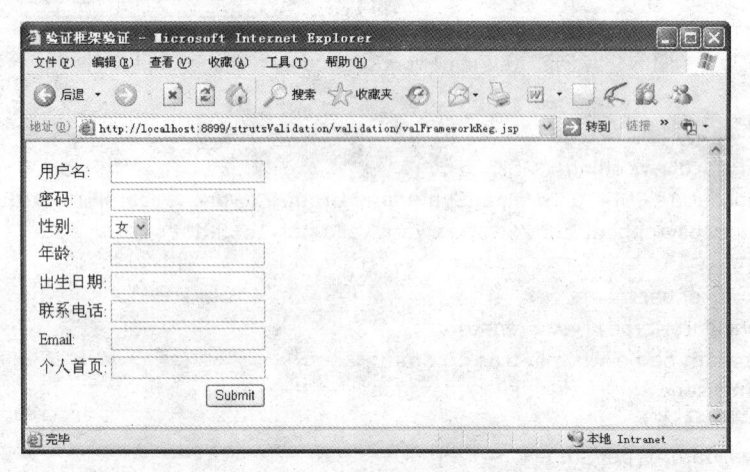

图 5-14 注册界面

在图 5-14 中不输入任何信息，单击 Submit 按钮，将显示校验信息，如图 5-15 所示。

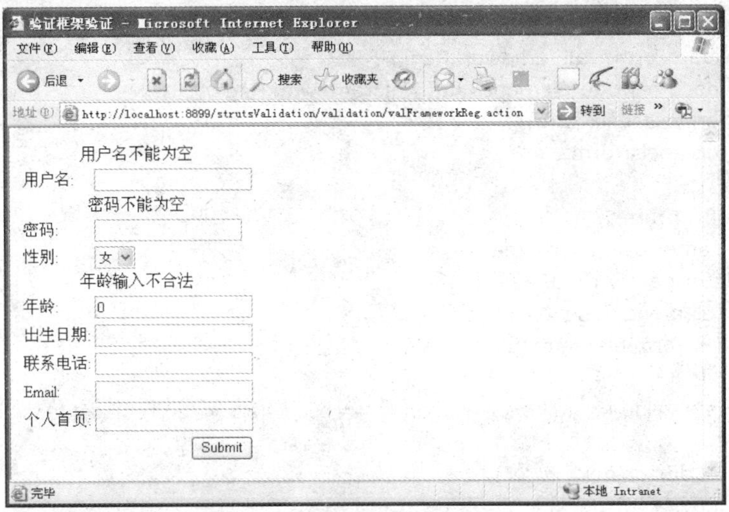

第 5 章　数据校验器

图 5-15　服务端校验失败界面

【例 5-4】使用 Struts 2 的验证框架完成客户端校验

〖实例需求〗

在 Struts 2 中，进行客户端校验将由框架在页面中自动生成 JavaScript 代码，在提交时调用自动生成的 JavaScript 代码中的函数：

validateForm_Action 名称()

本实例讲解如何使用 Struts 2 的验证框架完成客户端的验证。

〖开发过程〗

第一步：修改 valFrameworkReg.jsp 文件

在 struts 2 中进行客户端校验非常简单，只需要将 form 的 validate 属性设置为 true 即可。在此实例中，只需要将 valFrameworkReg.jsp 页面中的如下代码：

<s:form action="valFrameworkReg">

修改成：

<!-- validate 属性为 true 时表示进行客户端验证 -->
<s:form action="valFrameworkReg" validate="true">

第二步：运行结果

在浏览器中输入 valFrameworkReg.jsp 页面的地址，在出现的页面中单击鼠标右键，选择"查看源文件"，源文件的部分信息如下所示：

```
……
<script type="text/javascript" src="/strutsValidation/struts/xhtml/validation.js"></script>

<form namespace="/validation" id#"valFrameworkReg" name="valFrameworkReg" onsubmit="return validateForm_valFrameworkReg();" action="/strutsValidation/validation/valFrameworkReg.action" method="post">
……
```

```html
<script type="text/javascript">
    function validateForm_valFrameworkReg() {
        form = document.getElementById("valFrameworkReg");
        clearErrorMessages(form);
        clearErrorLabels(form);

        var errors = false;
        // field name: user.username
        // validator name: requiredstring
        if (form.elements['user.username']) {
            field = form.elements['user.username'];
            var error = "用户名不能为空";
            if (field.value != null && (field.value == "" || field.value.replace(/^\s+|\s+$/g,"").length == 0)) {
                addError(field, error);
                errors = true;
            }
        }
        ......
</script>
```

在该页面生成的源文件中可以看出，Struts 2 验证框架在进行客户端验证时，自动生成了 JavaScript 代码，该实例的运行结果与【例 5-3】相同，不再赘述。

【例 5-5】国际化校验的提示信息

〖实例需求〗

在前面的实例中，验证不通过时的提示信息都是通过中文直接显示的，显然这种方式不利用实现程序的国际化。本实例讲解如何国际化校验的提示信息。

〖开发过程〗

第一步：创建校验提示信息的配置文件

在 src 目录中建立配置文件：validationMessages.properties，该文件的内容如下所示：

```
user.username.requried=用户名不能为空
user.username.regex=用户名输入不合法，必须为长度为 5~50 之间的字母或数字
user.password.requried=密码不能为空
user.password.regex=密码输入不合法，必须为长度为 5~50 之间的字母或数字
user.age=年龄必须在${min}和${max}之间！
```

中文的配置文件 validationMessages_zh_CN.properties 需要通过编码后才能进行正常显示，为了简化编码过程，读者可在 src 目录中建立批处理文件 code.bat，该文件的内容如下：

```
// 删除 messages_zh_CN.properties 文件
del validationMessages_zh_CN.properties
// validationMessages.properties 到 validationMessages_zh_CN.properties.gbk 文件
copy validationMessages.properties validationMessages_zh_CN.properties.gbk
// 将 validationMessages_zh_CN.properties.gbk 文件进行 GBK 编码后将内容拷贝到 validationMessages_zh_CN.properties 中
native2ascii -encoding GBK validationMessages_zh_CN.properties.gbk validationMessages_zh_CN.
```

```
properties
    // 删除 validationMessages_zh_CN.properties.gbk 文件
    del validationMessages_zh_CN.properties.gbk
    // 删除所有后缀为.bak 的文件
    del *.bak
```

运行该文件后，可在 src 目录中生成中文的配置文件 validationMessages_zh_CN.properties，该文件的内容如下：

```
user.username.requried=\u7528\u6237\u540d\u4e0d\u80fd\u4e3a\u7a7a
user.username.regex=\u7528\u6237\u540d\u8f93\u5165\u4e0d\u5408\u6cd5\uff0c\u5fc5\u987b\u4e3a\u957f\u5ea6\u4e3a5~50\u4e4b\u95f4\u7684\u5b57\u6bcd\u6216\u6c49\u5b57
user.password.requried=\u5bc6\u7801\u4e0d\u80fd\u4e3a\u7a7a
user.password.regex=\u5bc6\u7801\u8f93\u5165\u4e0d\u5408\u6cd5\uff0c\u5fc5\u987b\u4e3a\u957f\u5ea6\u4e3a5~50\u4e4b\u95f4\u7684\u5b57\u6bcd\u6216\u6c49\u5b57
user.age=\u5e74\u9f84\u5fc5\u987b\u5728${min}\u548c${max}\u4e4b\u95f4!
```

第二步：修改 struts.xml 文件

接下来在 struts 的头部添加 validationMessages 配置文件的信息，并设置编码为 GBK，添加的配置信息如下所示：

```xml
<!-- 指定国际化配置文件 -->
<constant name="struts.custom.i18n.resources" value="validationMessages"/>
<constant name="struts.i18n.encoding" value="GBK"/>
```

第三步：修改校验文件 ValFrameworkRegAction-validation.xml

将 ValFrameworkRegAction-validation.xml 文件中的中文提示信息修改为如下代码：

```
${getText("配置文件中 key 的名称")}
```

来获取国际化文件中的信息，修改后的配置文件内容如下所示：

```xml
<?xml version="1.0" encoding="GBK"?>
<!DOCTYPE validators PUBLIC "-//OpenSymphony Group//XWork Validator 1.0.2//EN"
 "http://www.opensymphony.com/xwork/xwork-validator-1.0.2.dtd">

<validators>
 <field name="user.username">
     <field-validator type="requiredstring">
         <param name="trim">true</param>
         <message>${getText("user.username.requried")}</message>
         <!-- message>用户名不能为空</message-->
     </field-validator>
     <field-validator type="regex">
         <param name="expression"><![CDATA[(\w{5,50})]]></param>
         <message>${getText("user.username.regex")}</message>
         <!-- message>用户名输入不合法，必须为长度为 5~50 之间的字母或数字</message-->
     </field-validator>
 </field>
 <field name="user.password">
     <field-validator type="requiredstring">
         <param name="trim">true</param>
         <message>${getText("user.password.requried")}</message>
         <!-- message>密码不能为空</message-->
     </field-validator>
     <field-validator type="regex">
```

```xml
                <param name="expression"><![CDATA[(\w{5,50})]]></param>
                <message>${getText("user.password.regex")}</message>
                <!--message>密码输入不合法,必须为长度为 5~50 之间的字母或数字</message-->
            </field-validator>
        </field>
        <field name="user.age">
            <field-validator type="int">
                <param name="min">1</param>
                <param name="max">130</param>
                <message>${getText("user.age")}</message>
                <!-- message>年龄输入不合法</message-->
            </field-validator>
        </field>
</validators>
```

第四步：运行结果

该实例的运行结果与【例 5-3】和【例 5-4】类似，不再赘述。

【例 5-6】非字段校验器规则

〖实例需求〗

在配置校验规则时，Struts 2 提供了两种规则，即字段校验规则和非字段校验规则。上面实例所讲的是字段校验器，这种校验器的整体风格如下：

```xml
......
<validators>
    <!--0 到多个 field 元素-->
    <field name="被校验的属性名">
        <field-validator type="校验器名 1"-->
            <!--为校验器指定 0 到多个参数-->
            <param name="参数名">参数值</param>
            ......
            <message>提示信息</message>
        </field-validator>
        <field-validator type="校验器名 2">
            <param name="参数名">参数值</param>
            <message>提示信息</message>
        </field-validator>
    </field>
    ......
</validators>
```

其中 validators 是整个配置文件的根元素，它可包括 0 到多个 field 子元素，而 field 子元素可包括<field-validator/>元素，上例配置文件对 user.username 这个属性配置了两个校验器，一个非空字符串的校验器和一个正则表达式的校验器。

字段校验器是将<field.../>（字段）元素放在<field-validator.../>（校验器）元素之前，它是以字段优先，将属性的多个校验器配置在一起，而非字段校验器则与此不同，0 到多个<validator.../>作为<validators.../>的子元素进行配置，格式如下所示：

......

```xml
<validators>
 <!--0 到多个 validator 元素-->
 <validator type="校验器名">
        <param name="fieldname">被校验的属性名</param>
        <!--为校验器指定 0 到多个参数-->
        <param name="参数名">参数值</param>
        ......
        <message>提示信息</message>
 </validator>
        ......
</validators>
```

本实例通过对【例 5-3】、【例 5-4】、【例 5-5】的校验配置文件进行修改,将其由字段校验器修改成非字段校验器来达到同样的运行结果,从而使读者熟悉非字段校验器的配置。

〖开发过程〗

第一步:修改配置文件 ValFrameworkRegAction-validation.xml

将上面实例的 ValFrameworkRegAction-validation.xml 配置文件按照非字段校验器风格进行修改,修改后的配置文件如下所示:

```xml
<?xml version="1.0" encoding="GBK"?>
<!DOCTYPE validators PUBLIC "-//OpenSymphony Group//XWork Validator 1.0.2//EN">
 "http://www.opensymphony.com/xwork/xwork-validator-1.0.2.dtd">

<validators>
 <!-- 配置用户名的必填字符串校验 -->
 <validator type="requiredstring">
        <param name="fieldname">user.username</param>
        <param name="trim">true</param>
        <message>${getText("user.username.requried")}</message>
        <!-- message>用户名不能为空</message-->
 </validator>

 <!-- 配置用户名的正则表达式校验 -->
 <validator type="regex">
        <param name="fieldname">user.username</param>
        <param name="expression"><![CDATA[(\w{5,50})]]></param>
        <message>${getText("user.username.regex")}</message>
        <!-- message>用户名输入不合法,必须为长度为 5~50 之间的字母或数字</message-->
 </validator>

 <!-- 配置密码的必填字符串校验 -->
 <validator type="requiredstring">
        <param name="fieldname">user.password</param>
        <param name="trim">true</param>
        <message>${getText("user.password.requried")}</message>
        <!-- message>密码不能为空</message-->
 </validator>

 <!-- 配置密码的正则表达式校验 -->
 <validator type="regex">
```

```xml
        <param name="fieldname">user.password</param>
        <param name="expression"><![CDATA[(\w{5,50})]]></param>
        <message>${getText("user.password.regex")}</message>
        <!--message>密码输入不合法,必须为长度为 5~50 之间的字母或数字</message-->
    </validator>

    <!-- 配置年龄的整数范围校验 -->
    <validator type="int">
        <param name="fieldname">user.age</param>
        <param name="min">1</param>
        <param name="max">130</param>
        <message>${getText("user.age")}</message>
        <!-- message>年龄输入不合法</message-->
    </validator>
</validators>
```

在上面的配置中,当一个属性具有多个校验器时,例如用户名和密码都具有 requiredstring 和 regex 两个校验器,需要分开配置两个 validator,在这点上与字段校验器相比,非字段校验器不利于管理,因此建议开发人员使用字段校验器。

第二步:运行结果

按照【例 5-3】的方法进行测试,读者可看到运行结果并没有改变,即说明字段校验器和非字段校验器达到的效果是一样的,只不过配置的风格不同而已。

【例 5-7】常用内建的校验器

〖实例需求〗

为了简化 Web 开发人员的开发工作,Struts 2 中提供了一些内建的校验器,使用它们能够完成大部分的校验工作。常见的内建校验器有:必填字符串校验器、整数范围校验器、正则表达式校验器、必填校验器、字符串长度校验器、网址校验器、邮件地址校验器、日期校验器和表达式校验器。本实例讲解常用的内建校验器的使用。

〖开发过程〗

第一步:常用内建校验器简述

(1)必填字符串校验器。

必填字符串校验器的名称为 requiredstring。对于非字段校验器,它具有两个参数,即 fieldName 和 trim,而对于字段校验器,只有 trim 这个参数。fieldName 属性用于指定校验的属性名,而 trim 的值可为 true 和 false,它用于指定是否去除字符串前后的空格。

前面实例中的 user.username 和 user.password 两个属性都使用了该校验器,采用字段校验器风格时,配置信息如下:

```xml
<field name="user.username">
<field-validator type="requiredstring">
<param name="trim">true</param>
```

```
            <message>用户名不能为空</message>
        </field-validator>
</field>
```

采用非字段校验器风格时，配置信息如下：

```
<validator type="requiredstring">
<param name="fieldname">user.username</param>
<param name="trim">true</param>
<message>用户名不能为空</message>
</validator>
```

（2）整数范围校验器。

整数范围校验器的名称为int，该校验器用于校验整数是否在指定的最小值和最大值之间，可接受的参数如下所示：

- filedName：用于非字段校验器，指定需要验证的属性名。
- min：可选参数，用于指定整数最小值。当指定了该参数时，若属性小于这个值，则将提示错误信息。若未指定该属性，则表示不对最小值进行校验。
- max：可选参数，用于指定整数最大值。当指定了该参数时，若属性大于这个值，则将提示错误信息。若未指定该属性，则表示不对最大值进行校验。

前面实例对user.age进行校验时，使用的就是整数范围校验器。对于字段校验器，配置实例如下：

```
<field name="user.age">
 <field-validator type="int">
        <param name="min">1</param>
        <param name="max">130</param>
        <message>年龄输入不合法，必须在${min}到${max}之间</message>
 </field-validator>
</field>
```

非字段校验器的配置实例如下所示：

```
<validator type="int">
 <param name="fieldname">user.age</param>
 <param name="min">1</param>
 <param name="max">130</param>
 <message>年龄输入不合法，必须在${min}到${max}之间</message>
</validator>
```

（3）正则表达式校验器。

正则表达式校验器的名称为regex，它常常用于检测字符串是否匹配某一正则表达式，例如对用户名和密码等的验证。它具有如下属性：

- fieldname：非字段校验器具有该属性，指定Action属性名。
- expression：必填，指定正则表达式。
- caseSensitive：非必填，指定是否区分大小写，默认为true。

在上面的实例中，user.username采用的是正则表达式，对于字段校验器，配置实例如下：

```
<field name="user.username">
 <field-validator type="regex">
        <param name="expression"><![CDATA[(\w{5,50})]]></param>
        <message>用户名输入不合法，必须为长度为5~50之间的字母或数字</message>
 </field-validator>
</field>
```

对于非字段校验器风格，配置实例如下：

```xml
<validator type="regex">
 <param name="fieldname"> user.username </param>
 <param name="expression"><![CDATA[(\w{5,50})]]></param>
 <message>用户名输入不合法，必须为长度为 5~50 之间的字母或数字</message>
</validator>
```

（4）必填校验器。

必填校验器的名称为required，它用于检查校验的字段是否为空。对于非字段校验器配置风格，它接受fieldName参数，用于指定Action的属性名。

对于字段校验器风格，配置举例如下：

```xml
<field name="user.username">
 <field-validator type="required">
      <message>用户名不能为空</message>
 </field-validator>
</field>
```

对于非字段校验器风格，配置实例如下：

```xml
<validator type="required">
 <param name="fieldname">user.username</param>
 <message>用户名不能为空</message>
</validator>
```

（5）字符串长度校验器。

字符串长度校验器的名称为stringlength，它用于校验被校验字段的长度是否在指定范围内。它具有如下参数：

- fieldName：对于非字段校验器风格，需指定该属性，该属性用于指定Action的属性名。
- minLength：可选，用于指定字符串的最小长度，未指定时，不对最小长度进行限制。
- maxLength：可选，用于指定字符串的最大长度，未指定时，不对最大长度进行限制。

字符串长度校验器也是很常用的一种校验器，例如检测用户名的长度，对于字段校验器配置风格，配置举例如下：

```xml
<field name="user.username ">
 <field-validator type="stringlength">
     <param name="minLength">5</param>
     <param name="maxLength">50</param>
     <message>用户名长度必须在 5~50 之间</message>
 </field-validator>
</field>
```

对于非字段校验器配置风格，配置举例如下：

```xml
<validator type="required">
 <param name="fieldname">user.username</param>
<param name="minLength">5</param>
<param name="maxLength">50</param>
 <message>用户名长度必须在 5~50 之间</message>
</validator>
```

（6）日期校验器。

日期校验器的名称为date，它用于校验日期是否在某个范围之内，具有如下属性：

- fieldName：对于非字段校验器，需要设置该属性，它用于指定Action的属性名。
- min：可选，指定日期的最小值，未指定时，不检测最小值。

- max：可选，指定日期的最大值，未指定时，不检测最大值。

日期校验器可用于校验出生日期属性，对于字段校验器配置风格，配置举例如下：

```xml
<field name="user.birthDate">
 <field-validator type="date">
    <param name="min">1850-01-01</param>
    <param name="max">2008-7-20</param>
    <message>出生日期输入不合法</message>
  </field-validator>
</field>
```

对于非字段校验器配置风格，配置举例如下：

```xml
<validator type="date">
 <param name="fieldname">user.birthDate</param>
 <param name="min">1850-01-01</param>
 <param name="max">2008-7-20</param>
 <message>出生日期输入不合法</message>
</validator>
```

（7）网址校验器。

网址校验器的名称为url，它用于校验字段不为空时，是否为合法的URL地址，该校验器基于正则表达式校验器，对于非字段校验器风格，可指定fieldname参数，它用于指定Action属性名。

网址校验器可用于检测个人首页的合法性，对于字段校验器配置风格，配置信息举例如下：

```xml
<field name="user.url">
 <field-validator type="url">
     <message>个人首页输入不合法</message>
 </field-validator>
</field>
```

对于非字段校验器配置风格，配置信息举例如下：

```xml
<validator type="url">
 <param name="fieldname">user.url</param>
 <message>个人首页输入不合法</message>
</validator>
```

（8）邮件地址校验器。

邮件地址校验器用于校验邮件地址是否合法，校验器名称为email，它与网址校验器一样，都是基于正则表达式的校验器，对于非字段校验器配置风格，可指定fieldname参数，它用于指定Action属性名。

该校验器常用于校验用户输入的邮件地址的合法性，对于字段校验器配置风格，配置举例如下：

```xml
<field name="user.email">
 <field-validator type="email">
     <message>Email 地址不合法</message>
 </field-validator>
</field>
```

对于非字段校验器配置风格，配置举例如下：

```xml
<validator type="email ">
 <param name="fieldname">user.email</param>
 <message>Email 地址不合法</message>
</validator>
```

第二步：修改校验提示信息的配置文件

本实例在【例5-5】的基础上进行修改，添加对birthDate（出生日期）、email（Email）和url（个人首页）的验证，因此需要在提示信息的配置文件中添加这些属性验证失败的信息。在validationMessages.properties文件中添加的配置信息如下：

```
user.birthDate=出生日期输入不合法
user.email=Email 地址输入不合法
user.url=个人首页输入不合法
```

使用code.bat批处理文件进行处理后，在validationMessages_zh_CN.properties文件中通过编码后的配置信息如下：

```
user.birthDdate=\u51fa\u751f\u65e5\u671f\u8f93\u5165\u4e0d\u5408\u6cd5
user.email=Email\u5730\u5740\u8f93\u5165\u4e0d\u5408\u6cd5
user.url=\u4e2a\u4eba\u9996\u9875\u8f93\u5165\u4e0d\u5408\u6cd5
```

第三步：编写验证文件：ValFrameworkRegAction-validation.xml

接下来在ValFrameworkRegAction-validation.xml校验器配置文件中添加birthDate、email和url的校验，添加的校验信息如下所示：

```xml
<!-- 添加对出生日期的校验 -->
<field name="user.birthDate">
 <field-validator type="date">
     <param name="min">1850-01-01</param>
     <param name="max">2008-7-20</param>
     <message>${getText("user.birthDate")}</message>
     <!-- message>出生日期输入不合法</message-->
 </field-validator>
</field>

<!-- 添加对 Email 的校验 -->
<field name="user.email">
 <field-validator type="email">
     <message>${getText("user.email")}</message>
     <!-- message>Email 地址不合法</message-->
 </field-validator>
</field>

<!-- 添加对个人首页的校验 -->
<field name="user.url">
 <field-validator type="url">
     <message>${getText("user.url")}</message>
     <!-- message>个人首页输入不合法</message-->
 </field-validator>
</field>
```

第四步：运行结果

输入 valFrameworkReg.jsp 的请求地址，填写注册信息后，界面如图5-16所示。

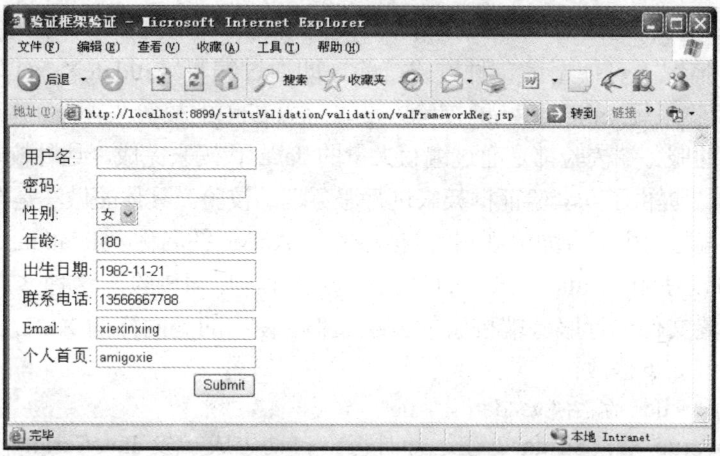

图 5-16　注册界面

单击图 5-16 中的 Submit 按钮，将提示错误信息，错误信息界面如图 5-17 所示。

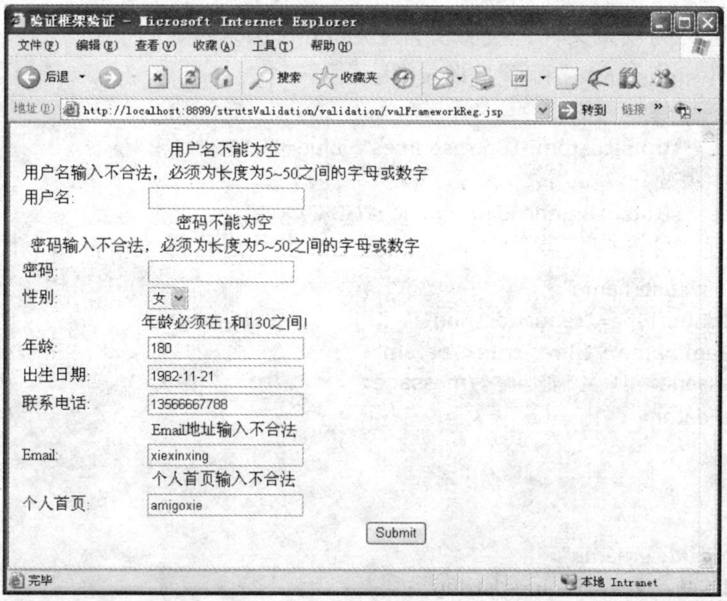

图 5-17　注册错误信息提示页

小结

在 Struts 2 中，提供了强大的客户端和服务端校验体系，它自身带了很多内建的校验器，而且还提供了良好的扩展性，允许开发人员在其基础上进行扩展。

本章讲述数据校验器，数据校验包括客户端校验和服务器端校验，其中客户端校验主要通过 JavaScript 实现，用于阻止合法用户的非法输入。而服务端校验是阻止非法输入进入系统的最后一道关卡，通过 Java 代码编程实现，它主要用于阻止非法用户的恶意进入。

在 Struts 2 中，服务器校验可通过几种方式实现。一是通过在 Action 中重写 validate()方法来实现，在 validate()方法中编写验证的代码，这种方式在当 Action 中包含多个方法（例如 reg()

方法和 login()方法）时都将通过 validate()方法来进行验证，很明显，这两个方法的校验是不一样的。因此在此种情况下可使用第二种方式校验，即通过编写 validateXxx()方法来分别进行校验，例如 reg()的校验采用 validateReg()校验方法，而 login()的校验采用 validateLogin()方法。

上述两种方式的服务端校验都是通过编写大量的 Java 代码来完成，这种校验重用性低，而且不利于管理。Struts 2 提供了一套验证框架来进行服务端的校验。具体的做法是在编写完 Action 类后，在其同目录下编写一个符合如下规则的校验文件：Action 的名称-validation.xml。

开发人员也可以使用 Struts 2 提供的验证框架进行客户端校验，这种客户端校验与前面所说的使用 XML 配置文件进行服务端校验的方法类似，使用的是同样的 XML 文件，不过需要在 JSP 页面对表单进行如下修改：

```
<s:form action="action 的路径" validate="true">
```

加上 validate="true"后，Struts 2 在运行时将会自动生成一段 JavaScript 代码，生成一个以 validateForm_Action()为名称的 JavaScript 函数，并且在表单提交时调用该方法进行校验。

在需要国际化的一些项目中，需要对校验提示信息也进行国际化，在 Struts 2 中提供了相应的方法，具体如下：

1）编写各个语种的校验文件：校验文件名称.properties 等。

2）在配置文件 struts.xml 中配置校验文件：

```xml
<!-- 指定国际化资源文件 -->
<constant name="struts.custom.i18n.resources" value="校验文件名称"/>
<!-- 指定资源文件编码 -->
<constant name="struts.i18n.encoding" value="GBK"/>
```

3）对校验配置文件：校验类名称-validation.xml 文件进行修改，将如下代码：

```xml
<field name="user.username">
    <field-validator type="requiredstring">
        <param name="trim">true</param>
        <message>用户名不能为空</message>
    </field-validator>
    ......
</field>
```

修改成：

```xml
<field name="user.username">
    <field-validator type="requiredstring">
        <param name="trim">true</param>
        <message>${getText("user.username.requried")}</message>
    </field-validator>
    ......
</field>
```

使用${getText("资源文件中的名称")}可以获得资源文件中的信息。

在配置校验规则时，Struts 2 提供了两种规则，即字段校验规则和非字段校验规则。其中字段校验器的整体风格如下：

```xml
......
<validators>
<!--0 到多个 field 元素-->
<field name="被校验的属性名">
    <field-validator type="校验器名 1">
        <!--为校验器指定 0 到多个参数-->
        <param name="参数名">参数值</param>
```

```
        ......
        <message>提示信息</message>
      </field-validator>
      <field-validator type="校验器名2">
        <param name="参数名">参数值</param>
        <message>提示信息</message>
      </field-validator>
   </field>
    ......
</validators>
```

字段校验器是将<field.../>（字段）元素放在<field-validator.../>（校验器）元素之前，它是以字段优先，将属性的多个校验器配置在一起。

非字段校验器将 0 到多个<validator.../>作为<validators.../>的子元素进行配置，配置格式如下所示：

```
......
<validators>
  <!--0 到多个 validator 元素-->
  <validator type="校验器名">
      <param name="fieldname">被校验的属性名</param>
      <!--为校验器指定 0 到多个参数-->
      <param name="参数名">参数值</param>
      ......
      <message>提示信息</message>
  </validator>
      ......
</validators>
```

这两种校验器配置方式不一样，但是效果差不多，开发人员可以自行选择。

为了简化 Web 开发人员的开发工作，Struts 2 中提供了一些内建的校验器，使用它们，能够完成大部分的校验工作。常用的内建校验器如下：

1）必填字符串校验器：名称为requiredstring，用于进行字符串的必填校验，采用字段校验器风格时，配置实例如下：

```
<field name="user.username">
<field-validator type="requiredstring">
<param name="trim">true</param>
    <message>用户名不能为空</message>
 </field-validator>
</field>
```

采用非字段校验器风格时，配置实例如下：

```
<validator type="requiredstring">
<param name="fieldname">user.username</param>
<param name="trim">true</param>
<message>用户名不能为空</message>
</validator>
```

2）整数范围校验器：名称为int，该校验器用于校验整数是否在指定的最小值和最大值之间。对于字段校验器，配置实例如下：

```
<field name="user.age">
 <field-validator type="int">
     <param name="min">1</param>
     <param name="max">130</param>
```

```
    <message>年龄输入不合法,必须在${min}到${max}之间</message>
  </field-validator>
</field>
```

非字段校验器的配置实例如下:

```
<validator type="int">
 <param name="fieldname">user.age</param>
 <param name="min">1</param>
 <param name="max">130</param>
 <message>年龄输入不合法,必须在${min}到${max}之间</message>
</validator>
```

3)正则表达式校验器:名称为regex,它常常用于检测字符串是否匹配某一正则表达式,例如对用户名和密码等的验证。对于字段校验器,配置实例如下:

```
<field name="user.age">
 <field-validator type="int">
    <param name="min">1</param>
    <param name="max">130</param>
    <message>年龄输入不合法,必须在${min}到${max}之间</message>
 </field-validator>
</field>
```

非字段校验器的配置实例如下:

```
<validator type="int">
 <param name="fieldname">user.age</param>
 <param name="min">1</param>
 <param name="max">130</param>
 <message>年龄输入不合法,必须在${min}到${max}之间</message>
</validator>
```

4)必填校验器:名称为required,它用于检查校验的字段是否为空。对于非字段配置风格,它接受fieldName参数,用于指定Action的属性名。

对于字段校验器风格,配置举例如下:

```
<field name="user.username">
 <field-validator type="required">
     <message>用户名不能为空</message>
 </field-validator>
</field>
```

对于非字段校验器风格,配置实例如下:

```
<validator type="required">
 <param name="fieldname">user.username</param>
 <message>用户名不能为空</message>
</validator>
```

5)字符串长度校验器:名称为stringlength,它用于校验被校验的字段的长度是否在指定范围之内。对于非字段校验器配置风格,配置实例如下:

```
<field name="user.username ">
 <field-validator type="stringlength">
     <param name="minLength">5</param>
     <param name="maxLength">50</param>
     <message>用户名长度必须在 5~50 之间</message>
 </field-validator>
</field>
```

对于非字段校验器配置风格,配置实例如下:

```xml
<validator type="required">
 <param name="fieldname">user.username</param>
 <param name="minLength">5</param>
 <param name="maxLength">50</param>
 <message>用户名长度必须在 5~50 之间</message>
</validator>
```

6）日期校验器：名称为 date，它用于校验日期是否在某个范围之内。对于字段校验器配置风格，配置实例如下：

```xml
<field name="user.birthDate">
 <field-validator type="date">
      <param name="min">1850-01-01</param>
      <param name="max">2008-7-20</param>
      <message>出生日期输入不合法</message>
 </field-validator>
</field>
```

对于非字段校验器配置风格，配置实例如下：

```xml
<validator type="date">
 <param name="fieldname">user.birthDate</param>
 <param name="min">1850-01-01</param>
 <param name="max">2008-7-20</param>
 <message>出生日期输入不合法</message>
</validator>
```

7）网址校验器：名称为 url，它用于校验字段不为空时，是否为合法的 URL 地址。对于字段校验器配置风格，配置实例如下：

```xml
<field name="user.url">
 <field-validator type="url">
      <message>个人首页输入不合法</message>
 </field-validator>
</field>
```

对于非字段校验器配置风格，配置实例如下：

```xml
<validator type="url">
 <param name="fieldname">user.url</param>
 <message>个人首页输入不合法</message>
</validator>
```

8）邮件地址校验器：名称为 email，该校验器用于校验邮件地址是否合法。对于字段校验器配置风格，配置实例如下：

```xml
<field name="user.email">
 <field-validator type="email">
      <message>Email 地址不合法</message>
 </field-validator>
</field>
```

对于非字段校验器配置风格，配置实例如下：

```xml
<validator type="email ">
 <param name="fieldname">user.email</param>
 <message>Email 地址不合法</message>
</validator>
```

学习数据校验对于构造健壮性高、安全性高的 Web 系统是很有必要的，对于各种非法输入系统都能做出有效的回应，从而将恶意输入拦截在外面。

第 6 章 类型转换

【本章导读语】

类型转换使用广泛,主要用在开发人员将一个字符串转换成更复杂些的对象类型时。因为 Web 中的类型非常单一(在 HTTP 中所有的信息都是 String 类型的),而 Java 是强类型的语言,因此 MVC 框架一般都会提供字符串类型到其他对象类型的转换,Struts 2 提供了基于 OGNL 表达式的功能强大的转换机制,而且还提供了良好的扩展性,允许开发人员创建自定义的类型转换器。

本章详细讲述在 Struts 2 中如何进行简单的类型转换和复杂的类型转换。另外,Struts 2 提供了内置的类型转换,包括简单的对象转换、数组类型转换、List 类型转换和 Map 类型转换等。

【例 6-1】不使用 Struts 2 的类型转换器进行类型转换

〖实例需求〗

本实例讲述在不使用 Struts 2 的类型转换时,如何通过代码实现强制类型转换。在注册页面中将注册信息传入 Action,在 Action 中获取表单的参数,并将某些参数信息进行强制类型转换后组装成 User 对象。

〖开发过程〗

第一步:建立工程

读者可参考前几章在 Eclipse 中新建 strutsTypeConvertion 动态 Web 工程,创建 amigo.struts.typeconversion 包,并在 WebRoot 中创建 typeConversion 子目录存放 JSP 页。最后在 web.xml 中配置 Struts 2 的 FilterDispatcher。完成后的工程结构如图 6-1 所示。

图 6-1 工程的目录结构

第二步：编写 POJO 类：User.java

该 POJO 类为包含用户信息的类，包括 username（用户名）、age（年龄）和 birthDate（出生日期）等信息，表单中的参数信息将最后组装成 User 对象。创建 User.java 类的操作步骤如图 6-2 所示。

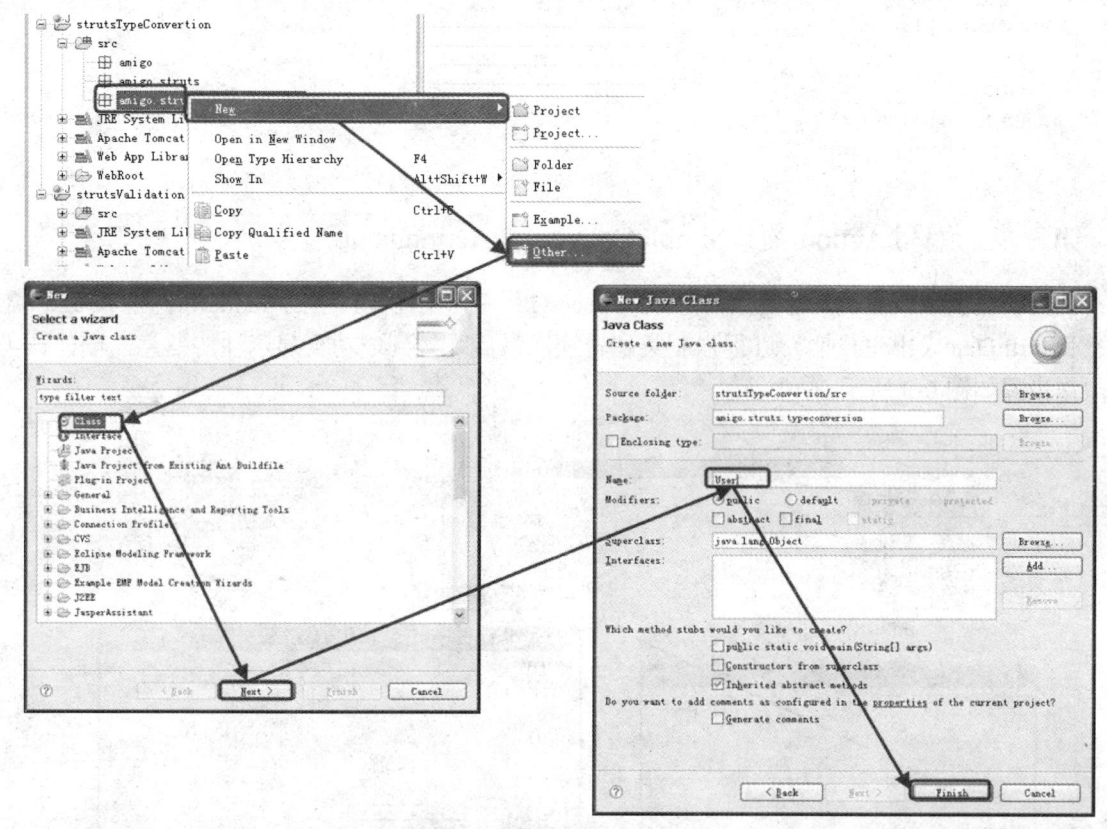

图 6-2 创建 User 类

该类的代码如下所示：

```java
package amigo.struts.typeconversion;

import java.util.Date;

/**
 * 用户的 POJO 类.
 */
public class User {
    /** 用户名. */
    private String username;

    /** 密码. */
    private String password;

    /** 性别. */
    private int gender;
```

```
/** 年龄. */
private int age;

/** 出生日期. */
private Date birthDate;

/** 联系电话. */
private String tel;

/** Email. */
private String email;
// 各属性的 getter/setter 方法
}
```

第三步：编写 Action 类：SimpleConvertionAction.java

该类获取参数信息后，将参数信息放入 user 对象中，并且将其中的 gender（性别）、age（年龄）和 birthDate（出生日期）进行强制类型转换，最后跳转到成功页显示注册信息。创建该类的操作步骤如图 6-3 所示。

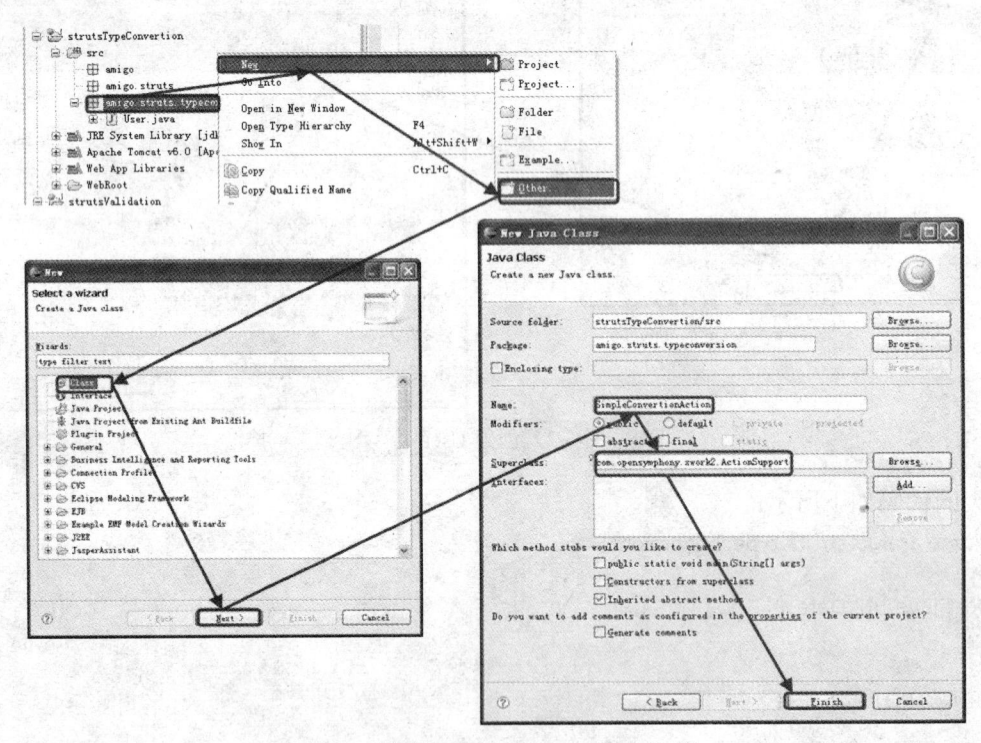

图 6-3 创建 SimpleConvertionAction 类

该类的代码如下所示：

```
package amigo.struts.typeconversion;

import java.text.SimpleDateFormat;
import javax.servlet.http.HttpServletRequest;
import org.apache.struts2.interceptor.ServletRequestAware;
import com.opensymphony.xwork2.ActionSupport;
```

```java
public class SimpleConvertionAction extends ActionSupport
            implements ServletRequestAware {
    private User user;
    private HttpServletRequest request;
    // 省略 user、request 的 getter/setter 方法

    /**
     * 完成用户的注册.
     * 在组装 User 对象时需要进行 gender、age 和 birthDate 属性的强制转换
     */
    public String execute() {
        try {
            String username = request.getParameter("username");
            String password = request.getParameter("password");
            String gender = request.getParameter("gender");
            String age = request.getParameter("age");
            String birthDate = request.getParameter("birthDate");
            String tel = request.getParameter("tel");
            String email = request.getParameter("email");

            user = new User();
            user.setUsername(username);
            user.setPassword(password);
            user.setTel(tel);
            user.setEmail(email);

            // gender、age 和 birthDate 进行强制类型转换
            SimpleDateFormat sdf = new SimpleDateFormat("yyyy-MM-dd");
            user.setGender(Integer.parseInt(gender));
            user.setAge(Integer.parseInt(age));
            user.setBirthDate(sdf.parse(birthDate));

            // 将用户信息保存，在此省略
            // ......
            return this.SUCCESS;
        } catch(Exception ex) {
            request.setAttribute("errorMessage", "操作失败：" + ex.getMessage());
            ex.printStackTrace();
            return this.ERROR;
        }
    }
}
```

第四步：编写注册页面：simpleReg.jsp

在 WebRoot\typeConversion 目录中建立注册页面：simpleReg.jsp，该页面让用户输入注册信息，单击 Submit 按钮后提交到 SimpleConvertionAction.java 这个 Action。创建该页面的操作步骤如图 6-4 所示。

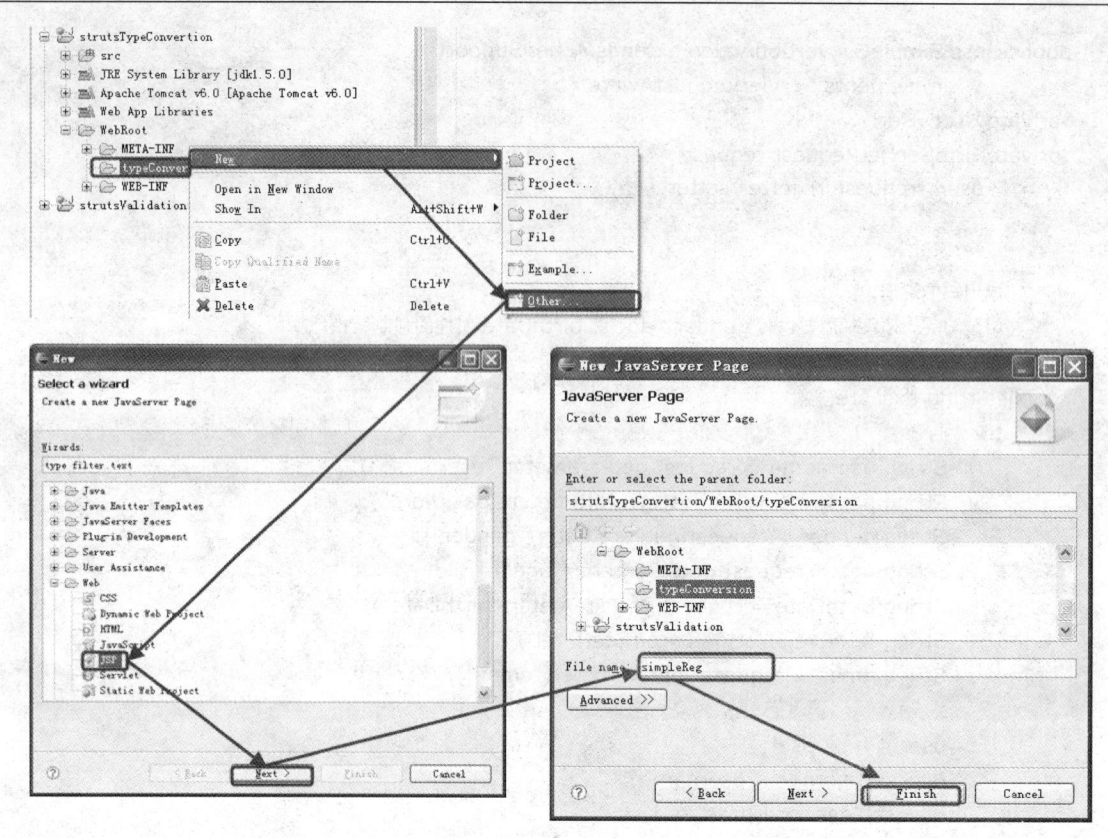

图 6-4 创建 simpleReg.jsp 页面

该页面的代码如下所示：

```jsp
<%@ page contentType="text/html; charset=UTF-8" %>
<%@ taglib prefix="s" uri="/struts-tags" %>
<html>
 <head>
     <title>注册用户</title>
     <meta http-equiv="Content-Type" content="text/html; charset=UTF-8"/>
 </head>
 <body>
     <s:form action="simpleConversion">
         <s:textfield name="username" label="用户名"></s:textfield>
         <s:password name="password" label="密码"></s:password>
         <s:select label="性别" name="gender"
             list="#{'1' : '男', '0' : '女'}"
             listKey="key"
             listValue="value" value="0"/>
         <s:textfield name="age" label="年龄"></s:textfield>
         <s:textfield name="birthDate" label="出生日期"></s:textfield>
         <s:textfield name="tel" label="联系电话"></s:textfield>
         <s:textfield name="email" label="Email"></s:textfield>
         <s:submit></s:submit>
     </s:form>
 </body>
</html>
```

第五步：注册成功页面：simpleRegSuccess.jsp

注册成功后，Action 将跳转到成功界面 simpleRegSuccess.jsp，该页面显示填写的注册信息，该界面的代码如下所示：

```
……
<html>
 <head>
     <title>注册成功</title>
     <meta http-equiv="Content-Type" content="text/html; charset=UTF-8"/>
 </head>
 <body>
     注册成功！注册信息如下：
     用户名：<s:property value="#user.username"/><br/>
     密码：<s:property value="user.password"/><br/>
     性别：<s:property value="user.gender"/><br/>
     年龄：<s:property value="user.age"/><br/>
     出生日期：<s:property value="user.birthDate"/><br/>
     联系电话：<s:property value="user.tel"/><br/>
     Email：<s:property value="user.email"/>
 </body>
</html>
```

第六步：注册失败页面：error.jsp

当注册失败或发生异常时，Action 将跳转到注册失败页面 error.jsp，显示错误信息，该页面的代码如下所示：

```
……
<html>
 <head>
     <title>操作失败界面</title>
     <meta http-equiv="Content-Type" content="text/html; charset=UTF-8"/>
 </head>
 <body>
     <s:property value="#request.errorMessage"/>
 </body>
</html>
```

第七步：Struts 2 配置文件：struts.xml

最后还需要在 struts.xml 文件中配置 Action 信息，在 src 目录中建立该文件后，添加 SimpleConversionAction 这个 Action，并配置操作成功界面和操作失败界面，该文件的内容如下所示：

```xml
<!DOCTYPE struts PUBLIC
    "-//Apache Software Foundation//DTD Struts Configuration 2.0//EN"
    "http://struts.apache.org/dtds/struts-2.0.dtd">

<struts>
    <include file="struts-default.xml"/>
    <package name="tags" extends="struts-default">
     <action name="simpleConversion" class="amigo.struts.typeconversion.SimpleConvertionAction">
         <result name="success">/typeConversion/simpleRegSuccess.jsp</result>
```

```xml
            <result name="error">/typeConversion/error.jsp</result>
        </action>
    </package>
</struts>
```

第八步：运行结果

在浏览器中输入地址 http://localhost:8899/strutsTypeConvertion/typeConversion/simpleReg.jsp 后填写如下注册信息，页面如图 6-5 所示。

图 6-5 注册界面

在图 6-5 中填写注册信息后，单击 Submit 按钮将信息提交到 Action，操作成功后，跳转到注册成功界面，如图 6-6 所示。

图 6-6 注册成功界面

【例 6-2】继承 DefaultTypeConverter 类进行类型转换

〖实例需求〗

Struts 2 的类型转换基于 OGNL，OGNL 中包括一个类型转换必须实现的接口：TypeConverter 接口。该接口定义了一个 convertValue(…)方法，OGNL 提供了一个该接口的实现类，即 DefaultTypeConverter 类，开发人员可以实现该类来定义自定义的类型转换器。convertValue(…) 包括 3 个参数：第一个参数 context 表示类型转换环境的上下文，第二个参数 value 是需要转换

第 6 章 类型转换

的参数,第三个参数 toType 是转换后的目标类型。

本实例讲解如何通过继承 Struts 2 的类型转换器 DefaultTypeConverter 类来进行类型转换。

〖开发过程〗

第一步:编写用户信息转换的类型转换器:UserConverter.java

该类型转换器用于将用户信息进行解析,解析后将其放置到 user 对象中,代码如下:

```java
package amigo.struts.typeconversion;

import java.util.Map;

import ognl.DefaultTypeConverter;

/**
 * User 对象转换器.
 */
public class UserConverter extends DefaultTypeConverter {
    public Object convertValue(Map context, Object value, Class toType) {
        if (toType == User.class) {
            String[] params = (String[]) value;
            User user = new User();
            String[] userInfo = params[0].split(",");
            user.setUsername(userInfo[0]);
            user.setPassword(userInfo[1]);
            return user;
        }
        return null;
    }
}
```

第二步:编写 Action 类:DefaultConvertionAction.java

该类包含一个 user 属性,user 对象的转换由转换器类 UserConverter.java 类完成,该类的代码如下所示:

```java
package amigo.struts.typeconversion;

import javax.servlet.http.HttpServletRequest;

import org.apache.struts2.interceptor.ServletRequestAware;

import com.opensymphony.xwork2.ActionSupport;

public class DefaultConvertionAction extends ActionSupport
            implements ServletRequestAware {
    private User user;
    private HttpServletRequest request;
    // 省略 user、request 的 getter/setter 方法

    /**
     * 完成用户的注册.
```

```
 * 使用 UserConverter 转换器.
 */
public String execute() {
    try {
        System.out.println(this.getUser().getUsername());
        System.out.println(this.getUser().getPassword());
        return this.SUCCESS;
    } catch(Exception ex) {
        request.setAttribute("errorMessage", "操作失败：" + ex.getMessage());
        ex.printStackTrace();
        return this.ERROR;
    }
}
}
```

第三步：编写 JSP 页面：defaultConversionReg.jsp

该页面提供给用户输入注册信息：用户名和密码，两者之间以英文逗号隔开。该页面将请求提供给 DefaultConvertionAction。该页面的代码如下所示：

```
<%@ page contentType="text/html; charset=UTF-8" %>
<%@ taglib prefix="s" uri="/struts-tags" %>

<html>
<head>
    <title>DefaultTypeConverter 扩展实例</title>
    <meta http-equiv="Content-Type" content="text/html; charset=UTF-8"/>
</head>
<body>
    <s:form action="defaultConvertion">
        说明：用户名、密码信息以英文逗号隔开<br/>
        <s:textfield name="user" label="用户信息"></s:textfield>
            <s:submit></s:submit>
    </s:form>
</body>
</html>
```

第四步：类型转换文件：DefaultConvertionAction-conversion.properties

在 Struts 2 中，可定义局部的类型转换器，即为特定类的特定属性配置类型转换器，还可以定义全局的类型转换器，即为某种类型的对象配置类型转换器。

局部的类型转换器放在需要进行转换的 Action 类的同一个包中，名称为：ActionName-conversion.properties，在本例中 ActionName 为 DefaultConversionAction，包为 amigo.struts.typeconversion，该文件由 key-value 对组成，格式为：

属性名=类型转换器类

在本实例中，在 DefaultConvertionAction-conversion.properties 中添加如下内容：

user = amigo.struts.typeconversion.UserConverter

若需要添加全局的类型转换器，对所有的 amigo.struts.typeconversion.User 的对象添加类型转换器，需要在 src 目录中建立 xwork-conversion.properties 文件，该文件的内容如下所示：

amigo.struts.typeconversion.User=amigo.struts.typeconversion.UserConverter

第五步：修改 struts.xml 文件

在 struts.xml 配置文件需要添加 DefaultConvertionAction 这个 Action 的配置信息，添加的配置信息如下所示：

```xml
<action name="defaultConvertion" class="amigo.struts.typeconversion.DefaultConvertionAction">
    <result name="success">/typeConversion/simpleRegSuccess.jsp</result>
    <result name="error">/typeConversion/error.jsp</result>
</action>
```

第六步：运行结果

在浏览器中输入地址：http://localhost:8899/strutsTypeConvertion/typeConversion/defaultConversionReg.jsp，输入用户信息后，页面如图 6-7 所示。

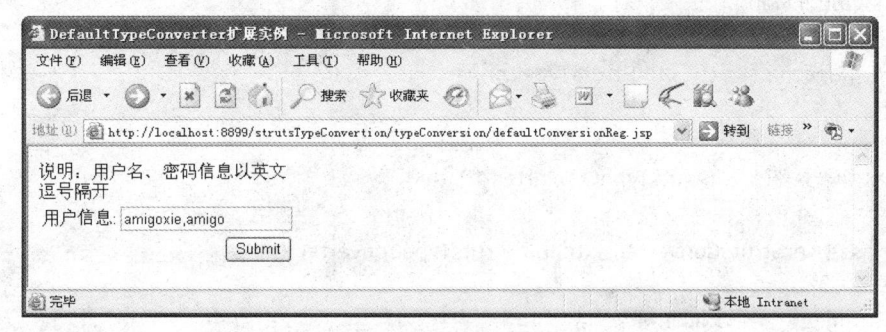

图 6-7 注册界面

在图 6-4 中单击 Submit 按钮后，经过转换器和 Action 处理后，成功获得用户名和密码信息，界面如图 6-8 所示。

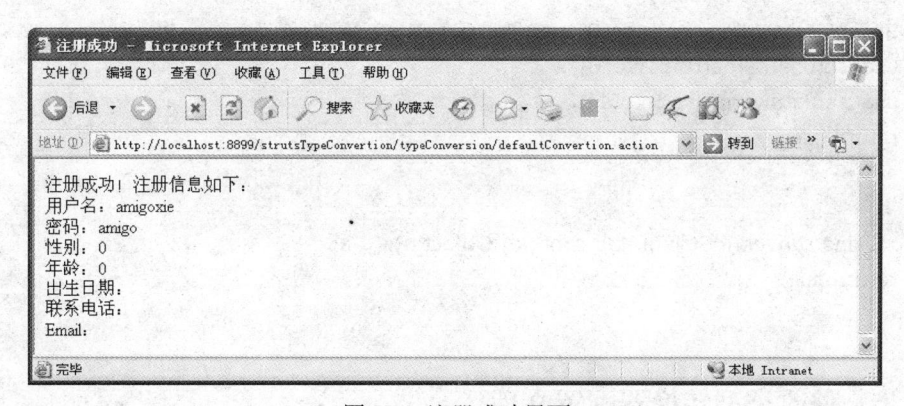

图 6-8 注册成功界面

【例 6-3】继承 StrutsTypeConverter 类进行类型转换

〖实例需求〗

Stuts 2 提供了 StrutsTypeConverter 这个抽象的类型转换器类来简化类型转换器的实现，该类为 DefaultTypeConverter 类的子类，继承该类的自定义类型转换器需要实现 convertFromString

(…)和 convertToString(…)两个方法，前者用于将字符串类型转换为复合类型，而后者用于将复合类型转换成字符串。

下面通过实例来讲解如何通过继承 StrutsTypeConverter 抽象类进行类型转换。

〖开发过程〗

第一步：编写类型转换器：UserStrutsConverter.java

在 amigo.struts.typeconversion 中建立 UserStrutsConverter.java 类，为了简便起见，该类只是提供了 convertFromString(…)方法的实现，该类的完整代码如下所示：

```java
package amigo.struts.typeconversion;

import java.util.Map;

import org.apache.struts2.util.StrutsTypeConverter;

/**
 * User 对象转换器(扩展 StrutsTypeConverter 类).
 */
public class UserStrutsConverter extends StrutsTypeConverter {
    /**
     * 从 String 类型转换为 User 对象.
     */
    public Object convertFromString(Map context, String[] values, Class toClass) {
        String[] params = (String[]) values;
        User user = new User();
        String[] userInfo = params[0].split(",");
        user.setUsername(userInfo[0]);
        user.setPassword(userInfo[1]);
        return user;
    }

    public String convertToString(Map context, Object o) {
        return null;
    }
}
```

第二步：修改类型转换器配置文件

将 User 对象的类型转换器修改为 amigo.struts.typeconversion.UserStrutsConverter，若要进行全局修改，可修改 xwork-conversion.properties 文件，若要进行局部修改，则修改 DefaultConvertionAction-conversion.properties 文件即可。

第三步：运行结果

此时输入地址：http://localhost:8899/strutsTypeConvertion/typeConversion/defaultConversion-Reg.jsp，运行结果与上例的结果一样，在此不再赘述。

【例 6-4】数组的类型转换

〖实例需求〗

在前面的内容中，讲解了当请求参数为单个值时如何进行类型转换，本实例讲解当属性的类型为数组（例如 User 数组）时如何进行转换。

〖开发过程〗

第一步：编写数组属性类型转换器：UserArrayStrutsConverter.java

在 amigo.struts.typeconversion 包中建立数组属性的类型转换器类 UserArrayStrtusConverter.java，该类实现了将字符串数组转换为 User 数组的方法，代码如下所示：

```java
package amigo.struts.typeconversion;

import java.util.Map;

import org.apache.struts2.util.StrutsTypeConverter;

/**
 * User 数组的类型转换器(扩展 StrutsTypeConverter 类).
 */
public class UserArrayStrutsConverter extends StrutsTypeConverter {
    /**
     * 从 String 类型转换为 User 数组对象.
     */
    public Object convertFromString(Map context, String[] values, Class toClass) {
        User[] userArray = new User[values.length];
        for (int i = 0; i < values.length; i++) {
            User user = new User();
            String[] userInfo = values[i].split(",");
            user.setUsername(userInfo[0]);
            user.setPassword(userInfo[1]);
            userArray[i] = user;
        }

        if (values.length == 1) {
            return userArray[0];
        } else {
            return userArray;
        }
    }

    /**
     * 从 User 数组转换为字符串，因为本实例没有用到，实现暂略。
     */
```

```java
    public String convertToString(Map context, Object o) {
        return null;
    }
}
```

第二步：编写 Action 类：UserArrayConvertionAction.java

在 amigo.struts.typeconversion 包中建立数组属性类型转换实例的 Action 类：UserArrayConvertionAction.java，该类有一个 User 数组属性 user，包含了 user 属性的 getter 和 setter 方法，该类的代码如下：

```java
package amigo.struts.typeconversion;

import javax.servlet.http.HttpServletRequest;

import org.apache.struts2.interceptor.ServletRequestAware;

import com.opensymphony.xwork2.ActionSupport;

public class UserArrayConvertionAction extends ActionSupport
        implements ServletRequestAware {
    private User[] user;
    private HttpServletRequest request;
    // 省略 user 的 getter/setter 方法，以及 request 的 setter 方法

    public String execute() {
        try {
            return this.SUCCESS;
        } catch(Exception ex) {
            request.setAttribute("errorMessage", "操作失败：" + ex.getMessage());
            ex.printStackTrace();
            return this.ERROR;
        }
    }
}
```

第三步：编写填写注册信息页面：userArrayReg.jsp

在 WebRoot/typeConversion 目录中建立多个用户注册的页面 userArrayReg.jsp，该页面包含两个名为 user 的输入框，代码如下所示：

```jsp
……
<body>
    <s:form action="userArrayConvertion">
        说明：用户名、密码信息以英文逗号隔开<br/>
        <s:textfield name="user" label="用户 0 信息"></s:textfield>
        <s:textfield name="user" label="用户 1 信息"></s:textfield>
        <s:submit></s:submit>
    </s:form>
</body>
</html>
```

第四步：编写注册成功页面：userArrayRegSuccess.jsp

在 WebRoot/typeConversion 目录中建立注册成功页面 userArrayRegSuccess.jsp，然后使用 <s:iterator…/>标签在页面循环输出用户数组信息，代码如下：

```
……
 <body>
      数组类型转换成功！
      <s:iterator value="user" status="st">
           <br/>用户<s:property value="#st.index"/>的信息：<br/>
           用户名：<s:property value="user[#st.index].username"/><br/>
           密码：<s:property value="user[#st.index].password"/>
      </s:iterator>
 </body>
</html>
```

第五步：配置类型转换器

接下来需要在 xwork-conversion.properties 中修改 User 的类型转换器为 UserArrayStrutsConverter，配置如下：

amigo.struts.typeconversion.User=amigo.struts.typeconversion.UserArrayStrutsConverter

第六步：配置 struts.xml

最后需要在 struts.xml 中配置 UserArrayConvertionAction 这个 Action，并配置其成功和失败的跳转页面，添加的配置内容如下所示：

```
<!-- 数组属性转换实例 -->
<action name="userArrayConvertion" class="amigo.struts.typeconversion.UserArrayConvertionAction">
    <result name="success">/typeConversion/userArrayRegSuccess.jsp</result>
    <result name="error">/typeConversion/error.jsp</result>
</action>
```

第七步：运行结果

在浏览器中输入地址：http://localhost:8899/strutsTypeConvertion/ typeConversion/ userArrayReg.jsp，填写用户信息后，界面如图 6-9 所示。

图 6-9 注册界面

在图 6-9 中单击 Submit 按钮，进行类型转换后跳转到成功页面，如图 6-10 所示。

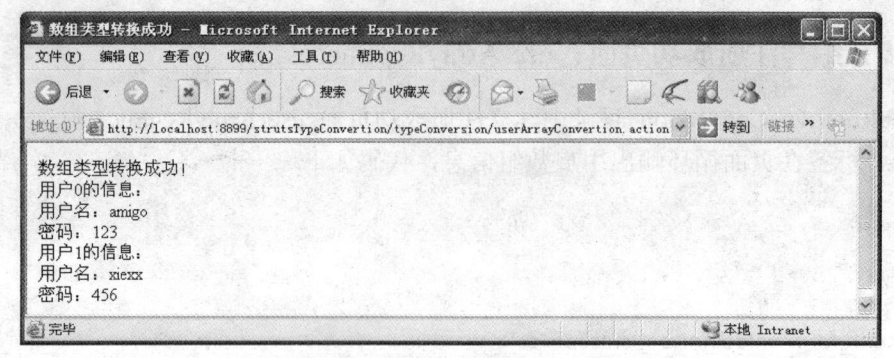

图 6-10 数组类型转换成功界面

【例 6-5】集合的类型转换

〖实例需求〗

常用的集合包括 List 和 Map，本实例讲解当 Action 中 user 为 List 集合时，如何实现类型转换。

〖开发过程〗

第一步：编写 List 集合类型转换器：UserListStrutsConverter.java

在 amigo.struts.typeconversion 包中建立 List 集合属性的类型转换器类 UserListStrtusConverter.java，该类实现了将字符串数组转换为 User 列表的方法，该类的核心方法 convertFromString()代码如下所示：

```java
public Object convertFromString(Map context, String[] values, Class toClass) {
    if (toClass == User.class) {
        List<User> userList = new ArrayList<User>();
        for (int i = 0; i < values.length; i++) {
            User user = new User();
            String[] userInfo = values[i].split(",");
            user.setUsername(userInfo[0]);
            user.setPassword(userInfo[1]);
            userList.add(user);
        }

        if (values.length == 1) {
            return userList.get(0);
        } else {
            return userList;
        }
    } else {
        return null;
    }
}
```

第二步：编写 Action 类：UserListStrutsConverter.java

在 amigo.struts.typeconversion 包中建立 List 属性类型转换实例的 Action 类：UserListConvertionAction.java，该类与 UserArrayConvertionAction.java 类的不同之处在于它的 user 属性为 List<User>类型，该段代码如下所示：

```java
private List<User> user;

public List<User> getUser() {
  return user;
}

public void setUser(List<User> user) {
  this.user = user;
}
```

第三步：编写填写注册信息页面：userListReg.jsp

在 WebRoot/typeConversion 目录中建立多个用户注册的页面 userListReg.jsp，该页面代码与上一步的 userArrayReg.jsp 相似，不过 form 表单的 action 修改为 userListConvertion，代码省略。

第四步：编写注册成功页面：userListRegSuccess.jsp

在 WebRoot/typeConversion 目录中建立注册成功页面 userListRegSuccess.jsp，使用 <s:iterator.../>标签在页面循环输出用户列表信息，代码如下：

```jsp
......
    <body>
        <table width="50%">
            <tr style="background-color:powderblue;font-weight:bold;">
                <td>序号</td>
                <td>用户名</td>
                <td>密码</td>
            </tr>
            <s:iterator value="user" status="st">
                <tr>
                    <td><s:property value="#st.index"/></td>
                    <td><s:property value="username"/></td>
                    <td><s:property value="password"/></td>
                </tr>
            </s:iterator>
        </table>
    </body>
</html>
```

第五步：配置类型转换器

在 amigo.struts.typeconversion 目录中建立 UserListConvertionAction.java 的类型转换文件 UserListConvertionAction-conversion.properties，配置 user 属性对应的类型转换器，配置如下：

```
user=amigo.struts.typeconversion.UserListStrutsConverter
```

第六步：配置 struts.xml

最后需要在 struts.xml 中配置 UserListConvertionAction 这个 Action，并配置其成功和失败的跳转页面，添加的配置内容如下所示：

```xml
<!-- List 集合属性转换实例 -->
<action name="userListConvertion" class="amigo.struts.typeconversion.UserListConvertionAction">
    <result name="success">/typeConversion/userListRegSuccess.jsp</result>
    <result name="error">/typeConversion/error.jsp</result>
</action>
```

第七步：运行结果

在浏览器中输入地址：http://localhost:8899/strutsTypeConvertion/typeConversion/userListReg.jsp，各步骤的显示界面与上一步的实例类似，在此不再赘述。

【例 6-6】Struts 2 中内置的类型转换

〖实例需求〗

本实例讲解如何利用 Struts 中内置的类型转换器来完成开发过程中的类型转换，本实例从简单的 User 对象转换入手，而后讲解了如何进行数组、List 和 Map 集合的类型转换。

〖开发过程〗

第一步：简单的对象转换

（1）编写 Action 类：DirectToUserConvertionAction.java。

在 amigo.struts.typeconversion 包中建立 DirectToUserConvertionAction 类，该类的内容如下所示：

```java
package amigo.struts.typeconversion;

import javax.servlet.http.HttpServletRequest;

import org.apache.struts2.interceptor.ServletRequestAware;

import com.opensymphony.xwork2.ActionSupport;

/**
 * 使用 Strus2 内置的转换器完成到对象 User 的类型转换实例.
 */
public class DirectToUserConvertionAction extends ActionSupport
        implements ServletRequestAware {
    private User user;
    private HttpServletRequest request;
    // 省略 user 的 getter/setter 方法，以及 request 的 setter 方法

    public String execute() {
        try {
```

```
                    System.out.println(this.getUser().getUsername());
                    System.out.println(this.getUser().getPassword());
                    return this.SUCCESS;
            } catch(Exception ex) {
                    request.setAttribute("errorMessage", "操作失败：" + ex.getMessage());
                    ex.printStackTrace();
                    return this.ERROR;
            }
        }
}
```

（2）编写注册页面：directToUserReg.jsp。

在 WebRoot/typeConversion 目录中建立注册页面 directToUserReg.jsp，使用语句：

```
<s:textfield name="user.username" label="用户名"></s:textfield>
```

该语句可在提交时将输入值关联到 Action 中 user 对象的 username 属性，该页面的代码如下所示：

```
……
    <body>
        <s:form action="directToUserConvertion">
            <!-- 对应 directToUserConvertion 这个 Action 的 user 对象的 username 属性 -->
            <s:textfield name="user.username" label="用户名"></s:textfield>
            <s:password name="user.password" label="密码"></s:password>
            <s:select label="性别" name="user.gender"
                list="#{'1' : '男', '0' : '女'}"
                listKey="key"
                listValue="value" value="0"/>
            <s:textfield name="user.age" label="年龄"></s:textfield>
            <s:textfield name="user.birthDate" label="出生日期"></s:textfield>
            <s:textfield name="user.tel" label="联系电话"></s:textfield>
            <s:textfield name="user.email" label="Email"></s:textfield>
            <s:submit></s:submit>
        </s:form>
    </body>
</html>
```

（3）配置 struts.xml。

最后在 struts.xml 中配置 DirectToUserConvertionAction，添加的配置信息如下所示：

```
<!-- 使用 Strus 2 内置的转换器完成到对象 User 的类型转换实例 -->
<action name="directToUserConvertion"  class="amigo.struts.typeconversion.DirectToUserConvertionAction">
    <result name="success">/typeConversion/simpleRegSuccess.jsp</result>
    <result name="error">/typeConversion/error.jsp</result>
</action>
```

（4）运行结果。

输入 directToUserReg.jsp 页面的地址，运行结果同【例 6-1】，在此不再赘述。

第二步：数组类型转换

当 Action 中某属性的类型为对象数组时，Struts 2 中也可在页面中指定文本元素等的 name 属性为：

```
Action 集合属性名['index 值'].集合元素属性名
```

例如下面的语句指定了该输入值对应 Action 中 user 属性（为 User 数组）的第一个元素的 username 属性：

```
<s:textfield name="user[0].username" label="用户名"></s:textfield>
```

这种转换都是 Struts 2 内置的类型转换器所完成的。

（1）编写 Action 类：DirectToUserArrayConvertionAction.java。

在 amigo.struts.typeconversion 包中建立 DirectToUserArrayConvertionAction 类，该类有一个 User 数组对象 user，该类通过打印 User 数组的信息来确认属性是否被正确赋值，该类的代码如下所示：

```java
……
public class DirectToUserArrayConvertionAction extends ActionSupport
            implements ServletRequestAware {
    private User[] user;
    private HttpServletRequest request;
    // 省略 user 的 getter 和 setter 方法，以及 request 的 setter 方法
    public String execute() {
        try {
            System.out.println("用户名 1：" + user[0].getUsername() + "，密码 1="+ user[0].getPassword());
            System.out.println("用户名 2：" + user[1].getUsername() + "，密码 ="+ user[1].getPassword());
            return null;
        } catch(Exception ex) {
            request.setAttribute("errorMessage", "操作失败：" + ex.getMessage());
            ex.printStackTrace();
            return this.ERROR;
        }
    }
}
```

（2）编写注册页面：directToUserArrayReg.jsp。

在 WebRoot/typeConversion 目录中建立注册页面 directToUserArrayReg.jsp，该页面输入多个用户数组信息，该页面的代码如下所示：

```jsp
……
  <body>
      <s:form action="directToUserArrayConvertion">
          <!-- 对应 directToUserConvertion 这个 Action 的 user 数组对象第一个元素的 username 属性 -->
          <s:textfield name="user[0].username" label="用户名 1"></s:textfield>
          <s:password name="user[0].password" label="密码 1"></s:password>

          <s:textfield name="user[1].username" label="用户名 2"></s:textfield>
          <s:password name="user[1].password" label="密码 2"></s:password>
          <s:submit></s:submit>
      </s:form>
  </body>
</html>
```

（3）配置 struts.xml。

在 strus.xml 文件中配置 DirectToUserArrayConvertionAction，添加的配置信息如下：

```xml
<!-- 使用 Strus 2 内置的转换器完成到对象 User 数组的类型转换实例 -->
<action name="directToUserArrayConvertion"
        class="amigo.struts.typeconversion.DirectToUserArrayConvertionAction">
```

```xml
        <result name="error">/typeConversion/error.jsp</result>
    </action>
```
（4）运行结果。

在浏览器中输入 directToUserArrayReg.jsp 的地址，填写信息后，页面如图 6-11 所示。

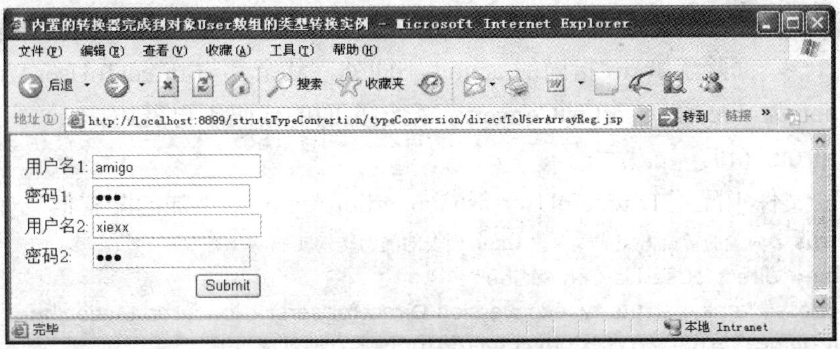

图 6-11　使用内置的类型转换器完成数组的转换实例

在图 6-11 中单击 Submit 按钮提交后，读者将在控制台看到输出了两个用户的用户名和密码信息。

第三步：List 类型转换

（1）编写 Action 类：DirectToUserListConvertionAction.java。

在 amigo.struts.typeconversion 包中建立 DirectToUserListConvertionAction 类，该类的内容如下所示：

```java
package amigo.struts.typeconversion;

import java.util.List;
import javax.servlet.http.HttpServletRequest;
import org.apache.struts2.interceptor.ServletRequestAware;
import com.opensymphony.xwork2.ActionSupport;

/**
 * 使用 Strus 2 内置的转换器完成到 User 列表的类型转换实例.
 */
public class DirectToUserListConvertionAction extends ActionSupport
        implements ServletRequestAware {
    private List<User> user;
    private HttpServletRequest request;
    // 省略 user、request 的 getter/setter 方法

    public String execute() {
        try {
            System.out.println("用户名 1：" + user.get(0).getUsername() + "，密码 1="+ user.get(1).getPassword());
            System.out.println("用户名 2：" + user.get(1).getUsername() + "，密码 2="+ user.get(1).getPassword());
            return null;
        } catch(Exception ex) {
            request.setAttribute("errorMessage", "操作失败：" + ex.getMessage());
            ex.printStackTrace();
```

```
            return this.ERROR;
        }
    }
}
```

（2）编写注册页面：directToUserListReg.jsp。

在 WebRoot/typeConversion 目录中建立注册页面 directToUserListReg.jsp，该页面输入多个用户列表信息。该页面除了 form 指向的 action 不同外，其余都与 directToUserArray.jsp 类似。它所指向的 action 为 directToUserListConvertion，该页面的代码不再赘述。

（3）配置 struts.xml。

在 strus.xml 文件中配置 DirectToUserListConvertionAction，添加的配置信息如下：

```xml
<!-- 使用 Strus 2 内置的转换器完成到对象 User 列表的类型转换实例 -->
<action name="directToUserListConvertion"
        class="amigo.struts.typeconversion.DirectToUserListConvertionAction">
    <result name="error">/typeConversion/error.jsp</result>
</action>
```

（4）运行结果。

该子实例的运行效果与第二步的运行结果类似。

第四步：Map 类型转换

（1）编写 Action 类：DirectToUserMapConvertionAction.java。

在 amigo.struts.typeconversion 包中建立 DirectToUserMapConvertionAction 类，该类的内容如下所示：

```java
package amigo.struts.typeconversion;

import java.util.Map;
import javax.servlet.http.HttpServletRequest;
import org.apache.struts2.interceptor.ServletRequestAware;
import com.opensymphony.xwork2.ActionSupport;

/**
 * 使用 Strus 2 内置的转换器完成到 User 列表的类型转换实例.
 */
public class DirectToUserMapConvertionAction extends ActionSupport
        implements ServletRequestAware {
    private Map<String, User> user;
    private HttpServletRequest request;
    // 省略 user 的 getter/setter 方法，以及 request 的 setter 方法

    public String execute() {
        try {
            System.out.println("用户名 1：" + user.get("one").getUsername() + "，密码 1="+ user.get(1).getPassword());
            System.out.println("用户名 2：" + user.get("two").getUsername() + "，密码 2="+ user.get(1).getPassword());
            return null;
        } catch(Exception ex) {
            request.setAttribute("errorMessage", "操作失败：" + ex.getMessage());
            ex.printStackTrace();
            return this.ERROR;
```

            }
        }
}

（2）编写注册页面：directToUserMapReg.jsp。

在 WebRoot/typeConversion 目录中建立注册页面 directToUserMapReg.jsp，该页面输入多个用户 Map 信息，该页面除了 form 指向的 action 不同外，其余都与 directToUserArray.jsp 类似。它所指向的 action 为 directToUserMapConvertion，该页面的代码不再赘述。

（3）配置 struts.xml。

在 strus.xml 文件中配置 DirectToUserMapConvertionAction，添加的配置信息如下：

```xml
<!-- 使用 Strus 2 内置的转换器完成到对象 User Map 的类型转换实例 -->
<action name="directToUserMapConvertion"
                class="amigo.struts.typeconversion.DirectToUserMapConvertionAction">
    <result name="error">/typeConversion/error.jsp</result>
</action>
```

（4）运行结果。

该子实例的运行效果与第二步的运行结果类似。

【例 6-7】类型转换的错误处理

〖实例需求〗

在用户输入数据时，可能出现正常用户输入错误的情况，或出现恶意用户的非法输入。其实，通过学习前一章的知识，读者可以知道解决非法输入可通过数据校验的方法实现。但是在进行数据校验前需要进行类型转换，满足类型转换的数据不一定合法，例如 age 字段为 int 类型，当用户输入 200 时也是满足类型转换的，但它还是非法数据，需要经过数据校验类进行校验。

本实例讲解在 Struts 2 中如何对类型转换时出现的错误进行处理。

〖开发过程〗

第一步：类型转换拦截器 conversionError 简介

Struts 2 提供了一个类型转换的拦截器：conversionError，读者可在解压 struts2-core-2.0.11.2.jar 后的根目录中的 struts-default.xml 文件中看到如下代码段：

```xml
<interceptor-stack name="defaultStack">
 <interceptor-ref name="exception"/>
 ……
    <interceptor-ref name="conversionError"/>
    <interceptor-ref name="validation">
            <param name="excludeMethods">input,back,cancel,browse</param>
    </interceptor-ref>
    ……
</interceptor-stack>
```

以上定义了默认的拦截器栈 defaultStack，该栈包含对类型转换拦截器 conversionError 的引用。conversionError 拦截器在 struts-default.xml 中的定义如下：

```xml
<interceptor name="conversionError" class="org.apache.struts2.interceptor.StrutsConversionErrorInterceptor"/>
```

conversionError 拦截器在执行转换出现异常时，将错误封装成表单域对象，并将错误信息放入 ActionContext 中。当该拦截器对转换异常进行处理后，系统会跳转到 input 视图。

【说明】为了让 Action 类处理类型转换的错误，以及进行数据校验，Action 类一般需要继承 ActionSupport 类，因为该类为完成类型转换和数据校验做了很多工作。

第二步：编写 Action 类：ExceptionConverter.java

在 amigo.struts.typeconversion 包中建立该例的 Action 类：ExceptionConvertionAction.java，该类的代码如下所示：

```java
package amigo.struts.typeconversion;

import java.util.Date;
import com.opensymphony.xwork2.ActionSupport;

/**
 * 演示 Struts 2 中类型转换的错误处理
 */
public class ExceptionConvertionAction extends ActionSupport {
    /** 用户名. */
    private String username;

    /** 年龄. */
    private int age;

    /** 出生日期. */
    private Date birthDate;
    // 省略各属性的 setter 方法

    public String execute() {
        return null;
    }
}
```

第三步：编写 JSP 页面：exceptionConversionReg.jsp

在 WebRoot/typeConversion 目录中建立该类的测试 JSP 页面：exceptionConversionReg.jsp，该页面包含 username、age、birthDate 的用户输入框，该页面的代码如下所示：

```jsp
<%@ page contentType="text/html; charset=UTF-8" %>
<%@ taglib prefix="s" uri="/struts-tags" %>
<html>
 <head>
    <title>演示 Struts 2 中类型转换的错误处理</title>
    <meta http-equiv="Content-Type" content="text/html; charset=UTF-8"/>
 </head>
 <body>
    <s:form action="exceptionConvertion">
        <s:textfield name="username" label="用户名"></s:textfield>
        <s:textfield name="age" label="年龄"></s:textfield>
        <s:textfield name="birthDate" label="出生日期"></s:textfield>
        <s:submit></s:submit>
    </s:form>
```

```
    </body>
</html>
```

第四步：修改 Struts 2 配置文件：struts.xml

接着在 Struts 2 的配置文件 struts.xml 中添加该 Action，并让其 input 指向 exceptionConversionReg.jsp，以便在类型转换失败时跳转至该页面，添加的配置信息如下：

```
<!-- 演示类型转换的错误处理实例 -->
<action name="exceptionConvertion"
 class="amigo.struts.typeconversion.ExceptionConvertionAction">
 <result name="input">/typeConversion/exceptionConversionReg.jsp</result>
</action>
```

第五步：运行结果

此时在浏览器中输入 exceptionConversionReg.jsp 页面的地址，运行结果如图 6-12 所示。

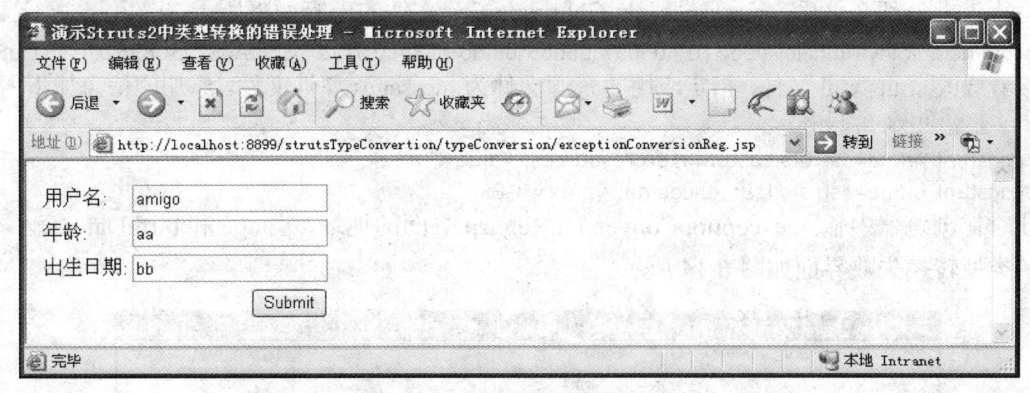

图 6-12 类型转换实例输入

在图 6-12 中 age（年龄）输入"aa"，birthDate（出生日期）输入"bb"，而 Action 中接收的 age 为 int 型，birthDate 为 Date 型，因此这两者的类型转换将告失败。单击图 6-12 中的 Submit 按钮，结果如图 6-13 所示。

图 6-13 类型转换失败默认提示信息

当出现类型转换失败的情况时，默认的转换失败信息为：
Invalid field value for field "字段名称"

第六步：编写应用的资源文件：messages.properties

上一步中出现的提示信息是英文的，如何将其变成中文呢？开发人员可在应用的国际化资源文件中添加如下信息来改变默认的类型转换失败后的提示信息：

```
xwork.default.invalid.fieldvalue={0}字段进行类型转换失败
```

读者可在 src 目录中建立资源文件：messages.properties 和 messages_zh_CN.properties，messages.properties 的内容为：

```
xwork.default.invalid.fieldvalue={0}字段进行类型转换失败
```

接着在 src 目录中建立批处理文件 code.bat，使用进行编码处理，该文件的处理如下所示：

```
del messages_zh_CN.properties
copy messages.properties messages_zh_CN.properties.gbk
native2ascii -encoding GBK messages_zh_CN.properties.gbk messages_zh_CN.properties
del messages_zh_CN.properties.gbk
del *.bak
```

运行该批处理文件后，messages_zh_CN.properties 文件的内容如下所示：

```
xwork.default.invalid.fieldvalue={0}\u5b57\u6bb5\u8fdb\u884c\u7c7b\u578b\u8f6c\u6362\u5931\u8d25
```

接着修改 struts.xml 文件，指定应用的资源文件为 messages 属性文件，添加的信息如下所示：

```xml
<!-- 指定应用的资源文件 -->
<constant name="struts.custom.i18n.resources" value="messages"/>
<constant name="struts.i18n.encoding" value="GBK"/>
```

此时在浏览器中输入 exceptionConversionReg.jsp 页面的地址，当 age 和 birthDate 输入不合法时，类型转换失败界面如图 6-14 所示。

图 6-14 修改类型转换失败默认提示信息

第七步：建立局部资源文件：ExceptionConvertionAction.properties

第六步演示了如何修改类型转换的默认信息，但是在某些情况下，若想为特定字段指定个性化的类型转换错误提示信息，应该如何做呢？在 Struts 2 中，可以为单个 Action 提供局部的资源文件，局部资源文件的命名为：Action 的名称.properties。在本步中，建立 ExceptionConvertionAction.java 类的局部资源文件：ExceptionConvertionAction.properties，该资源文件包含 age 和 birthDate 的类型转换错误信息。为某属性指定类型转换错误信息的格式如下所示：

```
invalid.fieldvalue.属性名称=类型转换失败提示信息
```

在本例中为 age 和 birthDate 的类型转换失败信息如下：

```
invalid.fieldvalue.age=年龄输入不合法，类型转换失败
invalid.fieldvalue.birthDate=出生日期应为 yyyy-MM-dd 格式
```

因为是中文的提示信息，因此也需要使用 native2ascii 命令进行编码处理，处理后 ExceptionConvertionAction.properties 文件的内容如下所示：

invalid.fieldvalue.age=\u5e74\u9f84\u8f93\u5165\u4e0d\u5408\u6cd5\uff0c\u7c7b\u578b\u8f6c\u6362\u5931\u8d25
invalid.fieldvalue.birthDate=\u51fa\u751f\u65e5\u671f\u5e94\u4e3ayyyy-MM-dd\u683c\u5f0f

此时在浏览器中输入 exceptionConversionReg.jsp 页面的地址，当 age 和 birthDate 输入不合法时，类型转换失败界面如图 6-15 所示。

图 6-15　为特定字段指定类型转换失败提示信息

小结

Struts 2 中提供了基于 OGNL 表达式的功能强大的转换机制。本章首先通过实例讲述不使用 Struts 2 的类型转换器时如何进行类型转换，此时需要通过代码对类型进行转换，当类型转换失败时，需要开发人员手动捕捉异常，并跳转到输入页面提示出错信息，显然这种方式繁琐而且可重用性差，不推荐开发人员使用。

OGNL 中包括一个类型转换必须实现的接口：TypeConverter 接口，OGNL 提供了一个该接口的实现类，即 DefaultTypeConverter 类，开发人员可以通过该类来定义自定义的类型转换器。继承该类时，开发人员需要实现该类定义的 convertValue()方法，该方法包括 3 个参数：第一个参数 context 表示类型转换环境的上下文，第二个参数 value 是需要转换的参数，第三个参数 toType 是转换后的目标类型。

在 Struts 2 中，可定义局部和全局的类型转换器。全局的类型转换器文件为：xwork-conversion.properties，该文件由 key-value 对组成，格式为：

属性名=类型转换器类

局部的类型转换器放在需要进行转换的 Action 类的同一个包中，名称为：ActionName-conversion.properties，该文件也由 key-value 对组成。

Stuts 2 提供了 StrutsTypeConverter 这个抽象的类型转换器类来简化类型转换器的实现，该类为 DefaultTypeConverter 类的子类，继承该类的自定义类型转换器需要实现 convertFromString(…)和 convertToString(…)两个方法，前者用于将字符串类型转换为复合类型，而后者用于将复合类型转换成字符串。

若要转换的类型为比较复杂的类型，例如数组类型时，需要在继承 StrutsTypeConverter 类的转换器类中的 convertFromString()中进行处理。处理集合类型时也与此类似。

Struts 2 中提供了内置的类型转换器，开发人员不需要进行处理，Struts 2 会自动地进行类型转换。在进行简单的对象转换时，只需要注意在 JSP 页面中进行少量修改即可，例如在 JSP 页面中编写"用户名"的输入文本框，该输入对应 Action 类的 user 对象的 username 属性，则代码为：

```
<s:textfield name="user.username" label="用户名"></s:textfield>
```

　　当 Action 中某属性的类型为对象数组时，Struts 2 中也可在页面中指定文本元素等的 name 属性为：

Action 集合属性名['index 值'].集合元素属性名

　　例如，下面的语句指定了该输入值对应 Action 中 user 属性（为 User 数组）的第一个元素的 username 属性：

```
<s:textfield name="user[0].username" label="用户名"></s:textfield>
```

　　类型转换可能会出现转换失败的情况，在 Struts 2 中如何进行此种情况的处理呢？

　　Struts 2 提供了一个类型转换的拦截器 conversionError 来进行类型转换失败的处理，默认的转换失败信息为：

Invalid field value for field "字段名称"

　　若想将默认的类型转换失败信息修改为中文，需要做如下三步操作：
- 建立中文的资源文件，在资源文件中写上中文的提示信息，例如：
  xwork.default.invalid.fieldvalue={0}字段进行类型转换失败
- 为避免中文出现乱码，需要使用 native2ascii 命令进行编码。
- 修改 struts.xml 文件，指定应用的资源文件。

　　若想为 Action 的特定属性指定类型转换失败信息，需要建立局部的资源文件，局部资源文件的命名为：Action 的名称.properties。在局部资源文件中为某属性指定类型转换错误信息的格式如下所示：

invalid.fieldvalue.属性名称=类型转换失败提示信息

第 7 章 拦截器

【本章导读语】

拦截器是 Struts 2 的一个重要的组成部分，甚至被人称为 Struts 2 框架的基石，它与 Servlet 中的过滤器类似，可在 Action 的方法之前或之后执行一些预先设置的方法。拦截器一般用于进行类型转换操作、进行权限控制、防止表单的双重提交和处理文件上传等功能，它将各 Action 执行前后的重复代码提取出来，因此在很大程度上减少了重复代码，增强了代码的复用。

Struts 2 框架中的拦截器是通过配置文件（struts.xml）进行动态配置的，Struts 2 框架提供了对拦截器的良好的扩展性，允许开发人员定义自定义的拦截器。

本章首先通过实例讲述拦截器的概念，使得读者对拦截器的概念有个清晰的理解。接着详细讲述 Struts 2 框架中拦截器和拦截器栈的配置，以及配置时需要注意的一些问题，为后续的实例打好基础。

Struts 2 提供了大量的内建拦截器，例如：

- exception：该拦截器负责处理异常，它将异常映射为结果。
- fileUpload：该拦截器主要用于文件上传，它负责解析表单中文件域的内容。
- params：最基本的拦截器，它负责解析 HTTP 请求中的参数，并将参数值设置成 Action 对应的属性值。

本章的内建拦截器的实例详细介绍了常用的内建拦截器的使用，详细讲解了其使用的场合，以及使用时需要注意的一些问题。

最后，本章讲述了如何利用 Struts 2 的良好的扩展性，实现自定义的拦截器，通过一个角色权限控制的实例来详细讲解在 Struts 2 中实现自定义的拦截器。

【例 7-1】理解拦截器

〖实例需求〗

拦截器在很多开源框架（例如 Struts 2、Spring 等）中使用广泛，它基于 AOP（Aspect Oriented Programming，面向切面编程）。AOP 是消除重复代码的一个很有用的方法，它从运行的角度取得业务处理过程的切面，在该切面处调用拦截器中定义的方法。在 AOP 中，有如下几个重要概念，其中"目标对象"和"被插入的处理方法"都与拦截器有很大关系：

- 被插入的处理方法：拦截器中定义的处理方法，在被拦截方法之前或之后执行。
- 目标对象：被拦截的对象。
- 代理对象：目标对象的代理对象，由系统创建。

在 Java 编程中，拦截器依赖的核心技术是 Java 的动态编程代理。本实例使用 Java 的动态代理技术来实现一个拦截器的模型，从而使读者从原理上理解拦截器。

【开发过程】

第一步：建立工程

读者可以参考前几章的方法在 Eclipse 中新建 strutsInterceptor 的动态 Web 工程，并将所需的 jar 包导入到 WEB-INF/lib 目录中，接着在 src 目录中建立 amigo.struts.interceptor 包，在 WebRoot 目录中建立 interceptor 子目录来存放本实例的 JSP 页面。最后在 web.xml 中配置 Struts 2 的 FilterDispatcher。操作完成后工程的目录结构如图 7-1 所示。

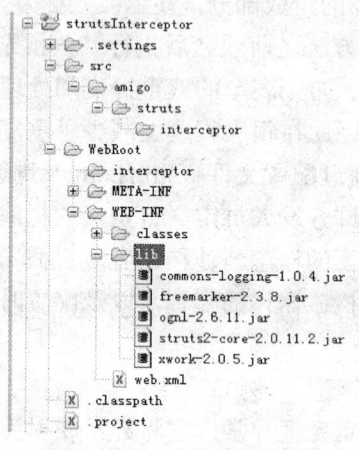

图 7-1 工程的目录结构

第二步：编写业务接口类：BusiInterface.java

在src目录中创建amigo.struts.interceptor.conception包，操作步骤如图7-2所示。

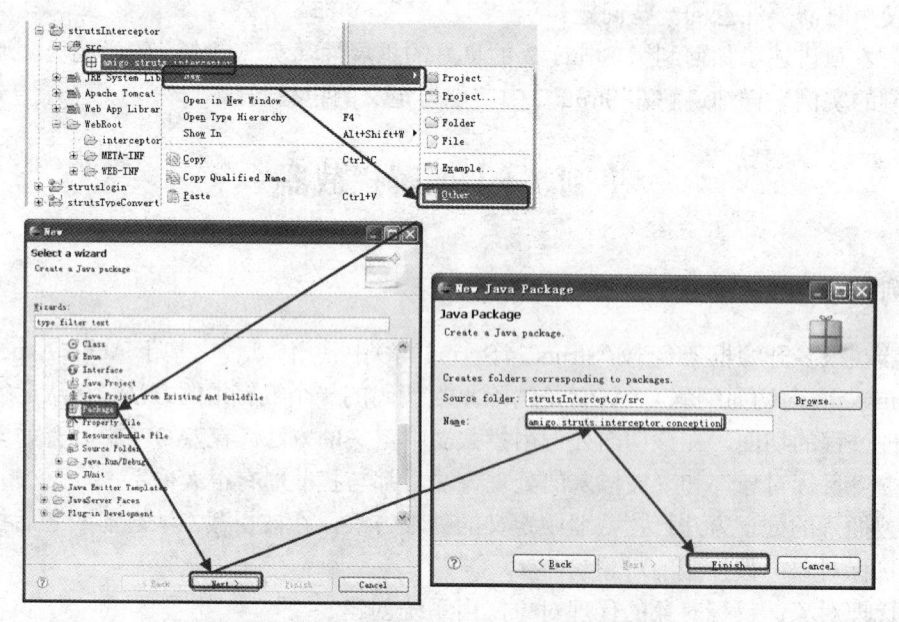

图 7-2 创建 amigo.struts.interceptor.conception 包

在amigo.struts.interceptor.conception包中建立业务接口类BusiInterface.java，该类定义了被拦

截的方法doSomeThing()，创建该接口的操作步骤如图7-3所示。

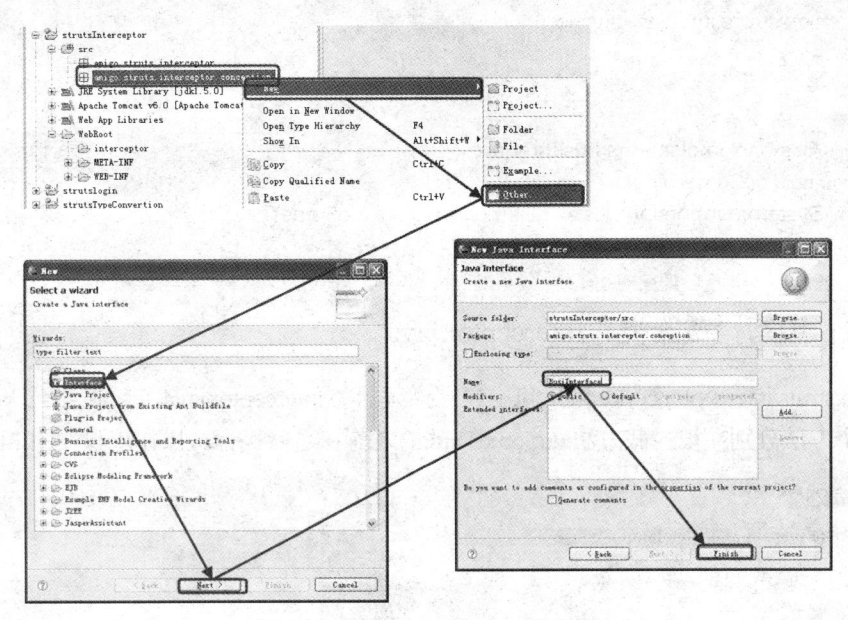

图 7-3 创建 BusiInterface 接口类

该类的代码如下所示：

```java
package amigo.struts.interceptor.conception;

public interface BusiInterface {
    public void doSomeThing();
}
```

第三步：编写业务实现类：BusiImpl.java

在amigo.struts.interceptor.conception包中创建BusiImpl类，该类模拟实现BusiInterface接口，用doSomeThing()方法中打印日志信息。创建BusiImpl类的操作步骤如图7-4所示。

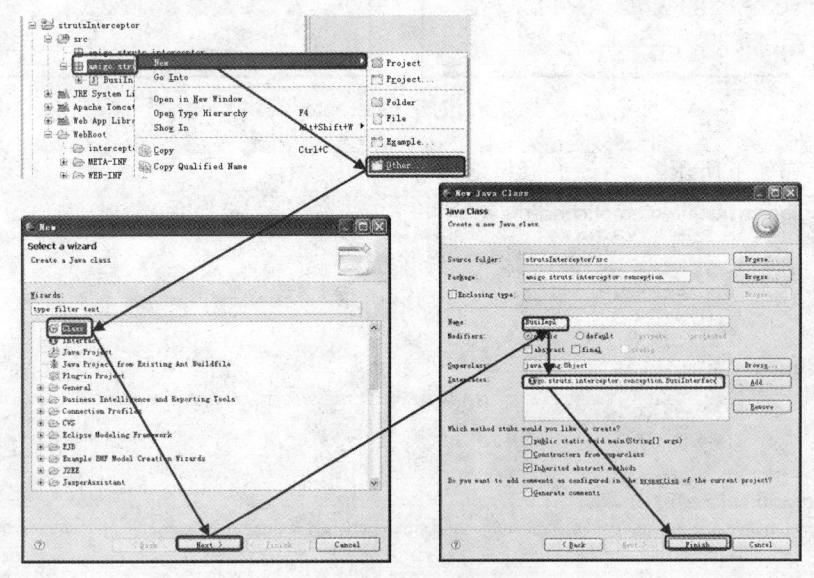

图 7-4 创建 BusiImpl 类

该类的代码如下所示:

```java
package amigo.struts.interceptor.conception;
/**
 * 业务实现类
 */
public class BusiImpl implements BusiInterface {
    public void doSomeThing() {
        System.out.println("class=BusiImpl, method=doSomeThing");
    }
}
```

第四步：编写拦截器类：Interceptor.java

在 amigo.struts.interceptor.conception 包中建立拦截器类 Interceptor.java，该类定义了 before() 和 after() 方法，这两个方法分别在被拦截方法 doSomeThing() 之前和之后执行。操作步骤如图 7-5 所示。

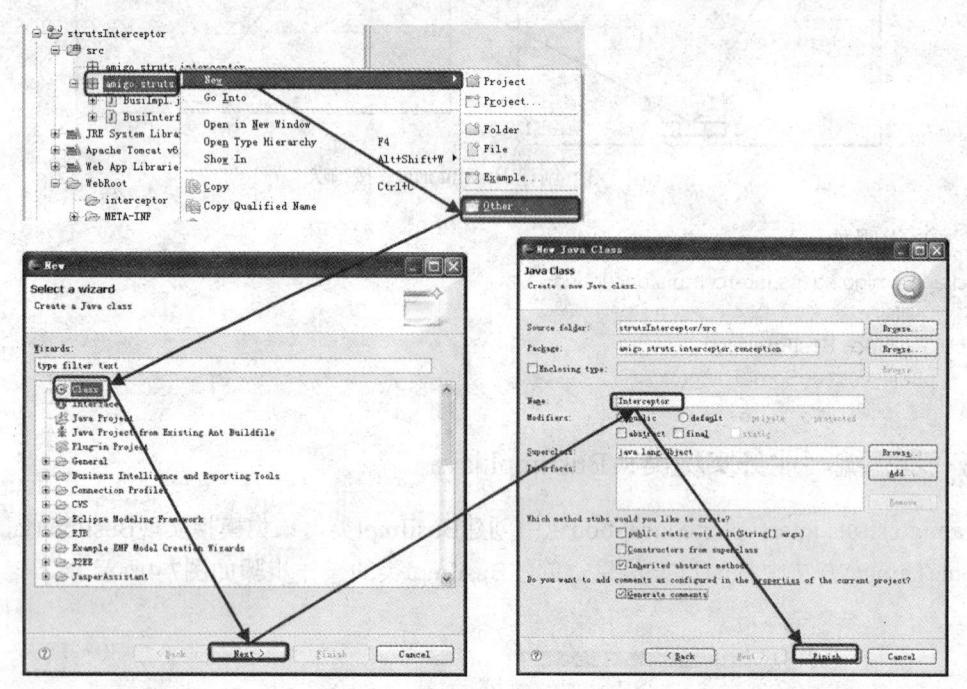

图 7-5　创建 Interceptor 类

该类的代码如下所示:

```java
package amigo.struts.interceptor.conception;

/**
 * 拦截器类
 */
public class Interceptor {
    /**
     * 在被拦截方法之前执行
     */
    public void before() {
        System.out.println("拦截器的方法，在 doSomeThing 之前执行");
    }
```

```java
    /**
     * 在被拦截方法之后执行
     */
    public void after() {
        System.out.println("拦截器的方法，在 doSomeThing 之后执行");
    }
}
```

第五步：编写动态代理类：DynamicProxyClass.java

在amigo.struts.interceptor.conception包中建立动态代理类DynamicProxyClass.java，该类实现InvocationHandler接口，该类的代码如下所示：

```java
package amigo.struts.interceptor.conception;

import java.lang.reflect.InvocationHandler;
import java.lang.reflect.Method;
import java.lang.reflect.Proxy;

/**
 * 动态代理类
 */
public class DynamicProxyClass implements InvocationHandler    {
    /** 被代理对象*/
    private Object busi;

    /** 拦截器*/
    private Interceptor interceptor = new Interceptor();

    /**
     * 动态生成一个代理类对象,并绑定被代理类和代理处理器
     * @param business
     * @return 代理类对象
     */
    public Object bind(Object busi) {
        this.busi = busi;
        return Proxy.newProxyInstance(
                busi.getClass().getClassLoader(), // 被代理类的 ClassLoader
                busi.getClass().getInterfaces(), // 要被代理的接口,本方法返回对象会自动声称实现了这些接口
                // 代理处理器对象
                this);
    }

    /**
     * 代理要调用的方法,并在方法调用前后调用拦截器的方法.
     * @param proxy 代理类对象
     * @param method 被代理的接口方法
     * @param args 被代理接口方法的参数
     * @return 方法调用返回的结果
     * @throws Throwable
     */
    public Object invoke(Object proxy, Method method, Object[] args)
            throws Throwable {
        Object result = null;
```

```
            interceptor.before();
            result = method.invoke(busi, args);
            interceptor.after();
            return null;
        }
}
```

第六步：编写测试类：Test.java

在amigo.struts.interceptor.conception包中建立测试类Test.java，该类用于测试拦截器是否能起作用，该类的代码如下所示：

```
package amigo.struts.interceptor.conception;
/**
 * 测试类
 */
public class Test {
    public static void main(String args[]) {
        // 创建动态代理处理类
        DynamicProxyClass proxyClass = new DynamicProxyClass();
        BusiInterface busi = new BusiImpl();
        // 创建代理对象
        BusiInterface busiProxy = (BusiInterface) proxyClass.bind(busi);
        busiProxy.doSomeThing();
    }
}
```

第七步：运行结果

运行Test.java类，控制台显示的信息如下所示：

```
拦截器的方法，在 doSomeThing 之前执行
class=BusiImpl, method=doSomeThing
拦截器的方法，在 doSomeThing 之后执行
```

从运行结果中可以看出，拦截器起了作用，通过动态代理处理器DynamicProxy类，在doSomeThing()方法之前调用了拦截器类的before()方法，在其后执行了拦截器类的after()方法。

【例 7-2】拦截器的配置

〖实例需求〗

Struts 2 提供的拦截器的框架是可插拔式的，这种可插拔式通过将拦截器配置在 struts.xml 中实现。

本实例详细讲解拦截器的配置，包括拦截器、拦截器栈的配置、多个拦截器执行的时序图和默认拦截器等。

〖开发过程〗

第一步：拦截器的配置

在struts.xml中配置拦截器时，只需要指定拦截器的名称和实现类，使用的元素为

<interceptor../>，<interceptor../>元素可包含一个或多个<param../>元素，拦截器都定义在<interceptors../>元素中，基本的格式如下所示：

```xml
<interceptors>
    <!--可定义0到多个拦截器-->
    <interceptor name="拦截器名称" class="拦截器实现类">
        <!--一个拦截器可定义0到多个参数-->
        <param name="参数名">参数值</param>
    </interceptor>
</interceptors>
```

使用举例如下所示：

```xml
<interceptors>
    <!-- interceptors 可配置0到多个拦截器子元素 -->
    <!-- 不带参数的拦截器配置举例 -->
    <interceptor name="myInterceptor" class="amigo.struts.interceptor.configure.myInterceptor">
    </interceptor>

    <!-- 带参数的拦截器配置举例 -->
    <interceptor name="sampleInterceptor"
 class="amigo.struts.interceptor.configure.sampleInterceptor">
        <!-- 可配置0到多个参数 -->
        <param name="username">amigo</param>
        <param name="password">amigo</param>
    </interceptor>
</interceptors>
```

第二步：拦截器栈的配置

Struts 2中可以将多个拦截器配置在一起形成拦截器栈，例如在进入Action的方法之前需要首先检查session、记录日志等拦截。拦截器栈语法格式如下：

```xml
<interceptor-stack name="拦截器栈名">
    <!-- interceptor-stack 可包含0到多个 interceptor-ref 元素，用来指明栈中的拦截器-->
    <interceptor-ref name="拦截器1" />
    <interceptor-ref name="拦截器2" />
    ……
</interceptor-stack>
```

下面的实例配置了一个session检查的拦截栈和一个日志记录的拦截栈后，将这两个拦截器组成一个栈，拦截器栈的名称为myStackInterceptor，配置信息如下所示：

```xml
<!-- 自定义的session 检查拦截栈 -->
<interceptor name="sessionInterceptor"
class="amigo.struts.interceptor.configure.sessionInterceptor"></interceptor>

<!-- 自定义的日志记录拦截栈 -->
<interceptor name="logInterceptor"
 class="amigo.struts.interceptor.configure.logInterceptor"></interceptor>

<!-- 配置拦截器栈1，它将sessionInterceptor 和 logInterceptor 两个拦截器组成一个栈 -->
<interceptor-stack name="myStackInterceptor">
<!-- interceptor-stack 可包含0到多个 interceptor-ref 元素，用来指明栈中的拦截器-->
    <interceptor-ref name="sessionInterceptor" />
    <interceptor-ref name="logInterceptor" />
</interceptor-stack>
```

另外，拦截器栈允许嵌套拦截器栈，即一个拦截器栈可包含另一个拦截器栈，例如我们在上面配置的基础上配置另一个拦截器栈actionStackInterceptor，它除了包含myStackInterceptor这个栈，还包含了一个securityInterceptor拦截器，修改后的配置信息如下所示：

```xml
<!-- 自定义的session 检查拦截栈 -->
<interceptor name="sessionInterceptor"
class="amigo.struts.interceptor.configure.sessionInterceptor"></interceptor>

<!-- 自定义的安全检查拦截栈 -->
<interceptor name="securityInterceptor"
 class="amigo.struts.interceptor.configure.securityInterceptor"></interceptor>

<!-- 自定义的日志记录拦截栈 -->
<interceptor name="logInterceptor"
class="amigo.struts.interceptor.configure.logInterceptor"></interceptor>

<!-- 配置拦截器栈1，它将sessionInterceptor 和logInterceptor 两个拦截器组成一个栈 -->
<interceptor-stack name="myStackInterceptor">
     <!-- interceptor-stack 可包含0到多个interceptor-ref 元素，用来指明栈中的拦截器-->
     <interceptor-ref name="sessionInterceptor" />
     <interceptor-ref name="logInterceptor" />
</interceptor-stack>

<!-- 配置拦截器栈2 actionStackInterceptor，它将sessionInterceptor、logInterceptor 和securityInterceptor 这3个拦截器组成一个栈 -->
<interceptor-stack name="actionStackInterceptor">
     <!-- interceptor-ref 可指定为另一个拦截器栈 -->
     <interceptor-ref name="myStackInterceptor" />
     <interceptor-ref name="securityInterceptor" />
</interceptor-stack>
```

第三步：为action指定拦截器或拦截器栈

若需要为某个action指定拦截器或拦截器栈，只需要在<action../>元素中配置一个或多个interceptor-ref元素即可，拦截器通常配置在result元素之后，若要为UserAction配置sessionInterceptor、sampleInterceptor和logInterceptor拦截器，配置示例如下：

```xml
<!-- 为action 配置拦截器实例 -->
<action name="user" class="amigo.struts.interceptor.configure.UserAction">
     <result name="success">userList.jsp</result>
     <result name="error">error.jsp</result>
     <!-- 为该action 指定拦截器：sessionInterceptor、sampleInterceptor 和logInterceptor -->
     <interceptor-ref name="sessionInterceptor" />
     <interceptor-ref name="sampleInterceptor">
           <!-- 动态设置参数值 -->
           <param name="username">amigo</param>
           <param name="password">amigo</param>
     </interceptor-ref>
     <interceptor-ref name="logInterceptor" />
</action>
```

若要动态设置拦截器的参数值，可通过<param../>子元素指定。若要为action指定拦截器栈，也使用<interceptor-ref...>元素，将name属性修改成拦截器栈的名称即可。

第四步：指定默认的拦截器或拦截器栈

当在struts.xml中配置一个<package../>包元素时，可为该包指定一个默认的拦截器或拦截器栈，进行这样的配置后，若某个Action没有显式地指定拦截器，则将使用默认拦截器。若Action显式地指定了拦截器，则默认拦截器将不再起作用。

默认拦截器使用<default-interceptor-ref../>指定，它是<package../>元素的子元素，若要为amigo这个包指定actionStackInterceptor这个拦截器栈，配置示例如下：

```xml
......
<struts>
    <package name="amigo" extends="struts-default">
        <interceptors>
            <!-- interceptors 可配置 0 到多个拦截器子元素 -->
            <!-- 自定义的 session 检查拦截栈 -->
            <interceptor name="sessionInterceptor"
 class="amigo.struts.interceptor.configure.sessionInterceptor"></interceptor>

            <!-- 自定义的安全检查拦截栈 -->
            <interceptor name="securityInterceptor"
 class="amigo.struts.interceptor.configure.securityInterceptor"></interceptor>

            <!-- 自定义的日志记录拦截栈 -->
            <interceptor name="logInterceptor"
 class="amigo.struts.interceptor.configure.logInterceptor"></interceptor>

            <!-- 配置拦截器栈 actionStackInterceptor，它将 sessionInterceptor、logInterceptor 和 securityInterceptor 这 3 个拦截器组成一个栈 -->
            <interceptor-stack name="actionStackInterceptor">
                <!-- interceptor-ref 可指定为另一个拦截器栈 -->
                <interceptor-ref name="myStackInterceptor" />
                <interceptor-ref name="securityInterceptor" />
            </interceptor-stack>
        </interceptors>

        <default-interceptor-ref name="actionStackInterceptor"></default-interceptor-ref>

        <!-- 为 action 配置拦截器实例 -->
        <action name="user" class="amigo.struts.interceptor.configure.UserAction">
            <result name="success">userList.jsp</result>
            <result name="error">error.jsp</result>
        </action>
    </package>
</struts>
```

在上面的配置中，未为UserAction指定拦截器，因此将使用默认的拦截器栈actionStackInterceptor。

【例7-3】内建拦截器

〖实例需求〗

Struts 2 框架提供了各种常用的拦截器来简化开发人员的编程工作，这些拦截器的定义存放在 struts-default.xml 文件中，该文件的拦截器部分的内容摘要如下：

```
<interceptors>
<interceptor name="alias" class="com.opensymphony.xwork2.interceptor.AliasInterceptor"/>
<interceptor name="autowiring"
 class="com.opensymphony.xwork2.spring.interceptor.ActionAutowiringInterceptor"/>
......
</interceptors>
```

当开发人员定义的包继承了 struts-default.xml 时，就可以使用这些内建的拦截器。本实例详细讲解如何使用这些内建的拦截器，以及在使用时需要注意的一些问题。

〖开发过程〗

第一步：常用内建拦截器简介

Struts 2框架提供了创建session、异常处理、重复提交等拦截器，下面对这些常用的拦截器进行简要介绍。

（1）alias。

这个拦截器实现在不同请求中相似参数别名的转换。它在struts-default.xml文件中的定义如下：

```
<interceptor name="alias" class="com.opensymphony.xwork2.interceptor.AliasInterceptor"/>
```

（2）exception。

这个拦截器负责处理异常，它将异常映射为结果。该拦截器定义如下：

```
<interceptor name="exception"
class="com.opensymphony.xwork2.interceptor.ExceptionMappingInterceptor"/>
```

（3）fileUpload。

这个拦截器主要用于文件上传，它负责解析表单中文件域的内容。该拦截器定义如下：

```
<interceptor name="fileUpload" class="org.apache.struts2.interceptor.FileUploadInterceptor"/>
```

（4）i18n。

这是支持国际化的拦截器，它负责把所选的语言、区域放入用户Session中。该拦截器定义如下：

```
<interceptor name="i18n" class="com.opensymphony.xwork2.interceptor.I18nInterceptor"/>
```

（5）params。

这是最基本的一个拦截器，它负责解析HTTP请求中的参数，并将参数值设置成Action对应的属性值。该拦截器定义如下：

```
<interceptor name="params" class="com.opensymphony.xwork2.interceptor.ParametersInterceptor"/>
```

（6）scope。

这是范围转换拦截器，它可以将Action状态信息保存到HttpSession范围，或者保存到ServletContext范围内。该拦截器定义如下：

```
<interceptor name="scope" class="org.apache.struts2.interceptor.ScopeInterceptor"/>
```

（7）timer。

这个拦截器负责输出Action的执行时间，这个拦截器在分析该Action的性能瓶颈时比较有用。该拦截器定义如下：

```
<interceptor name="timer" class="com.opensymphony.xwork2.interceptor.TimerInterceptor"/>
```

（8）token。

这个拦截器主要用于阻止重复提交，它检查传到Action中的token，从而防止多次提交。该拦截器定义如下：

```xml
<interceptor name="token" class="org.apache.struts2.interceptor.TokenInterceptor"/>
```

（9）validation。

这个拦截器通过执行在xxxAction-validation.xml中定义的校验器，从而完成数据校验。该拦截器定义如下：

```xml
<interceptor name="validation" class="org.apache.struts2.interceptor.validation.AnnotationValidationInterceptor"/>
```

（10）workflow。

这个拦截器负责调用Action类中的validate方法，如果校验失败，则返回input的逻辑视图。该拦截器定义如下：

```xml
<interceptor name="workflow" class="com.opensymphony.xwork2.interceptor.DefaultWorkflowInterceptor"/>
```

第二步：内建拦截器的使用方法

通常情况下，用户并不需要配置自定义的拦截器，只需要使用默认的拦截器即可。若想使用前面所描述的各种内建的拦截器中的一个或者多个时，并不需要一个一个引入，struts-default.xml文件中提供了一个默认的拦截器栈，可一次将这些拦截器引入进去，该栈在struts-default.xml文件中的定义如下所示：

```xml
<interceptor-stack name="defaultStack">
    <interceptor-ref name="exception"/>
    <interceptor-ref name="alias"/>
    <interceptor-ref name="servletConfig"/>
    <interceptor-ref name="prepare"/>
    <interceptor-ref name="i18n"/>
    <interceptor-ref name="chain"/>
    <interceptor-ref name="debugging"/>
    <interceptor-ref name="profiling"/>
    <interceptor-ref name="scopedModelDriven"/>
    <interceptor-ref name="modelDriven"/>
    <interceptor-ref name="fileUpload"/>
    <interceptor-ref name="checkbox"/>
    <interceptor-ref name="staticParams"/>
    <interceptor-ref name="params">
        <param name="excludeParams">dojo\..*</param>
    </interceptor-ref>
    <interceptor-ref name="conversionError"/>
    <interceptor-ref name="validation">
        <param name="excludeMethods">input,back,cancel,browse</param>
    </interceptor-ref>
    <interceptor-ref name="workflow">
        <param name="excludeMethods">input,back,cancel,browse</param>
    </interceptor-ref>
</interceptor-stack>
```

为某个Action类配置内建拦截器的方法如下：

首先需要将struts-default.xml文件包含进来，因为该文件定义了内建拦截器，读者可在struts.xml文件的struts根元素下添加如下配置：

```xml
<include file="struts-default.xml"/>
```

接着使用在struts.xml中需要指定内建拦截器的action元素添加如下配置：

```xml
<interceptor-ref name="内建拦截器的名称,例如: token" />
```

第三步:token 内建拦截器的使用

内建拦截器的使用方法都非常类似,所以本例通过token拦截器的使用来展示内建拦截器的使用。

(1)建立源码包和 JSP 文件目录。

在src目录中本实例的源码包为amigo.struts.interceptor.buildin。接着在WebRoot目录中建立interceptor/buildin目录,存放该实例的JSP文件token.jsp和success.jsp。

(2)建立 Action 类:TokenAction.java。

在amigo.struts.interceptor.buildin中建立该类的Action类TokenAction.java,该类的代码非常简单,只是接收从token.jsp传送过来的username参数后,跳转到操作成功界面,该类的代码如下所示:

```java
package amigo.struts.interceptor.buildin;

import com.opensymphony.xwork2.ActionSupport;

/**
 * 内建拦截器 token 的使用实例
 */
public class TokenAction extends ActionSupport {
    private static final long serialVersionUID = 1L;
    private String username;

    // 省略 username 的 getter/setter 方法

    public String execute(){
        System.out.println("token.jsp 传送过来的 username 参数: " + username);
        return SUCCESS;
    }
}
```

(3)建立 JSP 页面:token.jsp。

在WebRoot/interceptor/buildin目录中建立token.jsp页面,该页面将请求TokenAction这个类,它包含一个usernmae输入框,代码如下所示:

```jsp
<%@ page language="java" contentType="text/html; charset=utf-8" pageEncoding="utf-8" %>
<%@ taglib prefix="s" uri="/struts-tags" %>
<html>
    <head>
        <title>内建拦截器 token 的使用</title>
    </head>
    <body>
        <s:actionerror/>
        <s:form action="token" >
            <s:textfield name="username" label="用户名"></s:textfield>
            <s:token></s:token>
            <s:submit></s:submit>
        </s:form>
    </body>
</html>
```

（4）建立 JSP 页面：success.jsp。

当操作成功时，Action的成功界面为success.jsp，读者可在WebRoot/interceptor/buildin目录中建立该页面，该页面只是简单地输出"操作成功"的信息，该页面的代码如下所示：

```jsp
<%@ page contentType="text/html; charset=UTF-8" %>
<html>
    <head>
        <title>成功界面</title>
    </head>
    <body>
        <h3>操作成功！</h3>
    </body>
</html>
```

（5）配置 struts.xml。

最后还需要在struts.xml中配置TokenAction，并为其指定内建拦截器token，配置信息如下所示：

```xml
<!-- 使用内建拦截器 token -->
<action name="token" class="amigo.struts.interceptor.buildin.TokenAction">
    <interceptor-ref name="token"></interceptor-ref>
    <result name="invalid.token">/interceptor/buildin/token.jsp</result>
    <result>/interceptor/buildin/success.jsp</result>
</action>
```

（6）运行结果。

为了看到本例的运行结果，读者可以访问token.jsp页面，界面如图7-6所示。

图 7-6　输入界面

在图7-6中单击Submit按钮进行提交，此时将跳转到操作成功界面，如图7-7所示。

图 7-7　操作成功（第一次提交）

在图 7-7 中单击 IE 的 后退 按钮，后退到 token.jsp 页面，接着单击 Submit 按钮提交，此时将不能成功提交，token 拦截器起作用，界面如图 7-8 所示。

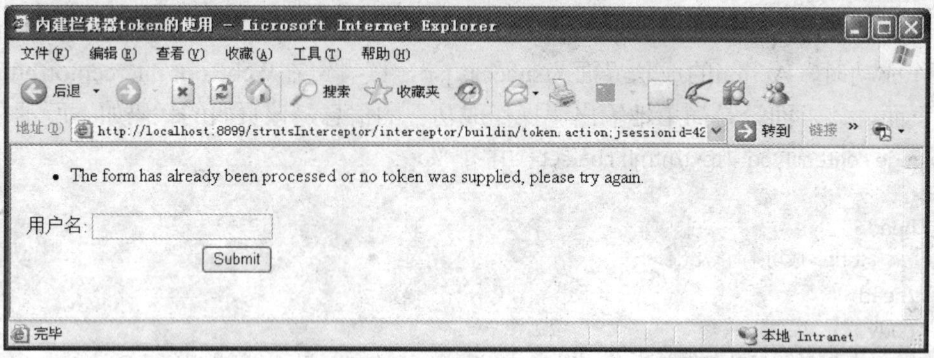

图 7-8 重复提交界面

当重复提交时，token拦截器起作用，将会跳转到struts.xml配置文件中invalid.token的指向界面：token.jsp，并输出提示信息：

The form has already been processed or no token was supplied, please try again

（7）输出中文提示信息。

该条提示信息是英文的提示信息，该提示信息在struts2-core-2.0.11.2/org/apache/struts2目录中的struts-messages.properties文件中，该文件的内容如下所示：

struts.messages.invalid.token=The form has already been processed or no token was supplied, please try again.

struts.internal.invalid.token=Form token {0} does not match the session token {1}.

struts.messages.bypass.request=Bypassing {0}/ {1}
struts.messages.current.file=File {0} {1} {2} {3}
struts.messages.invalid.file=Could not find a Filename for {0}. Verify that a valid file was submitted.
struts.messages.invalid.content.type=Could not find a Content-Type for {0}. Verify that a valid file was submitted.
struts.messages.removing.file=Removing file {0} {1}
struts.messages.error.uploading=Error uploading: {0}
struts.messages.error.file.too.large=File too large: {0} "{1}" {2}
struts.messages.error.content.type.not.allowed=Content-Type not allowed: {0} "{1}" {2}

devmode.notification=Developer Notification (set struts.devMode to false to disable this message):\n{0}

若读者想将发生重复提交时的提示信息转变成中文，可通过如下方式：

首先在src目录中建立messages.properties和经过编码的资源中文资源文件messages_zh_CN.properties，messages.properties文件的内容如下所示：

struts.messages.invalid.token=表单已提交过，不允许重复提交

使用native2ascii码进行编码后，messages_zh_CN.properties文件的内容如下所示：

struts.messages.invalid.token=\u8868\u5355\u5df2\u63d0\u4ea4\u8fc7\uff0c\u4e0d\u5141\u8bb8\u91cd\u590d\u63d0\u4ea4

接着在struts.xml文件中指定struts.custom.i18n.resources的值为messages资源文件，添加的信息如下所示：

<constant name="struts.custom.i18n.resources" value="messages" />

此时再按照上一步的方法重复提交，将显示中文的提示信息，如图7-9所示。

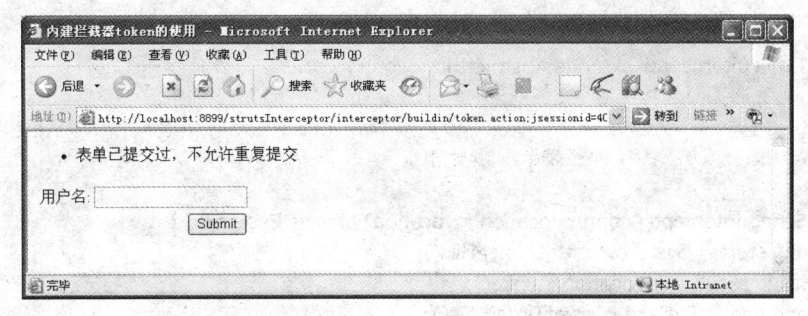

图 7-9 输出中文提示信息的重复提交界面

【例 7-4】自定义拦截器

〖实例需求〗

虽然 Struts 2 框架提供了大量的内建拦截器，但有时开发人员也需要定义自己的拦截器，Struts 2 中提供了 com.opensymphony.xwork2.Interceptor 接口来供用户实现自定义拦截器。Interceptor 包括如下 3 个方法：

- init()：在拦截器被初始化后，拦截方法执行之前调用。每个拦截器只执行一次 init() 方法，它一般用于申请资源。
- destroy()：在拦截器实例被销毁之前，系统将调用该方法，该方法一般用于销毁在 init() 方法中申请或打开的资源。
- intercept(ActionInvocation invocation)：定义拦截操作，该方法返回一个字符串，与 Action 类的 execute()方法一样返回的是逻辑视图字符串，该字符串表示跳转到的视图资源。

若自定义的拦截器不需要申请资源和销毁资源，则自定义的拦截器不需要实现 Interceptor 接口的 init()和 destory()方法，此时可以使用抽象类 com.opensymphony.xwork2.AbstractInterceptor，该类实现 Interceptor 接口，但是提供了 init()和 destroy()方法的空实现。

本实例详细讲解一个自定义的输出执行时间的拦截器 TimerInterceptor，学习如何利用 AbstractInterceptor 抽象类实现自定义的拦截器。

〖开发过程〗

第一步：编写拦截器类：TimerInterceptor.java

在 amigo.struts.interceptor 目录和 interceptor 目录中建立 custom 目录，这两个目录分别用于存放该实例的类文件和 JSP 文件。在 amigo.struts.interceptor.custom 包中建立拦截器类 TimerInterceptor.java，该类实现 AbstractInterceptor 抽象类，它的 intercept 方法打印被拦截方法的执行时间信息。该类的代码如下所示：

```
package amigo.struts.interceptor.custom;

import com.opensymphony.xwork2.ActionInvocation;
import com.opensymphony.xwork2.interceptor.AbstractInterceptor;

/**
 * 自定义的执行时间的拦截器
```

```java
*/
public class TimerInterceptor extends AbstractInterceptor{

    /**
     * 拦截方法，在该方法中打印被拦截方法的执行时间
     */
    public String intercept(ActionInvocation invocation) throws Exception {
        long start = System.currentTimeMillis();
        String result = invocation.invoke();
        long end = System.currentTimeMillis();
        System.out.println("执行被拦截方法的时间为=" + (end - start) + "毫秒");
        return null;
    }
}
```

第二步：编写 Action 类：LoginAction.java

该Action类用于检查在login.jsp中输入的用户名和密码是否输入正确，若输入成功，则跳转到loginSuccess.jsp页面，否则，跳转到error.jsp页面，该类的代码如下所示：

```java
package amigo.struts.interceptor.custom;

import com.opensymphony.xwork2.ActionSupport;

/**
 * 登录的 Action
 */
public class LoginAction extends ActionSupport {
    private String username;

    private String password;

    // 省略 username 和 password 的 getter/setter 方法

    public String execute() {
        if (username != null && "amigo".equals(username)
                && password != null && "amigo".equals(password)) {
            System.out.println("username=" + username + ", password=" + password);
            return this.SUCCESS;
        } else {
            return this.ERROR;
        }
    }
}
```

第三步：编写登录页面：login.jsp

在WebRoot/ interceptor/custom目录中建立login.jsp页面，该页面的表单包含用户名和密码信息，单击Submit按钮后，将表单信息提交到LoginAction，该页面的代码如下所示：

```html
......
<html>
    <head>
        <title>用户登录</title>
        <meta http-equiv="Content-Type" content="text/html; charset=UTF-8"/>
    </head>
```

```
        <body>
                <s:form action="login">
                        <s:textfield name="username" label="用户名"></s:textfield>
                        <s:password name="password" label="密码"></s:password>
                        <s:submit></s:submit>
                </s:form>
        </body>
</html>
```

第四步：编写登录成功和失败页面：loginSuccess.jsp 和 error.jsp

在WebRoot/ interceptor/custom目录中建立loginSuccess.jsp页面和error.jsp页面，这两个页面只是输出登录成功和登录失败的提示信息，内容不再赘述。

第五步：配置 struts.xml

最后还需要在struts.xml文件中配置LoginAction和TimerInterceptor拦截器，同时为LoginAction指定TimerInterceptor拦截器，配置信息如下所示：

```xml
<!DOCTYPE struts PUBLIC
    "-//Apache Software Foundation//DTD Struts Configuration 2.0//EN"
    "http://struts.apache.org/dtds/struts-2.0.dtd">
<struts>
    <include file="struts-default.xml"/>
    <package name="amigo" extends="struts-default">
      <interceptors>
          <interceptor name="timerInterceptor"
 class="amigo.struts.interceptor.custom.TimerInterceptor">
          </interceptor>
      </interceptors>

      <action name="login" class="amigo.struts.interceptor.custom.LoginAction">
          <result name="success">/interceptor/custom/loginSuccess.jsp</result>
          <result name="error">/interceptor/custom/error.jsp</result>
          <!-- 为 loginAction 配置 timerInterceptor 拦截器 -->
          <interceptor-ref name="timerInterceptor" />
      </action>
    </package>
</struts>
```

第六步：运行结果

在浏览器中输入login.jsp的请求地址，界面如图7-10所示。

图7-10 登录界面

在图7-10中单击Submit按钮提交表单后，读者可在控制台看到类似信息：

```
username=amigo, password=amigo
执行被拦截方法的时间为=47 毫秒
```

从运行结果中读者可以看出，拦截器类已经起了作用，输出了方法的执行时间。

小结

本章讲述的拦截器是 Struts 2 的一个重要的组成部分，它可在 Action 的方法之前或之后执行一些预先设置的方法。拦截器一般用于进行类型转换操作、进行权限控制、防止表单的双重提交和处理文件上传等，在 Web 项目中应用广泛。

拦截器在很多开源框架（例如 Struts 2、Spring 等）中使用广泛，它基于 AOP（Aspect Oriented Programming，面向切面编程）。AOP 是消除重复代码的一个很有用的方法，它从运行的角度取得业务处理过程的切面，在该切面处调用拦截器中定义的方法。在 AOP 中，有如下几个重要概念，其中"目标对象"和"被插入的处理方法"都与拦截器有很大关系：

- 被插入的处理方法：拦截器中定义的处理方法，在被拦截方法之前或之后执行。
- 目标对象：被拦截的对象。
- 代理对象：目标对象的代理对象，由系统创建。

拦截器所使用的核心技术是 Java 的动态代理技术。Java 的代理类 Proxy 的 newProxyInstance(…)方法可以获得代理对象，代码如下所示：

```
return Proxy.newProxyInstance(
    busi.getClass().getClassLoader(), // 被代理类的 ClassLoader
    busi.getClass().getInterfaces(), // 要被代理的接口,本方法返回对象会自动声称实现了这些接口
        // 代理处理器对象
        this);
}
```

另外自定义的动态代理类需要实现 java.lang.reflect.InvocationHandler 类，实现该类的类需要实现 invoke(Object proxy, Method method, Object[] args)方法，如下代码实现了该方法，拦截器的操作可在 method.invoke(busi, args)方法执行前后指定。例如，在下面的代码中，指定了执行业务逻辑方法之前调用拦截器的 before()方法，在其后执行拦截器的 after()方法，代码如下所示：

```
public Object invoke(Object proxy, Method method, Object[] args)
        throws Throwable {
    Object result = null;
    interceptor.before();
    result = method.invoke(busi, args);
    interceptor.after();
    return null;
}
```

拦截器需要在 Struts 2 的配置文件（eg. struts.xml）中进行配置，配置格式如下所示：

```
<interceptors>
        <!--可定义 0 到多个拦截器-->
<interceptor name="拦截器名称" class="拦截器实现类">
            <!—一个拦截器可定义 0 到多个参数-->
            <param name="参数名">参数值</param>
</interceptor>
</interceptors>
```

Struts 2 可以将多个拦截器配置在一起形成拦截器栈，拦截器栈的配置格式如下所示：

```xml
<interceptor-stack name="拦截器栈名">
    <!-- interceptor-stack 可包含 0 到多个 interceptor-ref 元素，用来指明栈中的拦截器-->
    <interceptor-ref name="拦截器 1" />
    <interceptor-ref name="拦截器 2" />
    ……
</interceptor-stack>
```

拦截器栈允许嵌套拦截器栈，即一个拦截器栈可包含另一个拦截器栈：

```xml
<interceptor-stack name="actionStackInterceptor">
    <!-- interceptor-ref 可指定为另一个拦截器栈 -->
    <interceptor-ref name="myStackInterceptor" />
    <interceptor-ref name="securityInterceptor" />
</interceptor-stack>
```

若要为 action 指定拦截器，可在 action 元素中指定 0～n 个<interceptor-ref/>子元素，例如在下面的配置中为 UserAction 配置了 sessionIntercetor 拦截器：

```xml
<action name="user" class="amigo.struts.interceptor.configure.UserAction">
    <result name="success">userList.jsp</result>
    <interceptor-ref name="sessionInterceptor" />
</action>
```

Struts 2 框架提供了各种常用的拦截器来简化开发人员的编程工作，这些拦截器的定义在 struts-default.xml 文件中。常用的内建拦截器包括 alias、exception、token 和 fileUpload 过滤器，本章的【例 7-3】通过一个 token 拦截器的使用展示了内建拦截器的使用。若需要为某个 Action 指定 token 拦截器，需要在 struts.xml 文件中为该 Action 指定 token 拦截器，配置信息如下：

```xml
<interceptor-ref name="token"></interceptor-ref>
```

并指定其 invalid.token 的页面指向，例如：

```xml
<result name="invalid.token">/interceptor/buildin/token.jsp</result>
```

接着还需要在 JSP 页面使用如下代码显示重复提交提示信息：

```jsp
<s:token></s:token>
```

默认提示信息为英文，若想输出中文的提示信息，需要在资源文件中配置该信息。

若需要开发自定义拦截器，可通过实现 com.opensymphony.xwork2.Interceptor 接口来供用户实现自定义拦截器。Interceptor 包括如下 3 个方法：

- init()：在拦截器被初始化后，拦截方法执行之前调用。每个拦截器只执行一次 init() 方法，它一般用于申请资源。
- destroy()：在拦截器实例被销毁之前，系统将调用该方法，该方法一般用于销毁在 init() 方法中申请或打开的资源。
- intercept(ActionInvocation invocation)：定义拦截操作，该方法返回一个字符串，与 Action 类的 execute()方法一样返回的是逻辑视图字符串，该字符串表示跳转到的视图资源。

若自定义的拦截器不需要申请资源和销毁资源，此时读者可以通过继承抽象类 com.opensymphony.xwork2.AbstractInterceptor，该类实现 Interceptor 接口，但是提供了 init()和 destroy()方法的空实现。

第 8 章　Struts 2 标签库

【本章导读语】

Struts 2 提供了丰富的标签供开发人员使用，它不再像 Struts 1.x 中一样，将种类标签进行分门别类，但可以根据其使用的用途加以区别。

与 Struts1.x 的标签库相比，Struts 2 的标签库使用 OGNL 表达式作为基础，其对集合和对象的访问功能很强大。同时，Struts 2 提供了很多额外的高级标签，例如树型结构、时期选择标签等。同时，Struts 2 提供了对 Dojo、DWR 和 Ajax 的支持，因此可以生成更多的页面效果。

本章详细讲述 Struts 2 的非 UI 标签（控制标签和数据标签）和 UI 标签的使用。Struts 2 提供了对主题和模板的支持，本章对 Struts 2 中主题和模板的使用进行了详细介绍，对如何使用主题和模板来简化视图页面的编写，以及如何利用主题和模板的扩展性来开发自定义的主题和模板进行了具体的讲述。

【例 8-1】控制标签

〖实例需求〗

Struts 2 的控制标签属于非 UI 标签，它主要用于完成流程的控制，例如循环和分支等操作。本实例对 Struts 2 的几个控制标签：iterator、if/elseif/else、append、generator、sort、merge 和 subset 的使用进行了详细讲解，并对使用时需要注意的一些问题进行了说明。

〖开发过程〗

第一步：建立工程

读者可以参考前几章建立工程的方法在 Eclipse 中新建一个名为 strutstag 的动态 Web 工程，并将所需的 jar 包导入到 WEB-INF/lib 目录中，并且在 src 目录中建立 amigo.struts.tag 包。操作完成后工程的目录结构如图 8-1 所示。

第二步：将 struts-tags.tld 文件复制到工程中

要使用标签库，需要将 struts-tags.tld 文件导入到工程中，解压缩导入到 WEB-INF/lib 目录中的 struts2-core-2.0.8.jar 包，其 struts2-core-2.0.8/META-INF 目录如图 8-2 所示。

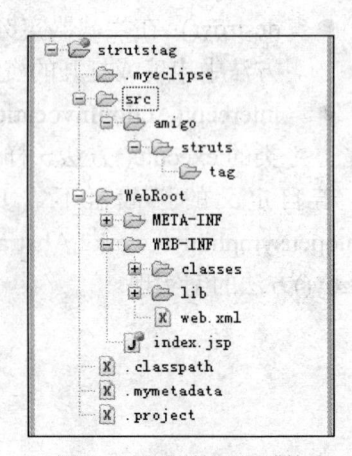

图 8-1　工程的目录结构

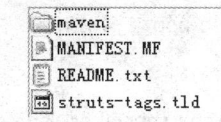

图 8-2 struts2-core-2.0.8/META-INF 目录

第三步：配置 web.xml

在工程中需要加入 Struts 2 的 FileterDispatcher 的 Filter，若 Web 应用使用的是 Servlet 2.3 及以下版本，需要在 web.xml 中定义 Struts 2 的标签库，例如对于 Servlet 2.3 版本的 web.xml 文件的配置如下：

```xml
<?xml version="1.0" encoding="UTF-8"?>
<!DOCTYPE web-app PUBLIC
 "-//Sun Microsystems, Inc.//DTD Web Application 2.3//EN"
 "http://java.sun.com/dtd/web-app_2_3.dtd">

<web-app>
    <!-- 配置 struts 2 的 Filter -->
    <filter>
      <filter-name>struts2</filter-name>
      <filter-class>org.apache.struts2.dispatcher.FilterDispatcher</filter-class>
    </filter>

    <filter-mapping>
      <filter-name>struts2</filter-name>
      <url-pattern>/*</url-pattern>
    </filter-mapping>

    <!-- 定义 Struts 2 的标签库 -->
    <taglib>
        <taglib-uri>/struts-tags</taglib-uri>
        <taglib-location>/WEB-INF/lib/struts2-core-2.0.8.jar</taglib-location>
    </taglib>
    <welcome-file-list>
    <welcome-file>index.jsp</welcome-file>
    </welcome-file-list>
</web-app>
```

其中`<taglib-uri.../>`元素指定了标签库的 URI，这个名称读者可以任意指定，在 JSP 页面中通过该 URI 来对标签库进行引用，"/struts-tags"是 struts-tags.tld 中默认的 URI，笔者建议使用该 URI。

`<taglib-location.../>`元素指定 tld 所在的位置，struts-tags.tld 文件位于 struts2-core-2.0.8.jar 的 META-INF 目录中。

对于 Servlet 2.4 或以上版本，可不在 web.xml 文件中增加标签库的定义，因为本章工程用的是 Servlet 2.4，所以不需要添加，本工程的 web.xml 文件的完整内容如下所示：

```xml
<?xml version="1.0" encoding="UTF-8"?>

<web-app version="2.4"
    xmlns="http://java.sun.com/xml/ns/j2ee"
    xmlns:xsi="http://www.w3.org/2001/XMLSchema-instance"
    xsi:schemaLocation="http://java.sun.com/xml/ns/j2ee
```

```xml
        http://java.sun.com/xml/ns/j2ee/web-app_2_4.xsd">
    <filter>
        <filter-name>struts2</filter-name>
        <filter-class>org.apache.struts2.dispatcher.FilterDispatcher</filter-class>
    </filter>

    <filter-mapping>
        <filter-name>struts 2</filter-name>
        <url-pattern>/*</url-pattern>
    </filter-mapping>

    <welcome-file-list>
        <welcome-file>index.jsp</welcome-file>
    </welcome-file-list>
</web-app>
```

第四步：在 JSP 页面中导入 Struts 2 标签库

在 JSP 页面可通过如下语句导入 Struts 2 标签库：

```
<%@ taglib prefix="s" uri="/struts-tags" %>
```

若使用的是 Servlet 2.3，URI 属性的值与 web.xml 中配置的对应标签库的<taglib-uri…/>对应；若使用的是 Servlet 2.4，则该 URI 可设置为 Struts 2 标签库的默认 URI。

prefix 属性的值用于表示标签库的前缀，例如当设置为 s 时，文本框标签的语句如下：

```
<s:textfield name="username" label="用户名"/>
```

通过<%@ taglib prefix="s" uri="/struts-tags" %>语句引入后，通过前缀关联，系统将会从 Struts 2 标签库中寻找 textfield 标签，若标签不存在时，将会出现错误信息。

第五步：创建文件夹

在 WebRoot 目录中创建名为 controlTags 的子目录，用来存放各种控制标签的 JSP 页面。

第六步：各种控制标签的使用

（1）iterator 标签。

首先在 WebRoot/controlTags 目录中建立 iteratorTag.jsp 文件，用来展示 iterator 标签的使用。该标签用于对 List、Map、ArrayList、Map 和 Set 等对象进行迭代，其属性如表 8-1 所示。

表 8-1　iterator 标签的属性

属性	是否必选	说明
id	可选	集合中引用的元素的 id，对于 UI 和表单标签可以用来做 HTML 的 id 属性
value	可选	需要进行迭代的迭代源，或者对象本身将会被放置到一个新的列表中
status	可选	指定迭代时的 IteratorStatus 实例。利用它可获得当前对象的索引

例 1　简要实例，在 iterator 的 value 属性中给定了水果集合，指定 id 后，迭代输出 fruitName（水果名称），完整代码如下所示：

```
<%@ page contentType="text/html; charset=UTF-8" %>
<%@ taglib prefix="s" uri="/struts-tags" %>
<!DOCTYPE HTML PUBLIC "-//W3C//DTD HTML 4.01 Transitional//EN">
<html>
    <head>
```

```
            <title>iterator 标签实例</title>
        </head>
        <body>
            <table border="1">
                <s:iterator value="{'banana', 'apple', 'orange', 'cherry'}" id="fruitName">
                <tr>
                    <td>
                        <s:property value="fruitName"/>
                    </td>
                </tr>
                </s:iterator>
            </table>
        </body>
</html>
```

该页面的运行效果如图 8-3 所示。

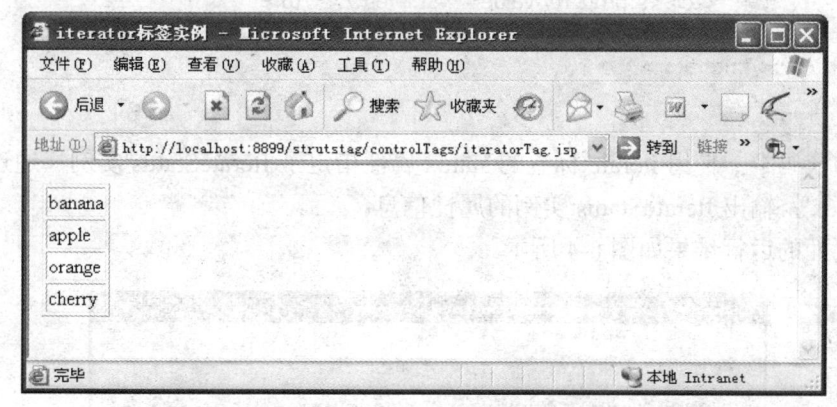

图 8-3 iterator 的简单实例

status 属性指定迭代时的 IteratorStatus 实例，包括的属性的说明如表 8-2 所示。

表 8-2 IteratorStatus 的属性

属性	说明
count	当前迭代的元素
index	当前迭代元素的索引
even	当前迭代元素的索引是否为偶数（第一条为1）
odd	当前迭代元素的索引是否为奇数（第一条为1）
first	当前迭代元素是否为第一个元素
last	当前迭代元素是否为最后一个元素

在上面的代码中进行修改，输出 status 的各属性信息，修改后的代码如下所示：

```
<%@ page contentType="text/html; charset=UTF-8" %>
<%@ taglib prefix="s" uri="/struts-tags" %>
<!DOCTYPE HTML PUBLIC "-//W3C//DTD HTML 4.01 Transitional//EN">
<html>
    <head>
        <title>iterator 标签实例</title>
    </head>
    <body>
        <table border="1">
```

```html
                <tr>
                    <td>索引</td>
                    <td>水果名称</td>
                    <td>是否为第一个</td>
                    <td>是否为最后一个</td>
                    <td>是否为奇数</td>
                    <td>是否为偶数</td>
                </tr>
                <s:iterator value="{'banana', 'apple', 'orange', 'cherry'}" id="fruitName" status="st">
                <tr>
                    <td><s:property value="#st.index"/></td>
                    <td><s:property value="fruitName"/></td>
                    <td><s:property value="#st.first"/></td>
                    <td><s:property value="#st.last"/></td>
                    <td><s:property value="#st.odd"/></td>
                    <td><s:property value="#st.even"/></td>
                </tr>
                </s:iterator>
        </body>
</html>
```

在上面的代码中，使用 iterate 标签的 status 属性指定了 IterateStatus 实例，通过<s:property value="#st.index"/>输出 IterateStatus 实例的属性信息。

此时该页面的运行结果如图 8-4 所示。

图 8-4　iterate 标签 status 属性的使用

iterator 标签还可以迭代 key-value 对的对象，例如 Map 对象，可在该标签的 value 属性中通过冒号（":"）指定 key-value 对，代码段如下所示：

```html
<table border="1">
    <tr>
        <td>水果 id</td>
        <td>水果名称</td>
    </tr>
    <s:iterator value="#{'1' : 'banana', '2' : 'apple', '3': 'orange', '4' : 'cherry'}">
    <tr>
        <td><s:property value="key"/></td>
        <td><s:property value="value"/></td>
    </tr>
    </s:iterator>
</table>
```

此时在运行页面可看到输出了水果的 ID 和名称信息，界面如图 8-5 所示。

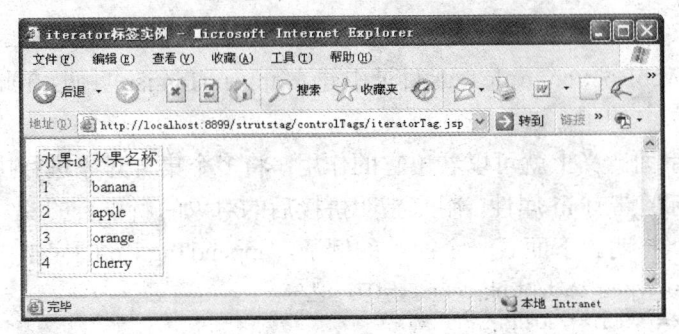

图 8-5 iterator 标签的 key-value 对实例

（2）if/elseif/else 标签。

首先在 controlTags 目录中建立 ifTag.jsp 文件，用来展示 if/elseif/else 3 个标签的使用。

if/elseif/else 标签都是用来做分支控制的，与 Java 中的 if/else if/else 类似，if/elseif 标签包括一个 test 属性，test 属性中返回一个 Boolean 值，用来决定是否进入分支。3 种标签混合使用的实例代码如下：

```jsp
<%@ page contentType="text/html; charset=UTF-8" %>
<%@ taglib prefix="s" uri="/struts-tags" %>
<!DOCTYPE HTML PUBLIC "-//W3C//DTD HTML 4.01 Transitional//EN">
<html>
    <head>
        <title>if/elseif/else 标签实例</title>
    </head>
    <body>
        <s:set name="score" value="87"/>
        <s:if test='${score < 60}'>
            您的分数小于 60，不及格
        </s:if>
        <s:elseif test='${score < 85}'>
            您的分数在 60 和 85 之间，良好
        </s:elseif>
        <s:else>
            您的分数在 85 分以上，优秀！
        </s:else>
    </body>
</html>
```

从上面的代码中可以看出，首先用 set 标签（在后续章节还会具体讲述）给 score 赋值为 87，接下来通过 if/elseif/else 标签根据判断表达式进入不同的条件分支，因为本例的 score 满足 else，所以本程序运行时将进入第三个分支，页面运行效果如图 8-6 所示。

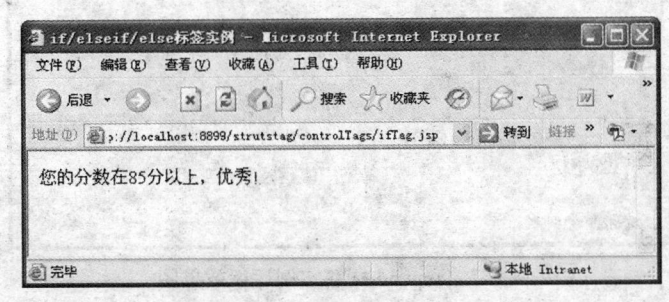

图 8-6 if/else/if 实例运行效果

（3）append 标签。

首先读者可在 WebRoot/controleTags 目录中建立 appendTag.jsp 页面，在此页面中展示 append 标签的使用。

append 标签从字面意义上就可以看出它的作用：将多个集合对象进行拼接，变成一个新的集合对象。append 标签带有 id 属性，用来指明拼接后的对象的新集合的 id，多个集合对象通过其子标签<s:param../>指明。下面看一个简单的例子，appendTag.jsp 的完整内容如下：

```jsp
<%@ page contentType="text/html; charset=UTF-8" %>
<%@ taglib prefix="s" uri="/struts-tags" %>
<!DOCTYPE HTML PUBLIC "-//W3C//DTD HTML 4.01 Transitional//EN">
<html>
    <head>
        <title>append 标签实例</title>
    </head>
    <body>
        <s:append id="totalFruitList">
            <s:param value="{'banana', 'apple', 'orange', 'cherry'}" id="fruitList1"/>
            <s:param value="{'香蕉', '苹果', '桔子', '樱桃'}" id="fruitList2"/>
        </s:append>
        <table border="1">
            <tr>
                <td>水果名称</td>
            </tr>
            <s:iterator value="#totalFruitList" id="fruitName">
            <tr>
                <td><s:property value="fruitName"/></td>
            </tr>
            </s:iterator>
        </table>
    </body>
</html>
```

在上面的代码中，使用 append 的子标签 param 确定了要加入到 append 标签定义的 totalFruitList 集合中的子集合，接下来的 table 中使用 iterate 标签遍历新集合的所有元素，该页面的运行效果如图 8-7 所示。

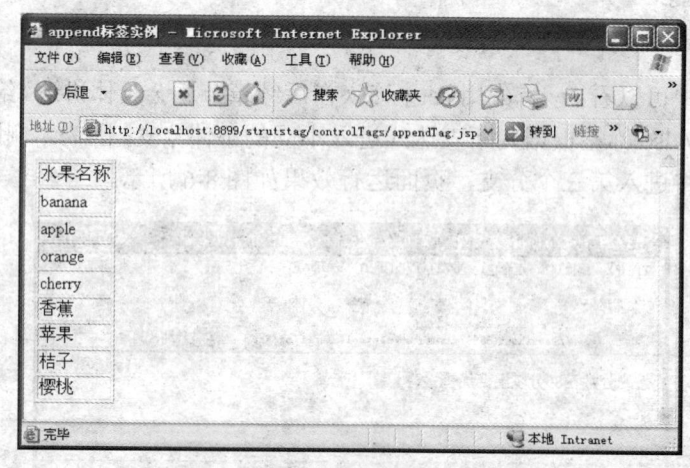

图 8-7 append 标签实例运行效果图

（4）generator 标签。

首先读者可在 WebRoot/controleTags 目录中建立 generatorTag.jsp 页面，在此页面中展示 generator 标签的使用。

该标签用于将字符串通过分隔符分隔后，转换为一个集合，它所包含的属性如表 8-3 所示。

表 8-3 generator 标签的属性

属性	说明
value	必填，指定需要被解析的字符串
separator	必填，分隔符，用于指定将字符串转换成集合所用的分隔符
count	可选，生成集合中元素的总数
id	可选，若指定，则生成集合被放置到 pageContext 属性中
converter	可选，指定一个转换器，将字符串转换为集合
last	当前迭代元素是否为最后一个元素

下面看一个简单的实例，generator.jsp 的代码如下所示：

```
<%@ page contentType="text/html; charset=UTF-8" %>
<%@ taglib prefix="s" uri="/struts-tags" %>
<!DOCTYPE HTML PUBLIC "-//W3C//DTD HTML 4.01 Transitional//EN">
<html>
    <head>
        <title>generator 标签实例</title>
    </head>
    <body>
        <s:generator val="'banana,apple,orange,cherry'" separator="," id="fruits" count="3">
            <table border="1">
                <tr>
                    <td>水果名称</td>
                </tr>
                <!-- 遍历水果，迭代临时生成的集合 -->
                <s:iterator>
                <tr>
                    <td><s:property/></td>
                </tr>
                </s:iterator>
            </table>
        </s:generator>
    </body>
</html>
```

在上面的代码中，iterator 标签取得位于 ValueStack 的顶端的集合对象，并将其遍历输出，因为在上例中指定了 generator 标签的 count 属性为 3，所以虽然 val 的值经分隔符（,）分隔后有 4 个元素，遍历对象读者将发现只输出了 3 个元素，iterator 遍历完毕后，集合对象被移出 ValueStack。该页面的运行效果如图 8-8 所示。

图 8-8 generator 标签实例的运行效果

若删除上面代码中的<table></table>中的所有内容，在 generator 标签后可通过如下 Java 代码获得集合对象：

```
<%
// 取出 pageContext 中的 fruits
java.util.Iterator ite = (java.util.Iterator) pageContext.getAttribute("fruits");
```

因为上例中的 generator 标签制定了 id 属性，所以 fruits 对象被放置到了 pageContext 中。

（5）sort 标签。

首先读者可在 WebRoot/controleTags 目录中建立 sortTag.jsp 页面，在此页面中展示 sort 标签的使用。

sort 标签用于对指定的集合进行排序，进行排序时，需要根据开发人员自己的排序规则进行排序，即需要实现自己的 Comparator 类，该类必须实现 java.util.Comparator 接口。

该标签包括两个属性：comparator（必填）和 source（可选），前者用于指定用于排序的 Comparator 实例，后者用于指定需要进行排序的集合，若未指定，默认对 ValueStack 顶端的元素进行排序。

在比较器中，compare(…)方法返回 int 型的值。若返回的值大于 0，则表示第一个元素大于第二个元素，等于 0 时，表示两者相等，小于 0，表示第一个元素小于第二个元素。下面在 amigo.struts.tag.controlTags 包中建立一个自己的 Comparator 类：NumComparator，该类对数字进行比较，该类的完整代码如下所示：

```java
package amigo.struts.tag.controlTags;

import java.util.Comparator;

/**
 * 自定义的数字比较器.
 * @author AmigoXie
 */
public class NumComparator implements Comparator {

    public int compare(Object element1, Object element2) {
        int resultCode = 0;
        int num1 = Integer.parseInt(element1.toString());
        int num2 = Integer.parseInt(element2.toString());
        if (num1 > num2) {
            resultCode = 1;
        } else if (num1 < num2) {
            resultCode = -1;
        }
```

```
            return resultCode;
        }
}
```

接下来在 sortTag.jsp 中使用 sort 标签，将 comparator 设置为该 NumComparator 的实例，该 JSP 页面的完整代码如下所示：

```
<%@ page contentType="text/html; charset=UTF-8" %>
<%@ taglib prefix="s" uri="/struts-tags" %>
<!DOCTYPE HTML PUBLIC "-//W3C//DTD HTML 4.01 Transitional//EN">
<html>
    <head>
        <title>sort 标签实例</title>
    </head>
    <body>
        <!-- 使用 bean 标签定义一个 NumComparator 实例 -->
        <s:bean id="numComparator" name="amigo.struts.tag.controlTages.NumComparator"/>
        <table border="1">
            <tr>
                <td>数字排序</td>
            </tr>
            <s:sort source="{2, 3, 7, 4, 1, 9, 5, 6, 8}"
                    comparator="numComparator">
                <s:iterator>
                    <tr>
                        <td><s:property/></td>
                    </tr>
                </s:iterator>
            </s:sort>
        </table>
    </body>
</html>
```

该页面的运行效果如图 8-9 所示。

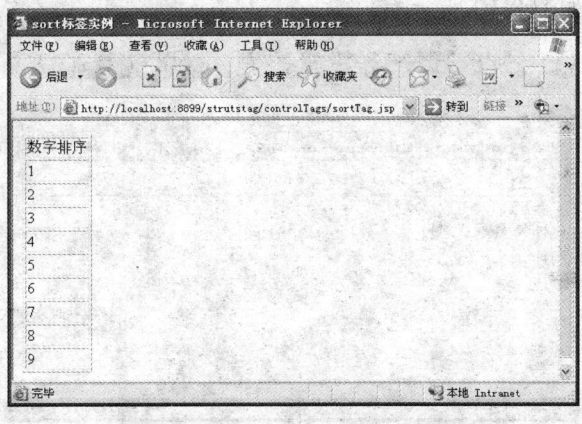

图 8-9　sort 标签实例的运行结果

从运行结果中可以看出，比较器已经起了作用，原来杂乱无章的数字排序已经按照数字大小的顺序进行了排列。

（6）merge 标签。

首先可在 WebRoot/controleTags 目录中建立 mergeTag.jsp 页面，在此页面中展示 merge 标

签的使用。

该标签与 append 标签类似,它也将多个集合拼接在一起,只是拼接方式不同而已,append 标签是将第一个集合的元素全部拼接完后,再开始拼接第二个集合中的所有元素,接着第三个、第四个……而 merge 标签则是先拼接第一个集合、第二个集合、第三个集合……中的第一个元素,接着开始拼接它们的第二个元素、第三个元素……下面来看一个 merge 标签的实例,mergeTag.jsp 页面的完整代码如下所示:

```jsp
<%@ page contentType="text/html; charset=UTF-8" %>
<%@ taglib prefix="s" uri="/struts-tags" %>
<!DOCTYPE HTML PUBLIC "-//W3C//DTD HTML 4.01 Transitional//EN">
<html>
    <head>
        <title>merge 标签实例</title>
    </head>
    <body>
        <s:merge id="totalFruitList">
            <s:param value="{'banana', 'apple', 'orange', 'cherry'}" id="fruitList1"/>
            <s:param value="{'香蕉', '苹果', '桔子', '樱桃'}" id="fruitList2"/>
        </s:merge>
        <table border="1">
            <tr>
                <td>水果名称</td>
            </tr>
            <s:iterator value="#totalFruitList" id="fruitName">
            <tr>
                <td><s:property value="fruitName"/></td>
            </tr>
            </s:iterator>
        </table>
    </body>
</html>
```

该页面的运行效果如图 8-10 所示。

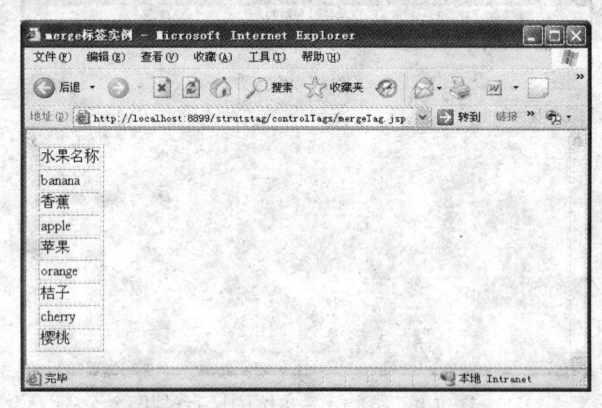

图 8-10 merge 标签实例的运行效果

从运行效果中可以看出,该标签与 append 标签的拼接方式不同。

(7) subset 标签。

首先可在 WebRoot/controleTags 目录中建立 subsetTag.jsp 页面,在此页面中展示 subset 标签的使用。

顾名思义，该标签用于取得集合的子集。它具有的属性如表 8-4 所示。

表 8-4 subset 标签的属性

属性	说明
source	可选，指定源集合，若没有指定，则取得 ValueStack 栈顶的集合
start	可选，指明从哪个元素开始抓取，第一个元素为 0
count	可选，子集中元素的个数，不指定时，取得从 start 开始的全部元素
decider	可选，指定由开发者自己决定是否选中该元素

下面的代码演示如何从集合中取得值，start 为 2，表示从第 3 个元素开始取，count 为 2，表示只取两个元素，subsetTag.jsp 页面的代码如下所示：

```
<%@ page contentType="text/html; charset=UTF-8" %>
<%@ taglib prefix="s" uri="/struts-tags" %>
<!DOCTYPE HTML PUBLIC "-//W3C//DTD HTML 4.01 Transitional//EN">
<html>
    <head>
        <title>subset 标签实例</title>
    </head>
    <body>
        <s:subset source="{'香蕉', '苹果', '桔子', '樱桃', '芒果', '葡萄'}"
                start="2"
                count="2">
            <table border="1">
                <tr>
                    <td>水果名称</td>
                </tr>
                <s:iterator>
                    <tr>
                        <td><s:property/></td>
                    </tr>
                </s:iterator>
            </table>
        </s:subset>
    </body>
</html>
```

该页面的运行效果如图 8-11 所示。

图 8-11 subset 标签实例的运行效果

【例 8-2】数据标签

〖实例需求〗

数据标签也是非 UI 标签，它主要用于提供各种数据访问的功能。常见的数据标签包括：action 标签、bean 标签、set 标签、property 标签、param 标签和 url 标签。本实例对所有数据标签的使用进行详细讲解，用于国际化的标签（i18n 标签、text 标签）因为在前续章节中有详细讲解，在此不再赘述。

〖开发过程〗

第一步：创建文件夹

在WebRoot目录中创建名为dataTags的子目录，用来存放各种数据标签的JSP页面。并在src目录中建立amigo.struts.tag.dataTags包，用来存放各数据标签实例的Java类。

第二步：使用 action 标签

顾名思义，该标签用来调用 Action，它可以指向具体某一命名空间的某一个 Action，该标签的属性如表 8-5 所示。

表 8-5 action 标签的属性

属性	说明
name	必填，指定标签调用的 Action
id	可选，指明该 Action 的引用 id
namespae	可选，指定该 Action 所在的 namespace
executeResult	可选，指定是否将 Action 的处理结果返回到该页面，默认为 false，即不将处理结果返回
ignoreContextParams	可选，表示是否将页面的请求参数传入到 Action 中，默认为 false，即不忽略页面的请求参数

（1）建立 Action 类：ActionTagAction.java。

下面来看一个 action 标签的使用实例，首先在 amigo.struts.tag.dataTags 包中建立 ActionTagAction.java 类，该类的代码如下所示：

```
package amigo.struts.tag.dataTags;

import com.opensymphony.xwork2.ActionContext;
import com.opensymphony.xwork2.ActionSupport;

/**
 * Action 标签的实例，在方法中验证用户名和密码.
 * @author AmigoXie
 */
public class ActionTagAction extends ActionSupport {
    private static final long serialVersionUID = 1L;
```

```java
/** 用户名. */
private String username;

/** 密码. */
private String passwd;

public String getUsername() {
    return username;
}

public void setUsername(String username) {
    this.username = username;
}

public String getPasswd() {
    return passwd;
}

public void setPasswd(String passwd) {
    this.passwd = passwd;
}

/**
 * 定义处理登录请求的 execute 方法.
 */
public String execute() {
    ActionContext ctx = ActionContext.getContext();
    if (this.getUsername() != null
            && "amigo".equals(this.getUsername())
            && this.getPasswd() != null
            && "amigo".equals(this.getPasswd())) {
        return this.SUCCESS;
    } else {
        return this.ERROR;
    }
}
}
```

在该 Action 中，判断 username 和 passwd 是否为 amigo，若都是 amigo，则跳转到登录成功页面，否则跳转到登录失败页面。

（2）编写登录成功页 success.jsp。

登录成功页位于 WebRoot/datatags 目录中，内容如下所示：

```jsp
<%@ page contentType="text/html; charset=UTF-8" %>
<%@ taglib prefix="s" uri="/struts-tags" %>
<!DOCTYPE HTML PUBLIC "-//W3C//DTD HTML 4.01 Transitional//EN">
<html>
    <head>
        <title>登录成功界面</title>
    </head>
    <body>
        登录成功!
    </body>
</html>
```

（3）编写登录失败页 error.jsp。

登录失败页位于 WebRoot/datatags 目录中，内容如下所示：

```jsp
<%@ page contentType="text/html; charset=UTF-8" %>
<%@ taglib prefix="s" uri="/struts-tags" %>
<!DOCTYPE HTML PUBLIC "-//W3C//DTD HTML 4.01 Transitional//EN">
<html>
    <head>
        <title>登录失败界面</title>
    </head>
    <body>
        登录失败！
    </body>
</html>
```

（4）配置 struts.xml。

接下来在 src 目录中建立 struts 2 的配置文件：struts.xml，并在该文件中添加 ActionTagAction 这个 Action，struts.xml 文件的内容如下所示：

```xml
<!DOCTYPE struts PUBLIC
    "-//Apache Software Foundation//DTD Struts Configuration 2.0//EN"
    "http://struts.apache.org/dtds/struts-2.0.dtd">

<struts>
    <include file="struts-default.xml"/>
    <package name="tags" extends="struts-default">
        <action name="Login" class="amigo.struts.tag.dataTags.ActionTagAction">
            <result name="success">/dataTags/success.jsp</result>
            <result name="error">/dataTags/error.jsp</result>
        </action>
    </package>
</struts>
```

（5）编写 action 标签的实例页面 actionTag.jsp。

位于 WebRoot/datatags 目录中的 actionTag.jsp 页面演示了 action 标签的使用，该页面的代码如下所示：

```jsp
<%@ page contentType="text/html; charset=UTF-8" %>
<%@ taglib prefix="s" uri="/struts-tags" %>
<!DOCTYPE HTML PUBLIC "-//W3C//DTD HTML 4.01 Transitional//EN">
<html>
    <head>
        <title>action 标签实例</title>
    </head>
    <body>
        展示 action 标签的使用<br/>
        （1）executeResult、ignoreContextParams 都为 false<br/>
        <s:action name="Login"/><br/>
        （2）executeResult 为 true、ignoreContextParams 为 false<br/>
        <s:action name="Login" executeResult="true" /><br/>
        （3）executeResult、ignoreContextParams 为 true<br/>
        <s:action name="Login" executeResult="true" ignoreContextParams="true" />
    </body>
</html>
```

（6）运行效果。

在浏览器中输入地址：http://localhost:8899/strutstag/dataTags/actionTag.jsp?username=amigo&passwd=amigo，可看到运行效果如图 8-12 所示。

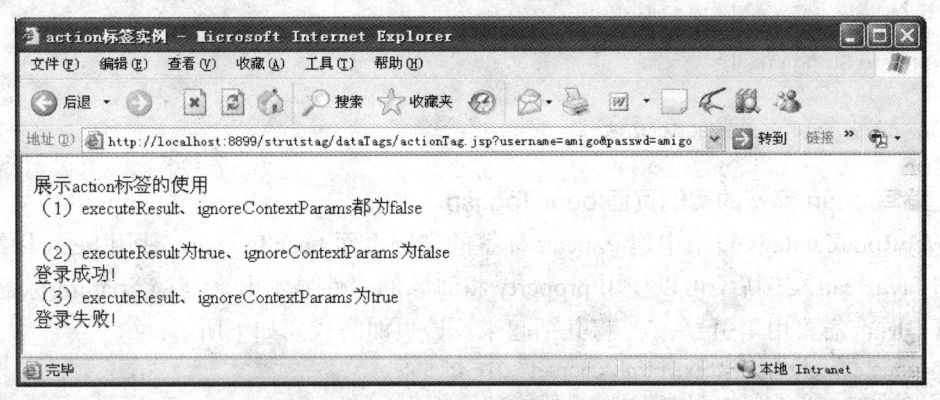

图 8-12 action 标签实例的运行效果

从图 8-12 中可以看出，若 executeResult 为 false 时，Action 的运行效果将不显示在页面中，当 executeResult 为 true，ignoreContextParams 为 false 时，Action 中接收了本页面的参数 username 和 passwd，因此登录成功。若 executeResult 和 ignoreContextParams 都为 true 时，因为参数没有传递到 Action 中，所以登录失败。

第三步：使用 bean 标签

bean 标签用于创建 JavaBean 实例，当 JavaBean 实例需要参数时，可以使用 param 标签将参数传递进去，不过 JavaBean 需要提供这个属性的 setter 方法。

bean 标签具有两个属性，即 name 和 id，其中 name 为必填属性，指定要实例化的 JavaBean 的实现类，而 id 为可选属性，若指定了该属性，bean 将会被放入 StackContext 中，在后续的代码中可以通过 id 来访问该 JavaBean 实例。

（1）编写 JavaBean 类 User.java。

首先建立一个用户信息的 JavaBean 类，该类包括 username、password 和 gender 等属性，并包括这些属性的 getter/setter 方法，该类的代码如下所示：

```
package amigo.struts.tag.dataTags;

/**
 * 用户的 JavaBean 类
 * @author AmigoXie
 */
public class User {
    /** 用户名. */
    private String username;

    /** 密码. */
    private String password;

    /** 性别. */
    private String gender;
```

```
    /** 联系电话. */
    private String tel;

    /** Email. */
    private String email;

    // 省略各属性的 getter/setter 方法
}
```

（2）编写 bean 标签的实例页面 beanTag.jsp。

在 WebRoot/datatags 目录中建立 bean 标签的实例页面 beanTag.jsp，使用 bean 标签创建一个用户的 JavaBean 实例后，可以使用 property 将对象的属性显示出来。注意 param 标签的 value 值为字符串时，需要用单引号（'）将其括起来。该页面的代码如下所示：

```jsp
<%@ page contentType="text/html; charset=UTF-8" %>
<%@ taglib prefix="s" uri="/struts-tags" %>
<!DOCTYPE HTML PUBLIC "-//W3C//DTD HTML 4.01 Transitional//EN">
<html>
    <head>
        <title>bean 标签实例</title>
    </head>
    <body>
        <!-- bean 标签指定 id 属性，用于后续用户信息的输出 -->
        <s:bean name="amigo.struts.tag.dataTags.User" id="user">
            <s:param name="username" value="'amigo'"/>
            <s:param name="password" value="'1234'"/>
            <s:param name="gender" value="'女'"/>
            <s:param name="tel" value="'13666666666'"/>
            <s:param name="email" value="'xiexingxing1121@126.com'"/>
        </s:bean>

        <!-- 输出用户信息 -->
        <table border="1" width="80%">
            <tr align="center">
                <td colspan="4">用户信息</td>
            </tr>
            <tr align="center">
                <td>用户名：</td>
                <td><s:property value="#user.username"/></td>
                <td>密码：</td>
                <td><s:property value="#user.password"/></td>
            </tr>
            <tr align="center">
                <td>性别：</td>
                <td><s:property value="#user.gender"/></td>
                <td>联系电话：</td>
                <td><s:property value="#user.tel"/></td>
            </tr>
            <tr align="center">
                <td>Email：</td>
                <td colspan="3"><s:property value="#user.email"/></td>
            </tr>
```

```
        </table>
    </body>
</html>
```

（3）运行结果。

该页面的运行结果如图 8-13 所示。

图 8-13　bean 标签实例的运行效果

从运行结果中可以看出，若 bean 指定了 id 的值（例如上例指定 id 为 user），则可通过 property 标签取得 bean 定义的对象的属性的值。若没有指定 id，则可将 property 属性包括在 bean 标签中，因为 bean 定义的对象被放置在了 StackContext 中，所以也可以达到上例同样的运行结果，代码片段如下所示：

```
<!-- bean 标签指定 id 属性，用于后续用户信息的输出 -->
<s:bean name="amigo.struts.tag.dataTags.User">
    <s:param name="username" value="'amigo'"/>
    <s:param name="password" value="'1234'"/>
    <s:param name="gender" value="'女'"/>
    <s:param name="tel" value="'13666666666'"/>
    <s:param name="email" value="'xiexingxing1121@126.com'"/>

    <!-- 输出用户信息 -->
    <table border="1" width="80%">
        <tr align="center">
            <td colspan="4">用户信息</td>
        </tr>
        <tr align="center">
            <td>用户名：</td>
            <td><s:property value="username"/></td>
            <td>密码：</td>
            <td><s:property value="password"/></td>
        </tr>
        <tr align="center">
            <td>性别：</td>
            <td><s:property value="gender"/></td>
            <td>联系电话：</td>
            <td><s:property value="tel"/></td>
        </tr>
        <tr align="center">
            <td>Email：</td>
```

```
            <td colspan="3"><s:property value="email"/></td>
        </tr>
    </table>
</s:bean>
```

第四步：使用 param 标签

（1）标签说明。

param 标签用于为其他标签提供参数，例如为 bean 标签提供参数等。该标签包括 3 个可选参数：id、name 和 value，其中 id 属性指定引用该元素的 ID，name 属性用于设置参数的参数名，value 用于设置参数的值。

param 标签常用的两种写法如下：

```
<s:param name="username" value="'amigo'"/>
```

和：

```
<s:param name="username">amigo</s:param>
```

使用第一种写法时，注意当 value 为字符串时，需要加上单引号（'），不然会去寻找名为 amigo 的对象，若对象不存在，则 username 将会被设为 null。

（2）编写 param 标签的实例页面 paramTag.jsp。

在 WebRoot/datatags 目录中建立 paramTag.jsp 文件，用来展示 param 标签的使用，该文件的代码如下所示：

```
<%@ page contentType="text/html; charset=UTF-8" %>
<%@ taglib prefix="s" uri="/struts-tags" %>
<!DOCTYPE HTML PUBLIC "-//W3C//DTD HTML 4.01 Transitional//EN">
<html>
    <head>
        <title>param 标签实例</title>
    </head>
    <body>
        <!-- 嵌套在 bean 标签中使用 -->
        <s:bean name="amigo.struts.tag.dataTags.User" id="user">
            <s:param name="username" value="'amigo'"/>
        </s:bean>
        <br/>

        嵌套在 include 标签中使用<br/>
        <s:include value="success.jsp">
            <s:param name="username" value="'amigo'"/>
            <s:param name="username" value="'amigo'"/>
        </s:include>
        <br/>

        嵌套在 componen 标签中使用<br/>
        <ui:component>
            <ui:param name="username">amigo</ui:param><br>
            <ui:param name="username">阿蜜果</ui:param><br>
            <ui:param name="username">谢星星</ui:param>
        </ui:component>
    </body>
</html>
```

从上面的代码中可以看出，param 标签可嵌入到 include、bean 和 UI 标签中的 component 标签中使用。

（3）运行结果。

该页面的运行结果如图 8-14 所示。

图 8-14　param 标签实例的运行效果

【说明】include 和 component 标签将在后续章节中详细讲解。

第五步：使用 set 标签

（1）标签说明。

该标签用于将属性值放在指定的范围内，例如 request、session 范围等。该标签的属性如表 8-6 所示。

表 8-6　set 标签的属性

属性	说明
name	必填，生成的新变量的名字
scope	可选，指明变量存放的范围，值可为 action、page、request、session 和 application，默认放在 Stack Context 中
value	可选，指定赋给变量的值，若没有该属性，则将 ValueStack 栈顶的值赋给新变量
id	可选，指定引用该变量时的引用 id

（2）编写 set 标签的实例页面 setTag.jsp。

在 WebRoot/datatags 目录中建立 setTag.jsp 页面，该页面的代码如下所示：

```jsp
<%@ page contentType="text/html; charset=UTF-8" %>
<%@ taglib prefix="s" uri="/struts-tags" %>
<!DOCTYPE HTML PUBLIC "-//W3C//DTD HTML 4.01 Transitional//EN">
<html>
    <head>
        <title>set 标签实例</title>
    </head>
    <body>
        <!-- bean 标签指定 id 属性，用于后续用户信息的输出 -->
        <s:bean name="amigo.struts.tag.dataTags.User" id="user">
            <s:param name="username" value="'amigo'"/>
            <s:param name="password" value="'1234'"/>
        </s:bean>
```

```html
未指定scope<br/>
<s:set name="newUsr" value="#user"/>
<table border="1" width="80%">
    <tr align="center">
        <td>用户名：</td>
        <td><s:property value="#newUsr.username"/></td>
        <td>密码：</td>
        <td><s:property value="#newUsr.password"/></td>
    </tr>
</table>

指定scope 为request<br/>
<s:set name="newUsr" value="#user" scope="request"/>
<table border="1" width="80%">
    <tr align="center">
        <td>用户名：</td>
        <td><s:property value="#attr.newUsr.username"/></td>
        <td>密码：</td>
        <td><s:property value="#attr.newUsr.password"/></td>
    </tr>
</table>
指定scope 为request 时的另一种属性获取方式<br/>
<table border="1" width="80%">
    <tr align="center">
        <td>用户名：</td>
        <td>${requestScope.newUsr.username}</td>
        <td>密码：</td>
        <td>${requestScope.newUsr.username}</td>
    </tr>
</table>
</body>
</html>
```

从上面的代码中可以看出，当指定了 scope 时（例如指定为 request），可通过<s:property value="#attr.newUsr.username"/> 的方法取得 username 的信息，也可通过 <s:property value="#attr.newUsr.username"/>取得 username 的信息。

（3）运行效果。

运行 setTag.jsp 页面，运行效果如图 8-15 所示。

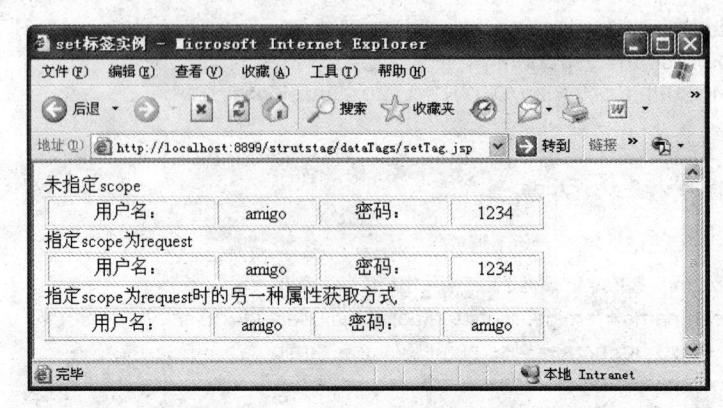

图 8-15　set 标签实例的运行效果

第六步：使用 property 标签

（1）标签说明。

该标签用于输出指定值，该标签的属性如表 8-7 所示。

表 8-7　property 标签的属性

属性	说明
default	可选，用于指定当属性为 null 时的输出值
escape	可选，值可为 true 或 false，用于指定是否 escape HTML 代码，默认为 false
value	可选，指定需要输出的属性值，没有指定时，输出 ValueStack 栈顶的值
id	可选，指定引用该元素时的引用 id

（2）编写 property 标签的实例页面 propertyTag.jsp。

在 WebRoot/datatags 目录中建立 propertyTag.jsp 文件，用来展示 property 标签的使用，该文件的代码如下所示：

```jsp
<%@ page contentType="text/html; charset=UTF-8" %>
<%@ taglib prefix="s" uri="/struts-tags" %>
<!DOCTYPE HTML PUBLIC "-//W3C//DTD HTML 4.01 Transitional//EN">
<html>
    <head>
        <title>property 标签实例</title>
    </head>
    <body>
    <s:bean name="amigo.struts.tag.dataTags.User" id="user">
        <s:param name="username">amigo</s:param>
        <s:property value="%{username}" /><br/>
    </s:bean>

    <s:property value="username" default="默认名称" /><br>
    获得 Stack Context 中的 username：<s:property value="#user.username"/><br/>

    获得 ValueStack 中的 fruitName：<br/>
    <s:iterator value="{'banana', 'apple', 'orange', 'cherry'}" id="fruitName">
        <s:property value="fruitName"/><br/>
    </s:iterator>
    </body>
</html>
```

从上面的代码中可以看出，property 标签的 value 中可以使用"#"作为前缀来输出 Stack Context 中的信息，也可以通过直接输出名称来输出 ValueStack 中的信息。

（3）运行结果。

运行 propertyTag.jsp 页面，运行结果如图 8-16 所示。

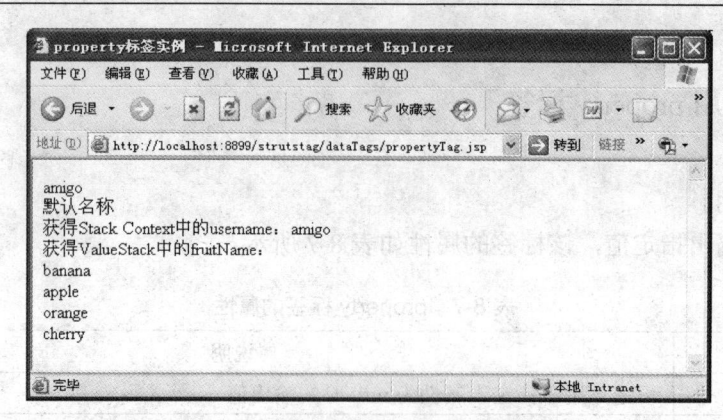

图 8-16　property 标签实例的运行结果

第七步：url 标签

（1）标签说明。

该标签用于输出 URL 地址，若需在 URL 地址后带上参数信息，可使用 param 标签作为其子元素。该标签的所有属性都为可选属性，属性说明如表 8-8 所示。

表 8-8　url 标签的属性

属性	说明
id	指定元素的引用 ID
anchor	指定 URL 的锚点
encode	指定是否需要对请求参数进行编码
includeContext	指定是否将当前的上下文路径包含在 URL 地址中，默认为 true，即包括上下文路径
value	指定生成的 URL 的地址值，若未指定时，使用 action 中的值
action	指定生成 URL 的地址为哪个 Action，如果没有时，使用 value 作为其值
method	指定使用 Action 的方法
namespace	指定命名空间
includeParams	指定是否包含请求的参数，值可为 none、get 或 all
scheme	设置 scheme

（2）编写 url 标签的实例页面 urlTag.jsp。

在 WebRoot/datatags 目录中建立 urlTag.jsp 文件，用来展示 url 标签的使用，该文件的代码如下所示：

```
<%@ page contentType="text/html; charset=UTF-8" %>
<%@ taglib prefix="s" uri="/struts-tags" %>
<!DOCTYPE HTML PUBLIC "-//W3C//DTD HTML 4.01 Transitional//EN">
<html>
    <head>
        <title>url 标签实例</title>
    </head>
    <body>
        指定 action 属性，不指定 value 属性<br/>
        <s:url action="Login">
            <s:param name="username" value="'amigo'"/>
            <s:param name="passwd" value="'amigo'"/>
```

```
            </s:url>

            <br/>
            指定action属性和value属性时，优先value属性<br/>
            <s:url action="Login" value="success.jsp">
                <s:param name="username" value="'amigo'"/>
                <s:param name="passwd" value="'amigo'"/>
            </s:url>

            <br/>
            action属性和value属性都不指定时，链接到本页面<br/>
            <s:url>
                <s:param name="username" value="'阿蜜果'"/>
                <s:param name="passwd" value="'amigo'"/>
            </s:url>
    </body>
</html>
```

（3）运行结果。

运行 urlTag.jsp 页面，该页面的运行结果如图 8-17 所示。

图 8-17　url 标签实例的运行效果

第八步：push 标签

（1）标签说明。

该标签用于将位于 ValueStack 的值放置到栈顶，该标签包括 value 和 id 两个属性，其中 value 属性为必填属性，该属性指定了需要放到 ValueStack 栈顶的值，id 表示该标签的引用 ID。

（2）编写 push 标签的实例页面 pushTag.jsp。

在 WebRoot/datatags 目录中建立 pushTag.jsp 文件，用来展示 push 标签的使用，该文件的代码如下所示：

```
<%@ page contentType="text/html; charset=UTF-8" %>
<%@ taglib prefix="s" uri="/struts-tags" %>
<!DOCTYPE HTML PUBLIC "-//W3C//DTD HTML 4.01 Transitional//EN">
<html>
    <head>
        <title>push 标签实例</title>
    </head>
    <body>
        <s:bean name="amigo.struts.tag.dataTags.User" id="user">
```

```
            <s:param name="username" value="'amigo'"/>
            <s:param name="password" value="'1234'"/>
        </s:bean>

        不使用 push 时对属性的访问<br/>
        <table border="1" width="80%">
            <tr align="center">
                <td>用户名：</td>
                <td><s:property value="#user.username"/></td>
                <td>密码：</td>
                <td><s:property value="#user.password"/></td>
            </tr>
        </table>

        使用 push 标签简化值的访问<br/>
        <s:push value="#user">
        <table border="1" width="80%">
            <tr align="center">
                <td>用户名：</td>
                <td><s:property value="username"/></td>
                <td>密码：</td>
                <td><s:property value="password"/></td>
            </tr>
        </table>
        </s:push>
    </body>
</html>
```

在上述代码中，在没有使用 push 标签前对象位于 Stack Context 中，需要通过<s:property value="#user.username"/>的方式来进行访问，当使用 push 标签将对象放置到 ValueStack 的栈顶后，可以通过<s:property value="username"/>的方式进行访问。

（3）运行结果。

运行 pushTag.jsp 页面，运行结果如图 8-18 所示。

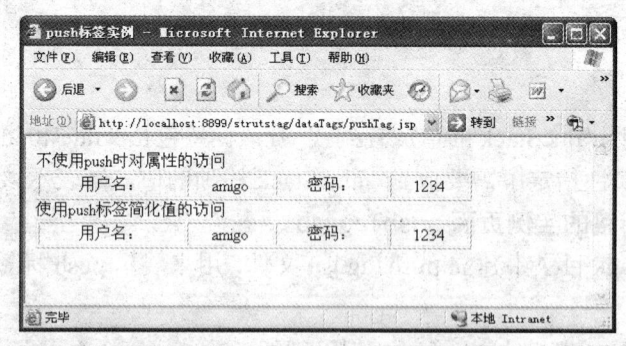

图 8-18　push 标签实例的运行效果

第九步：include 标签

（1）标签说明。

该标签用于将一个 JSP 页面或一个 Servlet 包含在页面中，它包含 value 和 id 两个属性，其中 value 为必填属性，它指定被包含的 JSP 页面或 Servlet，id 为可选属性，它表示用来引用该元素的 ID。

在 include 标签中，可使用 param 标签作为其子元素将参数传递到所包含的页面中。

（2）编写 include 标签的实例页面 includeTag.jsp。

在 WebRoot/datatags 目录中建立 includeTag.jsp 文件，用来展示 include 标签的使用，该文件的代码如下所示：

```jsp
<%@ page contentType="text/html; charset=UTF-8" %>
<%@ taglib prefix="s" uri="/struts-tags" %>
<!DOCTYPE HTML PUBLIC "-//W3C//DTD HTML 4.01 Transitional//EN">
<html>
    <head>
        <title>include 标签实例</title>
    </head>
    <body>
        <s:include value="includeFile.jsp" id="includeFile">
            <s:param name="username" value="'阿蜜果'"/>
            <s:param name="password" value="'1234'"/>
        </s:include>
    </body>
</html>
```

该页面使用 include 标签将 includeFile.jsp 页面包括到 includeTag.jsp 页面中，并将 username 和 password 参数信息传递到 includeFile.jsp 页面中。

（3）编写被包含的页面 includeFile.jsp。

includeTag.jsp 包含了 includeFile.jsp 页面，includeFile.jsp 页面使用 JSP 的表达式语言取得参数信息，该文件的代码如下所示：

```jsp
<%@ page contentType="text/html; charset=UTF-8" %>
<%@ taglib prefix="s" uri="/struts-tags" %>
<!DOCTYPE HTML PUBLIC "-//W3C//DTD HTML 4.01 Transitional//EN">
<html>
    <head>
        <title>include 标签实例-被包括的文件</title>
    </head>
    <body>
        <!-- 用 JSP 表达式语言输出参数信息 -->
        用户名：${param.username}<br/>
        密码：${param.password}<br/>
    </body>
</html>
```

（4）运行结果。

运行 includeTag.jsp 页面，该页面的运行结果如图 8-19 所示。

图 8-19　include 标签实例的运行效果

第十步：date 标签

（1）标签说明。

该标签用于格式化输出一个日期，还可以计算指定日期和当前日期的时差。该标签的属性如表 8-9 所示。

表 8-9 date 标签的属性

属性	说明
name	必填，指定需要进行格式化的日期值
id	可选，指定引用该元素的 ID
format	可选，指定特定的格式来格式化日期
nice	可选，值可为 true 或 false，指定是否输出指定日期和当前时间之间的时差，默认为 false，即不输出

（2）编写 date 标签的实例页面 dateTag.jsp。

在 WebRoot/datatags 目录中建立 dateTag.jsp 文件，用来展示 date 标签的使用，该文件的代码如下所示：

```jsp
<%@ page contentType="text/html; charset=UTF-8" %>
<%@ taglib prefix="s" uri="/struts-tags" %>
<!DOCTYPE HTML PUBLIC "-//W3C//DTD HTML 4.01 Transitional//EN">
<html>
    <head>
        <title>date 标签实例</title>
    </head>
    <body>
        <%
        java.util.Date now = new java.util.Date(2008 - 1900, 7 - 1, 13);
        pageContext.setAttribute("now", now);
        %>
        当前日期,格式化为 yyyy-MM-dd： <s:date name="#attr.now" format="yyyy-MM-dd"/><br/>
        当前日期,未指定 format 属性： <s:date name="#attr.now"/><br/>
        当前日期,指定了 nice 为 true，未指定 format： <s:date name="#attr.now" format="yyyy-MM-dd" nice="true"/><br/>
    </body>
</html>
```

（3）运行结果。

运行 dateTag.jsp 页面，运行结果如图 8-20 所示。

图 8-20 date 标签实例的运行效果

第十一步：debug 标签

（1）标签说明。

该标签用于辅助开发人员进行测试，它在页面上生成"[Debug]"的超级链接，点击该超级链接后，开发人员将可以查看 Stack Context 和 ValueStack 中的信息。

（2）编写 debug 标签的实例页面 debugTag.jsp。

在 WebRoot/datatags 目录中建立 debugTag.jsp 文件，用来展示 debug 标签的使用，该文件的代码如下所示：

```
<%@ page contentType="text/html; charset=UTF-8" %>
<%@ taglib prefix="s" uri="/struts-tags" %>
<!DOCTYPE HTML PUBLIC "-//W3C//DTD HTML 4.01 Transitional//EN">
<html>
    <head>
        <title>debug 标签实例</title>
    </head>
    <body>
        <s:debug/>
    </body>
</html>
```

（3）运行结果。

运行 debugTag.jsp 页面，该页面的运行效果如图 8-21 所示。

图 8-21 debug 标签实例的初始效果

点击上图的"[Debug]"超级链接，此时的界面如图 8-22 所示。

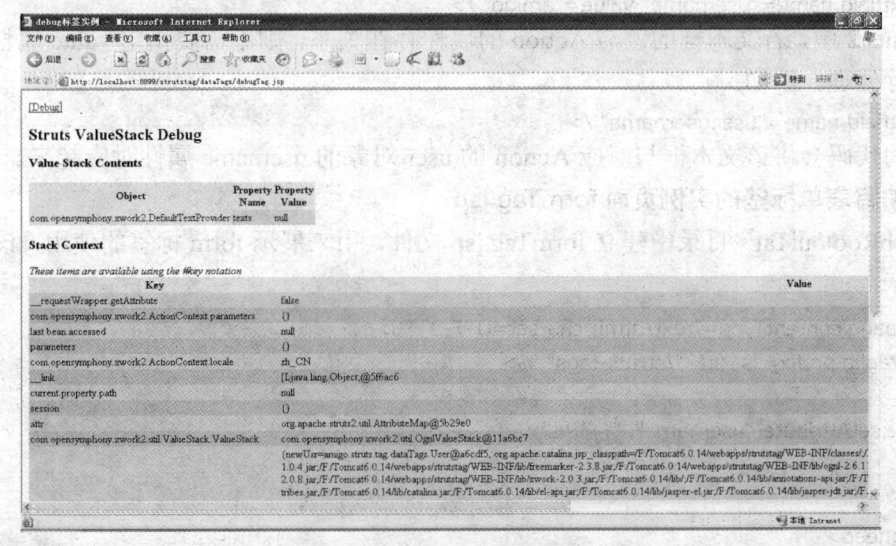

图 8-22 Struts 2 的调试界面

【例 8-3】UI 标签

〖实例需求〗

本实例讲解 Struts 2 中 UI 标签的使用，UI 标签包括表单标签（form 标签、textfield 标签、radio 标签和 select 标签等）和非表单标签（component 标签和 tree 标签等）。

〖开发过程〗

第一步：创建文件夹

在WebRoot目录中创建名为uiTags的标签，用来存放各种UI标签的JSP页面。并在src目录中建立amigo.struts.tag.uiTags包，用来存放各UI标签实例的Java类。

第二步：form 标签、textfield 标签

（1）标签说明。

表单标签包括 form 标签本身和单个表单元素的标签。

<form/>标签与 HTML 的<form/>标签类似，它用于创建表单。它比较常用的属性为 action 属性和 method 属性，其中 action 属性表示请求的路径，method 的值可为"POST"和"GET"，使用举例如下：

```
<s:form action="Login.action" method="post">
……
</s:form>
```

<s:textfield/>标签为输入标签，该标签与 HTML 的<input type="text" name="" value="" />作用相同。<s:textfield/>标签的使用举例如下：

```
<s:textfield name="username" />
```

若需要在文本框中显示值，需要加上 value 属性，例如：

```
<s: textfield name="username" value="amigo" />
```

在 Struts 2 中，若文本框的值与 Action 的属性存在关系，则不需要指定 value 属性，Struts 2 会自动进行处理。例如：

```
<s:textfield name="user.username" />
```

上面的代码会将该文本框与对应 Action 的 user 对象的 username 属性对应起来。

（2）编写表单标签的实例页面 formTag.jsp。

在 WebRoot/ uiTags 目录中建立 formTag.jsp 文件，用来展示 form 标签的使用，该文件的代码如下所示：

```
<%@ page contentType="text/html; charset=UTF-8" %>
<%@ taglib prefix="s" uri="/struts-tags" %>
<%
request.setAttribute("username", "阿蜜果");
%>
<html>
    <head>
        <title>表单标签实例</title>
```

```
        </head>
        <body>
            <s:form action="Login.action" method="post">
                <s:textfield name="username" label="没带 value 值的文本框"/>
                <s:textfield name="username" value="amigo" label="带 value 值的文本框" />
                <s:textfield name="username" value="${username}" label="value 值通过 el 表达式获得" />
            </s:form>
        </body>
</html>
```

（3）运行结果。

在浏览器中输入 formTag.jsp 页面的访问地址，运行结果如图 8-23 所示。

图 8-23　表单标签实例

从图 8-23 中看出，文本框的值的设置可直接设置，还可以通过 EL 表达式获得。

第三步：使用 select 标签

（1）标签说明。

该标签用于生成下拉列表框，该标签的 list 属性可指定集合，这个集合用于生成下拉列表框的选项。select 标签的常用属性如下所示：

- list：指定集合，集合可以是 Map 对象，还可以是对象的集合。
- listKey：指定集合中的某个元素作为复选框的 value。
- listValue：指定集合元素中的某个属性作为复选框的标签。
- multiple：设置列表框是否允许多选。

该标签与 HTML 的 select 标签的作用一样。例如下面的实例生成了一个单选的下拉列表，并且每个选项的 value 和显示值相同：

```
<s:select name="bookType"
          label="请选择图书类型"
          labelposition="top"
          list="{'计算机', '社会科学', '财经', '文学'}" />
```

生成的 HTML 代码如下所示：

```
<select name="bookType" id="Action 名称_bookType">
    <option value="计算机">计算机</option>
    <option value="社会科学">社会科学</option>
    <option value="财经">财经</option>
    <option value="文学">文学</option>
</select>
```

若想每个 option 的 value 属性的值与显示的值不一样，例如 value 属性需要设定为类型的 id，此时可使用如下代码实现：

```
<s:select name="bookType"
          label="请选择图书类型"
          labelposition="top"
          list="#{'1':'计算机', '2':'社会科学', '3':'财经', '4':'文学'}" />
```

此时每一个选项使用的都是 key-value 对的方式，中间以 ":" 隔开。此时运行后查看生成的源文件，可看到生成的 HTML 代码如下所示：

```
<select name="bookType" id="testAction_bookType">
    <option value="1">计算机</option>
    <option value="2">社会科学</option>
    <option value="3">财经</option>
    <option value="4">文学</option>
</select>
```

若要将下拉列表设置为可多选的，此时只需要将 select 标签的 multiple 设置为 true 即可，如下所示：

```
<s:select name="bookType"
          label="请选择图书类型"
          labelposition="top"
          list="{'计算机', '社会科学', '财经', '文学'}"
          multiple="true" />
```

此时生成的 HTML 代码为：

```
<select name="bookType" id="testAction_bookType" multiple="multiple">
    <option value="计算机">计算机</option>
    <option value="社会科学">社会科学</option>
    <option value="财经">财经</option>
    <option value="文学">文学</option>
</select>
```

可看出此时生成的 select 标签的 multiple 属性的值为 multiple。

（2）编写 select 标签的实例页面 selectTag.jsp。

在 WebRoot/uiTags 目录中建立 selectTag.jsp 文件，该页面最后的 select 标签使用实例需要使用 BookType 类，BookType 包含 typeId 和 typeName 两个属性。还需要使用 BookTypeService 这个类，该类包括了一个 getBookTypes()方法，该方法返回 BookType 对象数组。

selectTag.jsp 页面的代码如下所示：

```
<%@ page contentType="text/html; charset=UTF-8" %>
<%@ taglib prefix="s" uri="/struts-tags" %>

<html>
    <head>
        <title>select 标签实例</title>
    </head>
    <body>
        <s:form action="testAction" method="post">
            <!-- 选项的值与显示值一样的单选框： -->
            <s:select name="bookType"
                label="请选择图书类型"
                labelposition="top"
                list="{'计算机', '社会科学', '财经', '文学', '数学', '升学考试'}" />
```

```xml
<!-- 选项的值与显示值不一样的单选框： -->
<s:select name="bookType"
    label="请选择图书类型"
    labelposition="top"
    list="#{'1':'计算机', '2':'社会科学', '3':'财经', '4':'文学', '5':'数学', '6': '升学考试'}" />

<!-- 可多选框： -->
<s:select name="bookType"
    label="请选择图书类型"
    labelposition="top"
    list="{'计算机', '社会科学', '财经', '文学', '数学', '升学考试'}"
    multiple="true" />

<!-- 使用集合里放多个 JavaBean 实例来生成下拉列表框： -->
<s:bean name="amigo.struts.tag.uiTags.BookTypeService" id="typeService"/>
<s:select name="bookType"
    label="请选择图书类型"
    labelposition="top"
    list="#typeService.bookTypes"
    listKey="typeId"
    listValue="typeName" />
    </s:form>
  </body>
</html>
```

BookType 类的代码如下所示：

```java
package amigo.struts.tag.uiTags;

public class BookType {
    private String typeId;

    private String typeName;

    public BookType(String typeId, String typeName) {
        this.typeId = typeId;
        this.typeName = typeName;
    }
    // 省略 typeId 和 typeName 的 getter/setter 方法
}
```

BookTypeService 类的代码如下所示：

```java
package amigo.struts.tag.uiTags;

public class BookTypeService {
    public BookType[] getBookTypes() {
        return new BookType[] {
            new BookType("1", "计算机"),
            new BookType("2", "社会科学"),
            new BookType("3", "财经")
        };
    }
}
```

（3）运行结果。

在浏览器中输入 selectTag.jsp 页面的访问地址，运行结果如图 8-24 所示。

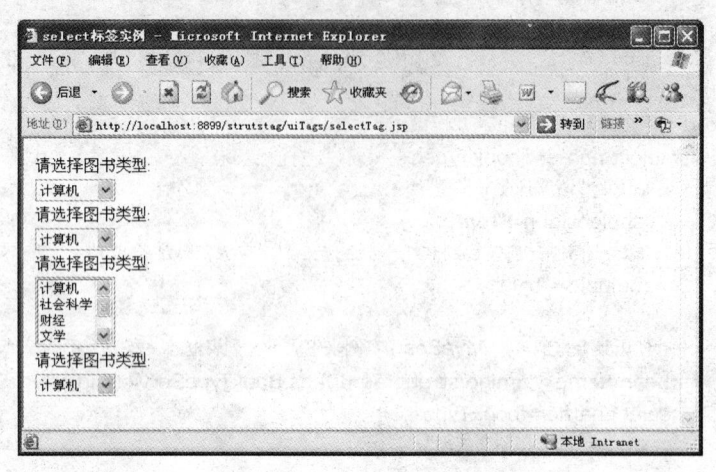

图 8-24　select 标签实例

第四步：使用 radio 标签

（1）标签说明。

该标签用于生成单选框，与 HTML 的 radio 标签作用相同。它与 select 标签类似，也可以指定 label、list、listkey 和 listValue 等属性。使用语法如下所示：

```
<s:radio name="bookType"
         label="请选择图书类型"
         labelposition="top"
         list="#{'1':'计算机', '2':'社会科学', '3':'财经'}" />
```

（2）编写 radio 标签的实例页面 radioTag.jsp。

在 WebRoot/uiTags 目录中建立 radioTag.jsp 文件，该标签与 select 标签相比，除了不能设置 multiple 属性之外，其余功能类似。实例代码如下所示：

```
<%@ page contentType="text/html; charset=UTF-8" %>
<%@ taglib prefix="s" uri="/struts-tags" %>
<html>
    <head>
        <title>radio 标签实例</title>
    </head>
    <body>
        <s:form action="testAction" method="post">
            <!-- 选项的值与显示值一样的单选框： -->
            <s:radio name="bookType"
                label="请选择图书类型"
                labelposition="top"
                list="{'计算机', '社会科学', '财经', '文学', '数学', '升学考试'}" />

            <!-- 选项的值与显示值不一样的单选框： -->
            <s:radio name="bookType"
                label="请选择图书类型"
                labelposition="top"
                list="#{'1':'计算机', '2':'社会科学', '3':'财经', '4':'文学', '5':'数学', '6': '升学考试'}" />
```

```
            <!-- 使用集合里放多个 JavaBean 实例来生成单选框： -->
            <s:bean name="amigo.struts.tag.uiTags.BookTypeService" id="typeService"/>
            <s:radio name="bookType"
                label="请选择图书类型"
                labelposition="top"
                list="#typeService.bookTypes"
                listKey="typeId"
                listValue="typeName" />
        </s:form>
    </body>
</html>
```

（3）运行结果。

在浏览器中输入 radioTag.jsp 页面的地址，可看到该实例的运行效果如图 8-25 所示。

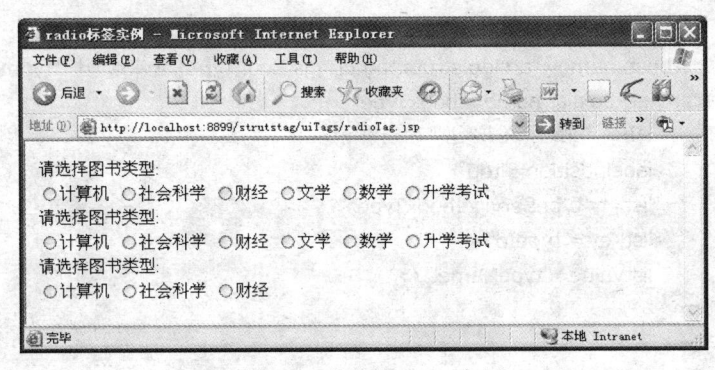

图 8-25 单选框 radio 实例

查看该页面的源文件，可看到单选框生成的 HTML 代码类似如下所示：

```
    <input    type="radio"    name="bookType"    id="testAction_bookType1"    value="1"/><label for="testAction_bookType1">计算机</label>
    <input    type="radio"    name="bookType"    id="testAction_bookType2"    value="2"/><label for="testAction_bookType2">社会科学</label>
    ……
    <input    type="radio"    name="bookType"    id="testAction_bookType6"    value="6"/><label for="testAction_bookType6">升学考试</label>
```

第五步：使用 checkboxlist 标签

（1）标签说明。

该标签可以一次创建多个复选框列表，它的属性与单选框类似，不再赘述。它与 HTML 的 checkbox 标签对应。

（2）编写 checkboxlist 标签的实例页面 checkboxlistTag.jsp。

在 WebRoot/uiTags 目录中建立 checkboxlistTag.jsp 文件，代码如下所示：

```
<%@ page contentType="text/html; charset=UTF-8" %>
<%@ taglib prefix="s" uri="/struts-tags" %>

<html>
    <head>
        <title>checkboxlist 标签实例</title>
    </head>
```

```
<body>
    <s:form action="testAction" method="post">
        <!-- 选项的值与显示值一样的复选框： -->
        <s:checkboxlist name="bookType"
            label="请选择图书类型"
            labelposition="top"
            list="{'计算机', '社会科学', '财经', '文学', '数学', '升学考试'}" />

        <!-- 选项的值与显示值不一样的复选框： -->
        <s:checkboxlist name="bookType"
            label="请选择图书类型"
            labelposition="top"
            list="#{'1':'计算机', '2':'社会科学', '3':'财经', '4':'文学', '5':'数学', '6': '升学考试'}" />

        <!-- 使用集合里放多个 JavaBean 实例来生成复选框： -->
        <s:bean name="amigo.struts.tag.uiTags.BookTypeService" id="typeService"/>
        <s:checkboxlist name="bookType"
            label="请选择图书类型"
            labelposition="top"
            list="#typeService.bookTypes"
            listKey="typeId"
            listValue="typeName" />
    </s:form>
</body>
</html>
```

（3）运行结果。

在浏览器中输入 checkboxlistTage.jsp 页面的请求地址，界面如图 8-26 所示。

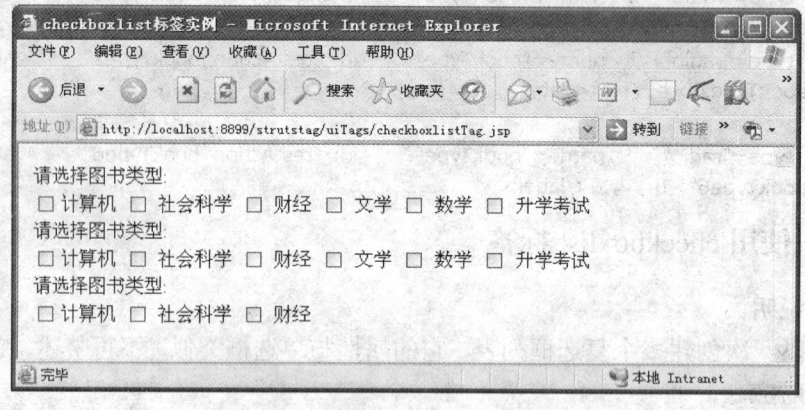

图 8-26 checkboxlist 标签使用实例

查看该文件生成的 HTML 源文件，将生成多个 checkbox 元素，如下所示：

```
<input type="checkbox" name="bookType" value="1" id="bookType-1"/>
<label for="bookType-1" class="checkboxLabel">计算机</label>
<input type="checkbox" name="bookType" value="2" id="bookType-2"/>
<label for="bookType-2" class="checkboxLabel">社会科学</label>
……
<input type="checkbox" name="bookType" value="6" id="bookType-6"/>
<label for="bookType-6" class="checkboxLabel">升学考试</label>
```

第六步：使用 combobox 标签

（1）标签说明。

该标签用于生成一个单行文本框和下拉列表框的组合，并且两个表单元素对应一个请求参数，例如 bookType。但是只有单行文本框中才包含请求参数，而下拉列表框只用于辅助输入，并没有 name 属性，当然也不会产生请求参数。

这个标签一般在如下这种场合使用：下拉框中选择了一些常用的选项，若读者想自行输入，也可在文本框中输入，若需要使用常用的选项，只需要下拉选择，该选项的值自动会被放入对应文本框中。

该标签需要设置 list 属性来指定集合，集合用于生成列表项目。

（2）编写 combobox 标签的实例页面 comboboxTag.jsp。

在 WebRoot/uiTags 目录中建立 comboboxTag.jsp 文件，代码如下所示：

```jsp
<%@ page contentType="text/html; charset=UTF-8" %>
<%@ taglib prefix="s" uri="/struts-tags" %>

<html>
    <head>
        <title>combobox 标签实例</title>
    </head>
    <body>
        <s:form action="testAction" method="post">
            <s:combobox name="bookType"
                label="请选择图书类型"
                labelposition="top"
                list="{'计算机', '社会科学', '财经', '文学', '数学', '升学考试'}" />
        </s:form>
    </body>
</html>
```

（3）运行结果。

在浏览器中输入 comboboxTag.jsp 页面的请求地址，界面如图 8-27 所示。

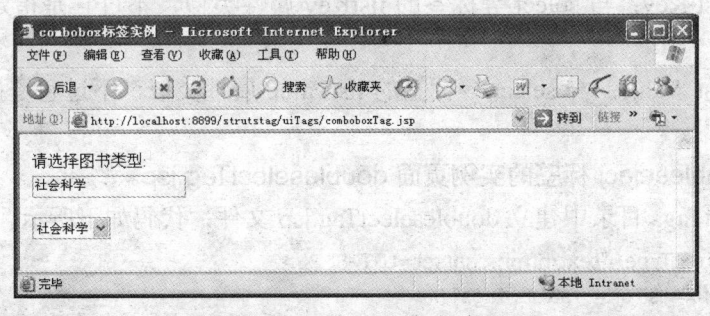

图 8-27　combobox 标签实例

当选择某个选项时，该选项的值将自动被置入文本框中，用户也可以在文本框中自行输入。查看该页面的源文件，可看到生成的 HTML 代码如下所示：

```html
<script type="text/javascript">
    function autoPopulate_testAction_bookType(targetElement) {
    targetElement.form.elements['bookType'].value=targetElement.options[targetElement.selectedIndex].value;
```

```html
        }
</script>
<input type="text" name="bookType" value="" id="testAction_bookType"/>
<br />
<select onChange="autoPopulate_testAction_bookType(this);">
    <option value="计算机">计算机</option>
    <option value="社会科学">社会科学</option>
    <option value="财经">财经</option>
    <option value="文学">文学</option>
    <option value="数学">数学</option>
    <option value="升学考试">升学考试</option>
</select>
```

从上面的代码可以看出，生成的下拉列表框并没有 name 属性，所以不会将请求参数带到提交页面。另外下拉列表框添加了一个 onChange 事件，当改变选项时，调用 Struts 2 自动生成的 JavaScript 方法改变 bookType 文本框的值。

第七步：使用 doubleselect 标签

（1）标签说明。

该标签会生成一个级联列表框，即生成两个下拉列表框，当选择一个下拉列表框改变时，另一个下拉列表框将会做出相应的改变。级联列表框在 Web 项目中使用广泛，例如在省市选择时就会用到级联列表框，当改变"省"的下拉选择时，"市"的下拉列表框也需要作出改变。

该标签具有如下常用的属性：

- name：指定第一个下拉列表框的 name 属性。
- list：指定用于输出第一个下拉列表框的选项的集合。
- listKey：与 select 等标签的该属性类似。
- listValue：与 select 等标签的该属性类似。
- doubleName：指定第二个下拉列表框的 name 属性。
- doubleList：指定用于输出第二个下拉列表框的选项的集合。
- doubleList Key：与 select 等标签的 listKey 属性类似，不过它是指定第二个下拉列表框的。
- doubleList Value：与 select 等标签的 listValue 属性类似，不过它是指定第二个下拉列表框的。

（2）编写 doubleselect 标签的实例页面 doubleselectTag.jsp。

在 WebRoot/uiTags 目录中建立 doubleselectTag.jsp 文件，代码如下所示：

```jsp
<%@ page contentType="text/html; charset=UTF-8" %>
<%@ taglib prefix="s" uri="/struts-tags" %>

<html>
    <head>
        <title>doubleselect 标签实例</title>
    </head>
    <body>
        <body>
            <s:form action="testAction" name="form0" method="POST">
```

```
            <s:set name="bookTypes" value="#{'计算机':{'Java', 'C#', 'Struts2'},
                 '文学':{'言情小说', '恐怖', '散文', '历史小说'},
                 '升学考试':{'考研', '考博','高考'}}">
                 <s:doubleselect label="请选择类别"
                     name="bookType"
                     list="#bookTypes.keySet()"
                     doubleName="subBookType"
                     doubleList="#bookTypes[top]"
                     label="请选择类别"> </s:doubleselect>
        </s:form>
      </body>
    </html>
```

【提示】在使用该标签时，记住要将标签放在<s:form../>标签中使用，并记住要为<s:form../>标签指定 name 属性。若没指定，运行该页面将会出现错误信息，如图 8-28 所示。

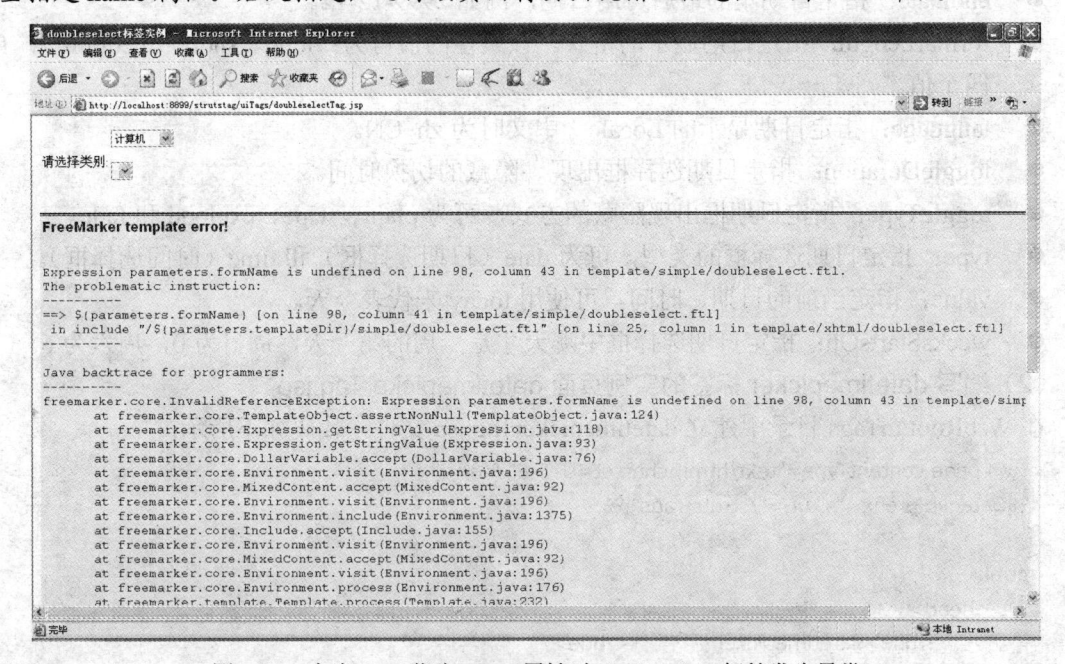

图 8-28　未为 form 指定 name 属性时 doubleselect 标签发生异常

（3）运行结果。

在浏览器中输入 doubleselectTag.jsp 页面的地址，界面如图 8-29 所示。

图 8-29　级联列表框

在图 8-29 中改变第一个列表的选项时，第二个列表框将相应作出改变。

第八步：使用 datetimepicker 标签

（1）标签说明。

该标签用于生成一个日期、时间下拉列表框，当选择好日期或时间后，选中的日期或时间的值将会自动放入文本框中。

该标签具有如下常用属性：

- displayFormat：该属性指定日期的显示格式，例如"yyyy-MM-dd"表示显示时期格式，其中"yyyy"表示年，"MM"表示月，"dd"表示日。"yyyy-MM-dd hh:mm:ss"表示日期时间格式，其中"hh"表示时，"mm"表示分，"ss"表示秒。
- displayWeeks：指定日历能显示星期数。
- startDate：指定最开始使用的日期，例如 1900-1-1。
- endDate：指定日期集的最后可用日期，例如 2999-12-12。
- formatLength：指定日期显示的格式。该属性的值可为：long、short、medium 和 full 四个值。
- language：指定日期显示的 Locale，中文时为 zh_CN。
- toggleDuration：指定日期选择框出现、隐藏的切换时间。
- toggleType：指定日期框出现隐藏的方式，可为 plain、wipe、explode 和 fade。
- type：指定日期选择框的类型，可为 date（日期选择框）和 time（时间选择框）。
- value：指定当前的日期、时间，可使用 today 来代表今天。
- weeksStartsOn：指定日期选择框中哪天才是一周的第一天，周日为 0，周六为 6。

（2）编写 datetimepicker 标签的实例页面 datetimepickerTag.jsp。

在 WebRoot/uiTags 目录中建立 datetimepickerTag.jsp 文件，代码如下所示：

```
<%@ page contentType="text/html; charset=UTF-8" %>
<%@ taglib prefix="s" uri="/struts-tags" %>

<html>
    <head>
        <title>datetimepicker 标签实例</title>
        <s:head />
    </head>
    <body>
        <s:form action="test" theme="simple" method="POST">
            日期选择,使用默认的 displayFormat(默认为 yyyy-MM-dd),指定 toggleType(默认为 plain)和 value 属性（值为 today，即今天）： <br>
            <s:datetimepicker name="birthDate" label="出生日期" toggleType="fade" value="today"/><hr>

            日期选择,指定了 format 属性<br>
            <s:datetimepicker name="birthDate" label="出生日期" displayFormat= "dddd/MM/dd"/><hr>

            日期选择,指定了 weekStartsOn 属性(不指定时默认为 0，即从周日开始)<br>
            <s:datetimepicker name="birthDate" label="出生日期" weekStartsOn="3"/><hr>

            时间选择（设置 type 为 time）<br>
```

```
                    <s:datetimepicker    name="start"    label="选 择 出 发 时 间 "    type="time"
value="13:00"/><hr>
            </s:form>
    </body>
</html>
```

【提示】需要<s:head />加上,若未加的话,打开该页面时,将会出现如图 8-30 所示的 JavaScript 错误。

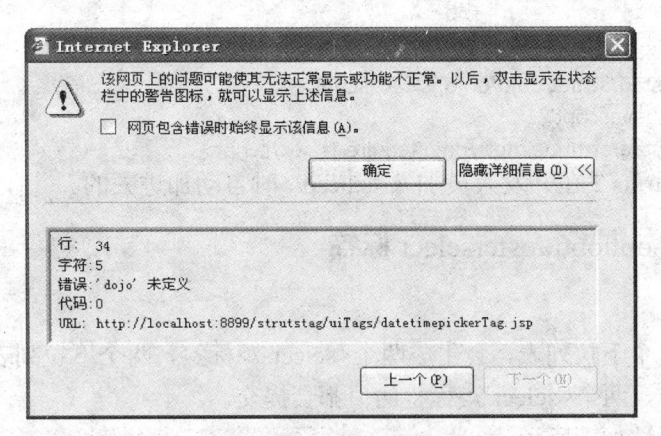

图 8-30 未加<s:head />出现的 JavaScript 错误

Struts 2 的日期控件是通过 DOJO 来实现的,所以在使用时,需要将相关的 JavaScript 文件(例如 dojo.js 和 dojoRequire.js)等引入。

(3) 运行结果。

在浏览器中输入 datetimepickerTag.jsp 页面的请求地址,界面如图 8-31 所示。

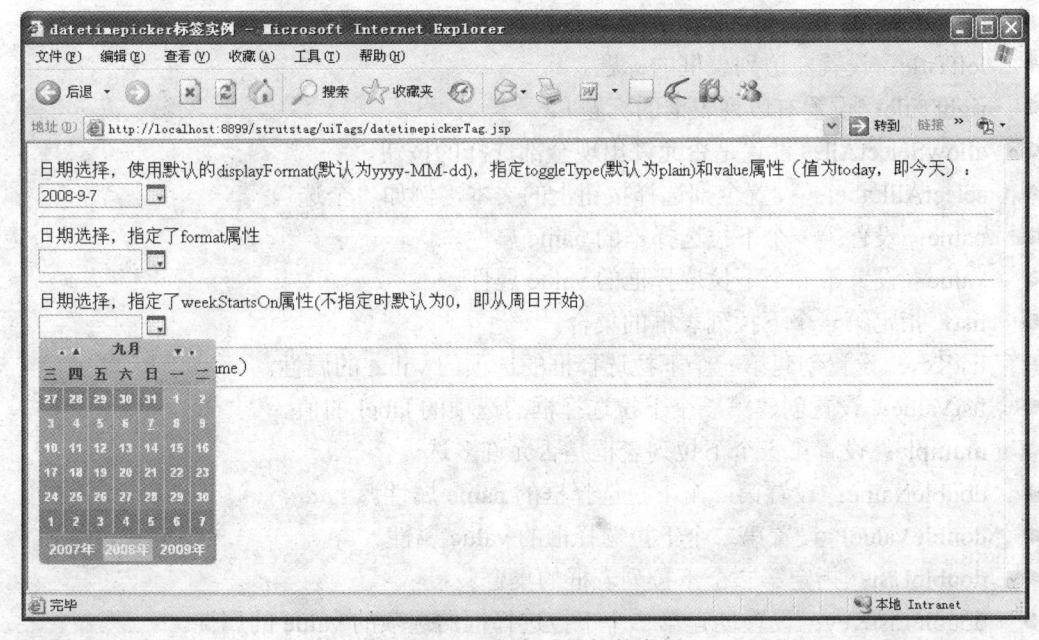

图 8-31 日期、时间控件实例

查看生成的源文件,可在头部看到如下代码:
```
<link rel="stylesheet" href="/strutstag/struts/xhtml/styles.css" type="text/css"/>
```

```
<script type="text/javascript">
    // Dojo configuration
    djConfig = {
        baseRelativePath: "/strutstag/struts/dojo",
        isDebug: false,
        bindEncoding: "UTF-8",
        debugAtAllCosts: true // not needed, but allows the Venkman debugger to work with the includes
    };
</script>
<script type="text/javascript"
    src="/strutstag/struts/dojo/dojo.js"></script>
<script type="text/javascript"
    src="/strutstag/struts/simple/dojoRequire.js"></script>
```

这些代码都是 Struts 2 在开发人员加入<s:head/>时自动加进去的。

第九步：使用 optiontransferselect 标签

（1）标签说明。

该标签会创建两个下拉列表，会生成两个<select../>标签，两个下拉列表中的元素能相互移动，提交表单的时候，两个<select../>标签的值都会提交。

该标签常用的属性如下所示：

- addAllToLeftLable：设置全部移动到左边按钮上的文本，例如"全部左移"。
- addAllToRightLable：设置全部移动到右边按钮上的文本，例如"全部右移"。
- addToLeftLable：设置向左移动按钮的文本，例如"左移"。
- addToRightLable：设置向右移动按钮的文本，例如"右移"。
- allowAddAllToLeft：设置是否允许出现全部左移的按钮。
- allowAddAllToRight：设置是否允许出现全部右移的按钮。
- leftTitle：设置左边列表框的标题。
- rightTitle：设置右边列表框的标题。
- allowSelectAll：设置是否允许出现全部选择的按钮。
- selectAllLabel：设置全部选择按钮上的文本，例如"全选"。
- name：设置第一个下拉选择框的 name 属性。
- value：设置第一个下拉选择框的 value 属性。
- list：指定第一个下拉列表框的集合。
- listKey：设置创建第一个下拉选择框的选项的 value 的属性。
- listValue：设置创建第一个下拉选择框的选项的 label 的值。
- multiple：设置第一个下拉列表框是否允许多选。
- doubleName：设置第二个下拉选择框的 name 属性。
- doubleValue：设置第二个下拉选择框的 value 属性。
- doubleList：指定第二个下拉列表框的集合。
- doubleListKey：设置创建第二个下拉选择框的选项的 value 的属性。
- doubleListValue：设置创建第二个下拉选择框的选项的 label 的值。
- doubleMultiple：设置第二个下拉列表框是否允许多选。

该标签也是很实用的一个标签，例如在修改某用户分配权限信息时，可在右边显示已具有的权限信息,在左边显示未具有的权限信息。

（2）编写 optiontransferselect 标签的实例页 optiontransferselectTag.jsp。

在 WebRoot/uiTags 目录中建立 optiontransferselectTag.jsp 文件,代码如下所示:

```jsp
<%@ page contentType="text/html; charset=UTF-8" %>
<%@ taglib prefix="s" uri="/struts-tags" %>

<html>
    <head>
        <title>optiontransferselect 标签实例</title>
        <s:head />
    </head>
    <body>
        <s:form>
            <!-- 使用简单集合对象来生成可移动的下拉列表框 -->
            <s:optiontransferselect
                label="请选择你喜欢的图书类型"
                name="bookType"
                leftTitle="---所有图书---"
                list="{'计算机', '社会科学', '财经', '文学', '数学'}"
                multiple="true"
                addToLeftLabel="左移"
                selectAllLabel="全部选择"
                addToRightLabel="右移"
                rightTitle="---喜欢图书---"
                doubleList="{'散文', '历史'}"
                doubleName="loveBookType"
                doubleMultiple="true" />
        </s:form>
    </body>
</html>
```

【提示】该标签也需要加上<s:head/>,不然也会出现 DOJO 未定义的 JavaScript 错误。

（3）运行结果。

在浏览器中输入该页面的地址,界面如图 8-32 所示。

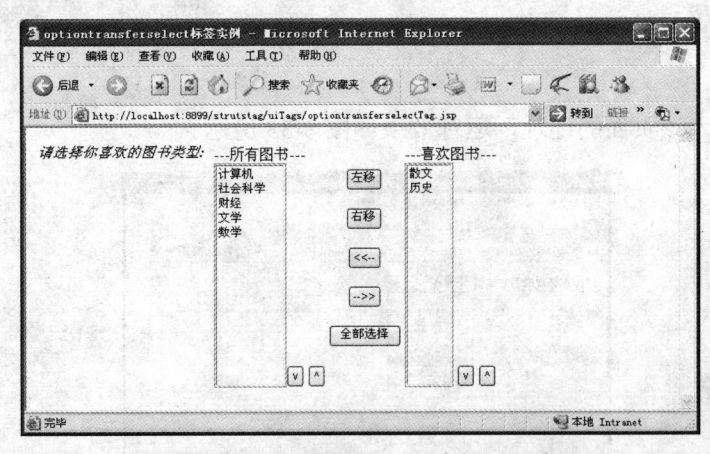

图 8-32 optiontransferselect 实例运行结果

第十步：使用 optgroup 标签

（1）标签说明。

该标签用于生成一个下拉列表框的选项组，因此，它需要放在<s:select../>标签中使用，可以在一个<s:select../>标签中添加多个<s:optgroup../>标签。

该标签的属性与<s:select../>标签类似，常用的属性有 list、listKey 和 listValue 等。不过它的 label 属性的意义与<s:select../>标签不同，表示的不是下拉列表框的 Label，而是选项组的组名。

（2）编写 optgroup 标签的实例页 optgroupTag.jsp。

在 WebRoot/uiTags 目录中建立 optgroupTag.jsp 文件，代码如下所示：

```
<%@ page contentType="text/html; charset=UTF-8" %>
<%@ taglib prefix="s" uri="/struts-tags" %>

<html>
    <head>
        <title>optgroup 标签实例</title>
    </head>
    <body>
        <s:form action="testAction" method="post">
            <s:select label="选择您喜欢的图书类型"
            name="bookType"
            list="#{'1':'计算机', '2':'社会科学', '3':'财经', '4':'数学'}"
                listKey="key"
                listValue="value">
            <s:optgroup label="小说"
            list="#{'5' : '言情小说', '6' : '武打小说', '7' : '恐怖小说'}"
                listKey="key"
                listValue="value"/>
            <s:optgroup label="升学考试"
            list="#{'8' : '考研', '9' : '考博', '10' : '高考'}"
                listKey="key"
                listValue="value"/>
            </s:select>
        </s:form>
    </body>
</html>
```

（3）运行结果。

在浏览器中输入该页面的地址，运行效果如图 8-33 所示。

图 8-33　optgroup 实例运行结果

从运行结果中可以看出，虽然笔者将两个选项组的元素都设置为 3 个，但却只显示了两个出来，如何解决这个问题呢？

此时读者可采用一种迂回的方式，不直接设置两个选项组的值，而通过如下方式设置。首先将该 JSP 页面修改为：

```
……
<s:bean name="amigo.struts.tag.uiTags.BookTypeService" id="typeService"/>
<s:select label="选择您喜欢的图书类型"
        name="bookType"
      list="#{'1':'计算机', '2':'社会科学', '3':'财经', '4':'数学'}"
        listKey="key"
        listValue="value">
        <s:optgroup label="小说"
       list="#typeService.novelBookTypes"
            listKey="typeId"
            listValue="typeName" />
        <s:optgroup label="升学考试"
       list="#typeService.examBookTypes"
            listKey="typeId"
            listValue="typeName" />
</s:select>
……
```

接着在 BookTypeService 类中添加如下两个方法，获得小说的图书种类和升学考试的图书种类，代码如下所示：

```
public BookType[] getNovelBookTypes() {
    return new BookType[] {
        new BookType("5", "言情小说"),
        new BookType("6", "武打小说"),
        new BookType("7", "恐怖小说")
    };
}

public BookType[] getExamBookTypes() {
    return new BookType[] {
        new BookType("8", "考研"),
        new BookType("9", "考博"),
        new BookType("20", "高考")
    };
}
```

此时运行 optgroupTag.jsp 页面，运行结果如图 8-34 所示。

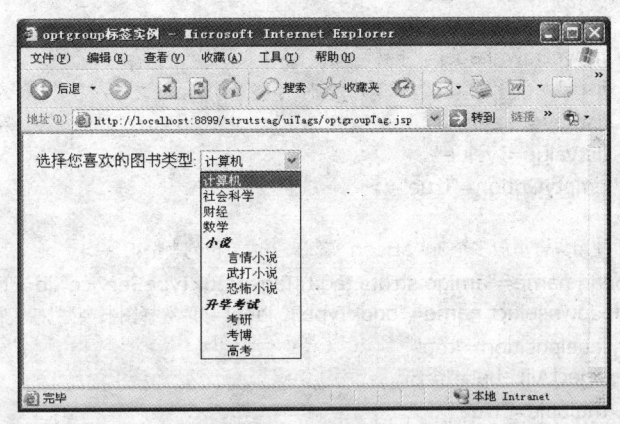

图 8-34　显示了全部 optgroup 选项的运行效果

【提示】选项组的组名用户不能选中。

第十一步：使用 updownselect 标签

（1）标签说明。

该标签的作用与 select 标签类似，它的属性也与之类似，常用属性为 list、listKey 和 listValue 等，不过它与 select 标签的不同之处在于：它支持选项的上下移动，针对这个特点，它还支持如下属性：

- allowMoveUp：是否显示向上移动的按钮，默认该值为 true。
- allowMoveDown：是否显示向下移动的按钮，默认该值为 true。
- allowSelectAll：是否显示全选按钮，默认为 true。
- moveUpLabel：向上移动的按钮的文本，例如"上移"，默认为"^"。
- moveDwonLabel：向下移动的按钮的文本，例如"下移"，默认为"v"。
- selectAllLabel：全选按钮的文本，例如"全选"，默认为"*"。

（2）编写 updownselect 标签的实例页 updownselectTag.jsp。

在 WebRoot/uiTags 目录中建立 updownselectTag.jsp 文件，代码如下所示：

```jsp
<%@ page contentType="text/html; charset=UTF-8" %>
<%@ taglib prefix="s" uri="/struts-tags" %>

<html>
    <head>
        <title>updownselect 标签实例</title>
        <s:head/>
    </head>
    <body>
        <s:form>
            <!-- 使用简单集合来生成可上下移动选项的下拉选择框 -->
            <s:updownselect name="bookType1" label="请选择图书类型"
                labelposition="top"
                list="{'计算机', '社会科学', '财经', '文学', '数学', '升学考试'}" />

            <!-- 使用简单 Map 对象来生成可上下移动选项的下拉选择框，且使用 emptyOption="true"增加一个空选项-->
            <s:updownselect name="bookType2" label="请选择图书类型"
                labelposition="top"
                moveUpLabel="上移"
                moveDownLabel="下移"
                list="#{'1':'计算机', '2':'社会科学', '3':'财经', '4':'文学', '5':'数学', '6': '升学考试'}"
                listKey="key"
                listValue="value"
                emptyOption="true" />

            <!-- 使用集合里放多个 JavaBean 实例来生成下拉列表框： -->
            <s:bean name="amigo.struts.tag.uiTags.BookTypeService" id="typeService"/>
            <s:updownselect name="bookType3" label="请选择图书类型"
                labelposition="top"
                selectAllLabel="全选"
                multiple="true"
                list="#typeService.bookTypes"
```

```
                    listKey="typeId"
                    listValue="typeName" />
        </s:form>
    </body>
</html>
```
该标签也需要加上<s:head/>，不然也会出现 DOJO 未定义的 JavaScript 错误。

（3）运行结果。

在浏览器中输入该页面的地址，界面如图 8-35 所示。

图 8-35 updownselect 标签实例运行结果

第十二步：使用 token 标签

该标签用于防止重复提交表单，避免刷新页面或通过后退来重复提交。如果需要该标签起作用，则需要为 Action 配置 token 拦截器。这在拦截器那章讲解内建拦截器的使用时已经详细说明了。

该标签的实现原理是在表单中添加一个隐藏域，每次加载页面时，该隐藏域的值都不相同，而 token 拦截器拦截所有用户请求，如果两次提交时该隐藏域的值相同，则认为是重复提交，Struts 2 将阻止该种情况的重复提交。

一般需要在 JSP 页面中添加如下语句：

```
<!-- 使用 token 标签生成一个防止重复提交的隐藏域 -->
<s:token/>
```

运行页面后，在生成的 HTML 源文件中可看到多出了如下一个隐含表单域：

```
<input type="hidden" name="struts.token" value="J7TF5EPLCCU644IELH7E9JQXUX0U8AB5" />
```

小结

本章主要讲述 Struts 2 的标签库，Struts 2 的标签库与 Struts 1.x 的标签库相比，它使用 OGNL 表达式作为基础，其对集合和对象的访问功能很强大。同时，Struts 2 提供了很多额外的高级标签，例如树型结构、时期选择标签等。同时，Struts 2 提供了对 DOJO、DWR 和 Ajax 的支持，因此可以生成更多的页面效果。

Struts 2 的标签分为两种：非 UI 标签（控制标签和数据标签）和 UI 标签。其中控制标签主要用于完成流程的控制，例如循环和分支等操作。常用的控制标签如下所示：

- iterator 标签：用于迭代，使用举例如下所示：
  ```
  <s:iterator value="{'banana', 'apple', 'orange', 'cherry'}" id="fruitName">
      <tr>
          <td>
              <s:property value="fruitName"/>
          </td>
      </tr>
  </s:iterator>
  ```

- if/elseif/else 标签：用来做分支控制的，与 Java 中的 if/else if/else 类似。例如：
  ```
  <s:set name="score" value="87"/>
  <s:if test='${score < 60}'>
      您的分数小于 60，不及格
  </s:if>
  <s:elseif test='${score < 85}'>
      您的分数在 60 和 85 之间，良好
  </s:elseif>
  <s:else>
      您的分数在 85 到以上，优秀！
  </s:else>
  ```

- append 标签：将多个集合对象进行拼接，变成一个新的集合对象，例如：
  ```
  <s:append id="totalFruitList">
      <s:param value="{'banana', 'apple', 'orange', 'cherry'}" id="fruitList1"/>
      <s:param value="{'香蕉', '苹果', '桔子', '樱桃'}" id="fruitList2"/>
  </s:append>
  ```

- generator 标签：用于将字符串通过分隔符分隔后，转换为一个集合，例如：
  ```
  <s:generator val="'banana,apple,orange,cherry'" separator="," id="fruits" count="3">
  ```

- sort 标签：用于对指定的集合进行排序，进行排序时，需要根据开发人员自己的排序规则进行排序，即需要实现自己的 Comparator 类，该类必须实现 java.util.Comparator 接口。

- merge 标签：与 append 标签类似，它也将多个集合拼接在一起，只是拼接方式不同而已。举例如下：
  ```
  <s:merge id="totalFruitList">
      <s:param value="{'banana', 'apple', 'orange', 'cherry'}" id="fruitList1"/>
      <s:param value="{'香蕉', '苹果', '桔子', '樱桃'}" id="fruitList2"/>
  </s:merge>
  ```

- subset 标签：用于取得集合的子集，举例如下：
  ```
  <s:subset source="{'香蕉', '苹果', '桔子', '樱桃', '芒果', '葡萄'}" start="2" count="2">
      <s:iterator>
          <s:property/>
      </s:iterator>
  </s:subset>
  ```

数据标签也是非 UI 标签，它主要用于提供各种数据访问的功能。常用的数据标签如下所示：

- action 标签：用来调用 Action，它可以指向具体某一命名空间的某一个 Action。举例如下：

```
<s:action name="Login"/><br/>
```

- bean 标签：用于创建 JavaBean 实例，当 JavaBean 实例需要参数时，可以使用 param 标签将参数传递进去，不过 JavaBean 需要提供这个属性的 setter 方法。使用举例如下：

```
<s:bean name="amigo.struts.tag.dataTags.User" id="user">
    <s:param name="username" value="'amigo'"/>
    <s:param name="password" value="'1234'"/>
</s:bean>
```

- param 标签：用于为其他标签提供参数，例如为 bean 标签提供参数等。
- set 标签：用于将属性值放在指定的范围内，例如 request、session 范围等。举例如下：

```
<s:bean name="amigo.struts.tag.dataTags.User" id="user">
    <s:param name="username" value="'amigo'"/>
    <s:param name="password" value="'1234'"/>
</s:bean>

<s:set name="newUsr" value="#user"/>
```

- property 标签：用于输出指定值，举例如下：

```
<s:property value="%{username}" /><br/>
```

- url 标签：用于输出 URL 地址，若需在 URL 地址后带上参数信息，可在其内使用 param 标签作为其子元素。举例如下：

```
<s:url action="Login" value="success.jsp">
    <s:param name="username" value="'amigo'"/>
    <s:param name="passwd" value="'amigo'"/>
</s:url>
```

- push 标签：用于将位于 ValueStack 的值放置到栈顶，举例如下：

```
<s:bean name="amigo.struts.tag.dataTags.User" id="user">
    <s:param name="username" value="'amigo'"/>
    <s:param name="password" value="'1234'"/>
</s:bean>
<s:push value="#user">
```

- include 标签：用于将一个 JSP 页面或一个 Servlet 包含在页面中，举例如下：

```
<s:include value="includeFile.jsp" id="includeFile">
    <s:param name="password" value="'1234'"/>
</s:include>
```

- date 标签：用于格式化输出日期，还可计算指定日期和当前日期的时差。举例如下：

```
<s:date name="#attr.now" format="yyyy-MM-dd" nice="true"/>
```

- debug 标签：该标签用于辅助开发人员进行测试，它在页面上生成"[Debug]"的超级链接，点击该超级链接后，开发人员将可以查看 Stack Context 和 ValueStack 中的信息。

UI 标签包括表单标签（如 form 标签、textfield 标签、radio 标签和 select 标签等）和非表单标签（component 标签和 tree 标签等）。

- form 标签：用于创建表单，与 HTML 的 form 标签对应，举例如下：

```
<s:form action="Login.action" method="post">
    ......
</s:form>
```

- textfield 标签：该标签与 HTML 的 <input type="text" name="" value="" /> 作用相同。<s:textfield/> 标签的使用举例如下：

```
<s:textfield name="username" />
```

- select 标签：用于生成下拉列表框，该标签的 list 属性可指定集合，这个集合用于生成下拉列表框的选项。举例如下：

```
<s:select name="bookType"
        label="请选择图书类型"
        labelposition="top"
        list="#{'1':'计算机', '2':'社会科学', '3':'财经', '4':'文学'}" />
```

- radio 标签：用于生成单选框，与 HTML 的 radio 标签作用相同，它与 select 标签类似，也可以指定 label、list、listkey 和 listValue 等属性。举例如下：

```
<s:bean name="amigo.struts.tag.uiTags.BookTypeService" id="typeService"/>
<s:radio name="bookType"
        label="请选择图书类型"
        labelposition="top"
        list="#typeService.bookTypes"
        listKey="typeId"
        listValue="typeName" />
```

- checkboxlist 标签：该标签可以一次创建多个复选框列表，举例如下：

```
<s:checkboxlist name="bookType"
        label="请选择图书类型"
        labelposition="top"
        list="#{'1':'计算机', '2':'社会科学', '3':'财经', '4':'文学', '5':'数学', '6': '升学考试'}" />
```

- combobox 标签：用于生成一个单行文本框和下拉列表框的组合，但是只有单行文本框中才包含请求参数，而下拉列表框只用于辅助输入。举例如下：

```
<s:combobox name="bookType"
        label="请选择图书类型"
        labelposition="top"
        list="{'计算机', '社会科学', '财经', '文学', '数学', '升学考试'}" />
```

- doubleselect 标签：用于生成一个级联列表框，即将生成两个下拉列表框，当选择一个下拉列表框改变时，另一个下拉列表框将会做出相应的改变。举例如下：

```
<s:set name="bookTypes" value="#{'计算机':{'Java', 'C#', 'Struts2'},
        '文学':{'言情小说', '恐怖', '散文', '历史小说'},
        '升学考试':{'考研', '考博','高考'}}">
<s:doubleselect label="请选择类别"
        name="bookType"
        list="#bookTypes.keySet()"
        doubleName="subBookType"
        doubleList="#bookTypes[top]"
        label="请选择类别"> </s:doubleselect>
```

- datetimepicker 标签：用于生成一个日期、时间下拉列表框，当选择好日期或时间后，选中的日期或时间的值将会自动放入文本框中。日期的选择如下所示：

```
<s:datetimepicker name="birthDate" label="出生日期" displayFormat="dddd/MM/dd"/>
```

时间选择的示例代码如下所示：

```
<s:datetimepicker name="start" label="选择出发时间" type="time" value="13:00"/>
```

- optiontransferselect 标签：该标签会创建两个下拉列表，会生成两个<select../>标签，两个下拉列表中的元素能相互移动，提交表单的时候，两个<select../>标签的值都会提交。使用举例如下：

```
<s:optiontransferselect
        label="请选择你喜欢的图书类型"
```

```
            name="bookType"
            leftTitle="---所有图书---"
            list="{'计算机', '社会科学', '财经', '文学', '数学'}"
            multiple="true"
            addToLeftLabel="左移"
            selectAllLabel="全部选择"
            addToRightLabel="右移"
            rightTitle="---喜欢图书---"
            doubleList="{'散文', '历史'}"
            doubleName="loveBookType"
            doubleMultiple="true" />
```

- optgroup 标签：用于生成一个下拉列表框的选项组，因此，它需要放在<s:select../>标签中使用，可以在一个<s:select../>标签中添加多个<s:optgroup../>标签。使用举例如下：

```
<s:bean name="amigo.struts.tag.uiTags.BookTypeService" id="typeService"/>
<s:select label="选择您喜欢的图书类型"
        name="bookType"
    list="#{'1':'计算机', '2':'社会科学', '3':'财经', '4':'数学'}"
        listKey="key"
        listValue="value">
        <s:optgroup label="小说"
    list="#typeService.novelBookTypes"
            listKey="typeId"
            listValue="typeName" />
        <s:optgroup label="升学考试"
    list="#typeService.examBookTypes"
            listKey="typeId"
            listValue="typeName" />
</s:select>
```

- updownselect 标签：它的作用与 select 标签类似，它的属性也与之类似，常用属性为 list、listKey 和 listValue 等，不过它与 select 标签的不同之处在于：它支持选项的上下移动。使用举例如下：

```
<s:updownselect name="bookType2" label="请选择图书类型"
            labelposition="top"
            moveUpLabel="上移"
            moveDownLabel="下移"
            list="#{'1':'计算机', '2':'社会科学', '3':'财经', '4':'文学', '5':'数学', '6': '升学考试'}"
            listKey="key"
            listValue="value"
            emptyOption="true" />
```

- token 标签：用于防止重复提交表单，避免刷新页面或通过后退来重复提交。使用举例如下：

```
<!-- 使用 token 标签生成一个防止重复提交的隐藏域 -->
<s:token/>
```

第 9 章 OGNL

【本章导读语】

OGNL（Object-Graph Navigation Language，对象图形导航语言）是一种功能强大的 EL（Expression Language，表达式语言），它简化了对数据的访问，使得开发人员能够通过非常简单的表达式访问对象层。OGNL 是 Struts 2 核心的表达式语言。在 Struts 2 的 OGNL 中，数据放在以下几个地方：ValueStack、request、session、application 和 attr（当从 attr 中取数据时，会按 page、request、session、application 的顺序进行遍历。通常不同的 tag 之间交换的数据都可以从 attr 中取到）。

本章详细讲解 OGNL 表达式语言的使用，以及 OGNL 表达式语言的相关知识，例如 EL 表达式和 Lambda 表达式。

【例 9-1】OGNL 的使用

〖**实例需求**〗

OGNL 极大地简化了 Struts 2 对数据的访问。本实例讲解如何通过 OGNL 取得存在不同地方的对象及其属性，例如 Context、ValueStack、parameters、request、session 中的对象。

〖**开发过程**〗

第一步：建立工程

读者可以参考前几章的方法在 Eclipse 中新建 strutsognl 的动态 Web 工程，并将所需的 jar 包导入到 WEB-INF/lib 目录中，在 src 目录中建立 amigo.struts.ognl 包，在 WebRoot 目录中建立 ognl 目录来存放本实例的 JSP 页面。工程的结构如图 9-1 所示。

图 9-1 工程的目录结构

第二步：通过 OGNL 获取各种属性

Action 实例总是被推入 ValueStack 中，因为 Action 在 Stack 中，而 Stack 是 OGNL 的根对象，若想访问 Action 中的属性，不使用"#"标记也是可以的。若开发人员需要访问 ActionContext 中的其他非根对象，如 request 和 session 中的对象时，需要使用"#"标记。

（1）编写 Action 类：OgnlAction.java。

在 amigo.struts.ognl 包中建立 OgnlAction 类，该类主要的任务是将各属性放入 request 等中，设置完成后，跳转到 ognl.jsp 页面。创建 OgnlAction 类的操作步骤如图 9-2 所示。

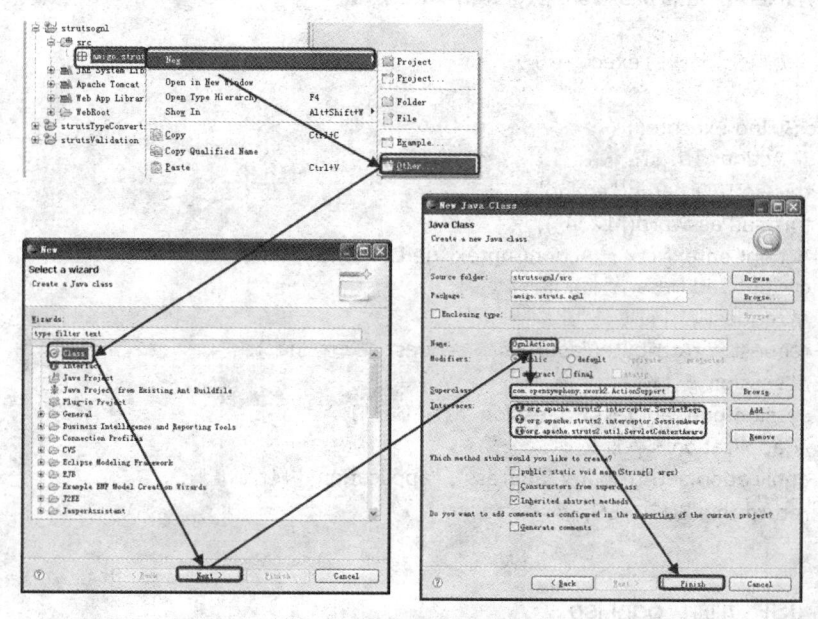

图 9-2 创建 OgnlAction 类

该类的代码如下所示：

```java
package amigo.struts.ognl;

import java.util.Map;

import javax.servlet.ServletContext;
import javax.servlet.http.HttpServletRequest;

import org.apache.struts2.interceptor.ServletRequestAware;
import org.apache.struts2.interceptor.SessionAware;
import org.apache.struts2.util.ServletContextAware;

import com.opensymphony.xwork2.ActionContext;
import com.opensymphony.xwork2.ActionSupport;

/**
 * OGNL 简单操作使用举例.
 */
public class OgnlAction extends ActionSupport implements ServletRequestAware,
            SessionAware, ServletContextAware {
    private static final long serialVersionUID = 1L;
```

```java
    private HttpServletRequest request;
    private Map<String,String> session;
    private ServletContext application;

    /** 用户名. */
    private String username;

    /** 密码. */
    private String password;
    // 省略 request、session 和 application 的 setter 方法
    // 省略 username 和 password 的 getter/setter 方法
    /**
     * 定义处理登录请求的 execute 方法.
     */
    public String execute() {
        // Action 属性设置
        this.setUsername("amigo");
        this.setPassword("1234");
        ActionContext ctx = ActionContext.getContext();
        ctx.put("address", "北京市海淀区");
        // request 属性设置
        request.setAttribute("address", "request 中属性的值");
        // session 属性设置
        session.put("address", "session 中属性的值");
        // application 属性设置
        application.setAttribute("address", "application 中属性的值");
        return this.SUCCESS;
    }
}
```

（2）编写 JSP 页面：ognl.jsp。

接着在 WebRoot/ognl 目录中建立 ognl.jsp 页面，该页面用于展示如何通过 OGNL 简单地获取各种属性。创建该页面的操作步骤如图 9-3 所示。

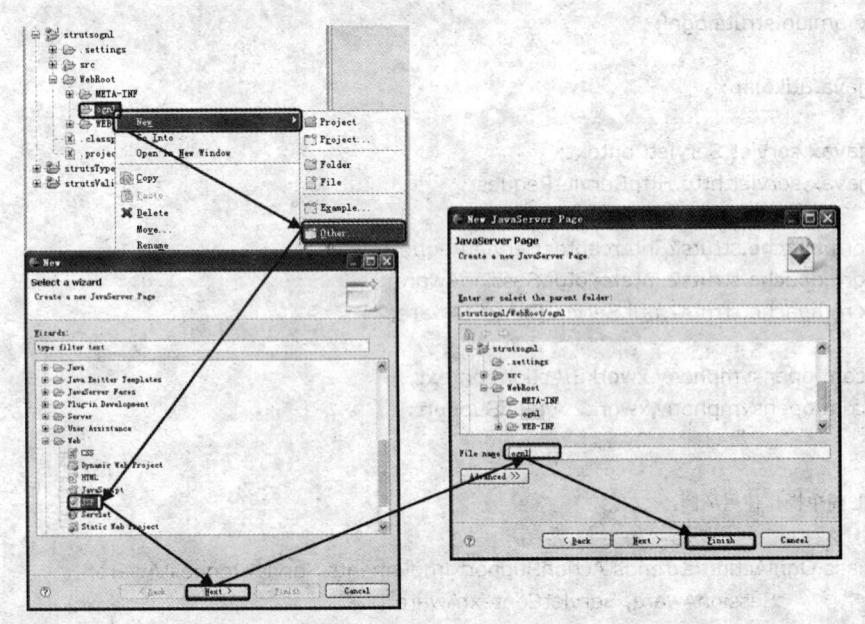

图 9-3 创建 ognl.jsp 页面

该页面的代码如下所示：

```html
......
<html>
    <head>
        <title>OGNL 简单操作实例</title>
    </head>
    <body>
        访问 Action 实例的属性时，使用和不使用"#"都是可以的：<br/>
        <s:property value="username"/><br/>
        <s:property value="password"/><br/>
        <s:property value="address"/><br/><br/>

        访问 parameter 中的信息，使用#parameters.paramName 或#parameters["paramName"]：<br/>
        <s:property value="#parameters.address"/><br/>
        <s:property value='#parameters["address"]'/><br/><br/>

        访问 request 中的信息，使用#request.paramName 或#request["paramName"]：<br/>
        <s:property value="#request.address"/><br/>
        <s:property value='#request["address"]'/><br/><br/>

        访问 session 中的信息，使用#session.paramName 或#session["paramName"]：<br/>
        <s:property value="#session.address"/><br/>
        <s:property value='#session["address"]'/><br/><br/>

        访问 application 中的信息，使用#application.paramName 或#application["paramName"]：<br/>
        <s:property value="#application.address"/><br/>
        <s:property value='#application["address"]'/><br/><br/>

        使用#attr.paramName 或#attr["paramName"]访问时，按 request > session > application 顺序访问属性<br/>
        <s:property value="#attr.address"/><br/>
        <s:property value='#attr["address"]'/>
    </body>
</html>
```

（3）编写 Struts 2 配置文件：struts.xml。

最后还需要在 struts.xml 文件中进行 Action 的配置，首先在 src 目录中建立 struts.xml 文件，接着将 OgnlAction 配置到其中，并指明其成功时的跳转页面为 ognl.jsp，内容如下：

```xml
......
<struts>
    <include file="struts-default.xml"/>
    <package name="tags" extends="struts-default">
        <action name="ognl"    class="amigo.struts.ognl.OgnlAction">
            <result name="success">/ognl/ognl.jsp</result>
        </action>
    </package>
</struts>
```

（4）运行结果。

在访问地址后加上 parameter 参数信息：address=paramAddress，运行效果如图 9-4 所示。

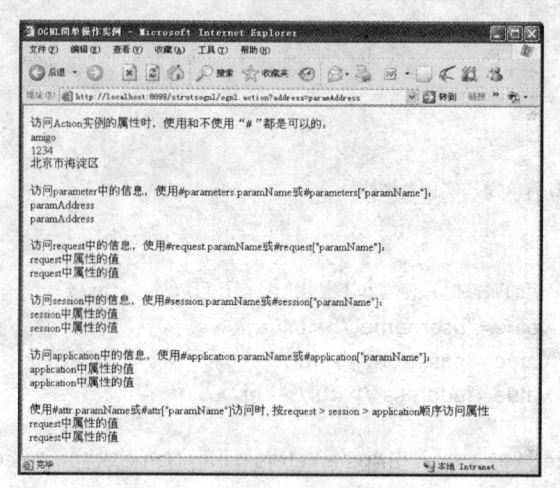

图 9-4　OGNL 简单操作实例

第三步：OGNL 中的集合操作

使用 OGNL 直接生成 List 类型集合的语法为：

{e1, e2, e3...}

List 中的多个元素使用英文逗号隔开。

使用 OGNL 直接生成 Map 类型（key-value 对）集合的语法为：

#{key1:value1, key2:value2, key3:value3...}

它使用"#"作为打头的字符，key-value 对之间以英文冒号隔开，多个 key-value 对之间使用英文逗号隔开。

＜s:iterator ../＞、＜s:select ../＞、＜s:radio ../＞等标签中都可能使用到 List 类型集合或 Map 类型集合，OGNL 的集合操作在 Web 应用中应用极其广泛。

（1）编写 JSP 页面：ognlCollection.jsp。

首先在 WebRoot/ognl 目录中建立 ognlCollection.jsp 文件，该页面展示在 OGNL 中如何进行各种集合的构建和操作。创建该页面的操作步骤如图 9-5 所示。

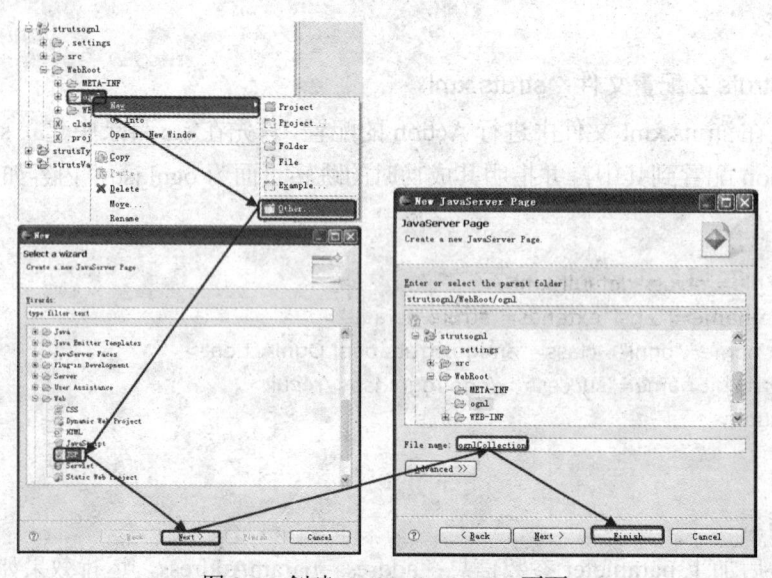

图 9-5　创建 ognlCollection.jsp 页面

该页面的代码如下所示：

```jsp
<%@ page contentType="text/html; charset=UTF-8" %>
<%@ taglib prefix="s" uri="/struts-tags" %>
<!DOCTYPE HTML PUBLIC "-//W3C//DTD HTML 4.01 Transitional//EN">
<html>
    <head>
        <title>OGNL 的集合操作实例</title>
    </head>
    <body>
        List 类型集合：
        <br/>(1)iterator 标签：<br/>
        <s:iterator value="{'香蕉', '苹果', '橘子', '樱桃'}" id="fruitName">
            <s:property value="fruitName"/>    
        </s:iterator>

        <br/>(2)select 标签（生成的 select 的各 option 的 value 属性与显示的名称相同）：<br/>
        <s:select label="userName" name="userName" list="{'阿蜜果', 'amigo', '谢星星'}" value="'谢星星'" />

        <br/><br/>Map 类型集合：
        <br/>(1)iterator 标签：<br/>
        <s:iterator value="#{'1' : '香蕉', '2' : '苹果', '3': '橘子', '4' : '樱桃'}">
            <s:property value="key"/>：<s:property value="value"/>     
        </s:iterator>

        <br/>(2)select 标签（生成的 select 的各 option 中的 value 值为各 key-value 对的 key）：<br/>
        <s:select label="userName" name="userName"
            list="#{'1' : '阿蜜果', '2' : 'amigo', '3' : '谢星星'}"
            listKey="key"
            listValue="value" value="3"/>
    </body>
</html>
```

（2）运行结果。

该页面的运行效果如图 9-6 所示。

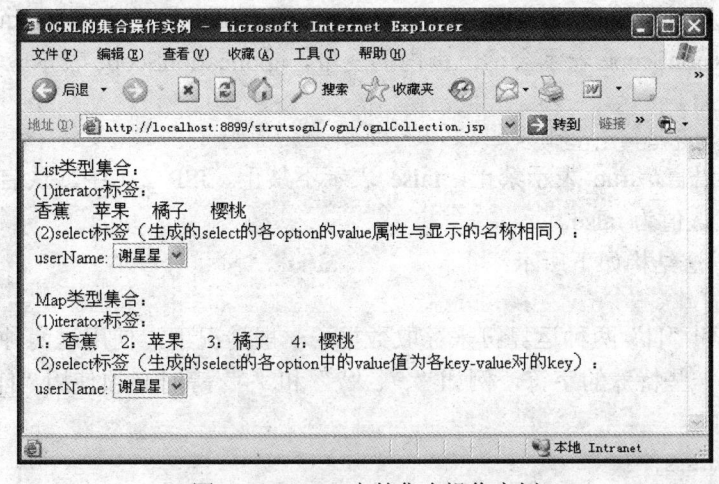

图 9-6　OGNL 中的集合操作实例

【例 9-2】EL 表达式

〖实例需求〗

表达式语言的灵感来自于 ECMAScript 和 XPath 表达式语言，它提供了在 JSP 中简化表达式的方法。它是一种简单的语言，基于可用的命名空间（PageContext 属性）、嵌套属性、对集合和操作符（算术型、关系型和逻辑型）的访问符、映射到 Java 类中静态方法的可扩展函数以及一组隐式对象。

EL 提供了在 JSP 脚本编制元素范围外使用运行时表达式的功能。脚本编制元素是指页面中能够用于在 JSP 文件中嵌入 Java 代码的元素。它们通常用于对象操作以及执行那些影响所生成内容的计算。JSP 2.0 将 EL 表达式添加为一种脚本编制元素。

Struts 2 在 2.0.11 版本前支持在标签中使用表达式语言 EL，而自此以后不再支持在标签中使用 EL，但在 Struts 2 标签之外使用 EL 表达式还是允许的。不再支持的原因在于使用 JSP 表达式语言可能会允许怀有恶意的 OGNL 表达式，详细信息请参见：
http://struts.apache.org/2.0.11/docs/release-notes-2011.html。

本实例只是简要地讲解如何在 JSP 中使用 EL 表达式，而不再讲解在 Struts 2.0.11 的以前版本中如何在标签中使用 EL 表达式。

〖开发过程〗

第一步：创建文件夹

首先在WebRoot目录中建立el文件夹，该目录用于存放该实例的JSP页面。

接着建立amigo.struts.el包，该包用于建立EL表达式实例的Java类。

第二步：在 JSP 页面中使用 EL

（1）表达式语言简介。

EL 表达式用${}表示，它可代替 JSP 页面中复杂的 Java 代码。EL 表达式可操作常量、变量和隐式对象。EL 表达式有 4 种范围，pageScope 表示页面范围的变量，requestScope 表示请求对象的变量，sessionScope 表示会话范围内的变量，applicationScope 表示应用范围的变量。

在 JSP 首部添加：

```
<%@ page isELIgnored="true"%>
```

表示是否禁用 EL 语言，true 表示禁止，false 表示不禁止。JSP 2.0 中默认启用 EL 语言，即 isELIgnored 属性默认值为 false。

EL 表达式的语法结构如下所示：

```
${expression}
```

EL 提供"."和"[]"两种运算符来存取数据，一般情况下，使用这两种运算符均可，但是当属性名称包括一些特殊的字符，例如"."、"?"和"-"等时必须使用"[]"运算符，例如如下表达式是错误的：

```
${staffer.My-Address}
```

正确写法应为：

```
${staffer.["My-Address"]}
```
还有一种非得使用"[]"操作符的情况是需要动态取值时，例如想要取得 request 范围中的对象 staffer 中属性名为变量 propertyName 的属性的名称时，下面的 EL 表达式是错误的：
```
${requestScope.staffer.propertyName}
```
正确的写法应为：
```
${requestScope.staffer[propertyName] }
```
在书写 EL 表达式时，可加上范围作为前缀，若未加，系统将按照 page→request→session→application 的范围查找。

使用 EL 表达式：
```
${requestScope.address}
```
可取的 request 范围内名称为 address 的变量，它的作用相当于代码：
```
request.getAttribute("address");
```
其他 3 种范围的变量的获取也与此类似。最常用的隐式对象有${param}和${paramValues}。其中${param}表示返回请求参数中单个字符串的值，${paramValues}表示返回请求参数的一组值。使用举例如下：
```
${param.address}
```
上面的 EL 表达式用于获取用户请求参数中名为 address 的参数，相当于 Java 代码：
```
request.getParameter("address");
```
返回请求参数中名为 address 的一组值的 EL 表达式为：
```
${paramValues.address}
```
上面的 EL 表达式相当于如下 Java 代码：
```
request.getParameterValues("address");
```
（2）编写 Action 类：ElAction.java。

首先读者可在 amigo.struts.el 包中建立 ElAction 类，该类将参数信息放到各种范围中，用于在后续的 el.jsp 页面中显示。创建 ElAction 类的操作步骤如图 9-7 所示。

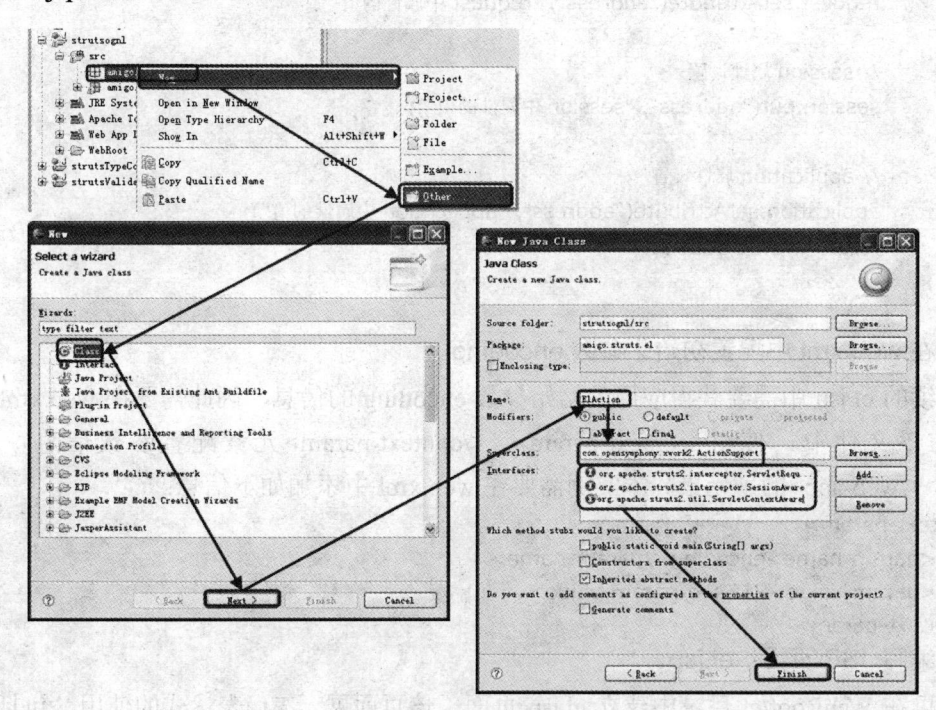

图 9-7　创建 ElAction 类

该类的代码如下：

```java
package amigo.struts.el;

import java.util.Map;

import javax.servlet.ServletContext;
import javax.servlet.http.HttpServletRequest;

import org.apache.struts2.interceptor.ServletRequestAware;
import org.apache.struts2.interceptor.SessionAware;
import org.apache.struts2.util.ServletContextAware;

import com.opensymphony.xwork2.ActionSupport;

/**
 * EL 表达式使用举例
 */
public class ElAction extends ActionSupport implements ServletRequestAware,
        SessionAware, ServletContextAware {
    private static final long serialVersionUID = 1L;
    private HttpServletRequest request;
    private Map<String,String> session;
    private ServletContext application;
    // 省略 request、session 和 application 的 setter 方法

    public String execute() {
        // request 属性设置
        request.setAttribute("address", "request 中属性的值");

        // session 属性设置
        session.put("address", "session 中属性的值");

        // application 属性设置
        application.setAttribute("address", "application 中属性的值");
        return this.SUCCESS;
    }
}
```

（3）在 web.xml 中配置初始化参数 encoding。

在后续的 el.jsp 中需要获得应用的初始参数 encoding 的信息，因此需要在 web.xml 中进行配置，在该文件中，使用<context-param>…</context-param>元素配置参数信息，它属于<web-app></web-app>的子元素。本实例需要在 web.xml 中添加如下信息：

```xml
<context-param>
    <param-name>encoding</param-name>
    <param-value>UTF-8</param-value>
</context-param>
```

（4）编写 JSP 页面：el.jsp。

读者可在 WebRoot/el 目录中建立 el.jsp 页面，该页面展示 EL 表达式的使用，包括 4 种范

围中变量、用户请求参数、cookie 中的变量、header 中的值、应用范围内的初始化参数、常用 request 信息和常用 session 信息的获取。创建该文件的操作步骤图如图 9-8 所示。

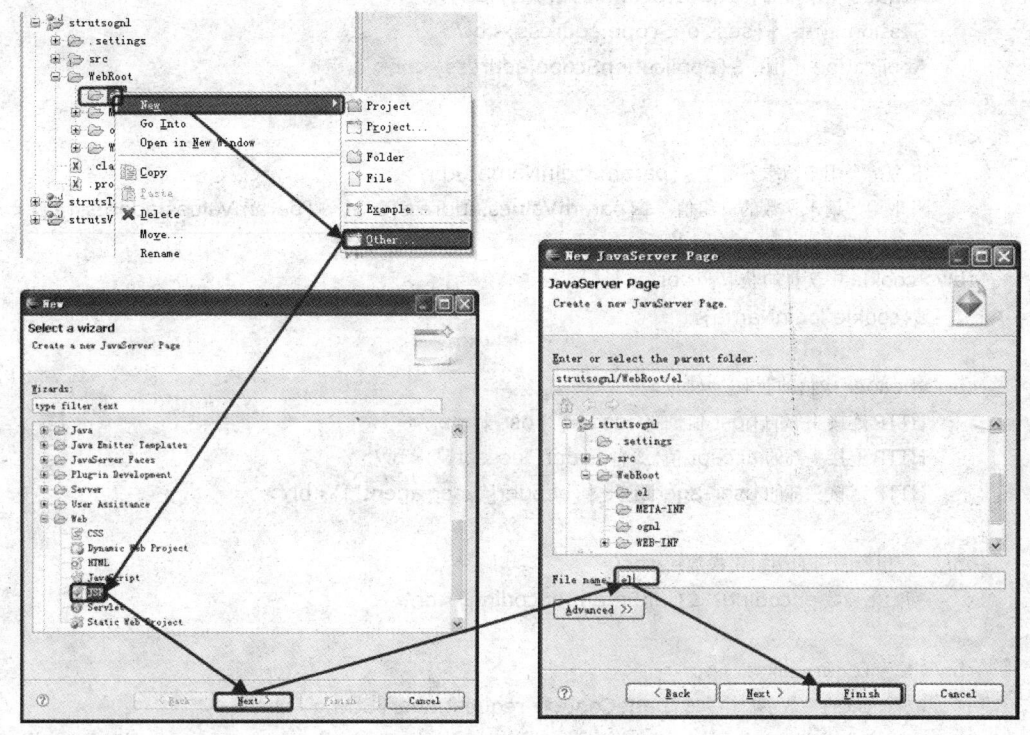

图 9-8 创建 el.jsp 页面

该页面的代码如下所示：

```jsp
<%@ page contentType="text/html; charset=UTF-8" %>
<%@ taglib prefix="s" uri="/struts-tags" %>
<!DOCTYPE HTML PUBLIC "-//W3C//DTD HTML 4.01 Transitional//EN">
<%
String address = "Page 范围中的 address 变量";
pageContext.setAttribute("address", address);
%>
<html>
    <head>
        <title>el 表达式使用实例</title>
        <meta http-equiv="Content-Type" content="text/html; charset=UTF-8"/>
        <meta http-equiv="pragma" content="no-cache">
        <meta http-equiv="cache-control" content="no-cache">
        <script language="javascript">
            var oneDay = 24*60*60*1000;
            var expDate = new Date();
            expDate.setTime(expDate.getTime() + oneDay);
            var cookieExpires = expDate.toGMTString();
            document.cookie="loginName=amigo;expires=" + cookieExpires;
        </script>
    </head>
    <body>
```

```
            四种范围中变量的获取：<br/>
                Page 范围：${pageScope.address}<br/>
                Request 范围：${requestScope.address}<br/>
                Session 范围：${sessionScope.address}<br/>
                Application 范围：${applicationScope.address}<br/>

            <br/>用户请求参数的获取：<br/>
                获取单个用户请求参数：${param.loginName}<br/>
                获取用户请求参数的一组值：${paramValues.address[0]}、${paramValues.address[1]}<br/>

            <br/>cookie 中变量的获取：<br/>
                ${cookie.loginName}

            <br/>header 中值的获取：<br/>
                HTTP 连接头部的 host 值：${header["host"]}<br/>
                HTTP 连接头部的 accept 值：${header["accept"]}<br/>
                HTTP 连接头部的 user-agent 值：${header["user-agent"]}<br/>

            <br/>应用范围内的初始化参数：<br/>
                初始化参数 encoding：${initParam.encoding}<br/>

            <br/>常用 request 信息：<br/>
                取得请求的参数字符串：${pageContext.request.queryString}<br/>
                取得请求的 URL，但不包括请求之参数字符串：${pageContext.request.requestURL}<br/>
                服务的 web application 的名称：${pageContext.request.contextPath}<br/>
                取得 HTTP 的方法(GET、POST)：${pageContext.request.method}<br/>
                取得使用的协议(HTTP/1.1、HTTP/1.0)：${pageContext.request.protocol}<br/>
                取得用户名称：${pageContext.request.remoteUser}<br/>
                取得用户的 IP 地址：${pageContext.request.remoteAddr}<br/>

            <br/>常用 session 信息：<br/>
                判断 session 是否为新的：${pageContext.session.new}<br/>
                取得 sessionID：${pageContext.session.id}
        </body>
</html>
```

（5）配置 struts.xml。

最后还需要将 ElAction.java 这个 Action 类配置到 struts.xml 中，需要在该文件中添加如下配置：

```
<action name="el" class="amigo.struts.el.ElAction">
    <result name="success">/el/el.jsp</result>
</action>
```

如上配置制定了该 Action 类的请求路径为 el.action，并且 success 的页面指向为 el/el.jsp 页面。

第三步：运行结果

在浏览器中输入地址：http://localhost:8899/strutsognl/el.action?loginName=amigo&address=paramAddress1&address=paramAddress2，运行结果如图 9-9 所示。

第 9 章 OGNL

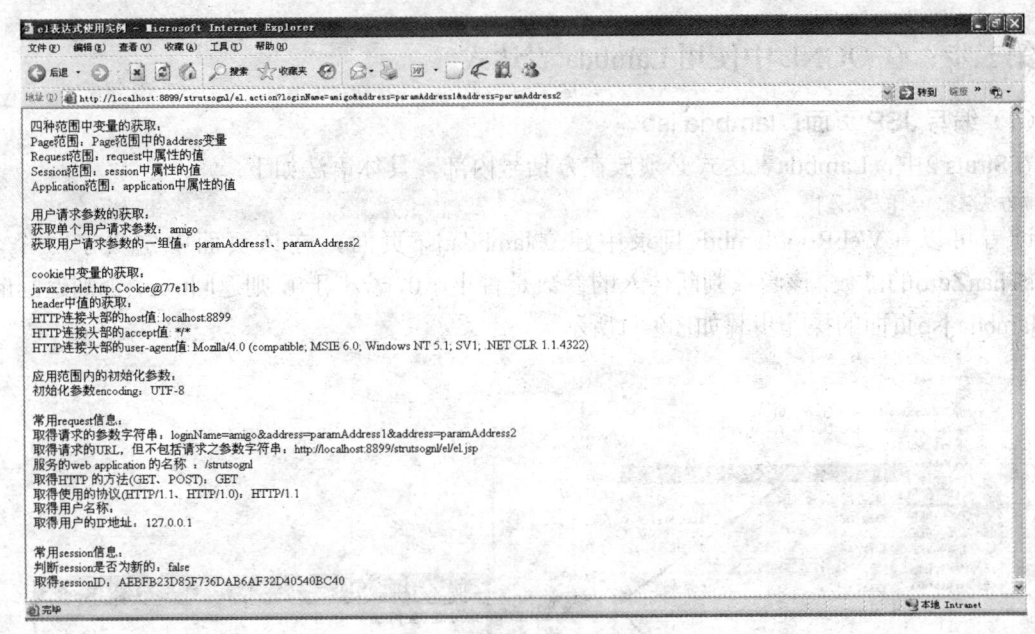

图 9-9 EL 表达式的使用举例

【例 9-3】Lambda 表达式

〖实例需求〗

OGNL 支持基本的 Lambda 表达式，因而允许在 OGNL 表达式中使用一些简单的函数。本实例讲述如何在 OGNL 中使用 Lambda 表达式。

〖开发过程〗

第一步：创建文件夹

首先在WebRoot目录中建立lambda文件夹，该目录用于存放该实例的JSP页面。创建lambda文件夹的操作步骤如图9-10所示。

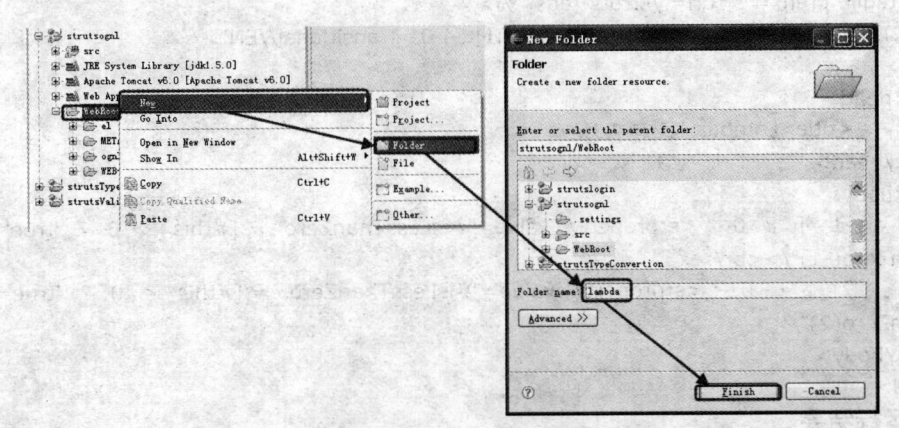

图 9-10 创建 lambda 文件夹

第二步：在 OGNL 中使用 Lambda 表达式

（1）编写 JSP 页面：lambda.jsp。

在 Struts 2 中，Lambda 表达式必须放在方括号内部，具体语法如下：

```
#方法名称 =:[方法体]
```

读者可以在 WebRoot/lambda 目录中建立 lambda.jsp 页面，在该页面中定义了一个名为 isLessThanZero 的函数，该函数判断传入的参数是否小于 0，若小于 0，则返回 true，否则返回 false。创建 lambda.jsp 页面的操作步骤如图 9-11 所示。

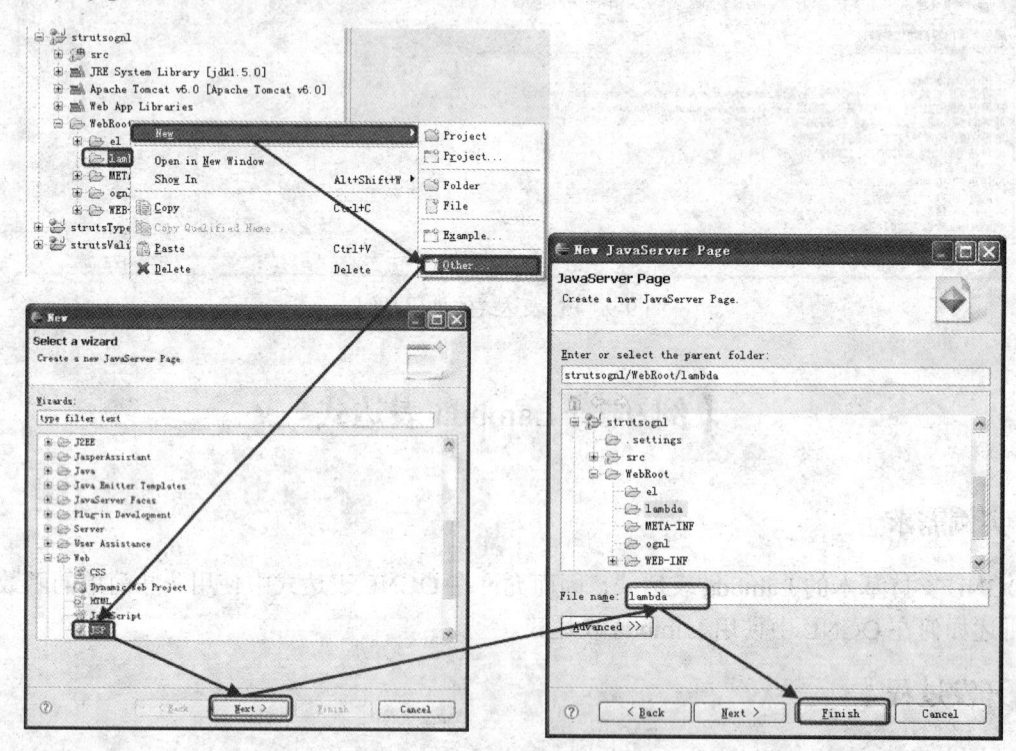

图 9-11　创建 lambda.jsp 页面

该页面的代码如下所示：

```jsp
<%@ page contentType="text/html; charset=UTF-8" %>
<%@ taglib prefix="s" uri="/struts-tags" %>
<!DOCTYPE HTML PUBLIC "-//W3C//DTD HTML 4.01 Transitional//EN">
<html>
    <head>
        <title>Lambda 表达式实例</title>
    </head>
    <body>
        -1 小于 0： <s:property value="#isLessThanZero =:[#this < 0 ? 'true' : 'false'], #isLessThanZero(-1)"/><br/>
        2 小于 0： <s:property value="#isLessThanZero =:[#this < 0 ? 'true' : 'false'], #isLessThanZero(2)"/>
    </body>
</html>
```

（2）运行结果。

在浏览器中运行该页面，运行结果如图 9-12 所示。

图 9-12 Lambda 表达式实例运行结果

小结

　　OGNL（Object-Graph Navigation Language，对象图导航语言）是 Struts 2 核心的表达式语言。它是一种功能强大的 EL（Expression Language，表达式语言），它简化了对数据的访问，使得开发人员能够通过非常简单的表达式访问对象层。

　　在 Struts 2 的 OGNL 中，数据放在以下几个地方：
- ValueStack：根路径(ROOT)。
- request：http 请求。
- session：会话。
- application：应用。

访问 Action 实例的属性时，使用和不使用"#"都是可以的，例如访问 Action 中 username 的值，可使用如下代码：

```
<s:property value="username"/>
```

访问 parameters 中的信息，可使用#parameters.paramName 或#parameters["paramName"]，例如如下两行代码都能用于访问 parameters 中的 address 参数：

```
<s:property value="#parameters.address"/>
<s:property value='#parameters["address"]'/>
```

访问 request 中的信息，可使用#request.paramName 或#request["paramName"]，例如访问 request 中的 address，如下两行代码都是可行的：

```
<s:property value="#request.address"/>
<s:property value='#request["address"]'/>
```

访问 session 中的信息，可使用#session.paramName 或#session["paramName"]，例如访问 session 中的 address 属性，如下两行代码都是可行的：

```
<s:property value="#session.address"/>
<s:property value='#session["address"]'/>
```

访问 application 中的信息，可使用#application.paramName 或#application["paramName"]，例如访问 session 中的 address 属性，如下两行代码都是可行的：

```
<s:property value="#application.address"/>
<s:property value='#application["address"]'/>
```

使用#attr.paramName 或#attr["paramName"]访问时，按 request > session > application 顺序访问属性，如下两行代码都是可行的：

```
<s:property value="#attr.address"/>
<s:property value='#attr["address"]'/>
```

　　EL 提供了在 JSP 脚本编制元素范围外使用运行时表达式的功能。脚本编制元素是指页面中能够用于在 JSP 文件中嵌入 Java 代码的元素。它们通常用于对象操作以及执行那些影响所生成内容的计算。JSP 2.0 将 EL 表达式添加为一种脚本编制元素。

Struts 2 在 2.0.11 版本前支持在标签中使用表达式语言 EL，而自此以后不再支持在标签中使用 EL，但在 Struts 2 标签之外使用 EL 表达式还是允许的。

使用 EL 表达式获得 pageContext、request、session、application 和 cookie 等中的变量的值的方法如下所示：

```
Page 范围：${pageScope.address}
Request 范围：${requestScope.address}
Session 范围：${sessionScope.address}
Application 范围：${applicationScope.address}
${cookie.loginName}
```

OGNL 支持基本的 Lambda 表达式，因而允许在 OGNL 表达式中使用一些简单的函数。例如下面使用的就是 Lambda 表达式：

```
-1 小于 0：<s:property value="#isLessThanZero =:[#this < 0 ? 'true' : 'false'], #isLessThanZero(-1)"/><br/>
2 小于 0：<s:property value="#isLessThanZero =:[#this < 0 ? 'true' : 'false'], #isLessThanZero(2)"/>
```

第 3 篇 Hibernate 篇

第 10 章 Hibernate 入门

【本章导读语】

Hibernate 是目前很流行的一个 ORM 框架，它将 SQL 操作优雅地包装成对象化的操作。目前，Hibernate 的文档丰富、开发者多，从而使得学习的难度得以降低。

要运用 Hibernate3 框架进行开发，第一步就是要将开发环境搭建起来，本章将采用 Hibernate 的最新版本 Hibernate3.2.6，并通过实例来详细讲解搭建环境的步骤，和读者一起来开发第一个使用 Hibernate 3 框架技术开发的数据查询实例。

【例 10-1】Java 对象持久化技术

〖实例需求〗

20 世纪 70 年代之前，一般采用文件系统存储数据，20 世纪 70 年代数据库技术得到普及，而在 80 年代数据库技术得到飞速发展。在初期编写程序时，一般将数据库操作的业务逻辑代码与用户界面的代码写在一起，后果是极大地加重了软件维护的负担，并且在可重用性方面需要改进。近年来由于分层技术的发展，一般的软件系统都被分成三到更多层，三层结构是最常用的一种结构，一般分为如下三层：

- 表现层：提供与用户进行交互的界面，该层的代码可为 JSP 和 HTML 页面等。
- 业务逻辑层：实现各种业务逻辑。
- 数据库层：负责存放和管理应用的持久化数据。

由于可持久化技术的发展，业务逻辑层又被划分成两层：业务逻辑层和持久化层。其中业务逻辑层与数据库打交道的操作都被交给持久化层去处理。

本实例讲述 Java 中的对象持久化技术。

〖开发过程〗

第一步：Java 应用的持久化层

持久化层封装数据访问的细节，为业务逻辑层提供了面向对象的 API，Hibernate 就是这样一种持久化技术。对于负责的数据模型，直接通过 JDBC 编程来实现健壮的持久化层需要很多高级的专业知识，企业开发自己的持久化层成本比较高。业界出现了很多优秀的 ORM 软件，Hibernate 就是其中的一种。Hibernate 可看成是连接 Java 应用和关系数据库的管道，它可为任何一个需要访问数据库的 Java 应用服务，数据库访问细节对于开发人员是透明的，开发人员只需要访问 Hibernate 的接口即可。

第二步：软件的概念模型

概念模型描述了每个实体的概念和属性，以及实体之间的关系，但是并不描述实体的行为，概念模型是根据对问题域进行详细的分析后确定的用例来创建的。而创建概念模型又可以帮助更好地理解问题域，识别系统中的实体。图 10-1 表示了权限系统的概念模型。

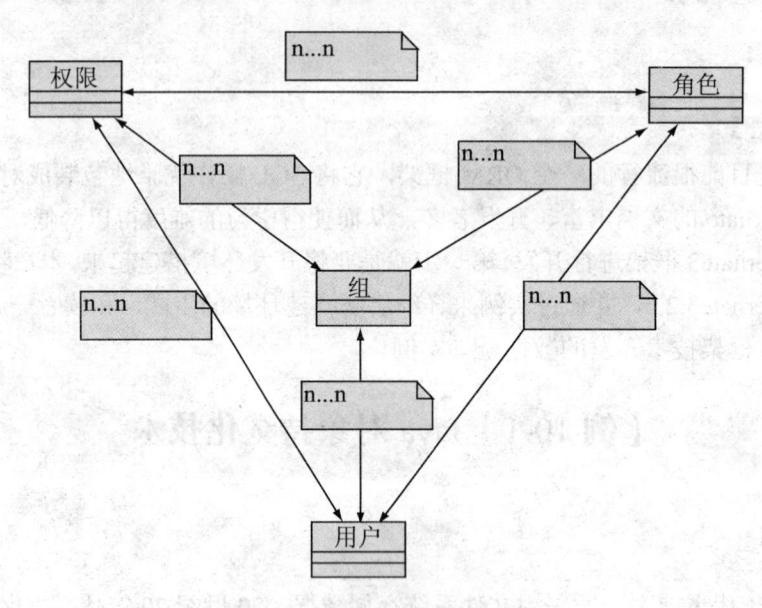

图 10-1　权限系统的概念模型

这个概念问题清晰地表示了问题域中的实体，这个图不管是技术人员还是非技术人员都可以看懂，因而可以很容易地找出模型中存在的问题。实体之间存在 3 种关系：一对一、一对多和多对多。在图 10-1 中，4 个实体之间的关系都是多对多关系。

一对多的实体关系也比较常见，例如部门与用户之间的关系就是一种常见的一对多关系，一个部门可包括多个用户。而用户与部门之间是一对一的关系，即一个用户只能隶属于一个部门。

第三步：关系数据模型

关系数据库到现在还是使用最广泛的数据库，它存储的是关系数据，本步所讲的关系数据模型是在上步的概念模型的基础上建立起来的，关系数据模型描述关系数据的静态结构，它由以下的内容组成：

- 一个或多个表
- 索引
- 视图
- 触发器
- 表与表之间的参照完整性

通常一个实体对应一个表，例如用户实体对应 USER 表，但是对于多对多关系的实体，在建立表时，一般要为这两者建立一个关联表。图 10-1 所示的概念模型对应的关系数据模型如图 10-2 所示。

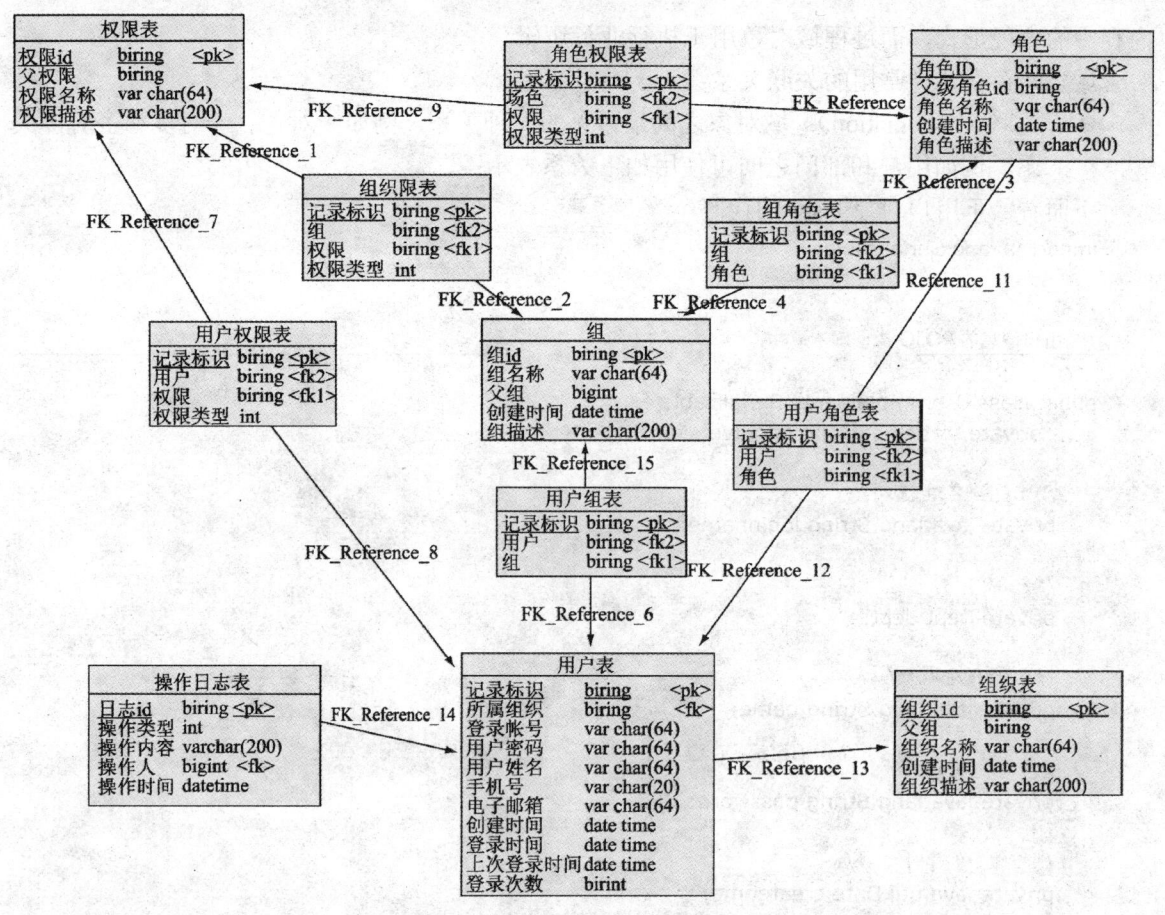

图 10-2 权限系统的关系数据模型

在关系数据库中，通常需要通过主键来保证每条记录的唯一性，一般在进行数据库设计时，最好不要给主键以业务意义，因为那样将会使得需要改变业务意义时，例如改变名称或字段的类型时，都会影响到与之存在外键关联的表。所以最好是设置代理主键。

在图 10-2 中，"用户表"与"权限表"、"用户表"与"角色表"等都是多对多的关系，所以都建立了关联表"用户权限表"、"用户角色表"等。

第四步：域模型

在软件设计阶段，需要在概念模型的基础上创建域模型，它是面向对象的。过程域模型的基本元素是域对象（DO，即 Domain Object），它是对真实世界的实体的软件抽象。域对象又被称为业务对象（BO，即 Business Object），域对象分为如下 3 种：

- 实体域对象：最常见的域对象，可代表人、事物或概念等。在图 10-1 中，用户、角色、权限和组等都属于实体域对象。采用 JavaBean 形式的实体域名对象也被称为 POJO （Plain Old Java Object）。
- 过程域对象：它代表应用中的业务逻辑和流程，它们通常依赖于实体域对象。在 J2EE 应用中，它们常常被称为会话 EJB 或消息驱动 EJB。
- 事件域对象：代表应用中的一些事件，这些事件由某些行为触发。

这 3 种对象在三层应用结构中，都位于业务逻辑层。实体域对象是应用的业务逻辑数据在内存中的表现形式，而过程域对象用于执行业务逻辑。

域之间存在几种常用的关联关系：

- 关联（Association）：域对象之间最常见的一种关系，例如一对一、一对多和多对多关系。例如用户和部门之间可使用如下关系表示：

下面看一下用户对象 User 的代码：

```java
import java.io.Serializable;

/**
 * 用户信息的 POJO 类.
 */
public class User implements Serializable {
    private static final long serialVersionUID = 1L;

    /** 用户名,主键. */
    private java.lang.String loginname;

    /** 部门. */
    private Dept dept;

    /** 帐户姓名. */
    private java.lang.String name;

    /** 登录密码. */
    private java.lang.String password;

    /** 帐户创建时间. */
    private java.util.Date createtime;

    // 省略各属性的 getter/setter 方法

    public User(String loginname, Dept dept,
            String name, String password, Date createTime) {
        this.loginname = loginname;
        this.dept = dept;
        this.name = name;
        this.password = password,
        this.createTime = createTime;
    }
}
```

用户与部门之间存在一对一关联，而部门表与用户表是多对一关系，因此部门类 Dept.java 中包含一个 User 的集合对象 users，该类的代码如下所示：

```java
import java.io.Serializable;
import java.util.HashSet;
import java.util.Set;

/**
 * 部门信息表对应的 pojo 类.
 */
public class Dept implements Serializable {
    private static final long serialVersionUID = 1L;

    /** 部门 id(自增). */
```

```
    private java.lang.Long deptid;

    /** 父级部门 id，最高层部门的父级部门 id 为 0. */
    private java.lang.Long parentdeptid;

    /** 部门名称. */
    private java.lang.String deptname;

    /** 部门全名. */
    private java.lang.String deptfullname;

    private Set<User> users = new HashSet<User>();


    // 省略其余属性的 getter/setter 方法
}
```

- 依赖（Dependency）：依赖关系指的是类之间的访问关系，如果类 A 访问类 B 的属性或方法，或类 A 负责实例化类 B，那么可说类 A 依赖类 B，例如用户的业务逻辑类负责对 User 对象进行增、删、改和查询功能，那么用户业务逻辑类与 User 对象存在的关系就是依赖关系。
- 聚集（Aggregation）：聚集指的是整体与部分的关系，例如人与手的关系，车子与轮子之间的关系，都是聚集关系。车子对象包含轮子对象的集合，如下所示：

```
public class Car implements Serializable {
    public Set<Wheel> wheels = new HashSet<Wheel>();
}
```

- 一般化（Generalization）：指的是类之间的继承关系，例如 Apple（苹果）类继承 Fruit（水果）类，所以 Apple 类和 Fruit 类之间的关系可用一般化（Generalization）来表示。

实体域在内存中创建后，不可能永远存在，要么会被删除，要么开发人员可将对象数据持久化到数据库中。一旦对象被持久化，它们就可以再被重新载入到内存中。当然，并不是所有对象都需要被持久化，显然大部分实体域对象是需要持久化的，但是过程域和事件域对象是可以不必持久化的。

持久化包括和数据库相关的各种操作：
- 保存：将域对象保存在数据库中。
- 修改：修改数据库中的数据。
- 删除：从数据库中删除对象。
- 查询：根据查询条件，查询出满足条件的数据。
- 加载：根据特定的主键，将一个域对象载入。

【例 10-2】搭建 Hibernate 3 开发环境

〖实例需求〗

本例需要搭建起利用 Hibernate 3 开发的工程环境，在 Eclipse 中新建一个工程，以方便本章此后的所有案例可以开发、运行在这个环境中。

〖开发过程〗

第一步：建立工程

读者可以参考前几章的方法在 Eclipse 中新建 hibernateAppWeb 的动态 Web 工程。在工程的 src 源码目录中创建 amigo.hibernate 工程的结构如图 10-3 所示。

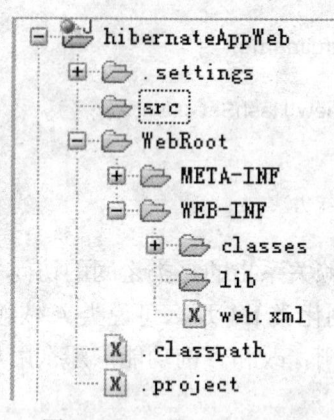

图 10-3　工程的目录结构

第二步：将 Hibernate 加入到工程中

（1）下载 Hibernate 3。

Hibernate 的首页为：http://www.hibernate.org/，界面如图 10-4 所示。

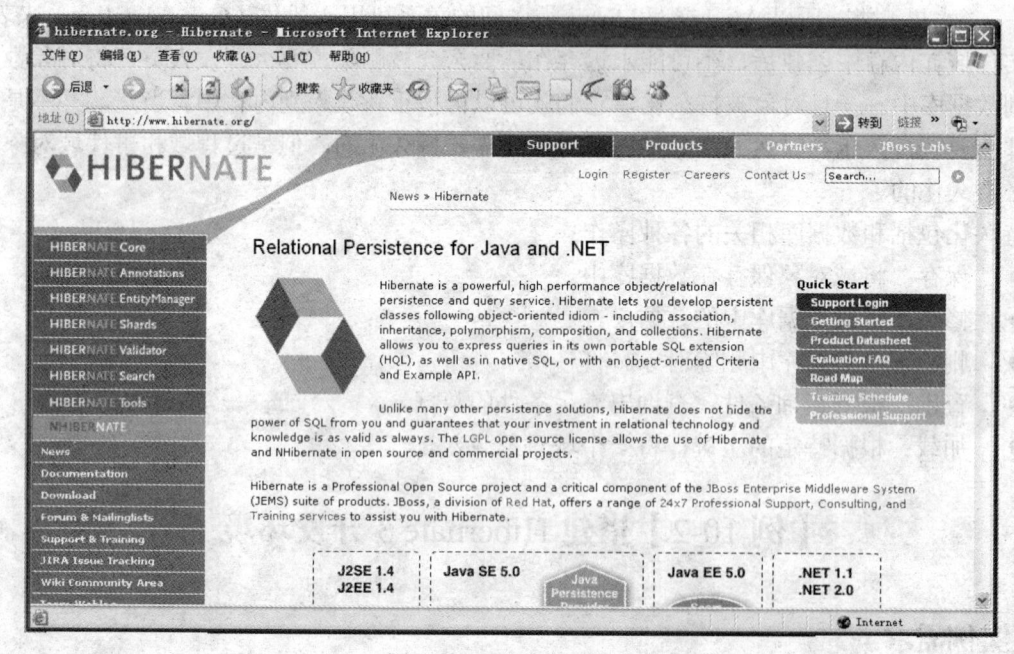

图 10-4　Hibernate 首页

在图 10-4 的首页左方单击 Download 按钮，进入下载主页面，如图 10-5 所示。

第 10 章 Hibernate 入门

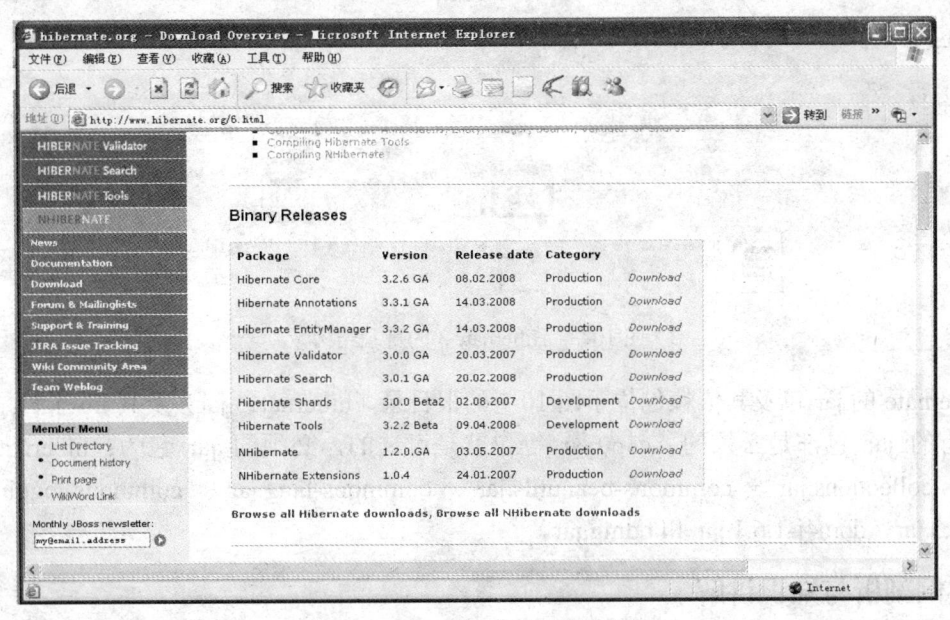

图 10-5 Hibernate 官方下载主界面

从图 10-5 中可以看出，Hibernate 当前的最新版本为 3.2.6，单击图 10-5 中 Hibernate Core 行的 Download 按钮，进入 Hibernate 在 Sourceforge 上的下载页面，下载地址为：http://sourceforge.net/project/showfiles.php?group_id=40712&package_id=127784&release_id=574498 下载界面如图 10-6 所示。

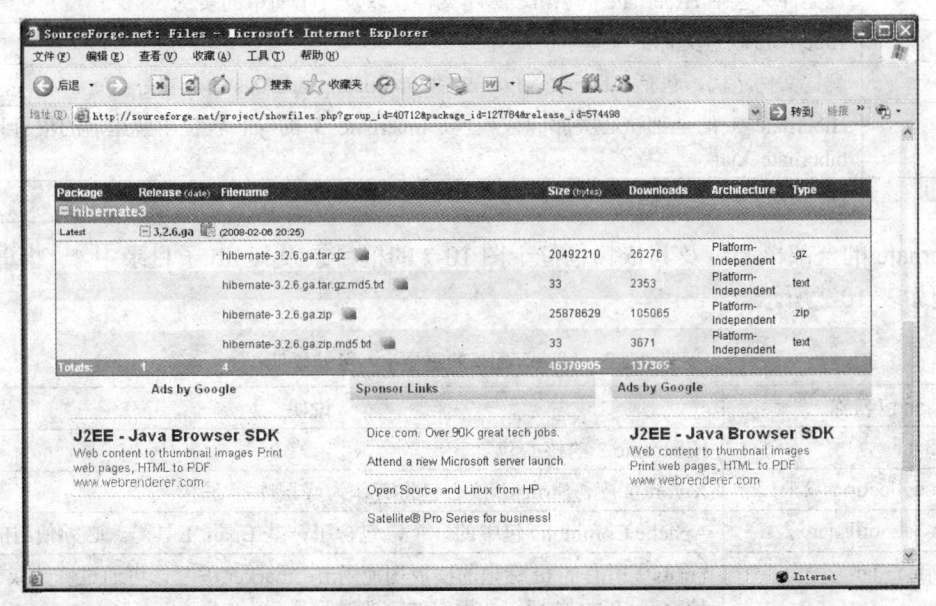

图 10-6 Hibernate 在 Sourceforge 上的下载界面

对于 Windows 用户，读者可以下载 hibernate-3.2.6.ga.zip 这个组件包，对于 Linux 等用户，可下载 hibernate-3.2.6.ga.tar.gz 这个下载包。

【提示】访问此页时，可能显示的界面会稍有不同，读者可自行下载最新的版本应用。

（2）安装 Hibernate 3。

下载完毕后得到一个 ZIP 压缩文件，解压缩即可得到 Hibernate 3 的所有相关资料，包括源码、jar 包等，解压后的目录如图 10-7 所示。

图 10-7　Hibernate 3 的目录结构

Hibernate 的 jar 包及其依赖包位于图 10-7 的根目录（hibernate3.jar）及其 lib 子目录中，并不是所有的 jar 包都是必须的，c3p0.jar 等包就是可选的，必须的 jar 包为：hibernate3.jar、commons-collections.jar、commons-beanutils.jar、commons-lang.jar、commons-logging.jar、cglib-2.1.3.jar、dom4j-1.6.1.jar 和 odmg.jar。

〖实例剖析与知识讲解〗

Hibernate 软件包中包括 jar 组件包、API 手册、示例代码等。图 10-7 中各文件夹的内容描述如表 10-1 所示。

表 10-1　Hibernate 3 压缩包中文件夹的内容

文件夹名称	文件夹内容
doc	该文件夹包括 Hibernate 的 API、参考文档，以及一个简单的实例
eg	Hibernate 映射文件的一些示例配置
etc	配置文件示例，包括 hibernate.cfg.xml 和 hibernate.properties 的配置等
lib	Hibernate 3 的全部核心类库和依赖包，hibernate 3 的 jar 包位于解压后的根目录中，即 hibernate3.jar
src	Hibernate 3 的源代码

Hibernate 的全部核心包及其依赖包位于图 10-7 的根目录及其 lib 子目录中，一些重要的 jar 包的说明如表 10-2 所示。

表 10-2　Hibernate 的重要 jar 包的说明

jar 包名称	说明
hibernate3.jar	Hibernate 3 的核心包
commons-collections-2.1.1.jar	Xwork 2 库，Struts 2 核心包将其作为底层库存在
commons-beanutils.jar	Apache Commons 包中的一个，包含了一些 Bean 工具类。必须使用的 jar 包
commons-lang.jar	Struts 2 所有的 ui 标记的模板均使用 freemarker 编写，可通过修改或重写模板使 struts 2 的 ui 标记按用户的需要进行显示
commons-logging-1.0.4.jar	Apache Commons 包中的一个，包含了日志功能，必须使用的 jar 包。这个包本身包含了一个 Simple Logger，但是功能很弱。在运行的时候它会先在 CLASSPATH 找 log4j，强烈建议使用 log4j，因为 log4j 性能很高，log 输出信息时间几乎等于 System.out，而处理一条 log 平均只需要 5μs。可以在 Hibernate 的 src 目录中找到 Hibernate 已经准备好了的 log4j 的配置文件，只需要到 Apache 网站去下载 log4j 就可以了。commons-logging.jar 也是必须的 jar 包

jar 包名称	说明
cglib-2.1.3.jar	CGLIB 库，Hibernate 用它来实现 PO 字节码的动态生成，非常核心的库，必须使用的 jar 包
dom4j-1.6.1.jar	dom4j 是一个 Java 的 XML API，类似于 jdom，用来读写 XML 文件。dom4j 是一个非常优秀的 Java XML API，具有性能优异、功能强大和极端易用的特点，看到越来越多的 Java 软件都在使用 dom4j 来读写 XML，特别值得一提的是连 Sun 的 JAXM 也在用 dom4j。这是必须使用的 jar 包，Hibernate 用它来读写配置文件
odmg.jar	ODMG 是一个 ORM 的规范，Hibernate 实现了 ODMG 规范，这是一个核心的库，必须使用的 jar 包

以上包是使用 Hibernate 必须的包，lib 包下的很多其他的包都是可选的，例如：

- c3p0.jar：C3P0 是一个数据库连接池，Hibernate 可以配置为使用 C3P0 连接池。如果准备用这个连接池，就需要这个 jar 包。
- proxool.jar：也是一个连接池，同上。
- commons-pool.jar, commons-dbcp.jar：DBCP 数据库连接池，Apache 的 Jakarta 组织开发的，Tomcat4 的连接池也是 DBCP。

【例 10-3】用 Hibernate 实现用户信息查询

〖实例需求〗

创建一个用户信息表，而后使用 Hibernate 完成用户信息的查询。

〖开发过程〗

第一步：创建数据库

首先需要创建一个数据库 test，并在该数据库中创建用户信息表 user，创建数据库和脚本的代码如下：

```
CREATE DATABASE 'test';
USE 'test';

CREATE TABLE 'user' (
  'id' int(11) NOT NULL auto_increment,
  'username' varchar(100) default NULL,
  'password' varchar(100) default NULL,
  PRIMARY KEY  ('id')
) ENGINE=InnoDB DEFAULT CHARSET=gb2312;

INSERT INTO 'user' ('id', 'username', 'password') VALUES (1,'amigo','123');
INSERT INTO 'user' ('id', 'username', 'password') VALUES (2,'xiexingxing','12345678');
```

第二步：创建 Hibernate 配置文件 Hibernate.cfg.xml

Hibernate 的配置文件可以是一个属性文件（hibernate.properties），也可以是一个 xml 文件

（Hibernate.cfg.xml），而采用 xml 方式配置比较常见。

读者可以复制图 10-7 中的 doc/tutorial/src 目录中的 Hibernate.cfg.xml 文件到工程的 src 目录中，稍加修改即可。

修改后的文件内容如下：

```xml
<?xml version='1.0' encoding='utf-8'?>
<!DOCTYPE hibernate-configuration PUBLIC
    "-//Hibernate/Hibernate Configuration DTD 3.0//EN"
    "http://hibernate.sourceforge.net/hibernate-configuration-3.0.dtd">
<hibernate-configuration>
    <session-factory>
        <!-- properties -->
        <property name="connection.url">jdbc:mysql://localhost:3306/test</property>
        <property name="connection.username">root</property>
        <property name="connection.password">root</property>
        <property name="dialect">org.hibernate.dialect.MySQL5Dialect</property>
        <property name="connection.driver_class">com.mysql.jdbc.Driver</property>

        <!-- mapping files -->
        <mapping resource="com/amigo/hibernate/model/User.hbm.xml"/>
    </session-factory>
</hibernate-configuration>
```

第三步：创建包：**amigo.hibernate.model**

在 src 源码目录中创建包：amigo.hibernate.model，操作步骤如图 10-8 所示。

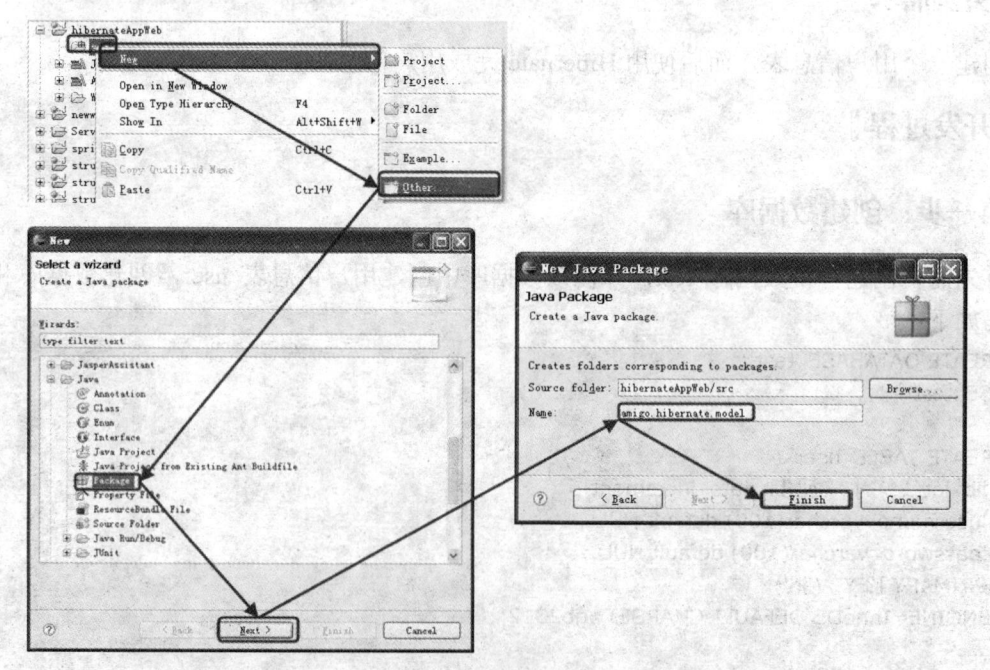

图 10-8　创建 amigo.hibernate.model 包

第四步：编写 Hibernate 映射文件 User.hbm.xml

Hibernate 之所以能够智能地判断实体类和数据表之间的对应关系，就是因为有 XML 映射文件。读者可以在工程 amigo.hibernate.model 包中创建 user 表的映射文件 User.hbm.xml。创建 User.hbm.xml 文件的操作步骤如图 10-9 所示。

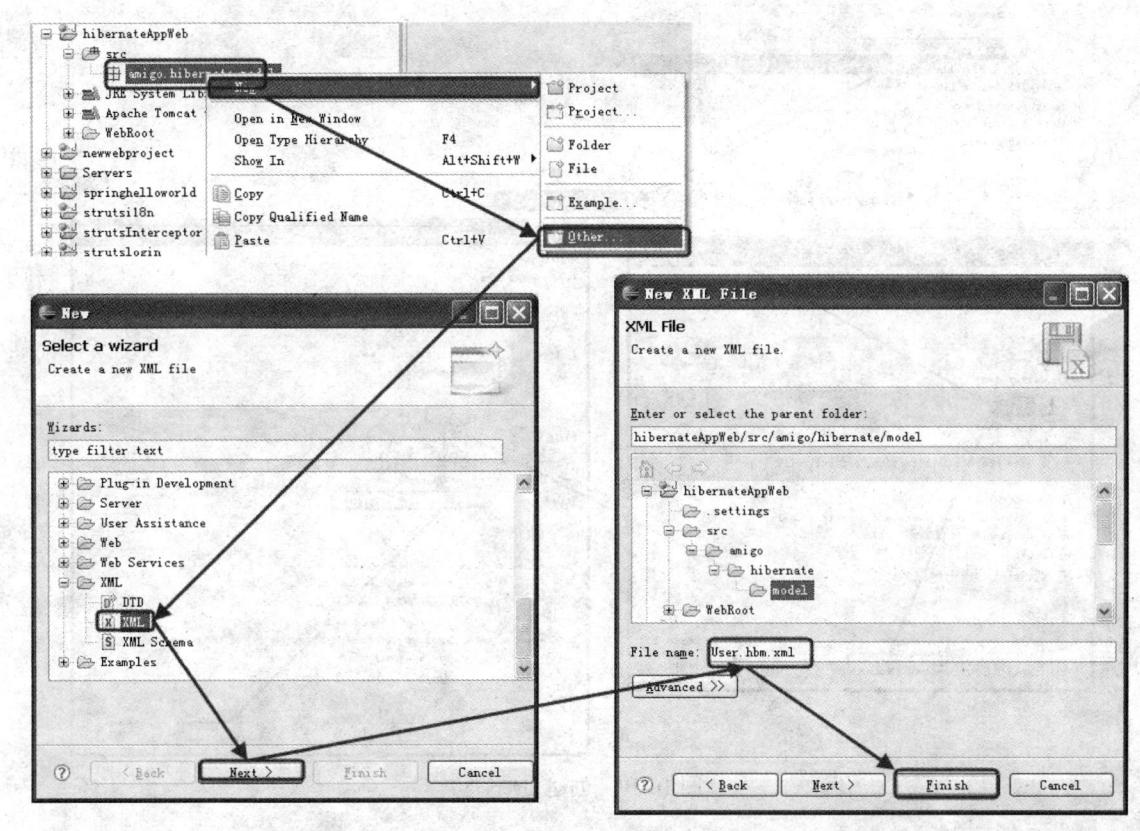

图 10-9 创建 User.hbm.xml 文件

User.hbm.xml 文件的内容如下所示：

```xml
<?xml version="1.0" encoding='UTF-8'?>
<!DOCTYPE hibernate-mapping PUBLIC
                "-//Hibernate/Hibernate Mapping DTD 3.0//EN"
                "http://hibernate.sourceforge.net/hibernate-mapping-3.0.dtd" >

<hibernate-mapping package="amigo.hibernate.model">
   <class name="User" table="user">
      <id name="id" column="id" type="java.lang.Integer">
         <generator class="native"/>
      </id>

      <property name="username" column="username" type="java.lang.String"  not-null="true" />
      <property name="password" column="password" type="java.lang.String"  not-null="true" />
   </class>
</hibernate-mapping>
```

第五步：编写 POJO 文件 User.java

每一个对应的表都有一个映射文件（.hbm.xml 文件）和一个 POJO 文件，User.java 为使用

Hibernate 进行数据的增、删、改和查操作的对象。读者可在 amigo.hibernate.model 包下创建 User.java 类，创建该类的操作步骤图如图 10-10 所示。

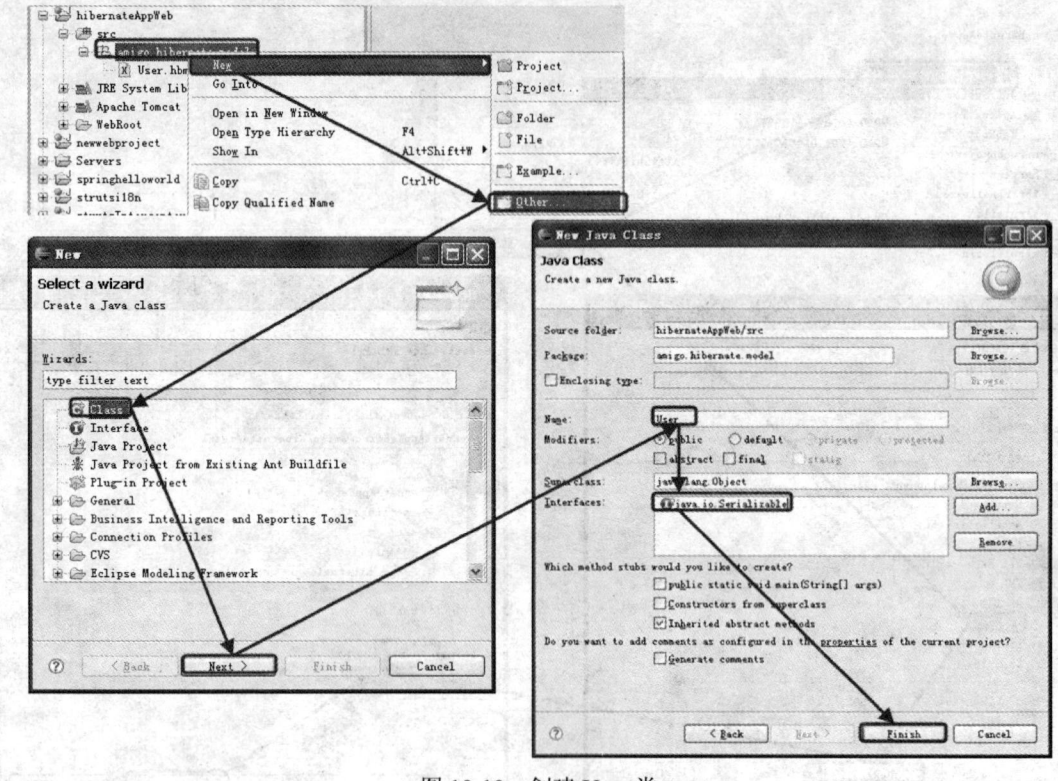

图 10-10　创建 User 类

该类的代码如下：

```java
package amigo.hibernate.model;

import java.io.Serializable;

/**
 * 用户的 pojo 对象.
 */
public class User implements Serializable {
    private static final long serialVersionUID = 1L;

    /** 用户 id. */
    private Integer id;

    /** 用户名 */
    private String username;

    /** 密码. */
    private String password;

    // 省略各属性的 getter/setter 方法
}
```

第六步：编写 Hibernate 工具类 HibernateUtil.java

类 HibernateUtil.java 文件用于获得当前的 Session，该类包括获得当前的 session 的方法和获得 SessionFactory 的方法。读者可在 amigo.hibernate 包中创建 HibernateUtil 类，操作步骤如图 10-11 所示。

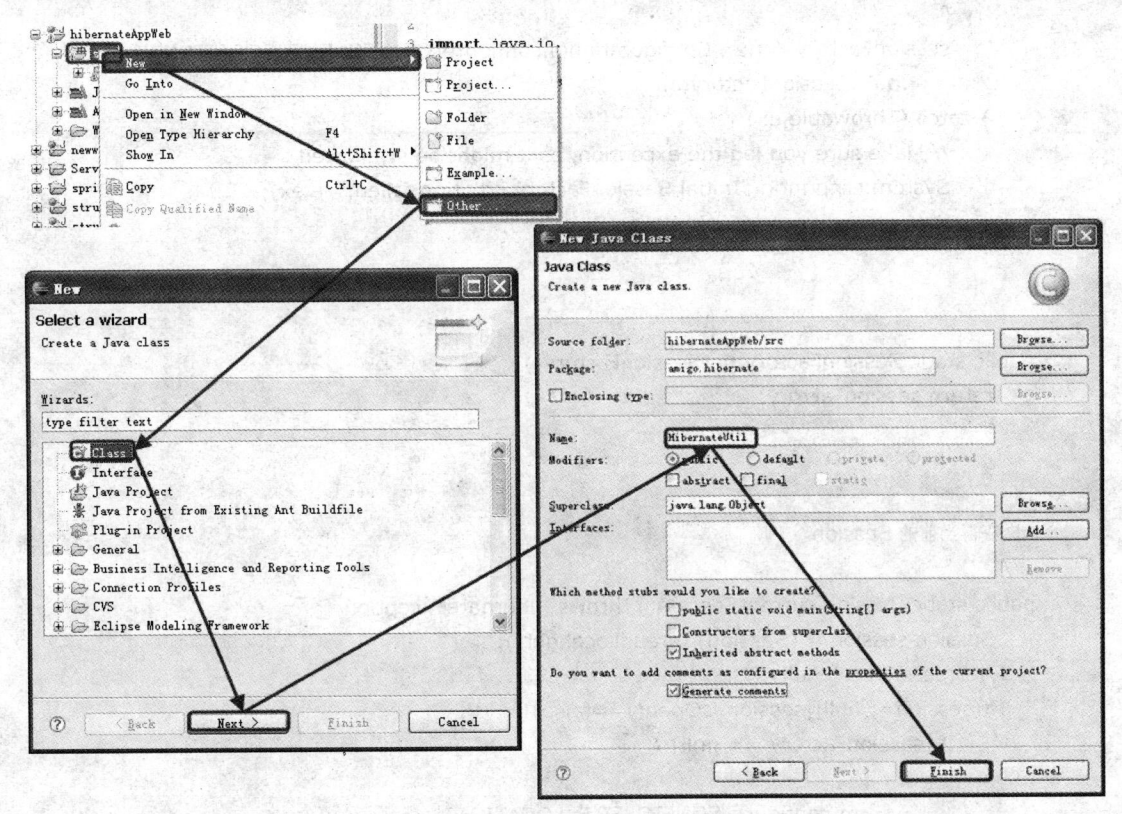

图 10-11 创建 HibernateUtil 类

该类的代码如下：

```java
package amigo.hibernate;

import org.hibernate.HibernateException;
import org.hibernate.Session;
import org.hibernate.SessionFactory;
import org.hibernate.cfg.Configuration;

/**
 * Hibernate 的工具类.
 */
public class HibernateUtil {
    private static SessionFactory sessionFactory;

    /** 持有一个单态的 Session 实例. */
    private static final ThreadLocal threadLocal = new ThreadLocal();
```

```java
/** 持有一个单态的 configuration 实例. */
private static final Configuration cfg = new Configuration();

private static String CONFIG_FILE_LOCATION = "/hibernate.cfg.xml";

static {
    try {
        sessionFactory = new Configuration().configure(CONFIG_FILE_LOCATION)
            .buildSessionFactory();
    } catch (Throwable ex) {
        // Make sure you log the exception, as it might be swallowed
        System.err.println("Initial SessionFactory creation failed." + ex);
        throw new ExceptionInInitializerError(ex);
    }
}

public static SessionFactory getSessionFactory() {
    return sessionFactory;
}

/**
 * 获得当前的 Session 实例.
 */
public static Session currentSession() throws HibernateException {
    Session session = (Session) threadLocal.get();
    //if (session == null) {
    if(session==null||session.isOpen()==false){
        if (sessionFactory == null) {
            try {
                cfg.configure(CONFIG_FILE_LOCATION);
                sessionFactory = cfg.buildSessionFactory();
            }
            catch (Exception e) {
                System.err.println("%%%% Error Creating SessionFactory %%%%"
                    + e.getMessage());
            }
        }
        session = sessionFactory.openSession();
        threadLocal.set(session);
    }

    return session;
}
```

第七步：编写测试类：HibernateTest.java

在 amigo.hibernate 包中创建测试类：HibernateTest.java，操作步骤如图 10-12 所示。

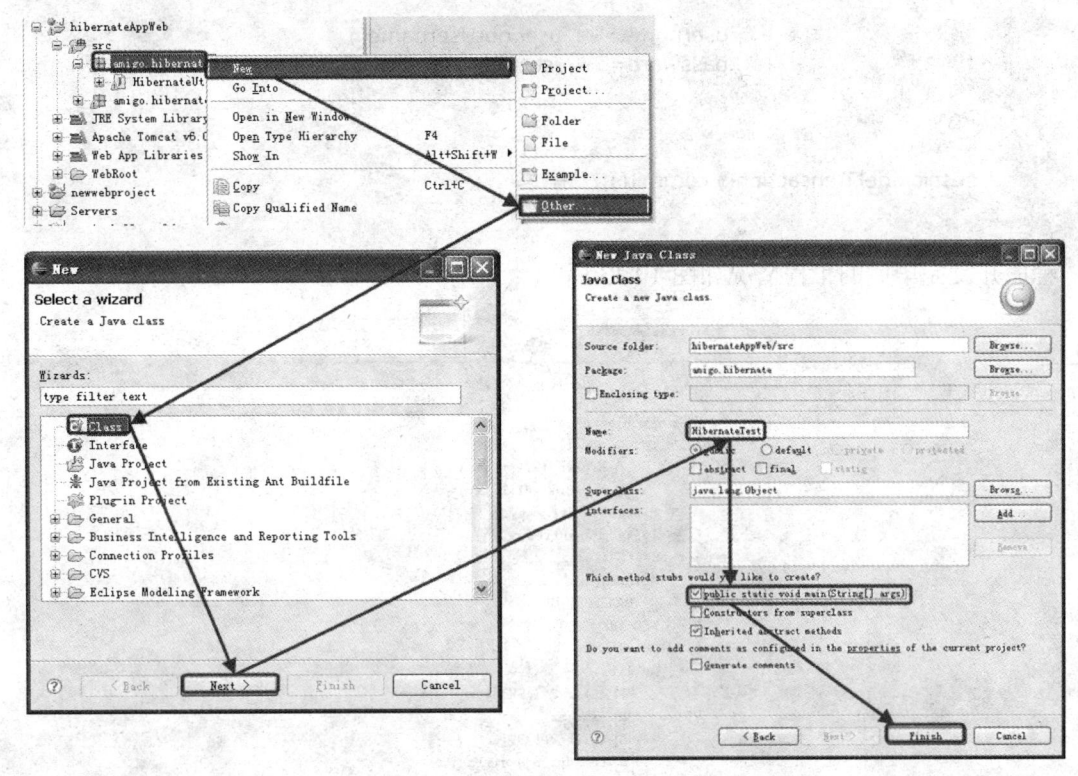

图 10-12　创建 HibernateTest 类

该类的代码如下所示：

```java
package amigo.hibernate;

import java.util.List;

import org.hibernate.Query;
import org.hibernate.Session;

import amigo.hibernate.model.User;

/**
 * Hibernate 简要测试,
 * 获得用户信息表（user）中的用户信息，并打印出来
 */
public class HibernateTest {
    public static void main(String[] args) throws Exception {
        Session session = HibernateUtil.currentSession();
        session.beginTransaction();
        // 创建查询对象
        Query query = session.createQuery("from User");
        // 获得用户列表
        List<User> userList = query.list();

        User user = null;
        if (userList != null && userList.size() > 0) {
            for (int i = 0; i < userList.size(); i++) {
                user = (User) userList.get(i);
                System.out.println("i=" + i
                        + ", id=" + user.getId()
```

```
                   + ", username=" + user.getUsername()
                   + ", password=" + user.getPassword());
        }
    }
    session.getTransaction().commit();// 提交
   }
}
```

程序开发完毕后的工程情况如图 10-13 所示。

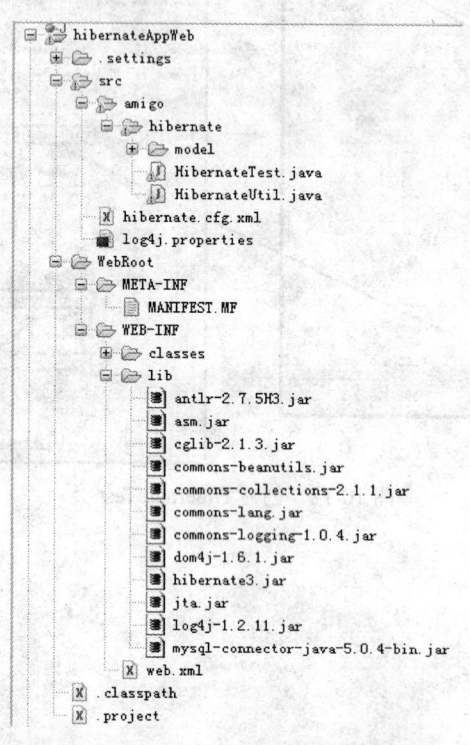

图 10-13 开发完毕后的工程情况

在 HibernateTest.java 文件中单击鼠标右键，选择 Run As→Java Application 命令，运行该文件的 main 方法，运行结果如图 10-14 所示。

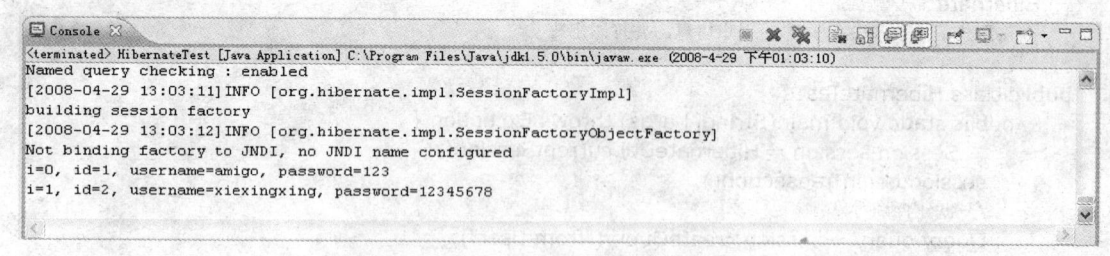

图 10-14 查询用户列表运行结果

从图 10-14 中可以看出，通过 Hibernate 很简便地查询出了 user 表初始化的两条数据。

〖实例剖析与知识讲解〗

本实例通过一个简单的 Hibernate 查询数据的实例，讲解了 Hibernate 的核心配置文件 Hibernate.cfg.xml 的基本配置，并讲解了映射文件（.hbm.xml）的配置，以及 Hibernate 的查询

API 的使用。

本例中的 hibernate.cfg.xml 配置的数据库连接是 MySQL 的 JDBC 连接，读者还可以配置其他各种数据库的连接，以及配置 C3P0 和 DBCP 等数据源的连接。

Hibernate 是一种很常用的 ORM（Object Relation Mapping）的解决方案，ORM 产品都是对 JDBC 的对象持久层封装。Hibernate 对 JDBC 进行了轻量级的对象封装，使得 Java 程序员能很简便地使用面向对象编程思想来对数据库进行操作。

Hibernate 提供了 Java 类到数据表之间的映射，并且相对于 JDBC，它大大减少了操作数据库的工作量。

下面介绍一下重要的几个概念。

何谓持久层？

"持久"简单来讲就是把数据保存到可掉电式存储设备中供之后使用，特别是企业应用中，数据持久化也就意味着将内存中的数据保存到硬盘上加以"固化"，持久化的过程大多通过关系型数据库完成。

何谓 ORM（Object Relation Mapping）？

由于 J2EE 持久化标准对于处理对象与关系的尴尬，而且持久化问题的解决方案是由关系—对象映射（ORM）来解决的，它可以透明地持久化普通 Java 对象（POJO）。因此，ORM 框架得以产生。1990 年，一些商业的 ORM 工具（例如 TopLink）出现了，而后，涌现出很多 ORM 工具，例如 JDO 和 Hibernate 等。

小结

搭建 Hibernate 的开发环境需要两个步骤：第一步是建立起一个动态工程，第二步是要在工程中加入所要用到的 jar 组件包，实现一个简单的 Hibernate 查询所需要的 jar 包包括：antlr-2.7.6.jar、asm.jar、cglib-2.1.3.jar、commons-collections-2.1.1.jar、commons-logging-1.0.4.jar、dom4j-1.6.1.jar、hibernate3.jar、jta.jar、log4j-1.2.11.jar 和 mysql-connector-java-5.0.4-bin.jar。

要实现用户信息的查询功能，需要 5 个步骤，分别为：

1）编写 Hibernate 的核心配置文件 hibernate.cfg.xml，在该文件中配置数据库连接等信息。

2）编写 user 表的映射文件 User.hbm.xml 文件及其对应的 POJO 文件 User.java。

3）编写 Hibernate 的工具类 HibernateUtil.java 文件，该类中包括了获得 Session 等的方法。

4）编写实现 Hibernate 查询的测试类 HibernateTest.java 文件。

5）通过使用 Hibernate，使得 Java 开发人员不必使用烦琐的 SQL 语句来完成数据库的操作，而只需要简便地使用面向对象编程思想来对数据库进行操作，减轻了开发人员的工作。

第 11 章 Hibernate 配置文件

【本章导读语】

使用 Hibernate 时，需要配置不少配置文件，例如 hibernate.cfg.xml 文件，该文件用于设置数据库的基本信息、数据库的 URL、用户名和密码、驱动等信息。另外 Hibernate 的映射文件.hbm.xml 也有很多需要注意的地方，一对一、一对多、多对多这三种关联关系是 Hibernate 的重点，需要读者着重理解。

虽然这些配置文件都可以通过 IDE（例如 MyEclipse、JBuilder 等）自动生成，但是学习其基本用法还是很有必要的。

【例 11-1】配置 hibernate.cfg.xml

〖实例需求〗

Hibernate 运行时需要获取一些数据库的基本信息，包括数据库 URL、数据库用户名、数据库用户密码、数据库 JDBC 驱动类和数据库 dialect 等。

Hibernate 支持以 XML 格式和 properties 文件两种方式配置数据库的基本信息。本实例讲解如何对 Hibernate 默认的 XML 格式配置文件 hibernate.cfg.xml 进行配置。并对各种常用的数据库的驱动类进行说明。

〖开发过程〗

第一步：建立工程

读者可在 Eclipse 中按照前一章的方式建立一个名为 hibernateConfigure 的 Java 工程，接着将 hibernate 的相关 jar 包、常用数据库驱动的 jar 包等复制到 hibernateConfigure 工程的 lib 目录中，并将这些 jar 包加入到工程的 CLASSPATH 路径中。jar 包清单如下所示：

- c3p0-0.9.0.4.jar：c3p0 连接池包。
- cglib-2.1.3.jar。
- commons-beanutils.jar。
- commons-collections-2.1.1.jar。
- commons-lang.jar。
- commons-logging-1.0.4.jar。
- dom4j-1.6.1.jar。
- hibernate3.jar。
- jtds-1.2.jar：SQL Server 的数据库驱动包。

- log4j-1.2.11.jar：log4j 日志包。
- mysql-connector-java-5.0.4-bin.jar：MySQL 的数据库驱动包。
- ojdbc14.jar：Oracle 的数据库驱动包。

创建完成后工程的目录结构如图 11-1 所示。

图 11-1　工程的目录结构

第二步：hibernate.cfg.xml 配置格式

下面讲述一下 hibernate.cfg.xml 配置连接数据库的具体格式及其说明：

```
<?xml version="1.0" encoding="UTF-8"?>
<!--指定该文件的官方 dtd-->
<!DOCTYPE hibernate-configuration PUBLIC "-//Hibernate/Hibernate Configuration DTD 3.0//EN"
"http://hibernate.sourceforge.net/hibernate-configuration-3.0.dtd" >
<hibernate-configuration>
    <session-factory>
    <!--是否在后台打印 sql 语句，默认为 false -->
    <property name="show_sql">值为 true 或 false</property>
    <!--指定 SQL 的本地方言，根据连接的数据库确定-->
    <property name="dialect">sql 方言</property>
    <!--指定 jdbc 驱动程式 -->
    <property name="connection.driver_class">驱动类</property>
    <!--指定 jdbc url -->
    <property name="connection.url">jdbc 的 url</property>
    <!--指定数据库用户名 -->
    <property name="connection.username">数据库用户名</property>
    <!-- 指定数据库密码 -->
    <property name="connection.password">数据库密码</property>
    <!-- C3P0 连接池设定 -->
    <!--设定最小连接数-->
    <property name="c3p0.min_size">最小连接数</property>
    <!--设定最大连接数-->
    <property name="c3p0.max_size">最大连接数</property>
    <!--设定延迟所允许的时间（ms）-->
    <property name="c3p0.timeout">延迟所允许的时间</property>
    <!--设定缓存所允许的最大连接数-->
```

```xml
        <property name="c3p0.max_statements">缓存所允许的最大连接数</property>
        <!--设定每隔多少比笔资料送入资料库，清除缓存（定期清除缓存，减小压力） -->
    <property name="hibernate.jdbc.batch_size">多少比</property>
        <!-- 设定事务管理的工厂类 -->
        <property name="hibernate.transaction.factiory_class">事务管理的工厂类</property>
        <!--指定 0 到多个 hbm.xml 映射文件-->
        <mapping resource="映射文件全路径"/>
    </session-factory>
</hibernate-configuration>
```

其中重要属性的说明如下：

- show_sql：是否在后台打印 SQL，默认为不打印，如果需要打印则设置为 true，如果是在程序的调试阶段，可以将其设置为 true。但是如果程序已经到了产品化阶段，为了提高程序的效率，建议还是设置为 false。
- dialect：SQL 的本地方言，根据连接的数据库确定。
- connection.driver_class：连接数据库所要用到的驱动程序。
- connection.url：数据库连接地址。
- connection.username：数据库用户名。
- connection.password：数据库密码。
- connection.pool_size：连接池大小。
- current_session_context_class：确定以何种方式产生 Session，如 thread 或 jta。
- cache.provider_class：hibernate 对缓存的支持。
- mapping resource：对象配置所在地址。

第三步：几种常用数据库的 hibernate.cfg.xml 配置

（1）MySQL。

若系统所用的数据库为 MySQL 时，需要将 MySQL 的驱动类的 jar 包加入到工程的 CLASSPATH 路径中。MySQL 驱动的下载地址为：http://mysql.ntu.edu.tw/Downloads/Connector-J/

驱动类为：com.mysql.jdbc.Driver。若需要连接 192.168.1.124 机器的 testhibernate 数据库，数据库用户名和密码都为 root，并且需要将 amigo/hibernate 目录中的 User.hbm.xml 和 Dept.hbm.xml 两个映射文件加入到 hibernate.cfg.xml 文件中，配置示例如下所示：

```xml
<?xml version='1.0' encoding='UTF-8'?>
<!DOCTYPE hibernate-configuration PUBLIC
        "-//Hibernate/Hibernate Configuration DTD 3.0//EN"
        "http://hibernate.sourceforge.net/hibernate-configuration-3.0.dtd">
<hibernate-configuration>
    <session-factory>
        <!-- 在后台打印 sql 语句 -->
        <property name="show_sql">true</property>
        <!-- 指定 sql 的本地方言，根据连接的数据库确定-->
        <property name="dialect">org.hibernate.dialect.MySQLDialect</property>
        <!-- 指定 jdbc url,MySql 的默认端口为 3306，192.168.1.124 为需要连接的主机，testhibernate 为连接的数据库 -->
        <property name="connection.url">jdbc:mysql://192.168.1.124:3306/testhibernate</property>
        <!-- 数据库的用户名 -->
```

```xml
            <property name="connection.username">root</property>
            <!-- 数据库的密码 -->
            <property name="connection.password">root</property>
            <!-- 设定数据库的驱动类，MySql 的驱动 jar 包为 mysql-connector-java-5.0.4-bin.jar，驱动类为 com.mysql.jdbc.Driver -->
            <property name="connection.driver_class">com.mysql.jdbc.Driver</property>
            <!-- 设定事务管理的工厂类 -->
            <property name="transaction.factory_class">org.hibernate.transaction.JDBCTransactionFactory</property>

            <!--指定 0 到多个 hbm.xml 映射文件-->
            <mapping resource="amigo/hibernate/User.hbm.xml" />
            <mapping resource="amigo/hibernate/Dept.hbm.xml" />
        </session-factory>
    </hibernate-configuration>
```

（2）SQLServer。

若系统所用的数据库为 SQLServer 时，需要将 SQLServer 的驱动类 jar 包 jtds-1.2.jar 加入到工程的 CLASSPATH 路径中。SQLServer 驱动 jar 包的下载地址为：

http://sourceforge.net/project/showfiles.php?group_id=33291&package_id=25350&release_id=369359

驱动类为：net.sourceforge.jtds.jdbc.Driver。若需要连接 192.168.1.124 机器的 testhibernate 数据库，数据库用户名和密码都为 sa，并且需要将 amigo/hibernate 目录中的 User.hbm.xml 和 Dept.hbm.xml 两个映射文件加入到 hibernate.cfg.xml 文件中，配置示例如下所示：

```xml
<?xml version='1.0' encoding='UTF-8'?>
<!DOCTYPE hibernate-configuration PUBLIC
        "-//Hibernate/Hibernate Configuration DTD 3.0//EN"
        "http://hibernate.sourceforge.net/hibernate-configuration-3.0.dtd">
<hibernate-configuration>
    <session-factory>
        <!-- 在后台打印 sql 语句 -->
        <property name="show_sql">true</property>
        <!-- 指定 sql 的本地方言，根据连接的数据库确定-->
        <property name="dialect">org.hibernate.dialect.SQLServerDialect</property>
        <!-- 指定 jdbc url，SqlServer 的默认端口为 1433，192.168.1.124 为需要连接的主机，testhibernate 为连接的数据库 -->
        <property name="connection.url">jdbc:jtds:sqlserver://localhost:1433/testhibernate</property>
        <!-- 数据库的用户名 -->
        <property name="connection.username">sa</property>
        <!-- 数据库的密码 -->
        <property name="connection.password">sa</property>
        <!-- 设定数据库的驱动类，SqlServer 的驱动 jar 包为 jtds-1.2.jar，驱动类为 net.sourceforge.jtds.jdbc.Driver -->
        <property name="connection.driver_class">net.sourceforge.jtds.jdbc.Driver</property>
        <!-- 设定 JDBC 连接池的大小(使用内置的连接池) -->
        <property name="connection.pool_size">1</property>
        <!-- 确定以何种方式产生 Session,可为 jdbc 和 jta -->
        <property name="current_session_context_class">thread</property>
        <!-- 不使用缓存 -->
        <property name="cache.provider_class">org.hibernate.cache.NoCacheProvider</property>
```

```xml
        <!--指定 0 到多个 hbm.xml 映射文件-->
        <mapping resource="amigo/hibernate/User.hbm.xml" />
        <mapping resource="amigo/hibernate/Dept.hbm.xml" />
    </session-factory>
</hibernate-configuration>
```

（3）Oracle。

若系统所用的数据库为 Oracle10g 时，需要将 Oracle 的驱动类的 jar 包 ojdbc14.jar 加入到工程的 CLASSPATH 路径中。Oracle 的驱动类为：oracle.jdbc.driver.OracleDriver。若需要连接 192.168.1.124 机器的 testhibernate 数据库，数据库用户名和密码都为 test，并且需要将 amigo/hibernate 目录中的 User.hbm.xml 和 Dept.hbm.xml 两个映射文件加入到 hibernate.cfg.xml 文件中，配置示例如下所示：

```xml
<?xml version='1.0' encoding='UTF-8'?>
<!DOCTYPE hibernate-configuration PUBLIC
    "-//Hibernate/Hibernate Configuration DTD 3.0//EN"
    "http://hibernate.sourceforge.net/hibernate-configuration-3.0.dtd">
<hibernate-configuration>
    <session-factory>
        <!-- 在后台打印 sql 语句 -->
        <property name="show_sql">true</property>
        <!-- 指定 sql 的本地方言，根据连接的数据库确定-->
        <property name="dialect">org.hibernate.dialect.Oracle10gDialect</property>
        <!-- 指定 jdbc url，Oracle 的默认端口为 1521，192.168.1.124 为需要连接的主机，testhibernate 为连接的数据库 -->
        <property name="connection.url">jdbc:oracle:thin:@192.168.1.124:1521:testhibernate</property>
        <!-- 数据库的用户名 -->
        <property name="connection.username">test</property>
        <!-- 数据库的密码 -->
        <property name="connection.password">test</property>
        <!-- 设定数据库的驱动类，Oracle 的驱动 jar 包为 ojdbc14.jar，驱动类为 oracle.jdbc.driver.OracleDriver -->
        <property name="connection.driver_class">oracle.jdbc.driver.OracleDriver</property>
        <!-- 设定 JDBC 连接池的大小(使用内置的连接池) -->
        <property name="connection.pool_size">1</property>
        <!-- 确定以何种方式产生 Session,可为 jdbc 和 jta -->
        <property name="current_session_context_class">thread</property>
        <!-- 不使用缓存 -->
        <property name="cache.provider_class">org.hibernate.cache.NoCacheProvider</property>

        <!--指定 0 到多个 hbm.xml 映射文件-->
        <mapping resource="amigo/hibernate/User.hbm.xml" />
        <mapping resource="amigo/hibernate/Dept.hbm.xml" />
    </session-factory>
</hibernate-configuration>
```

第四步：hibernate.cfg.xml **连接池配置**

在 hibernate.cfg.xml 中可使用 connection.datasource 属性来配置 JNDI 连接池，还可以在配置文件中配置 c3p0 和 dpcp 连接池，接下来讲述一下这三者的配置。

第 11 章 Hibernate 配置文件

（1）JNDI 连接池。

若需要在 hibernate.cfg.xml 文件中配置外置的连接池，例如在 Tomcat 容器中配置连接池时，只需要使用 connection.datasource 指定数据源的名称即可。例如，在 Tomcat 容器中指定了名为 testhibernate 的 MySQL 数据源，则只需要在 hibernate.cfg.xml 中进行如下类似的设置即可取得数据库连接。

```xml
<?xml version='1.0' encoding='UTF-8'?>
<!DOCTYPE hibernate-configuration PUBLIC
        "-//Hibernate/Hibernate Configuration DTD 3.0//EN"
        "http://hibernate.sourceforge.net/hibernate-configuration-3.0.dtd">
<hibernate-configuration>
    <session-factory>
      <!-- 在后台打印 SQL 语句 -->
      <property name="show_sql">true</property>
      <!-- 指定 SQL 的本地方言，根据连接的数据库确定-->
      <property name="dialect">org.hibernate.dialect.MySQLDialect</property>
      <!-- 一次读的数据库记录数 -->
         <property name="jdbc.fetch_size">50</property>
         <!-- 设定对数据库进行批量删除 -->
      <property name="jdbc.batch_size">30</property>
         <!-- 配置 JNDI 数据源，其中 jdbc/testhibernate 为 JDNI 数据源的名称 -->
         <property name="connection.datasource">java:comp/env/jdbc/testhibernate</property>
         <!-- Hibernate 的连接加载类 -->
         <property name="connection.provider_class">org.hibernate.connection.DatasourceConnectionProvider</property>

         <!--指定 0 到多个 hbm.xml 映射文件-->
         <mapping resource="amigo/hibernate/User.hbm.xml" />
         <mapping resource="amigo/hibernate/Dept.hbm.xml" />
    </session-factory>
</hibernate-configuration>
```

（2）C3P0 连接池。

C3P0 连接池是 Hibernate 推荐使用的连接池，若需要使用该连接池时，需要将 C3P0 的 jar 包加入到 CLASSPATH 中。若需要配置一个 C3P0 连接池，连接的主机为 192.168.1.124，数据库的类型为 MySQL，数据库的名称为 testhibernate，数据库用户名和密码都为 root，且需要将 User.hbm.xml 和 Dept.hbm.xml 加入到配置中，则配置信息如下所示：

```xml
<?xml version='1.0' encoding='UTF-8'?>
<!DOCTYPE hibernate-configuration PUBLIC
        "-//Hibernate/Hibernate Configuration DTD 3.0//EN"
        "http://hibernate.sourceforge.net/hibernate-configuration-3.0.dtd">
<hibernate-configuration>
    <session-factory>
        <!-- 在后台打印 SQL 语句 -->
        <property name="show_sql">true</property>
        <!-- SQL 方言，设定的是 MySQL 方言 -->
        <property name="dialect">org.hibernate.dialect.MySQLDialect</property>
        <!--MySQL 驱动程序，sqlserver 和 Oracle 驱动类的配置请参考前面的内容 -->
        <property name="connection.driver_class">com.mysql.jdbc.Driver</property>
        <!-- JDBC URL -->
        <property name="connection.url">jdbc:mysql://192.168.1.124:3306/testhibernate</property>
```

```xml
        <!-- 数据库用户名 -->
        <property name="connection.username">root</property>
        <!-- 数据库密码 -->
        <property name="connection.password">root</property>
        <!-- 设定最小连接数-->
        <property name="c3p0.min_size">5</property>
        <!-- 设定最大连接数-->
        <property name="c3p0.max_size">20</property>
        <!-- 设定延迟所允许的时间（ms）-->
        <property name="c3p0.timeout">1800</property>
        <!-- 设定缓存所允许的最大连接数-->
        <property name="c3p0.max_statements">50</property>

        <!--指定 0 到多个 hbm.xml 映射文件-->
        <mapping resource="amigo/hibernate/User.hbm.xml" />
        <mapping resource="amigo/hibernate/Dept.hbm.xml" />
    </session-factory>
</hibernate-configuration>
```

（3）dpcp 连接池。

在 Hibernate 3.0 中，已经不再支持 dbcp 了。Hibernate 的作者在 hibernate.org 中明确指出在实践中发现 dbcp 有 BUG，在某些情况下会产生很多空连接不能释放，所以抛弃了对 dbcp 的支持。

若需要使用 dbcp，开发人员还需要将 commons-pool-1.2.jar 和 commons-dbcp-1.2.1.jar 两个 jar 包加入到 classpath 中。dbcp 与 C3P0 一样，都是由 hibernate 建立连接的。

下面看一个 Hibernate 2.0 中 dbcp 连接池的配置实例，该实例连接的是 192.168.1.124 主机的 MySQL，数据库为 testhibernate，数据库的用户名和密码都为 root，并指定 User.hbm.xml 和 Dept.hbm.xml 这两个文件为 Hibernate 的配置文件，实例配置如下所示：

```xml
<?xml version='1.0' encoding='UTF-8'?>
<!DOCTYPE hibernate-configuration PUBLIC
        "-//Hibernate/Hibernate Configuration DTD 2.0//EN"
        "http://hibernate.sourceforge.net/hibernate-configuration-2.0.dtd">
<hibernate-configuration>
    <session-factory>
        <!-- 在后台打印 SQL 语句 -->
        <property name="show_sql">true</property>
        <!-- SQL 方言，设定的是 MySQL 方言 -->
        <property name="dialect">net.sf.hibernate.dialect.MySQLDialect</property>
        <!-- 指定驱动类，本配置实例 MySql，SqlServer 和 Oracle 的配置请参考前续内容 -->
        <property name="connection.driver_class">com.mysql.jdbc.Driver</property>
        <!-- JDBC URL -->
        <property name="connection.url">jdbc:mysql://192.168.1.124:3306/testhibernate</property>
        <!-- 数据库用户名 -->
        <property name="connection.username">root</property>
        <!-- 数据库密码-->
        <property name="connection.password">root</property>
        <!-- 设定 dbcp 数据源的最大连接数 -->
        <property name="dbcp.maxActive">50</property>
        <property name="dbcp.whenExhaustedAction">1</property>
        <!-- 设定 dbcp 数据源的最大等待数 -->
```

```xml
            <property name="dbcp.maxWait">500</property>
            <!-- 设定 dbcp 数据源的最大闲置数 -->
            <property name="dbcp.maxIdle">10</property>

            <!--指定 0 到多个 hbm.xml 映射文件-->
            <mapping resource="amigo/hibernate/User.hbm.xml" />
            <mapping resource="amigo/hibernate/Dept.hbm.xml" />
    </session-factory>
</hibernate-configuration>
```

【例 11-2】.hbm.xml 文件基本配置

〖实例需求〗

Hibernate 采用 XML 格式的文件来指定对象到关系数据库表之间的映射，在系统运行的时候，Hibernate 会根据这些配置来生成对应的 SQL 语句。本实例首先详细讲解映射文件.hbm.xml 的文档类型定义（DTD），接着通过一个用户信息表（tbl_user）和部门信息表（tbl_dept）的.hbm.xml 映射文件的配置来详细描述.hbm.xml 的基本配置。

〖开发过程〗

第一步：映射文件的文档类型定义（DTD）

映射文件的文档类型定义（DTD）可参考 hibernate\src\org\hibernate 目录中的 hibernate-mapping-3.0.dtd 文件。

为了使读者清楚地理解 hibernate-mapping-3.0.dtd 文件，首先讲述一下 DTD 文件中特殊符号的使用说明，如表 11-1 所示。

表 11-1 DTD 文件特殊符号说明

符号	说明
无符号	在子元素在父元素内必须存在且只能存在一次
+	在子元素在父元素内必须存在，但是可能存在一次或多次
*	在子元素在父元素内可以存在 0 到多次
?	在子元素在父元素内可以存在 0 到 1 次

（1）hibernate-mapping 根元素。

映射文件的根元素为 hibernate-mapping，在 DTD 文件中的定义如下所示：

```
<!ELEMENT hibernate-mapping (
    meta*,
    typedef*,
    import*,
    (class|subclass|joined-subclass|union-subclass)*,
    resultset*,
    (query|sql-query)*,
    filter-def*,
    database-object*
```

```
    )>
    <!ATTLIST hibernate-mapping schema CDATA #IMPLIED>
<!-- default: none -->
        <!ATTLIST hibernate-mapping catalog CDATA #IMPLIED>
<!-- default: none -->
        <!ATTLIST hibernate-mapping default-cascade CDATA "none">
        <!ATTLIST hibernate-mapping default-access CDATA "property">
        <!ATTLIST hibernate-mapping default-lazy (true|false) "true">
        <!ATTLIST hibernate-mapping auto-import (true|false) "true">
        <!ATTLIST hibernate-mapping package CDATA #IMPLIED>
<!-- default: none -->
```

根元素中可存在0到多个meta、typedef、import等元素。hibernate-mapping具有如下属性：

- catalog。
- default-cascade：设置默认的层叠样式。
- default-access。
- default-lazy：设定默认的延迟加载方式。
- auto-import。
- package：该属性用于设置包的类名，在默认情况下，hibernate-mapping的子元素class需要提供完整的类名，当有多个class文件或class中包含了很多关联映射时，这种方式很烦琐。若设定了hibernate-mapping的package的值，则将简化一部分工作。

（2）class元素。

hibernate-mapping根元素可以有0到多个class子元素，class在DTD文件中的定义如下所示：

```
<!ELEMENT class (
    meta*,
    subselect?,
    cache?,
    synchronize*,
    comment?,
    tuplizer*,
    (id|composite-id),
    discriminator?,
    natural-id?,
    (version|timestamp)?,
    (property|many-to-one|one-to-one|component|dynamic-component|properties|any|map|set|list|bag|idbag|array|primitive-array)*,
    ((join*,subclass*)|joined-subclass*|union-subclass*),
    loader?,sql-insert?,sql-update?,sql-delete?,
    filter*,
    resultset*,
    (query|sql-query)*
)>
        <!ATTLIST class entity-name CDATA #IMPLIED>
        <!ATTLIST class name CDATA #IMPLIED>
 <!-- this is the class name -->
        <!ATTLIST class proxy CDATA #IMPLIED>
<!-- default: no proxy interface -->
        <!ATTLIST class lazy (true|false) #IMPLIED>
        <!ATTLIST class table CDATA #IMPLIED>
<!-- default: unqualified classname -->
```

```
        <!ATTLIST class schema CDATA #IMPLIED>
<!-- default: none -->
        <!ATTLIST class catalog CDATA #IMPLIED>
<!-- default: none -->
        <!ATTLIST class subselect CDATA #IMPLIED>
        <!ATTLIST class discriminator-value CDATA #IMPLIED>
<!-- default: unqualified class name | none -->
        <!ATTLIST class mutable (true|false) "true">
        <!ATTLIST class abstract (true|false) #IMPLIED>
        <!ATTLIST class polymorphism (implicit|explicit) "implicit">
        <!ATTLIST class where CDATA #IMPLIED>
<!-- default: none -->
        <!ATTLIST class persister CDATA #IMPLIED>
        <!ATTLIST class dynamic-update (true|false) "false">
        <!ATTLIST class dynamic-insert (true|false) "false">
        <!ATTLIST class batch-size CDATA #IMPLIED>
        <!ATTLIST class select-before-update (true|false) "false">
        <!ATTLIST class optimistic-lock (none|version|dirty|all) "version">
        <!ATTLIST class check CDATA #IMPLIED>
<!-- default: none -->
        <!ATTLIST class rowid CDATA #IMPLIED>
        <!ATTLIST class node CDATA #IMPLIED>
```

从上面的定义中可以看出，class 元素可包括 0 到多个 meta、synchronize、tuplizer、property|many-to-one|one-to-one|component|dynamic-component|properties|any|map|set|list|bag|idbag|array|primitive-array 元素、join、subclass|joined-subclass|union-subclass、filter、resultset、query 和 sql-query 元素。

可包含 0 到 1 个 subselect、cache、comment、discriminator、natural-id、version|timestamp、loader、sql-insert、sql-update 和 sql-delete 元素。

可包含 0 到 1 个 id|composite-id 元素。

它常用的属性如下所示：

- name：类名，当未指定 package 时，类名需要将包的全路径包含在内，否则只需给出类名。
- table：对应的数据库表的名称，例如 SEC_USER。
- schema：设置命名空间，例如 test。

（3）id 元素。

在关系数据库的表中，需要使用主键来识别记录并保持每条记录的唯一性，主键需要满足如下条件：

- 主键不能为空。
- 主键必须唯一。
- 主键值永远不会改变。

例如管理员信息表中的用户名是唯一的，因此可以将用户名作为其主键。若现在定义的主键有可能在将来设计变更时变成非主键时，开发人员可设置一定自增的主键作为代理主键。在表的设计中，读者可能还会遇到两个键一起形成组合主键的情况，例如"用户表"和"权限表"的关联表可使用"用户 id"和"权限 id"作为复合主键。

映射文件的一个 class 元素必须包含一个 id（主键）或一个 composite-id（复合主键）子元

素。其中 id 在 DTD 文件中的定义如下所示：

```
<!ELEMENT id (meta*,column*,type?,generator?)>
    <!ATTLIST id name CDATA #IMPLIED>
    <!ATTLIST id node CDATA #IMPLIED>
    <!ATTLIST id access CDATA #IMPLIED>
    <!ATTLIST id column CDATA #IMPLIED>
    <!ATTLIST id type CDATA #IMPLIED>
    <!ATTLIST id length CDATA #IMPLIED>
    <!ATTLIST id unsaved-value CDATA #IMPLIED>           <!-- any|none|null|undefined|0|-1|... -->
```

元素可包括 0 到多个 meta、column 元素，0 到一个 type 元素和 generator 元素。常用的属性如下所示：

- name：在映射的 pojo 类中的名称。
- column：在数据库的表中对应的字段名称。
- type：对应的 pojo 类中的类型。

MySQL 中自增主键的配置实例如下所示：

```xml
<id name="roleid" column="roleId" type="java.lang.Integer">
<generator class="native"/>
</id>
```

generator 的 class 指定为 native，表示将根据本地数据库的设置来创建 roleid，若 MySQL 中将其表的 roleId 字段设置为自增，则在保存记录时，roleid 将自动增长。

对于需要在程序中指定主键的值，可将 generator 的 class 属性设置为 assigned，例如 User 表的 loginName 可按照此种方式设置，配置实例如下所示：

```xml
<id name="loginname" column="loginName" type="java.lang.String">
<generator class="assigned"/>
</id>
```

对于 Oracle 数据库，需要通过设定序列来实现主键的自增，若数据库中设置了一个名为 SEQ_ALL 的自增序列，需要为某表指定 id 为该序列，配置实例如下所示：

```xml
<id name="id" column="ID" unsaved-value="null">
<generator class="sequence">
<param name="sequence">USER_SEQ</param>
</generator>
</id>
```

（4）composite-id 元素。

composite-id 元素用于设定组合 id 构成的主键，该元素在 DTD 文件中的定义如下所示：

```
<!ELEMENT composite-id ( meta*, (key-property|key-many-to-one)+ )>
    <!ATTLIST composite-id class CDATA #IMPLIED>
    <!ATTLIST composite-id mapped (true|false) "false">
    <!ATTLIST composite-id name CDATA #IMPLIED>
    <!ATTLIST composite-id node CDATA #IMPLIED>
    <!ATTLIST composite-id access CDATA #IMPLIED>
    <!ATTLIST composite-id unsaved-value (undefined|any|none) "undefined">
```

该元素可包含 0 到多个 meta 元素、1 到多个 key-property 或 key-many-to-one 元素。例如若在用户和权限的关联表中需要指定将 userId（用户 id）和 roleId（角色 id）作为该表的复合主键，则配置实例如下所示：

```xml
<composite-id>
```

```
        <key-property name="userId" column="USER_ID" type="java.lang.Long" />
        <key-property name="roleId" column="ROLE_ID" type="java.lang.Long" />
</composite-id>
```

（5）property 元素。

property 元素用于配置某个属性，它是使用最多的一个元素，在 DTD 文件中的定义如下所示：

```
<!ELEMENT property (meta*,(column|formula)*,type?)>
     <!ATTLIST property name CDATA #REQUIRED>
     <!ATTLIST property node CDATA #IMPLIED>
     <!ATTLIST property access CDATA #IMPLIED>
     <!ATTLIST property type CDATA #IMPLIED>
     <!ATTLIST property column CDATA #IMPLIED>
     <!ATTLIST property length CDATA #IMPLIED>
     <!ATTLIST property precision CDATA #IMPLIED>
     <!ATTLIST property scale CDATA #IMPLIED>
     <!ATTLIST property not-null (true|false) #IMPLIED>
     <!ATTLIST property unique (true|false) "false">
     <!ATTLIST property unique-key CDATA #IMPLIED>
     <!ATTLIST property index CDATA #IMPLIED>
<!-- include the columns spanned by this property in an index -->
     <!ATTLIST property update (true|false) #IMPLIED>
     <!ATTLIST property insert (true|false) #IMPLIED>
     <!ATTLIST property optimistic-lock (true|false) "true">
<!-- only supported for properties of a class (not component) -->
     <!ATTLIST property formula CDATA #IMPLIED>
     <!ATTLIST property lazy (true|false) "false">
     <!ATTLIST property generated (never|insert|always) "never">
```

该属性可有 0 到多个 meta 元素、0 到多个 column 或 formula 元素、0 到 1 个 type 元素。它常用的属性如下所示：

- name：该属性表示 pojo 对应的属性名称。
- column：在数据库表中对应的字段名称。
- type：在 pojo 类中的类型。
- not-null：指定是否可为空，值可为 true 或 false，默认为 false，即允许为空。
- length：当为 String 类型的属性时，指定字符串的长度。
- insert：指定该字段是否永远不能被插入，值可为 true 和 false，默认为 true，即该字段可被插入。
- update：指定该字段是否永远不能被更新，值可为 true 和 false，默认为 true，即该字段可被更新。

例如在 User 表中包含了一个 password（密码）字段，它的类型为 String，不能为空，且长度只能小于 50，则该属性的配置实例如下所示：

```
<property name="password" column="PASSWORD" type="java.lang.String" not-null="true" length="50"/>
```

若需要为某表的 cy 字段指定 property 属性，配置实例如下所示：

```
<property name="cy" type="java.math.BigDecimal">
<column name="CY" precision="22" scale="0" />
</property>
```

第二步：tbl_user、tbl_dept 表的表结构

本实例中的 tbl_dept（部门信息）表用于存储系统的部门信息，它包含部门 ID、部门名称、部门全称等信息，其中部门 ID 采用 MySQL 数据库中的自动增长主键。

tbl_user（用户信息）表用于存储系统的用户信息，它包含用户名、姓名、所属部门和密码等信息。用户隶属于某个部门，tbl_user 表和 tbl_dept 表存在外键关联。创建表结构的 SQL 语句如下所示：

```sql
CREATE DATABASE `testhibernate`;
USE `testhibernate`;

#创建部门信息表
CREATE TABLE `tbl_dept` (
  `deptId` bigint(20) NOT NULL auto_increment COMMENT '部门id(自增)',
  `parentDeptId` bigint(20) NOT NULL COMMENT '父级部门id，最高层部门的父级部门id 为0',
  `deptName` varchar(50) NOT NULL COMMENT '部门名称',
  `deptFullName` varchar(100) default NULL COMMENT '部门全名',
  `state` tinyint(1) NOT NULL COMMENT '状态(0:未启用，1:启用)',
  `description` varchar(255) default NULL COMMENT '描述信息',
  `creator` varchar(50) default NULL COMMENT '创建人',
  `createTime` datetime default NULL COMMENT '创建时间',
  PRIMARY KEY (`orgId`)
) ENGINE=InnoDB DEFAULT CHARSET=gb2312 COMMENT='部门信息表';

#创建用户信息表
CREATE TABLE `tbl_user` (
  `loginName` varchar(50) NOT NULL COMMENT '帐户id，用户登录名',
  `deptId` bigint(20) NOT NULL COMMENT '所属组织id',
  `name` varchar(50) NOT NULL COMMENT '帐户姓名',
  `password` varchar(50) NOT NULL COMMENT '登录密码',
  `mobile` varchar(20) default NULL COMMENT '帐户手机号',
  `telephone` varchar(20) default NULL COMMENT '电话号码',
  `email` varchar(100) default NULL COMMENT '邮箱地址',
  `createTime` datetime NOT NULL COMMENT '帐户创建时间',
  `lastLoginTime` datetime default NULL COMMENT '最后登录时间',
  `loginTimes` bigint(20) NOT NULL COMMENT '登录次数',
  `state` tinyint(1) NOT NULL COMMENT '用户状态(0:未启用，1:启用)',
  `description` varchar(255) default NULL COMMENT '帐户简述',
  PRIMARY KEY (`loginName`),
  KEY `FK_orgId_user_organization` (`orgId`)
) ENGINE=InnoDB DEFAULT CHARSET=gb2312 COMMENT='帐户信息表';

#将用户信息表的 deptId 与部门信息表的主键 id 建立外键关联
ALTER TABLE `tbl_user`
ADD FOREIGN KEY (`deptId`) REFERENCES `tbl_dept` (`deptId`);
```

【说明】数据库脚本请参考 chapter11/example2/数据库脚本中的 scripts.sql 文件。

第三步：编写 tbl_dept 表对应的 POJO 类：Dept.java

在 amigo.hibernate.configure 包中建立 tbl_dept 表的 pojo 类 Dept.java，该类包含各属性，以及各属性的 getter/setter 方法，该类的代码如下所示：

```java
package amigo.hibernate.configure;

import java.io.Serializable;

/**
 * 部门信息表对应的 pojo 类.
 */
public class Dept implements Serializable {
    private static final long serialVersionUID = 1L;

    /** 部门 id(自增). */
    private java.lang.Long deptid;

    /** 父级部门 id，最高层部门的父级部门 id 为 0. */
    private java.lang.Long parentdeptid;

    /** 部门名称. */
    private java.lang.String deptname;

    /** 部门全名. */
    private java.lang.String deptfullname;

    /** 状态(0:未启用，1:启用). */
    private java.lang.Byte state;

    /** 描述信息. */
    private java.lang.String description;

    /** 创建人. */
    private java.lang.String creator;

    /** 创建时间. */
    private java.util.Date createtime;

    //省略各 getter/setter 方法
}
```

第四步：编写 tbl_dept 表映射文件：Dept.hbm.xml

在 amigo.hibernate.configure 包中建立 tbl_dept 表和 POJO 类 Dept.java 的 hibernate 映射文件 Dept.hbm.xml，编写完成后，该文件的内容如下所示：

```xml
<?xml version="1.0" encoding='UTF-8'?>
<!DOCTYPE hibernate-mapping PUBLIC
                    "-//Hibernate/Hibernate Mapping DTD 3.0//EN"
                    "http://hibernate.sourceforge.net/hibernate-mapping-3.0.dtd" >

<hibernate-mapping package="amigo.hibernate.configure">
    <class name="Dept" table="tbl_dept">
        <id name="deptd" column="deptId" type="java.lang.Long">
            <generator class="native"/>
        </id>

        <property name="parentdeptid" column="parentDeptId" type="java.lang.Long"  not-null="true" />
```

```xml
                <property name="deptname" column="deptName" type="java.lang.String" not-null="true" />
                <property name="deptfullname" column="deptFullName" type="java.lang.String" />
                <property name="state" column="state" type="java.lang.Byte" not-null="true" />
                <property name="description" column="description" type="java.lang.String" />
                <property name="creator" column="creator" type="java.lang.String" />
                <property name="createtime" column="createTime" type="java.util.Date" />
        </class>
</hibernate-mapping>
```

第五步：编写 tbl_user 表对应的 POJO 类：User.java

在 amigo.hibernate.configure 包中建立 tbl_user 表的 pojo 类 User.java，该类包含各属性，以及各属性的 getter/setter 方法，该类的代码如下所示：

```java
package amigo.hibernate.configure;

import java.io.Serializable;

/**
 * 用户信息的 POJO 类.
 */
public class User implements Serializable {
    private static final long serialVersionUID = 1L;

    /** 用户名,主键. */
    private java.lang.String loginname;

    /** 部门 Id. */
    private long deptId;

    /** 账户姓名. */
    private java.lang.String name;

    /** 登录密码. */
    private java.lang.String password;

    /** 账户手机号. */
    private java.lang.String mobile;

    /** 电话号码. */
    private java.lang.String telephone;

    /** 邮箱地址. */
    private java.lang.String email;

    /** 账户创建时间. */
    private java.util.Date createtime;

    /** 最后登录时间. */
    private java.util.Date lastlogintime;
```

```java
    /** 登录次数. */
    private java.lang.Long logintimes;

    /** 用户状态(0:未启用，1:启用)*/
    private java.lang.Byte state;

    /** 账户简述. */
    private java.lang.String description;

    // 省略各属性的 getter/setter 方法
}
```

第六步：编写 tbl_user 表映射文件：User.hbm.xml

在 amigo.hibernate.configure 包中建立 tbl_user 表和 POJO 类 User.java 的 hibernate 映射文件 User.hbm.xml，编写完成后，该文件的内容如下所示：

```xml
<?xml version="1.0" encoding='UTF-8'?>
<!DOCTYPE hibernate-mapping PUBLIC
                    "-//Hibernate/Hibernate Mapping DTD 3.0//EN"
                    "http://hibernate.sourceforge.net/hibernate-mapping-3.0.dtd" >

<hibernate-mapping package="amigo.hibernate.configure">
    <class name="User" table="tbl_user">
        <id name="loginname" column="loginName" type="java.lang.String">
            <generator class="assigned"/>
        </id>
        <property name="name" column="name" type="java.lang.String"   not-null="true" />
        <property name="deptId" column="deptId" type="java.lang.Long"   not-null="true" />
        <property name="password" column="password" type="java.lang.String"   not-null="true" />
        <property name="mobile" column="mobile" type="java.lang.String" />
        <property name="telephone" column="telephone" type="java.lang.String" />
        <property name="email" column="email" type="java.lang.String" />
        <property name="createtime" column="createTime" type="java.util.Date"   not-null="true" />
        <property name="lastlogintime" column="lastLoginTime" type="java.util.Date" />
        <property name="logintimes" column="loginTimes" type="java.lang.Long"   not-null="true" />
        <property name="state" column="state" type="java.lang.Byte"   not-null="true" />
        <property name="description" column="description" type="java.lang.String" />
    </class>
</hibernate-mapping>
```

【例 11-3】配置一对多关联

〖实例需求〗

一对多关联是关系数据库中最常见的一种关联。本实例首先讲解一对多关联关系的概念，接着通过 tbl_user（部门信息表）和 tbl_user（用户信息表）的例子详细讲述如何在 Hibernate 中配置这种关联关系，以及对应的 POJO 类应该做怎样的变化。

【开发过程】

第一步：一对多关联关系介绍

一对多关联是关系数据库中最常见的一种关联，例如在【例 11-2】中，部门信息表和用户信息表就存在这种一对多的关联关系，因为一个部门信息对象可关联 0 到多个用户信息对象。另外，客户信息与订单信息也是一种很常见的一对多关联，每个客户信息对象可引用一组订单信息对象，即一个客户可能有 0 到多个订单。

在关系数据库中，这种关系一般采用外键来体现，即"多"的一方建立到"一"的一方的外键关联，在上面两个举例中，tbl_user（用户信息表）存在到 tbl_dept（部门信息表）的外键关联，通过 deptId 关联 tbl_dept 表的主键。

在 Hibernate 中，支持"单向关联"和"双向关联"，当只存在一对多的关联或只存在多对一的关联时，属于"单向关联"，若同时包含两种关联时，称为"双向关联"。而关系数据库中，只能通过外键体现单向关联，即"多对一"的关联，将"多"的一方建立到"一"的一方的外键。

第二步：多对一关联关系配置——配置 User.java 和 User.hbm.xml

在类与类的关系中，多对一的关系对应关系数据库中的外键关联关系。要建立 User 和 Dept 之间的关联，可选择单向关联或双向关联。若选择的是单向关联，一般是建立 User 到 Dept 的多对一关系。User.java 类需要将 long 类型的 deptId 属性修改为 Dept 类型的 dept 属性，并添加其 getter/setter 方法，修改后的代码如下所示：

```java
package amigo.hibernate.configure;

import java.io.Serializable;

/**
 * 用户信息的 POJO 类
 */
public class User implements Serializable {
    private static final long serialVersionUID = 1L;

    /** 用户名,主键. */
    private java.lang.String loginname;

    /** 部门. */
    private Dept dept;

    /** 账户姓名. */
    private java.lang.String name;

    /** 登录密码. */
    private java.lang.String password;

    /** 账户手机号. */
    private java.lang.String mobile;

    /** 电话号码 */
```

```java
    private java.lang.String telephone;

    /** 邮箱地址 */
    private java.lang.String email;

    /** 账户创建时间 */
    private java.util.Date createtime;

    /** 最后登录时间 */
    private java.util.Date lastlogintime;

    /** 登录次数. */
    private java.lang.Long logintimes;

    /** 用户状态(0:未启用，1:启用)*/
    private java.lang.Byte state;

    /** 账户简述 */
    private java.lang.String description;

    // 省略各属性的 getter/setter 方法
}
```

在 Hibernate 的映射文件中多对一的关系采用<many-to-one../>元素来定义，在 DTD 文件中其定义如下所示：

```
<!ELEMENT many-to-one (meta*,(column|formula)*)>
    <!ATTLIST many-to-one name CDATA #REQUIRED>
    <!ATTLIST many-to-one access CDATA #IMPLIED>
    <!ATTLIST many-to-one class CDATA #IMPLIED>
    <!ATTLIST many-to-one entity-name CDATA #IMPLIED>
    <!ATTLIST many-to-one column CDATA #IMPLIED>
    <!ATTLIST many-to-one not-null (true|false) #IMPLIED>
    <!ATTLIST many-to-one unique (true|false) "false">
    <!ATTLIST many-to-one unique-key CDATA #IMPLIED>
    <!ATTLIST many-to-one index CDATA #IMPLIED>
    <!ATTLIST many-to-one cascade CDATA #IMPLIED>
    <!ATTLIST many-to-one outer-join (true|false|auto) #IMPLIED>
    <!ATTLIST many-to-one fetch (join|select) #IMPLIED>
    <!ATTLIST many-to-one update (true|false) "true">
    <!ATTLIST many-to-one insert (true|false) "true">
    <!ATTLIST many-to-one optimistic-lock (true|false) "true">   <!-- only supported for properties of a class (not component) -->
    <!ATTLIST many-to-one foreign-key CDATA #IMPLIED>
    <!ATTLIST many-to-one property-ref CDATA #IMPLIED>
    <!ATTLIST many-to-one formula CDATA #IMPLIED>
    <!ATTLIST many-to-one lazy (false|proxy|no-proxy) #IMPLIED>
    <!ATTLIST many-to-one not-found (exception|ignore) "exception">
    <!ATTLIST many-to-one node CDATA #IMPLIED>
    <!ATTLIST many-to-one embed-xml (true|false) "true">
```

该元素的常用属性如下所示：

- name：持久化类中的属性名，在本例中为 User.java 中的 dept 属性。
- column：设定与持久化类的属性对应的关系数据库表中的关键，在本例中为 deptId。

- class：对应的持久化类，在本例中为 Dept。
- not-null：该属性是否允许为空，值可为 true 或 false。当为 true 时，表示该属性不允许为 null，默认为 false。

在本例中，需要在 User.hbm.xml 映射文件中删除如下语句：

```xml
<property name="deptId" column="deptId" type="java.lang.Long" not-null="true" />
```

而修改为使用<many-to-one.../>元素来代替，内容如下：

```xml
<many-to-one name="dept"
             column="deptId"
             class="Dept"
             not-null="true" />
```

第三步：一对多关联关系配置——配置 Dept.java 和 Dept.hbm.xml

为了使得一个对象能够更方便地导航到一组关联对象，还需要将一对多的关系建立起来。例如，在本例中，对于一个 Dept 对象，可关联出一组用户对象。要增加一对多的关联，"一"的一方需要在持久化类中添加一个到"多"的一方的一个属性的集合，Dept.java 类需要添加的内容如下所示：

```java
/** 该部门关联的用户对象 */
private Set<User> users = new HashSet<User>();

public Set<User> getUsers() {
    return users;
}

public void setUsers(Set<User> users) {
    this.users = users;
}
```

在映射关系中，一对多的关联关系采用<set../>元素体现，该标签在 DTD 文件中的定义如下所示：

```
<!ELEMENT set (
    meta*,
    subselect?,
    cache?,
    synchronize*,
    comment?,
    key,
    (element|one-to-many|many-to-many|composite-element|many-to-any),
    loader?,sql-insert?,sql-update?,sql-delete?,sql-delete-all?,
    filter*
)>
    <!ATTLIST set name CDATA #REQUIRED>
    <!ATTLIST set access CDATA #IMPLIED>
    <!ATTLIST set table CDATA #IMPLIED>
             <!-- default: name -->
    <!ATTLIST set schema CDATA #IMPLIED>
             <!-- default: none -->
    <!ATTLIST set catalog CDATA #IMPLIED>
             <!-- default: none -->
```

```
<!ATTLIST set subselect CDATA #IMPLIED>
<!ATTLIST set lazy (true|false|extra) #IMPLIED>
<!ATTLIST set sort CDATA "unsorted">
        <!-- unsorted|natural|"comparator class" -->
<!ATTLIST set inverse (true|false) "false">
<!ATTLIST set mutable (true|false) "true">
<!ATTLIST set cascade CDATA #IMPLIED>
<!ATTLIST set order-by CDATA #IMPLIED>
        <!-- default: none -->
<!ATTLIST set where CDATA #IMPLIED>
        <!-- default: none -->
<!ATTLIST set batch-size CDATA #IMPLIED>
<!ATTLIST set outer-join (true|false|auto) #IMPLIED>
<!ATTLIST set fetch (join|select|subselect) #IMPLIED>
<!ATTLIST set persister CDATA #IMPLIED>
<!ATTLIST set collection-type CDATA #IMPLIED>

<!ATTLIST set check CDATA #IMPLIED>
        <!-- default: none -->
<!ATTLIST set optimistic-lock (true|false) "true">        <!-- only supported for properties of a class (not component) -->
<!ATTLIST set node CDATA #IMPLIED>
<!ATTLIST set embed-xml (true|false) "true">
```

其常用属性如下所示：

- name：设定持久化类的属性名，在本例中为 users。
- cascade：表示级联的属性，若设置为 "save-update"，表示级联保存和更新。
- order-by：设定取得的集合的排序方式，若设置为 loginName，表示按照用户对象的 loginName 属性进行排序。
- lazy：是否为立即加载，值可为 true 或 false，当设置为 true 时，表示立即加载集合对象，默认值为 false。

在 set 元素中，一般包含一个 one-to-many 的子元素，该子元素在 DTD 文件中的定义如下所示：

```
<!ELEMENT one-to-many EMPTY>
    <!ATTLIST one-to-many class CDATA #IMPLIED>
    <!ATTLIST one-to-many not-found (exception|ignore) "exception">
    <!ATTLIST one-to-many node CDATA #IMPLIED>
    <!ATTLIST one-to-many embed-xml (true|false) "true">
    <!ATTLIST one-to-many entity-name CDATA #IMPLIED>
    <!-- No column declaration attributes required in this case. The primary
    key column of the associated class is already mapped elsewhere.-->
```

one-to-many 常用的属性为 class，该属性用于指定一对多关系中"多"的一方对应的类。
本例中一对多关联关系添加的配置信息如下所示：

```
<set name="users" cascade ="save-update">
<key>
        <column name="deptId" />
    </key>
    <one-to-many class="User" />
</set>
```

上面的配置表明 Dept 对象中的 users 集合属性通过字段 deptId 与 User 对象关联起来。

【例 11-4】配置一对一关联

〖实例需求〗

一对一的关联也是关系数据库中比较常见的一种关联关系。本实例通过一个用户表（tbl_user）和用户附加信息表（tbl_user_ext）的关联配置实例来讲解在 Hibernate 中如何配置一对一的关联。

〖开发过程〗

第一步：一对一关联关系介绍

一对一的关联关系在关系数据库中也比较常见。这种关系一般通过一个表的主键去外键关联另一个表的主键来实现，称为"主键关联"。另一种叫做"唯一外键关联"，即一个表的外键去唯一关联另一个表的主键。

本实例的用户表（tbl_user）有一个附加表 tbl_user_ext，表 tbl_user_ext 与 tbl_user 表存在着一对一的关系，本实例讲解如何配置这两个表的一对一的"主键关联"和"唯一外键关联"。

（1）一对一"主键关联"。

一对一"主键关联"关系采用的是 one-to-one 元素，它在 hibernate 的映射文件的 DTD 中的定义如下所示：

```
<!ELEMENT one-to-one (meta*,formula*)>
    <!ATTLIST one-to-one name CDATA #REQUIRED>
    <!ATTLIST one-to-one formula CDATA #IMPLIED>
    <!ATTLIST one-to-one access CDATA #IMPLIED>
    <!ATTLIST one-to-one class CDATA #IMPLIED>
    <!ATTLIST one-to-one entity-name CDATA #IMPLIED>
    <!ATTLIST one-to-one cascade CDATA #IMPLIED>
    <!ATTLIST one-to-one outer-join (true|false|auto) #IMPLIED>
    <!ATTLIST one-to-one fetch (join|select) #IMPLIED>
    <!ATTLIST one-to-one constrained (true|false) "false">
    <!ATTLIST one-to-one foreign-key CDATA #IMPLIED>
    <!ATTLIST one-to-one property-ref CDATA #IMPLIED>
    <!ATTLIST one-to-one lazy (false|proxy|no-proxy) #IMPLIED>
    <!ATTLIST one-to-one node CDATA #IMPLIED>
    <!ATTLIST one-to-one embed-xml (true|false) "true">
```

常用的属性如下所示：

- name：在 pojo 中对应的属性名。
- class：属性对应的类型。
- cascade：在一对一"主键关联"关系映射中，在主动的一方一般设置为 all，在本例中表示当保存、更新和删除 User 对象时，级联保存、更新和删除 UserExt 对象。在从属的一方（本例为 UserExt）一般不进行该属性的设置，默认为 none。
- constrained：在从属的一方（本例为 UserExt）一般需要进行该属性的设置，表明从属一方（本例为 UserExt）的主键同时作为外键关联主动的一方（本例为 User）。

（2）一对一"唯一外键关联"。

一对一的"唯一外键关联"关系需要 many-to-one 和 one-to-one 元素配合实现。在主动的对象（本例为 User）建立到从属的对象（本例为 UserExt）的 many-to-one 的唯一映射。而在从属的对象（本例为 UserExt）建立到主动的对象（本例为 User）的 one-to-one 的映射。不过要注意在 many-to-one 配置时，需要设置属性 unique 为 true。

在关系数据库表的设计中，一般是在从属表（本例为 tbl_user_ext）中建立主动表（本例为 tbl_user）的唯一外键。

第二步：配置一对一"主键关联"——数据库脚本

（1）编写数据库脚本 scripts-one-to-one-way1.sql。

建立 amigo.hibernate.configure.onetoone.way1 包，并在该目录中建立数据库脚本，该脚本创建了 tbl_user 和 tbl_user_ext 两个表，并指定了这两个表的主键都为 loginName，并将用户附加信息表 tbl_user_ext 的 loginName 建立到 tbl_user 的主键 loginName 的关联。数据库脚本的内容如下所示：

```sql
CREATE DATABASE `testhibernate`;
USE `testhibernate`;

#创建用户信息表
CREATE TABLE `tbl_user` (
  `loginName` varchar(50) NOT NULL COMMENT '用户登录名',
  `name` varchar(50) NOT NULL COMMENT '姓名',
  `password` varchar(50) NOT NULL COMMENT '登录密码',
  `createTime` datetime NOT NULL COMMENT '创建时间',
  PRIMARY KEY  (`loginName`)
) ENGINE=InnoDB DEFAULT CHARSET=gb2312 COMMENT='用户信息表';

#创建用户附加信息表
CREATE TABLE `tbl_user_ext` (
  `loginName` varchar(50) NOT NULL COMMENT '用户登录名',
  `mobile` varchar(20) default NULL COMMENT '帐户手机号',
  `telephone` varchar(20) default NULL COMMENT '电话号码',
  `email` varchar(100) default NULL COMMENT '邮箱地址',
  `address` varchar(100) default NULL COMMENT '地址',
  `fax` varchar(100) default NULL COMMENT '传真',
  `blog` varchar(100) default NULL COMMENT 'blog 地址'
  PRIMARY KEY  (`loginName`),
  KEY `FK_loginName_user_userext` (`loginName`)
) ENGINE=InnoDB DEFAULT CHARSET=gb2312 COMMENT='用户附加信息表';

#将用户附加信息表的主键 loginName 与用户信息表的主键 loginName 建立外键关联
ALTER TABLE `tbl_user_ext`
ADD FOREIGN KEY (`loginName`) REFERENCES `tbl_user` (`loginName`);
```

（2）编写 User.java。

在 amigo.hibernate.configure.onetoone.way1 包中建立 User.java 类，该类包括 loginname、name、password、createtime 和 userExt 属性，该类的代码如下所示：

```java
package amigo.hibernate.configure.onetoone.way1;

import java.io.Serializable;
```

```java
/**
 * 用户信息的POJO类.
 */
public class User implements Serializable {
    private static final long serialVersionUID = 1L;

    /** 用户名,主键. */
    private java.lang.String loginname;

    /** 账户姓名. */
    private java.lang.String name;

    /** 登录密码. */
    private java.lang.String password;

    /** 创建时间. */
    private java.util.Date createtime;

    /** 与用户附加信息存在一对的关联关系. */
    private UserExt userExt;

    // 省略各属性的getter/setter方法
}
```

（3）配置 User.hbm.xml。

在 amigo.hibernate.configure.onetoone.way1 包中建立 User.hbm.xml 映射文件，该文件通过配置 one-to-one 元素配置了到 UserExt 的一对一的关系，该文件的内容如下：

```xml
<?xml version="1.0" encoding='UTF-8'?>
<!DOCTYPE hibernate-mapping PUBLIC
                    "-//Hibernate/Hibernate Mapping DTD 3.0//EN"
                    "http://hibernate.sourceforge.net/hibernate-mapping-3.0.dtd" >

<hibernate-mapping package="amigo.hibernate.configure.onetoone.way1">
    <class name="User" table="tbl_user">
        <id name="loginname" column="loginName" type="java.lang.String">
            <generator class="assigned"/>
        </id>
        <property name="name" column="name" type="java.lang.String"    not-null="true" />
        <property name="password" column="password" type="java.lang.String"    not-null="true" />
        <property name="createtime" column="createTime" type="java.util.Date"    not-null="true" />

        <one-to-one name="userExt"
            class="UserExt"
            cascade="all" />
    </class>
</hibernate-mapping>
```

其中代码：

```xml
<one-to-one name="userExt"
        class="UserExt"
        cascade="all" />
```

是一对一"主键关联"关系中主动方常用的配置。

(4) 编写 UserExt.java。

UserExt.java 是用户附加信息表映射的 pojo 类，该类包括 user、mobile 和 telephone 等属性，该类的代码如下所示：

```java
package amigo.hibernate.configure.onetoone.way1;

import java.io.Serializable;

/**
 * 用户附加信息的 POJO 类.
 */
public class UserExt implements Serializable {
    private static final long serialVersionUID = 1L;

    /** 用户信息，UserExt 与 User 存在一对一的"主键关联"关系. */
    private User user;

    /** 手机号. */
    private java.lang.String mobile;

    /** 电话号码. */
    private java.lang.String telephone;

    /** 邮箱地址. */
    private java.lang.String email;

    /** 地址. */
    private String address;

    /** 传真. */
    private String fax;

    /** blog 地址. */
    private String blog;

    // 省略各属性的 getter/setter 方法
}
```

(5) 配置 UserExt.hbm.xml。

在 amigo.hibernate.configure.onetoone.way1 包中建立表 tbl_user_ext 的 hibernate 映射文件为 UserExt.hbm.xml，该文件的内容如下：

```xml
<?xml version="1.0" encoding='UTF-8'?>
<!DOCTYPE hibernate-mapping PUBLIC
                    "-//Hibernate/Hibernate Mapping DTD 3.0//EN"
                    "http://hibernate.sourceforge.net/hibernate-mapping-3.0.dtd" >

<hibernate-mapping package="amigo.hibernate.configure.onetoone.way1">
    <class name="UserExt" table="tbl_user_ext">
        <id name="id" column="id">
            <generator class="foreign">
                <param name="property">user</param>
            </generator>
        </id>
```

```xml
            <property name="mobile" column="mobile" type="java.lang.String" />
            <property name="telephone" column="telephone" type="java.lang.String" />
            <property name="email" column="email" type="java.lang.String" />
            <property name="address" column="address" type="java.lang.String" />
            <property name="fax" column="fax" type="java.lang.String" />
            <property name="blog" column="blog" type="java.lang.String" />

            <one-to-one name="user"
                class="User"
                constrained="true" />
    </class>
</hibernate-mapping>
```

一对一"主键关联"关系的从属方的核心的配置如上述代码中的黑体字，其中 id 是采用外键方式生成的，生成的方式是通过后面的 one-to-one 元素的 user 属性的设置。

第三步：一对一"唯一外键关联"配置

（1）数据库脚本 scripts-one-to-one-way2.sql。

建立 amigo.hibernate.configure.onetoone.way2 包，并在该目录中建立数据库脚本，该脚本创建了 tbl_user 和 tbl_user_ext 两个表，并指定 tbl_user 表的主键为 loginName，tbl_user_ext 表的主键为 extId，该主键为自增主键。将用户附加信息表 tbl_user_ext 的 loginName 建立到 tbl_user 的主键 loginName 的关联。数据库脚本的内容如下所示：

```sql
#创建用户信息表
CREATE TABLE `tbl_user` (
    `loginName` varchar(50) NOT NULL COMMENT '用户登录名',
    `name` varchar(50) NOT NULL COMMENT '姓名',
    `password` varchar(50) NOT NULL COMMENT '登录密码',
    `createTime` datetime NOT NULL COMMENT '创建时间',
    PRIMARY KEY (`loginName`)
) ENGINE=InnoDB DEFAULT CHARSET=gb2312 COMMENT='用户信息表';

#创建用户附加信息表
CREATE TABLE `tbl_user_ext` (
    `extId` bigint(20) NOT NULL auto_increment COMMENT '主键ID(自增)',
    `loginName` varchar(50) unique NOT NULL COMMENT '用户登录名',
    `mobile` varchar(20) default NULL COMMENT '帐户手机号',
    `telephone` varchar(20) default NULL COMMENT '电话号码',
    `email` varchar(100) default NULL COMMENT '邮箱地址',
    `address` varchar(100) default NULL COMMENT '地址',
    `fax` varchar(100) default NULL COMMENT '传真',
    `blog` varchar(100) default NULL COMMENT 'blog 地址'
    PRIMARY KEY (`extId`),
    KEY `FK_loginName_user_userext` (`loginName`)
) ENGINE=InnoDB DEFAULT CHARSET=gb2312 COMMENT='用户附加信息表';

#将用户附加信息表的主键 loginName 与用户信息表的主键 loginName 建立外键关联
ALTER TABLE `tbl_user_ext`
ADD FOREIGN KEY (`loginName`) REFERENCES `tbl_user` (`loginName`);
```

为了确保 tbl_user_ext 表中的每条记录的 loginName 是唯一的，给 tbl_user_ext 表中的 loginName 设定了 unique 约束。

（2）编写 UserExt.java。

在 amigo.hibernate.configure.onetoone.way2 包中建立 UserExt.java 文件，该类的代码如下所示：

```java
package amigo.hibernate.configure.onetoone.way2;

import java.io.Serializable;

/**
 * 用户附加信息的 POJO 类.
 */
public class UserExt implements Serializable {
    private static final long serialVersionUID = 1L;

    /** 附加信息的 id. */
    private Long extId;

    /** 用户信息，UserExt 与 User 存在一对一的关联关系. */
    private User user;

    // 省略 mobile、blog 等属性

    // 省略各属性的 getter/setter 方法
}
```

（3）配置 UserExt.hbm.xml。

在 amigo.hibernate.configure.onetoone.way2 包中建立 user 表的映射文件 UserExt.hbm.xml，表 tbl_user_ext 的 loginName 与表 tbl_user 的主键建立唯一外键关联，配置信息如下所示：

```xml
......
<hibernate-mapping package="amigo.hibernate.configure.onetoone.way2">
    <class name="UserExt" table="tbl_user_ext">
        <id name="extId" column="extId" type="java.lang.Long">
            <generator class="native"/>
        </id>
        ......
        <many-to-one name="user"
            class="User"
            column="loginName"
            unique="true" />
    </class>
</hibernate-mapping>
```

如上配置表明 UserExt 对象的 user 属性关联到 User 对象，通过 tbl_user_ext 表的 loginName 进行关联。

unique 属性为核心配置，设置为 true 表示每个 User 对象都有唯一的 UserExt 对象。

（4）编写 User.java。

在 amigo.hibernate.configure.onetoone.way2 包中建立 User.java 文件，该文件的内容除了所在包与第二步的 User.java 不一样外，其余都是一样的，内容不再赘述。

（5）配置 User.hbm.xml。

在 amigo.hibernate.configure.onetoone.way2 包中建立 user 表的映射文件 User.hbm.xml，该文

件的其余配置都与上一步的实例相同，但是 userExt 属性的配置需要进行修改，修改后的该属性的配置如下所示：

```xml
<one-to-one name="userExt"
    class="UserExt"
    property-ref="user"
cascade="all"/>
```

one-to-one 元素的 property-ref 指定为 user，表明 tbl_user_ext 表引用了 tbl_user 的主键作为它的外键。cascade 属性设置为 all，表示在保存、更新或删除 User 对象时，级联保存、更新或删除 UserExt 对象。

【例 11-5】配置多对多关联

〖实例需求〗

在进行数据库设计时，多对多关系是一种很常见的表与表之间的关系，而这种关系常被分解为两个一对多的关系，使用一个关联表在这两个表之间"搭桥"。

本实例将通过讲解用户表与角色表之间的多对多关系来讲述在 Hibernate 中如何配置多对多关系，以及在配置时需要注意的一些问题。

〖开发过程〗

第一步：多对多关联关系介绍

多对多关系也是比较常见的一种关联关系。例如在基于角色的权限系统中，若允许一个用户具有多个角色，则用户与角色的关系就是一种多对多关系。即一个用户可以具有多个角色信息，而一个角色信息可以关联出多个具有该角色的用户对象。

在关系数据库中，无法直接表达多对多的关联关系，需要通过附加表方式将其转换为两个到附加表的多对一关联关系。例如 tbl_user（用户表）和 tbl_role（角色表）通过其关联表 tbl_user_role 表建立多对多的关联，关联表中一般只包含多对多关系的两个表的主键。

多对多关联关系映射需要使用<set../>和<many-to-many../>两个元素来配合实现。<set../>元素在前面的内容中有详细介绍，本实例只介绍<many-to-many../>元素的 DTD 定义，该元素的定义如下：

```
<!ELEMENT many-to-many (meta*,(column|formula)*,filter*)>
    <!ATTLIST many-to-many class CDATA #IMPLIED>
    <!ATTLIST many-to-many node CDATA #IMPLIED>
    <!ATTLIST many-to-many embed-xml (true|false) "true">
    <!ATTLIST many-to-many entity-name CDATA #IMPLIED>
    <!ATTLIST many-to-many column CDATA #IMPLIED>
    <!ATTLIST many-to-many formula CDATA #IMPLIED>
    <!ATTLIST many-to-many not-found (exception|ignore) "exception">
    <!ATTLIST many-to-many outer-join (true|false|auto) #IMPLIED>
    <!ATTLIST many-to-many fetch (join|select) #IMPLIED>
    <!ATTLIST many-to-many lazy (false|proxy) #IMPLIED>
    <!ATTLIST many-to-many foreign-key CDATA #IMPLIED>
    <!ATTLIST many-to-many unique (true|false) "false">
```

```
<!ATTLIST many-to-many where CDATA #IMPLIED>
<!ATTLIST many-to-many order-by CDATA #IMPLIED>
<!ATTLIST many-to-many property-ref CDATA #IMPLIED>
```

该属性的常用属性如下：
- class：该对象多对多关联的另一方的对象的类。
- column：该对象多对多关联的另一方的表的对应字段。

第二步：数据库脚本 scripts-many-to-many.sql

建立 amigo.hibernate.configure.manytomany 包，在该目录中创建数据库脚本文件 scripts-many-to-many.sql，该文件创建 tbl_user、tbl_role 及两者的关联表 tbl_user_role，该文件的内容如下：

```sql
CREATE DATABASE `testhibernate`;
USE `testhibernate`;

#创建用户信息表
CREATE TABLE `tbl_user` (
  `loginName` varchar(50) NOT NULL COMMENT '用户登录名',
  `name` varchar(50) NOT NULL COMMENT '姓名',
  `password` varchar(50) NOT NULL COMMENT '登录密码',
  `createTime` datetime NOT NULL COMMENT '创建时间',
  PRIMARY KEY  (`loginName`)
) ENGINE=InnoDB DEFAULT CHARSET=gb2312 COMMENT='用户信息表';

#创建角色信息表
CREATE TABLE `tbl_role` (
  `roleId` bigint(20) NOT NULL auto_increment COMMENT '角色ID(自增)',
  `roleName` varchar(50) unique NOT NULL COMMENT '角色名称',
  `description` varchar(100) default NULL COMMENT '描述'
  PRIMARY KEY  (`roleId`)
) ENGINE=InnoDB DEFAULT CHARSET=gb2312 COMMENT='角色信息表';

#创建用户与角色关联表
CREATE TABLE `tbl_user_role` (
    `loginName` varchar(50) NOT NULL COMMENT '用户登录名',
  `roleId` bigint(20) NOT NULL COMMENT '角色ID'
  PRIMARY KEY  (`loginName`, `roleId`)
) ENGINE=InnoDB DEFAULT CHARSET=gb2312 COMMENT='用户与角色关联表';

#将关联表的 loginName 与用户信息表的主键 loginName 建立外键关联
ALTER TABLE `tbl_user_role`
ADD FOREIGN KEY (`loginName`) REFERENCES `tbl_user` (`loginName`);

#将关联表的 loginName 与用户信息表的主键 loginName 建立外键关联
ALTER TABLE `tbl_user_role`
ADD FOREIGN KEY (`roleId`) REFERENCES `tbl_role` (`roleId`);
```

第三步：配置单向多对多关联

在映射多对多的关联关系时，可将关联关系配置成单向的，即只配置其中一方。也可配置成双向的，即关联关系的两方都需要进行配置。本步骤将详细讲述 User 到 Role 的单向多对多关联。

（1）编写 User.java。

建立 amigo.hibernate.configure.manytomany.unilateralism 包，并在该包中建立 User.java 类，该类包含一个 Role 的集合。该类的代码如下所示：

```java
package amigo.hibernate.configure.manytomany.unilateralism;

import java.io.Serializable;
import java.util.HashSet;
import java.util.Set;

/**
 * 用户信息的POJO类.
 */
public class User implements Serializable {
    private static final long serialVersionUID = 1L;

    /** 用户名,主键. */
    private java.lang.String loginname;

    /** 账户姓名. */
    private java.lang.String name;

    /** 登录密码. */
    private java.lang.String password;

    /** 创建时间. */
    private java.util.Date createtime;

    /** 角色集合. */
    private Set<Role> roles = new HashSet<Role>();

    // 省略各属性的 getter/setter 方法
}
```

（2）配置 User.hbm.xml。

在 tbl_user 表的映射文件中需要建立到 tbl_role 的多对多关联，该文件的配置信息如下所示：

```xml
<?xml version="1.0" encoding='UTF-8'?>
<!DOCTYPE hibernate-mapping PUBLIC
                    "-//Hibernate/Hibernate Mapping DTD 3.0//EN"
                    "http://hibernate.sourceforge.net/hibernate-mapping-3.0.dtd" >

<hibernate-mapping package="amigo.hibernate.configure.manytomany.unilateralism">
    <class name="User" table="tbl_user">
        <id name="loginname" column="loginName" type="java.lang.String">
            <generator class="assigned"/>
        </id>
        <property name="name" column="name" type="java.lang.String"   not-null="true" />
        <property name="password" column="password" type="java.lang.String"   not-null="true" />
        <property name="createtime" column="createTime" type="java.util.Date"   not-null="true" />
```

```xml
        <set name="roles" table="tbl_user_role"
            lazy="true"
            cascade="save-update">
                <key>
                    <column name="loginname" not-null="true"/>
                </key>
                <many-to-many class="Role" column="roleid"/>
        </set>
    </class>
</hibernate-mapping>
```

<set../>元素的 cascade 属性设置为 save-update,表示保存和更新 User 对象时,级联保存和更新 Role 对象。若将该属性设置为 all、delete 或 all-delete-orphans,显然是不合理的,因为如果进行这样的设置,将导致在删除 User 对象时,也将级联删除 Role 对象,而 Role 对象还可能跟其他的 User 有关联关系。

<set../>元素的 table 属性指定多对多关系的关联表。

<set../>元素的子元素<key../>表示关联表 tbl_user_role 与 tbl_user 表建立关联的外键为 loginname。

<set../>元素的子元素<many-to-many../>表示 User 对象的 roles 集合属性存放的对象的类型,以及与关联的 Role 通过何键关联。

(3) 编写 Role.java。

角色信息对象包括角色 id、角色名称和描述信息,该类的代码如下所示:

```java
package amigo.hibernate.configure.manytomany.unilateralism;

import java.io.Serializable;

/**
 * 角色信息的 POJO 类
 */
public class Role implements Serializable {
    private static final long serialVersionUID = 1L;

    /** 角色 id(自增) */
    private java.lang.Long roleId;

    /** 角色名称 */
    private String roleName;

    /** 角色描述 */
    private String description;

    // 省略各属性的 getter/setter 方法
}
```

(4) 配置 Role.hbm.xml。

Role.hbm.xml 为表 tbl_role 的 hibernate 映射文件,该文件的内容如下所示:

```xml
<?xml version="1.0" encoding='UTF-8'?>
<!DOCTYPE hibernate-mapping PUBLIC
```

```xml
              "-//Hibernate/Hibernate Mapping DTD 3.0//EN"
              "http://hibernate.sourceforge.net/hibernate-mapping-3.0.dtd" >

<hibernate-mapping package="amigo.hibernate.configure.manytomany.unilateralism">
    <class name="Role" table="tbl_role">
        <id name="roleId" column="roleId" type="java.lang.Long">
            <generator class="native"/>
        </id>

        <property name="roleName" column="roleName" type="java.lang.String" not-null="true" />
        <property name="description" column="description" type="java.lang.String" />
    </class>
</hibernate-mapping>
```

第四步：配置双向多对多关联

（1）编写 User.java。

建立 amigo.hibernate.configure.manytomany.bidirectional 包，并在该包中建立 User.java 类，该类包含一个 Role 的集合。该类的代码与上一步骤类似，在此不再赘述。

（2）配置 User.hbm.xml。

在 amigo.hibernate.configure.manytomany.bidirectional 包中建立 User.hbm.xml 文件，该文件除了包文件与上一步骤的不同外，其余的配置都是一样的，内容不再赘述。

（3）编写 Role.java。

因为要建立的是双向关联，所以 Role.java 中也需要配置 User 的集合属性 users，在上一步的基础上添加的内容如下：

```java
/** 用户集合*/
private Set<User> users = new HashSet<User>();

public Set<User> getUsers() {
    return users;
}

public void setUsers(Set<User> users) {
    this.users = users;
}
```

（4）配置 Role.hbm.xml。

在 tbl_role 表的映射文件中也需要建立多对多的关联，在上一步的基础上添加了如下配置信息：

```xml
<set name="users" table="tbl_user_role"
     lazy="true"
     inverse="true"
     cascade="save-update">
    <key>
        <column name="roleid" not-null="true"/>
    </key>
    <many-to-many class="User" column="loginname"/>
</set>
```

【注意】在进行双向多对多关联时，需要将其中一方的 inverse 属性设置为 true，本例中 Role.hbm.xml 的 users 属性的 inverse 设置为 true。

小结

Hibernate 支持以 XML 格式和 properties 文件两种方式配置数据库的基本信息。基本信息包括数据库 URL、数据库用户名、数据库用户密码、数据库 JDBC 驱动类和数据库 dialect 等。

最常用的是使用 XML 格式的文件进行配置，将 hibernate.cfg.xml 文件作为该 XML 配置文件。MySQL、SQLServer 和 Oracle 三种数据库的 hibernate.cfg.xml 文件配置格式类似，基本格式如下所示：

```xml
<?xml version="1.0" encoding="UTF-8"?>
<!--指定该文件的官方dtd-->
<!DOCTYPE hibernate-configuration PUBLIC "-//Hibernate/Hibernate Configuration DTD 3.0//EN"
"http://hibernate.sourceforge.net/hibernate-configuration-3.0.dtd" >
<hibernate-configuration>
<session-factory>
    <!--是否在后台打印sql语句，默认为false -->
    <property name="show_sql">值为true或false</property>
    <!--指定sql的本地方言，根据连接的数据库确定-->
    <property name="dialect">sql方言</property>
    <!--指定jdbc驱动程序 -->
    <property name="connection.driver_class">驱动类</property>
    <!--指定jdbc url -->
    <property name="connection.url">jdbc的url</property>
    <!--指定数据库用户名 -->
    <property name="connection.username">数据库用户名</property>
    <!-- 指定数据库密码 -->
    <property name="connection.password">数据库密码</property>
    <!-- C3P0连接池设定 -->
    <!--设定最小连接数-->
    <property name="c3p0.min_size">最小连接数</property>
    <!--设定最大连接数-->
    <property name="c3p0.max_size">最大连接数</property>
    <!--设定延迟所允许的时间（ms）-->
    <property name="c3p0.timeout">延迟所允许的时间</property>
    <!--设定缓存所允许的最大连接数-->
    <property name="c3p0.max_statements">缓存所允许的最大连接数</property>
    <!--设定每隔多少比笔资料送入资料库，清除缓存（定期清除缓存，减小压力） -->
    <property name="hibernate.jdbc.batch_size">多少比</property>
    <!-- 设定事务管理的工厂类 -->
    <property name="hibernate.transaction.factiory_class">事务管理的工厂类</property>
    <!--指定0到多个hbm.xml映射文件-->
    <mapping resource="映射文件全路径"/>
</session-factory>
</hibernate-configuration>
```

MySQL 数据库的驱动类为：com.mysql.jdbc.Driver，默认端口为 3306，连接字串类似为：jdbc:mysql://192.168.1.124:3306/testhibernate

SQLServer 数据库的驱动类为：net.sourceforge.jtds.jdbc.Driver，默认端口为 1433，连接串类似为：

jdbc:jtds:sqlserver://localhost:1433/testhibernate

Oracle 数据库的驱动类为：oracle.jdbc.driver.OracleDriver，默认端口为 1433，连接串类似为：

jdbc:oracle:thin:@192.168.1.124:1521:testhibernate

在 hibernate.cfg.xml 中可使用 connection.datasource 属性来配置 JNDI 连接池，还可以在配置文件中配置 C3P0 和 dpcp 连接池。JNDI 连接池是在别处设置的连接池（例如 Tomcat），配置 JNDI 连接池的方法如下所示：

```
<property name="connection.datasource">java:comp/env/jdbc/testhibernate</property>
```

第 12 章　Hibernate 查询

【本章导读语】

数据库查询是数据库操作中最常用的一种，Hibernate 提供了 HQL 来进行数据库查询，另外还提供条件查询（Criteria Queries）SQL 查询和连接查询等方式。

Hibernate 提供了一种功能强大的查询语言——HQL，这种查询语言虽然在语法结构上与 SQL 类似，但是它与 SQL 的原理不同，它是一种面向对象的查询，它可以理解继承、多态和关联之类的概念。本章将详细介绍 HQL 查询语言，包括它的各种子句，例如 from 子句、select 子句和 where 子句等，以及在 Hibernate 进行查询时如何使用占位符 "?" 和 ":" 进行参数绑定。

条件查询（Criteria Queries）提供了另一种查询方式，它直观而且具有可扩展性，它主要由 Criteria 接口、Criterion 接口和 Expression 类组成。本章将对条件查询的使用进行详细讲解。

HQL 查询是跨平台的，但是有些应用程序需要数据库底层的数据库方言，来执行一些特殊的或复杂的 SQL 语句。对于此种情况，Hibernate 的 Session 接口提供了 createSQLQuery() 方法来执行本地的 SQL 语句。本章的【例 12-3】将通过实例讲解如何在 Hibernate 中使用 SQL 查询。

【例 12-1】Hibernate 查询语言：HQL

〖实例需求〗

HQL（Hibernate Query Language）是 Hibernate 中使用最广泛的一种查询方式，它的语法与 SQL 类似，本实例详细讲解 HQL 的语法，并通过编码实例讲解 HQL 的使用，以及在使用时应该注意的一些问题。

〖开发过程〗

第一步：HQL 概述

Hibernate 提供了一种强大的查询语言：HQL（Hibernate Query Language），它虽然看上去很像 SQL，但却是一种面向对象的查询语言，在其中可以应用继承、多态和关联等知识。它是 Hibernate 提供的查询方式中使用最广泛的一种。下面来看一些 HQL 的知识。

（1）大小写敏感问题。

在 HQL 语言中，Java 类和属性的名称是大小写敏感的，但是 select、from、group by、order by 和 where 等查询关键字大小写不敏感，开发人员可以自行使用，不过笔者建议这些关键字要么全使用大写，要么全使用小写，大小写混用会导致易读性变差。

（2）from 子句。

在 SQL 语句中，from 后紧跟表的名称，而在 HQL 查询语言中，from 后跟随的是实体的名称。例如执行如下 HQL 语句将查询返回 User 以及 User 子类的所有实例：

```
from User
```

而执行如下语句将返回数据库中所有表对应的 POJO 实例：

```
from java.lang.Object
```

一般情况下，需要使用 as 为实体执行一个别名，例如如下语句：

```
from User as obj
```

上句的关键字 as 是可选的，因此上句与下句是等价的：

```
from User obj
```

若需要在多个实体中联合查询对象时，from 后紧跟的实体名称之间可使用英文逗号（,）隔开，例如：

```
from User as user, Department as dept
```

或：

```
from User user, Department dept
```

这两条语句的作用一样，其查询结果都将产生一个笛卡尔积或产生跨表的连接。

（3）select 子句。

select 子句用于选择将哪些属性或哪些对象放入查询结果集中，例如如下语句将 User 实例的 username 和 password 属性查询出来，每条记录的属性被存放在 Object[]数组中：

```
select user.username, user.password from User as user
```

select 语句还可以将查询的信息组装成一个实际的 Java 对象，例如在下面的语句中，对 username 和 password 属性的封装，组装成新的 User 对象，其他属性均未赋值，所以不能用它来进行更新操作：

```
select new User(user.username, user.password) from User as user
```

在 HQL 的 select 子句中也可以使用统计函数，如 count()、min()、max()和 sum()等。例如下面的语句查询年龄最大值、最小值以及记录总数：

```
select max(age) as max, min(age) as min, count(*) as count from User as user
```

在如上语句中，使用 as 关键字给被选择的表达式指定别名。

开发人员还可以使用 select 查询单个或多个对象，例如如下语句查询出用户对应的所有部门信息：

```
select dept from User as user inner join user.dept as dept;
```

若查询的是多个对象时，将被存放在 Object[]数组中。

在开发程序时，有时需要删除重复记录，这时候可在 select 子句中使用 distinct 关键字，例如如下 HQL 语句将取出 username 重复的记录：

```
select distinct user.username from User as user
```

（4）where 子句。

where 子句用于限定查询条件，例如如下语句查询属性名 username 为 amigo 的记录：

```
from User where username= 'amigo'
```

若给定了别名，则对应语句为：

```
from User as user where user.username= 'amigo'
```

where 子句中，我们可以通过比较运算符设定条件，如：=, <>, >, <, >=, <=, between, not between, in, not in, is, like 等。

下面来看一个使用 like 实现模糊查询的实例。如下实例查询 User 中属性名 username 包含 amigo 字符串的所有记录：

```
from User as user where user.username like '%amigo%'
```

接下来看一个使用 ">=" 和 "<=" 来限定查询条件的 where 实例，如下 HQL 语句查询所有 age 在 20～30（包括边界）之间的记录：

from User as user where user.age >= 20 and user.age <= 30

is 比较运算符使用也比较广泛，例如查询 password 属性为空的记录的对应语句为：

from User as user where user.password is null

与此类似，查询 password 属性不为空的记录的 HQL 语句为：

from User as user where user.password is not null

in 和 not in 使用情况也很多，例如如下语句查询 userid 不为 1、2、3、4、5 的记录：

from User as user where user.userid not in(1, 2, 3, 4, 5)

in 和 not in 也常被使用在子查询中。

（5）order by 子句。

开发人员可使用 order by 子句对查询结果按照类中的任何属性进行升序或降序排列，例如在如下的语句中对查询出的 User 实例按照 age 属性降序排列：

from User as user order by user.age desc

desc 指明按照降序排列，若要按照升序排列，可使用如下语句：

from User as user order by user.age asc

因为默认是按照升序排列，所以如上语句可修改成：

from User as user order by user.age

开发人员还可以按照多个属性组合排序，排序的属性之间以英文逗号（,）隔开，优先按照排在前面的属性排序。例如如下语句首先按照 age 升序排列，若 age 属性值相同，则再按照创建时间属性 createTime 降序排列，对应的 HQL 语句为：

from User as user order by user.age asc, user.createTime desc

（6）group by 子句。

返回聚集值的查询可以按照返回的类或组件的任何属性进行分组，例如如下 HQL 语句按照登录次数（loginTimes）属性进行分组：

select user.age from User as user group by user.loginTimes

【提示】带有分组的 HQL 语句必须返回聚集值，如下语句将返回错误信息：

select user.name, user.age from User as user group by user.loginTimes

在运行时，Hibernate 将会出现如下错误：

Exception in thread "main" org.hibernate.QueryException: could not resolve property: name of: amigo.hibernate.query.User [select user.name, user.age from amigo.hibernate.query.User as user group by loginTimes]
　　at　　org.hibernate.persister.entity.AbstractPropertyMapping.propertyException(AbstractPropertyMapping.java:44)
……

带有 group by 子句的 HQL 语句在 select 中可带有多个聚集函数信息，例如：

select user.age, count(user), sum(user.loginTimes) from User as user group by user.age

（7）聚集函数。

在 HQL 语句中，支持如下聚集函数：

- avg()：求平均值。
- sum()：求和。
- max()：求最大值。
- min()：求最小值。
- count()：求记录数。

聚集函数一般出现在 select 子句中，例如如下的语句用于查询记录总数：

```
select count(*) from User
```

count()函数还可以与 distinct 组合使用，例如如下语句查询记录总数以及 username 属性不重复的记录数：

```
select count(*), count(distinct username) from User user
```

如下语句求各用户的登录次数的总和：

```
select sum(user.loginTimes) from User as user
```

下面的语句使用 max()和 min()聚集函数分别求得登录次数的最大值和最小值：

```
select max(user.loginTimes), min(user.loginTimes) from User as user
```

如下语句使用 avg()函数求出 loginTimes 的平均值：

```
select avg(user.loginTimes) from User as user
```

（8）子查询。

对于支持子查询的数据库，例如 Oracle、MySQL 等，Hibernate 支持使用子查询。子查询使用英文圆括号（()）括起来。

例如如下语句查询年龄（age）大于平均年龄的所有记录：

```
from User as user where user.age > (
    select avg(obj.age) from User as obj
)
```

在上面的查询语句中，子查询：select avg(obj.age) from User as obj 查询出平均年龄。

接下来再看一个子查询的实例，在下面的查询语句中使用了 not in 表达式查询用户 amigo 不具有的角色信息：

```
from Role role where role.roleId not in (
    select roleId from UserRole where username = 'amigo'
)
```

子查询除了出现在 where 子句中外，还可以出现在 select 子句中，下面来看一个子查询出现在 select 子句的情况，如下的 HQL 语句查询各用户所具有的角色数量：

```
select user.username,
    (select count(*) from UserRole as obj where obj.username = user.username)
from User as user
```

（9）join 子句。

开发人员可以使用 join 关键字为相关联的实体甚至是一个集合的全部元素指定一个别名，join 包括如下方式：

- inner join：内连接，inner join 语句使用举例如下：

```
select details.detailId, details.owner, card.type
from CREDIT_CARD card
    inner join BILLING_DETAILS details on
        details.cardId = card.cardId
```

- left outer join：左外连接。
- right outer join：右外连接。
- full join：全连接。

第二步：参数绑定

（1）通过顺序占位符"?"来填充参数。

在 HQL 语句中，可使用顺序占位符"?"来填充参数信息。在 Hibernate 2 中，使用 Session

对象的 find()方法来查询需要参数绑定的查询。

例如如下的语句在 Hibernate 2 中，查询 username 模糊匹配：amigo，并且年龄大于 25 的用户记录：

```
Object[] args = new Object[] {
        "%amigo%",
        new Integer(25)};
Type[] types = new Type{
        Hibernate.STRING,
        Hibernate.INTEGER};
session.find("from User user where user.username like ? and user.age > ?",
        args,
        types);
```

在 Hibernate 3 中，改用 Query 进行查询，下面的代码完成上面代码同样的功能：

```
Query query = session.createQuery(
        "from User user where user.username like ? and user.age > ?");
query.setParameter(0, "%amigo%");
query.setParameter(1, new Integer(25));
List userList = query.list();
```

（2）通过占位符":"来填充参数。

开发人员也可以使用占位符来填充参数，因为采用 key-value 的方式对应，所以可以不按照顺序设置，上面的查询若改成占位符":"的方式，可将代码修改为：

```
Query query = session.createQuery(
        "from User user where user.username like :username and user.age > :age");
query.setParameter("username", "%amigo%");
query.setParameter("age", new Integer(25));
List userList = query.list();
```

【提示】占位符后的名称与 query.setParameter(String arg0, Object arg1)方法的第一个参数对应，若没找到对应的参数，将会抛出异常信息。

（3）分页查询。

在数据量比较大时，一般不会一次查出所有数据，因为这样会因查询结果集太大，而导致查询速度慢，更有甚者会导致内存溢出的异常，Hibernate 中也提供了分页查询的方法。

Query 接口提供了 setFirstResult()方法来设定第一条被查询的记录的 index 值，另外它还提供了 setMaxResults()方法限制每页查询的最大数量。例如若想查询 User 中的第一页的记录，每页为 5 条数据，可使用如下语句：

```
Query query = session.createQuery("from User user");
query.setFirstResult(0);
query.setMaxResults(5);
List userList = query.list();
```

【提示】maxResults 被设置为 5，若数据库中该表的记录少于 5 条也是可以的。

第三步：建立工程

按照第 11 章的方式建立一个名为 hibernatequery 的 Java 工程，将 Hibernate 的 jar 复制到 lib 目录，并将其加入 CLASSPATH 路径中。接着在 src 源码目录中创建 amigo.hibernate.query 的包，并将 log4j 的配置文件 log4j.properties 复制到 src 源码目录。完成后，目录结构如图 12-1 所示。

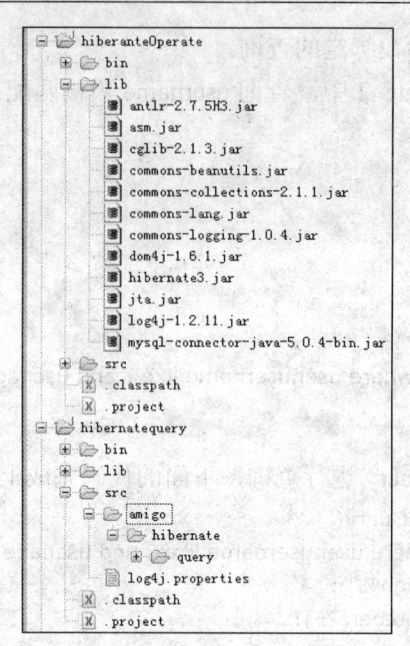

图 12-1 工程的目录结构

第四步：创建数据库和表

为了演示 HQL 语句的使用，读者可在 MySQL 中建立名为 hibernatequery 的数据库，并在其中建立表：tbl_user 和 tbl_dept，对应的 SQL 脚本如下所示：

```sql
CREATE DATABASE 'hibernatequery' /*!40100 DEFAULT CHARACTER SET gb2312 */;
USE 'hibernatequery';

CREATE TABLE 'tbl_dept' (
  'deptId' int(11) NOT NULL auto_increment COMMENT '部门 id',
  'deptName' varchar(50) default NULL COMMENT '部门名称',
  PRIMARY KEY  ('deptId')
) ENGINE=InnoDB DEFAULT CHARSET=gb2312 COMMENT='部门信息表';

INSERT INTO 'tbl_dept' ('deptId', 'deptName') VALUES (1,'软件研发部');

CREATE TABLE 'tbl_user' (
  'userid' int(11) NOT NULL auto_increment COMMENT '用户 id',
  'username' varchar(50) NOT NULL COMMENT '用户名',
  'password' varchar(50) NOT NULL COMMENT '密码',
  'loginTimes' int(11) NOT NULL default '0' COMMENT '登录次数',
  'createTime' datetime default NULL COMMENT '创建时间',
  'deptId' int(11) default NULL COMMENT '所属部门',
  PRIMARY KEY  ('userid'),
  KEY 'deptId' ('deptId')
) ENGINE=InnoDB DEFAULT CHARSET=gb2312 COMMENT='用户信息表';

INSERT INTO 'tbl_user' ('userid', 'username', 'password', 'loginTimes', 'createTime', 'deptId') VALUES (1,'amigo','1111',2,'2008-09-15 12:00:00',1);
INSERT INTO 'tbl_user' ('userid', 'username', 'password', 'loginTimes', 'createTime', 'deptId') VALUES (2,'xiexx','2222',5,'2008-09-15 13:05:00',1);
```

INSERT INTO 'tbl_user' ('userid', 'username', 'password', 'loginTimes', 'createTime', 'deptId') VALUES (3,'test','3333',3,'2008-09-15 12:40:30',1);
INSERT INTO 'tbl_user' ('userid', 'username', 'password', 'loginTimes', 'createTime', 'deptId') VALUES (4,'test4','4444',2,'2008-09-15 14:00:00',1);

ALTER TABLE 'tbl_user'
ADD FOREIGN KEY ('deptId') REFERENCES 'tbl_dept' ('deptId');

第五步：编写 Hibernate 配置文件：hibernate.cfg.xml

在 src 目录中建立 Hibernate 配置文件：hibernate.cfg.xml，该文件配置连接 hibernatequery 数据库，并将映射文件 User.hbm.xml 和 Dept.hbm.xml 加入其中，该文件的内容如下所示：

```xml
<?xml version='1.0' encoding='UTF-8'?>
<!DOCTYPE hibernate-configuration PUBLIC
        "-//Hibernate/Hibernate Configuration DTD 3.0//EN"
        "http://hibernate.sourceforge.net/hibernate-configuration-3.0.dtd">
<hibernate-configuration>
    <session-factory>
      <property name="show_sql">true</property>
      <property name="dialect">org.hibernate.dialect.MySQLDialect</property>
        <property name="connection.url">jdbc:mysql://localhost:3306/hibernatequery</property>
        <property name="connection.username">root</property>
        <property name="connection.password">root</property>
        <property name="connection.driver_class">com.mysql.jdbc.Driver</property>

        <!--指定 0 到多个 hbm.xml 映射文件-->
        <mapping resource="amigo/hibernate/query/User.hbm.xml" />
        <mapping resource="amigo/hibernate/query/Dept.hbm.xml" />
    </session-factory>
</hibernate-configuration>
```

第六步：编写 Hibernate 映射文件：Dept.hbm.xml 和 Dept.java

在 amigo.hibernate.query 包中创建 tbl_dept 表的 Hibernate 映射文件 Dept.hbm.xml 及其对应的 POJO 类 Dept.java，Dept.java 类的代码如下所示：

```java
package amigo.hibernate.query;

import java.io.Serializable;
import java.util.HashSet;
import java.util.Set;

/**
 * 部门信息表对应的 pojo 类
 */
public class Dept implements Serializable {
    private static final long serialVersionUID = 1L;

    /** 部门 id(自增). */
    private java.lang.Integer deptId;

    /**部门名称. */
    private java.lang.String deptName;
```

```
    /** 该部门关联的用户对象. */
    private Set<User> users = new HashSet<User>();

    // 省略各属性的 getter/setter 方法
}
```

映射文件 Dept.hbm.xml 的内容如下所示:

```xml
<?xml version="1.0" encoding='UTF-8'?>
<!DOCTYPE hibernate-mapping PUBLIC
                "-//Hibernate/Hibernate Mapping DTD 3.0//EN"
                "http://hibernate.sourceforge.net/hibernate-mapping-3.0.dtd" >

<hibernate-mapping package="amigo.hibernate.query">
    <class name="Dept" table="tbl_dept">
        <id name="deptId" column="deptId" type="java.lang.Integer">
            <generator class="native"/>
        </id>
        <property name="deptName" column="deptName" type="java.lang.String"  not-null="true" />
        <set name="users" cascade ="save-update">
            <key>
                <column name="deptId" />
            </key>
            <one-to-many class="User" />
        </set>
    </class>
</hibernate-mapping>
```

第七步：编写 Hibernate 映射文件：User.hbm.xml 和 User.java

在 amigo.hibernate.query 包中创建 tbl_user 表的 Hibernate 映射文件 User.hbm.xml 及其对应的 POJO 类 User.java，User.java 类的代码如下所示：

```java
package amigo.hibernate.query;

import java.io.Serializable;
import java.util.Date;

/**
 * 用户信息的 POJO 类.
 */
public class User implements Serializable {
    private static final long serialVersionUID = 1L;

    /** 用户 id. */
    private Integer userid;

    /** 用户名. */
    private java.lang.String username;

    /** 密码. */
    private java.lang.String password;

    /** 登录次数. */
```

```
    private Integer loginTimes;

    /** 创建时间. */
    private Date createTime;

    /** 部门. */
    private Dept dept;

    // 省略各属性的 getter/setter 方法
}
```

映射文件 User.hbm.xml 的内容如下所示：

```xml
......
<hibernate-mapping package="amigo.hibernate.query">
    <class name="User" table="tbl_user">
        <id name="userid" column="userid" type="java.lang.Integer">
            <generator class="native"/>
        </id>
        <property name="username" column="username" type="java.lang.String"  not-null="true" />
        <property name="password" column="password" type="java.lang.String"  not-null="true" />
        <property name="loginTimes" column="loginTimes" type="java.lang.Integer"  not-null="true" />
        <property name="createtime" column="createTime" type="java.util.Date" />
        <many-to-one name="dept"
                column="deptId"
                class="Dept" />
    </class>
</hibernate-mapping>
```

第八步：编写 Session 工厂类：HibernateSessionFactory.java

在 amigo.hibernate.query 包中创建 Session 工厂类，该类提供获得当前 Session 和关闭 Session 的方法，该类的代码如下所示：

```java
package amigo.hibernate.query;

import org.hibernate.HibernateException;
import org.hibernate.Session;
import org.hibernate.SessionFactory;
import org.hibernate.cfg.Configuration;
import org.apache.log4j.*;

/**
 * Hibernate 的 session 获取类.
 */
public class HibernateSessionFactory {
    public static Logger log = (Logger)Logger.getLogger(HibernateSessionFactory.class);

    private static String CONFIG_FILE_LOCATION = "/hibernate.cfg.xml";

    /** Holds a single instance of Session */
    private static final ThreadLocal threadLocal = new ThreadLocal();

    /** The single instance of hibernate configuration */
    private static final Configuration cfg = new Configuration();
```

```java
/** The single instance of hibernate SessionFactory */
private static SessionFactory sessionFactory;


/**
 * 返回 ThreadLocal 中的 Session 实例.
 * 采用懒加载的方式
 */
public static Session currentSession() throws HibernateException {
    Session session = (Session) threadLocal.get();

    if(session==null || session.isOpen()==false){
        if (sessionFactory == null) {
            try {
                cfg.configure(CONFIG_FILE_LOCATION);
                sessionFactory = cfg.buildSessionFactory();
            } catch (Exception e) {
                log.error(e);
                log.error("Error Creating SessionFactory %%%%"+ session.isOpen());
            }
        }
        session = sessionFactory.openSession();
        threadLocal.set(session);
    }

    return session;
}

/**
 * 关闭 session.
 */
public static void closeSession() throws HibernateException {
    Session session = (Session) threadLocal.get();
    threadLocal.set(null);

    if (session != null) {
        session.close();
    }
}

private HibernateSessionFactory() {
}
}
```

第九步：编写 HQL 查询测试类：HqlTest.java

在 amigo.hibernate.query.hql 包中创建 HQL 查询测试类：HqlTest.java，该类展示 HQL 语句的查询，代码如下所示：

```java
package amigo.hibernate.query.hql;

import java.util.List;
```

```java
import org.apache.log4j.Logger;
import org.hibernate.Query;
import org.hibernate.Session;

import amigo.hibernate.query.HibernateSessionFactory;
import amigo.hibernate.query.User;

/**
 * hql 语句使用实例.
 */
public class HqlTest {
    private static Logger log = Logger.getLogger(HqlTest.class);

    public static void main(String[] args) throws Exception {
        Session session = HibernateSessionFactory.currentSession();

        log.info("==========查询所有数据，最简单的hql=========");
        List allUserList = session.createQuery("from User").list();
        printUserInfo(allUserList);

        log.info("=======带有 where 查询子句的HQL，查询用户名为 amigo 的信息=======");
        List userList = session.createQuery(
                "from User as user where user.username = 'amigo'").list();
        printUserInfo(userList);

        log.info("======= 带有 select 子句的 HQL 查询用户的 username 和 loginTimes 信息 =======");
        List userProList = session.createQuery(
                "select user.username, user.loginTimes from User as user").list();
        for (int i = 0; i < userProList.size(); i++) {
            // 获得的是一个数组
            Object[] array = (Object[]) userProList.get(i);
            String username = (String) array[0];
            Integer loginTimes = (Integer) array[1];
            log.info("i=" + i + ", username=" + username + ", loginTimes=" + loginTimes);
        }

        log.info("=======带有 order by 子句的HQL，按照 loginTimes 进行降序排列=======");
        List userOrderByList = session.createQuery(
                "from User as user order by loginTimes desc").list();
        printUserInfo(userOrderByList);

        log.info("=======带有 group by 子句的HQL，按照 loginTimes 进行分组=======");
        List userGroupByList = session.createQuery(
                "select user.loginTimes, count(user.loginTimes), max(user.loginTimes) " +
                "from User as user group by user.loginTimes").list();
        for (int i = 0; i < userGroupByList.size(); i++) {
            // 获得的是一个数组
            Object[] array = (Object[]) userGroupByList.get(i);
            Integer loginTimes = (Integer) array[0];
            Long countLoginTimes = (Long) array[1];
            Integer maxLoginTimes = (Integer) array[2];
```

```java
                log.info("i=" + i + ", loginTimes=" + loginTimes
                        + ", countLoginTimes=" + countLoginTimes
                        + ", maxLoginTimes=" + maxLoginTimes);
            }

            log.info("=======带有子查询的的 HQL，查询登录次数大于平均登录次数的记录=======");
            List userSubQueryList = session.createQuery(
                    "from User as user where user.loginTimes > " +
                    "(" +
                    "   select avg(obj.loginTimes) from User as obj" +
                    ")").list();
            printUserInfo(userSubQueryList);


            log.info("=====通过顺序占位符\"?\"来填充参数，查询用户名中含有 test，并且 loginTimes 大于 2 的记录");
            Query query1 = session.createQuery(
                    "from User user where user.username like ? and user.loginTimes > ?");
            query1.setParameter(0, "%test%");
            query1.setParameter(1, new Integer(2));
            List userList1 = query1.list();
            printUserInfo(userList1);

            log.info("=====通过占位符\":\"来填充参数，查询用户名中含有 test，并且 loginTimes 大于 2 的记录");
            Query query2 = session.createQuery(
                    "from User user where user.username like :username and user.loginTimes > :loginTimes");
            query2.setParameter("username", "%test%");
            query2.setParameter("loginTimes", new Integer(2));
            List userList2 = query2.list();
            printUserInfo(userList2);


            log.info("=============分页查询，查询两条记录=============");
            Query query3 = session.createQuery("from User user");
            query3.setFirstResult(0);
            query3.setMaxResults(2);
            List userList3 = query3.list();
            printUserInfo(userList3);


        // 关闭 Session
        HibernateSessionFactory.closeSession();
    }

    private static void printUserInfo(List userList) throws Exception {
        for (int i = 0; i < userList.size(); i++) {
            User user = (User) userList.get(i);
            log.info("i=" + i + ", username=" + user.getUsername()
                    + ",password=" + user.getPassword() + ", loginTimes=" + user.getLoginTimes());
        }
    }
}
```

第十步：运行结果

运行测试类 HqlTest.java，该类的运行结果如下所示：

amigo.hibernate.query.hql.HqlTest - ==========查询所有数据，最简单的 hql=========
Hibernate: select user0_.userid as userid0_, user0_.username as username0_, user0_.password as password0_, user0_.loginTimes as loginTimes0_, user0_.createTime as createTime0_, user0_.deptId as deptId0_ from tbl_user user0_
amigo.hibernate.query.hql.HqlTest - i=0, username=amigo,password=1111, loginTimes=2
amigo.hibernate.query.hql.HqlTest - i=1, username=xiexx,password=2222, loginTimes=5
amigo.hibernate.query.hql.HqlTest - i=2, username=test,password=3333, loginTimes=3
amigo.hibernate.query.hql.HqlTest - i=3, username=test4,password=4444, loginTimes=2
amigo.hibernate.query.hql.HqlTest - =======带有 where 查询子句的 HQL，查询用户名为 amigo 的信息=======
Hibernate: select user0_.userid as userid0_, user0_.username as username0_, user0_.password as password0_, user0_.loginTimes as loginTimes0_, user0_.createTime as createTime0_, user0_.deptId as deptId0_ from tbl_user user0_ where user0_.username='amigo'
amigo.hibernate.query.hql.HqlTest - i=0, username=amigo,password=1111, loginTimes=2
amigo.hibernate.query.hql.HqlTest - =======带有 select 子句的 HQL 查询用户的 username 和 loginTimes 信息=======
Hibernate: select user0_.username as col_0_0_, user0_.loginTimes as col_1_0_ from tbl_user user0_
amigo.hibernate.query.hql.HqlTest - i=0, username=amigo, loginTimes=2
amigo.hibernate.query.hql.HqlTest - i=1, username=xiexx, loginTimes=5
amigo.hibernate.query.hql.HqlTest - i=2, username=test, loginTimes=3
amigo.hibernate.query.hql.HqlTest - i=3, username=test4, loginTimes=2
amigo.hibernate.query.hql.HqlTest - =======带有 order by 子句的 HQL，按照 loginTimes 进行降序排列=======
Hibernate: select user0_.userid as userid0_, user0_.username as username0_, user0_.password as password0_, user0_.loginTimes as loginTimes0_, user0_.createTime as createTime0_, user0_.deptId as deptId0_ from tbl_user user0_ order by user0_.loginTimes desc
amigo.hibernate.query.hql.HqlTest - i=0, username=xiexx,password=2222, loginTimes=5
amigo.hibernate.query.hql.HqlTest - i=1, username=test,password=3333, loginTimes=3
amigo.hibernate.query.hql.HqlTest - i=2, username=amigo,password=1111, loginTimes=2
amigo.hibernate.query.hql.HqlTest - i=3, username=test4,password=4444, loginTimes=2
amigo.hibernate.query.hql.HqlTest - =======带有 group by 子句的 HQL，按照 loginTimes 进行分组=======
Hibernate: select user0_.loginTimes as col_0_0_, count(user0_.loginTimes) as col_1_0_, max(user0_.loginTimes) as col_2_0_ from tbl_user user0_ group by user0_.loginTimes
amigo.hibernate.query.hql.HqlTest - i=0, loginTimes=2, countLoginTimes=2, maxLoginTimes=2
amigo.hibernate.query.hql.HqlTest - i=1, loginTimes=3, countLoginTimes=1, maxLoginTimes=3
amigo.hibernate.query.hql.HqlTest - i=2, loginTimes=5, countLoginTimes=1, maxLoginTimes=5
amigo.hibernate.query.hql.HqlTest - =======带有子查询的的 HQL，查询登录次数大于平均登录次数的记录=======
Hibernate: select user0_.userid as userid0_, user0_.username as username0_, user0_.password as password0_, user0_.loginTimes as loginTimes0_, user0_.createTime as createTime0_, user0_.deptId as deptId0_ from tbl_user user0_ where user0_.loginTimes>(select avg(user1_.loginTimes) from tbl_user user1_)
amigo.hibernate.query.hql.HqlTest - i=0, username=xiexx,password=2222, loginTimes=5
amigo.hibernate.query.hql.HqlTest - =====通过顺序占位符"?"来填充参数，查询用户名中含有 test，并且 loginTimes 大于 2 的记录
Hibernate: select user0_.userid as userid0_, user0_.username as username0_, user0_.password as password0_, user0_.loginTimes as loginTimes0_, user0_.createTime as createTime0_, user0_.deptId as

```
deptId0_ from tbl_user user0_ where (user0_.username like ?) and user0_.loginTimes>?
    amigo.hibernate.query.hql.HqlTest    - i=0, username=test,password=3333, loginTimes=3
    amigo.hibernate.query.hql.HqlTest    - =====通过占位符":"来填充参数，查询用户名中含有 test，并且
loginTimes 大于 2 的记录
    Hibernate: select user0_.userid as userid0_, user0_.username as username0_, user0_.password as
password0_, user0_.loginTimes as loginTimes0_, user0_.createTime as createTime0_, user0_.deptId as
deptId0_ from tbl_user user0_ where (user0_.username like ?) and user0_.loginTimes>?
    amigo.hibernate.query.hql.HqlTest    - i=0, username=test,password=3333, loginTimes=3
    amigo.hibernate.query.hql.HqlTest    - =============分页查询，查询两条记录============
    Hibernate: select user0_.userid as userid0_, user0_.username as username0_, user0_.password as
password0_, user0_.loginTimes as loginTimes0_, user0_.createTime as createTime0_, user0_.deptId as
deptId0_ from tbl_user user0_ limit ?
    amigo.hibernate.query.hql.HqlTest    - i=0, username=amigo,password=1111, loginTimes=2
    amigo.hibernate.query.hql.HqlTest    - i=1, username=xiexx,password=2222, loginTimes=5
```

【例 12-2】条件查询（Criteria Queries）

〖实例需求〗

采用 HQL 查询语言进行查询时，需要定义 HQL 查询语句，条件查询（Criteria Queries）提供了另一种查询方式，它直观而且具有可扩展性，它主要由 Criteria 接口、Criterion 接口和 Expression 类组成。

本实例讲解条件查询（Criteria Queries）的使用，以及在使用时需要注意的一些问题。

〖开发过程〗

第一步：创建包：amigo.hibernate.query.criteria

在 src 源码目录中创建包：amigo.hibernate.query.criteria，该包用于存放本实例的类文件。

第二步：条件查询概述

org.hibernate.Criteria 接口是条件查询的核心接口，它表示特定持久类的一个查询，其创建方法如下所示：

```
Criteria criteria = session.createCriteria(User.class);
```

使用 org.hibernate.Criteria 接口的 setMaxResults(...)方法可设置记录大小，使用 list()方法可获得查询到的记录列表。

若要限定查询条件，可使用 Criterion 添加查询限制。例如需要查询 username 中含有 test，并且 loginTimes 大小 2 的用户记录，可使用如下语句：

```
Criteria criteria = session.createCriteria(User.class);

// 限定查询条件
Criterion criterion1 = Expression.like("username", "%test%");
Criterion criterion2 = Expression.gt("loginTimes", new Integer(2));
criteria.add(criterion1);
criteria.add(criterion2);
List userList = criteria.list();
```

org.hibernate.criterion.Expression 类定义了某些内置的 Criterion 类型的工厂方法，它提供等于（eq(...)）、大于（gt(...)）、模糊匹配（like(...)）、或（or）、为空（isNull(...)）等方法。如上的句子，运行时产生的 SQL 语句如下所示：

Hibernate: select this_.userid as userid0_0_, this_.username as username0_0_, this_.password as password0_0_, this_.loginTimes as loginTimes0_0_, this_.createTime as createTime0_0_, this_.deptId as deptId0_0_ from tbl_user this_ where this_.username like ? and this_.loginTimes>?

若要对结果集进行排序，可使用一个或多个 addOrder(...)方法添加排序的列，例如若要首先按照 loginTimes 降序排列，而后按照 createTime 升序排列，可使用如下语句来实现：

```
Criteria criteria = session.createCriteria(User.class);
criteria.addOrder(Order.desc("loginTimes"));
criteria.addOrder(Order.desc("createTime"));
List userList = criteria3.list();
```

使用条件查询（Criteria Queries）也可以实现分页查询，Criteria 接口提供了 setFirstResult()方法来设置需要取得第一条记录，setMaxResults()方法用于设置最多取得的记录数。例如如下语句获得从第 6 条记录开始的 10 条记录：

```
Criteria criteria = session.createCriteria(User.class);
criteria.setFirstResult(5);
criteria.setMaxResults(10);
List userList = criteria.list();
```

第三步：编写条件查询测试类：CriteriaTest.java

在 amigo.hibernate.query.criteria 包中创建测试类：CriteriaTest.java，用于展示条件查询的使用，该类的代码如下所示：

```java
package amigo.hibernate.query.criteria;

import java.util.List;

import org.apache.log4j.Logger;
import org.hibernate.Criteria;
import org.hibernate.Session;
import org.hibernate.criterion.Criterion;
import org.hibernate.criterion.Expression;
import org.hibernate.criterion.Order;

import amigo.hibernate.query.HibernateSessionFactory;
import amigo.hibernate.query.User;

public class CriteriaTest {
    private static Logger log = Logger.getLogger(CriteriaTest.class);

    public static void main(String[] args) throws Exception {
        Session session  = HibernateSessionFactory.currentSession();

        log.info("========查询所有用户记录======");
        Criteria criteria1 = session.createCriteria(User.class);
        List allUserList = criteria1.list();
        printUserInfo(allUserList);
```

```java
        log.info("========查询username 中含有test，则loginTimes 大于2 的记录======");
        Criteria criteria2 = session.createCriteria(User.class);
        // 限定查询条件
        Criterion criterion1 = Expression.like("username", "%test%");
        Criterion criterion2 = Expression.gt("loginTimes", new Integer(2));
        criteria2.add(criterion1);
        criteria2.add(criterion2);
        List userList = criteria2.list();
        printUserInfo(userList);

        log.info("========添加排序,首先按照loginTimes 降序,而后按照createTime 升序======");
        Criteria criteria3 = session.createCriteria(User.class);
        criteria3.addOrder(Order.desc("loginTimes"));
        criteria3.addOrder(Order.desc("createTime"));
        List userList3 = criteria3.list();
        printUserInfo(userList3);

        log.info("========分页查询，查出从2（第3 条开始）的2 条数据======");
        Criteria criteria4 = session.createCriteria(User.class);
        criteria4.setFirstResult(3);
        criteria4.setMaxResults(10);
        List userList4 = criteria4.list();
        printUserInfo(userList4);

        // 关闭Session
        HibernateSessionFactory.closeSession();
    }

    private static void printUserInfo(List userList) throws Exception {
        for (int i = 0; i < userList.size(); i++) {
            User user = (User) userList.get(i);
            log.info("i=" + i + ", username=" + user.getUsername()
                    + ",password=" + user.getPassword() + ", loginTimes=" + user.getLoginTimes());
        }
    }
}
```

第四步：运行结果

运行类 CriteriaTest.java，运行结果如下所示：

```
amigo.hibernate.query.criteria.CriteriaTest  - ========查询所有用户记录======
Hibernate: select this_.userid as userid0_0_, this_.username as username0_0_, this_.password as password0_0_, this_.loginTimes as loginTimes0_0_, this_.createTime as createTime0_0_, this_.deptId as deptId0_0_ from tbl_user this_
amigo.hibernate.query.criteria.CriteriaTest  - i=0, username=amigo,password=1111, loginTimes=2
amigo.hibernate.query.criteria.CriteriaTest  - i=1, username=xiexx,password=2222, loginTimes=5
amigo.hibernate.query.criteria.CriteriaTest  - i=2, username=test,password=3333, loginTimes=3
amigo.hibernate.query.criteria.CriteriaTest  - i=3, username=test4,password=4444, loginTimes=2
amigo.hibernate.query.criteria.CriteriaTest  - ========查询username 中含有test，则loginTimes 大于2 的记录======
Hibernate: select this_.userid as userid0_0_, this_.username as username0_0_, this_.password as password0_0_, this_.loginTimes as loginTimes0_0_, this_.createTime as createTime0_0_, this_.deptId as
```

deptId0_0_ from tbl_user this_ where this_.username like ? and this_.loginTimes>?
    amigo.hibernate.query.criteria.CriteriaTest   - i=0, username=test,password=3333, loginTimes=3
    amigo.hibernate.query.criteria.CriteriaTest   - ========添加排序，首先按照 loginTimes 降序，而后按照 createTime 升序======
    Hibernate: select this_.userid as userid0_0_, this_.username as username0_0_, this_.password as password0_0_, this_.loginTimes as loginTimes0_0_, this_.createTime as createTime0_0_, this_.deptId as deptId0_0_ from tbl_user this_ order by this_.loginTimes desc, this_.createTime desc
    amigo.hibernate.query.criteria.CriteriaTest   - i=0, username=xiexx,password=2222, loginTimes=5
    amigo.hibernate.query.criteria.CriteriaTest   - i=1, username=test,password=3333, loginTimes=3
    amigo.hibernate.query.criteria.CriteriaTest   - i=2, username=test4,password=4444, loginTimes=2
    amigo.hibernate.query.criteria.CriteriaTest   - i=3, username=amigo,password=1111, loginTimes=2
    amigo.hibernate.query.criteria.CriteriaTest   - ========分页查询，查出从 2（第 3 条开始）的 2 条数据======
    Hibernate: select this_.userid as userid0_0_, this_.username as username0_0_, this_.password as password0_0_, this_.loginTimes as loginTimes0_0_, this_.createTime as createTime0_0_, this_.deptId as deptId0_0_ from tbl_user this_ limit ?, ?
    amigo.hibernate.query.criteria.CriteriaTest   - i=0, username=test4,password=4444, loginTimes=2

【例 12-3】SQL 查询

〖实例需求〗

采用 HQL 和条件查询（Criteria Queries）进行查询时，Hibernate 会生成适用于各种数据库平台的标准的 SQL 查询语句，这两种检索方式是跨平台的，但是有些应用程序需要数据库底层的数据库方言来执行一些特殊的或复杂的 SQL 语句。

对于此种情况，Hibernate 的 Session 接口提供了 createSQLQuery()方法来执行本地的 SQL 语句。本实例讲解如何在 Hibernate 中进行本地的 SQL 查询。

〖开发过程〗

第一步：创建包：amigo.hibernate.query.sql

在 src 源码目录中创建包：amigo.hibernate.query.sql，该包用于存放本实例的类文件。

第二步：说明

Session 接口的 createSQLQuery()方法返回一个 SQLQuery 查询，该类继承 org.hibernate.Query 类，因此具有该类的方法。使用该类的：

    setParameter(String arg0, String arg1)

方法可设置占位符参数的信息，而使用该类的：

    addEntity(String arg0, Class arg1)

方法设置查询返回的实体。例如如下语句查询 tbl_user 表中 username 字段中包括 test，且 loginTimes 大于 2 的记录：

    SQLQuery query = session.createSQLQuery(
            "select * from tbl_user as user " +
            "where username like :username and loginTimes > :loginTimes");

```
query.setParameter("username", "%test%");
query.setParameter("loginTimes", new Integer(2));
query.addEntity("user", User.class);
List userList = query.list();
```

在上面的代码中，使用"*"代表所有属性，当然开发人员也可以显式地列出所需要的字段，但是此时需要让 Hibernate 为每个属性加上字段别名，这些字段的占位符以字段别名为前导，再加上属性名。例如下面的例子，作用与前面的 SQL 查询实例类似，但是在写法上有些不同：

```
SQLQuery query = session.createSQLQuery(
    "select userid as {user.userid}, username as {user.username} from tbl_user as user " +
    "where username like :username and loginTimes > :loginTimes");
query.setParameter("username", "%test%");
query.setParameter("loginTimes", new Integer(2));
query.addEntity("user", User.class);
List userList = query1.list();
```

第三步：编写 SQL 查询测试类：SqlTest.java

在 amigo.hibernate.query.sql 包中创建测试类：SqlTest.java，用于展示 SQL 查询的使用，该类的代码如下所示：

```java
package amigo.hibernate.query.sql;

import java.util.List;

import org.apache.log4j.Logger;
import org.hibernate.SQLQuery;
import org.hibernate.Session;

import amigo.hibernate.query.HibernateSessionFactory;
import amigo.hibernate.query.User;

/**
 * 在 Hibernate 中使用 SQL 查询.
 * @author <a href="mailto:xiexingxing1121@126.com">AmigoXie</a>
 * @Creation date: Sep 15, 2008 - 4:41:21 PM
 */
public class SqlTest {
    private static Logger log = Logger.getLogger(SqlTest.class);

    public static void main(String[] args) throws Exception {
        Session session = HibernateSessionFactory.currentSession();

        log.info("============查询所有记录================");
        SQLQuery query = session.createSQLQuery(
                "select * from tbl_user as user");
        query.addEntity("user", User.class);
        List userList = query.list();
        printUserInfo(userList);

        log.info("======查询 username 字段中包括 test，则 loginTimes 大于 2 的记录======");
        SQLQuery query1 = session.createSQLQuery(
                "select * from tbl_user as user " +
                "where username like :username and loginTimes > :loginTimes");
```

```java
            query1.setParameter("username", "%test%");
            query1.setParameter("loginTimes", new Integer(2));
            query1.addEntity("user", User.class);
            List userList1 = query1.list();
            printUserInfo(userList1);

            log.info("===查询 username 字段中包括 test，则 loginTimes 大于 2 的记录的另一种写法===");
            SQLQuery query2 = session.createSQLQuery(
                    "select userid as {user.userid}, username as {user.username} from tbl_user as user " +
                    "where username like :username and loginTimes > :loginTimes");
            query2.setParameter("username", "%test%");
            query2.setParameter("loginTimes", new Integer(2));
            query2.addEntity("user", User.class);
            List userList2 = query2.list();
            printUserInfo(userList2);

            log.info("==========分页查询，查询从第 2 条记录开始的 5 条记录======");
            SQLQuery query3 = session.createSQLQuery(
                    "select * from tbl_user as user");
            query3.setFirstResult(1);
            query3.setMaxResults(5);
            query3.addEntity("user", User.class);
            List userList3 = query3.list();
            printUserInfo(userList3);

            // 关闭 Session
        HibernateSessionFactory.closeSession();
    }

    private static void printUserInfo(List userList) throws Exception {
        for (int i = 0; i < userList.size(); i++) {
            User user = (User) userList.get(i);
            log.info("i=" + i + ", username=" + user.getUsername()
                    + ",password=" + user.getPassword() + ", loginTimes=" + user.getLoginTimes());
        }
    }
}
```

第四步：运行结果

运行类 SqlTest.java，运行结果如下所示：

```
amigo.hibernate.query.sql.SqlTest    - ============查询所有记录====================
Hibernate: select * from tbl_user as user
amigo.hibernate.query.sql.SqlTest    - i=0, username=amigo,password=1111, loginTimes=2
amigo.hibernate.query.sql.SqlTest    - i=1, username=xiexx,password=2222, loginTimes=5
amigo.hibernate.query.sql.SqlTest    - i=2, username=test,password=3333, loginTimes=3
amigo.hibernate.query.sql.SqlTest    - i=3, username=test4,password=4444, loginTimes=2
amigo.hibernate.query.sql.SqlTest    - =========查询 username 字段中包括 test，则 loginTimes 大于 2 的记录======
```

```
Hibernate: select * from tbl_user as user where username like ? and loginTimes > ?
amigo.hibernate.query.sql.SqlTest    - i=0, username=test,password=3333, loginTimes=3
amigo.hibernate.query.sql.SqlTest    - =====查询 username 字段中包括 test，则 loginTimes 大于 2 的记录
的另一种写法===
Hibernate: select userid as userid0_0_, username as username0_0_ from tbl_user as user where
username like ? and loginTimes > ?
amigo.hibernate.query.sql.SqlTest    - i=0, username=test,password=3333, loginTimes=3
amigo.hibernate.query.sql.SqlTest    - =======分页查询，查询从第 2 条记录开始的 5 条记录====
Hibernate: select * from tbl_user as user limit ?, ?
amigo.hibernate.query.sql.SqlTest    - i=0, username=xiexx,password=2222, loginTimes=5
amigo.hibernate.query.sql.SqlTest    - i=1, username=test,password=3333, loginTimes=3
amigo.hibernate.query.sql.SqlTest    - i=2, username=test4,password=4444, loginTimes=2
```

【例 12-4】连接查询

〖实例需求〗

HQL 和条件查询（Criteria Queries）支持内连接、外连接和交叉连接等连接查询。本实例首先介绍映射文件中的检索策略，而后讲述如何使用 Hibernate 进行连接查询。

〖开发过程〗

第一步：检索策略说明

在进行关联时，Hibernate 中有如下 3 种检索策略：
- 立即检索：立即加载和检索指定的对象关联的对象。
- 延迟检索：延迟加载和检索指定的对象关联的对象。
- 迫切左外连接检索：通过左外连接加载和检索指定的对象关联的对象。

在存在关联的 Hibernate 映射文件中，可使用如下属性设定检索策略：
- lazy：值可为 true 或 false，默认为 false，用于指定是否使用延迟加载策略，为 true 表示使用延迟加载，为 false 表示立即加载。
- outer-join：值可为 auto、true 和 false。在<set/>元素中，默认值为 false，在<one-to-one/>和<many-to-one/>元素中默认值为 auto。true 表示使用迫切左外连接检索策略，false 表示不使用。
- batch-size：该属性用于设置批量检索的数量，默认值为 1，参考的合理值为 3~10。

例如在一个部门信息关联多个用户信息，有些情况下，需要通过部门信息 Dept 关联出用户信息 User，而有的情况下又不需要。在 Hibernate 中除了可以通过映射文件配置检索策略，还能通过编码显式的设定检索策略。

第二步：创建包：amigo.hibernate.query.join

在 src 源码目录中创建包：amigo.hibernate.query.join，该包用于存放本实例的类文件。

第三步：编写连接查询测试类：JoinTest.java

首先在 amigo.hibernate.query.join 包中创建本实例的测试类：JoinTest.java，该类的代码如下

所示：

```java
package amigo.hibernate.query.join;

import org.apache.log4j.Logger;
import org.hibernate.Session;

import amigo.hibernate.query.Dept;
import amigo.hibernate.query.HibernateSessionFactory;

/**
 * 连接查询测试类.
 */
public class JoinTest {
    private static Logger log = Logger.getLogger(JoinTest.class);

    public static void main(String[] args) throws Exception {
        Session session = HibernateSessionFactory.currentSession();

        // 使用 load()方法加载 deptId 为 1 的部门信息
        Dept dept = (Dept) session.load(Dept.class, new Integer(1));

        // 关闭 Session
        HibernateSessionFactory.closeSession();
    }
}
```

此时 Dept.hbm.xml 的<class/>元素中未定义 lazy 元素，运行该类，可看到控制台没有输出查询语句信息，由此可看出<class/>元素的 lazy 的默认值为 true。使用 load()方法时将延迟加载，它返回的是 Dept 类的代理类的实例，Hibernate 在创建代理类实例时，仅仅初始化了其 OID 属性，其余属性都为空。若在该句后：

```java
Dept dept = (Dept) session.load(Dept.class, new Integer(1));
```

加上如下语句来获得对象的属性，将会使得 Hibernate 初始化 Dept 的代理类实例，因而在控制台打出 Hibernate 查询语句信息：

```java
log.info("deptName=" + dept.getDeptName());
```

【提示】若在 lazy 为 true 时将打印信息放入关闭 session 的语句后执行会是怎样的呢？

因为在 session 关闭之前 Dept 一直是代理类的实例，没有被初始化，因此在 session 关闭之后打印该对象的属性信息时，将会不能初始化代理并引发如下异常信息提示：

```
org.hibernate.LazyInitializationException: could not initialize proxy - no Session
    at org.hibernate.proxy.AbstractLazyInitializer.initialize(AbstractLazyInitializer.java:57)
    at org.hibernate.proxy.AbstractLazyInitializer.getImplementation(AbstractLazyInitializer.java:111)
    at org.hibernate.proxy.pojo.cglib.CGLIBLazyInitializer.invoke(CGLIBLazyInitializer.java:150)
    at amigo.hibernate.query.Dept$$EnhancerByCGLIB$$8e9f1d30.getDeptName(<generated>)
    ......
```

接下来读者可将 Dept.hbm.xml 文件的<class/>元素修改成：

```xml
<class name="Dept" table="tbl_dept" lazy="false">
```

因为此时 lazy 属性被设置成 false，即不使用延迟加载，因此再次运行该测试类，可在控制台看到如下信息：

```
Hibernate: select dept0_.deptId as deptId1_0_, dept0_.deptName as deptName1_0_ from tbl_dept dept0_ where dept0_.deptId=?
```

Dept.hbm.xml 具有一个到 User 的一对多关联，配置信息如下所示：

```xml
<set name="users" cascade ="save-update">
    <key>
        <column name="deptId" />
    </key>
    <one-to-many class="User" />
</set>
```

<set/>元素可设置 lazy 和 outer-join 两个属性，在此处都使用默认设置。这两个属性中只有一者为 true 时，表示采用这种检索策略；当两者都为 false 时，采用立即检索；当两者都为 true 时，没有任何意义。

若将 set 的 lazy 属性修改成 false，即采用立即加载：

```xml
<set name="users" cascade ="save-update" lazy="false">
```

此时运行连接查询测试类：JoinTest.java，控制台输出信息如下所示：

```
Hibernate: select dept0_.deptId as deptId1_0_, dept0_.deptName as deptName1_0_ from tbl_dept dept0_ where dept0_.deptId=?
Hibernate: select users0_.deptId as deptId1_, users0_.userid as userid1_, users0_.userid as userid0_0_, users0_.username as username0_0_, users0_.password as password0_0_, users0_.loginTimes as loginTimes0_0_, users0_.createTime as createTime0_0_, users0_.deptId as deptId0_0_ from tbl_user users0_ where users0_.deptId=?
```

从上面的运行结果中可以看出，在查询到部门信息后，还是用了一条 SQL 语句来查询该部门相关的用户信息。

继续修改 Dept.hbm.xml 的 set，将其 lazy 属性设置为 false，outer-join 属性设置为 true，代码如下所示：

```xml
<set name="users" cascade ="save-update" lazy="false" outer-join="true">
```

此时将使用迫切左外连接检索，控制台输出结果与前面不同，它使用 left outer join 来关联查处 tbl_user 表的信息，如下所示：

```
Hibernate: select dept0_.deptId as deptId1_1_, dept0_.deptName as deptName1_1_, users1_.deptId as deptId3_, users1_.userid as userid3_, users1_.userid as userid0_0_, users1_.username as username0_0_, users1_.password as password0_0_, users1_.loginTimes as loginTimes0_0_, users1_.createTime as createTime0_0_, users1_.deptId as deptId0_0_ from tbl_dept dept0_ left outer join tbl_user users1_ on dept0_.deptId=users1_.deptId where dept0_.deptId=?
```

在 User.hbm.xml 中，多条用户信息关联一条部门信息，因此 User 到 Dept 的关联为多对一的关联，配置信息如下所示：

```xml
<many-to-one name="dept"
        column="deptId"
        class="Dept" />
```

<many-to-one/>元素有一个 outer-join 属性，用于设置连接策略，它的 3 个可选值的说明如下所示：

- auto：默认值，若 Dept 对象的 lazy 属性为 true，则与 User 关联的 Dept 采用延迟加载，否则采用迫切左外连接检索策略。
- true：采用迫切左外连接检索策略。
- false：不采用迫切左外连接检索策略。若 Dept.hbm.xml 中 lazy 属性的值为 true，则采用延迟检索策略，否则采用立即检索策略。

下面来看<many-to-one/>中 outer-join 属性的设置效果，首先在测试类中添加如下代码：

```java
User user = (User) session.get(User.class, new Integer(1));
```

当 User.hbm.xml 文件的<many-to-one/>元素未设置 outer-join 属性，即采用默认设置 auto 时，此时 Dept.hbm.xml 文件的对应<set/>元素配置如下：

```
<set name="users" cascade ="save-update" lazy="false" outer-join="true">
```

此时按照上面所述，应该采用迫切左外连接检索策略，运行测试类后，该部分的输出信息如下所示：

```
Hibernate: select user0_.userid as userid0_1_, user0_.username as username0_1_, user0_.password as password0_1_, user0_.loginTimes as loginTimes0_1_, user0_.createTime as createTime0_1_, user0_.deptId as deptId0_1_, dept1_.deptId as deptId1_0_, dept1_.deptName as deptName1_0_ from tbl_user user0_ left outer join tbl_dept dept1_ on user0_.deptId=dept1_.deptId where user0_.userid=?
......
```

若将<many-to-one/>元素修改为：

```
<many-to-one name="dept" column="deptId" class="Dept" outer-join="false"/>
```

此时无论怎样都不会使用迫切左外连接检索策略，运行测试类，可看到如下输出信息：

```
Hibernate: select user0_.userid as userid0_0_, user0_.username as username0_0_, user0_.password as password0_0_, user0_.loginTimes as loginTimes0_0_, user0_.createTime as createTime0_0_, user0_.deptId as deptId0_0_ from tbl_user user0_ where user0_.userid=?
```

小结

Hibernate 提供了一种强大的面向对象的查询语言：HQL（Hibernate Query Language）。它与 SQL 相似，在其中可以应用继承、多态和关联等知识，它是 Hibernate 使用最广泛的一种检索方式。

在 HQL 语言中，Java 类和属性的名称是大小写敏感的，但是 select、from、group by、order by 和 where 等查询关键字大小写不敏感。from 子句后紧跟一到多个实体的名称，多个实体名称以英文逗号隔开。使用举例如下所示：

```
from User as user, Department as dept
```

select 子句用于选择将哪些属性或哪些对象放入查询结果集中，使用举例如下：

```
select user.username, user.password from User as user
```

在 select 子句中还可以使用聚集函数，例如如下 HQL 语句：

```
select max(age) as max, min(age) as min, count(*) as count from User as user
```

where 子句用于限定查询条件，例如如下语句查询属性名 username 为 amigo 的记录：

```
from User where username= 'amigo'
```

order by 子句对查询结果按照类中的任何属性进行升序或降序排列，例如在如下的语句中对查询出的 User 实例按照 age 属性降序排列：

```
from User as user order by user.age desc
```

group by 子句用于对返回聚集值的查询可以按照返回的类或组件的任何属性进行分组，例如如下 HQL 语句按照登录次数（loginTimes）属性进行分组：

```
select user.age from User as user group by user.loginTimes
```

聚集函数一般出现在 select 子句和 where 子句中。在 HQL 语句中，支持如下聚集函数：

- avg()：求平均值。
- sum()：求和。
- max()：求最大值。
- min()：求最小值；
- count()：求记录数。

例如如下语句用于查询记录总数：

```
select count((*) from User
```

对于支持子查询的数据库，例如 Oracle、MySQL 等，Hibernate 支持使用子查询。子查询使用英文圆括号（()）括起来。例如如下语句查询年龄（age）大于平均年龄的所有记录：

```
from User as user where user.age > (
    select avg(obj.age) from User as obj
)
```

在 Hibernate 中，提供几种方式来进行参数绑定，一是使用占位符"?"，二是使用占位符":"。第一种有顺序要求，而第二种没有顺序要求。使用占位符"?"限定查询的实例如下所示，该实例查询 User 中 username 属性包含 amigo 字符串，age 属性大于 25 的用户列表：

```
Query query = session.createQuery(
        "from User user where user.username like ? and user.age > ?");
query.setParameter(0, "%amigo%");
query.setParameter(1, new Integer(25));
List userList = query.list();
```

同样看一个使用占位符":"的实例，该实例与前面的实例作用类似，但是写法上有一些区别，实例如下：

```
Query query = session.createQuery(
        "from User user where user.username like :username and user.age > :age");
query.setParameter("username", "%amigo%");
query.setParameter("age", new Integer(25));
List userList = query.list();
```

Hibernate 也支持分页查询，Query 接口提供了 setFirstResult()方法来设定第一条被查询的记录的 index 值，另外它还提供了 setMaxResults()方法限制了每页查询的最大数量。例如若想查询 User 中第一页的记录，每页为 5 条数据，可使用如下语句：

```
Query query = session.createQuery("from User user");
query.setFirstResult(0);
query.setMaxResults(5);
List userList = query.list();
```

Hibernate 还提供了条件查询（Criteria Queries）方式，它主要由 Criteria 接口、Criterion 接口和 Expression 类组成。使用举例如下所示：

```
Criteria criteria = session.createCriteria(User.class);

// 限定查询条件
Criterion criterion1 = Expression.like("username", "%test%");
Criterion criterion2 = Expression.gt("loginTimes", new Integer(2));
criteria.add(criterion1);
criteria.add(criterion2);
List userList = criteria.list();
```

若要对结果集进行排序，可实现类似语句：

```
criteria.addOrder(Order.desc("loginTimes"));
```

开发人员也可使用条件查询（Criteria Queries）来实现分页查询，提供的方法与 HQL 查询方式类似，使用举例如下所示：

```
Criteria criteria = session.createCriteria(User.class);
criteria.setFirstResult(5);
criteria.setMaxResults(10);
List userList = criteria.list();
```

有些应用程序需要数据库底层的数据库方言来执行一些特殊的或复杂的 SQL 语句。对于此种情况，Hibernate 的 Session 接口提供了 createSQLQuery()方法来执行本地的 SQL 语句。使用举例如下所示：

```
SQLQuery query = session.createSQLQuery(
                "select * from tbl_user as user " +
                "where username like :username and loginTimes > :loginTimes");
query.setParameter("username", "%test%");
query.setParameter("loginTimes", new Integer(2));
query.addEntity("user", User.class);
List userList = query.list();
```

在进行关联时，Hibernate 中有如下 3 种检索策略：
- 立即检索：立即加载和检索指定的对象关联的对象。
- 延迟检索：延迟加载和检索指定的对象关联的对象。
- 追切左外连接检索：通过左外连接加载和检索指定的对象关联的对象。

在存在关联的 Hibernate 映射文件中，可使用如下属性设定检索策略：
- lazy：值可为 true 或 false，默认为 false，用于指定是否使用延迟加载策略，为 true 表示使用延迟加载，为 false 表示立即加载。
- outer-join：值可为 auto、true 和 false。在<set/>元素中，默认值为 false，在<one-to-one/>和<many-to-one/>元素中默认值为 auto。true 表示使用追切左外连接检索策略，false 表示不使用。
- batch-size：该属性用于设置批量检索的数量，默认值为 1，参考的合理值为 3~10。

开发人员可根据使用情况设置 lazy、outer-join 以及 batch-size 属性。

第 13 章　操纵实体对象

【本章导读语】

在对数据库记录进行操作时，最常见的操作除了查询之外，还有添加、修改和删除记录。本章首先讲述 Hibernate 对象的 3 种状态，即瞬时态（Transient）、持久态（Persistent）和脱管态（Detached），并详细讲述了这 3 种状态在何种状态下进行状态转换。接着将讲述如何利用 Hibernate 提供的 API 来保存、更新和删除对象。对于一些复杂的操作，例如复杂查询等，需要绕过 Hibernate 的 API 来进行操作。本章还将讲述如何绕过 Hibernate API 进行操作。

若系统使用了存储过程，则开发人员还需要通过 Hibernate 调用存储过程。本章还提供了使用 Hibernate 调用存储过程的实例。

【例 13-1】解说 Hibernate 对象的 3 种状态

〖实例需求〗

Hibernate 的对象有 3 种状态：瞬时态（Transient）、持久态（Persistent）和脱管态（Detached）。处于持久态的对象也称为 PO（Persistence Object），瞬时对象和脱管对象也称为 VO（Value Object）。本实例详细解说 Hibernate 对象的 3 种状态，为后续的各实例打下基础。

〖开发过程〗

第一步：建立工程

读者可在 Eclipse 中按照前面几章的方式建立一个名为 hibernateOperate 的 Java 工程，接着将 hibernate 的相关 jar 包、MySQL 数据库驱动的 jar 包等复制到该工程的 lib 目录中，并将这些 jar 包加入到工程的 CLASSPATH 路径中。jar 包清单如下所示：

- cglib-2.1.3.jar。
- commons-beanutils.jar。
- commons-collections-2.1.1.jar。
- commons-lang.jar。
- commons-logging-1.0.4.jar。
- dom4j-1.6.1.jar。
- hibernate3.jar。
- log4j-1.2.11.jar：log4j 日志包。
- mysql-connector-java-5.0.4-bin.jar：MySQL 的数据库驱动包。
- asm.jar。

- jta.jar：事务管理的 jar 包。
- antlr-2.7.5H3.jar。

接着在 src 目录中建立 log4j 的配置文件 log4j.properties，并在 src 目录中建立 amigo.hibernate.operate 包，用来存放本章各实例的源码。

创建完成后工程的目录结构如图 13-1 所示。

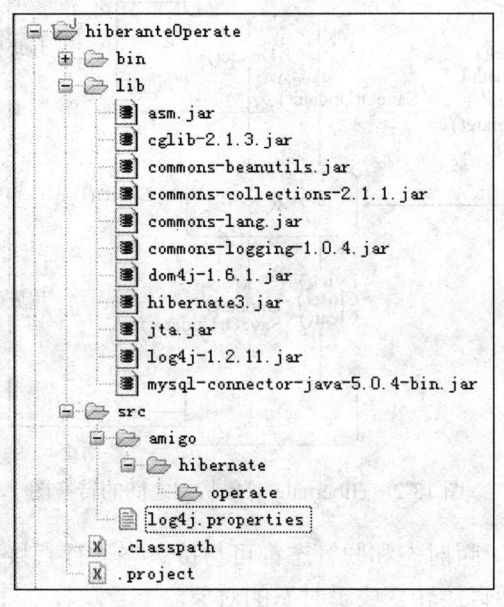

图 13-1 工程的目录结构

第二步：持久态

处于持久态的对象在数据库中具有对应的记录，并拥有一个持久化标识。若这两个条件都不满足，该对象将变成瞬时态的对象。当只满足第一个条件时，该对象将变成脱管态对象。

持久对象具有如下特点：
- 和 session 实例关联。
- 在数据库中有与之关联的记录。

第三步：瞬时态

由 new 开辟内存空间的 java 对象，如 User user = new User（"amigo","女", "25"）；如果没有变量对该对象进行引用，它将被 JVM（Java 虚拟机）回收。处于瞬间态的对象在内存中孤立存在，它是携带信息的载体，但是不和数据库的数据存在任何关联关系。

第四步：脱管态

当与某持久对象关联的 session 被关闭后，该持久对象转变为脱管对象。

脱管对象具有如下特点：
- 本质上与瞬时对象相同，在没有任何变量引用它时，JVM 会在适当的时候将它回收。
- 比瞬时对象多了一个数据库记录标识值。

第五步：各种状态对象在 Hibernate 中的转换

Hibernate 中对象的 3 种状态可进行转换，转换的图示如图 13-2 所示。

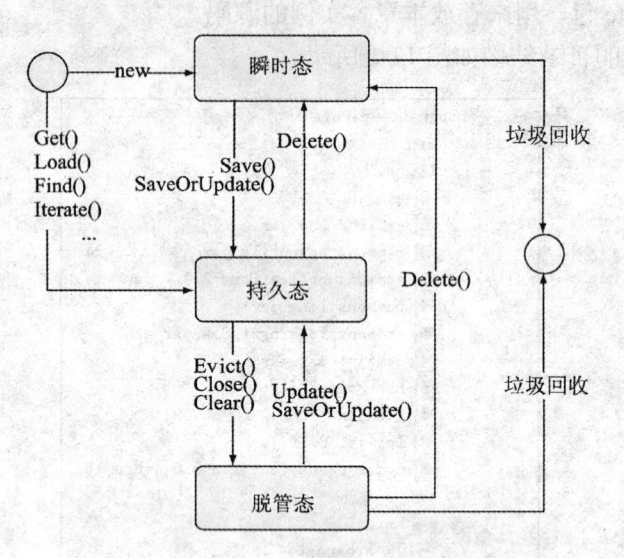

图 13-2 Hibernate 对象状态之间的转换图

从图 13-2 中可以看出，瞬时态和脱管态都可与持久态进行直接互转，脱管态的对象也可以在执行 session 的 delete()后直接转变成瞬时态的对象。

（1）瞬时态 → 持久态。

瞬时态的对象可转换为持久态的对象，具体方法是通过 session 的 save()或 saveOrUpdate()方法将瞬时对象与数据库相关联，并将数据对应地插入数据库中，此时该瞬时对象转变成持久化对象。

例如，在如下代码中，可以将处于瞬时态的对象 user 转变为持久态的对象：

```
User user = new User(); // 瞬时态
user.setLoginName("amigo");
user.setGender("女");
user.setAge(25);
......
session.save(user); // 将 user 对象持久化
......
```

（2）持久态 → 瞬时态。

当对一个持久态的对象（在数据库中有对应的记录）使用 Hibernate 的 delete()方法时，将使得处于持久态的对象转变成瞬时态的对象，因为数据库中的对应数据已被删除，该对象不再与数据库的记录关联，该对象不再满足持久态对象的条件。

（3）持久态 → 脱管态。

当一个处于持久态的对象执行 session 的 close()或 clear()、evict()之后，该对象将变成脱管态对象，此时该对象虽然具有数据库识别值，但它已不在 Hibernate 持久层的管理之下。

（4）脱管态 → 持久态。

当脱管态的对象被重新关联到 session 上时，将使得该对象转变成持久态的对象。脱管对象拥有数据库的识别值，可通过update()、saveOrUpdate()等方法转变成持久对象。

（5）脱管态 → 瞬时态。

处于脱管态的对象执行session的delete()方法后，可变成瞬时态的对象。

【例13-2】保存实体对象

〖实例需求〗

在进行关系数据库的操作中，查询、保存、更新和删除记录都是很常用的操作，在Hibernate中，提供这几个方法的都是Session接口。本实例讲解如何使用Session接口的方法进行数据库记录的保存。本实例以及其后的几个实例都使用的是MySQL数据库，因此需要将MySQL数据库驱动放入到工程的CLASSPATH中。

〖开发过程〗

第一步：创建hibernate.cfg.xml文件

在src目录中建立Hibernate的配置文件hibernate.cfg.xml，该文件配置连接本地的MySQL，并加上了映射文件User.hbm.xml，该文件的内容如下所示：

```
......
<hibernate-configuration>
    <session-factory>
        <!-- 在后台打印sql语句 -->
        <property name="show_sql">true</property>
        <!-- 指定sql的本地方言，根据连接的数据库确定-->
        <property name="dialect">org.hibernate.dialect.MySQLDialect</property>
        <!-- 指定jdbc url,MySql的默认端口为3306，192.168.1.124为需要连接的主机，testhibernate为连接的数据库 -->
        <property name="connection.url">jdbc:mysql://localhost:3306/testhibernate</property>
        <!-- 数据库的用户名 -->
        <property name="connection.username">root</property>
        <!-- 数据库的密码 -->
        <property name="connection.password">root</property>
        <!-- 设定数据库的驱动类，MySql的驱动jar包为mysql-connector-java-5.0.4-bin.jar -->
        <property name="connection.driver_class">com.mysql.jdbc.Driver</property>

        <!--指定0到多个hbm.xml映射文件-->
        <mapping resource="amigo/hibernate/operate/User.hbm.xml" />
    </session-factory>
</hibernate-configuration>
```

第二步：编写Session工厂类：HibernateSessionFactory.java

在amigo.hibernate.operate包中建立Session的工厂类，该类提供了获取当前session和关闭session的方法，该类的代码如下所示：

```
package amigo.hibernate.operate;

import org.hibernate.HibernateException;
```

```java
import org.hibernate.Session;
import org.hibernate.SessionFactory;
import org.hibernate.cfg.Configuration;
import org.apache.log4j.*;

/**
 * Hibernate 的 session 获取类.
 */
public class HibernateSessionFactory {
    public static Logger log = (Logger)Logger.getLogger(HibernateSessionFactory.class);

    private static String CONFIG_FILE_LOCATION = "/hibernate.cfg.xml";

    /** Holds a single instance of Session */
    private static final ThreadLocal threadLocal = new ThreadLocal();

    /** The single instance of hibernate configuration */
    private static final Configuration cfg = new Configuration();

    /** The single instance of hibernate SessionFactory */
    private static SessionFactory sessionFactory;


    /**
     * 返回 ThreadLocal 中的 Session 实例.
     * 采用懒加载的方式
     * @return Session
     * @throws HibernateException
     */
    public static Session currentSession() throws HibernateException {
        Session session = (Session) threadLocal.get();

        if(session==null || session.isOpen()==false){
            if (sessionFactory == null) {
                try {
                    cfg.configure(CONFIG_FILE_LOCATION);
                    sessionFactory = cfg.buildSessionFactory();
                } catch (Exception e) {
                    log.error("Error Creating SessionFactory %%%%"+ session.isOpen());
                }
            }
            session = sessionFactory.openSession();
            threadLocal.set(session);
        }

        return session;
    }

    /**
     * 关闭 session.
     * @throws HibernateException
     */
    public static void closeSession() throws HibernateException {
```

```java
        Session session = (Session) threadLocal.get();
        threadLocal.set(null);

        if (session != null) {
            session.close();
        }
    }

    private HibernateSessionFactory() {
    }
}
```

第三步:编写数据库脚本 scripts.sql

在 amigo.hibernate.operate 包中建立数据库脚本文件,该脚本文件创建 testhibernate 文件,并创建了表 tbl_user,脚本文件的内容如下所示:

```sql
CREATE DATABASE 'testhibernate';
USE 'testhibernate';

#创建用户信息表
CREATE TABLE 'tbl_user' (
  'loginName' varchar(50) NOT NULL COMMENT '用户登录名',
  'name' varchar(50) NOT NULL COMMENT '姓名',
  'password' varchar(50) NOT NULL COMMENT '登录密码',
  'createTime' datetime NOT NULL COMMENT '创建时间',
  PRIMARY KEY  ('loginName')
) ENGINE=InnoDB DEFAULT CHARSET=gb2312 COMMENT='用户信息表';
```

第四步:编写 User.java

在 amigo.hibernate.operate 包中建立 tbl_user 表的 POJO 文件,该文件的内容如下所示:

```java
package amigo.hibernate.operate;

import java.io.Serializable;

/**
 * 用户信息的 POJO 类.
 */
public class User implements Serializable {
    private static final long serialVersionUID = 1L;

    /** 登录名,主键. */
    private String loginname;

    /** 姓名. */
    private java.lang.String name;

    /** 密码. */
    private String password;

    /** 创建时间. */
    private java.util.Date createtime;
```

```
        // 省略各属性的 getter/setter 方法
}
```

第五步：配置 User.hbml.xml

在 amigo.hibernate.operate 包中建立 tbl_user 表的映射文件，该文件的内容如下所示：

```
......
<hibernate-mapping package="amigo.hibernate.operate">
    <class name="User" table="tbl_user">
        <id name="loginname" column="loginName" type="java.lang.String">
            <generator class="assigned"/>
        </id>
        <property name="name" column="name" type="java.lang.String"  not-null="true" />
        <property name="password" column="password" type="java.lang.String"  not-null="true" />
        <property name="createtime" column="createTime" type="java.util.Date"  not-null="true" />
    </class>
</hibernate-mapping>
```

第六步：编写保存实体对象测试类：SaveTest.java

在 amigo.hibernate.operate 包中建立 SaveTest.java 文件，该类用于测试 Session 接口的 save() 方法，注意保存操作需要放置在事务中，在执行完 session 的 save()方法后，需要执行事务的 commit()方法才能真正地将数据提交到数据库。在关闭事务后，要记得关闭 session。该类的代码如下所示：

```
package amigo.hibernate.operate;

import java.util.Date;

import org.hibernate.Session;
import org.hibernate.Transaction;

/**
 * 测试利用 Session 接口的方法保存对象.
 */
public class SaveTest {
    public static void main(String[] args) throws Exception {
        // 瞬时态对象
        User user = new User();
        // 设置对象的属性
        user.setLoginname("amigo");
        user.setName("阿蜜果");
        user.setPassword("198211");
        user.setCreatetime(new Date());

        // 获得 session
        Session session = HibernateSessionFactory.currentSession();
        // 获得事务
        Transaction ts = session.beginTransaction();
        // 调用 Session 接口的 save()方法保存对象
        // 将对象从瞬时态变成持久态
        session.save(user);
        // 在提交事务之前，数据并没有保存到数据库中，还是脏数据
```

```
        // 执行如下这句后，会将数据提交到数据库
        ts.commit();
        // 执行完毕后，关闭 session
        HibernateSessionFactory.closeSession();
        System.out.println("保存成功!");
    }
}
```

【说明】本实例的 tbl_user 的主键 loginName 是开发人员指定的，在很多常用的情况中，主键是自动增长的，在 User.hbm.xml 中进行了配置后，不用执行 setter 方法进行自增主键的设置。

第七步：运行结果

运行 SaveTest.java 类，可在控制台看到如下信息：

```
Hibernate: insert into tbl_user (name, password, createTime, loginName) values (?, ?, ?, ?)
保存成功!
```

在数据库中进行查看时，tbl_user 表的记录列表如图 13-3 所示。

loginName	name	password	createTime
amigo	阿蜜果	198211	2008-08-02 18:57:38

图 13-3　保存记录成功后的 tbl_user 表

从图 13-3 中可以看出，记录保存成功。

【说明】保存对象除了可调用 Session 接口的 save()方法外，还可以调用该接口的 saveOrUpdate()方法，该方法首先使用 select 语句查询是否有 loginName 与之相同的记录存在，若存在，则执行 update 语句对该记录进行更新操作，若不存在，则执行 insert 语句进行记录的插入。

若将 SaveTest.java 中的代码：

```
session.save(user);
```

修改成：

```
session.saveOrUpdate(user);
```

则在数据库中不存在对应记录时，打印的 SQL 语句如下所示：

```
Hibernate: select user_.loginName, user_.name as name0_, user_.password as password0_, user_.createTime as createTime0_ from tbl_user user_ where user_.loginName=?
Hibernate: insert into tbl_user (name, password, createTime, loginName) values (?, ?, ?, ?)
保存成功!
```

若存在 loginName 与之相同的记录时，打印的 SQL 语句如下所示：

```
Hibernate: select user_.loginName, user_.name as name0_, user_.password as password0_, user_.createTime as createTime0_ from tbl_user user_ where user_.loginName=?
Hibernate: update tbl_user set name=?, password=?, createTime=? where loginName=?
保存成功!
```

【例 13-3】更新实体对象

〖实例需求〗

Session 接口提供了 update()和 saveOrUpdate()方法来更新单个实体对象。在更新实体对象

前，一般需要通过 load()或 get()方法获得对象后再执行更新。本实例讲解如何在 Hibernate 中更新实体对象。

【开发过程】

第一步：编写更新单个实体对象测试类：UpdateTest.java

在 amigo.hibernate.operate 包中建立 UpdateTest.java 文件，该类用于演示在 Hibernate 中如何对对象进行更新。在执行更新前，可通过 load()或 get()方法来获得对象，而后更新属性后，通过 Session 接口的 update()方法进行更新。

【注意】更新操作需要包括在事务中，执行 update()方法后，需要调用事务的 commit()方法来提交事务。

该测试类的代码如下所示：

```java
package amigo.hibernate.operate;

import org.hibernate.Session;
import org.hibernate.Transaction;

/**
 * 测试利用 Session 接口的方法更新对象.
 */
public class UpdateTest {
    public static void main(String[] args) throws Exception {
        // 获得 session
        Session session = HibernateSessionFactory.currentSession();
        // 获得事务
        Transaction ts = session.beginTransaction();

        // 获得持久化对象
        String loginname = "amigo";
        User user = (User) session.get(User.class,
                loginname);
        // 更新对象的属性
        user.setName("谢星星");
        user.setPassword("19821121");

        // 调用 Session 接口的方法更新对象
        session.update(user);
        // 在提交事务之前，数据并没有更新到数据库中，还是脏数据
        // 执行如下这句后，会将数据提交到数据库
        ts.commit();
        // 执行完毕后，关闭 session
        HibernateSessionFactory.closeSession();
        System.out.println("更新成功!");
    }
}
```

【提示】Session 接口的 load()和 get()方法都可以根据给定的 OID 从数据库中加载对象，两者的不同是当对象不存在时，get()方法返回 null，而 load()方法将抛出 org.hibernate.ObjectNotFoundException 异常。在开发过程中，通过 get()方法获得对象比 load()方法常用。

第二步：更新单个对象运行结果

运行 UpdateTest.java 类，控制台的结果如下所示：

Hibernate: select user0_.loginName as loginName0_0_, user0_.name as name0_0_, user0_.password as password0_0_, user0_.createTime as createTime0_0_ from tbl_user user0_ where user0_.loginName=?
Hibernate: update tbl_user set name=?, password=?, createTime=? where loginName=?
更新成功!

读者也可以通过 saveOrUpdate()方法来对对象进行更新，例如将上述代码修改成：

```
.......
User user = new User();
user.setLoginname("amigo");
// 更新对象的属性
user.setName("谢星星");
user.setPassword("198211");
user.setCreatetime(new Date());
.......
```

通过如上的代码也可以达到类似的效果，不过要注意的是，使用 saveOrUpdate()方法执行更新有一个问题，就是需要将所有的必填属性都填上，本来在进行更新操作时，不需要更新 createTime 这个必填属性，但是若不设置该值，执行代码时将出现如下异常：

org.hibernate.PropertyValueException: not-null property references a null or transient value: amigo.hibernate.operate.User.createtime

所以建议读者在执行更新操作时，还是使用比较明确的 update()方法。

第三步：编写批量更新的测试类：BatchUpdateTest.java

在 amigo.hibernate.operate 包中建立批量更新的测试类 BatchUpdateTest.java 文件。批量可采取如下几种方式：

- 使用存储过程进行批量更新。
- 绕过 Hibernate API，直接通过 JDBC API 进行数据的批量更新。
- 查询出需要更新的对象后，遍历这些对象，循环使用 update()方法进行更新。
- 使用 createQuery(String hql)方法获得 Query 对象后，设置参数后，执行 executeUpdate()方法更新记录。

第一种和第二种都必须绕过 Hibernate API，直接通过 JDBC API，因此效率很高，但笔者不推荐使用。第三种方式当需要更新 1 万条数据时，需要执行 1 万次 update 语句，效率很低，因此笔者推荐使用第四种方式。

BatchUpdateTest 类提供了第 3、4 种方式的实现。BatchUpdateTest 类首先使用第 3 种方式将所有 loginname 中包含 amigo 的记录的 name 都修改为"阿蜜果"，接着使用第 4 种方式将所有 loginname 中包含 xiexx 的记录的 name 都修改为"谢星星"，该类的代码如下所示：

```
package amigo.hibernate.operate;

import java.util.Iterator;

import org.hibernate.Query;
import org.hibernate.Session;
import org.hibernate.Transaction;
```

```java
/**
 * 批量更新对象.
 */
public class BatchUpdateTest {
    public static void main(String[] args) throws Exception {
        // 获得 session
        Session session = HibernateSessionFactory.currentSession();
        // 获得事务
        Transaction ts = session.beginTransaction();

        // 第 3 种方式批量更新数据
        // 将所有 loginname 中包含 amigo 的记录的 name 都修改为 "阿蜜果"
        Query queryUpdate = session.createQuery(
                "from User where loginname like ?");
        queryUpdate.setParameter(0, "%amigo%");
        // 循环更新数据
        Iterator users = queryUpdate.list().iterator();
        int count = 0;
        while(users.hasNext()){
            User user = (User) users.next();
            user.setName("阿蜜果");
            session.flush();
            session.evict(user);
            count++;
        }
        System.out.println("使用第 3 种方式批量更新记录条数为=" + count);

        // 第 4 种方式批量更新数据
        // 将所有 loginname 中包含 xiexx 的记录的 name 都修改为 "谢星星"
        String hqlUpdate = "update User set name=? where loginname like ?";
        Query query = session.createQuery(hqlUpdate);
        query.setParameter(0, "谢星星");
        query.setParameter(1, "%xiexx%");
        int updateCount = query.executeUpdate();
        System.out.println("使用第 4 种方式批量更新记录条数为=" + updateCount);

        ts.commit();
        // 执行完毕后，关闭 session
        HibernateSessionFactory.closeSession();
    }
}
```

在以上程序中，第 3 种方式更新了一个 User 对象的 name 属性后，就立即调用 Session 的 flush()方法和 evict()方法。

flush()方法使 Hibernate 立刻根据这个 User 对象的状态变化同步更新数据库，从而立即执行相关的 update 语句；evict()方法用于把这个 Customer 对象从缓存中清除出去，从而及时释放它占用的内存。

但 evict()方法只能稍微提高批量操作的性能，因为不管有没有使用 evict()方法，Hibernate 都必须执行 N 条 update 语句，才能更新 N 个 User 对象，这是影响批量操作性能的重要因素。

第四步：批量更新对象运行结果

在运行前，数据库中的记录如图 13-4 所示。

loginName	name	password	createTime
amigo1	amgo1	198211	2008-08-03 13:37:37
amigo2	amigo2	19821121	2008-08-03 00:00:00
amigo3	amigo3	198211	2008-08-03 00:00:00
xiexx	xiexx	198211	2008-08-03 13:25:00
xiexx1	xiexx1	eeeee	2008-08-03 00:00:00
xiexx2	xiexx2	xxxx	2008-08-03 00:00:00
xiexx3	xiexx3	xxx3	2008-08-03 00:00:00

图 13-4　运行前数据库中的记录

运行 BatchUpdateTest.java 类，控制台的信息如下所示：

Hibernate: select user0_.loginName as loginName0_, user0_.name as name0_, user0_.password as password0_, user0_.createTime as createTime0_ from tbl_user user0_ where user0_.loginName like ?
Hibernate: update tbl_user set name=?, password=?, createTime=? where loginName=?
Hibernate: update tbl_user set name=?, password=?, createTime=? where loginName=?
Hibernate: update tbl_user set name=?, password=?, createTime=? where loginName=?
使用第 3 种方式批量更新记录条数为=3
Hibernate: update tbl_user set name=? where loginName like ?
使用第 4 种方式批量更新记录条数为=4

从打印的 SQL 语句可以看出，使用第 3 种方式进行批量更新时，若查到 N 条记录，将执行 N 次 update 语句。而使用第 4 种方式更新时，只执行一次 update 语句，因此第 4 种方式的效率更高。

执行完毕后，数据库中的记录如图 13-5 所示。

loginName	name	password	createTime
amigo1	阿蜜果	198211	2008-08-03 13:37:37
amigo2	阿蜜果	19821121	2008-08-03 00:00:00
amigo3	阿蜜果	198211	2008-08-03 00:00:00
xiexx	谢星星	198211	2008-08-03 13:25:00
xiexx1	谢星星	eeeee	2008-08-03 00:00:00
xiexx2	谢星星	xxxx	2008-08-03 00:00:00
xiexx3	谢星星	xxx3	2008-08-03 00:00:00

图 13-5　执行后 tbl_user 表中的记录

从图 13-5 中可以看出，数据被成功更新。

【例 13-4】删除实体对象

〖实例需求〗

Session 接口提供了 delete() 方法来删除单个实体对象。在使用 delete(Object obj) 方法进行单个对象的删除时，需要使用 load() 方法或 get() 方法获得需要删除的对象。Hibernate 还提供了批量删除对象的方法。

本实例将详细讲述如何使用 Session 接口的方法来进行删除操作。

【开发过程】

第一步：编写删除实体对象测试类：DeleteTest.java

在 amigo.hibernate.operate 包中建立 DeleteTest.java 类，该类展示了在 Hibernate 中如何删除单个对象和批量删除对象。

删除单个对象的方法是在取得要删除的对象后，使用 Session 接口的 delete(Object obj)方法进行对象的删除。

批量删除对象时，需要将构造好的删除的 hql 语句传入到 session 接口的 createQuery(String hql)方法中，将参数设置好后，执行 Query 对象的 executeUpdate()方法，该方法将返回删除的记录条数。

该类的代码如下所示：

```java
package amigo.hibernate.operate;

import org.hibernate.Query;
import org.hibernate.Session;
import org.hibernate.Transaction;

/**
 * 测试利用 Session 接口的方法删除对象.
 */
public class DeleteTest {
    public static void main(String[] args) throws Exception {
        // 获得 session
        Session session = HibernateSessionFactory.currentSession();
        // 获得事务
        Transaction ts = session.beginTransaction();

        // 获得持久化对象
        String loginname = "amigo";
        User user = (User) session.get(User.class,
                loginname);
        // 删除单个对象
        session.delete(user);
        System.out.println("删除 amigo 成功!");

        // 删除所有 loginname 包含 xiexx 的记录
        String hqlDelete = "delete User where loginname like ?";
        Query query = session.createQuery(hqlDelete);
        query.setParameter(0, "%xiexx%");
        int deleteCount = query.executeUpdate();
        System.out.println("批量删除记录条数为=" + deleteCount);

        ts.commit();
        // 执行完毕后，关闭 session
        HibernateSessionFactory.closeSession();
    }
}
```

第二步：运行结果

在 tbl_user 表中添加如下记录，如图 13-6 所示。

loginName	name	password	createTime
amigo	谢星星	198211	2008-08-02 19:38:04
xiexingxing	xiexingxing	xiexingxing	2008-08-02 19:17:00
xiexx1	xiexx1	xiexx1	2008-08-02 00:00:00
xiexx2	xiexx2	xiexx2	2008-08-02 19:17:00

图 13-6　删除前 tbl_user 表中的记录

此时执行 DeleteTest 类，运行结果如下所示：

```
Hibernate: select user0_.loginName as loginName0_0_, user0_.name as name0_0_, user0_.password as password0_0_, user0_.createTime as createTime0_0_ from tbl_user user0_ where user0_.loginName=?
删除 amigo 成功!
Hibernate: delete from tbl_user where loginName=?
Hibernate: delete from tbl_user where loginName like ?
批量删除记录条数为=2
```

此时到数据库中查看记录，可看到 amigo 记录被成功地单个删除，而记录 xiexx1 和 xiexx2 满足批量删除的条件，也已被删除。

【例 13-5】绕过 Hibernate API 对数据进行操作

〖实例需求〗

Hibernate 中提供了获得 Connection 对象的方法，有了该对象，开发人员就可以绕过 Hibernate API，而使用 JDBC API 来进行对数据的增、删、改和查的功能，虽然不推荐使用这种方式来操作数据库，但在某些特殊场合还可以使用这种方法来进行一些特定数据库的操作。

本实例通过对 tbl_user 表进行增、删、改和查操作的类的讲解，学习如何绕过 Hibernate API 来进行数据的操作。

〖开发过程〗

第一步：编写使用 JDBC API 进行数据操作的类：JdbcTest.java

在 amigo.hibernate.operate 包中建立 JdbcTest.java 类，该类通过 Session 对象获得 Connection 对象，有了对象后，就可以使用 JDBC API 来进行数据操作了。不过 Session 接口的 connection() 方法已不推荐使用，对于一般的数据操作，只需要使用 Hibernate API 即可，对于一些特殊情况，才考虑绕过 Hibernate API 来进行操作。

该类的代码如下所示：

```java
package amigo.hibernate.operate;

import java.sql.Connection;
import java.sql.PreparedStatement;

import org.hibernate.Session;
import org.hibernate.Transaction;
```

```java
/**
 * 使用 JDBC API 进行数据操作.
 */
public class JdbcTest {
    public static void main(String[] args) throws Exception {
        // 获得 session
        Session session = HibernateSessionFactory.currentSession();
        // 获得事务
        Transaction ts = session.beginTransaction();
        // 通过 session 的 connection()方法获得 Connection 对象
        // 该方法已不推荐使用
        Connection con = session.connection();

        // 添加数据
        String insertSql = "insert into tbl_user (loginname, name, password, createTime) " +
                "value ('amigoxie', 'amigoxie', '123', '2008-8-3')";
        PreparedStatement stmtInsert = con.prepareStatement(insertSql);
        stmtInsert.executeUpdate(insertSql);
        System.out.println("添加成功!");

        // 修改数据
        // 将所有 loginname 为 amigo 的数据的 name 字段修改为：amigo
        String updateSql = "update tbl_user set name='amigo' where loginname like '%amigo%'";
        PreparedStatement stmtUpdate = con.prepareStatement(insertSql);
        stmtUpdate.executeUpdate(updateSql);
        System.out.println("修改成功!");

        // 删除数据
        // 删除所有 loginname 为 xiexx 的数据
        String deleteSql = "delete from tbl_user where loginname like '%xiexx%'";
        PreparedStatement stmtDelete = con.prepareStatement(insertSql);
        stmtDelete.executeUpdate(deleteSql);
        System.out.println("删除成功!");

        // 提交事务
        ts.commit();
        // 执行完毕后，关闭 session
        HibernateSessionFactory.closeSession();
    }
}
```

第二步：运行结果

在未运行前，tbl_user 表中的记录如图 13-7 所示。

loginName	name	password	createTime
amigo1	阿蜜果	198211	2008-08-03 13:37:37
amigo2	阿蜜果	19821121	2008-08-03 00:00:00
amigo3	阿蜜果	198211	2008-08-03 00:00:00
xiexx	谢星星	198211	2008-08-03 13:25:00
xiexx1	谢星星	eeeee	2008-08-03 00:00:00
xiexx2	谢星星	xxxx	2008-08-03 00:00:00
xiexx3	谢星星	xxx3	2008-08-03 00:00:00

图 13-7　未运行前 tbl_user 表中的数据

运行 JdbcTest.java 后，控制台显示如下信息：

```
添加成功!
修改成功!
删除成功!
```

此时 tbl_user 中将添加 loginname 为 amigoxie 的记录，所有 loginname 中包含 amigo 的记录的 name 字段都被更新为 amigo，并且所有 loginname 中包含 xiexx 的记录都将被删除，运行完毕后，tbl_user 表中的记录如图 13-8 所示。

loginName	name	password	createTime
amigo1	amigo	198211	2008-08-03 13:37:37
amigo2	amigo	19821121	2008-08-03 00:00:00
amigo3	amigo	198211	2008-08-03 00:00:00
amigoxie	amigo	123	2008-08-03 00:00:00

图 13-8 操作完毕后 tbl_user 表中的记录

【例 13-6】使用 Hibernate 调用存储过程

〖实例需求〗

如果底层数据库（如 Oracle、mySQL、SQL Server）等支持存储过程，可通过存储过程执行批量删除、更新等操作。本文以实例说明在 hibernate3.x 中如何调用存储过程。本实例展示了 hibernate3.x 中调用存储过程的各步骤，从建立测试表、存储过程的建立、工程的建立以及类的编写和测试一步一步引导读者学习 hibernate3.x 中调用存储过程的方法。

〖开发过程〗

第一步：在 MySQL 中建立存储过程

（1）建立获取用户列表的存储过程——getUserList。

使用如下脚本建立获取用户列表的存储过程 getUserList：

```sql
DROP PROCEDURE IF EXISTS 'getUserList';
CREATE PROCEDURE 'getUserList' ()
begin
    select * from tbl_user;
end;
```

该存储过程使用 select 语句查询出 tbl_user 表中的所有记录。

（2）建立创建用户的存储过程——createUser。

使用如下脚本建立创建用户的存储过程 createUser：

```sql
DROP PROCEDURE IF EXISTS 'createUser';
CREATE PROCEDURE 'createUser' (IN loginname varchar(50), IN name varchar(50), IN password varchar(50))
begin
    insert into tbl_user values(loginname, name, password, sysdate());
end;
```

在该存储过程中，使用"IN"指定存储过程的参数，createUser() 有 3 个参数，分别为 loginname

（登录名）、name（姓名）和 password（密码），在 insert 语句中，将这 3 个参数插入到对应的字段，并且给 createTime 字段插入了 sysdate()，即当前时间。

（3）建立修改用户的存储过程——updateUser。

使用如下脚本建立修改用户的存储过程 updateUser：

```
DROP PROCEDURE IF EXISTS 'updateUser';
CREATE PROCEDURE 'updateUser' (IN nameValue varchar(50), IN passwordValue varchar(50), IN loginnameValue varchar(50))
  begin
    update tbl_user set name = nameValue, password = passwordValue where loginname = loginnameValue;
  end;
```

该存储过程传入了 nameValue（姓名）、passwordValue（密码）和 loginnameValue（登录名）3 个参数。使用 update 语句更新 loginname 字段为 loginnameValue 的记录的 name 和 password 字段。

（4）建立删除用户的存储过程——deleteUser。

使用如下脚本建立删除用户的存储过程 deleteUser：

```
DROP PROCEDURE IF EXISTS 'deleteUser';
CREATE PROCEDURE 'deleteUser' (IN loginnameValue varchar(50))
begin
    delete from tbl_user where loginname = loginnameValue;
end;
```

该存储过程只传入一个 loginnameValue 参数，delete 语句删除用户登录名为 loginnameValue 的记录。

第二步：在 User.hbm.xml 映射文件中配置存储过程

在 User.hbm.xml 中配置存储过程，在 hibernate-mapping 元素下添加子元素 sql-query，修改后的 User.hbm.xml 文件的内容如下所示：

```xml
......
<hibernate-mapping package="amigo.hibernate.operate">
  <class name="User" table="tbl_user">
    <id name="loginname" column="loginName" type="java.lang.String">
      <generator class="assigned"/>
    </id>
    <property name="name" column="name" type="java.lang.String"  not-null="true" />
    <property name="password" column="password" type="java.lang.String"  not-null="true" />
    <property name="createtime" column="createTime" type="java.util.Date"  not-null="true" />
  </class>

  <sql-query name="getUserList" callable="true">
    <return alias="user" class="User">
      <return-property name="loginname" column="loginName"/>
      <return-property name="name" column="name"/>
      <return-property name="password" column="password" />
      <return-property name="createtime" column="createTime" />
    </return>
    {call getUserList()}
```

```
    </sql-query>
</hibernate-mapping>
```

第三步：编写调用存储过程测试类：ProcTest.java

在 amigo.hibernate.operate 包中建立存储过程测试类 ProcTest.java 类，该类的代码如下所示：

```java
package amigo.hibernate.operate;

import java.sql.CallableStatement;
import java.sql.Connection;
import java.sql.PreparedStatement;
import java.text.SimpleDateFormat;

import java.util.List;

import org.hibernate.Session;
import org.hibernate.Transaction;

/**
 * 使用 Hibernate 调用存储过程
 */
public class ProcTest {
    public static void main(String[] args) throws Exception {
        Session session = HibernateSessionFactory.currentSession();
        Transaction ts = session.beginTransaction();

        // 查询用户列表
        List list = session.getNamedQuery("getUserList").list();
        SimpleDateFormat sdf = new SimpleDateFormat("yyyy-MM-dd hh:mm:ss");
        for (int i = 0; i < list.size(); i++) {
            User user = (User) list.get(i);
            System.out.print("序号: " + (i + 1));
            System.out.print("，登录名: " + user.getLoginname());
            System.out.print("，姓名: " + user.getName());
            System.out.print("，密码: " + user.getPassword());
            System.out.println("，创建时间: " + sdf.format(user.getCreatetime()));
        }

        // 添加用户信息
        // 添加数据为：loginname(amigo)、name(阿蜜果)、密码(123).
        PreparedStatement st = session.connection().prepareStatement(
                "{call createUser(?, ?, ?)}");
        st.setString(1, "amigo");
        st.setString(2, "阿蜜果");
        st.setString(3, "123");
        st.execute();
        System.out.println("添加成功!");

        // 更新用户信息
        // 更新 loginname 为 xiexx 的数据，将其 name 修改为：谢星星，将密码修改为：1234
        Connection con = session.connection();
        String procedure = "{call updateUser(?, ?, ?)}";
        CallableStatement cstmt = con.prepareCall(procedure);
```

```
            cstmt.setString(1, "谢星星");
            cstmt.setString(2, "1234");
            cstmt.setString(3, "xiexx");
            cstmt.executeUpdate();
            System.out.println("修改成功!");

            // 删除用户信息
            // 删除 loginname 为 xiexingxing 的数据
            PreparedStatement deleteSt = session.connection().prepareStatement(
                    "{call deleteUser(?)}");
            deleteSt.setString(1, "xiexingxing");
            deleteSt.execute();
            System.out.println("删除成功");

            // 提交事务
            ts.commit();
            // 关闭 session
            session.close();
        }
    }
```

在本类中，调用查询类存储过程时，调用 session.getNamedQuery("...")方法来获得 User.hbm.xml 中配置的查询存储过程。在其余的存储过程调用的测试中，首先通过 hibernate 的 session 获得 connection，然后调用 connection 对象的相应方法来实现存储过程的调用。

第四步：运行结果

在开始运行 ProcTest 类前，tbl_user 中存在 loginName 为 xiexx 和 xiexingxing 的两条记录，如图 13-9 所示。

loginName	name	password	createTime
xiexingxing	xiexingxing	xiexingxing	2008-08-03 16:07:00
xiexx	xiexx	198211	2008-08-03 13:37:37

图 13-9　执行前 tbl_user 表的记录

ProcTest 类将插入一条用户名为 amigo 的记录，并更新 loginName 为 xiexx 的记录的 name 字段为"谢星星"，最后删除 loginName 为 xiexingxing 的记录，执行后，控制台的输出信息如下所示：

```
Hibernate: {call getUserList()}
序号: 1, 登录名: xiexingxing, 姓名: xiexingxing, 密码: xiexingxing, 创建时间: 2008-08-03 04:07:00
序号: 2, 登录名: xiexx, 姓名: xiexx, 密码: 198211, 创建时间: 2008-08-03 01:37:37
添加成功!
修改成功!
删除成功
```

此时数据库中应该有两条记录，loginName 分别为 amigo 和 xiexx，如图 13-10 所示。

loginName	name	password	createTime
amigo	阿蜜果	123	2008-08-03 16:22:45
xiexx	谢星星	1234	2008-08-03 13:37:37

图 13-10　执行完毕后 tbl_user 表中的记录

小结

Hibernate 的对象有 3 种状态：瞬时态（Transient）、持久态（Persistent）和脱管态（Detached）。处于持久态的对象也称为 PO（Persistence Object），瞬时对象和脱管对象也称为 VO（Value Object）。

处于持久态的对象在数据库中具有对应的记录，并拥有一个持久化标识。处于瞬时态的对象在内存中孤立存在，它是携带信息的载体，但是不和数据库的数据存在任何关联关系。当与某持久对象关联的 session 被关闭后，该持久对象转变为脱管对象。瞬时态和脱管态都可与持久态进行直接互转，脱管态的对象也可以在执行 session 的 delete()后直接转变成瞬时态的对象。

在 Hibernate 中，保存实体对象使用的方法是 Session 对象的 save()方法，例如在下面的代码中，首先创建一个名为 user 的瞬时态对象，接着通过 Session 对象的 save()方法将对象保存，代码如下所示：

```
// 瞬时态对象
User user = new User();
// 设置对象的属性
user.setLoginname("amigo");
user.setName("阿蜜果");
user.setPassword("198211");
user.setCreatetime(new Date());

// 获得session
Session session = HibernateSessionFactory.currentSession();
// 获得事务
Transaction ts = session.beginTransaction();
// 调用 Session 接口的 save()方法保存对象
session.save(user);
ts.commit();
```

不过在保存对象时，需要注意的一点是，保存实体对象时需要将其包含在事务中，调用 save(…)方法后，需要调用 Transaction 对象的 commit()方法提交事务。

Session 对象的 update(…)方法用于更新对象，不过在更新对象前，一般需要调用 Session 对象的 get(…)方法获得对象后，再进行更新操作。在如下的代码中，首先通过 Session 的 get(…)方法获得主键值为 amigo 的对象，而后更新其"name"（姓名）和"password"（密码）信息，接着调用 Session 的 update(…)方法保存对象，最后提交事务，关闭 Session，实例代码如下所示：

```
// 获得session
Session session = HibernateSessionFactory.currentSession();
// 获得事务
Transaction ts = session.beginTransaction();

// 获得持久化对象
String loginname = "amigo";
User user = (User) session.get(User.class,
                    loginname);
// 更新对象的属性
user.setName("谢星星");
user.setPassword("19821121");

// 调用 Session 接口的方法更新对象
```

```
session.update(user);
// 提交事务
ts.commit();
// 执行完毕后，关闭session
HibernateSessionFactory.closeSession();
```

在批量更新对象时，可以通过 HQL 语句查询出对象列表后，再逐条更新，但是此种更新方式在更新数据较多时效率低下，因为它执行了一次查询和若干次更新操作。Hibernate 提供了一种通过 HQL 语句批量更新记录的方法。例如在下面的代码中，通过 Session 对象的 createQuery(...)方法将所有 loginname 中包含 xiexx 的记录的 name 都修改为"谢星星"。在此种方式下，只会生成一句 SQL，因此效率很高，代码如下所示：

```
// 获得session
Session session = HibernateSessionFactory.currentSession();
// 获得事务
Transaction ts = session.beginTransaction();

// 将所有loginname中包含xiexx的记录的name都修改为"谢星星"
String hqlUpdate = "update User set name=? where loginname like ?";
Query query = session.createQuery(hqlUpdate);
query.setParameter(0, "谢星星");
query.setParameter(1, "%xiexx%");
int updateCount = query.executeUpdate();
// 提交事务
ts.commit();
// 关闭session
HibernateSessionFactory.closeSession();
```

Session 接口提供了 delete()方法来删除单个实体对象和批量删除对象。在使用 delete(Object obj)方法进行单个对象的删除时，需要使用 load()方法或 get()方法获得需要删除的对象。删除单个对象的实例代码如下所示：

```
// 获得session
Session session = HibernateSessionFactory.currentSession();
// 获得事务
Transaction ts = session.beginTransaction();

// 获得持久化对象
String loginname = "amigo";
User user = (User) session.get(User.class,
                    loginname);
// 删除单个对象
session.delete(user);
// 提交事务
ts.commit();
// 执行完毕后，关闭session
HibernateSessionFactory.closeSession();
```

批量删除对象的方法与批量更新数据的方法类似，都是通过 Session 对象的 createQuery(...)方法来实现，例如下面的代码将实现删除所有 loginname 包含 xiexx 的记录，代码如下所示：

```
// 获得session
Session session = HibernateSessionFactory.currentSession();
// 获得事务
Transaction ts = session.beginTransaction();
```

```
// 删除所有 loginname 包含 xiexx 的记录
String hqlDelete = "delete User where loginname like ?";
Query query = session.createQuery(hqlDelete);
query.setParameter(0, "%xiexx%");
int deleteCount = query.executeUpdate();
// 提交事务
ts.commit();
// 执行完毕后，关闭 session
HibernateSessionFactory.closeSession();
```

虽然在 Hibernate 中不推荐使用绕过 Hibernate API 来操作数据库，但在某些特殊场合还需要采用此法。Hibernate 中提供了获得 Connection 对象的方法，有了该对象，开发人员就可以绕过 Hibernate API，而使用 JDBC API 来进行对数据的增、删、改和查的功能。例如在下面的代码中使用了一个复杂的查询语句来获得 infokind（类别表）中 infokindid 为 1001 的记录的最父级的记录的 id，其中"connect by prior…start with"是 Oracle 中支持的查询语句，但是在有些数据库中不支持，因此需要绕过 Hibernate API 来做操作，代码如下所示：

```
// 获得 session
Session session = HibernateSessionFactory.currentSession();
// 获得事务
Transaction ts = session.beginTransaction();
// 通过 session 的 connection()方法获得 Connection 对象，该方法已不推荐使用
Connection con = session.connection();
// 查询数据
String sql = "select infokindid from infokind where infokindid in(select infokindid from infokind infokind connect by prior parentid=infokindid start with infokindid=1001)";
PreparedStatement stmt = con.prepareStatement(sql);
ResultSet rs = stmt.executeQuery();
Long parentId = new Long(0);
if (rs.next()) {
    parented = new Long(rs.getInt(1));
}
// 提交事务
ts.commit();
// 执行完毕后，关闭 session
HibernateSessionFactory.closeSession();
```

如果底层数据库（如 Oracle、MySQL、SQL Server）等支持存储过程，可通过存储过程执行批量删除、更新等操作。本章讲述了在 Hibernate 中如何调用 MySQL 数据库中的存储过程，例如在下面的代码中，调用 createUser(…)存储过程，并将所需要的 3 个参数传入，代码如下所示：

```
Session session = HibernateSessionFactory.currentSession();
Transaction ts = session.beginTransaction();
PreparedStatement st = session.connection().prepareStatement(
        "{call createUser(?, ?, ?)}");
st.setString(1, "amigo");
st.setString(2, "阿蜜果");
st.setString(3, "123");
st.execute();
// 提交事务
ts.commit();
// 执行完毕后，关闭 session
HibernateSessionFactory.closeSession();
```

需要注意的是，对实体对象的保存、更新和删除操作，需要包含在事务控制中，在执行完相应的方法后，需要使用事务对象的 commit()方法提交事务。

第 14 章　Hibernate 的事务控制

【本章导读语】

数据库事务是指作为单个逻辑工作单元执行的一系列操作。它由一个或多个 SQL 语句组成，当其中的一个 SQL 语句执行失败时，整个逻辑工作单元的操作都应该被撤销。

本章将介绍数据库的事务、事务的隔离级别、悲观锁和乐观锁等概念，并通过实例讲述如何在 Hibernate 中使用事务。

【例 14-1】解说数据库事务

〖实例需求〗

本实例讲解数据库事务的概念，并讲述事务的隔离级别、悲观锁和乐观锁等概念。为后续讲述如何在 Hibernate 中进行事务控制打下基础。

〖开发过程〗

第一步：数据库事务

（1）介绍。

在实际情况中，常常会出现一组互相依赖的操作行为，例如在网上进行交易时，其付款过程一般包括以下几步数据库操作：

1）更新客户所购商品的库存信息。
2）保存客户付款信息。
3）生成订单并且保存到数据库中。
4）更新用户的购物数量等信息。

正常情况下，这一组操作将顺利进行，最终交易成功。但是，如果在这组操作中任何一个步骤出了差错，例如在更新商品库存信息时发生异常、该顾客银行账户存款不足等，都将导致交易失败。一旦交易失败，数据库中的所有信息都需要回退到交易之前的状态；否则，数据库的信息将会一片混乱而不可预测。数据库事务正是用来保证这种情况下交易的平稳性和可预测性的技术。

在进行银行转账时，例如张三需要从账户上转 5000 元给李四，这个过程一般包括以下几个操作：

1）从张三的账户上减去 5000 元。
2）给李四的账户上增加 5000 元。

这个过程就可以看做一个事务，若在第二步骤发生异常时，也即李四账户上的金额没有添加成功时，张三账户上的金额应该回退到之前的状态，此时整个事务失败。

（2）ACID 属性。

ACID（Atomic（原子性）、Consistency（一致性）、Isolation（隔离性）和 Durability（持久性）是数据库事务必须具有的特征，下面分别对其进行介绍：

- Atomic（原子性）：事务必须是原子工作单元；对于其数据修改，要么全都执行，要么全都不执行。通常，与某个事务关联的操作具有共同的目标，并且是相互依赖的。如果系统只执行这些操作的一个子集，则可能会破坏事务的总体目标。原子性消除了系统处理操作子集的可能性。
- Consistency（一致性）：事务在完成时，必须使所有的数据都保持一致状态。在相关数据库中，所有规则都必须应用于事务的修改，以保持所有数据的完整性。事务结束时，所有的内部数据结构（如 B 树索引或双向链表）都必须是正确的。某些维护一致性的责任由应用程序开发人员承担，他们必须确保应用程序已强制所有已知的完整性约束。例如，当开发用于转账的应用程序时，应避免在转账过程中任意移动小数点。
- Isolation（隔离性）：由并发事务所做的修改必须与任何其他并发事务所做的修改隔离。事务查看数据时数据所处的状态，要么是另一并发事务修改它之前的状态，要么是另一事务修改它之后的状态，事务不会查看中间状态的数据。这称为可串行性，因为它能够重新装载起始数据，并且重播一系列事务，以使数据结束时的状态与原始事务执行的状态相同。当事务可序列化时将获得最高的隔离级别。在此级别上，从一组可并行执行的事务获得的结果与通过连续运行每个事务所获得的结果相同。由于高度隔离会限制可并行执行的事务数，所以一些应用程序降低隔离级别以换取更大的吞吐量。
- Durability（持久性）：事务完成之后，它对于系统的影响是永久性的。该修改即使出现致命的系统故障也将一直保持。

数据库管理系统通过日志记录来保证 Atomic（原子性）、Consistency（一致性）和 Durability（持久性），当过程中的某个操作发生异常时，数据库管理系统将根据日志记录的操作来撤销已做的修改，将状态回滚到之前的状态。

数据库管理系统通过锁机制来保证 Isolation（隔离性），当多个事务同时更新数据库中的相同数据时，只允许持有锁的事务更新该条数据。只有当该事务执行完毕后，其余的事务才能对该记录进行更新。

（3）事务边界。

事务边界包括如下内容：

- 开始边界：在 Hibernate 中使用 Session 接口的 beginTransaction()方法开始事务。
- 正常结束边界（Commit）：在 Hibernate 中，Transaction 提供了 commit()方法来提交事务。
- 异常结束边界（Rollback）：在 Hibernate 中，Transaction 提供了 rollback()方法来回滚事务。

数据库系统支持"自动提交"和"手工提交"两种模式来提交事务。其中"自动提交"模式将每一条 SQL 语句都看成是一个独立的事务，在执行完毕后，将自动对数据库记录进行更新。而"手动提交"模式必须由开发人员手动开始和结束事务。

在前面的章节中大家可以看到，在创建数据库表时，数据库的脚本都写上了 type=INNODB，INNODB 表示表支持事务。type 可设置为如下 3 种类型：

- INNODB：该类型的表支持事务。

- MyISAM：该类型的表不支持事务，默认为该类型。
- BOB：该类型的表支持事务。

若在创建表时 type 被设置成 MyISAM 类型，而后因为需要该表支持事务，可以通过如下语句修改其 type 类型：

```
alter table 表的名称 type= INNODB;
```

第二步：事务隔离级别

（1）事务并发问题。

当同时运行多个事务时，可能出现如下并发问题：

- 脏读：一个事务（事务甲）读取到另一个事务（事务乙）未提交的更新数据，并且事务甲在数据上进行了更新操作，接着事务乙撤销了更新操作，此时事务甲操作的就是脏数据。
- 虚读：一个事务（事务甲）读到另一个事务（事务乙）已提交的新插入的数据。事务甲在事务的执行过程中，对数据进行了两次查询，第一次查询时，事务乙未插入数据，因此查出的数量是 count1，第二次查询时，事务乙提交了插入数据，因此查出的数量是 count2，此时 count1 和 count2 的数量不相等。在一般情况下，允许虚读的情况发生，但是对于一些要根据这个查询的结果进行重要决策的场合，需要采取隔离措施，不允许虚读的情况发生。
- 不可重复读：一个事务（事务甲）读到另一个事务（事务乙）已提交的更新数据。事务甲在进行第一次查询时，查询到某条记录，此时事务乙尚未对该条记录进行更新。事务甲在进行第二次查询时，事务乙已提交了对该条记录的更新，导致此次查询结果与上一次有所不同，因此事务甲无法确定根据哪一次查询的结果作为操作的基准来进行数据的更新。
- 第一类丢失更新：一个事务在撤销事务时，将其他事物已提交的更新数据覆盖。这类问题是由于完全没有使用事务引起的，若使用了事务，不允许两个事物同时更新相同的数据资源。
- 第二类丢失更新：一个事务覆盖另一个事务已提交的更新数据。该类并发问题是不可重复读的特例，不可重复读进行了两次查询，而第二类丢失更新只在进行了第一次查询后，直接执行了更新，导致事务甲的更新被丢失。

（2）事务隔离级别。

数据库提供了如下 4 种事务隔离级别：

- 串行化（Serializable）：该级别中一个事务完全看不到其他事务所做的更新，操纵相同数据时，一个事务只有在另一个事务执行完毕后，才允许进行操作，因此所有的并发问题在这种情况下都不会发生。该级别是最高的隔离级别，因此也是并发性能最低的隔离级别。
- 可重复读（Repeatable Read）：该级别可看到其他事务已经提交的新插入的记录，但是不能看到其他事务对已有记录的更新。
- 读已提交数据（Read Commited）：该级别可看到其他事务已经提交的新插入的记录，而且能看到其他事务对已有记录的更新。

- 读未提交的数据（Read Uncommited）：该级别的事务可以看到其他事务没有提交的新插入的记录，而且能看到其他事务没有提交的对已有记录的更新。

4 种事务隔离级别避免的并发问题如表 14-1 所示。

表 14-1　隔离级别能避免的并发问题

隔离级别	脏读	虚读	不可重复读	第一类丢失更新	第二类丢失更新
串行化	否	否	否	否	否
可重复读	否	是	否	否	否
读已提交数据	否	是	是	否	是
读未提交的数据	是	是	是	否	是

串行化→可重复读→读已提交数据→读未提交的数据的事务隔离级别是递减的，而并发性能是递增的。

在 Hibernate 中，可通过属性设置事务的隔离级别。属性 hibernate.connection.isolation 可设置 JDBC 事务隔离级别，取值可为 1、2、4 和 8。注意，很多数据库都不支持所有的隔离级别。

第三步：数据库的锁

（1）概念。

在前面已经提到，ACID 属性的隔离性是通过数据库的锁机制来保证的。许多数据库管理系统都提供了自动管理锁的功能，对普通的并发性事务，使用自动管理锁即可，但是如果对数据安全等有特别的要求的话，需要由事务本身控制对数据资源的锁定和解锁。

根据锁定资源的粒度，锁可分为如下类型：
- 数据库级锁：锁定整个数据库。
- 表级锁：锁定一个表。
- 区域级锁：锁定数据库的指定区域。
- 页面级锁：锁定数据库的特定页面。
- 键值级锁：锁定带有索引的一行数据。
- 行级锁：锁定表中的单行数据。

锁定资源的粒度越大，隔离性越高，但是并发性越低。

根据锁的封锁程度来分，可分为如下类型：
- 共享锁：用于读数据操作，允许其他事务同时读取锁定的资源，但不允许其他事务对锁定的资源进行更新。
- 独占锁：适用于更新数据的场合，不允许其他事务读取或修改其锁定的资源。
- 更新锁：在更新操作的初始化阶段用来锁定可能要修改的资源。

（2）死锁。

在数据库系统中，当多个事务锁定了一个资源，而又试图请求锁定对方已锁定的资源时，将会引起死锁。

例如事务 1 锁定了 ID 为 1001 的记录，事务 2 锁定了 ID 为 1002 的记录，事务 1 在等待锁定 1002 的记录，因此需要事务 2 解锁。而事务 2 在等待锁定 1001 的记录，因此需要事务 1 解锁，这种相互等待就是一种死锁现象。

很多数据库系统使用自动定期搜索来处理死锁问题，当发现死锁现象时，将结束死锁优先级低的事务,并且撤销该事务。

开发人员可使用如下手段来尽量避免死锁:
- 合理安排访问顺序。
- 使用短事务。
- 对数据一致性要求不高的场合,可允许脏读,脏读不对资源加锁,不会出现死锁。
- 使用尽可能低的隔离级别。

【例 14-2】在 Hibernate 中进行事务控制

〖实例需求〗

Hibernate 中提交了方法来开始事务、提交事务和回滚事务。本实例讲解如何在 Hibernate 中进行事务控制。

〖开发过程〗

第一步:获得 Session

在进行事务操作前,首先需要获得 Session,读者可看到上一章 HibernateSessionFactory 类的 currentSession()方法中通过如下方式打开 Session,获得 Session 对象:

```
session = sessionFactory.openSession();
```

SessionFactory 类中的 openSession()方法从数据库连接池中获得连接,Session 将这个连接设置为手动提交的方式。

第二步:开始事务

Session 接口中提供了 beginTransaction()方法来开始事务,如下语句可获得事务对象:

```
// 获得事务
Transaction ts = session.beginTransaction();
```

第三步:提交事务

Transaction 接口提供了 commit()方法来提交事务,当在操作执行完毕后,可使用 commit()方法来提交事务,提交事务后,数据将更新到数据库中。语句如下所示:

```
ts.commit();
```

第四步:回滚事务

当在事务的执行过程中发生异常时,需要对已做的工作进行回滚,Transaction 接口提供了 rollback()方法来回滚事务,语句如下所示:

```
ts.rollback()
```

第五步:关闭 Session

不管事务是否执行成功,最后都需要调用 Session 接口的 close()方法来关闭事务。读者可参见上一章 HibernateSessionFactory 类的 closeSession()方法,关闭 Session 的语句如下所示:

```
session.close();
```

第六步：Hibernate 的异常

当 Session 抛出异常时，开发人员必须调用 Transaction 接口的 rollback() 方法回滚事务，并调用 Session 对象的 close() 方法关闭 Session。

Hibernate 的 HibernateException 异常封装了 Hibernate 持久层可能出现的大多数错误，这些异常通常是无法恢复的，当出现这些异常时，常常需要在后台记录异常日志，并提供一个人性化的错误信息返回给用户。

在和数据库进行交互时，Hibernate 将 SQLException 封装成 Hibernate 的 JDBCException，为了让开发人员更加清楚地知道发生的异常类型，Hibernate 提供了更能表示异常类型的 JDBCException 的子类。标准的 JDBCException 子类型如下所示：

- JDBCConnectionException：底层 JDBC 通信出现异常。
- SQLGrammarException：SQL 语句的语法或格式发生异常，这种错误是一种很常见的错误。
- ConstraintViolationException：出现某种类型的约束异常，例如主键和外键错误，这种错误比较常见。
- LockAcquisitionException：获取所需的锁级别时发生异常。
- GenericJDBCException：不属于任何其他种类的原生异常。

第七步：编写 Hibernate 事务控制类：TransactionTest.java

接下来在上一章的例子上编写 Hibernate 的事务控制类 TransactionTest.java，该类位于 amigo.hibernate.operate 包中，内容如下所示：

```java
package amigo.hibernate.operate;

import java.util.Date;

import org.hibernate.Session;
import org.hibernate.Transaction;

/**
 * 测试 Hibernate 的事务控制.
 */
public class TransactionTest {
    public static void main(String[] args) {
        // 获得 session
        Session session = HibernateSessionFactory.currentSession();
        Transaction ts = null;

        try {
            // 获得事务
            ts = session.beginTransaction();
            // 设置对象的属性
            User user = new User();
            user.setLoginname("amigo");
            user.setName("阿蜜果");
```

```java
                    user.setPassword("198211");
                    user.setCreatetime(new Date());

                    // 保存对象
                    session.save(user);

                    // 在保存 loginname 为 amigo 的对象成功后,继续更新 loginname 为 xiexx 的对象
                    User otherUser = (User) session.get(
                            User.class,
                            "xiexx");
                    otherUser.setName("谢星星");
                    session.update(otherUser);

                    // 将更新提交到数据库
                    ts.commit();
                    System.out.println("保存成功!");
            } catch(Exception ex) {
                    ex.printStackTrace();
                    if (ts != null) {
                            try {
                                    // 回滚事务
                                    ts.rollback();
                            } catch(Exception e) {
                                    // 处理异常...
                            }
                    }

                    // 处理异常...
            } finally {
                    // 不论事务是否成功,都需要关闭 Session
                    try {
                            HibernateSessionFactory.closeSession();
                    } catch(Exception e) {
                            // 处理异常
                    }
            }
    }
}
```

该类首先添加 loginname 为 amigo 的记录,而后获得 loginname 为 xiexx 的记录,并将它的 name 更新为:xiexx,若更新记录的操作失败时,将使用 rollback()方法进行回滚,添加 amigo 记录也将操作不成功。

第八步:运行结果

当数据库中不存在记录时,otherUser 对象将为空,对其 name 属性设值将失败,此时运行 TransactionTest 类,运行结果如下所示:

```
Hibernate: select user0_.loginName as loginName0_0_, user0_.name as name0_0_, user0_.password as password0_0_, user0_.createTime as createTime0_0_ from tbl_user user0_ where user0_.loginName=?
java.lang.NullPointerException
    at amigo.hibernate.operate.TransactionTest.main(TransactionTest.java:35)
```

此时查看数据库，可看到该表还是没有记录，添加 amigo 记录的操作被回滚。

若当前数据库中 tbl_user 表的记录如图 14-1 所示时：

loginName	name	password	createTime
xiexx	xiexx	198211	2008-08-03 13:25:00

图 14-1　当前 tbl_user 表中的记录

此时运行 TransactionTest 类，控制台的信息如下所示：

> Hibernate: select user0_.loginName as loginName0_0_, user0_.name as name0_0_, user0_.password as password0_0_, user0_.createTime as createTime0_0_ from tbl_user user0_ where user0_.loginName=?
> Hibernate: insert into tbl_user (name, password, createTime, loginName) values (?, ?, ?, ?)
> Hibernate: update tbl_user set name=?, password=?, createTime=? where loginName=?
> 保存成功！

此时查看数据库的记录，如图 14-2 所示。

loginName	name	password	createTime
amigo	阿蜜果	198211	2008-08-03 13:37:37
xiexx	谢星星	198211	2008-08-03 13:25:00

图 14-2　运行后 tbl_user 表中的记录

从图 14-2 可看到，保存和更新记录操作成功。

小结

在日常生活中，常常会遇到一组互相依赖的操作行为，例如在网上进行交易时，它分为多个步骤，当其中一个步骤发生异常时，视为整个操作不成功，因此需要将状态变到最初始的状态，这种情况可称为事务。

数据库事务必须具有 ACID（Atomic（原子性）、Consistency（一致性）、Isolation（隔离性）和 Durability（持久性）的缩写）特征，这 4 个特征描述如下：

- Atomic（原子性）：事务必须是原子工作单元；对于其数据修改，要么全都执行，要么全都不执行。
- Consistency（一致性）：事务在完成时，必须使所有的数据都保持一致状态。
- Isolation（隔离性）：由并发事务所做的修改必须与任何其他并发事务所做的修改隔离。
- Durability（持久性）：事务完成之后，它对于系统的影响是永久性的。该修改即使出现致命的系统故障也将一直保持。

事务边界分为如下 3 种：
- 开始边界：开始事务。
- 正常结束边界：提交事务。
- 异常结束边界：回滚事务。

在 Hibernate 中，提供了这 3 种边界的操作方法，开始边界使用的是 Session 接口的 beginTransaction()方法，正常结束边界使用的是 Transaction 提供的 commit()方法，异常结束边界使用的是 Transaction 接口提供的 rollback()方法。在 MySQL 中，INNODB 和 BOB 类型的表是支持事务的，而默认的表类型 MyISAM 并不支持事务，所以开发人员在创建表时需要执行表类型为 INNODB 或 BOB，或通过：

    alter table 表的名称 type= INNODB;

修改表的类型为支持事务的类型。

    常见的事务并发问题为脏读、虚读、不可重复读、第一类丢失更新和第二类丢失更新。数据库提供了串行化（Serializable）、可重复读（Repeatable Read）、读已提交数据（Read Commited）和读未提交的数据（Read Uncommited）4 种事务隔离级别。4 种事务隔离级别避免的并发问题如表 14-2 所示。

表 14-2

隔离级别	脏读	虚读	不可重复读	第一类丢失更新	第二类丢失更新
串行化	否	否	否	否	否
可重复读	否	是	否	否	否
读已提交数据	否	是	是	否	是
读未提交的数据	是	是	是	否	是

ACID 属性的隔离性是通过数据库的锁机制来保证的。根据锁定资源的粒度，锁可分为如下类型：

- 数据库级锁：锁定整个数据库。
- 表级锁：锁定一个表。
- 区域级锁：锁定数据库的指定区域。
- 页面级锁：锁定数据库的特定页面。
- 键值级锁：锁定带有索引的一行数据。
- 行级锁：锁定表中的单行数据。

根据锁的封锁程度来分，可分为如下类型：

- 共享锁：用于读数据操作，允许其他事务同时读取锁定的资源，但不允许其他事务对锁定的资源进行更新。
- 独占锁：适用于更新数据的场合，不允许其他事务读取或修改其锁定的资源。
- 更新锁：在更新操作的初始化阶段用来锁定可能要修改的资源。

在 Hibernate 中，提供了相应的方法类操作事务，例如如下代码展示了在 Hibernate 中使用事务的方法：

```
Session session = HibernateSessionFactory.currentSession();
Transaction ts = null;
try {
    // 获得事务
    ts = session.beginTransaction();
    ... // 进行一连串数据库操作
    // 将更新提交到数据库
    ts.commit();
} catch(Exception ex) {
    ex.printStackTrace();
    if (ts != null) {
        try {
            ts.rollback();// 回滚事务
        } catch(Exception e) {
            // 处理异常...
```

```
            }
        }
    } finally {
        // 不论事务是否成功，都需要关闭 Session
        try {
            HibernateSessionFactory.closeSession();
        } catch(Exception e) {
            // 处理异常
        }
    }
}
```

需要注意的地方是，开发人员使用 session.beginTransaction()开启事务，使用 Transaction 类型对象的 commit()方法提交事务，使用 Transaction 类型对象的 rollback()方法回滚事务。

第 4 篇 Spring 2 篇

第 15 章 Spring 入门

【本章导读语】

Spring 是一种非侵入式的开发模型，它为企业应用的开发提供了一种轻量级的解决方案。它的核心机制是依赖注入和基于 AOP 的声明式事务管理。本章讲解 Spring 的入门知识，包括如何下载和安装 Spring 2，并通过讲解 Spring 的 HelloWorld 实例来使 Spring 更快地进入读者的视野。

【例 15-1】SPRING 2 简介

〖实例需求〗

本例介绍 Spring 2，并重点讲述 SPRING 2 的一些突出的新特性，以及开发人员从 Spring 1.2.x 升级到 Spring 2 需要注意的一些问题。

〖开发过程〗

第一步：Spring 介绍

Spring 是一种轻量级的 J2EE 应用程序开源框架。它是为了解决企业应用开发的复杂性而创建的，Spring 使用基本的 JavaBean 来完成以前只可能由 EJB 完成的事情。

Spring 的核心即是个 IoC/DI 的容器，它可以帮程序设计人员完成组件之间的依赖关系注入，使得组件之间的依赖达到最小，进而提高组件的重用性。

Spring 最为人重视的另一方面是支持 AOP（Aspect-Oriented Programming），AOP 框架是 Spring 支持的一个子框架。

Spring 也提供其他方面的整合，包括持久层的整合，如 JDBC、O/R Mapping 工具（Hibernate、iBATIS）、事务处理等，Spring 做了对多方面整合的努力。

第二步：Spring 2 的新特性

Spring 2 于 2005 年 12 月在佛罗里达召开的 Spring 经验交流会上问世。对比它的前续版本，其最大的改进在于控制反转（IOC）容器，其次面向切面编程（AOP）方面也进行了少量修改等。

它具有如下新特性：

（1）更简单、更易扩展的 XML 配置。

因为 Spring 2 使用了 XML Schema 的 XML 配置语法，所以使配置更加简单。在 Spring 的配置文件中使用 Spring 2 的 DTD 文档类型定义如下：

```
<!DOCTYPE beans PUBLIC "-//SPRING//DTD BEAN 2.0//EN" "http://www.springframework.org/dtd/spring-beans-2.0.dtd">
```

在 SPRING 2 中，AOP 和声明性事务控制的 XML 配置都得到简化。

有关 Spring 配置的更易扩展，指的是开发人员、第三方框架或产品供应商能开发自定义的标签，并将这些标签嵌入到自己的 Spring 配置文件中。

（2）新的 bean 作用域。

这又是 SPRING 2 的 IoC 容器的又一大改进之处。

SPRING 2 的以前版本的 IoC 容器支持两个不同的 bean 作用域：单例与原型。而 SPRING 2 除了支持两个作用域外，还提供了一些依赖于 Spring 部署环境（例如，在 Web 环境中的 request 和 session 作用域 bean）的额外的作用域，而且提供了所谓的"钩子"（"hooks"）使 Spring 用户可以创造自己的作用域。

（3）对@AspectJ 切面的支持。

SPRING 2 也支持使用@AspectJ 注解定义的切面，这些切面可以在 AspectJ 与 Spring AOP 中共享。

（4）其他特性。

Spring 自带的 Web 层的表单标签库和 Portlet 框架等都进行了改进，但是因为本书所讲述的 MVC 框架为 Struts 2.0，所以在此不再讲述。

另外，SPRING 2 还提供了对动态语言（例如 JRuby、Groovy 和 BeanShell 等）的支持，还提供了对 Java 5（Tiger）的支持等。

第三步：从 Spring1.2.x 移植到 SPRING 2

从 Spring 1.2.x 移植到 SPRING 2 比较简单，一般情况下，只需要更换 jar 包即可。但是有几点需要开发人员注意：

（1）XML 配置。

SPRING 2 的 XSD 在描述 Spring XML 元数据格式方面比先前的 DTD 更丰富，但是旧的 DTD 仍然得到支持。

如果读者使用的是 Spring 1.2 DTD，那么能继续用**'singleton'**属性。如果读者通过如下语句：

```
<!DOCTYPE beans PUBLIC "-//SPRING//DTD BEAN 2.0//EN" "http://www.springframework.org/dtd/spring-beans-2.0.dtd">
```

选择引用新的 SPRING 2 DTD，它不允许使用'singleton'属性，例如此时下面的 bean 定义就是非法的：

```
<bean name="/test" class="amigo.spring.TestAction" singleton="false"/>
```

此时可以用'scope'属性来定义 bean 的生命周期作用域，上面的 bean 定义可修改为：

```
<bean name="/test" class="amigo.spring.TestAction" scope="singleton"/>
```

（2）JAR 包。

Spring 1.2.x 和 SPRING 2 的 jar 文件有很多不同之处。JDO、Hibernate 2/3、TopLink 的 ORM 集成类不再被打包在核心文件 spring.jar 中，它们都有专门的 jar 文件。

（3）Deprecated 的类和方法。

一些以前被标记为@deprecated 的类和方法 SPRING 2 代码库中被完全删除了。

（4）Apache OJB。

请注意 Spring 主代码中的 Apache OJB 支持被完全删除了；但仍然可以在 Spring Modules 项目中找到 Apache OJB 的集成库。

（5）iBATIS。

iBATIS SQL Maps 1.3 支持被完全去除了。需升级到 iBATIS SQL Maps 2.0/2.1。

【例 15-2】下载 SPRING 2

〖实例需求〗

本例讲解如何下载 Spring 2。

〖开发过程〗

第一步：访问主页

Spring 的主页地址为：http://www.springframework.org/，界面如图 15-1 所示。

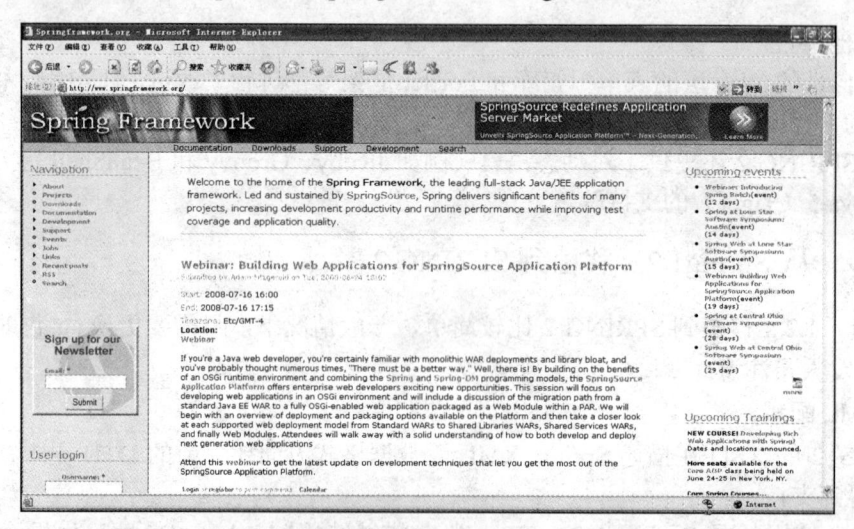

图 15-1　Spring 首页

第二步：下载 Spring

点击图 15-1 左侧的 Downloads 链接，进入 Spring 的下载界面，如图 15-2 所示。

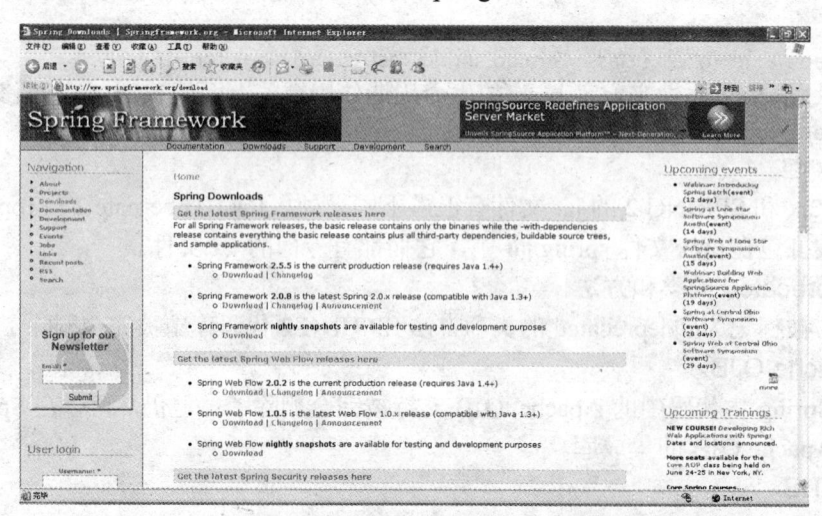

图 15-2　Spring 下载主页面

从图 15-2 中可以看到，Spring 的最新版本为 2.5.5，该版本需要 JDK1.4 及以上版本。单击该版本的 Download 按钮，读者将进入 Spring 在 http://sourceforge.net/网站上的镜像下载页面。建议下载 spring-framework-2.5.5-with-dependencies.zip 包，该压缩包不仅包括 Spring 的开发包和源码，还包括所依赖的第三方类库。

第三步：Spring 的目录结构

解压缩该压缩包后，目录结构如图 15-3 所示。

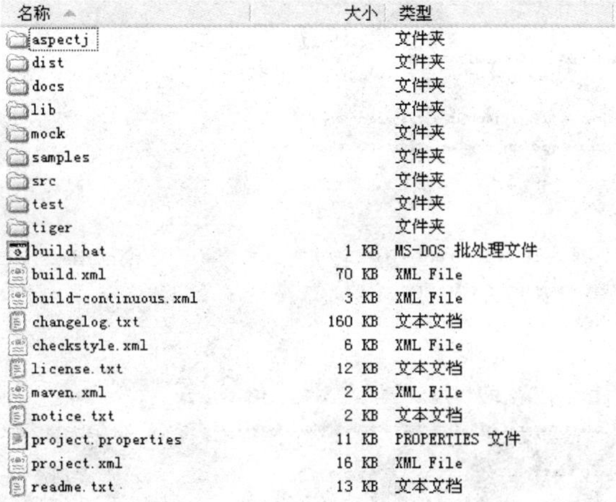

图 15-3 Spring 2.5.5 解压缩目录结构

目录下包括 9 个文件夹，其中：

- aspectj：AspectJ 5 主要的重点是对 Java 5 中引入的新 Java 语言特性（包括注释和泛型）提供支持。该目录包括 Spring 中提供的一些事务的注释。
- dist：该文件夹包括 Spring 的 jar 包，spring-xxx.jar 包是 Spring.jar 的子模块的压缩包，一般读者只需要将 spring.jar 拷贝到工程中即可，若工程只用到 spring 的一部分功能，可选择将对应的分模块包导入。
- docs：该文件夹包括 Spring 的开发文档，包括 API 参考文档、MVC 开发指南和 Spring 的标签说明。
- lib：该文件夹包括 Spring 所依赖的第三方类库。
- mock：该文件夹包括 Spring 的测试代码。
- samples：该文件夹包括 Spring 的简单实例，读者可以将其作为入门实例来学习。
- src：该文件夹包含 Spring 的全部源文件。
- test：该文件夹包含 Spring 的测试用例。
- tiger：该文件夹存放 JDK1.5 的相关内容。

【例 15-3】搭建 Spring 2 开发环境

〖实例需求〗

本例讲解如何搭建 Spring 2 的开发环境。

【开发过程】

第一步：建立工程

新建一个 springhelloworld 项目，如图 15-4 所示。

图 15-4　新建 springhelloworld 项目

在图 15-4 中单击 Next 按钮后，在而后出现的对话框中单击 Finish 按钮，完成工程的创建。

第二步：建立 lib 文件夹

在左侧的导航窗口中在 springhelloworld 工程上单击鼠标右键，弹出如图 15-5 所示的 New 菜单项。

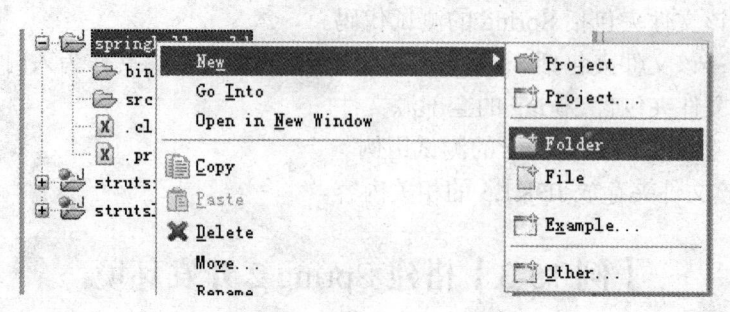

图 15-5　建立 lib 文件夹（1）

在图 15-5 中，选择 New→Folder 命令，弹出的对话框如图 15-6 所示。

图 15-6　建立 lib 文件夹（2）

在图 15-6 中的 Folder name 中输入 lib 后，单击 Finish 按钮，完成 lib 文件夹的创建。此时的工程结构如图 15-7 所示。

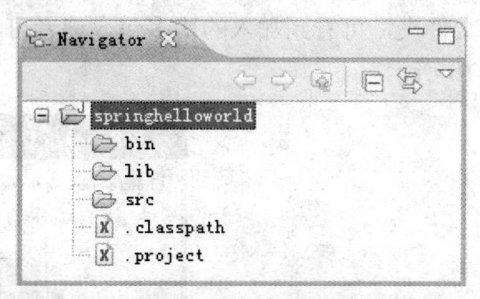

图 15-7　添加完 lib 目录后的目录结构

第三步：将 Spring 集成到工程中

（1）拷贝包到 lib 目录。

要将 Spring 集成到工程中，建议读者将 spring-framework-2.5.5\dist 文件夹中的 spring.jar 复制到工程 lib 目录中，而不是采用分模块将 spring-xxx.jar 拷贝。

另外 Spring 还需要使用 commons-logging.jar 和 log4j.jar 来输出日志，因此读者还需要将 log4j.jar 和 commons-logging.jar 复制到 lib 目录下。log4j.jar 位于 spring-framework-2.5.5\lib\log4j 文件夹下。commons-logging.jar 位于 spring-framework-2.5.5\lib\jakarta-commons 目录下。

在使用 Spring 时，还需要依赖 jakarta-commons 里面的诸多包，读者可以将 spring-framework-2.5.5\lib\jakarta-commons 目录下的所有包都复制到 springhelloworld 工程的 lib 目录中。

（2）添加包到编译路径。

在图 15-7 中，选择工程节点后单击鼠标右键，在弹出的菜单中选择 Properties，弹出工程的属性对话框，选择 Java Build Path，在其页签中选择 Libraries，如图 15-8 所示。

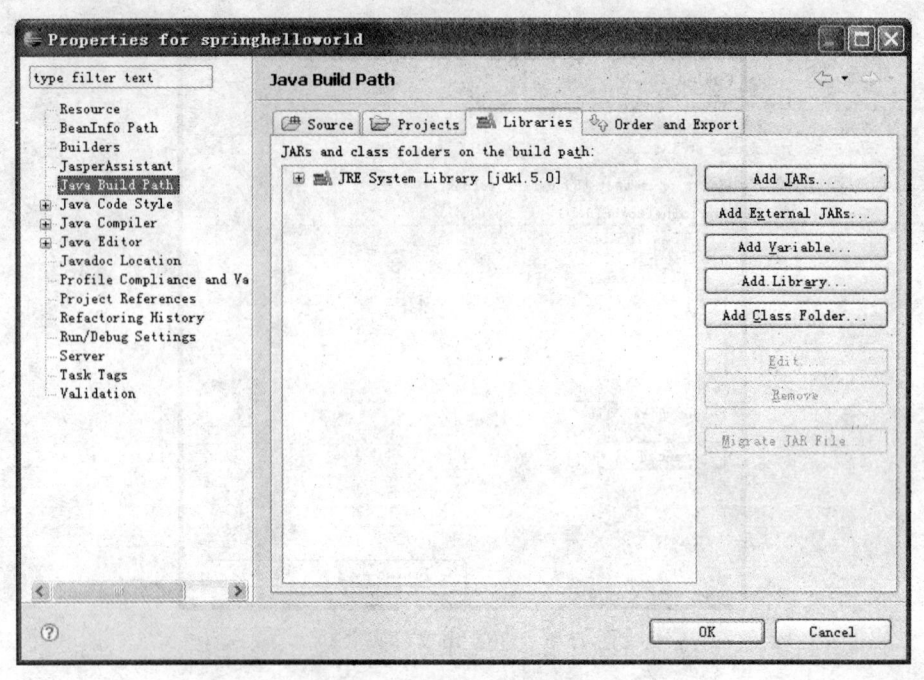

图 15-8 工程的编译路径设置

在图 15-8 中，单击 Add JARs 按钮，弹出的添加 jar 包的对话框如图 15-9 所示。

在图 15-9 中，点开 lib 文件夹，可看到加入的诸多包，读者可将其全选后，单击 OK 按钮完成 jar 包的加入，如图 15-10 所示。

图 15-9 添加 jar 包的对话框

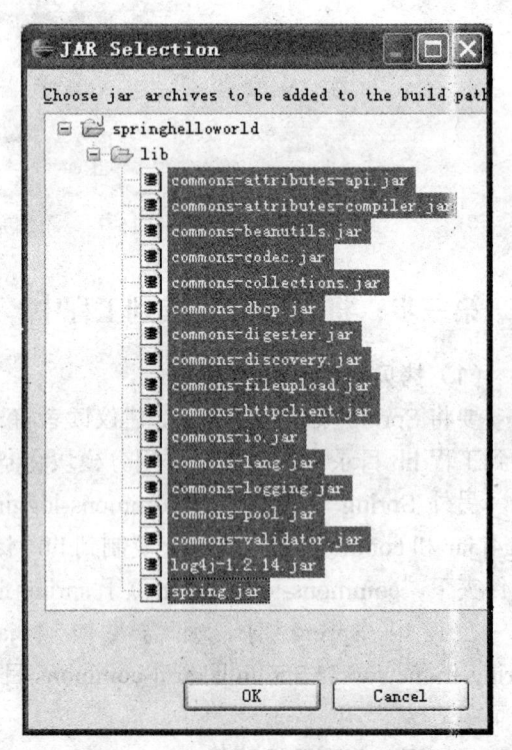

图 15-10 添加 jar 包

添加完 jar 包后的包结构视图如图 15-11 所示。

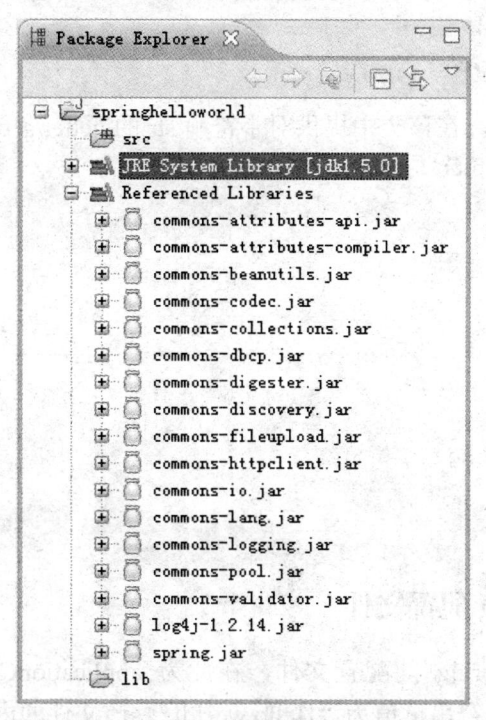

图 15-11 添加包到编译路径后的包结构

（3）配置 log4j。

为了保证工程日志的正常输出，还需要配置 log4j.properties 文件，在 src 源码目录中建立 log4j.properties 文件，其内容如下：

```
#定义日志输出级别为 DEBUG
log4j.rootLogger=DEBUG, CONSOLE
#输出源采用输出到控制台
log4j.appender.CONSOLE=org.apache.log4j.ConsoleAppender
#定义输出日志的布局采用的类是 org.apache.log4j.PatternLayout
log4j.appender.CONSOLE.layout=org.apache.log4j.PatternLayout
#定义日志输出的布局
log4j.appender.CONSOLE.layout.ConversionPattern=%c %x - %m%n
```

【例 15-4】使用 Spring 2 开发 HelloWorld

〖实例需求〗

本例讲解如何使用Spring 2进行简单的开发，通过依赖注入的方式输出字符串信息：helloworld。

〖开发过程〗

第一步：建立包目录

在本实例中，首先需要建立业务类和测试类所在的包目录，HelloBean 放在 amigo.spring.chapter15 包中，TestSpring 这个测试类放在 amigo.spring.chapter15.test 包中。

第二步：编写 HelloBean

首先编写 HelloBean 类，在该类中提供对字符串 str 的 getter/setter 方法。该类的内容如下：

```java
package amigo.spring.chapter15;

public class HelloBean {
    private String str;

    public String getStr() {
        return str;
    }

    public void setStr(String str) {
        this.str = str;
    }
}
```

第三步：编写 Spring 配置文件

在 src 目录下建立 Spring 的配置文件，在此为 applicationContext.xml，在该文件中给 HelloBean 的实例中的 str 字符串赋值为 "Hello world!"，该文件的内容如下所示：

```xml
<?xml version="1.0" encoding="UTF-8"?>
<beans xmlns="http://www.springframework.org/schema/beans"
    xmlns:xsi="http://www.w3.org/2001/XMLSchema-instance"
    xmlns:aop="http://www.springframework.org/schema/aop"
    xmlns:tx="http://www.springframework.org/schema/tx"
    xsi:schemaLocation="http://www.springframework.org/schema/beans
http://www.springframework.org/schema/beans/spring-beans-2.0.xsd
    http://www.springframework.org/schema/aop
http://www.springframework.org/schema/aop/spring-aop-2.0.xsd
    http://www.springframework.org/schema/tx
http://www.springframework.org/schema/tx/spring-tx-2.0.xsd"
    default-autowire="byName" default-lazy-init="true">
    <bean id="HelloBean" class="amigo.spring.chapter15.HelloBean">
        <property name="str">
            <value>Hello world!</value>
        </property>
    </bean>
</beans>
```

第四步：编写测试类

接着在 amigo.spring.chapter15.test 包下建立 TestSpring 类，在该类中，获得 Spring 的 BeanFactory，该类的代码如下所示：

```java
package amigo.spring.chapter15.test;

import org.springframework.beans.factory.xml.XmlBeanFactory;
import org.springframework.core.io.ClassPathResource;

import amigo.spring.chapter15.HelloBean;
```

```
public class TestSpring {
    public static void main(String[] args) {
        ClassPathResource res = new ClassPathResource(
                "applicationContext.xml");
        XmlBeanFactory factory = new XmlBeanFactory(res);
        HelloBean bean = (HelloBean) factory.getBean("HelloBean");
        System.out.println(bean.getStr());
    }
}
```

第五步：运行结果

在 TestSpring 类中单击鼠标右键，选择 Run As→Java Application 命令，可看到控制台输出了如下信息：

> ……
> org.springframework.beans.factory.xml.XmlBeanFactory - Creating instance of bean 'HelloBean' with merged definition [Root bean: class [amigo.spring.chapter15.HelloBean]; scope=singleton; abstract=false; lazyInit=true; autowireCandidate=true; autowireMode=1; dependencyCheck=0; factoryBeanName=null; factoryMethodName=null; initMethodName=null; destroyMethodName=null; defined in class path resource [applicationContext.xml]]
> org.springframework.beans.factory.xml.XmlBeanFactory - Eagerly caching bean 'HelloBean' to allow for resolving potential circular references
> Hello world!

读者可以看到，输出的 str 字符串的内容是：Hello world!，这个字符串值是在 Spring 配置文件中注入的。

小结

本章为 Spring 的入门章，笔者首先简要地介绍了 Spring，它是一种轻量级的 J2EE 应用程序开源框架，它的核心部分为其 IOC 容器以及 AOP 面向切面编程，这些知识都将在后续的章节进行讲解。SPRING 2 与其前续版本对比，比较突出的新特性包括：

- 更简单、更易扩展的 XML 配置：因为 SPRING 2 使用了 XML Schema 的 XML 配置语法，所以使得 XML 配置得以简化。另外 SPRING 2 允许开发人员、第三方框架或产品供应商能开发自定义的标签，提供了易扩展性。
- 新的 bean 作用域：支持了更多的作用域，提供了一些依赖于 Spring 部署环境（例如，在 Web 环境中的 request 和 session 作用域 bean）的额外的作用域。
- 对@AspectJ 切面的支持：支持使用@AspectJ 注解定义的切面。

从 Spring 1.2.x 升级到 SPRING 2 比较简单，一般只需要更换 jar 包即可，但还有一些需要重点注意的问题：

- XML 配置中作用域属性的改变。
- Deprecated 的类和方法已被完全去除。

Spring 的首页地址为：http://www.springframework.org/，读者可在对应的链接地址上下载 SPRING 2 框架。

在项目中加入 SPRING 2 的支持时，只需加入对应的 jar 包即可。在项目中使用 Spring 进行开发时，关键点在于配置 Spring 的配置文件，这些内容都将在后续章节详细讲述。

第 16 章 核心机制——IoC

【本章导读语】

Spring 框架所提供的众多功能之所以能成为一个整体正是建立在 IoC 的基础之上，IoC 是 Spring 中极其重要的一部分，可谓是 Spring 的灵魂。

本章将讲述 IoC 的知识，包括 IoC 的相关概念（例如实现的基本原理、IoC 容器的概念等），另外还将讲述实例化容器和 bean 的几种方式，以及 Spring 中注入的几种方式（构造注入、setter 方法注入以及接口注入）。另外，Spring 一般采用 XML 格式来配置，因此笔者还讲述了 Spring 的基本配置，并重点讲述了 bean 属性及构造器参数的配置。

【例 16-1】解说 IoC 的相关概念

〖实例需求〗

Spring 框架提供的众多功能都是建立在 IoC 基础上的，其外延非常丰富，它是 Spring 框架极为重要的一部分。本实例要达到的目的是使读者对 IoC 实现的基本原理有比较清晰的理解。另外，还需掌握 Spring 中容器的概念，以及在 Spring 中如何实例化容器。

〖开发过程〗

第一步：建立工程

按照第 15 章的方式建立一个名为 springioc 的 Web 工程，并将 Spring 的 jar 复制到 WebRoot/WEB-INF/lib 目录中。接着在 src 源码目录中创建 amigo.spring.ioc.conception 包，并将 log4j 的配置文件 log4j.properties 复制到 src 源码目录。完成后，目录结构如图 16-1 所示。

第二步：控制反转的基本原理

（1）IoC 的概念。

IoC（Inversion of Control）被称为"控制反转"，它又有一个比较让人好理解的概念：DI（Dependency Injection），即依赖注入。

IoC 指的就是由容器控制程序之间的关系，而非传统实现中，由程序代码直接控制。即组件之间的依赖关系由容器在运行期决定。

为了让读者更好地了解 IoC 的概念，笔者举一个国外网站看到的一个可运行的简单实例来帮助读者理解。在下面的实例中，在类 MovieLister 中提供一个根据导演的名称获取他所导演的影片的方法，在该类中，需要调用一个影片查找器获得所有影片信息。在该类中调用影片查找器的工厂类来获得具体的影片查找器。

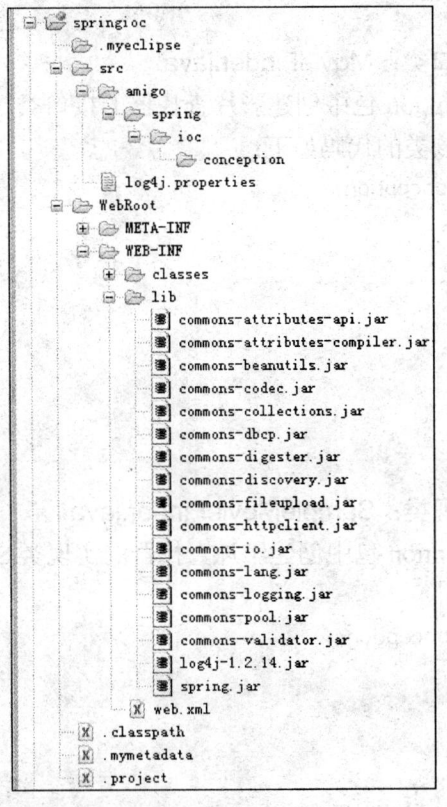

图 16-1　工程的目录结构

（2）编写影片类：Movie.java。

在 amigo.spring.ioc.conception 包下创建影片类 Movie.java，该类包括对影片的 ID、名称、女演员、男演员和导演属性，该类的代码如下所示：

```java
package amigo.spring.ioc.conception;

/**
 * 影片类.
 */
public class Movie {
    /** 影片 ID. */
    private long id;

    /** 影片名称. */
    private String name;

    /** 导演. */
    private String director;

    /** 男演员. */
    private String actor;

    /** 女演员. */
    private String actress;
```

```
    // 省略 getter/setter 方法
}
```

（3）编写影片查找器接口类：MovieFinder.java。

在 amigo.spring.ioc.conception 包中创建影片查找器的接口类 MovieFinder.java，该接口包括获取所有影片信息的方法，该类的代码如下：

```java
package amigo.spring.ioc.conception;

import java.util.List;

/**
 * 影片查找器接口类.
 */
public interface MovieFinder {
    List findAll();
}
```

（4）编写影片查找器实现类：SampleMovieFinder.java。

在 amigo.spring.ioc.conception 包中创建影片查找器的实现类 SampleMovieFinder.java，该类的代码如下所示：

```java
package amigo.spring.ioc.conception;

import java.util.ArrayList;
import java.util.List;

/**
 * 影片查找器实现类.
 */
public class SampleMovieFinder implements MovieFinder {
    public List findAll() {
        List movieList = new ArrayList();

        Movie movie1 = new Movie();
        movie1.setId(1);
        movie1.setName("花样年华");
        movie1.setActress("张曼玉");
        movie1.setActor("梁朝伟");
        movie1.setDirector("王家卫");
        movieList.add(movie1);

        Movie movie2 = new Movie();
        movie2.setId(2);
        movie2.setName("茉莉花");
        movie2.setActress("章子怡");
        movieList.add(movie2);

        Movie movie3 = new Movie();
        movie3.setId(3);
        movie3.setName("玉观音");
        movie3.setActress("孙俪");
        movie3.setActor("佟大为");
        movieList.add(movie3);
```

```
            Movie movie4 = new Movie();
            movie4.setId(4);
            movie4.setName("2046");
            movie4.setActress("张曼玉");
            movieList.add(movie4);

            return movieList;
        }
    }
```

（5）编写影片查找器工厂类：SampleMovieFinder.java。

在 amigo.spring.ioc.conception 包中创建影片查找器的工厂类 MovieFinderFactory.java，该类提供一个输入查找器名称获取具体的查找器的方法，该类的代码如下所示：

```
package amigo.spring.ioc.conception;

/**
 * 影片查找器的工厂类.
 */
public class MovieFinderFactory {
    public static MovieFinder getFinder(String finderName) {
        MovieFinder finder = null;
        if ("sampleFinder".equals(finderName)) {
            finder = new SampleMovieFinder();
        } else {
            // ...
        }
        return finder;
    }
}
```

（6）编写测试类：MovieLister.java。

在 amigo.spring.ioc.conception 包下创建测试类 MovieLister.java，该类引用了 MovieFinder 接口，但并没有引入具体的影片查找器实现类，具体查找器实现类是通过查找器工厂类获得的。该类的代码如下所示：

```
package amigo.spring.ioc.conception;

import java.util.Iterator;
import java.util.List;

/**
 * 测试类.
 */
class MovieLister {
    private MovieFinder finder;

    public MovieLister() {
        finder = MovieFinderFactory.getFinder("sampleFinder");
    }

    public Movie[] moviesActressBy(String arg) {
        List allMovies = finder.findAll();
        for (Iterator it = allMovies.iterator(); it.hasNext();) {
```

```java
            Movie movie = (Movie) it.next();
            if (!movie.getActress().equals(arg))
                it.remove();
        }
        return (Movie[]) allMovies.toArray(new Movie[allMovies.size()]);
    }

    public static void main(String[] args) {
        MovieLister lister = new MovieLister();
        Movie[] movies = lister.moviesActressBy("张曼玉");
        System.out.println("有" + movies.length + "部电影");
        for (int i = 0; i < movies.length; i++) {
            Movie movie = movies[i];
            System.out.println("影片ID=" + movie.getId() + ",影片名称=" + movie.getName());
        }
    }
}
```

（7）运行结果。

该实例的运行结果如下所示：

```
有 2 部电影
影片 ID=1,影片名称=花样年华
影片 ID=4,影片名称=2046
```

Spring 中的 IoC 所起的作用就相当于 MovieFinderFactory 类，它负责给需要某接口的实现类的某个类注入实现类。在这些类中，只需引入实现类即可，而不需要将实现类也引入到类中。

第三步：Spring 的 IoC 容器

org.springframework.beans.factory.BeanFactory 是 Spring IoC 容器的实际代表者，IoC 容器负责容纳此前所描述的 bean，并对 bean 进行管理。

在 Spring 中，BeanFactory 是 IoC 容器的核心接口。它的职责包括：实例化、定位、配置应用程序中的对象及建立这些对象间的依赖。Spring 为开发人员提供了许多易用的 BeanFactory 实现，而这些实现中，XmlBeanFactory 最为常用，它以 XML 方式描述组成应用的对象以及对象间的依赖关系。

Spring 支持 3 种配置元数据格式：XML 格式、Java 属性文件格式或使用 Spring 公共 API 编程实现。其中 XML 格式是其中最常用的一种。Spring IoC 容器具有 1 到多个 bean 的定义。bean 定义与应用程序中实际使用的对象一一对应。bean 的定义可包括：业务逻辑对象、数据访问层对象（DAO）、表示层（例如 Struts 的 Action）对象等。

【例 16-2】XML 格式配置元数据

〖实例需求〗

本实例讲解 XML 元数据的配置，对常用的 XML 元数据：<beans>、<bean>和<property>的配置通过简单实例的方式进行详细讲解。

第 16 章 核心机制——IoC

〖开发过程〗

第一步：基本结构

当使用基于 XML 的配置元数据时，将在顶层的<beans/>元素中配置一个或多个<bean/>元素。以下是其基本结构：

```xml
<?xml version="1.0" encoding="UTF-8"?>
<beans xmlns="http://www.springframework.org/schema/beans"
       xmlns:xsi="http://www.w3.org/2001/XMLSchema-instance"
       xsi:schemaLocation="http://www.springframework.org/schema/beans
http://www.springframework.org/schema/beans/spring-beans-2.0.xsd">
    <bean id="..." class="...">
        ......
    </bean>

    <bean id="..." class="...">
        ......
    </bean>
</beans>
```

第二步：<beans>元素的配置

<beans>为配置文件的根元素，它可包含 0 到多个<bean>元素。它有如下属性：

- **default-autowire**：该属性用于指定默认的 bean 自动装配模式。
- **default-dependency-check**：该属性用于指定默认的依赖检查模式。该属性有如下 4 个值：
  - **none** ：不进行依赖检查。没有指定值的 bean 属性仅仅是没有设值。
  - **Simple**：对基本类型和集合（除了合作者外，比如其他的 bean，所有东西）进行依赖检查。
  - **Object**：对合作者进行依赖检查。
  - **all** ：对合作者，基本类型和集合都进行依赖检查。
- **default-lazy-init**：该属性用于指定是否默认延迟加载。值为 true 表示延迟加载，为 false 表示非延迟加载。

第三步：<bean>元素的基本配置

<bean>元素为<beans>元素的子元素，它用于指明 Spring 容器一个类以及指明它是如何配置的。它具有如下属性：

- **class**：该属性用于指定类的全路径，例如 amigo.spring.chapter16.SMSSender。
- **id**：class 属性对应的类在 BeanFactory 中的唯一标识，代码中可通过该名称在 BeanFactory 获取类实例。
- **name**：同上，如果给 bean 增加别名，可以通过 name 属性指定一个或多个 id。
- **scope**：用于指定 bean 的作用域。Spring 支持 5 种作用域（其中 request、session 和 global session 三种只能用在基于 Web 的 Spring ApplicationContext）。5 种作用域及其描述如表 16-1 所示。

表 16-1 bean 的作用域及其描述

作用域	描述
singleton	在每个 Spring IoC 容器中一个 bean 定义对应一个对象实例
prototype	一个 bean 定义对应多个对象实例
request	在一次 HTTP 请求中，一个 bean 定义对应一个实例；即每次 HTTP 请求将会有各自的 bean 实例，它们依据某个 bean 定义创建而成。该作用域仅在基于 Web 的 Spring ApplicationContext 情形下有效
session	在一个 HTTP Session 中，一个 bean 定义对应一个实例。该作用域仅在基于 Web 的 Spring ApplicationContext 情形下有效
global session	在一个全局的 HTTP Session 中，一个 bean 定义对应一个实例。典型情况下，仅在使用 portlet context 的时候有效。该作用域仅在基于 Web 的 Spring ApplicationContext 情形下有效

- abstract：设定 ApplicationContext 是否对 bean 进行预先的初始化。
- parent：定义一个模板。
- autowire：bean 自动装配模式。具体的值可参考<beans>元素的 default-autowire 属性。
- dependency-check：依赖检查模式，同<beans>元素的 default-dependency-check 属性。
- lazy-init：延迟加载。值同<beans>元素的 default-lazy-init 属性。
- init-method：该属性用于指定初始化方法，此方法将在 BeanFactory 创建 JavaBean 实例之后，在向应用层返回引用之前执行。一般用于一些资源的初始化工作。
- destroy-method：该属性用于指定销毁方法。此方法将在 BeanFactory 销毁的时候执行，一般用于资源释放。
- factory-bean：该属性用于指定通过实例工厂方法创建 bean，class 属性必须为空，factory-bean 属性必须指定一个 bean 的名字，这个 bean 一定要在当前的 bean 工厂或者父 bean 工厂中，并包含工厂方法。而工厂方法本身通过 factory-method 属性设置。
- factory-method：该属性用于设定工厂类的工厂方法。
- depends-on：该属性用于指定 Bean 依赖关系。一般情况下无需设定。通过 depends-on 指定其依赖关系可保证在此 Bean 加载之前，首先对 depends-on 所指定的资源进行加载。

第四步：<property>元素的基本配置

<property>属性为<bean>元素的子元素，它用于设置一个属性。它包括如下属性：
- name：该属性用于指定属性的名称。
- value：用于指定 bean 的属性值。
- ref：指定了属性对 BeanFactory 中其他 Bean 的引用关系。

该属性的使用举例如下：

例 1：<property name="msgType" value="0" />

例 2：<property name="userSampleBean" ref="userBean" />

【例 16-3】实例化容器的几种方式

〖实例需求〗

在 Spring 中，可通过多种方式实例化容器，本实例将讲解常用的实例化容器的方式。

【开发过程】

第一步：创建包 amigo.spring.ioc.container

首先在 src 目录中创建本实例的包 amigo.spring.ioc.container，用于包含本实例的类文件。

第二步：编写辅助测试 Bean：HelloBean.java

为了辅助实例化容器的测试，读者可在包 amigo.spring.ioc.container 中创建一个辅助类 HelloBean.java，该类的代码非常简单，只是提供了一个 sayHelloWorld() 方法显示简单的信息，该类的代码如下所示：

```java
package amigo.spring.ioc.container;

/**
 * 实例化容器实例辅助类，用于输出 Hello 信息.
 */
public class HelloBean {
    public void sayHelloWorld() {
        System.out.println("hello,阿蜜果");
    }
}
```

第三步：编写 Spring 配置文件：container.xml

在 src 目录中创建 Spring 的配置文件 container.xml，该文件定义了一个 bean：helloBean，指定的类为 amigo.spring.ioc.container.HelloBean，该文件的内容如下所示：

```xml
<?xml version="1.0" encoding="UTF-8"?>
<beans xmlns="http://www.springframework.org/schema/beans"
       xmlns:xsi="http://www.w3.org/2001/XMLSchema-instance"
       xsi:schemaLocation="http://www.springframework.org/schema/beans
http://www.springframework.org/schema/beans/spring-beans-2.0.xsd">

    <bean id="helloBean" class="amigo.spring.ioc.container.HelloBean" />
</beans>
```

第四步：方式一：在 CLASSPATH 路径下获取 XMLBeanFactory 实例

在本步中讲解如何在 CLASSPATH 路径下获取 Spring 配置文件，并获得 XMLBeanFactory 实例。

首先在包 amigo.spring.ioc.container 中创建测试类 Test.java，该类的代码如下所示：

```java
package amigo.spring.ioc.container;

import org.springframework.beans.factory.xml.XmlBeanFactory;
import org.springframework.core.io.ClassPathResource;

/**
 * 实例化容器测试类.
 */
public class Test {
```

```java
public static void main(String[] args) {
    // 方式一：在 CLASSPATH 路径下获取 XMLBeanFactory 实例
    ClassPathResource res = new ClassPathResource(
            "container.xml");
    XmlBeanFactory factory = new XmlBeanFactory(res);
    HelloBean helloBean = (HelloBean) factory.getBean("helloBean");
    helloBean.sayHelloWorld();
}
```

运行该类后，读者可在控制台看到输出了信息：hello,阿蜜果，即表示成功地从 XmlBeanFactory 对象中获得了 HelloBean 对象。

【提示】若 CLASSPATH 路径下无 applicationContext.xml 文件时，将会出现如下异常信息：

```
……
Caused by: java.io.FileNotFoundException: class path resource [container.xml] cannot be opened because it does not exist
        at org.springframework.core.io.ClassPathResource.getInputStream(ClassPathResource.java:135)
        at org.springframework.beans.factory.xml.XmlBeanDefinitionReader.loadBeanDefinitions(XmlBeanDefinitionReader.java:297)
        at org.springframework.beans.factory.xml.XmlBeanDefinitionReader.loadBeanDefinitions(XmlBeanDefinitionReader.java:280)
        at org.springframework.beans.factory.xml.XmlBeanFactory.<init>(XmlBeanFactory.java:73)
        at org.springframework.beans.factory.xml.XmlBeanFactory.<init>(XmlBeanFactory.java:61)
……
```

第五步：方式二：指定绝对路径创建 ApplicationContext 实例

在 Test.java 类中添加如下代码：

```java
// 方式二：指定绝对路径创建 ApplicationContext 实例
FileSystemXmlApplicationContext context = new FileSystemXmlApplicationContext(
        "E:\\springioc\\src\\container.xml");
BeanFactory factory2 = (BeanFactory) context;
HelloBean helloBean2 = (HelloBean) factory2.getBean("helloBean");
helloBean2.sayHelloWorld();
```

此时运行该类，依然能看到该段代码成功地输出了信息。

在构造 FileSystemApplicationContext 实例时，若需要的是多个 Spring 的配置文件，它的构造函数也可传入配置文件的路径数组。

第六步：方式三：通过 ClassPathXmlApplicationContext 创建 BeanFactory 实例

使用 ClassPathXmlApplicationContext 类可以在 CLASSPATH 路径下的 Spring 配置文件中创建 ApplicationContext，在 Test.java 类中添加如下代码，它所完成的功能与前两步完成的功能一样：

```java
// 方式三：通过 ClassPathXmlApplicationContext 创建 BeanFactory 实例
ClassPathXmlApplicationContext context3 = new ClassPathXmlApplicationContext(
        "container.xml");
BeanFactory factory3 = (BeanFactory) context3;
HelloBean helloBean3 = (HelloBean) factory3.getBean("helloBean");
helloBean3.sayHelloWorld();
```

此时运行该类，依然能看到该段代码成功地输出了信息。

构造 ClassPathXmlApplicationContext 对象时，也可以传入 Spring 配置文件数组，举例如下：

```
// 多个 Spring 配置文件
String[] paths = new String[]{
        "applicationContext.xml",
        "applicationContext2.xml"};
ClassPathXmlApplicationContext context = new ClassPathXmlApplicationContext(
        paths);
BeanFactory factory = (BeanFactory) context;
```

第七步：容器的使用

上面讲述了实例化容器的几种方式。下面讲述一下获得容器对象后，如何使用容器对象，容器接口类 BeanFactory 包括如下方法：

- containsBean(String)：如果 BeanFactory 包含给定名称的 bean 定义（或 bean 实例），则返回 true。
- getBean(String)：该方法在前面各步时都被使用到，它返回以给定名字注册的 bean 实例。根据 bean 的配置情况，如果为 singleton 模式将返回一个共享的实例，否则将返回一个新建的实例。如果没有找到指定的 bean，该方法可能会抛出 BeansException 异常。
- getBean(String, Class)：返回以给定名称注册的 bean 实例，并转换为给定 class 类型的实例，如果转换失败，相应的异常（BeanNotOfRequiredTypeException）将被抛出。上面的 getBean(String)方法也遵循该规则。
- getType(String name)：返回给定名称的 bean 的 Class。如果没有找到指定的 bean 实例，则抛出 NoSuchBeanDefinitionException 异常。
- isSingleton(String)：判断给定名称的 bean 定义（或 bean 实例）是否为 singleton 模式（singleton 将在 bean 的作用域中讨论），如果 bean 没找到，则抛出 NoSuchBeanDefinitionException 异常。
- getAliases(String)：返回给定 bean 名称的所有别名的数组。

为了讲述其使用，读者可在包 amigo.spring.ioc.container 中创建 ContainerUser.java 类，该类的代码如下所示：

```
package amigo.spring.ioc.container;

import org.springframework.beans.factory.xml.XmlBeanFactory;
import org.springframework.core.io.ClassPathResource;

/**
 * 展示容器对象 BeanFactory 的使用
 */
public class ContainerUse {
    public static void main(String[] args) {
        ClassPathResource res = new ClassPathResource(
                "container.xml");
        XmlBeanFactory factory = new XmlBeanFactory(res);
        boolean containFlag = factory.containsBean("helloBean");
        System.out.println("是否包含名为 helloBean 的 bean：" + containFlag);

        if (containFlag) {
```

```java
            HelloBean helloBean = (HelloBean) factory.getBean("helloBean");
            helloBean.sayHelloWorld();
            System.out.println("成功通过 getBean(String)获得 Bean 实例");

            HelloBean helloBean2 = (HelloBean) factory.getBean("helloBean", HelloBean.class);
            helloBean2.sayHelloWorld();
            System.out.println("成功通过 getBean(String, Class)获得 Bean 实例");

            boolean isSingleton = factory.isSingleton("helloBean");
            System.out.println("helloBean 是否为 Singleton：" + isSingleton);

            Class type = factory.getType("helloBean");
            System.out.println("helloBean 的类的类型为：" + type.getName());

            String[] aliases = factory.getAliases("helloBean");
            System.out.println("helloBean 的类的别名个数为：" + aliases.length);
        }
    }
}
```

运行该类后可看到控制台输出如下信息：

```
……
是否包含名为 helloBean 的 bean：true
……
成功通过 getBean(String)获得 Bean 实例
org.springframework.beans.factory.xml.XmlBeanFactory   - Returning cached instance of singleton bean 'helloBean'
hello,阿蜜果
成功通过 getBean(String, Class)获得 Bean 实例
helloBean 是否为 Singleton：true
helloBean 的类的类型为：amigo.spring.ioc.container.HelloBean
helloBean 的类的别名个数为：0
……
```

【例 16-4】实例化 bean 的 3 种方式

〖实例需求〗

就 Spring IoC 容器而言，bean 定义基本上描述了创建一个或多个实际 bean 对象的内容。当需要的时候，容器会从 bean 定义列表中取得一个指定的 bean 定义，并根据 bean 定义里面的配置元数据使用反射机制来创建一个实际的对象。

Spring 提供了 3 种方式来实例化 bean，本实例讲解这 3 种实例化 bean 的方式。

〖开发过程〗

第一步：创建包 amigo.spring.ioc.bean

首先在 src 目录中创建本实例的包 amigo.spring.ioc.bean，用于包含本实例的类文件。

第二步：编写用户对象类：UserBean.java

在包 amigo.spring.ioc.bean 中创建用户对象类：UserBean.java。该类的代码如下所示：

```java
package amigo.spring.ioc.bean;

/**
 * 用户对象.
 */
public class UserBean {
    private String username;

    private String password;

    // 省略 username 和 password 的 getter/setter 方法

    /**
     * 创建 UserBean 对象.
     * @return 返回 UserBean 对象，
     *         设置其 username 为：阿蜜果，密码为：123
     */
    public static UserBean createUserBean() {
        UserBean user = new UserBean();
        user.setUsername("阿蜜果");
        user.setPassword("123");
        return user;
    }
}
```

第三步：编写 UserBean 的工厂类：UserBeanFactory.java

在包 amigo.spring.ioc.bean 中创建 UserBean 的工厂类：UserBeanFactory.java，该类包含 createUserBean()方法，用户创建 UserBean 对象。该类的代码如下所示：

```java
package amigo.spring.ioc.bean;

/**
 * UserBean 的工厂类.
 */
public class UserBeanFactory {
    /**
     * 创建 UserBean 对象.
     * @return 返回 UserBean 对象，
     *         设置其 username 为：谢星星，密码为：xiexx
     */
    public UserBean createUserBean() {
        UserBean user = new UserBean();
        user.setUsername("谢星星");
        user.setPassword("xiexx");
        return user;
    }
}
```

第四步：编写测试类：Test.java

在包 amigo.spring.ioc.bean 中创建测试类：Test.java，该类获得 UserBean 对象后，显示其 username 和 password 属性。该类的代码如下所示：

```java
package amigo.spring.ioc.bean;

import org.springframework.beans.factory.xml.XmlBeanFactory;
import org.springframework.core.io.ClassPathResource;

/**
 * bean 实例化测试类.
 */
public class Test {
    public static void main(String[] args) {
        // 使用"构造器实例化"
        ClassPathResource res1 = new ClassPathResource(
                "bean1.xml");
        XmlBeanFactory factory1 = new XmlBeanFactory(res1);
        UserBean userBean1 = (UserBean) factory1.getBean("userBean");
        System.out.println("使用"构造器实例化", username=" + userBean1.getUsername()
                + ", password=" + userBean1.getPassword());

        // 使用"静态工厂方法实例化"
        ClassPathResource res2 = new ClassPathResource(
                "bean2.xml");
        XmlBeanFactory factory2= new XmlBeanFactory(res2);
        UserBean userBean2 = (UserBean) factory2.getBean("userBean");
        System.out.println("使用"静态工厂方法实例化", username=" + userBean2.getUsername()
                + ", password=" + userBean2.getPassword());

        // 使用"实例工厂方法实例化"
        ClassPathResource res3 = new ClassPathResource(
                "bean3.xml");
        XmlBeanFactory factory3= new XmlBeanFactory(res3);
        UserBean userBean3 = (UserBean) factory3.getBean("userBean");
        System.out.println("使用"实例工厂方法实例化", username=" + userBean3.getUsername()
                + ", password=" + userBean3.getPassword());
    }
}
```

第五步：用构造器实例化

当采用构造器来创建 bean 实例时，Spring 对 class 并没有特殊的要求，被创建的类并不需要实现任何特定的接口，只要指定 bean 的 class 属性即可。不过根据所采用的 IoC 类型，class 可能需要一个默认的空构造器。下面来看一下使用构造器实例化时的配置。

在 src 目录中建立 bean1.xml 文件，该文件的内容如下所示：

```xml
<?xml version="1.0" encoding="UTF-8"?>
<beans xmlns="http://www.springframework.org/schema/beans"
       xmlns:xsi="http://www.w3.org/2001/XMLSchema-instance"
       xsi:schemaLocation="http://www.springframework.org/schema/beans
http://www.springframework.org/schema/beans/spring-beans-2.0.xsd">

    <bean id="userBean" class="amigo.spring.ioc.bean.UserBean" />
</beans>
```

只需在 Spring 的配置文件中配置 userBean，并指定其 class 属性为该 UserBean 类即可。

第六步：使用静态工厂方法实例化

当采用静态工厂方法创建 bean 时，除了需要指定 class 属性外，还需要通过 factory-method 属性来指定创建 bean 实例的工厂方法。Spring 将调用此方法返回实例对象。

可在 src 目录中建立静态工厂方法实例化的 Spring 配置文件：bean2.xml，该文件的内容如下：

```xml
<?xml version="1.0" encoding="UTF-8"?>
<beans xmlns="http://www.springframework.org/schema/beans"
    xmlns:xsi="http://www.w3.org/2001/XMLSchema-instance"
    xsi:schemaLocation="http://www.springframework.org/schema/beans
http://www.springframework.org/schema/beans/spring-beans-2.0.xsd">

    <bean id="userBean"
     class="amigo.spring.ioc.bean.UserBean"
     factory-method="createUserBean"/>
</beans>
```

【提示】 需要注意的是，使用静态工厂方法实例化时，对应的工厂方法一定需要声明为 static 的。

若将 amigo.spring.ioc.bean.UserBean 类的：

```java
public static UserBean createUserBean() {
    ……
}
```

修改成：

```java
public UserBean createUserBean() {
    ……
}
```

此时运行测试类 Test.java 时，控制台将会报如下错误：

```
aused by: org.springframework.beans.factory.BeanDefinitionStoreException: No matching factory method found: factory method 'createUserBean'
    at org.springframework.beans.factory.support.ConstructorResolver.instantiateUsingFactoryMethod(ConstructorResolver.java:324)
    at org.springframework.beans.factory.support.AbstractAutowireCapableBeanFactory.instantiateUsingFactoryMethod(AbstractAutowireCapableBeanFactory.java:785)
    ……
```

该错误表明 Spring 在 amigo.spring.ioc.bean.UserBean 类中找不到名为 createUserBean 的静态方法。

第七步：使用实例工厂方法实例化

与使用静态工厂方法实例化类似，不过用来进行实例化的实例工厂方法位于另外一个已有的 bean 中，容器将调用该 bean 的工厂方法来创建一个新的 bean 实例。

在进行配置时，class 属性必须为空，而 factory-bean 属性必须指定为当前（或其祖先）容器中包含工厂方法的 bean 的名称，而该工厂 bean 的工厂方法本身必须通过 factory-method 属性来设定。可在 src 目录中建立使用实例工厂方法实例化的 Spring 的配置文件：bean3.xml，该文件的内容如下所示：

```xml
<?xml version="1.0" encoding="UTF-8"?>
<beans xmlns="http://www.springframework.org/schema/beans"
    xmlns:xsi="http://www.w3.org/2001/XMLSchema-instance"
```

```xml
    xsi:schemaLocation="http://www.springframework.org/schema/beans
http://www.springframework.org/schema/beans/spring-beans-2.0.xsd">

    <bean id="userBeanFactory" class="amigo.spring.ioc.bean.UserBeanFactory" />

    <bean id="userBean"
        factory-bean="userBeanFactory"
        factory-method="createUserBean" />
</beans>
```

【提示】需要注意的是，使用实例工厂方法实例化时，对应的工厂方法与静态工厂方法实例化不同，它不能声明为 static 的，若声明为 static，将会报如下错误：

```
Exception in thread "main" org.springframework.beans.factory.BeanCreationException: Error creating bean with name 'userBean' defined in class path resource [bean3.xml]: Instantiation of bean failed; nested exception is org.springframework.beans.factory.BeanDefinitionStoreException: No matching factory method found: factory bean 'userBeanFactory'; factory method 'createUserBean'
    Caused by: org.springframework.beans.factory.BeanDefinitionStoreException: No matching factory method found: factory bean 'userBeanFactory'; factory method 'createUserBean'
    ......
```

第八步：运行结果

在 Eclipse 中运行测试类 Test.java，运行结果如下所示：

```
使用"构造器实例化", username=null, password=null
......
使用"静态工厂方法实例化", username=阿蜜果, password=123
......
使用"实例工厂方法实例化", username=谢星星, password=xiexx
```

从上述运行结果中可以看出，使用构造器进行实例化时，使用的是默认的构造器，因此输出的 username 和 password 信息都为空。

使用静态工厂方法实例化时，使用的是 amigo.spring.ioc.bean.UserBean 类的 public static UserBean createUserBean()方法进行实例化，因此 username 被设置为"阿蜜果"，而 password 属性被设置为：123。

使用实例工厂方法实例化时，使用 amigo.spring.ioc.bean.UserBeanFactory 类的 public UserBean createUserBean()进行实例化，因此 username 属性被设置为"谢星星"，密码被设置为"xiexx"。

【例 16-5】注入方式——构造子注入

【实例需求】

构造子输入指的是通过构造函数完成依赖关系的设定。本实例讲解如何使用构造注入。

【开发过程】

第一步：建立包目录

在 springioc 工程中建立 amigo.spring 包，用来存放构造注入实例的相关类，另外建立

amigo.spring.test 目录，用来存放构造输入实例的测试类。

第二步：编写短信类 SMSSender1.java

SMSSender1.java 类用于发送短信，所需要的参数采用构造函数的方式注入，本例只是演示 Spring 构造函数注入的方式，所以发送短信的方法并没有给出实现。该类的代码如下所示：

```java
package amigo.spring.chapter16;

/**
 * 短信发送.
 */
public class SMSSender1 {
    public SMSSender1(
            int msgType,
            int needReport,
            int msgLevel,
            String serviceID,
            int msgFormat,
            String feeType,
            int feeUserType,
            String feeCode,
            String validTime,
            String atTime,
            String srcTermID) {
        this.msgType = msgType;
        this.needReport = needReport;
        this.msgLevel = msgLevel;
        this.serviceID = serviceID;
        this.msgFormat = msgFormat;
        this.feeType = feeType;
        this.feeUserType = feeUserType;
        this.feeCode = feeCode;
        this.validTime = validTime;
        this.atTime = atTime;
        this.srcTermID = srcTermID;
    }
    /** 0 消息类型. */
    int msgType;

    /** 1 是否需要状态报告. */
    int needReport;

    /** 1 消息发送优先级别. */
    int msgLevel;

    /** 11111 业务代码. */
    String serviceID;

    /** 15 消息格式. */
    int msgFormat;

    /** 01 计费类型. */
    String feeType;
```

```java
/** 00 用户类型. */
int feeUserType;

/** 123456 计费代码. */
String feeCode;

/** "" 有效期 */
String validTime;

/** "" 定时发送时间. */
String atTime;

/** 11111 源用户号码. */
String srcTermID;

//...省略了各属性的getter/setter方法

/**
 * 以二进制发送短信.
 * @param chargeTermID 计费手机号
 * @param destTermID 目的手机号
 * @param content 字节内容
 * @return 返回完整的返回信息, 操作成功时返回: "发送成功", 其余都为错误的情况.
 */
public String send(
        final String chargeTermID,
        final String destTermID,
        final byte[] content) {
    String resultInfo = "100";
    //.....
    return resultInfo;
}
}
```

第三步: 编写 Spring 配置文件

在 src 目录中建立 Spring 的配置文件 applicationContext.xml, 构造注入使用子标签 constructor-arg, 例如:

```xml
<bean id="SMSSender1" class=" amigo.spring.chapter16.SMSSender1">
    <constructor-arg>
        <value>13555555555</value>
    </constructor-arg>
</bean>
```

当构造函数有多个参数时, 可以使用 constructor-arg 标签的 index 属性, index 属性的值从 0 开始。本例就使用了 constructor-arg 标签的 index 属性。

当构造器中的参数需要用到另外的 bean 时, 可以使用 ref 标签。例如:

```xml
<bean id="SMSSender1" class=" amigo.spring.chapter16.SMSSender1">
    <constructor-arg>
        <ref bean="otherBean">otherBean</value>
    </constructor-arg>
</bean>
```

Spring 的配置文件 applicationContext.xml 的内容如下所示：

```xml
<?xml version="1.0" encoding="UTF-8"?>
<beans xmlns="http://www.springframework.org/schema/beans"
       xmlns:xsi="http://www.w3.org/2001/XMLSchema-instance"
       xmlns:aop="http://www.springframework.org/schema/aop"
       xmlns:tx="http://www.springframework.org/schema/tx"
       xsi:schemaLocation="http://www.springframework.org/schema/beans      http://www.springframework.org/schema/beans/spring-beans-2.0.xsd
        http://www.springframework.org/schema/aop  http://www.springframework.org/schema/aop/spring-aop-2.0.xsd
        http://www.springframework.org/schema/tx http://www.springframework.org/schema/tx/spring-tx-2.0.xsd"
       default-autowire="byName" default-lazy-init="true">
    <!-- 构造方式注入 -->
    <bean id="SMSSender1" class="amigo.spring.chapter16.SMSSender1">
        <constructor-arg index="0">
            <value>0</value>
        </constructor-arg>
        <constructor-arg index="1">
            <value>1</value>
        </constructor-arg>
        <constructor-arg index="2">
            <value>1</value>
        </constructor-arg>
        <constructor-arg index="3">
            <value>11111</value>
        </constructor-arg>
        <constructor-arg index="4">
            <value>15</value>
        </constructor-arg>
        <constructor-arg index="5">
            <value>01</value>
        </constructor-arg>
        <constructor-arg index="6">
            <value>01</value>
        </constructor-arg>
        <constructor-arg index="7">
            <value>000001</value>
        </constructor-arg>
        <constructor-arg index="8">
            <value></value>
        </constructor-arg>
        <constructor-arg index="9">
            <value></value>
        </constructor-arg>
        <constructor-arg index="10">
            <value>13555555555</value>
        </constructor-arg>
    </bean>
</beans>
```

第四步： 编写测试类 TestSMSSender1.java

在包 amigo.spring.chapter16 中建立 TestSMSSender1.java 类，该类的内容如下所示：

```java
package amigo.spring.chapter16.test;
```

```java
import org.springframework.beans.factory.xml.XmlBeanFactory;
import org.springframework.core.io.ClassPathResource;

import amigo.spring.chapter16.SMSSender1;

public class TestSMSSender1 {
    public static void main(String[] args) {
        ClassPathResource res = new ClassPathResource(
                "applicationContext.xml");
        XmlBeanFactory factory = new XmlBeanFactory(res);
        SMSSender1 sender1 = (SMSSender1) factory.getBean("SMSSender1");
        System.out.println(sender1.getSrcTermID());
    }
}
```

运行该类，读者可以看到输出了通过构造子注入的源号码信息。

【例 16-6】注入方式——setter 方法注入

第一步：编写短信类 SMSSender2.java

SMSSender2.java 类与 SMSSender1.java 略有不同，它去掉了构造函数，与后者一样提供了对各属性的 getter/setter 方法。该类的内容如下所示：

```java
package amigo.spring.chapter16;

/**
 * 短信发送.
 */
public class SMSSender2 {
    /** 0 消息类型. */
    int msgType;

    /** 1 是否需要状态报告. */
    int needReport;

    /** 1 消息发送优先级别. */
    int msgLevel;

    /** 11111 业务代码. */
    String serviceID;

    /** 15 消息格式. */
    int msgFormat;

    /** 01 计费类型. */
    String feeType;

    /** 00 用户类型. */
    int feeUserType;
```

```java
/** 123456 计费代码. */
String feeCode;

/** "" 有效期 */
String validTime;

/** "" 定时发送时间. */
String atTime;

/** 11111 源用户号码. */
String srcTermID;

// 省略各属性的 getter/setter 方法

/**
 * 以二进制发送短信.
 * @param chargeTermID 计费手机号
 * @param destTermID 目的手机号
 * @param content 字节内容
 * @return 返回完整的返回信息，操作成功时返回："发送成功"，其余都为错误的情况.
 */
public String send(
        final String chargeTermID,
        final String destTermID,
        final byte[] content) {
    String resultInfo = "100";
    //.....
    return resultInfo;
}
}
```

第二步：修改配置文件 applicationContext.xml

修改例 16-2 中的配置文件，添加如下 bean：

```xml
<!-- 构造方式注入 -->
<bean id="SMSSender2" class="amigo.spring.chapter16.SMSSender2">
    <property name="msgType" value="0" />
    <property name="needReport" value="1" />
    <property name="msgLevel" value="1" />
    <property name="serviceID" value="11111" />
    <property name="msgFormat" value="15" />
    <property name="feeType" value="01" />
    <property name="feeUserType" value="01" />
    <property name="feeCode" value="000001" />
    <property name="validTime" value="" />
    <property name="atTime" value="" />
    <property name="srcTermID" value="13555555555" />
</bean>
```

第三步：编写测试类

在 amigo.spring.test 包中新建 TestSMSSender2.java 类，该类的内容与 TestSMSSender1.java 差不多，取得 SMSSender2 类后，显示其某个属性。该类的代码如下所示：

```
package amigo.spring.chapter16.test;

import org.springframework.beans.factory.xml.XmlBeanFactory;
import org.springframework.core.io.ClassPathResource;

import amigo.spring.chapter16.SMSSender2;

public class TestSMSSender2 {
    public static void main(String[] args) {
        ClassPathResource res = new ClassPathResource(
                "applicationContext.xml");
        XmlBeanFactory factory = new XmlBeanFactory(res);
        SMSSender2 sender2 = (SMSSender2) factory.getBean("SMSSender2");
        System.out.println(sender2.getSrcTermID());
    }
}
```

运行后读者可以发现，该类的输出与例16-2是一样的。

【例16-7】注入方式——接口注入

【实例需求】

在日常的开发过程中，开发人员常常会借助接口来将调用者与实现者分离。例如：

```
public class ClassA {
    private InterfaceB classB;
    public init() {
        classB = (InterfaceB) Class.forName("amigo.spring.interfaceBImpl").newInstance();
    }
    ......
}
```

上面的代码中，ClassA 依靠于 InterfaceB 实现，传统的方法一般是通过 Class.forName("实现类的全路径")来反射出 InterfaceB 实现类的实例。本例讲解如何在 Spring 中实现接口注入，以及接口注入在 Spring 配置文件中如何进行配置。

在开发过程中，常常需要编写业务逻辑类，但开发人员又想业务逻辑实现可以根据情况来进行灵活的配置，此时可以采用 Spring 将业务逻辑实现类注入。

在本例中，InterfaceInject.java 类需要用到 UserBean 的实现类，它的实现类是通过 Spring 来注入的。

【开发过程】

第一步：编写接口类 UserBean.java

本例的用户管理业务逻辑接口类 UserBean.java 的代码如下所示：

```
package amigo.spring.chapter16;

import java.util.List;

/**
```

```
 * 用户管理业务逻辑接口
 */
public interface UserBean {
    public List getUserList();

    public void saveUser(String loginName, String password);

    public void updateUser(String loginName, String password);

    public void deleteUser(String loginName);
}
```

第二步：编写实现类 UserBeanImpl.java

本例提供了业务逻辑接口类 UserBean.java 的一个示意性实现类 UserBeanImpl.java，该类的代码如下所示：

```
package amigo.spring.chapter16;

import java.util.ArrayList;
import java.util.HashMap;
import java.util.List;
import java.util.Map;

public class UserBeanImpl implements UserBean {
    public List getUserList() {
        List userList = new ArrayList();

        Map userMap1 = new HashMap();
        userMap1.put("loginName", "amigo");
        userMap1.put("password", "xiexingxing");

        Map userMap2 = new HashMap();
        userMap2.put("loginName", "xiexingxing");
        userMap2.put("password", "xiexingxing");

        userList.add(userMap1);
        userList.add(userMap2);
        return userList;
    }

    public void saveUser(String loginName, String password) {
        // TODO Auto-generated method stub
    }

    public void updateUser(String loginName, String password) {
        // TODO Auto-generated method stub
    }

    public void deleteUser(String loginName) {

    }
}
```

第三步：编写接口注入类 InterfaceInject.java

接下来还需要编写一个接口注入类InterfaceInject.java，该类需要使用UserBean的实现类，为了让Spring能进行正常的接口注入，所以该类需要提供userBean的setter方法，该类的代码如下所示：

```java
package amigo.spring.chapter16.test;

import amigo.spring.chapter16.UserBean;

public class InterfaceInject {
private UserBean userBean;

    public void setUserBean(UserBean userBean) {
        this.userBean = userBean;
    }

    public void printUserListSize() {
        System.out.println("userList's size is: " + userBean.getUserList().size());
    }
}
```

第四步：编写 Spring 配置文件

在 Spring 配置文件 applicationContext.xml 中添加一个名为 UserBean 的 bean，该 bean 指向 UserBeanImpl 这个 UserBean 的实现类，相应的配置如下所示：

```xml
<bean id="UserBean" class="amigo.spring.chapter16.UserBeanImpl" />

<bean id="InterfaceInject" class="amigo.spring.chapter16.test.InterfaceInject">
    <property name="userBean">
        <ref local="UserBean"/>
    </property>
</bean>
```

第五步：编写测试类

最后编写测试类 TestInterfaceInject.java，在该类中在 Spring 中获得 UserBean 的一个实现类，可将其强制转换为 UserBean 类，但是 TestInterfaceInject 类中不需要引入 UserBean 的实现类 UserBeanImpl。TestInterfaceInject 类的代码如下所示：

```java
package amigo.spring.chapter16.test;

import org.springframework.beans.factory.xml.XmlBeanFactory;
import org.springframework.core.io.ClassPathResource;

/**
 * 测试接口注入.
 */
public class TestInterfaceInject {
    public static void main(String[] args) {
        ClassPathResource res = new ClassPathResource(
                "applicationContext.xml");
```

```
            XmlBeanFactory factory = new XmlBeanFactory(res);
            InterfaceInject inject = (InterfaceInject) factory.getBean("InterfaceInject");
            inject.printUserListSize();
    }
}
```

运行后，读者可以看到输出了用户列表的用户数量：2，由此可知InterfaceInject.java类的userBean属性已被成功地注入了实现类UserBeanImpl.java。

【例 16-8】bean 属性及构造器参数

〖实例需求〗

bean的属性及构造器参数既可以引用容器中的其他bean，也可以是内联（inline，在Spring的XML配置中使用<property/>和<constructor-arg/>元素定义）bean。

本实例讲解在Spring的配置文件中配置直接量、如何引用其他的bean、内部bean的配置，以及如何在配置文件中配置集合等知识。

〖开发过程〗

第一步：创建源码包：amigo.spring.ioc.beanproperties

首先在 src 目录中建立该实例的源码包：amigo.spring.ioc.beanproperties。

第二步：配置直接量

（1）说明。

当需要设置 bean 的某个属性或构造器参数的值时，可使用 Spring 提供的<value/>元素，它通过字符串来指定属性或构造器参数的值。<value/>元素既可以指向一个简单的字符串，还可以指向另一个 bean，例如：

```xml
<bean id="anotherBean" class="..."/>
<bean id="testBean" class="...">
    <property name="targetBean">
        <value>anotherBean</value>
    </property>
</bean>
```

此时可以采用一种更好的可替换的方式：使用 idref 元素。idref 元素用来将容器内其他 bean 的 id 传给<constructor-arg/> 或 <property/>元素，同时提供在部署时进行错误验证的功能。而使用<value/>元素是不会进行此种验证的。上面的代码可使用如下代码代替：

```xml
<bean id="anotherBean" class="..."/>
  <bean id="testBean" class="...">
    <property name="targetBean">
        <idref bean="anotherBean" />
    </property>
</bean>
```

下面来看一个直接量使用的举例，在 DbConnection 类中，driverClassName（驱动器类名）、url（数据库连接路径）、username（数据库用户名）和 password（数据库密码）属性都需要在

Spring 中进行配置。

（2）编写测试类：DataSource.java。

读者可在 amigo.spring.ioc.beanproperties 包中建立直接量<value/>元素使用的测试类：DataSource.java，该类具有 driverClassName（驱动器类名）、url（数据库连接路径）、username（数据库用户名）和 password（数据库密码）等属性，并提供了这些属性的 setter 方法，以便 Spring 通过 setter 注入方法将这些属性注入，该类的代码如下所示：

```java
package amigo.spring.ioc.beanproperties;

import org.springframework.beans.factory.xml.XmlBeanFactory;
import org.springframework.core.io.ClassPathResource;

/**
 * 演示直接量的使用
 */
public class DataSource {
    /** 驱动器类名. */
    private String driverClassName;

    /** 数据库连接路径. */
    private String url;

    /** 数据库用户名. */
    private String username;

    /** 数据库密码. */
    private String password;

    // 省略各属性的 getter/setter 方法

    public Object getConnection() {
        //...省略实现
        return null;
    }

    public void close() {
        //...省略实现
    }

    /**
     * 测试方法.
     */
    public static void main(String[] args) {
        ClassPathResource res1 = new ClassPathResource(
                "beanproperties.xml");
        XmlBeanFactory factory = new XmlBeanFactory(res1);
        DataSource dbConnection = (DataSource) factory.getBean("dataSource");
        System.out.println("driverClassName=" + dbConnection.getDriverClassName());
        System.out.println("url=" + dbConnection.getUrl());
        System.out.println("username=" + dbConnection.getUsername());
        System.out.println("password=" + dbConnection.getPassword());
    }
}
```

第 16 章 核心机制——IoC

(3) 编写配置文件：beanproperties.xml。

在src目录中建立本实例的Spring配置文件：beanproperties.xml，该文件定义了dataSource这个bean，并设置了其driverClassName和url等属性，该文件的内容如下所示：

```xml
<?xml version="1.0" encoding="UTF-8"?>
<beans xmlns="http://www.springframework.org/schema/beans"
       xmlns:xsi="http://www.w3.org/2001/XMLSchema-instance"
       xsi:schemaLocation="http://www.springframework.org/schema/beans
http://www.springframework.org/schema/beans/spring-beans-2.0.xsd">

    <bean id="dataSource"
              destroy-method="close"
          class="amigo.spring.ioc.beanproperties.DataSource">
    <!-- 需要在 amigo.spring.ioc.beanproperties.DataSource 类中有相应的 setter 方法. -->
        <property name="driverClassName">
        <value>com.mysql.jdbc.Driver</value>
        </property>
        <property name="url">
        <value>jdbc:mysql://localhost:3306/test</value>
        </property>
        <property name="username">
        <value>root</value>
        </property>
        <property name="password">
        <value>123</value>
        </property>
    </bean>
</beans>
```

(4) 运行结果。

在Eclipse中运行DataSource类，控制台输出的运行结果信息如下所示：

```
……
org.springframework.beans.factory.xml.XmlBeanFactory  - Creating instance of bean 'dataSource' with merged definition [Root bean: class [amigo.spring.ioc.beanproperties.DataSource]; scope=singleton; abstract=false; lazyInit=false; autowireCandidate=true; autowireMode=0; dependencyCheck=0; factoryBeanName=null; factoryMethodName=null; initMethodName=null; destroyMethodName=close; defined in class path resource [beanproperties.xml]]
org.springframework.beans.factory.xml.XmlBeanFactory  - Eagerly caching bean 'dataSource' to allow for resolving potential circular references
driverClassName=com.mysql.jdbc.Driver
url=jdbc:mysql://localhost:3306/test
username=root
password=123
```

读者可看到driverClassName和url等属性被成功注入。

第三步：引用其他的 bean

(1) 说明。

在<property/>或<constructor-arg/>内部可以使用ref元素将bean中指定属性的值设置为对容器中的另外一个bean的引用。该引用bean将被作为依赖注入，而且在注入之前会被初始化（如果是单态的bean则已被容器初始化）。

可使用3种方式指向另外一个对象，不同的形式将决定如何处理作用域及验证。

第1种形式是通过使用<ref/>标记指定bean属性的目标bean，通过该标签可以引用同一容器或父容器内的任何bean。XML 'bean'元素的值既可以是指定bean的id值，也可以是其name值。

第2种形式是使用ref的local属性指定目标bean，它可以利用XML解析器来验证所引用的bean是否存在同一文件中。local属性值必须是目标bean的id属性值。如果在同一配置文件中没有找到引用的bean，XML解析器将抛出一个异常。如果目标bean是在同一文件内，最好使用local方式，因为它能尽早地发现错误。

第3种方式是通过使用ref的parent属性来引用当前容器的父容器中的bean。parent属性值既可以是目标bean的id值，也可以是name属性值。而且目标bean必须在当前容器的父容器中。这种方式不太常见，因此在此不做详细讲述。

本实例用于展示第1、2种方式的使用。

（2）编写测试类：User.java。

读者可在amigo.spring.ioc.beanproperties包中建立User.java类，该类包含了一个dept属性，该类依赖Dept（部门信息类），该属性通过Spring注入，该类的代码如下所示：

```java
package amigo.spring.ioc.beanproperties;

import org.springframework.beans.factory.xml.XmlBeanFactory;
import org.springframework.core.io.ClassPathResource;

/**
 * 展示在 Spring 配置文件中如何引用其他的 bean.
 */
public class User {
    /** 用户名.*/
    private String username;

    /** 密码. */
    private String password;

    /** 所属部门. */
    private Dept dept;

    // 省略各属性的 getter/setter 方法

    /**
     * 测试方法.
     */
    public static void main(String[] args) {
        ClassPathResource res1 = new ClassPathResource(
                "beanproperties.xml");
        XmlBeanFactory factory = new XmlBeanFactory(res1);
        User user = (User) factory.getBean("user");
        System.out.println("用户所属部门名称=" + user.getDept().getName());
    }
}
```

（3）编写依赖类：Dept.java。

接下来读者可在amigo.spring.ioc.beanproperties包中建立User.java所依赖的类Dept.java（部门信息类），该类的代码如下所示：

```java
package amigo.spring.ioc.beanproperties;
```

第 16 章 核心机制——IoC

```
public class Dept {
    /** 部门名称. */
    private String name;

    /** 状态. */
    private int status;

    // 省略各属性的 getter/setter 方法
}
```

（4）修改配置文件：beanproperties.xml。

接着在配置文件beanproperties.xml中添加如下配置信息，并使用<ref bean="..."/>指定引用其他的bean，添加的配置信息如下所示：

```xml
<!-- 引用其他的 bean. -->
<bean id="dept" class="amigo.spring.ioc.beanproperties.Dept">
    <property name="name">
        <value>软件研发部</value>
    </property>
</bean>

<bean id="user" class="amigo.spring.ioc.beanproperties.User">
<property name="dept">
        <ref bean="dept" />
    </property>
</bean>
```

（5）运行结果。

在Eclipse中运行User.java类，可在控制台看到输出如下信息：

```
……
org.springframework.beans.factory.xml.XmlBeanFactory  - Creating shared instance of singleton bean 'dept'
org.springframework.beans.factory.xml.XmlBeanFactory  - Creating instance of bean 'dept' with merged definition [Root bean: class [amigo.spring.ioc.beanproperties.Dept]; scope=singleton; abstract=false; lazyInit=false; autowireCandidate=true; autowireMode=0; dependencyCheck=0; factoryBeanName=null; factoryMethodName=null; initMethodName=null; destroyMethodName=null; defined in class path resource [beanproperties.xml]]
org.springframework.beans.factory.xml.XmlBeanFactory  - Eagerly caching bean 'dept' to allow for resolving potential circular references
用户所属部门名称=软件研发部
```

从运行结果中读者可以看出，dept属性被成功注入。上面演示的是第一种方式对其他的bean进行引用，在此种方式下，若dept定义在另外一个Spring配置文件中也是可行的。若将beanproperties.xml文件中的：

```xml
<ref bean="dept" />
```

修改成：

```xml
<ref local="dept" />
```

此时再运行User.java类，运行结果与之前是一样的。若将dept这个bean的定义移到另一个配置文件中，则将报如下异常信息：

```
……
Caused by: org.xml.sax.SAXParseException: cvc-id.1: There is no ID/IDREF binding for IDREF 'dept'.
……
```

第四步：内部 bean

（1）说明。

内部bean（inner bean）是指在一个bean的<property/>或 <constructor-arg/>元素中使用<bean/>元素定义的bean。

内部bean定义不需要有id或name属性，即使指定id 或name属性值也将会被容器忽略。内部bean中的singleton标记也将被忽略。内部bean总是匿名和prototype模式的，并且不能将内部bean注入到包含该内部bean之外的bean。内部bean的定义格式如下：

```xml
<bean id="testBean" class="...">
  <property name="targetBean">
    <bean class="...">
      <property name="name" value="软件研发部"/>
      <property name="status" value="1"/>
    </bean>
  </property>
</bean>
```

（2）编写测试类：OuterBean.java。

读者可在amigo.spring.ioc.beanproperties包中建立外部bean对应的类：OuterBean.java，该类依赖类：InnerBean，对应的属性为innerBean，innerBean通过Spring注入。该类的代码如下所示：

```java
package amigo.spring.ioc.beanproperties;

import org.springframework.beans.factory.xml.XmlBeanFactory;
import org.springframework.core.io.ClassPathResource;

/**
 * 演示 Spring 中内部 bean 的配置.
 */
public class OuterBean {
    private InnerBean innerBean;

    // 省略 innerBean 的 getter/setter 方法

    /**
     * 测试方法.
     */
    public static void main(String[] args) {
        ClassPathResource res1 = new ClassPathResource(
                "beanproperties.xml");
        XmlBeanFactory factory = new XmlBeanFactory(res1);
        OuterBean outerBean = (OuterBean) factory.getBean("outerBean");
        System.out.println("内部 bean 的 name 属性值为=" + outerBean.getInnerBean().getName());
    }
}
```

（3）编写内部 bean 类：InnerBean.java。

接下来在amigo.spring.ioc.beanproperties包中建立内部bean对应的类：InnerBean.java。该类的代码如下所示：

```java
package amigo.spring.ioc.beanproperties;
```

第16章 核心机制——IoC

```java
/**
 * 内部 bean.
 */
public class InnerBean {
    private String name;

    // 省略 name 属性的 getter/setter 方法
}
```

（4）修改配置文件：beanproperties.xml。

接着在配置文件beanproperties.xml中添加内部bean和外部bean的配置信息，添加的配置信息如下所示：

```xml
<!-- 内部 bean -->
<bean id="outerBean" class="amigo.spring.ioc.beanproperties.OuterBean">
  <property name="innerBean">
    <bean class="amigo.spring.ioc.beanproperties.InnerBean">
      <property name="name">
        <value>我是内部 bean</value>
      </property>
    </bean>
  </property>
</bean>
```

（5）运行结果。

在Eclipse中运行User.java类，可在控制台看到输出如下信息：

```
……
org.springframework.beans.factory.xml.XmlBeanFactory   -   Creating   instance   of   bean
'amigo.spring.ioc.beanproperties.InnerBean#1b60280' with merged definition [Root bean: class
[amigo.spring.ioc.beanproperties.InnerBean];    scope=singleton;    abstract=false;    lazyInit=false;
autowireCandidate=true;      autowireMode=0;      dependencyCheck=0;      factoryBeanName=null;
factoryMethodName=null; initMethodName=null; destroyMethodName=null; defined in class path resource
[beanproperties.xml]]
内部 bean 的 name 属性值为=我是内部 bean
```

从运行结果中可以看出，内部bean被成功注入到外部bean中，内部bean的name属性被成功获得。

第五步：在配置文件中配置集合

（1）说明。

在进行注入时，有时需要将集合信息注入到某属性中，此时可以在Spring配置文件中通过<list/>、<set/>、<map/>及<props/>元素定义和设置与Java Collection类型对应的List、Set、Map及Properties的值。

接下来讲解如何配置List、Set、Map及Properties的值。

（2）编写测试类：CollectionTest.java。

读者可在amigo.spring.ioc.beanproperties包中建立集合配置的测试类：CollectionTest.java，该类包含userList（List类型）、emailSet（Set类型）、typeMap（Map类型）和configProperties（Properties类型）。该类的代码如下所示：

```java
package amigo.spring.ioc.beanproperties;

import java.util.*;
```

```java
import org.springframework.beans.factory.xml.XmlBeanFactory;
import org.springframework.core.io.ClassPathResource;

/**
 * Spring 配置集合.
 */
public class CollectionTest {
    private List userList;

    private Set emailSet;

    private Map typeMap;

    private Properties configProperties;

    // 省略各属性的 getter/setter 方法

    /**
     * 测试方法.
     */
    public static void main(String[] args) {
        ClassPathResource res1 = new ClassPathResource(
                "beanproperties.xml");
        XmlBeanFactory factory = new XmlBeanFactory(res1);
        CollectionTest test = (CollectionTest) factory.getBean("collectionTest");

        // List 类型
        List userList =  test.getUserList();
        for (int i = 0, len = userList.size(); i < len; i++) {
            System.out.println("用户信息：" + (String) userList.get(i));
        }

        // Set 类型
        Set emailSet = test.getEmailSet();
        Iterator ite = emailSet.iterator();
        while(ite.hasNext()) {
            System.out.println("Email 信息：" + ite.next());
        }

        // Map 类型
        Map typeMap = test.getTypeMap();
        System.out.println("id 为 1000 的类型的名称为=" + typeMap.get("1000"));

        // Properties 类型
        Properties configProperties = test.getConfigProperties();
        System.out.println("usernmae 属性为：" + configProperties.getProperty("username"));
    }
}
```

（3）修改配置文件：beanproperties.xml。

接着在配置文件beanproperties.xml中添加各种集合的配置信息，添加的配置信息如下所示：

```xml
<!-- 集合 -->
```

```xml
<bean id="collectionTest" class="amigo.spring.ioc.beanproperties.CollectionTest">
    <!-- List 类型 -->
    <property name="userList">
        <list>
            <value>阿蜜果</value>
            <value>amigo</value>
            <value>谢星星</value>
        </list>
    </property>

    <!-- Set 类型 -->
    <property name="emailSet">
    <set>
        <value>administrator@amigo.com</value>
        <value>xiexingxing1121@126.com</value>
        <value>amigo@126.com</value>
    </set>
    </property>

    <!-- Map 类型 -->
    <property name="typeMap">
        <map>
            <entry>
                <key>
                    <value>1000</value>
                </key>
                <value>时尚购物</value>
            </entry>
            <entry>
                <key>
                    <value>1001</value>
                </key>
                <value>精彩旅游</value>
            </entry>
        </map>
    </property>

    <property name="configProperties">
        <props>
            <prop key="username">阿蜜果</prop>
            <prop key="password">3344</prop>
        </props>
    </property>
</bean>
```

（4）运行结果。

在Eclipse中运行User.java类，可在控制台看到输出如下信息：

```
……
用户信息：阿蜜果
用户信息：amigo
用户信息：谢星星
Email 信息：administrator@amigo.com
Email 信息：xiexingxing1121@126.com
```

Email 信息：amigo@126.com
id 为 1000 的类型的名称为=时尚购物
usernmae 属性为：阿蜜果

从上面的运行结果中可以看到，各种集合被成功注入。

小结

Spring 框架提供的众多功能都是建立在 IoC 基础上的，它是 Spring 框架极为重要的一部分。IoC（Inversion of Control）被称为"控制反转"，又被称为 DI（Dependency Injection），即依赖注入。IoC 指的就是由容器控制程序之间的关系，而非传统实现中，由程序代码直接控制，即组件之间的依赖关系由容器在运行期决定。

Spring 支持 3 种配置元数据格式：XML 格式、Java 属性文件格式或使用 Spring 公共 API 编程实现，最常用的是 XML 格式。XML 格式配置的基本结构如下所示：

```xml
<?xml version="1.0" encoding="UTF-8"?>
<beans xmlns="http://www.springframework.org/schema/beans"
       xmlns:xsi="http://www.w3.org/2001/XMLSchema-instance"
       xsi:schemaLocation="http://www.springframework.org/schema/beans
http://www.springframework.org/schema/beans/spring-beans-2.0.xsd">
    <bean id="..." class="...">
        ......
    </bean>

    <bean id="..." class="...">
        ......
    </bean>
</beans>
```

其中<beans/>为其根元素，可包含一到多个 bean 子元素。在使用时，需要在<beans/>元素中指定使用 SPRING 2 的 schema 文件。

实例化容器有多种方式，例如在 CLASSPATH 路径中获得，或者通过指定绝对的文件地址来实例化。最常用的一种是通过如下方式实例化容器：

```
ClassPathResource res = new ClassPathResource(
            "配置文件名称");
XmlBeanFactory factory = new XmlBeanFactory(res);
```

可通过 3 种方式实例化 bean，如下所示：

- 使用构造器实例化：这是 bean 的一种最常见的实例化方式，一般使用默认构造器来进行实例化。
- 使用静态工厂方式实例化：当采用静态工厂方法创建 bean 时，除了需要指定 class 属性外，还需要通过 factory-method 属性来指定创建 bean 实例的工厂方法。使用举例如下所示：

```xml
<bean id="userBean"
      class="amigo.spring.ioc.bean.UserBean"
      factory-method="createUserBean"/>
```

注意：指定的"factory-method"方法必须声明为 static 类型的。

- 使用实例工厂方法实例化：用来进行实例化的实例工厂方法位于另外一个已有的 bean 中，容器将调用该 bean 的工厂方法来创建一个新的 bean 实例。配置时，class 属性必须为空，而 factory-bean 属性必须指定为当前（或其祖先）容器中包含工厂方法的 bean 的名称，而该工厂 bean 的工厂方法本身必须通过 factory-method 属性来设定。使用举例如下所示：

```
<bean id="userBeanFactory" class="amigo.spring.ioc.bean.UserBeanFactory" />
<bean id="userBean"
        factory-bean="userBeanFactory"
        factory-method="createUserBean" />
```

Spring 在进行注入时，提供了多种方式：构造子注入、setter 方法注入和接口注入。其中构造子注入指的是通过构造函数完成依赖关系的设定。setter 方法注入需要被注入类提供对应属性的 setter 方法，Spring 将通过调用对应属性的 setter 方法将依赖关系注入进去。

bean 的属性及构造器参数既可以引用容器中的其他 bean，也可以是内联（inline，在 Spring 的 XML 配置中使用<property/>和<constructor-arg/>元素定义）bean。

当需要设置 bean 的某个属性或构造器参数的值时，可使用 Spring 提供的<value/>元素来设置直接量，它通过字符串来指定属性或构造器参数的值。使用举例如下所示：

```
<bean id="dataSource"
        destroy-method="close"
        class="amigo.spring.ioc.beanproperties.DataSource">
    <property name="driverClassName">
        <value>com.mysql.jdbc.Driver</value>
    </property>
    <property name="url">
        <value>jdbc:mysql://localhost:3306/test</value>
    </property>
    ……
</bean>
```

<value/>元素既可指向一个简单的字符串，还可以指向另一个 bean，此种情况下，可使用 idref 元素，该元素用来将容器内其他 bean 的 id 传给<constructor-arg/> 或 <property/>元素，同时提供在部署时进行错误验证的功能。使用举例如下所示：

```
<bean id="anotherBean" class="..."/>
<bean id="testBean" class="...">
    <property name="targetBean">
        <idref bean="anotherBean" />
    </property>
</bean>
```

在<property/>或<constructor-arg/>内部可以使用 ref 元素将 bean 中指定属性的值设置为对容器中的另外一个 bean 的引用。该引用 bean 将被作为依赖注入，而且在注入之前会被初始化（如果是单态的 bean 则已被容器初始化）。使用举例如下所示：

```
<bean id="dept" class="amigo.spring.ioc.beanproperties.Dept">
    ……
</bean>

<bean id="user" class="amigo.spring.ioc.beanproperties.User">
    <property name="dept">
        <ref bean="dept" />
    </property>
</bean>
```

内部 bean（inner bean）是指在一个 bean 的<property/>或 <constructor-arg/>元素中使用

<bean/>元素定义的 bean。内部 bean 的使用举例如下所示：

```xml
<bean id="outerBean" class="amigo.spring.ioc.beanproperties.OuterBean">
    <property name="innerBean">
        <bean class="amigo.spring.ioc.beanproperties.InnerBean">
            <property name="name">
                <value>我是内部 bean</value>
            </property>
        </bean>
    </property>
</bean>
```

在进行注入时，有时需要将集合信息注入到某属性中，此时可以在 Spring 配置文件中通过 <list/>、<set/>、<map/> 及 <props/> 元素定义和设置与 Java Collection 类型对应的 List、Set、Map 及 Properties 的值。List 类型的注入举例如下所示：

```xml
<bean id="..." class="... ">
    <property name="userList">
        <list>
            <value>阿蜜果</value>
            <value>amigo</value>
            <value>谢星星</value>
        </list>
    </property>
</bean>
```

Set 类型的注入举例如下所示：

```xml
<bean id="..." class="... ">
    <property name="emailSet">
        <set>
            <value>administrator@amigo.com</value>
            <value>xiexingxing1121@126.com</value>
            <value>amigo@126.com</value>
        </set>
    </property>
</bean>
```

Map 类型的注入举例如下所示：

```xml
<bean id="..." class="... ">
    <property name="typeMap">
        <map>
            <entry>
                <key>
                    <value>1000</value>
                </key>
                <value>时尚购物</value>
            </entry>
            <entry>
                <key>
                    <value>1001</value>
                </key>
                <value>精彩旅游</value>
            </entry>
        </map>
    </property>
</bean>
```

Properties 类型的注入举例如下所示：

```xml
<bean id="..." class="... ">
    <property name="configProperties">
        <props>
            <prop key="username">阿蜜果</prop>
            <prop key="password">3344</prop>
        </props>
    </property>
</bean>
```

第 17 章　Spring 的 AOP

【本章导读语】

面向切面编程（Aspect Oriented Programming，AOP）是 OOP 的延续。AOP 实际是 GoF 设计模式的延续，设计模式孜孜不倦追求的是调用者和被调用者之间的解耦，AOP 可以说也是这种目标的一种实现。

本章介绍 Spring 中除了 IoC 之外的另一个重要的概念——AOP，AOP 在 Java EE 项目中使用广泛，例如，使用它定义的切面来完成异常拦截、日志处理和事务管理等。本章首先向读者解说 AOP 的相关概念，而后更进一步，通过代码讲解 AOP 的实现原理，而后讲解在 Spring 2.0 中对@AspectJ 的支持，最后通过使用 Spring AOP 实现异常拦截的实例讲解 AOP 的使用，向读者展现了 Spring 的 AOP 的独特魅力。

【例 17-1】解说 AOP 的概念

〖实例需求〗

本实例讲解如何在工程中配置 Spring 的多种数据源，它支持 JDBC、C3P0、DBCP 数据源等。为了简便起见，本例中采用的数据库为 MySQL，其他数据库配置与此类似。

〖开发过程〗

第一步：AOP 的相关概念

面向切面编程（AOP）弥补了面向对象编程（OOP）的不足，它提供另外一种角度来思考程序结构。AOP 提供了切面。切面对关注点进行模块化，例如横切多个类型和对象的事务管理。除了 IoC 外，Spring 的另一个关键的组件就是 AOP 框架。Spring 的 IoC 容器不依赖 AOP 框架，从而开发人员能自由选择是否使用 AOP，AOP 提供强大的中间件解决方案，这使得 Spring IoC 容器更加完善。

在 Spring 2 中，用户可以选择使用基于模式（schema-based）的方式或者使用@AspectJ 注解。这两种风格都完全支持通知（Advice）类型和 AspectJ 的切入点语言，虽然实际上仍然使用 Spring AOP 进行织入（Weaving）。AOP 允许开发人员自定义切面，用 AOP 来完善 OOP 的使用。

在讲述 AOP 的知识之前，笔者首先讲述一下 AOP 的一些重要的概念：

- 切面（Aspect）：一个关注点的模块化，这个关注点可能会横切多个对象。例如事务管理、异常处理等都可视为切面。在 Spring AOP 中，可以使用通用类（基于模式的风格），或者在普通类中以 @Aspect 注解（@AspectJ 风格）来实现切面。

- 连接点（Joinpoint）：在程序执行过程中某个特定的点，比如某方法调用的时候或者处理异常的时候。在 Spring AOP 中，一个连接点总代表一个方法的执行。
- 通知（Advice）：在切面的某个特定的连接点（Joinpoint）上执行的动作。包括"around"、"before"和"after"等类型的通知。
- 切入点（Pointcut）：匹配连接点（Joinpoint）的断点。通知和一个切入点表达式关联，并在满足这个切入点的连接点上运行。切入点表达式如何和连接点匹配是 AOP 的核心，Spring 缺省使用 AspectJ 切入点语法。
- 引入（Introduction）：（也被称为内部类型声明（inter-type declaration））。声明额外的方法或者某个类型的字段。Spring 允许引入新的接口（以及一个对应的实现）到任何被代理的对象。例如，你可以使用一个引入来使 bean 实现 IsModified 接口，以便简化缓存机制。
- 目标对象（Target Object）：被一个或者多个切面（aspect）所通知（advise）的对象。又被称为通知（advised）对象。
- AOP 代理（AOP Proxy）：AOP 框架创建的对象，用来实现切面契约（aspect contract）（包括通知方法执行等功能）。在 Spring 中，AOP 代理可以是 JDK 动态代理或者 CGLIB 代理。

第二步：通知的类型

在上一步中，讲述了 AOP 中重要的概念：通知。通知的类型如下所示：

- 前置通知（Before advice）：在某连接点（join point）之前执行的通知，但这个通知不能阻止连接点前的执行（除非它抛出一个异常）。
- 返回后通知（After returning advice）：在某连接点（join point）正常完成后执行的通知。例如，一个方法没有抛出任何异常，正常返回。
- 抛出异常后通知（After throwing advice）：在方法抛出异常退出时执行的通知。
- 后通知（After (finally) advice）：当某连接点退出的时候执行的通知（不论是正常返回还是异常退出）。
- 环绕通知（Around Advice）：包围一个连接点（join point）的通知，如方法调用。这是最强大的一种通知类型。环绕通知可以在方法调用前后完成自定义的行为。它也会选择是否继续执行连接点或直接返回它们自己的返回值或抛出异常来结束执行。环绕通知是最常用的一种通知类型。

【例 17-2】AOP 实现原理

〖实例需求〗

AOP 实现原理使用的是 Java 的反射和动态代理机制。本实例通过一个使用 Java 反射和动态代理实现 AOP 的实例来展现 AOP 的实现原理。

〖开发过程〗

第一步：建立工程

按照第 15 章的方式建立一个名为 springaop 的 Web 工程，并将 SPRING 2 的 jar 复制到 WebRoot/WEB-INF/lib 目录中。接着在 src 源码目录下创建 amigo.spring.aop.conception 包，并将 log4j 的配置文件 log4j.properties 复制到 src 源码目录。

完成后的目录结构如图 17-1 所示。

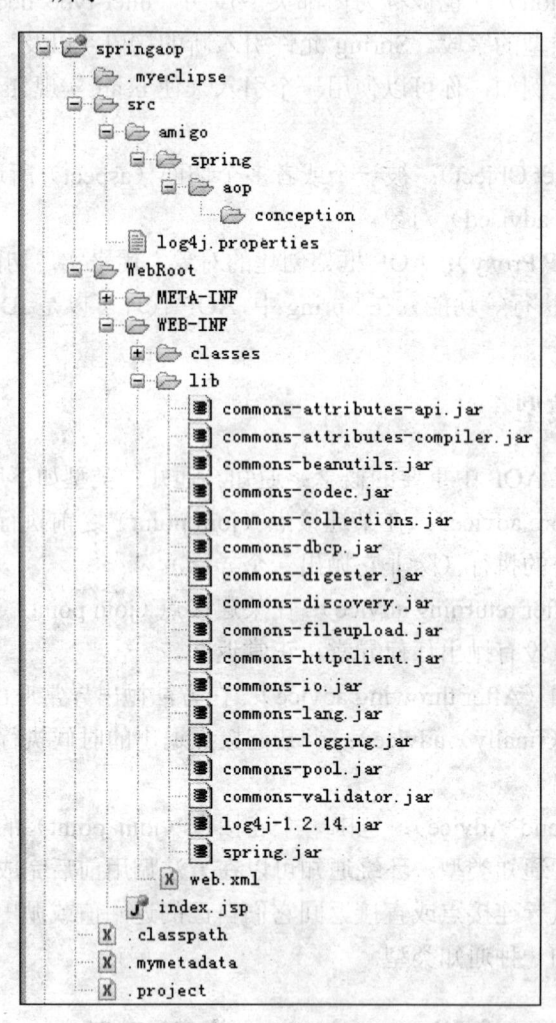

```
springaop
    .myeclipse
    src
        amigo
            spring
                aop
                    conception
        log4j.properties
    WebRoot
        META-INF
        WEB-INF
            classes
            lib
                commons-attributes-api.jar
                commons-attributes-compiler.jar
                commons-beanutils.jar
                commons-codec.jar
                commons-collections.jar
                commons-dbcp.jar
                commons-digester.jar
                commons-discovery.jar
                commons-fileupload.jar
                commons-httpclient.jar
                commons-io.jar
                commons-lang.jar
                commons-logging.jar
                commons-pool.jar
                commons-validator.jar
                log4j-1.2.14.jar
                spring.jar
            web.xml
        index.jsp
    .classpath
    .mymetadata
    .project
```

图 17-1 工程的目录结构

第二步：创建包：amigo.spring.aop.principle

在 src 目录中创建包目录：amigo.spring.aop.principle，该包用于存放本实例的源码。

第三步：编写业务逻辑接口类：BusinessObj.java

在包 amigo.spring.aop.principle 中建立业务逻辑接口类：BusinessObj.java，该类的代码如下所示：

```java
package amigo.spring.aop.principle;

/**
 * 业务逻辑接口.
 */
public interface BusinessObj {
    /**
     * 执行业务.
     */
    public void process();
}
```

第四步：编写业务逻辑实现类：BusinessObjImpl.java

接着在包 amigo.spring.aop.principle 中建立业务逻辑实现类，该类实现 BusinessObj 接口，此为模拟实现，该类的 process()方法只是简单地输出了日志信息，代码如下所示：

```java
package amigo.spring.aop.principle;

/**
 * 业务逻辑实现类.
 */
public class BusinessObjImpl implements BusinessObj {
    public void process() {
        try {
            System.out.println("执行业务逻辑");
        } catch (Exception e) {
            System.err.println("发生异常:" + e.toString());
        }
    }
}
```

第五步：编写 Advisor 接口：Advisor.java

Advisor 接口定义了 doInAdvisor(…)方法，该方法由其前置或后置的 Advisor 类来实现。该类的代码如下所示：

```java
package amigo.spring.aop.principle;

import java.lang.reflect.Method;

/**
 * Advisor 接口类.
 */
public interface Advisor {
    public void doInAdvisor(Object proxy, Method method, Object[] args);
}
```

第六步：编写方法前置 Advisor 类：BeforeMethodAdvisor.java

接下来在 amigo.spring.aop.principle 包中创建方法前置 Advisor 类，该类实现 Advisor 接口，在 doInAdvisor(…)方法中显示简单的信息，该类的代码如下所示：

```java
package amigo.spring.aop.principle;
```

```java
import java.lang.reflect.Method;

/**
 * 方法前置 Advisor.
 */
public class BeforeMethodAdvisor implements Advisor {
    /**
     * 在方法执行前所进行的操作.
     */
    public void doInAdvisor(Object proxy, Method method, Object[] args) {
        System.out.println("处理前: " + method);
    }
}
```

第七步：编写方法后置 Advisor 类：AfterMethodAdvisor.java

接下来在 amigo.spring.aop.principle 包中创建方法后置 Advisor 类：AfterMethodAdvisor，该类实现 Advisor 接口，在 doInAdvisor(...)方法中显示简单的信息，该类的代码如下所示：

```java
package amigo.spring.aop.principle;

import java.lang.reflect.Method;

/**
 * 方法的后置 Advisor，它完成方法的后置操作.
 */
public class AfterMethodAdvisor implements Advisor {

    /**
     * 在方法执行后所进行的操作.
     */
    public void doInAdvisor(Object proxy, Method method, Object[] args) {
        System.out.println("after process " + method);
    }
}
```

第八步：编写 AOP 处理类：AopHandler.java

在 amigo.spring.aop.principle 包中创建 AOP 处理类 AopHandler.java，该类为本实例的核心类，在该类中使用了 Java 的反射和动态代理技术，来模拟实现 AOP 的功能，该类的代码如下所示：

```java
package amigo.spring.aop.principle;

import java.lang.reflect.InvocationHandler;
import java.lang.reflect.Method;
import java.lang.reflect.Proxy;

/**
 * AOP 处理器.
 */
public class AopHandler implements InvocationHandler {
    //需要代理的目标对象
    private Object target;
    //方法前置顾问
```

```java
Advisor beforeAdvisor;
//方法后置顾问
Advisor afterAdvisor;

/**
 * 设置代理目标对象,并生成动态代理对象.
 * @param target 代理目标对象
 * @return 返回动态代理对象
 */
public Object setObject(Object target) {
    //设置代理目标对象
    this.target = target;
    //根据代理目标对象生成动态代理对象
    Object obj = Proxy.newProxyInstance(
            target.getClass().getClassLoader(),
            target.getClass().getInterfaces(), this);
    return obj;
}

/**
 * 若定义了前置处理,则在方法执行前执行前置处理
 * 若定义了后置处理,则在方法调用后调用后置处理.
 * @param proxy 代理对象
 * @param method 调用的业务方法
 * @param args 方法的参数
 * @return 返回结果信息
 * @throws Throwable
 */
public Object invoke(Object proxy, Method method, Object[] args) throws Throwable {
    //进行业务方法的前置处理
    if (beforeAdvisor != null) {
        beforeAdvisor.doInAdvisor(proxy, method, args);
    }

    //执行业务方法
    Object result = method.invoke(target, args);
    //进行业务方法的后置处理
    if (afterAdvisor != null) {
        afterAdvisor.doInAdvisor(proxy, method, args);
    }
    //返回结果对象
    return result;
}

/**
 * 设置方法的前置顾问.
 * @param advisor 方法的前置顾问
 */
public void setBeforeAdvisor(Advisor advisor) {
    this.beforeAdvisor = advisor;
}

/**
```

```
         * 设置方法的后置顾问.
         * @param advisor  方法的后置顾问
         */
        public void setAfterAdvisor(Advisor advisor) {
            this.afterAdvisor = advisor;
        }
}
```

第九步：编写 Bean 工厂：BeanFactory.java

在 amigo.spring.aop.principle 包中创建 bean 工厂类，在该类中从 XML 文件中获得配置信息，并使用 DOM4J 来对 XML 文件进行解析，并根据配置信息调用 AOP 的对应方法进行处理，该类的代码如下所示：

```java
package amigo.spring.aop.principle;

import java.io.InputStream;
import java.lang.reflect.Method;
import java.util.*;
import org.dom4j.*;
import org.dom4j.io.SAXReader;

/**
 * bean 工厂类.
 */
public class BeanFactory {
    private Map<String, Object> beanMap = new HashMap<String, Object>();

    /**
     * bean 工厂的初始化.
     * @param   xml 配置文件
     */
    public void init(String xml) {
        try {
            //读取指定的配置文件
            SAXReader reader = new SAXReader();
            ClassLoader classLoader = Thread.currentThread().getContextClassLoader();
            InputStream ins = classLoader.getResourceAsStream(xml);
            Document doc = reader.read(ins);
            Element root = doc.getRootElement();
            Element foo;

            //创建 AOP 处理器
            AopHandler aopHandler = new AopHandler();

            //遍历 bean
            for (Iterator i = root.elementIterator("bean"); i.hasNext();) {
                foo = (Element) i.next();
                //获取 bean 的属性 id、class、aop 以及 aopType
                Attribute id = foo.attribute("id");
                Attribute cls = foo.attribute("class");
                Attribute aop = foo.attribute("aop");
                Attribute aopType = foo.attribute("aopType");
```

```java
//配置了 aop 和 aopType 属性时，需进行拦截操作
if (aop != null && aopType != null) {
    //根据 aop 字符串获取对应的类
    Class advisorCls = Class.forName(aop.getText());
    //创建该类的对象
    Advisor advisor = (Advisor) advisorCls.newInstance();

    //根据 aopType 的类型来设置前置或后置顾问
    if ("before".equals(aopType.getText())) {
        aopHandler.setBeforeAdvisor(advisor);
    } else if ("after".equals(aopType.getText())) {
        aopHandler.setAfterAdvisor(advisor);
    }
}

//利用 Java 反射机制，通过 class 的名称获取 Class 对象
Class bean = Class.forName(cls.getText());

//获取对应 class 的信息
java.beans.BeanInfo info = java.beans.Introspector.getBeanInfo(bean);
//获取其属性描述
java.beans.PropertyDescriptor pd[] = info.getPropertyDescriptors();
//设置值的方法
Method mSet = null;
//创建一个对象
Object obj = bean.newInstance();
//遍历该 bean 的 property 属性
for (Iterator ite = foo.elementIterator("property"); ite.hasNext();) {
    Element foo2 = (Element) ite.next();
    //获取该 property 的 name 属性
    Attribute name = foo2.attribute("name");
    String value = null;

    //获取该 property 的子元素 value 的值
    for(Iterator ite1 = foo2.elementIterator("value"); ite1.hasNext();) {
        Element node = (Element) ite1.next();
        value = node.getText();
        break;
    }

    for (int k = 0; k < pd.length; k++) {
        if (pd[k].getName().equalsIgnoreCase(name.getText())) {
            mSet = pd[k].getWriteMethod();
            //利用 Java 的反射机制调用对象的某个 set 方法，并将值设置进去
            mSet.invoke(obj, value);
        }
    }
}

//为对象增加前置或后置顾问
obj = (Object) aopHandler.setObject(obj);

//将对象放入 beanMap 中，其中 key 为 id 值，value 为对象
beanMap.put(id.getText(), obj);
}
```

```java
        } catch (Exception e) {
            System.out.println(e.toString());
        }
    }

    /**
     *通过 bean 的 id 获取 bean 的对象.
     *@param beanName bean 的 id
     *@return 返回对应对象
     */
    public Object getBean(String beanName) {
        Object obj = beanMap.get(beanName);
        return obj;
    }

    /**
     * 测试方法.
     * @param args
     */
    public static void main(String[] args) {
        BeanFactory factory = new BeanFactory();
        factory.init("amigo/spring/aop/principle/config.xml");
        BusinessObj obj = (BusinessObj) factory.getBean("businessObj");
        obj.process();
    }
}
```

第十步：编写配置文件：config.xml

在 amigo.spring.aop.principle 包中创建本实例的配置文件，在该文件中添加名为 businessObj 的 bean，并为其配置 aop 和 aopType 属性，增加了方法的前置顾问。该文件的内容如下所示：

```xml
<?xml version="1.0" encoding="UTF-8"?>
<beans>
    <bean id="businessObj"
        class="amigo.spring.aop.principle.BusinessObjImpl"
        aop="amigo.spring.aop.principle.BeforeMethodAdvisor"
        aopType="before"/>
</beans>
```

第十一步：运行结果

在 Eclipse 中运行 BeanFactory.java 类，运行结果如下所示：

```
处理前: public abstract void amigo.spring.aop.principle.BusinessObj.process()
执行业务逻辑
```

由运行结果可以看出，前置处理已经生效。

【例 17-3】@AspectJ 支持

第一步：创建包：amigo.spring.aop.aspectj

在 src 源码目录中创建本实例的包目录：amigo.spring.aop.aspectj。

第二步：@AspectJ 介绍

@AspectJ使用了Java 5的注解，可以将切面声明为普通的Java类，其历史悠久，@AspectJ项目已经交给Eclipse组织维护和开发，访问地址为：http://www.eclipse.org/aspectj，界面如图17-2所示。

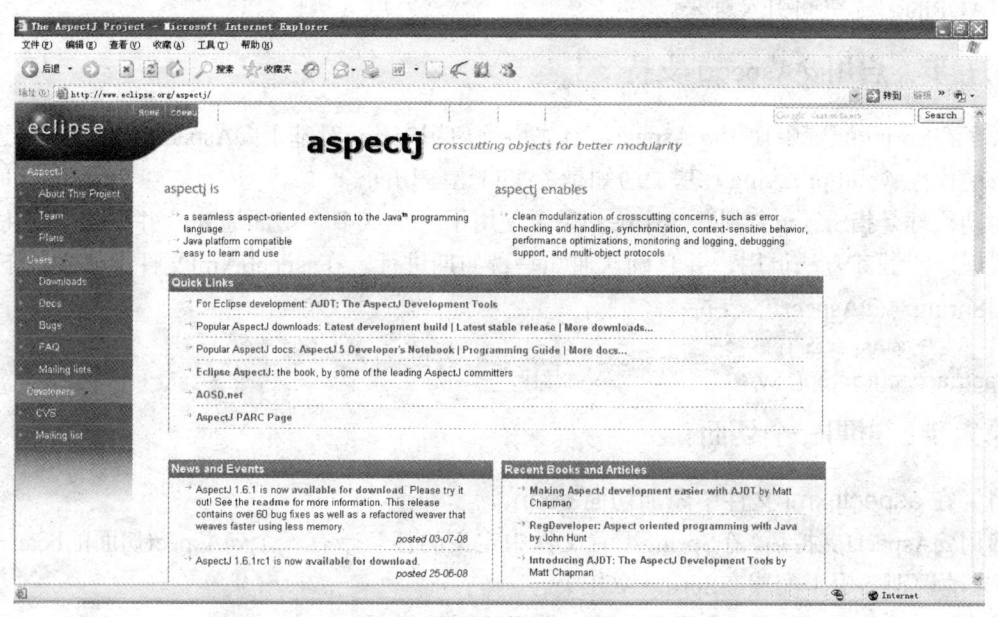

图 17-2 @AspectJ 首页

AspectJ开发的切入点（pointcut）表达语言非常简单，但是功能强大。AspectJ的最新版本为AspectJ 5，SPRING 2 使用了和AspectJ 5一样的注解，使用了AspectJ 提供的一个库来做切点（pointcut）解析和匹配。但是，AOP在运行时仍旧是纯的Spring AOP，并不依赖于AspectJ 的编译器或者织入器（weaver）。

第三步：添加 jar 包：aspectjrt.jar 和 aspectjweaver.jar

若要在Spring中使用@AspectJ，首先需要在应用程序的classpath中引入两个AspectJ库：aspectjweaver.jar 和 aspectjrt.jar。这些库可以在Spring解压目录：spring-framework-2.x\lib\aspectj中找到。

第四步：创建 Spring 配置文件：aspectj.xml

在amigo.spring.aop.aspectj中创建本实例的配置文件：aspectj.xml。初始内容如下所示：

```
<?xml version="1.0" encoding="UTF-8"?>
<?xml version="1.0" encoding="UTF-8"?>
<beans xmlns="http://www.springframework.org/schema/beans"
       xmlns:xsi="http://www.w3.org/2001/XMLSchema-instance"
       xmlns:aop="http://www.springframework.org/schema/aop"
       xsi:schemaLocation="http://www.springframework.org/schema/beans
http://www.springframework.org/schema/beans/spring-beans-2.0.xsd
          http://www.springframework.org/schema/aop
http://www.springframework.org/schema/aop/spring-aop-2.0.xsd"
```

```
            default-autowire="byName" default-lazy-init="true">
</beans>
```
如下两句：

```
xmlns:aop=http://www.springframework.org/schema/aop
http://www.springframework.org/schema/aop
http://www.springframework.org/schema/aop/spring-aop-2.0.xsd
```
将AOP的名称空间引入进来。

第五步：启用@AspectJ 支持

为了在Spring配置中使用@Aspect，首先必须启用Spring对基于@AspectJ aspects的配置支持，自动代理（autoproxying）基于通知是否来自这些切面。

自动代理是指Spring会判断一个bean是否使用了一个或多个切面通知，并据此自动生成相应的代理以拦截其方法调用，并且确认通知是否如期进行。在aspectj.xml文件中添加如下信息来启用Spring对@AspectJ的支持：

```xml
<!-- 支持 @AspectJ 标记-->
<aop:aspectj-autoproxy/>
```

第六步：声明一个切面

（1）在 aspectj.xml 文件中添加切面 bean。

启用@AspectJ支持后，在Spring配置文件中定义的任意带有一个@Aspect切面的bean都将被Spring自动识别并用于配置在Spring AOP中。

读者可在aspectj.xmlSpring配置文件中进行如下配置，这个bean指向一个使用了@Aspect 注释的类：

```xml
<!-- 自定义切面 -->
<bean id="myAspect" class="amigo.spring.aop.aspectj.MyAspect" />
```

（2）编写自定义切面类：MyAspect.java。

接着在amigo.spring.aop.aspect包中创建myAspect这个bean对应的类：MyAspect.java，它使用org.aspectj.lang.annotation.Aspect 注解，代码如下所示：

```java
package amigo.spring.aop.aspectj;

import org.aspectj.lang.annotation.Aspect;

/**
 * 自定义的切面类
 */
@Aspect
public class MyAspect {

}
```

切面（用 @Aspect 注解的类）和其他类一样有方法和字段定义。它们也可能包括切入点、通知和引入（inter-type）声明。

第七步：声明一个切入点

（1）说明。

切入点决定了连接点关注的内容，使得开发人员可以控制通知什么时候执行。

Spring AOP 只支持 Spring bean 方法执行连接点。所以可以把切入点看成是匹配 Spring bean 上方法的执行。

一个切入点声明有两个部分：一个包含名字和任意参数的签名，还有一个切入点表达式，该表达式决定了我们关注那个方法的执行。

在@AspectJ 注解风格的 AOP 中，一个切入点签名通过一个普通的方法定义来提供，并且切入点表达式使用@Pointcut 注解来表示（作为切入点签名的方法必须返回 void 类型）。

（2）实例，修改 MyAspect.java 类。

下面的实例定义了一个切入点：anyProcess，这个切入点将匹配任何名为 process 的方法的执行，修改后的 MyAspect.java 类的代码如下：

```java
package amigo.spring.aop.aspectj;

import org.aspectj.lang.annotation.Aspect;
import org.aspectj.lang.annotation.Pointcut;

/**
 * 自定义的切面类
 */
@Aspect
public class MyAspect {
    @Pointcut("execution(* process(..))") // 切入点表达式
    private void anyProcess() { // 嵌入点签名
    }
}
```

其中切入点表达式，也就是@Pointcut 注解的值，是正规的 AspectJ 5 切入点表达式。

可以使用 Spring 统一管理事务。例如，有些情况下需要对以 Manager 或 BeanImpl 等结尾的类统一配置事务，例如下面的配置：

```xml
<!-- 支持 @Transactional 标记 -->
<tx:annotation-driven/>

<!-- 支持 @AspectJ 标记 -->
<aop:aspectj-autoproxy/>

<!-- 以 AspectJ 方式 定义 AOP -->
<aop:config proxy-target-class="true">
    <aop:advisor pointcut="execution(* amigo.spring.aop..*Manager.*(..))" advice-ref="txAdvice"/>
</aop:config>


<!-- 基本事务定义,使用 transactionManager 作事务管理,默认 get*方法的事务为 readonly-->
<tx:advice id="txAdvice">
    <tx:attributes>
        <tx:method name="get*" read-only="true"/>
        <tx:method name="find*" read-only="true"/>
        <tx:method name="*"/>
    </tx:attributes>
</tx:advice>
```

在如上配置中，定义了如下嵌入点表达式中的方法，采用 txAdvice 中定义的事务属性：

pointcut="execution(* amigo.spring.aop..*Manager.*(..))"

该句表示将 amigo.spring.aop 包及其子包中的所有以 Manager 结尾的类文件作为切入点，统一配置事务属性。

接下来看几个切入点的实例：

- execution(public * *(..))：任何声明为 public 的方法都执行。
- execution(* amigo.spring.aop.aspectj.UserService.*(..))：UserService 类的任意方法执行。
- execution(* amigo.spring.aop.aspectj.*.*(..))：amigo.spring.aop.aspectj 包的任意类的任意方法执行。
- execution(*amigo.spring.aop.aspectj..*.*(..))：amigo.spring.aop.aspectj 包及其子包的任意类的任意方法执行。

第八步：声明通知

通知是跟一个切入点表达式关联起来的，并且在切入点匹配的方法执行之前或者之后或者之前和之后运行。切入点表达式可能是指向已命名的切入点的简单引用或者是一个已经声明过的切入点表达式。

（1）前置通知（Before advice）。

前置通知在方法执行之前执行，一个切面里使用@Before 注解声明前置通知。

读者可在 amigo.spring.aop.aspectj 包中创建 Manager 类：UserManager.java，该类用于协助进行各种通知的测试，该类的代码如下所示：

```java
package amigo.spring.aop.aspectj;

/**
 * 业务逻辑类（用户测试各种通知）
 */
public class UserManager {
    public void saveUser(
            String username,
            String password) throws Exception {
        if (username == null) {
            throw new Exception("username 为空");
        }
        System.out.println("用户名=" + username);
        System.out.println("密码=" + password);
    }
}
```

读者可在 amigo.spring.aop.aspectj 包中建立 BeforeAdviceExample 类，该类的代码如下所示：

```java
package amigo.spring.aop.aspectj;

/**
 * 前置通知实例。
 */
public class BeforeAdviceExample {
    public void beforeAspect() {
        System.out.println("测试前置通知");
    }

    /**
     * 测试方法。
```

```
    */
    public static void main(String[] args) throws Exception {
        ClassPathResource res = new ClassPathResource(
                    "amigo/spring/aop/aspectj/aspectj.xml");
        XmlBeanFactory factory = new XmlBeanFactory(res);
        UserManager userManager = (UserManager) factory.getBean("userManager");
        userManager.saveUser("阿蜜果", "1234");
    }
}
```

该类的 befroeAspect() 方法输出简单的打印信息。

接着在 Spring 配置文件 aspectj.xml 中添加如下前置通知的配置：

```xml
<!-- 前置通知实例 -->
<bean id="userManager" class="amigo.spring.aop.aspectj.UserManager" />
<bean id="beforeAdviceExample" class="amigo.spring.aop.aspectj.BeforeAdviceExample" />
<aop:config proxy-target-class="false">
    <!-- 定义切入点 -->
    <aop:pointcut type="aspectj" id="beforePointcut"
        expression="execution(* amigo.spring.aop.aspectj..*Manager.*(..))" />
    <!-- 定义切面 -->
    <aop:aspect ref="beforeAdviceExample">
        <aop:before pointcut-ref="beforePointcut" method="beforeAspect" />
    </aop:aspect>
</aop:config>
```

上述的前置通知表示在执行 amigo.spring.aop.aspectj 包及其子包的任意方法前，调用 amigo.spring.aop.aspectj.BeforeAdviceExample 类的 beforeApect() 方法进行前置处理。其中 pointcut-ref 表明引用的是其他的切入点（pointcut），pointcut 用于定义全新的切入点。

在上面的 <config/> 中，在配置文件中直接配置了切入点表达式，若开发人员希望 XML 文件使用定义在 @AspectJ 中定义的切入点表达式，则可参考如下实现：可在 amigo.spring.aop.aspectj 包中建立 AdviceAspectJ.java 类，在该类中定义切入点表达式。该类的代码如下所示：

```java
package amigo.spring.aop.aspectj;

import org.aspectj.lang.annotation.Aspect;
import org.aspectj.lang.annotation.Pointcut;

@Aspect
public class AdviceAspectJ {
    @Pointcut("execution(* amigo.spring.aop.aspectj..*Manager*(..))")
    public void before() {};
}
```

接着修改 aspectj.xml 文件的部分内容，将文件中的如下内容：

```xml
<aop:pointcut type="aspectj" id="beforePointcut"
        expression="execution(* amigo.spring.aop.aspectj..*Manager.*(..))
            and args(str) and target(obj) and this(proxy)" />
```

修改成：

```xml
<aop:pointcut type="aspectj" id="beforePointcut"
        expression="amigo.spring.aop.aspectj.AdviceAspectJ.before()
            and args(str) and target(obj) and this(proxy)" />
```

（2）返回后通知（After returning advice）。

返回后通知通常在一个匹配的方法返回的时候执行，使用@AfterReturning 注释来声明。使用 aop:aspect 在 Spring 配置文件中进行配置。读者首先可在本实例的包中建立 AfterReturningAdviceExample 类，该类用于测试返回后通知实例，代码如下所示：

```java
package amigo.spring.aop.aspectj;

import org.aspectj.lang.JoinPoint;
import org.springframework.beans.factory.xml.XmlBeanFactory;
import org.springframework.core.io.ClassPathResource;

/**
 * 返回后通知实例.
 */
public class AfterReturningAdviceExample {
    public void afterReturningAspect(JoinPoint jp, Object returnValue) {
        System.out.println("测试返回后通知");
    }

    /**
     * 测试方法.
     */
    public static void main(String[] args) throws Exception {
        //...同 BeforeAdviceExample 类的该方法
    }
}
```

接着在 Spring 配置文件 aspectj.xml 中添加如下配置信息：

```xml
<!-- 返回后通知实例 -->
<bean id="afterReturningAdviceExample"
    class="amigo.spring.aop.aspectj.AfterReturningAdviceExample" />
<aop:config proxy-target-class="false">
    <!-- 定义切入点 -->
    <aop:pointcut type="aspectj" id="afterReturningPointcut"
        expression="execution(* amigo.spring.aop.aspectj..*Manager.*(..))" />
    <!-- 定义切面 -->
    <aop:aspect ref="afterReturningAdviceExample">
        <aop:after-returning pointcut-ref="afterReturningPointcut"
            method="afterReturningAspect"
            returning="returnValue"/>
    </aop:aspect>
</aop:config>
```

返回后通知使用<after-returning/>，其属性与<before/>类似。若要将从 XML 方式配置切入点表达式修改成通过声明的方式定义切入点表达式，方法与前置通知类似。

（3）抛出后通知（After throwing advice）。

抛出后通知在一个方法抛出异常后执行。采用声明式方法定义切入点时，可使用@AfterThrowing 注释来声明。若采用XML方式来配置，可使用<after-throwing/>元素的pointcut-ref来定义切入点表达式。

首先在本实例的包中建立AfterThrowingAdviceExample.java类，该类定义如下方法来进行抛出后的后置处理：

```java
public void afterThrowingAspect(JoinPoint jp, RuntimeException ex)
```

该类的代码如下所示:

```java
package amigo.spring.aop.aspectj;

import org.aspectj.lang.JoinPoint;
import org.springframework.beans.factory.xml.XmlBeanFactory;
import org.springframework.core.io.ClassPathResource;

/**
 * 抛出后通知实例.
 */
public class AfterThrowingAdviceExample {
    public void afterThrowingAspect(JoinPoint jp, RuntimeException ex) {
        System.out.println("测试抛出后通知");
        System.err.println(ex);
    }

    /**
     * 测试方法.
     */
    public static void main(String[] args) throws Exception{
        ClassPathResource res = new ClassPathResource(
                    "amigo/spring/aop/aspectj/aspectj.xml");
        XmlBeanFactory factory = new XmlBeanFactory(res);
        UserManager userManager = (UserManager) factory.getBean("userManager");
        userManager.saveUser(null, "1234");
    }
}
```

接着在Spring的配置文件中配置抛出后通知信息,添加的配置内容如下所示:

```xml
<!-- 抛出后通知实例 -->
<bean id="afterThrowingAdviceExample"
    class="amigo.spring.aop.aspectj.AfterThrowingAdviceExample" />
<aop:config proxy-target-class="false">
    <!-- 定义切入点 -->
    <aop:pointcut type="aspectj" id="afterThrowingPointcut"
        expression="execution(* amigo.spring.aop.aspectj..*Manager.*(..))" />
    <!-- 定义切面 -->
    <aop:aspect ref="afterThrowingAdviceExample">
        <aop:after-throwing pointcut-ref="afterThrowingPointcut"
            method="afterThrowingAspect"
                throwing="ex"/>
    </aop:aspect>
</aop:config>
```

其中<after-throwing/>元素用来定义抛出后通知,point-ref和method属性与前置通知一样,throwing属性指定抛出的异常对象名称。

(4) 后通知(After (finally) advice)。

不论一个方法是如何结束的,在它结束后后通知都会运行。若使用声明式时,可使用@After注释来声明。这个通知必须做好处理正常返回和异常返回两种情况,通常用来释放资源。

读者可在该实例的包中建立AfterAdviceExample.java类,该类的代码如下所示:

```java
package amigo.spring.aop.aspectj;
```

```java
import org.aspectj.lang.JoinPoint;
import org.springframework.beans.factory.xml.XmlBeanFactory;
import org.springframework.core.io.ClassPathResource;

/**
 * 后通知实例.
 */
public class AfterAdviceExample {
    public void afterAspect(JoinPoint jp, Object returnValue) {
        System.out.println("测试后通知");
    }

    public static void main(String[] args) throws Exception {
        // 同前置通知的该方法，略
    }
}
```

后通知在 Spring 配置文件中使用 aop:after 元素来声明，读者需在 aspectj.xml 中添加如下配置信息：

```xml
<!-- 后通知实例 -->
<bean id="afterAdviceExample" class="amigo.spring.aop.aspectj.AfterAdviceExample" />
<aop:config proxy-target-class="false">
    <!-- 定义切入点 -->
    <aop:pointcut type="aspectj" id="afterPointcut"
        expression="execution(* amigo.spring.aop.aspectj..*Manager.*(..))" />
    <!-- 定义切面 -->
    <aop:aspect ref="afterAdviceExample">
        <aop:after pointcut-ref="afterPointcut" method="afterAspect"/>
    </aop:aspect>
</aop:config>
```

（5）环绕通知（Around Advice）。

环绕通知在一个方法执行之前和之后执行，并且，它可以决定这个方法在什么时候执行，如何执行，甚至是否执行。

环绕通知经常在某线程安全的环境下，开发人员需要在一个方法执行之前和之后共享某种状态的时候使用。请尽量使用最简单的满足需求的通知，如果在前置通知也可以适用的情况下不要使用环绕通知。

声明式的环绕通知使用@Around 注释来声明。Around 通知使用 aop:around 元素来声明。通知方法的第一个参数的类型必须是 ProceedingJoinPoint 类型。在通知的主体中，调用 ProceedingJoinPoint 的 proceed() 方法来执行真正的方法。proceed 方法也可能会被调用并且传入一个 Object[] 对象。

首先在本实例的包 amigo.spring.aop.aspectj 中创建 AroundAdviceExample.java 类，该类的代码如下所示：

```java
package amigo.spring.aop.aspectj;

import org.aspectj.lang.ProceedingJoinPoint;
import org.springframework.beans.factory.xml.XmlBeanFactory;
import org.springframework.core.io.ClassPathResource;

/**
```

```java
 * 环绕通知实例.
 */
public class AroundAdviceExample {
    public void aroundAspect(
            ProceedingJoinPoint pjp,
            String str) throws Throwable{
        System.out.println("测试环绕通知");
        System.out.println("str=" + str);
        pjp.proceed(new Object[]{str});
    }

    /**
     * 测试方法.
     */
    public static void main(String[] args) throws Exception {
        // 同前置通知的该方法，略
    }
}
```

接着在Spring的配置文件aspectj.xml中添加环绕通知的配置信息，如下所示：

```xml
<!-- 环绕通知实例 -->
<bean id="aroundAdviceExample" class="amigo.spring.aop.aspectj.AroundAdviceExample" />
<aop:config proxy-target-class="false">
    <!-- 定义切入点 -->
    <aop:pointcut type="aspectj" id="aroundPointcut"
        expression="execution(* amigo.spring.aop.aspectj..*Manager.*(..))" />
    <!-- 定义切面 -->
    <aop:aspect ref="aroundAdviceExample">
        <aop:after pointcut-ref="aroundPointcut" method="aroundAspect"/>
    </aop:aspect>
</aop:config>
```

【例 17-4】使用 Spring AOP 实现异常拦截

〖实例需求〗

若读者在项目中有过这样的需求：想在某种异常抛出时进行一些记录操作，例如记录错误日志到数据库或日志文件中，但把这些代码分布到项目各处不但难于管理，并且代码量巨大，用 Spring 的 AOP 来实现拦截不失为一个比较好的方法。

本实例讲解如何使用 Spring 的 ThrowsAdvice 来实现异常拦截。ThrowsAdvice 是一个标示接口，开发人员可以在类中定义一个或多个，来捕获定义异常通知的 bean 抛出的异常，并在抛出异常前执行相应的方法。

〖开发过程〗

第一步：创建包：amigo.spring.aop.exception

在src源码目录中创建包：amigo.spring.aop.exception，该包用于存放本实例的Java类代码。

第二步：复制jar包

在运行该例时，需要将cglib-2.1.jar和asm.jar复制到工程的WEB-INF/lib目录中。

【提示】若未复制cglib-2.1.jar，则在运行ExceptionAdvisor.java类时，将会出现如下异常：

```
org.springframework.util.ClassUtils    - Class [net.sf.cglib.proxy.Enhancer] or one of its dependencies is not present: java.lang.ClassNotFoundException: net.sf.cglib.proxy.Enhancer
Exception in thread "main" org.springframework.aop.framework.AopConfigException: Cannot proxy target class because CGLIB2 is not available. Add CGLIB to the class path or specify proxy interfaces.
……
```

若未复制asm.jar，则在运行ExceptionAdvisor.java类时，将会出现如下异常信息：

```
Exception in thread "main" java.lang.NoClassDefFoundError: org/objectweb/asm/Type
    at net.sf.cglib.core.TypeUtils.parseType(TypeUtils.java:180)
    at net.sf.cglib.core.KeyFactory.<clinit>(KeyFactory.java:66)
    at net.sf.cglib.proxy.Enhancer.<clinit>(Enhancer.java:69)
    at org.springframework.aop.framework.Cglib2AopProxy.createEnhancer(Cglib2AopProxy.java:224)
……
```

第三步：编写异常拦截处理类：ExceptionAdvisor

在amigo.spring.aop.exception中创建异常拦截处理类：ExceptionAdvisor，该类演示了如何对未知的异常进行处理，以及如何对特定的异常进行处理。该类的代码如下所示：

```java
package amigo.spring.aop.conception;

import org.springframework.aop.ThrowsAdvice;
import org.springframework.aop.framework.ProxyFactory;

import java.lang.reflect.Method;

/**
 * 异常拦截类.
 */
public class ExceptionAdvisor implements ThrowsAdvice {
    public static void main(String[] args) {
        TestBean bean = new TestBean();
        ProxyFactory pf = new ProxyFactory();
        pf.setTarget(bean);
        pf.addAdvice(new ExceptionAdvisor());

        TestBean proxy = (TestBean) pf.getProxy();
        try {
            proxy.method1();
        } catch (Exception ignore) {
        }

        try {
            proxy.changeToNumber("amigo");
        } catch (Exception ignore) {
        }
    }
```

```java
/**
 * 对未知异常的处理.
 */
public void afterThrowing(Method method, Object[] args, Object target,
        Exception ex) throws Throwable {
    System.out.println("***************************************");
    System.out.println("Error happened in class: " + target.getClass().getName());
    System.out.println("Error happened in method: " + method.getName());

    for (int i = 0; i < args.length; i++) {
        System.out.println("arg[" + i + "]: " + args[i]);
    }

    System.out.println("Exception class: " + ex.getClass().getName());
    System.out.println("***************************************");
}

/**
 * 对 NullPointerException 异常的处理
 */
public void afterThrowing(Method method, Object[] args, Object target,
        NullPointerException ex) throws Throwable {
    System.out.println("***************************************");
    System.out.println("Error happened in class: " + target.getClass().getName());
    System.out.println("Error happened in method: " + method.getName());

    for (int i = 0; i < args.length; i++) {
        System.out.println("args[" + i + "]: " + args[i]);
    }

    System.out.println("Exception class: " + ex.getClass().getName());
    System.out.println("***************************************");
}
}
```

第四步：编写产生异常的类：TestBean.java

接着在 amigo.spring.aop.exception 中编写产生异常的类：TestBean.java，该类的代码如下所示：

```java
package amigo.spring.aop.conception;

/**
 * 产生异常的类.
 */
public class TestBean {
    public void method1() throws Exception {
        throw new Exception("Exception happened!");
    }

    /**
     * 将字符串转换为整数.
     * @param number 需转换的字符串
     * @return 转换成的字符串
     * @throws NumberFormatException
```

```java
    */
    public int changeToNumber(String number) throws NumberFormatException {
        //当number为空或非数字时，将抛出NumberFormatException
        int num = Integer.parseInt(number);
        return num;
    }
}
```

第五步：运行结果

在Eclipse中运行类ExceptionAdvisor.java，运行结果如下所示：

```
……
***********************************
Error happened in class: amigo.spring.aop.conception.TestBean
Error happened in method: method1
Exception class: java.lang.Exception
***********************************
……
Error happened in class: amigo.spring.aop.conception.TestBean
Error happened in method: changeToNumber
arg[0]: amigo
Exception class: java.lang.NumberFormatException
***********************************
```

小结

本章讲解了Spring的另一个关键的组件即AOP框架，AOP弥补了面向对象编程（OOP）的不足，它提供了另外一种角度来思考程序结构。在SPRING 2中，用户可以选择使用基于模式（schema-based）的方式或者使用@AspectJ注释。这两种风格都完全支持通知（Advice）类型和AspectJ的切入点语言。

AOP具有如下重要的概念：

- 切面（Aspect）：一个关注点的模块化，这个关注点可能会横切多个对象。例如事务管理、异常处理等都可视为切面。
- 连接点（Joinpoint）：在程序执行过程中某个特定的点，比如某方法调用的时候或者处理异常的时候。
- 通知（Advice）：在切面的某个特定的连接点（Joinpoint）上执行的动作。
- 切入点（Pointcut）：匹配连接点（Joinpoint）的断点。
- 引入（Introduction）：声明额外的方法或者某个类型的字段。
- 目标对象（Target Object）：被一个或者多个切面（aspect）所通知（advise）的对象。又被称为通知（advised）对象。
- AOP代理（AOP Proxy）：AOP框架创建的对象，在Spring中，AOP代理可以是JDK动态代理或者CGLIB代理。

通知的类型如下所示：

- 前置通知（Before advice）
- 返回后通知（After returning advice）

- 抛出异常后通知（After throwing advice）
- 后通知（After (finally) advice）
- 环绕通知（Around Advice）

AOP 实现的原理是采用 Java 提供的反射、动态代理机制以及 AspectJ 技术。@AspectJ 使用了 Java 5 的注解，可以将切面声明为普通的 Java 类，目前最新版本为 AspectJ 5，在 Spring 2.0 中加入@AspectJ 支持，首先需要通过如下配置信息启用@AspectJ 的支持：

```xml
<aop:aspectj-autoproxy/>
```

前置通知在方法执行之前执行，参考配置实例如下所示：

```xml
<bean id="beforeAdviceExample" class="amigo.spring.aop.aspectj.BeforeAdviceExample" />
<aop:config proxy-target-class="false">
    <!-- 定义切入点 -->
    <aop:pointcut type="aspectj" id="beforePointcut"
        expression="execution(* amigo.spring.aop.aspectj..*Manager.*(..))" />
    <!-- 定义切面 -->
    <aop:aspect ref="beforeAdviceExample">
        <aop:before pointcut-ref="beforePointcut" method="beforeAspect" />
    </aop:aspect>
</aop:config>
```

返回后通知通常在一个匹配的方法返回的时候执行，使用@AfterReturning 注释来声明。使用 aop:aspect 在 Spring 配置文件中进行配置，配置实例如下所示：

```xml
<aop:config proxy-target-class="false">
    <!-- 定义切入点 -->
    <aop:pointcut type="aspectj" id="afterReturningPointcut"
        expression="execution(* amigo.spring.aop.aspectj..*Manager.*(..))" />
    <!-- 定义切面 -->
    <aop:aspect ref="afterReturningAdviceExample">
        <aop:after-returning pointcut-ref="afterReturningPointcut"
            method="afterReturningAspect"
                returning="returnValue"/>
    </aop:aspect>
</aop:config>
```

抛出后通知在一个方法抛出异常后执行。采用声明式方法定义切入点时，可使用@AfterThrowing 注释来声明。若采用 XML 方式来配置，可使用<after-throwing/>元素的 pointcut-ref 来定义切入点表达式。配置实例如下所示：

```xml
<aop:config proxy-target-class="false">
    <!-- 定义切入点 -->
    <aop:pointcut type="aspectj" id="afterThrowingPointcut"
        expression="execution(* amigo.spring.aop.aspectj..*Manager.*(..))" />
    <!-- 定义切面 -->
    <aop:aspect ref="afterThrowingAdviceExample">
        <aop:after-throwing pointcut-ref="afterThrowingPointcut"
            method="afterThrowingAspect"
                throwing="ex"/>
    </aop:aspect>
</aop:config>
```

后通知指的是不论一个方法是如何结束的，在它结束后后通知都会运行。配置实例如下所示：

```xml
<bean id="afterAdviceExample" class="amigo.spring.aop.aspectj.AfterAdviceExample" />
<aop:config proxy-target-class="false">
    <!-- 定义切入点 -->
```

```xml
        <aop:pointcut type="aspectj" id="afterPointcut"
            expression="execution(* amigo.spring.aop.aspectj..*Manager.*(..))" />
        <!-- 定义切面 -->
        <aop:aspect ref="afterAdviceExample">
            <aop:after pointcut-ref="afterPointcut" method="afterAspect"/>
        </aop:aspect>
    </aop:config>
```

环绕通知在一个方法执行之前和之后执行，并且，它可以决定这个方法在什么时候执行，如何执行，甚至是否执行。配置实例如下所示：

```xml
<!-- 环绕通知实例 -->
<bean id="aroundAdviceExample" class="amigo.spring.aop.aspectj.AroundAdviceExample" />
<aop:config proxy-target-class="false">
    <!-- 定义切入点 -->
    <aop:pointcut type="aspectj" id="aroundPointcut"
        expression="execution(* amigo.spring.aop.aspectj..*Manager.*(..))" />
    <!-- 定义切面 -->
    <aop:aspect ref="aroundAdviceExample">
        <aop:after pointcut-ref="aroundPointcut" method="aroundAspect"/>
    </aop:aspect>
</aop:config>
```

Spring 的 AOP 使用比较广泛，例如事务管理（在下一章将进行详细讲述）、日志管理和异常拦截等情况都可以使用 Spring AOP 来实现，因为这些情况都可以使用 Spring AOP 来方便地进行统一配置。

第 18 章　Spring 的高级配置

【本章导读语】

Spring 中具有很多高级功能，例如很方便地集成了事务、邮件服务和定时任务等。本章讲解这些实用功能的配置。

Spring 提供 JDBC 数据源、C3P0、DBCP 数据源等的支持，各种数据源的配置类似，不过参数方面有些细微的区别，本章实例将对各种数据源的参考配置进行说明。

Spring 提供了 org.springframework.transaction 包来解决事务问题，本章的 Hibernate 事务配置实例将对 Spring 的事务属性进行讲解，并将讲解在 Spring 的配置文件中如何配置 Hibernate 的事务，包括 sessionFactory、transactionManager（事务管理器）和 transactionInterceptor（事务拦截器）的配置。另外 Spring 2 还提供了更加方便的事务配置方法：使用 tx:advice 进行配置。

Java SE 提供了 JavaMail API，它能够构建邮件和消息应用。Spring 2 提供了邮件服务抽象，使得开发人员不需要处理底层邮件系统的具体细节，也不用管理底层的 Transport 等资源，从而使得代码简单化。邮件服务实例将讲解如何在 Spring 2 中通过配置来集成 JavaMail 邮件服务来发送简单邮件和复杂邮件。

定时任务在各种工程中应用广泛，例如定时去 FTP 取文件、定时进行数据表的状态更新、定时删除过时文件等。在定时任务实例中，将讲解如何在 Spring 中进行定时任务的配置。

【例 18-1】数据源配置

〖实例需求〗

本实例讲解如何在工程中配置所需要的多种数据源，Spring 提供 JDBC、C3P0、DBCP 等数据源。为了简便起见，本例中采用的数据库为 MySQL，其他数据库配置与此类似。

〖开发过程〗

第一步：创建工程

按照第 15 章的方式建立一个名为 springconfig 的 Web 工程，并将 Spring 2 的 jar 复制到 WebRoot/WEB-INF/lib 目录中。接着在 src 源码目录中创建 amigo.spring.config.datasource 包，并将 log4j 的配置文件 log4j.properties 复制到 src 源码目录。

完成后的目录结构如图 18-1 所示。

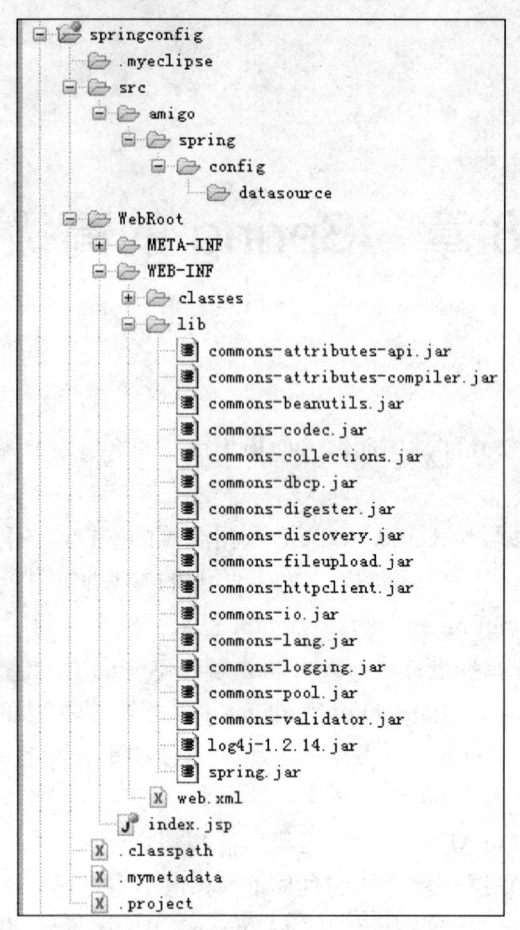

```
springconfig
  .myeclipse
  src
    amigo
      spring
        config
          datasource
  WebRoot
    META-INF
    WEB-INF
      classes
      lib
        commons-attributes-api.jar
        commons-attributes-compiler.jar
        commons-beanutils.jar
        commons-codec.jar
        commons-collections.jar
        commons-dbcp.jar
        commons-digester.jar
        commons-discovery.jar
        commons-fileupload.jar
        commons-httpclient.jar
        commons-io.jar
        commons-lang.jar
        commons-logging.jar
        commons-pool.jar
        commons-validator.jar
        log4j-1.2.14.jar
        spring.jar
      web.xml
    index.jsp
  .classpath
  .mymetadata
  .project
```

图 18-1　工程的目录结构

第二步：配置 Spring 中的 JDBC 数据源

（1）创建数据库和表。

通过如下数据库脚本，在 MySQL 中创建一个名为 springtest 的数据库，并在其中创建一个 user 表，数据库脚本如下所示：

```sql
CREATE DATABASE 'springtest';
USE 'springtest';

CREATE TABLE 'user' (
  'id' int(11) NOT NULL auto_increment,
  'username' varchar(100) NOT NULL,
  'password' varchar(100) NOT NULL,
  PRIMARY KEY  ('id')
) ENGINE=InnoDB DEFAULT CHARSET=gb2312;

INSERT INTO 'user' ('id', 'username', 'password') VALUES (1,'amigo','123');
INSERT INTO 'user' ('id', 'username', 'password') VALUES (2,'xiexingxing','12345678');
```

（2）编写 user 表对应的 POJO 类 User.java。

在 amigo.spring.config.datasource 包下创建 User.java 类，该类包含属性 id、username 和 password 的 getter/setter 方法，该类的代码如下所示：

```java
package amigo.spring.config.datasource;

/**
 * user 表的 POJO 对象
 */
public class User {
    /** 用户 ID. */
    private int id;

    /** 用户名. */
    private String username;

    /** 密码. */
    private String password;

    // 省略各属性的 getter/setter 方法
}
```

（3）编写 user 表的 DAO 接口类 UserDao.java。

UserDao.java 位于 amigo.spring.chapter16.example2 包中，在该例中，为了简便起见，只提供获取用户列表和通过 ID 获取某个用户的方法，该类的代码如下所示：

```java
package amigo.spring.config.datasource;

import java.util.List;

/**
 * 用户 DAO 接口类.
 */
public interface UserDao {
    public abstract List getUserList() throws Exception;

    public abstract User getUserById(int id) throws Exception;
}
```

（4）编写 user 表的 DAO 实现类 UserDaoImpl.java。

UserDaoImpl.java 类实现 UserDao.java 接口，在该类中，需要用到 DataSource 对象，DataSource 对象将在后续的 Spring 配置中提及。

```java
package amigo.spring.config.datasource;

import java.sql.Connection;
import java.sql.ResultSet;
import java.sql.Statement;
import java.util.ArrayList;
import java.util.List;

import javax.sql.DataSource;

/**
 * UserDao 的实现类.
 */
public class UserDaoImpl implements UserDao {
    private DataSource dataSource;
```

```java
public void setDataSource(DataSource dataSource) {
    this.dataSource = dataSource;
}

/**
 * 获取用户列表.
 * @return 返回用户列表
 */
public List<User> getUserList() throws Exception {
    List<User> userList = new ArrayList<User>();
    User user = null;
    Connection conn = null;
    Statement stmt = null;
    conn = dataSource.getConnection();
    stmt = conn.createStatement();

    try {
        // 获取用户列表
        ResultSet userSet = stmt.executeQuery(
                "SELECT * FROM user");
        while (userSet.next()) {
            user = new User();
            user.setId(userSet.getInt("id"));
            user.setUsername(userSet.getString("username"));
            user.setPassword(userSet.getString("password"));
            userList.add(user);
        }
    } catch(Exception e) {
        e.printStackTrace();
    } finally {
        // 关闭资源
        if (stmt != null) {
            try {
                stmt.close();
            } catch(Exception ex) {
                ex.printStackTrace();
            }
        }

        if (conn != null) {
            try {
                conn.close();
            } catch(Exception e) {
                e.printStackTrace();
            }
        }
    }
    return userList;
}

/**
 * 通过 ID 获取用户对象.
 * @param id 用户 id
```

```java
     * @return 返回用户对象，不存在时，返回 null
     */
    public User getUserById(int id) throws Exception {
        User user = null;
        Connection conn = null;
        Statement stmt = null;
        conn = dataSource.getConnection();
        stmt = conn.createStatement();

        try {
            ResultSet userSet = stmt.executeQuery(
                    "SELECT * FROM user WHERE id=" + id);
            if (userSet.next()) {
                user = new User();
                user.setId(userSet.getInt("id"));
                user.setUsername(userSet.getString("username"));
                user.setPassword(userSet.getString("password"));
            }
        } catch(Exception e) {
            e.printStackTrace();
        } finally {
            // 关闭资源
            if (stmt != null) {
                try {
                    stmt.close();
                } catch(Exception ex) {
                    ex.printStackTrace();
                }
            }

            if (conn != null) {
                try {
                    conn.close();
                } catch(Exception e) {
                    e.printStackTrace();
                }
            }
        }
        return user;
    }
}
```

（5）在 Spring 中配置 JDBC 数据源和 userDao。

Spring 框架中的 org.springframework.jdbc.datasource.DriverManagerDataSource 类提供了进行 JDBC 操作的数据源。因为需要用到 JDBC 数据源驱动 com.mysql.jdbc.Driver，所以读者还需要将 mysql-connector-java-5.0.4-bin.jar 包复制到 springconfig 工程的 lib 目录中，并将其引入到 CLASSPATH 路径中。

接着在 src/amigo/spring/chapter18/example2 目录中配置 JDBC 数据源配置文件 jdbcDataSource.xml，在该配置文件中配置了 dataSource 和 userDao 两个 bean，userDao 对 dataSource 进行了引用，该文件的完整内容如下所示：

```xml
<?xml version="1.0" encoding="UTF-8"?>
```

```xml
<beans xmlns="http://www.springframework.org/schema/beans"
    xmlns:xsi="http://www.w3.org/2001/XMLSchema-instance"
    xsi:schemaLocation="http://www.springframework.org/schema/beans
http://www.springframework.org/schema/beans/spring-beans-2.0.xsd">
    <!-- jdbc 数据源的配置 -->
    <bean id="dataSource"
        class="org.springframework.jdbc.datasource.DriverManagerDataSource">
        <property name="driverClassName">
            <value>com.mysql.jdbc.Driver</value>
        </property>
        <property name="url">
            <value>jdbc:mysql://localhost/springtest</value>
        </property>
        <property name="username">
            <value>root</value>
        </property>
        <property name="password">
            <value>root</value>
        </property>
    </bean>

    <!-- userDao 的配置 -->
    <bean id="userDao" class=" amigo.spring.config.datasource.UserDaoImpl">
        <property name="dataSource">
            <ref bean="dataSource"/>
        </property>
    </bean>
</beans>
```

（6）编写 JDBC 数据源的测试类 JdbcDataSourceTest.java。

在 amigo.spring.chapter18.example2 包中建立 JdbcDataSourceTest.java 类，在该类中获得 userDao 这个 bean，并测试 JDBC 数据源是否成功获取，是否能正确地获取用户信息。该类的代码如下所示：

```java
package amigo.spring.config.datasource;

import java.util.List;

import org.springframework.beans.factory.xml.XmlBeanFactory;
import org.springframework.core.io.ClassPathResource;

/**
 * JDBC 数据源配置.
 */
public class JdbcDataSourceTest {

    /**
     * @param args
     */
    public static void main(String[] args) throws Exception {
        ClassPathResource res = new ClassPathResource(
                " amigo/spring/config/datasource/jdbcDataSource.xml");
        XmlBeanFactory factory = new XmlBeanFactory(res);
        UserDao userDao = (UserDao) factory.getBean("userDao");
```

```java
            List<User> userList = userDao.getUserList();
            System.out.println("user 表中共有" + userList.size() + "个用户");
            for (int i = 0; i < userList.size(); i++) {
                User user = (User) userList.get(i);
                System.out.println("id=" + user.getId() +
                        ", username=" + user.getUsername() +
                        ", password=" + user.getPassword());

            }

            User user = userDao.getUserById(1);
            if (user == null) {
                System.out.println("不存在 id 为 1 的用户");
            } else {
                System.out.println("存在 id 为 1 的用户,username=" + user.getUsername() +
                        ",password=" + user.getPassword());
            }
        }
    }
```

（7）运行结果。

在 Eclipse 中运行 JdbcDataSourceTest 类,运行结果如下所示:

```
……
org.springframework.jdbc.datasource.DriverManagerDataSource  - Loaded JDBC driver: com.mysql.jdbc.Driver
org.springframework.jdbc.datasource.DriverManagerDataSource  - Creating new JDBC Connection to [jdbc:mysql://localhost/springtest]
user 表中共有 2 个用户
id=1, username=amigo, password=123
id=2, username=xiexingxing, password=12345678
org.springframework.jdbc.datasource.DriverManagerDataSource  - Creating new JDBC Connection to [jdbc:mysql://localhost/springtest]
存在 id 为 1 的用户,username=amigo,password=123
```

第三步:配置 C3P0 数据源

（1）在 Spring 中配置 C3P0 数据源和 userDao。

配置 C3P0 数据源使用 com.mchange.v2.c3p0.ComboPooledDataSource 类,因此需要读者将 c3p0-0.9.0.jar 拷贝到 springconfig 工程的 lib 目录中,并将其引入到工程的 CLASSPATH 路径中。

接下来在 src/amigo/spring/chapter18/example2 目录中配置 C3P0 数据源配置文件 c3p0DataSource.xml,该配置文件的完整内容如下所示:

```xml
<?xml version="1.0" encoding="UTF-8"?>
<beans xmlns="http://www.springframework.org/schema/beans"
    xmlns:xsi="http://www.w3.org/2001/XMLSchema-instance"
    xsi:schemaLocation="http://www.springframework.org/schema/beans
http://www.springframework.org/schema/beans/spring-beans-2.0.xsd">
    <!-- c3p0 数据源的配置 -->
    <bean id="dataSource"
        class="com.mchange.v2.c3p0.ComboPooledDataSource">
        <property name="driverClass">
            <value>com.mysql.jdbc.Driver</value>
```

```xml
            </property>
            <property name="jdbcUrl">
                <value>jdbc:mysql://localhost/springtest</value>
            </property>
            <property name="user">
                <value>root</value>
            </property>
            <property name="password">
                <value>root</value>
            </property>
            <property name="maxPoolSize">
                <value>80</value>
            </property>
            <property name="minPoolSize">
                <value>1</value>
            </property>
            <property name="initialPoolSize">
                <value>1</value>
            </property>
            <property name="maxIdleTime">
                <value>20</value>
            </property>
    </bean>

    <!-- userDao 的配置 -->
    <bean id="userDao" class="amigo.spring.config.datasource.UserDaoImpl">
        <property name="dataSource">
            <ref bean="dataSource"/>
        </property>
    </bean>
</beans>
```

（2）编写 C3P0 数据源的测试类 C3P0DataSourceTest.java。

在 src/amigo/spring/chapter18/example2 目录中创建 C3P0DataSourceTest.java 类，用它来进行 C3P0 数据源的配置，该类与 JdbDataSourceTest.java 类似，只是将以下这句：

```
ClassPathResource res = new ClassPathResource(
            "amigo/spring/config/datasource/jdbcDataSource.xml");
```

替换成：

```
ClassPathResource res = new ClassPathResource(
            "amigo/spring/config/datasource/c3p0DataSource.xml");
```

在此不再赘述该类的全部内容。

（3）运行结果。

在 Eclipse 中运行 C3P0DataSourceTest 类，运行结果如下：

```
……
user 表中共有 2 个用户
id=1, username=amigo, password=123
id=2, username=xiexingxing, password=12345678
com.mchange.v2.resourcepool.BasicResourcePool    - resource age is okay: com.mchange.v2.c3p0.impl.NewPooledConnection@14acfcd ---> age: 15    max: 20000 [com.mchange.v2.resourcepool.BasicResourcePool@15c07d8]
com.mchange.v2.resourcepool.BasicResourcePool    - trace com.mchange.v2.resourcepool. BasicResourcePool@15c07d8 [managed: 2, unused: 0, excluded: 0] (e.g. com.mchange.v2. c3p0.impl.New
```

PooledConnection@979e8b)
　　com.mchange.v2.resourcepool.BasicResourcePool　　- trace com.mchange.v2.resourcepool. Basic ResourcePool@15c07d8 [managed: 2, unused: 1, excluded: 0] (e.g. com.mchange.v2.c3p0. impl.New PooledConnection@979e8b)
　　存在 id 为 1 的用户，username=amigo,password=123
　　com.mchange.v2.resourcepool.BasicResourcePool　　- trace com.mchange.v2.resourcepool. Basic ResourcePool@15c07d8 [managed: 3, unused: 3, excluded: 0] (e.g. com.mchange.v2. c3p0.impl. NewPooledConnection@979e8b)

第四步：配置 DBCP 数据源

（1）在 Spring 中配置 DBCP 数据源和 userDao。

配置 DBCP 数据源使用 org.apache.commons.dbcp.BasicDataSource 类，因此需要读者将 commons-dbcp.jar 复制到 springconfig 工程的 lib 目录中，并将其引入到工程的 CLASSPATH 路径中。

接下来在 src/amigo/spring/config/datasource 目录中配置 DBCP 数据源配置文件 dbcpDataSource.xml，该配置文件的完整内容如下：

```xml
<?xml version="1.0" encoding="UTF-8"?>
<beans xmlns="http://www.springframework.org/schema/beans"
       xmlns:xsi="http://www.w3.org/2001/XMLSchema-instance"
       xsi:schemaLocation="http://www.springframework.org/schema/beans http://www.springframework.org/schema/beans/spring-beans-2.0.xsd">
    <!--dbcp 数据源的配置 -->
    <bean id="dataSource"
        class="org.apache.commons.dbcp.BasicDataSource">
        <property name="driverClassName">
            <value>com.mysql.jdbc.Driver</value>
        </property>
        <property name="url">
            <value>jdbc:mysql://localhost/springtest</value>
        </property>
        <property name="username">
            <value>root</value>
        </property>
        <property name="password">
            <value>root</value>
        </property>
        <property name="maxActive">
            <value>2</value>
        </property>
    </bean>

    <!-- userDao 的配置 -->
    <bean id="userDao" class="amigo.spring.config.datasource.UserDaoImpl">
        <property name="dataSource">
            <ref bean="dataSource"/>
        </property>
    </bean>
</beans>
```

（2）编写 DBCP 数据源的测试类 DbcpDataSourceTest.java。

在 src/amigo/spring/config/datasource 目录中创建 DbcpDataSourceTest.java 类，用它来进行 DBCP 数据源的配置，该类与 JdbcDataSourceTest.java 类似，只是将以下这句：

```
        ClassPathResource res = new ClassPathResource(
                 "amigo/spring/config/datasource/jdbcDataSource.xml");
```
替换成：
```
        ClassPathResource res = new ClassPathResource(
                 "amigo/spring/config/datasource/dbcpDataSource.xml");
```
在此不再赘述该类的全部内容。

（3）运行结果。

在 Eclipse 中运行 DbcpDataSourceTest 类，运行结果如下：

```
……
org.springframework.beans.factory.xml.XmlBeanFactory   - Eagerly caching bean 'dataSource' to allow for resolving potential circular references
user 表中共有 2 个用户
id=1, username=amigo, password=123
id=2, username=xiexingxing, password=12345678
存在 id 为 1 的用户，username=amigo,password=123
```

【例 18-2】Hibernate 事务配置

〖实例需求〗

Spring 提供了 org.springframework.transaction 包来解决事务问题。Spring 对 Hibernate Session 和 JDBC Connection 等独立的事务策略进行了抽象，提供了统一的 PlatformTransactionManager 接口。Spring 提供了该接口的若干实现，其中 HibernateTransactionManager 即是为 Hibernate 提供的一种事务实现。

本实例讲解 Spring 的事务属性（包括传播策略、隔离性、超时、只读事务、设定提交或回滚事务），并讲解了在 Spring 的配置文件中如何配置 Hibernate 的事务，包括 sessionFactory、transactionManager（事务管理器）和 transactionInterceptor（事务拦截器）的配置。

〖开发过程〗

第一步：Spring 的事务属性

Spring 常用的事务属性包括：

- **传播策略**：以"PROPAGATION_"开头，TransactionDefiniton 的事务传播策略说明如表 18-1 所示。

表 18-1 事务传播策略

传播策略	说明
PROPAGATION_REQUIRED	当前方法必须处于事务中，如果已处于事务中，则直接使用该事务，否则，开启新的事务
PROPAGATION_SUPPORTS	当前方法可运行也可不运行在事务中，如果调用时已在客户中，则当前方法处于事务中，否则，不处于事务中
PROPAGATION_MANDATORY	当前方法必须处于事务中，如果调用的客户不在事务中，则抛出异常
PROPAGATION_REQUIRES_NEW	当前方法必须在新事务中，无论何种情况，都将开启新事务

传播策略	说明
PROPAGATION_NOT_SUPPORTED	当前方法不能在事务中,如果调用其客户处于事务中,则在执行它时,活动事务必须挂起
PROPAGATION_NEVER	调用当前方法的客户不能够处于事务中,否则,抛出异常
PROPAGATION_NESTED	当前方法支持嵌入式事务,即以内需事务嵌套

- 隔离性:以"ISOLATION_"开头,值可为 ISOLATION_DEFAULT、ISOLATION_READ_UNCOMMITTED、ISOLATION_READ_COMMITTED、ISOLATION_REPEATABLE_READ 和 ISOLATION_SERIALIZABLE。
- 超时:以"TIMEOUT_"开头,它表示事务的有效时限,默认时,使用事务系统的超时设置,即 TIMEOUT_DEFAULT = -1。TIMEOUT_30 表示事务的有效时限为 30s。
- 只读:为 readOnly,用于将事务标记为只读事务。在只进行读取操作的时候,可设置为 readOnly,这样能提高效率,因为避免了不必要的 flush 操作。

第二步:创建包:amigo.spring.config.transaction

在src源码目录中创建该实例的源码包:amigo.spring.config.transaction。

第三步:创建 Hibernate 事务配置文件:transaction.xml

在amigo.spring.config.transaction中创建Hibernate的事务配置文件,本实例采用的数据库为MySQL,使用的还是【例18-1】的数据库和表。

在进行Hibernate的事务配置时,首先需要配置数据源(dataSource),接着根据数据源信息配置Session工厂(sessionFactory),接着再根据Session工厂信息创建事务管理器(transactionManager),最后配置事务拦截器(transactionInterceptor),在事务拦截器中定义事务属性(传播策略、只读和隔离性等信息)。

该文件的内容如下所示:

```xml
<?xml version="1.0" encoding="UTF-8"?>
<beans xmlns="http://www.springframework.org/schema/beans"
       xmlns:xsi="http://www.w3.org/2001/XMLSchema-instance"
       xsi:schemaLocation="http://www.springframework.org/schema/beans      http://www.springframework.org/schema/beans/spring-beans-2.0.xsd">

    <!-- jdbc 数据源的配置 -->
    <bean id="dataSource"
        class="org.springframework.jdbc.datasource.DriverManagerDataSource">
        <property name="driverClassName">
            <value>com.mysql.jdbc.Driver</value>
        </property>
        <property name="url">
            <value>jdbc:mysql://localhost/springtest</value>
        </property>
        <property name="username">
            <value>root</value>
        </property>
        <property name="password">
            <value>root</value>
```

```xml
        </property>
    </bean>

    <!--定义了 Hibernate 的 SessionFactory -->
    <bean id="sessionFactory" class="org.springframework.orm.hibernate3.LocalSessionFactoryBean">
        <property name="dataSource">
            <ref local="dataSource" />
        </property>
        <property name="mappingResources">
            <list>
                <!--加载的 Hibernate 配置文件-->
                <!--value>amigo/spring/config/transaction/User.hbm.xml</value-->
            </list>
        </property>
        <property name="hibernateProperties">
            <props>
                <prop key="hibernate.dialect">org.hibernate.dialect.MySQLDialect</prop>
                <prop key="show_sql">true</prop>
                <prop key="hibernate.jdbc.batch_size">20</prop>
            </props>
        </property>
    </bean>

    <bean id="transactionManager"
            class="org.springframework.orm.hibernate3.HibernateTransactionManager">
        <property name="sessionFactory" ref="sessionFactory" />
    </bean>

    <bean id="transactionInterceptor"
            class="org.springframework.transaction.interceptor.TransactionInterceptor">
        <!-- 事务拦截器 bean 需要依赖注入一个事务管理器 -->
        <property name="transactionManager" ref="transactionManager" />
        <property name="transactionAttributes">
            <!-- 下面定义事务传播策略-->
            <props>
                <prop key="save*">PROPAGATION_REQUIRED</prop>
                <prop key="update*">PROPAGATION_REQUIRED</prop>
                <prop key="delete*">PROPAGATION_REQUIRED</prop>
                <prop key="query*">PROPAGATION_REQUIRED,readOnly</prop>
                <prop key="find*">PROPAGATION_REQUIRED,readOnly</prop>
            </props>
        </property>
    </bean>

    <!-- 定义 BeanNameAutoProxyCreator-->
    <bean class="org.springframework.aop.framework.autoproxy.BeanNameAutoProxyCreator">
        <!-- 指定对满足哪些 bean name 的 bean 自动生成业务代理 -->
        <property name="beanNames">
            <list>
                <!-- 需要自动创建事务代理的 bean-->
                <!-- value>userManager</value-->
            </list>
```

```xml
            <!-- 此处可增加其他需要自动创建事务代理的 bean-->
        </property>
        <!-- 下面定义 BeanNameAutoProxyCreator 所需的事务拦截器-->
        <property name="interceptorNames">
            <list>
                <value>transactionInterceptor</value>
            </list>
        </property>
    </bean>
</beans>
```

其中dataSource这个bean在【例18-1】中已详细讲述，在此不再赘述。

名为sessionFactory的bean用于定义Session工厂，对应的类为：

    org.springframework.orm.hibernate3.LocalSessionFactoryBean

其中dataSource属性用于指定数据源，mappingResources属性用于指定需要加入配置的Hibernate映射文件列表。hibernateProperties属性用于设置Hibernate的属性信息，例如show_sql（是否显示SQL语句），参考配置如下所示：

```xml
<bean id="sessionFactory"
        class="org.springframework.orm.hibernate3.LocalSessionFactoryBean">
    <property name="dataSource">
        <ref local="dataSource" />
    </property>
    <property name="mappingResources">
        <list>
            <!--加载的 Hibernate 配置文件-->
            <!--value>amigo/spring/config/transaction/User.hbm.xml</value-->
        </list>
    </property>
    <property name="hibernateProperties">
        <props>
            <prop key="hibernate.dialect">org.hibernate.dialect.MySQLDialect</prop>
            <prop key="show_sql">true</prop>
            <prop key="hibernate.jdbc.batch_size">20</prop>
        </props>
    </property>
</bean>
```

transactionManager这个bean用于定义事务管理器，对应的类为：

    org.springframework.orm.hibernate3.HibernateTransactionManager

需要为该bean指定Session工厂，属性名称为：sessionFactory。

transactionInterceptor这个bean为事务拦截器，需要为该拦截器指定事务管理器，并可以在transactionInterceptor这个bean中指定事务管理器，在此处指定的是在其前面定义的transactionManager这个事务管理器。另外还可以在事务拦截器中指定事务属性，例如如下配置：

```xml
<property name="transactionAttributes">
    <!-- 下面定义事务传播策略-->
    <props>
        <prop key="save*">PROPAGATION_REQUIRED</prop>
        <prop key="update*">PROPAGATION_REQUIRED</prop>
        <prop key="delete*">PROPAGATION_REQUIRED</prop>
        <prop key="query*">PROPAGATION_REQUIRED,readOnly</prop>
        <prop key="find*">PROPAGATION_REQUIRED,readOnly</prop>
    </props>
```

```
</property>
```
如上的事务策略表示save、update和delete开头的方法都必须处于事务中，query和find开头的方法也需要处于事务中，但是为只读事务。

BeanNameAutoProxyCreator用于为bean指定事务拦截器，在此处可为系统的各业务逻辑器指定事务拦截器transactionManager。

第四步：Spring 2 中的 tx:advice

（1）说明。

为了使应用能够使用注释（Annotation）技术带来的优势，Spring 2.x大量使用了注释技术，例如它引用了@Transactional注释来简化事务的应用。

要在Srping 2.0中启用@Transactional来管理事务，开发人员需要在Spring 2的配置文件中引入tx的命名空间，需要将beans元素改成：

```
<beans xmlns="http://www.springframework.org/schema/beans"
       xmlns:xsi="http://www.w3.org/2001/XMLSchema-instance"
       xmlns:tx="http://www.springframework.org/schema/tx"
       xsi:schemaLocation="http://www.springframework.org/schema/beans
http://www.springframework.org/schema/beans/spring-beans-2.0.xsd
       http://www.springframework.org/schema/tx
http://www.springframework.org/schema/tx/spring-tx-2.0.xsd">
```

其中如下两句是新加的：

```
xmlns:tx=http://www.springframework.org/schema/tx
    http://www.springframework.org/schema/tx
http://www.springframework.org/schema/tx/spring-tx-2.0.xsd
```

要启动Spring 2的自动代理机制，在运行时，Spring 2会自动寻找那些直接或间接使用了@Transactional注释的受管理的POJO。还需要在配置文件中添加如下内容：

```
<!-- 支持 @Transactional 标记 -->
<tx:annotation-driven/>
```

`<tx:annotation-driven/>`能够自动代理受管业务对象，但是它将事务信息内置在 Java 源代码中，属于声明式事务，不能够享受 Spring 2 引入的 AspectJ 5 pointcut 表达式语言。

Spring 2 通过 spring-tx-2.0.xsd 引进了`<tx:advice/>`内容模式来解决这个问题，例如如下定义：

```
<!-- 以 AspectJ 方式定义 AOP -->
<aop:config proxy-target-class="true">
    <aop:advisor    pointcut="execution(*    amigo.spring.config.transaction..*Manager.*(..))"
advice-ref="txAdvice"/>
</aop:config>

<!--事务定义,默认query和find开头的方法的事务为readonly,其余方法按默认设置. -->
<tx:advice id="txAdvice">
    <tx:attributes>
        <tx:method name="query*" read-only="true"/>
        <tx:method name="find*" read-only="true"/>
        <tx:method name="*"/>
    </tx:attributes>
</tx:advice>
```

如上定义了amigo.spring.config.transaction包下所有以"Manager"结尾的类都使用txAdvice，txAdvice定义的事务属性为：使用query或find开头的方法都为只读事务，而其余的方法采用的是默认设置（read-only属性为false）。

<method/>的属性如表18-2所示。

表 18-2 <method/>的属性

属性	说明
name	方法名，可使用通配符（*）来匹配若干方法，例如：query*表示以 query 开头的方法
propagation	传播策略，可参见表 18-1，取值可为 REQUIRED、SUPPORTS、MANDATORY、REQUIRES_NEW、NOT_SUPPORTED、NEVER 和 NESTED，默认为 REQUIRED
isolation	隔离性，值可为 DEFAULT、READ_UNCOMMITTED、READ_COMMITTED、REPEATABLE_READ 和 SERIALIZABLE，默认为 DEFAULT
timeout	事务超时，见【第一步：Spring 的事务属性】
read-only	是否为只读事务，默认为 false，即不是只读事务
rollback-for	触发回滚的异常类，若为多个异常类，使用逗号隔开
no-rollback-for	触发提交的异常类，若为多个异常类，使用逗号隔开

（2）编写 tx:advice 配置参考 Spring 文件：adviceTransaction.xml。

若要采用tx:advice，大家来看一下如何对transaction.xml进行改造，可在amigo.spring.config.transaction建立adviceTransaction.xml文件，该文件的内容如下所示：

```xml
<?xml version="1.0" encoding="UTF-8"?>
<beans xmlns="http://www.springframework.org/schema/beans"
       xmlns:xsi="http://www.w3.org/2001/XMLSchema-instance"
       xmlns:aop="http://www.springframework.org/schema/aop"
       xmlns:tx="http://www.springframework.org/schema/tx"
       xsi:schemaLocation="http://www.springframework.org/schema/beans   http://www.springframework.org/schema/beans/spring-beans-2.0.xsd
       http://www.springframework.org/schema/aop   http://www.springframework.org/schema/aop/spring-aop-2.0.xsd
       http://www.springframework.org/schema/tx http://www.springframework.org/schema/tx/spring-tx-2.0.xsd"
       default-autowire="byName" default-lazy-init="true">

    <!--数据源和 sessionFactory 的配置与第三步一样，故此省略-->

    <bean id="transactionManager"
        class="org.springframework.orm.hibernate3.HibernateTransactionManager">
        <property name="sessionFactory" ref="sessionFactory" />
    </bean>

    <!-- 支持 @Transactional 标记 -->
    <tx:annotation-driven/>

    <!-- 支持 @AspectJ 标记-->
    <aop:aspectj-autoproxy/>

    <!-- 以 AspectJ 方式 定义 AOP -->
    <aop:config proxy-target-class="true">
        <aop:advisor   pointcut="execution(*   amigo.spring.config.transaction..*Manager.*(..))" advice-ref="txAdvice"/>
```

```xml
        </aop:config>

        <!-- 基本事务定义,使用transactionManager作事务管理,默认get*方法的事务为readonly,其余方法按默认
设置.-->
        <tx:advice id="txAdvice">
            <tx:attributes>
                <tx:method name="get*" read-only="true"/>
                <tx:method name="find*" read-only="true"/>
                <tx:method name="*"/>
            </tx:attributes>
        </tx:advice>
</beans>
```

【例 18-3】邮件服务配置

〖实例需求〗

Java SE 提供了 JavaMail API,它能够构建邮件和消息应用。开发者在使用 JavaMail 进行邮件收发时,需要自己编写代码来获得 Session、创建和关闭 Transport,而这些代码是与业务功能无关的代码,Spring 2 提供了邮件服务抽象,使得开发人员不需要处理底层邮件系统的具体细节,也不用管理底层的 Transport 等资源,从而使得代码简单化。

本实例讲解如何在 Spring 2 中通过配置来集成 JavaMail 邮件服务来发送简单邮件和复杂邮件(例如含有附件的邮件和含有 HTML 和内嵌资源的邮件)。

〖开发过程〗

第一步:加入 mail.jar 包

首先需要将JavaMail的jar包拷贝到工程的WEB-INF/lib目录中。
JavaMail的下载地址如下所示:http://java.sun.com/products/javamail/downloads/index.jsp

第二步:创建包目录:amigo.spring.config.mail

在src目录中创建本实例的包目录:amigo.spring.config.mail,用于存放本实例的类文件和Spring配置文件。

第三步:编写邮件发送类:SpringMail.java

在amigo.spring.config.mail包中建立发送邮件的类:SpringMail.java,该类包含了发送简单文本邮件和发送带附件的邮件的方法,该类的代码如下所示:

```java
package amigo.spring.config.mail;

import org.springframework.beans.factory.xml.XmlBeanFactory;
import org.springframework.core.io.ClassPathResource;
import org.springframework.mail.SimpleMailMessage;
import org.springframework.mail.javamail.JavaMailSender;
import org.springframework.mail.javamail.MimeMessagePreparator;
```

```java
import javax.mail.internet.MimeMessage;
import javax.mail.MessagingException;
import javax.mail.Message;
import javax.mail.internet.InternetAddress;
import javax.activation.FileDataSource;
import javax.activation.DataHandler;
import javax.mail.internet.MimeMultipart;
import javax.mail.internet.MimeBodyPart;
import javax.mail.Multipart;

import java.util.List;
import java.util.ArrayList;
import java.util.Date;
import java.util.Iterator;

/**
 * spring 的邮件发送例子.
 */
public class SpringMail {

    public static void main(String[] args) throws Exception {
        ClassPathResource res = new ClassPathResource(
                    "amigo/spring/config/mail/mail.xml");
        XmlBeanFactory factory = new XmlBeanFactory(res);
        JavaMailSender sender = (JavaMailSender) factory.getBean("mailSender");
        SpringMail springMail = new SpringMail();

        //测试发送只有文本信息的简单测试
        springMail.sendTextMail(
                sender, "xiexingxing1121@126.com",
                "xiexingxing1121@126.com", "test by amigo",
                "spring Mail 的简单测试");

        //测试发送带附件的邮件
        springMail.sendMimeMessage(sender);
    }

    /**
     * 测试发送只有文本信息的简单测试.
     * @param sender  邮件发送器
     * @param sendTo  发送的目标邮箱
     * @param sendFrom  发送的源邮箱
     * @param subject  邮件标题
     * @param mailText  邮件内容
     * @throws Exception
     */
    private void sendTextMail(JavaMailSender sender,
            String sendTo,
            String sendFrom,
            String subject,
            String mailText) throws Exception {
        SimpleMailMessage mail = new SimpleMailMessage();
        mail.setTo(sendTo);
```

```java
        mail.setFrom(sendFrom);
        mail.setSubject(subject);
        mail.setText(mailText);
        sender.send(mail);

        System.out.println("成功发送文本文件！");
    }

    /**
     * 发送带附件的邮件.
     * @param sender  邮件发送器
     * @throws Exception
     */
    private void sendMimeMessage(final JavaMailSender sender) throws Exception {
        //附件文件集合
        final List files = new ArrayList();
        MimeMessagePreparator mimeMail = new MimeMessagePreparator() {
            public void prepare(MimeMessage mimeMessage) throws MessagingException {
                mimeMessage.setRecipient(Message.RecipientType.TO,
                    new InternetAddress("xiexingxing1121@126.com"));
                mimeMessage.setFrom(new InternetAddress("xiexingxing1121@126.com"));
                mimeMessage.setSubject("Spring 发送带附件的邮件", "gb2312");

                Multipart mp = new MimeMultipart();

                //向 Multipart 添加正文
                MimeBodyPart content = new MimeBodyPart();
                content.setText("内含 spring 邮件发送的例子，请查收!");

                //向 MimeMessage 添加（Multipart 代表正文）
                mp.addBodyPart(content);

                sun.misc.BASE64Encoder enc = new sun.misc.BASE64Encoder();
                files.add("src/amigo/spring/config/mail/SpringMail.java");
                files.add("src/amigo/spring/config/mail/mail.xml");
                files.add("src/amigo/spring/config/mail/阿蜜果.xml");

                //向 Multipart 添加附件
                Iterator it = files.iterator();
                while (it.hasNext()) {
                    MimeBodyPart attachFile = new MimeBodyPart();
                    String filename = it.next().toString();
                    FileDataSource fds = new FileDataSource(filename);
                    attachFile.setDataHandler(new DataHandler(fds));

                attachFile.setFileName("=?GBK?B?"+enc.encode(fds.getName().getBytes())+"?=");
                    mp.addBodyPart(attachFile);
                }

                files.clear();

                //向 Multipart 添加 MimeMessage
                mimeMessage.setContent(mp);
```

```
                mimeMessage.setSentDate(new Date());
            }
        };

        //发送带附件的邮件
        sender.send(mimeMail);

        System.out.println("成功发送带附件邮件!");
    }
}
```

第四步：编写 Spring 配置文件：mail.xml

在amigo.spring.config.mail包中建立该实例的Spring配置文件：mail.xml，在该文件中配置一个名为mailSender的bean，它对应的类为：

　　　　org.springframework.mail.javamail.JavaMailSenderImpl

在该bean中指定邮件发送的源host、源邮箱的用户名和密码信息。该文件的内容如下所示：

```xml
<?xml version="1.0" encoding="UTF-8"?>
<beans xmlns="http://www.springframework.org/schema/beans"
    xmlns:xsi="http://www.w3.org/2001/XMLSchema-instance"
    xsi:schemaLocation="http://www.springframework.org/schema/beans     http://www.springframework.org/schema/beans/spring-beans-2.0.xsd">
    <bean id="mailSender" class="org.springframework.mail.javamail.JavaMailSenderImpl">
        <property name="host">
            <value>smtp.126.com</value>
        </property>
        <property name="javaMailProperties">
            <props>
                <prop key="mail.smtp.auth">true</prop>
                <prop key="mail.smtp.timeout">25000</prop>
            </props>
        </property>
        <property name="username">
            <value>xiexingxing1121</value>
        </property>
        <property name="password">
            <value><!--此处为邮箱密码--></value>
        </property>
    </bean>
</beans>
```

第五步：创建中文名称文件：阿蜜果.xml

最后在amigo.spring.config.mail包中创建中文名称文件：阿蜜果.xml，该文件用于测试传送中文文件名的附件是否能成功。该文件的内容如下：

```
<info>
    Hello
</info>
```

第六步：运行结果

在Eclipse中运行SpringMail类，运行结果如下所示：

……
　　org.springframework.mail.javamail.JavaMailSenderImpl - Creating new MIME message using the following mail properties: SimpleMailMessage: from=xiexingxing1121@126.com; replyTo=null; to=xiexingxing1121@126.com; cc=; bcc=; sentDate=null; subject=test by amigo; text=spring Mail 的简单测试
　　成功发送文本文件！
　　成功发送带附件邮件！

在邮箱中可以看到新收的邮件信息。

【例 18-4】定时任务配置

〖实例需求〗

定时任务在各种工程中应用广泛，例如定时去 FTP 取文件、定时进行数据表的状态更新、定时删除过时文件等。

在本实例中，讲解如何在 Spring 中进行定时任务的配置。为了简便起见，在该实例中，只是提供 Spring 定时任务的示范实例，打出简单的日志信息，重点在于演示 Spring 中定时任务如何进行配置。

〖开发过程〗

第一步：准备工作

（1）创建包目录。

读者可在springconfig工程的源码目录中建立amigo.spring.config.timer包。

（2）导入包。

在Spring中添加定时任务需要使用quartz-1.5.2.jar包，因此需要将该包复制到springconfig工程的WebContent\WEB-INF\lib目录中。

（3）创建 Spring 配置文件 timerConfig.xml。

在本实例中，使用的配置文件timerConfig.xml作为Spring的定时任务的配置文件，在springconfig工程的src目录中建立该文件。该文件初始时的内容如下所示：

```xml
<?xml version="1.0" encoding="UTF-8"?>
<beans xmlns="http://www.springframework.org/schema/beans"
       xmlns:xsi="http://www.w3.org/2001/XMLSchema-instance"
       xsi:schemaLocation="http://www.springframework.org/schema/beans    http://www.springframework.org/schema/beans/spring-beans-2.0.xsd">
</beans>
```

（4）修改 web.xml 文件。

在本实例中，需要在web.xml中配置Spring的ContextLoaderListener，修改完成后web.xml文件的内容如下所示：

```xml
<?xml version="1.0" encoding="UTF-8"?>
<web-app version="2.4"
    xmlns="http://java.sun.com/xml/ns/j2ee"
    xmlns:xsi="http://www.w3.org/2001/XMLSchema-instance"
    xsi:schemaLocation="http://java.sun.com/xml/ns/j2ee
```

```xml
        http://java.sun.com/xml/ns/j2ee/web-app_2_4.xsd">
    <welcome-file-list>
        <welcome-file>index.jsp</welcome-file>
    </welcome-file-list>

    <listener>
            <listener-class>
                    org.springframework.web.context.ContextLoaderListener
            </listener-class>
    </listener>

    <context-param>
            <param-name>contextConfigLocation</param-name>
            <param-value>
            /WEB-INF/classes/amigo/spring/config/timer/timerConfig.xml
            </param-value>
    </context-param>
</web-app>
```

第二步：创建定时任务类 PrintJobTask.java

在amigo.spring.config.timer包下建立PrintJobTask.java类，该类的print(…)方法打印信息。该类的完整代码如下：

```java
package amigo.spring.config.timer;

import java.text.SimpleDateFormat;
import java.util.Date;

/**
 * 定时打印任务.
 */
public class PrintJobTask  {
    public void print()  {
        SimpleDateFormat sdf = new SimpleDateFormat("yyyy-MM-dd HH:mm:ss");
        Date now = new Date();

        System.out.println("==========begin print==========");
        System.out.println("time:" + sdf.format(now));
        System.out.println("==========end print==========");
    }
}
```

第三步：配置 timerConfig.xml 文件

timerConfig.xml文件中需要配置工作任务，并通过触发器来启动定时任务。该文件的完整内容如下所示：

```xml
<?xml version="1.0" encoding="UTF-8"?>
<beans xmlns="http://www.springframework.org/schema/beans"
       xmlns:xsi="http://www.w3.org/2001/XMLSchema-instance"
       xsi:schemaLocation="http://www.springframework.org/schema/beans
http://www.springframework.org/schema/beans/spring-beans-2.0.xsd">
```

```xml
<!-- begin 定时打印任务配置 -->
<bean id="printJobTask" class="amigo.spring.config.timer.PrintJobTask" />
<bean id="printJob" class="org.springframework.scheduling.quartz.MethodInvokingJobDetailFactoryBean">
    <property name="targetObject">
        <ref bean="printJobTask"/>
    </property>
    <property name="targetMethod">
        <value>print</value>
    </property>
</bean>

<bean id="printJobTaskTrigger" class="org.springframework.scheduling.quartz.CronTriggerBean">
    <property name="jobDetail">
        <ref bean="printJob"/>
    </property>
    <property name="cronExpression">
        <!-- "0 0 22 * * ?"表示晚上 10 点执行-->
        <value>0 0 22 * * ?</value>
    </property>
</bean>

<bean id="doScheduler" class="org.springframework.scheduling.quartz.SchedulerFactoryBean">
    <property name="triggers">
        <list>
            <ref local="printJobTaskTrigger"/>
        </list>
    </property>
</bean>
<!-- end 定时打印任务配置 -->
</beans>
```

cronExpression的值的配置分为7段，字段顺序如表18-3所示。

表18-3　cronExpression 的值的配置

字段顺序	允许值	允许的特殊字符
秒	0-59	, - * /
分	0-59	, - * /
小时	0-23	, - * /
日期	1-31	, - * ? / L W C
月份	1-12 或者 JAN-DEC	, - * /
星期	1-7 或者 SUN-SAT	, - * ? / L C #
年（可选）	留空, 1970-2099	, - * /

下面举一个 cronExpression 配置的例子：

0 0 22 * * ?：表示晚上 10 点执行

第四步：运行结果

在 Eclipse 中启动该工程，则在晚上 10 点时将会打出如下信息：

==========begin print==========
time=2008-9-13 22:00:00
==========end print==========

小结

　　在进行项目开发时，常常需要配置各种数据源，其中 JDBC 数据源、C3P0、DBCP 数据源比较常见。JDBC 的数据源配置（使用的是 MySQL 数据库）举例如下所示：

```
<bean id="dataSource"
    class="org.springframework.jdbc.datasource.DriverManagerDataSource">
    <property name="driverClassName">
        <value>com.mysql.jdbc.Driver</value>
    </property>
    <property name="url">
        <value>jdbc:mysql://localhost/springtest</value>
    </property>
    <property name="username">
        <value>root</value>
    </property>
    <property name="password">
        <value>root</value>
    </property>
</bean>
```

JDBC 数据源对应的驱动类为：

org.springframework.jdbc.datasource.DriverManagerDataSourc

　　其中 driverClassName 属性用于设置数据库驱动，MySQL 数据库对应为 com.mysql.jdbc.Driver，url 表示数据库的连接字符串，username 表示数据库的用户名，password 表示数据库的密码。

　　在配置 C3P0 数据源时，首先需要将 C3P0 的 jar 包 c3p0-x.jar 拷贝到工程中。C3P0 的数据源配置参考如下：

```
<bean id="dataSource"
    class="com.mchange.v2.c3p0.ComboPooledDataSource">
    <property name="driverClass">
        <value>com.mysql.jdbc.Driver</value>
    </property>
    <property name="jdbcUrl">
        <value>jdbc:mysql://localhost/springtest</value>
    </property>
    <property name="user">
        <value>root</value>
    </property>
    <property name="password">
        <value>root</value>
    </property>
    <property name="maxPoolSize">
        <value>80</value>
    </property>
    <property name="minPoolSize">
        <value>1</value>
```

```xml
        </property>
        <property name="initialPoolSize">
            <value>1</value>
        </property>
        <property name="maxIdleTime">
            <value>20</value>
        </property>
    </bean>
```

C3P0 数据源对应的类为：

`com.mchange.v2.c3p0.ComboPooledDataSource`

driverClass 属性表示数据库驱动类，jdbcUrl 表示数据库连接串，user 表示数据库名称，password 表示数据库密码，maxPoolSize 表示最大连接池大小，minPoolSize 表示最小连接池大小，initialPoolSize 表示初始时连接池大小。

若要配置 DBCP 数据源，首先需要将 DBCP 的 jar 包 commons-dbcp.jar 拷贝到工程中，DBCP 的数据库配置如下所示：

```xml
<bean id="dataSource"
    class="org.apache.commons.dbcp.BasicDataSource">
    <property name="driverClassName">
        <value>com.mysql.jdbc.Driver</value>
    </property>
    <property name="url">
        <value>jdbc:mysql://localhost/springtest</value>
    </property>
    <property name="username">
        <value>root</value>
    </property>
    <property name="password">
        <value>root</value>
    </property>
    <property name="maxActive">
        <value>2</value>
    </property>
</bean>
```

对应的数据源类为：

`org.apache.commons.dbcp.BasicDataSource`

其属性与 JDBC 数据源类似。

Spring 提供了 org.springframework.transaction 包来解决事务问题。Spring 对 Hibernate Session 和 JDBC Connection 等独立的事务策略进行了抽象，提供了统一的 PlatformTransactionManager 接口。Spring 提供了该接口的若干实现，其中 HibernateTransactionManager 就是为 Hibernate 提供的一种事务实现。

Spring 常用的事务属性包括：

- 传播策略：以"PROPAGATION_"开头，只可为 PROPAGATION_REQUIRED、PROPAGATION_SUPPORTS、PROPAGATION_MANDATORY、PROPAGATION_REQUIRES_NEW、PROPAGATION_NOT_SUPPORTED、PROPAGATION_NEVER 和 PROPAGATION_NESTED。
- 隔离性：以"ISOLATION_"开头，值可为 ISOLATION_DEFAULT、ISOLATION_READ_UNCOMMITTED、ISOLATION_READ_COMMITTED、ISOLATION_

REPEATABLE_READ 和 ISOLATION_SERIALIZABLE；
- 超时：以"TIMEOUT_"开头，它表示事务的有效时限，默认时，使用事务系统的超时设置，即 TIMEOUT_DEFAULT = -1。TIMEOUT_30 表示事务的有效时限为 30s。
- 只读：为 readOnly，用于将事务标记为只读事务。

在 Spring 1.x 中，可这样进行事务配置：

```xml
<?xml version="1.0" encoding="UTF-8"?>
<beans xmlns="http://www.springframework.org/schema/beans"
    xmlns:xsi="http://www.w3.org/2001/XMLSchema-instance"
    xsi:schemaLocation="http://www.springframework.org/schema/beans
http://www.springframework.org/schema/beans/spring-beans-2.0.xsd">

    <!-- jdbc 数据源的配置 -->
    <bean id="dataSource"
        class="org.springframework.jdbc.datasource.DriverManagerDataSource">
        ……
    </bean>

    <!--定义了 Hibernate 的 SessionFactory -->
    <bean id="sessionFactory" class="org.springframework.orm.hibernate3.LocalSessionFactoryBean">
        <property name="dataSource">
            <ref local="dataSource" />
        </property>
        <property name="mappingResources">
            <list>
                <!—加载的 Hibernate 配置文件-->
            </list>
        </property>
        <property name="hibernateProperties">
            <props>
                ……
            </props>
        </property>
    </bean>

    <bean id="transactionManager"
        class="org.springframework.orm.hibernate3.HibernateTransactionManager">
        <property name="sessionFactory" ref="sessionFactory" />
    </bean>

    <bean id="transactionInterceptor"
        class="org.springframework.transaction.interceptor.TransactionInterceptor">
        <!-- 事务拦截器 bean 需要依赖注入一个事务管理器 -->
        <property name="transactionManager" ref="transactionManager" />
        <property name="transactionAttributes">
            <props>
                <prop key="save*">PROPAGATION_REQUIRED</prop>
                …
            </props>
        </property>
    </bean>
```

```xml
<!-- 定义BeanNameAutoProxyCreator-->
<bean class="org.springframework.aop.framework.autoproxy.BeanNameAutoProxyCreator">
    <!-- 指定对满足哪些bean name 的bean 自动生成业务代理 -->
    <property name="beanNames">
        <list>
            <!-- 需要自动创建事务代理的bean-->
        </list>
    </property>
    <!-- 下面定义BeanNameAutoProxyCreator 所需的事务拦截器-->
    <property name="interceptorNames">
        <list>
            <value>transactionInterceptor</value>
        </list>
    </property>
</bean>
</beans>
```

在 Spring 2 中，通过使用 tx:advice 简化了事务配置，参考配置如下所示：

```xml
<?xml version="1.0" encoding="UTF-8"?>
<beans xmlns="http://www.springframework.org/schema/beans"
    xmlns:xsi="http://www.w3.org/2001/XMLSchema-instance"
    xmlns:aop="http://www.springframework.org/schema/aop"
    xmlns:tx="http://www.springframework.org/schema/tx"
    xsi:schemaLocation="http://www.springframework.org/schema/beans
http://www.springframework.org/schema/beans/spring-beans-2.0.xsd
    http://www.springframework.org/schema/aop
http://www.springframework.org/schema/aop/spring-aop-2.0.xsd
    http://www.springframework.org/schema/tx
http://www.springframework.org/schema/tx/spring-tx-2.0.xsd"
    default-autowire="byName" default-lazy-init="true">
    <!--数据源和sessionFactory 的配置与第三步一样，故此省略-->
    <bean id="transactionManager"
        class="org.springframework.orm.hibernate3.HibernateTransactionManager">
        <property name="sessionFactory" ref="sessionFactory" />
    </bean>

    <tx:annotation-driven/>
    <aop:aspectj-autoproxy/>

    <aop:config proxy-target-class="true">
        <aop:advisor    pointcut="execution(*   amigo.spring.config.transaction..*Manager.*(..))"
advice-ref="txAdvice"/>
    </aop:config>

    <tx:advice id="txAdvice">
        <tx:attributes>
            <tx:method name="get*" read-only="true"/>
            <tx:method name="find*" read-only="true"/>
            <tx:method name="*"/>
        </tx:attributes>
    </tx:advice>
</beans>
```

Java SE 提供了 JavaMail API，它能够构建邮件和消息应用。Spring 2 提供了邮件服务抽象，使得开发人员不需要处理底层邮件系统的具体细节，也不用管理底层的 Transport 等资源，从而使得代码简单化。在使用 Spring 配置邮件服务时，首先需要将 JavaMail 的 jar 包 mail.jar 拷贝到工程中。邮件发送的参考配置如下：

```xml
<bean id="mailSender" class="org.springframework.mail.javamail.JavaMailSenderImpl">
    <property name="host">
        <value>smtp.126.com</value>
    </property>
    <property name="javaMailProperties">
        <props>
            <prop key="mail.smtp.auth">true</prop>
            <prop key="mail.smtp.timeout">25000</prop>
        </props>
    </property>
    <property name="username">
        <value>xiexingxing1121</value>
    </property>
    <property name="password">
        <value><!--此处为邮箱密码--></value>
    </property>
</bean>
```

mailSender 这个 bean 可获得用于发送邮件的 JavaMailSender 对象，开发人员可在此基础上进行操作。

定时任务在各种工程中应用广泛，例如定时去 FTP 取文件、定时进行数据表的状态更新、定时删除过时文件等。定时任务需要使用 quartz-x.jar 包，因此需要将该 jar 包拷贝到工程中。定时任务的参考配置如下所示：

```xml
<bean id="printJobTask" class="amigo.spring.config.timer.PrintJobTask" />
<bean id="printJob"
        class="org.springframework.scheduling.quartz.MethodInvokingJobDetailFactoryBean">
    <property name="targetObject">
        <ref bean="printJobTask"/>
    </property>
    <property name="targetMethod">
        <value>print</value>
    </property>
</bean>

<bean id="printJobTaskTrigger"
        class="org.springframework.scheduling.quartz.CronTriggerBean">
    <property name="jobDetail">
        <ref bean="printJob"/>
    </property>
    <property name="cronExpression">
        <!-- "0 0 22 * * ?"表示晚上 10 点执行-->
        <value>0 0 22 * * ?</value>
    </property>
</bean>

<bean id="doScheduler"
```

```xml
              class="org.springframework.scheduling.quartz.SchedulerFactoryBean">
    <property name="triggers">
        <list>
            <ref local="printJobTaskTrigger"/>
        </list>
    </property>
</bean>
```

在进行定时任务配置时,在创建触发 bean 时,cronExpression 可设置触发事件的时间,例如设置为 0 0 22 * * ?表示晚上 10 点执行。

第 5 篇 实战篇

第 19 章 Struts、Hibernate 和 Spring 整合

【本章导读语】

Struts 2 作为 MVC2 的 Web 框架，自推出以来不断受到开发者的喜爱，得到广泛的应用。Spring 在某些方面方便了 Struts 的开发。Hibernate 作为对象持久化的框架，能显著地提高在数据库操作层软件开发的效率与生产力。这 3 种流行框架的整合应用，可以发挥各自的优势，高效率地开发出 Web 系统。

本章通过一个用户注册的实例讲解这三者如何进行整合。本章首先只使用 Struts2 完成用户注册，而后的实例中加入 Hibernate，持久层的数据库操作交给 Hibernate 去完成。最后将 Spring 集成进来，完成了 Struts+Hibernate+Spring 的整合。

【例 19-1】使用 Struts 实现用户注册

〖实例需求〗

本实例采用 Struts 完成 MVC 框架中视图和控制层之间的代码，包括 JSP 页面的编写和 Action 的实现。

〖开发过程〗

第一步：建立工程

读者可以参考前几章建立 Web 工程的方法在 Eclipse 中新建一个名为 ssh 的动态 Web 工程，并将 Struts 所需的 jar 包导入到 WEB-INF/lib 目录中，接着在 src 目录中建立 amigo.ssh 包。最后在 web.xml 中配置 Struts 2 的 FilterDispatcher。

操作完成后工程的结构如图 19-1 所示。

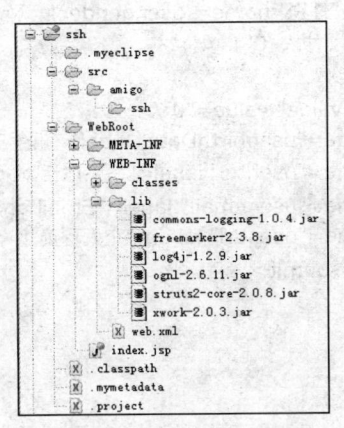

图 19-1 工程的目录结构

此时 web.xml 文件的内容如下所示：

```xml
<?xml version="1.0" encoding="UTF-8"?>
<web-app version="2.4"
    xmlns="http://java.sun.com/xml/ns/j2ee"
    xmlns:xsi="http://www.w3.org/2001/XMLSchema-instance"
    xsi:schemaLocation="http://java.sun.com/xml/ns/j2ee
    http://java.sun.com/xml/ns/j2ee/web-app_2_4.xsd">
    <filter>
        <filter-name>struts2</filter-name>
        <filter-class>org.apache.struts2.dispatcher.FilterDispatcher</filter-class>
    </filter>

    <filter-mapping>
        <filter-name>struts2</filter-name>
        <url-pattern>/*</url-pattern>
    </filter-mapping>

    <welcome-file-list>
        <welcome-file>index.jsp</welcome-file>
    </welcome-file-list>
</web-app>
```

第二步：编写注册界面：reg.jsp

在 WebRoot 目录中建立 reg.jsp 页面，该页面用于供用户填写注册信息，包括用户名、密码、性别和出生日期等信息，该页面的属性与 Action 的 user 对象的属性对应，该页面的代码如下所示：

```jsp
<%@ page contentType="text/html; charset=UTF-8" %>
<%@ taglib prefix="s" uri="/struts-tags" %>

<html>
    <head>
        <title>注册用户</title>
        <meta http-equiv="Content-Type" content="text/html; charset=UTF-8"/>
    </head>
    <body>
        <s:form action="reg">
            <s:textfield name="user.username" label="用户名"></s:textfield>
            <s:password name="user.password" label="密码"></s:password>
            <s:select label="性别" name="user.gender"
                list="#{'1' : '男', '0' : '女'}"
                listKey="key"
                listValue="value" value="0"/>
            <s:textfield name="user.birthDate" label="出生日期"></s:textfield>
            <s:textfield name="user.tel" label="联系电话"></s:textfield>
            <s:textfield name="user.email" label="Email"></s:textfield>
            <s:textfield name="user.url" label="个人首页"></s:textfield>
            <s:submit></s:submit>
        </s:form>
    </body>
</html>
```

第三步：编写注册成功和失败界面：success.jsp 和 error.jsp

在 WebRoot 目录下建立注册成功和失败的界面 success.jsp 和 error.jsp，这两个页面只是简单地输出"注册成功"和"注册失败"的信息，内容不再详述。

第四步：编写用户信息的表单类：UserForm.java

在 amigo.ssh 包中建立用户信息的表单类 UserForm.java，该类包含的属性如下所示：

```java
package amigo.ssh;

import java.util.Date;

/**
 * 用户信息的 POJO 对象.
 */
public class UserForm {
    /** 用户名. */
    private String username;

    /** 密码. */
    private String password;

    /** 性别*/
    private int gender;

    /** 出生日期. */
    private Date birthDate;

    /** 联系电话.*/
    private String tel;

    /** Email. */
    private String email;

    /** 个人首页.*/
    private String url;

    // 省略各属性的 getter/setter 方法
}
```

第五步：编写注册的 Action 类：RegAction.java

在 amigo.ssh 包中建立注册的 Action 类 RegAction.java，它接收表单中的信息，并调用业务逻辑类保存注册信息，成功后跳转到成功界面。该类的代码如下所示：

```java
package amigo.ssh;

import com.opensymphony.xwork2.ActionSupport;

/**
 * 注册的业务逻辑类.
 */
public class RegAction extends ActionSupport {
```

```java
/** 用户表单对象. */
private UserForm user;

/** 用户管理的业务逻辑类. */
private UserManager userManager;

// user 的 getter/setter 方法和 userManager 的 setter 方法省略

public String execute() {
    try {
        // 设置业务逻辑实现类
        this.setUserManager(new UserManagerImpl());
        // 用户注册
        userManager.userReg(user);
        return this.SUCCESS;
    } catch(Exception ex) {
        ex.printStackTrace();
        return this.ERROR;
    }
}
```

第六步：编写业务逻辑接口和实现类

在 amigo.ssh 目录中建立业务逻辑接口和实现类 UserManager.java 和 UserManagerImpl.java 类，在这里并不提供注册的详细实现，在后面的实例中将实现注册方法。UserManager.java 接口定义了一个用户注册的方法 userReg(...)，该方法传入用户表单，该类的代码如下所示：

```java
package amigo.ssh;

/**
 * 用户注册的业务逻辑接口类.
 */
public interface UserManager {
    /**
     * 用户注册.
     * @param form 用户表单
     */
    public void userReg(UserForm form) throws Exception ;
}
```

UserManagerImpl.java 类实现 UserManager.java 接口，该类的实现将会在后续的实例中给出，该类的代码如下所示：

```java
package amigo.ssh;

/**
 * 用户注册的业务逻辑实现类.
 */
public class UserManagerImpl implements UserManager {

    public void userReg(UserForm form) throws Exception {
        // 在后续的整合中将会实现
    }
}
```

第七步：编写验证文件：RegAction-validation.xml

在注册用户信息的表单中，用户名、密码都是非空字段，需要进行验证，而且出生日期、Email、个人首页等也需要进行输入是否规则的验证，在此，可以利用 Struts 提供的强大的验证机制，在 amigo.ssh 包下建立 RegAction.java 的验证文件 RegAction-validation.xml，该文件的内容如下所示：

```xml
<?xml version="1.0" encoding="GBK"?>
<!DOCTYPE validators PUBLIC "-//OpenSymphony Group//XWork Validator 1.0.2//EN"
    "http://www.opensymphony.com/xwork/xwork-validator-1.0.2.dtd">

<validators>
    <!-- 添加对用户名的校验 -->
    <field name="user.username">
        <field-validator type="requiredstring">
            <param name="trim">true</param>
            <message>${getText("user.username.requried")}</message>
            <!-- message>用户名不能为空</message-->
        </field-validator>
        <field-validator type="regex">
            <param name="expression"><![CDATA[(\w{5,50})]]></param>
            <message>${getText("user.username.regex")}</message>
        </field-validator>
    </field>

    <!-- 添加对密码的校验 -->
    <field name="user.password">
        <field-validator type="requiredstring">
            <param name="trim">true</param>
            <message>${getText("user.password.requried")}</message>
        </field-validator>
        <field-validator type="regex">
            <param name="expression"><![CDATA[(\w{5,50})]]></param>
            <message>${getText("user.password.regex")}</message>
        </field-validator>
    </field>

    <!-- 添加对出生日期的校验 -->
    <field name="user.birthDate">
        <field-validator type="date">
            <param name="min">1850-01-01</param>
            <param name="max">2008-7-20</param>
            <message>${getText("user.birthDate")}</message>
        </field-validator>
    </field>

    <!-- 添加对 Email 的校验 -->
    <field name="user.email">
        <field-validator type="email">
            <message>${getText("user.email")}</message>
        </field-validator>
    </field>
```

```xml
        <!-- 添加对个人首页的校验 -->
        <field name="user.url">
            <field-validator type="url">
                <message>${getText("user.url")}</message>
            </field-validator>
        </field>
</validators>
```

第八步：编写验证信息的国际化文件

在 src 目录中建立验证信息国际化的属性文件，该文件的内容如下：

```
user.username.requried=用户名不能为空
user.username.regex=用户名输入不合法，必须为长度为 5~50 之间的字母或数字
user.password.requried=密码不能为空
user.password.regex=密码输入不合法，必须为长度为 5~50 之间的字母或数字
user.birthDate=出生日期输入不合法
user.email=Email 地址输入不合法
user.url=个人首页输入不合法
```

在 src 目录中复制前面 struts 验证章节的批处理文件 code.bat，运行该文件后，可在 src 目录下建立经过编码后的验证文件 validationMessages_zh_CN.properties，该文件的内容如下所示：

```
user.username.requried=\u7528\u6237\u540d\u4e0d\u80fd\u4e3a\u7a7a
user.username.regex=\u7528\u6237\u540d\u8f93\u5165\u4e0d\u5408\u6cd5\uff0c\u5fc5\u987b\u4e3a\u957f\u5ea6\u4e3a5~50\u4e4b\u95f4\u7684\u5b57\u6bcd\u6216\u6570\u5b57
user.password.requried=\u5bc6\u7801\u4e0d\u80fd\u4e3a\u7a7a
user.password.regex=\u5bc6\u7801\u8f93\u5165\u4e0d\u5408\u6cd5\uff0c\u5fc5\u987b\u4e3a\u957f\u5ea6\u4e3a5~50\u4e4b\u95f4\u7684\u5b57\u6bcd\u6216\u6570\u5b57
user.birthDate=\u51fa\u751f\u65e5\u671f\u8f93\u5165\u4e0d\u5408\u6cd5
user.email=Email\u5730\u5740\u8f93\u5165\u4e0d\u5408\u6cd5
user.url=\u4e2a\u4eba\u9996\u9875\u8f93\u5165\u4e0d\u5408\u6cd5
```

第九步：配置 struts.xml

最后还需要配置 struts 2 的配置文件 struts.xml。读者可在 src 目录中建立 struts.xml 文件，该文件配置了 RegAction 这个 Action，并指定了其验证失败以及注册成功和失败的走向，还指定了 struts 的国际化文件的基本名称为 validationMessages。该文件的内容如下所示：

```xml
<!DOCTYPE struts PUBLIC
    "-//Apache Software Foundation//DTD Struts Configuration 2.0//EN"
    "http://struts.apache.org/dtds/struts-2.0.dtd">

<struts>
    <!-- 指定国际化配置文件 -->
    <constant name="struts.custom.i18n.resources" value="validationMessages"/>
    <constant name="struts.i18n.encoding" value="GBK"/>

    <include file="struts-default.xml"/>
    <package name="amigo" extends="struts-default">
        <!-- 配置注册用户的 Action -->
        <action name="reg"  class="amigo.ssh.RegAction">
            <result name="input">/reg.jsp</result>
            <result name="success">/success.jsp</result>
            <result name="error">/error.jsp</result>
        </action>
    </package>
</struts>
```

第十步：运行结果

在 Eclipse 中部署 ssh 工程后，接着在浏览器中输入地址：http://localhost:8899/ssh/reg.jsp 用户可在注册界面输入注册信息，界面如图 19-2 所示。

图 19-2　注册界面运行结果

填写完信息后，单击 Submit 按钮，将会将信息提交到 RegAction，并跳转到注册成功界面。

【例 19-2】在 Struts 项目中整合 Hibernate

〖实例需求〗

Hibernate 主要用来完成与数据库有关的操作，在【例 19-1】中，并没有实现将用户输入的注册信息插入到数据库中，该本实例中，将使用 Hibernate 实现数据库操作，完成用户信息的插入。

〖开发过程〗

第一步：将 Hibernate 的 jar 包复制到 WEB-INF/lib 目录中

因为在该实例中需要将 Hibernate 集成进去，所以首先需要将 Hibernate 的 jar 包复制到工程的 WEB-INF/lib 目录中，加入完毕后 WEB-INF/lib 目录中的 jar 包如图 19-3 所示。

图 19-3　加入了 Hibernate 的 jar 包后的 lib 列表

第二步：编写数据操作的 Dao 接口和实现类

建立 amigo.ssh.dao 包，在该文件中建立 Hibernate 数据操作的 Dao 接口类和实现类：BaseDao.java 和 BaseDaoImpl.java。

接口类 BaseDao.java 定义了对数据的增、删、改和查方法，该类的代码如下所示：

```java
package amigo.ssh.dao;

import java.io.Serializable;
import java.util.List;

import org.hibernate.HibernateException;

/**
 * Hibernate 数据库操作接口.
 */
public interface BaseDao {
    /**
     * 删除传入的对象
     * @param obj 需删除的对象
     * @throws HibernateException
     */
    public void deleteObject(Object obj) throws HibernateException;

    /**
     * 根据主键和类信息删除某 POJO 对象
     * @param class1 对象所属的 POJO 类
     * @param serializable 主键
     * @throws HibernateException
     */
    public void deleteObject(Class class1, Serializable serializable) throws HibernateException;

    /**
     * 更新某个对象
     * @param obj 需更新的对象
     * @throws HibernateException
     */
    public void updateObject(Object obj) throws HibernateException;

    /**
     * 保存某个对象
     * @param obj 需保存的对象
     * @throws HibernateException
     */
    public void saveObject(Object obj) throws HibernateException;

    /**
     * 获得某个对象
     * @param class1
     * @param serializable
     * @throws HibernateException
     */
```

```java
    public Object getObject(Class class1, Serializable serializable) throws HibernateException;

    /**
     * 根据查询语句获得满足该查询条件的对象列表
     * @param hsql hql 语句
     * @return 查询出的对象列表
     */
    public List hqlQuery(String hsql) throws HibernateException;

    /**
     * 根据查询语句获得满足该查询条件的对象列表
     * @param hsql: hql 语句
     * @param obj: 参数信息(类型可为 Map 或者 Object[])
     * @return 对象列表
     */
    public List hqlQuery(String hsql, Object obj) throws HibernateException;

    public Session getSession();

        public void setSession(Session session);
}
```

其实现类 BaseDaoImpl.java 类调用 Hibernate 的方法实现了数据的增、删、改和查功能，该类的代码如下所示：

```java
package amigo.ssh.dao;

import java.io.Serializable;
import java.util.List;
import java.util.Map;

import org.hibernate.HibernateException;
import org.hibernate.Session;

/**
 * Hibernate 数据库操作实现类.
 */
public class BaseDaoImpl implements BaseDao {
    protected Session session;

    public void deleteObject(Object obj) throws HibernateException {
        session.delete(obj);
    }

    public void deleteObject(Class class1,
            Serializable serializable) throws HibernateException {
        session.delete(this.getObject(class1, serializable));
    }

    public void updateObject(Object obj) throws HibernateException {
        session.update(obj);
        return;
    }
```

```java
    public void saveObject(Object obj) throws HibernateException {
        session.save(obj);
    }

    public Object getObject(Class class1,
            Serializable serializable) throws HibernateException {
        return session.get(class1, serializable);
    }

    public List hqlQuery(String hsql) throws HibernateException {
        return query(hsql, null);
    }

    public List hqlQuery(String hsql, Object obj) throws HibernateException {
        return query(hsql, obj);
    }

    private List query(String sql, Object obj) throws HibernateException {
        org.hibernate.Query query = session.createQuery(sql);

        if (obj != null) {
            if (obj instanceof Map) {
                String as[] = query.getNamedParameters();
                for (int k1 = 0; k1 < as.length; k1++)
                    query.setParameter(as[k1], ((Map) obj).get(as[k1]));

            } else if (obj instanceof Object[]) {
                for (int i1 = 0; i1 < ((Object[]) obj).length; i1++)
                    query.setParameter(i1, ((Object[]) obj)[i1]);

            } else {
                query.setParameter(0, obj);
            }
        }

        return query.list();
    }

    public Session getSession() {
        return session;
    }

    public void setSession(Session session) {
        this.session = session;
    }
}
```

第三步：编写数据库脚本

要将注册的用户信息存储起来，需要将其保存到数据库中。因此首先需要建立数据库和用户信息表，开发人员可在 amigo.ssh.dao 包下建立 MySQL 的数据库脚本文件 scripts.sql，该文件创建了数据库 ssh，并在其下建立了用户表 tbl_user，该文件的内容如下所示：

```sql
CREATE DATABASE 'ssh';
USE 'ssh';

CREATE TABLE 'tbl_user' (
  'username' varchar(50) NOT NULL COMMENT '用户名',
  'password' varchar(50) NOT NULL COMMENT '密码',
  'gender' int(11) default '0' COMMENT '性别',
  'birthDate' date default NULL COMMENT '出生日期',
  'tel' varchar(255) default NULL COMMENT '联系电话',
  'email' varchar(255) default NULL COMMENT 'Email',
  'url' varchar(255) default NULL COMMENT '个人首页',
  PRIMARY KEY  ('username')
) ENGINE=InnoDB DEFAULT CHARSET=gb2312 COMMENT='用户信息表';
```

在 MySQL 中通过这个数据库脚本创建 ssh 数据库，并在该数据库下建立用户信息表 tbl_user。

第四步：建立 tbl_user 表的 Hibernate 映射文件

在 amigo.ssh.dao 包中建立 tbl_user 表的 POJO 文件 User.java 和 Hibernate 映射文件 User.hbm.xml，User.java 文件与【例 19-1】中的 UserForm.java 类似，该文件的内容如下所示：

```java
package amigo.ssh.dao;

import java.io.Serializable;
import java.util.Date;

/**
 * 用户信息表对应的 POJO 对象.
 */
public class User implements Serializable {
    private static final long serialVersionUID = 1L;

    /** 用户名. */
    private String username;

    // 省略其余属性，与 UserForm.java 相同

    // 省略各属性的 getter/setter 方法
}
```

tbl_user 表的 Hibernate 映射文件 User.hbm.xml 如下所示：

```xml
<?xml version="1.0" encoding='UTF-8'?>
<!DOCTYPE hibernate-mapping PUBLIC
                    "-//Hibernate/Hibernate Mapping DTD 3.0//EN"
                    "http://hibernate.sourceforge.net/hibernate-mapping-3.0.dtd" >

<hibernate-mapping package="amigo.ssh.dao">
    <class name="User" table="tbl_user">
        <id name="username" column="username" type="java.lang.String" length="50">
            <generator class="assigned"/>
        </id>
        <property name="password" column="password" type="java.lang.String"  not-null="true" length="50"/>
        <property name="gender" column="gender" length="2" />
        <property name="birthDate" column="birthDate" type="java.util.Date" />
```

```xml
        <property name="tel" column="tel" type="java.lang.String" length="255"/>
        <property name="email" column="email" type="java.lang.String" length="255"/>
        <property name="url" column="url" type="java.lang.String" length="255"/>
    </class>
</hibernate-mapping>
```

第五步：建立 Hibernate 配置文件 hibernate.cfg.xml

接下来需要在 src 目录中建立 Hibernate 的配置文件 hibernate.cfg.xml，该文件中将映射文件 User.hbm.xml 配置进来，并配置连接的数据库是 ssh，该文件的信息如下所示：

```xml
......
<hibernate-configuration>
    <session-factory>
        <!-- 在后台打印 sql 语句 -->
        <property name="show_sql">true</property>
        <!-- 指定 sql 的本地方言，根据连接的数据库确定-->
        <property name="dialect">org.hibernate.dialect.MySQLDialect</property>
        <!-- 指定 jdbc url -->
        <property name="connection.url">jdbc:mysql://localhost:3306/ssh</property>
        <!-- 数据库的用户名 -->
        <property name="connection.username">root</property>
        <!-- 数据库的密码 -->
        <property name="connection.password">root</property>
        <!-- 设定数据库的驱动类，MySql 的驱动 jar 包为 mysql-connector-java-5.0.4-bin.jar，驱动类为 com.mysql.jdbc.Driver -->
        <property name="connection.driver_class">com.mysql.jdbc.Driver</property>

        <!--指定 0 到多个 hbm.xml 映射文件-->
        <mapping resource="amigo/ssh/dao/User.hbm.xml" />
    </session-factory>
</hibernate-configuration>
```

第六步：编写 Session 工厂类：HibernateSessionFactory.java

在 amigo.ssh.dao 包中建立 Hibernate 的 Session 工厂类 HibernateSessionFactory.java，该类提供打开和关闭 Session 的方法，该类的内容如下所示：

```java
......
public class HibernateSessionFactory {
    public static Logger log = (Logger)Logger.getLogger(HibernateSessionFactory.class);

    private static String CONFIG_FILE_LOCATION = "/hibernate.cfg.xml";

    /** Holds a single instance of Session */
    private static final ThreadLocal threadLocal = new ThreadLocal();

    /** The single instance of hibernate configuration */
    private static final Configuration cfg = new Configuration();

    /** The single instance of hibernate SessionFactory */
    private static SessionFactory sessionFactory;
```

```java
/**
 * 返回 ThreadLocal 中的 Session 实例.
 * 采用懒加载的方式
 * @return Session
 * @throws HibernateException
 */
public static Session currentSession() throws HibernateException {
    Session session = (Session) threadLocal.get();

    if(session==null || session.isOpen()==false){
        if (sessionFactory == null) {
            try {
                cfg.configure(CONFIG_FILE_LOCATION);
                sessionFactory = cfg.buildSessionFactory();
            } catch (Exception e) {
e.printStackTrace();
                log.error("Error Creating SessionFactory %%%%"+ session.isOpen());
            }
        }
        session = sessionFactory.openSession();
        threadLocal.set(session);
    }

    return session;
}

/**
 * 关闭 session.
 * @throws HibernateException
 */
public static void closeSession() throws HibernateException {
    Session session = (Session) threadLocal.get();
    threadLocal.set(null);

    if (session != null) {
        session.close();
    }
}

private HibernateSessionFactory() {
}
}
```

第七步：修改业务逻辑实现类 UserManagerImpl.java

在【例 19-1】中，并没有实现业务逻辑实现类 UserManagerImpl.java，在本实例中，需要实现该类，实现将用户表单中的信息保存到数据库的 tbl_user 表中。

该类的代码如下所示：

```java
package amigo.ssh;

import org.apache.commons.beanutils.BeanUtils;
import org.hibernate.Session;
```

```java
import org.hibernate.Transaction;

import amigo.ssh.dao.BaseDao;
import amigo.ssh.dao.BaseDaoImpl;
import amigo.ssh.dao.HibernateSessionFactory;
import amigo.ssh.dao.User;

/**
 * 用户注册的业务逻辑实现类.
 */
public class UserManagerImpl implements UserManager {

    private BaseDao dao = null;

    private Session session = null;

    public UserManagerImpl()  {
        dao = new BaseDaoImpl();
    }

    public void userReg(UserForm form) throws Exception  {
        session = HibernateSessionFactory.currentSession();
        dao.setSession(session);
        // 获得事务
        Transaction ts = session.beginTransaction();

        // 构造 User 对象
        User user = new User();
        BeanUtils.copyProperties(user, form);

        // 保存 user 对象
        dao.saveObject(user);

        // 提交事务
        ts.commit();

        // 关闭 Session
        HibernateSessionFactory.closeSession();
    }
}
```

从代码中可以看出，在 UserManagerImpl.java 的构造函数中，需要实例化 dao 对象。而在用户注册方法 userReg(…)中，首先通过 HibernateSessionFactory 的 currentSession()方法获得当前的 Session，而后将该 Session 设置到 dao 对象中，而后开始事务、保存 user 对象、提交事务，最后关闭 Session。

第八步：运行结果

工程部署完成后，在浏览器中输入地址：
http://localhost:8899/ssh/reg.jsp
在运行前，tbl_user 表中的记录为空。

填写图 19-4 所示的注册信息后，单击 Submit 按钮提交表单，数据将会保存到数据库 ssh 的 tbl_user 表中。

图 19-4 注册界面

单击 Submit 按钮后，将数据提交到 Action，而后通过 Hibernate 将数据保存到 tbl_user 表中，并跳转到操作成功界面，此时 ssh 数据库中 tbl_user 表的内容如图 19-5 所示。

图 19-5 注册完成后 tbl_user 表的数据

【例 19-3】Struts+Hibernate 中整合 Spring

〖实例需求〗

前面的两个实例实现了 Struts 和 Hibernate 的集成，在本实例中读者将学习如何将 Spring 集成到 Struts+Hibernate 的项目中去。

在本实例中，Spring 主要完成数据库事务的管理、业务逻辑类的管理等。在上面的实例中，当需要使用构造某接口的实例时，需要将实现类也引入到类中，造成了紧耦合，而 Spring 很好地解决了这个问题，将具体由哪个实现类实现接口改为配置在 Spring 配置文件中。在进行数据库操作时，【例 19-2】中需要类来进行事务管理，加入 Spring 后，事务的管理将交给 Spring 去管理。

〖开发过程〗

第一步：将 Spring 的 jar 包复制到 WEB-INF/lib 目录下

因为在该实例中需要将 Spring 集成进去，所以首先需要将 Spring 的 jar 包及其相关的 jar 包复制到工程的 WEB-INF/lib 目录中，添加完成后 lib 目录中的 jar 包如图 19-6 所示。

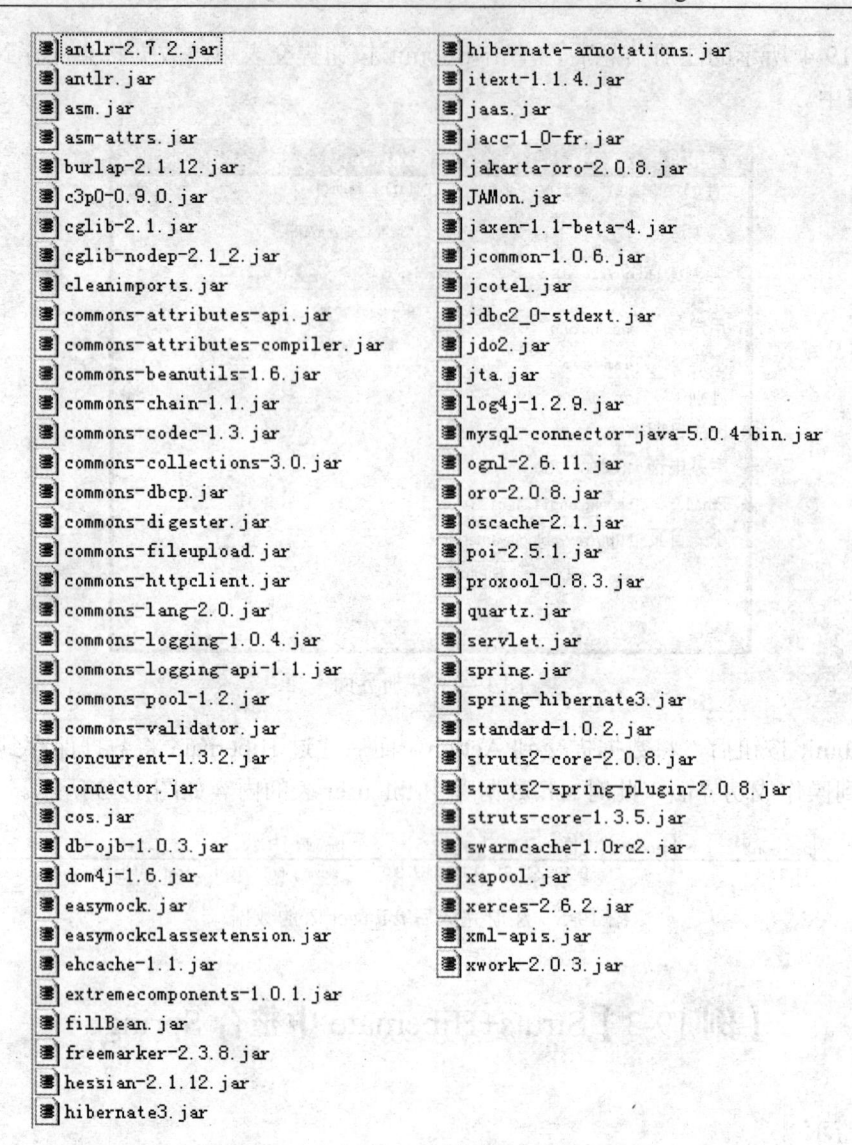

antlr-2.7.2.jar	hibernate-annotations.jar
antlr.jar	itext-1.1.4.jar
asm.jar	jaas.jar
asm-attrs.jar	jacc-1_0-fr.jar
burlap-2.1.12.jar	jakarta-oro-2.0.8.jar
c3p0-0.9.0.jar	JAMon.jar
cglib-2.1.jar	jaxen-1.1-beta-4.jar
cglib-nodep-2.1_2.jar	jcommon-1.0.6.jar
cleanimports.jar	jcotel.jar
commons-attributes-api.jar	jdbc2_0-stdext.jar
commons-attributes-compiler.jar	jdo2.jar
commons-beanutils-1.6.jar	jta.jar
commons-chain-1.1.jar	log4j-1.2.9.jar
commons-codec-1.3.jar	mysql-connector-java-5.0.4-bin.jar
commons-collections-3.0.jar	ognl-2.6.11.jar
commons-dbcp.jar	oro-2.0.8.jar
commons-digester.jar	oscache-2.1.jar
commons-fileupload.jar	poi-2.5.1.jar
commons-httpclient.jar	proxool-0.8.3.jar
commons-lang-2.0.jar	quartz.jar
commons-logging-1.0.4.jar	servlet.jar
commons-logging-api-1.1.jar	spring.jar
commons-pool-1.2.jar	spring-hibernate3.jar
commons-validator.jar	standard-1.0.2.jar
concurrent-1.3.2.jar	struts2-core-2.0.8.jar
connector.jar	struts2-spring-plugin-2.0.8.jar
cos.jar	struts-core-1.3.5.jar
db-ojb-1.0.3.jar	swarmcache-1.0rc2.jar
dom4j-1.6.jar	xapool.jar
easymock.jar	xerces-2.6.2.jar
easymockclassextension.jar	xml-apis.jar
ehcache-1.1.jar	xwork-2.0.3.jar
extremecomponents-1.0.1.jar	
fillBean.jar	
freemarker-2.3.8.jar	
hessian-2.1.12.jar	
hibernate3.jar	

图 19-6　加入了 Spring 的 jar 包后的 lib 列表

第二步：编写 Spring 的配置文件：applicationContext.xml

在 src 目录中建立 Spring 的配置文件 applicationContext.xml，在该文件中配置事务管理的策略，并定义 dao、业务逻辑类、action 的 bean。

该文件的内容如下所示：

```xml
<?xml version="1.0" encoding="UTF-8"?>
<!DOCTYPE beans PUBLIC "-//SPRING//DTD BEAN//EN"
    "http://www.springframework.org/dtd/spring-beans.dtd">

<beans>
    <bean id="dataSource" class="com.mchange.v2.c3p0.ComboPooledDataSource" destroy-method=
      "close">
        <property name="driverClass">
            <value>com.mysql.jdbc.Driver</value>
        </property>
```

```xml
        <property name="jdbcUrl">
            <value>jdbc:mysql://localhost/ssh</value>
        </property>
        <property name="user">
            <value>root</value>
        </property>
        <property name="password">
            <value>root</value>
        </property>
        <property name="maxPoolSize">
            <value>80</value>
        </property>
        <property name="minPoolSize">
            <value>1</value>
        </property>
        <property name="initialPoolSize">
            <value>1</value>
        </property>
        <property name="maxIdleTime">
            <value>20</value>
        </property>
    </bean>

    <!--定义了 Hibernate 的 SessionFactory -->
    <bean id="sessionFactory" class="org.springframework.orm.hibernate3.LocalSessionFactoryBean">
        <property name="dataSource">
            <ref local="dataSource" />
        </property>
        <property name="mappingResources">
            <list>
                <value>amigo/ssh/dao/User.hbm.xml</value>
            </list>
        </property>
        <property name="hibernateProperties">
            <props>
                <prop key="hibernate.dialect">org.hibernate.dialect.MySQLDialect</prop>
                <prop key="show_sql">true</prop>
                <prop key="hibernate.jdbc.batch_size">20</prop>
            </props>
        </property>
    </bean>

    <bean id="transactionManager"
          class="org.springframework.orm.hibernate3.HibernateTransactionManager">
        <property name="sessionFactory" ref="sessionFactory" />
    </bean>

    <bean id="transactionInterceptor"
          class="org.springframework.transaction.interceptor.TransactionInterceptor">
        <!-- 事务拦截器 bean 需要依赖注入一个事务管理器 -->
        <property name="transactionManager" ref="transactionManager" />
        <property name="transactionAttributes">
            <!-- 下面定义事务传播属性-->
```

```xml
            <props>
                <prop key="save*">PROPAGATION_REQUIRED</prop>
                <prop key="update*">PROPAGATION_REQUIRED</prop>
                <prop key="delete*">PROPAGATION_REQUIRED</prop>
                <prop key="*">PROPAGATION_REQUIRED,readOnly</prop>
            </props>
        </property>
    </bean>

    <!-- 定义BeanNameAutoProxyCreator-->
    <bean class="org.springframework.aop.framework.autoproxy.BeanNameAutoProxyCreator">
        <!-- 指定对满足哪些bean name的bean自动生成业务代理 -->
        <property name="beanNames">
            <list>
                <!-- 需要自动创建事务代理的bean-->
                <value>userManager</value>
            </list>
            <!-- 此处可增加其他需要自动创建事务代理的bean-->
        </property>
        <!-- 下面定义BeanNameAutoProxyCreator所需的事务拦截器-->
        <property name="interceptorNames">
            <list>
                <value>transactionInterceptor</value>
            </list>
        </property>
    </bean>

    <bean id="baseDao" class="amigo.ssh.dao.BaseDaoImpl">
        <property name="sessionFactory">
            <ref bean="sessionFactory" />
        </property>
    </bean>

    <!--用户注册业务逻辑类 -->
    <bean id="userManager" class="amigo.ssh.UserManagerImpl">
        <property name="dao">
            <ref bean="baseDao" />
        </property>
    </bean>

    <!-- 用户注册的Action-->
    <bean id="regAction" class="amigo.ssh.RegAction">
        <property name="userManager">
            <ref bean="userManager" />
        </property>
    </bean>

</beans>
```

上面的配置中，如下配置信息指定了数据源的信息，指定了连接的驱动类，JDBC连接串、数据库用户名和密码等信息：

```xml
<bean id="dataSource" class="com.mchange.v2.c3p0.ComboPooledDataSource" destroy-method=
```

```xml
"close">
    <property name="driverClass">
        <value>com.mysql.jdbc.Driver</value>
    </property>
    <property name="jdbcUrl">
        <value>jdbc:mysql://localhost/ssh</value>
    </property>
    <property name="user">
        <value>root</value>
    </property>
    ......
</bean>
```

接下来 sessionFactory 的配置指定了 sessionFactory 使用的数据源为上面的数据源,并指定了 Hibernate 映射文件。配置信息如下:

```xml
<bean id="sessionFactory" class="org.springframework.orm.hibernate3.LocalSessionFactoryBean">
    <property name="dataSource">
        <ref local="dataSource" />
    </property>
    <property name="mappingResources">
        <list>
            <value>amigo/ssh/dao/User.hbm.xml</value>
        </list>
    </property>
    ......
</bean>
```

transactionInterceptor 这个 bean 指定了事务管理的策略,以 save、update、delete 开头的方法以及中间包含 Reg 的方法采用的策略都为 PROPAGATION_REQUIRED,即都必须包含在事务中,而其余的方法也都包含在事务中,但是是只读状态的。

配置信息如下所示:

```xml
<bean id="transactionManager"
        class="org.springframework.orm.hibernate3.HibernateTransactionManager">
    <property name="sessionFactory" ref="sessionFactory" />
</bean>

<bean id="transactionInterceptor"
        class="org.springframework.transaction.interceptor.TransactionInterceptor">
    <!-- 事务拦截器 bean 需要依赖注入一个事务管理器 -->
    <property name="transactionManager" ref="transactionManager" />
    <property name="transactionAttributes">
        <!-- 下面定义事务传播属性-->
        <props>
            <prop key="save*">PROPAGATION_REQUIRED</prop>
            <prop key="update*">PROPAGATION_REQUIRED</prop>
            <prop key="delete*">PROPAGATION_REQUIRED</prop>
<prop key="*Reg*">PROPAGATION_REQUIRED</prop>
            <prop key="*">PROPAGATION_REQUIRED,readOnly</prop>
        </props>
    </property>
</bean>
```

接下来需要指定将哪些 bean 放入事务管理中,这项工作在本实例中是由

BeanNameAutoProxyCreator 来完成的,它指定自动事务代理的 bean 为业务逻辑类 userManager,事务拦截器为 transactionInterceptor。具体配置如下所示:

```xml
<bean class="org.springframework.aop.framework.autoproxy.BeanNameAutoProxyCreator">
    <property name="beanNames">
        <list>
            <value>userManager</value>
        </list>
    </property>
    <property name="interceptorNames">
        <list>
            <value>transactionInterceptor</value>
        </list>
    </property>
</bean>
```

接下来需要定义 baseDao 这个 bean,指定其实现类为:amigo.ssh.dao.BaseDaoImpl。该类需要 sessionFactory,因此需要在 Spring 的配置文件中注入,具体配置如下所示:

```xml
<bean id="baseDao" class="amigo.ssh.dao.BaseDaoImpl">
    <property name="sessionFactory">
        <ref bean="sessionFactory" />
    </property>
</bean>
```

接着配置用户的业务逻辑类,其实现类为 amigo.ssh.UserManagerImpl,在该类中需要使用 dao,因此需要将 BaseDao 接口的实例注入,配置信息如下所示:

```xml
<bean id="userManager" class="amigo.ssh.UserManagerImpl">
    <property name="dao">
        <ref bean="baseDao" />
    </property>
</bean>
```

为了进行统一管理,需要将 Action 也交给 Spring 进行管理,RegAction 类需要使用业务逻辑类来完成用户注册,因此需要将用户业务逻辑类注入到其中,该 Action 的配置信息如下所示:

```xml
<bean id="regAction" class="amigo.ssh.RegAction">
    <property name="userManager">
        <ref bean="userManager" />
    </property>
</bean>
```

第三步:修改 BaseDao.java 和 BaseDaoImpl.java

在引入了 Spring 后,需要使用 Spring 进行统一的事务管理,数据源和 sessionFactory 都交给 Spring 去生成,因此 BaseDao 的实现类 BaseDaoImpl.java 需要进行相应的修改。

Spring 提供了 HibernateDaoSupport 类来完成对数据的操作,因此 BaseDaoImpl 类在实现 BaseDao 接口的同时,还需要继承 HibernateDaoSupport 类,并将先前对 session 的操作修改成对 HibernateTemplate 的操作,HibernateTemplate 对象可通过 HibernateDaoSupport 类的 getHibernateTemplate()方法获得。

在做修改时,BaseDao.java 类只需要删除 getSession()和 setSession()方法即可。

BaseDaoImpl.java 类需要做较大的修改,修改后该类的代码如下所示:

```java
package amigo.ssh.dao;
```

```java
import java.io.Serializable;
import java.sql.SQLException;
import java.util.List;
import java.util.Map;

import org.hibernate.HibernateException;
import org.hibernate.Query;
import org.hibernate.Session;
import org.springframework.orm.hibernate3.HibernateCallback;
import org.springframework.orm.hibernate3.support.HibernateDaoSupport;

/**
 * Hibernate 数据库操作实现类.
 */
public class BaseDaoImpl extends HibernateDaoSupport implements BaseDao {
    public void deleteObject(Object obj) throws HibernateException {
        this.getHibernateTemplate().delete(obj);
    }

    public void deleteObject(Class class1,
            Serializable serializable) throws HibernateException {
        getHibernateTemplate().delete(getObject(class1, serializable));
        getHibernateTemplate().flush();
    }

    public void updateObject(Object obj) throws HibernateException {
        this.getHibernateTemplate().update(obj);
    }

    public void saveObject(Object obj) throws HibernateException {
        this.getHibernateTemplate().save(obj);
    }

    public Object getObject(Class class1,
            Serializable serializable) throws HibernateException {
        return getHibernateTemplate().get(class1, serializable);
    }

    public List hqlQuery(String hsql) throws HibernateException {
        return query(hsql, null);
    }

    public List hqlQuery(String hsql, Object obj) throws HibernateException {
        return query(hsql, obj);
    }

    private List query(final String hsql, final Object obj) throws HibernateException {
        int count = 0;
        List queryList =   (List)getHibernateTemplate().execute(
                //创建匿名内部类
                new HibernateCallback() {
                    public Object doInHibernate(Session session)
                            throws HibernateException, SQLException {
```

```java
                        Query query = session.createQuery(hsql);

                        if (obj != null) {
                            if (obj instanceof Map) {
                                String as[] = query.getNamedParameters();
                                for (int k1 = 0; k1 < as.length; k1++) {
                                    query.setParameter(as[k1],
                                            ((Map) obj).get(as[k1]));
                                }
                            } else if (obj instanceof Object[]) {
                                for (int i1 = 0;
                                        i1 < ((Object[]) obj).length; i1++) {
                                    query.setParameter(i1,
                                            ((Object[]) obj)[i1]);

                                }
                            } else {
                                query.setParameter(0, obj);
                            }
                        }
                        return query.list();
                    }
                }
            );

        return queryList;
    }
}
```

【提示】读者可能会有疑问，在 Spring 的配置文件中，指定了为 BaseDaoImpl 注入 sessionFactory，但是为什么在 BaseDaoImpl 类中并没有提供该属性及其 setter 方法？原因在于该方法在其所继承的父类 HibernateDaoSupport 中提供。

第四步：修改业务逻辑实现类：UserManagerImpl.java

在【例 19-2】中，业务逻辑实现类的 Session 的获得、dao 的实例化，以及事务的管理都是该类自行管理的，加入 Spring 后，这些工作都将交给 Spring 去管理，该类的 dao 的实例化由 Spring 注入，该业务逻辑实现类只需要提供对应的 setter 方法即可。修改后该类的代码如下所示：

```java
package amigo.ssh;

import org.apache.commons.beanutils.BeanUtils;

import amigo.ssh.dao.BaseDao;
import amigo.ssh.dao.User;

/**
 * 用户注册的业务逻辑实现类.
 */
public class UserManagerImpl implements UserManager {

    private BaseDao dao;
```

```java
    public void setDao(BaseDao dao) {
        this.dao = dao;
    }

    public void userReg(UserForm form) throws Exception {
        // 构造 User 对象
        User user = new User();
        BeanUtils.copyProperties(user, form);

        // 保存 user 对象
        dao.saveObject(user);
    }
}
```

第五步：修改用户注册的 Action：RegAction.java

因 RegAction 被交给 Spring 管理，其所需要的业务逻辑类的实例化也将交给 Spring 进行管理，因此【例 19-2】中实例化 userManager 对象的语句可以删除，修改后 execute(…)方法如下所示：

```java
public String execute() {
    try {
        // 用户注册
        userManager.userReg(user);
        return this.SUCCESS;
    } catch(Exception ex) {
        ex.printStackTrace();
        return this.ERROR;
    }
}
```

第六步：删除文件 hibernate.cfg.xml 和 HibernateSessionFactory.java

加入 Spring 后，数据源的创建和 sessionFactory 的创建都被交给 Spring 去管理，因此【例 19-2】中的 hibernate.cfg.xml 文件和 HibernateSessionFactory.java 类都已不再有用，读者可以将其删除。

第七步：修改 web.xml：加载 Spring

要想在启动时加载 Spring 的配置文件，需要在 web.xml 中配置对应的监听器（listener），并指定 Spring 的配置文件。配置信息如下所示：

```xml
……
<context-param>
    <param-name>contextConfigLocation</param-name>
    <param-value>classpath*:applicationContext*.xml</param-value>
</context-param>

<listener>
    <listener-class>org.springframework.web.context.ContextLoaderListener</listener-class>
</listener>
……
```

context-param 指定了 Spring 的配置文件为 classpath 路径下以 applicationContext 开头的文件，listener 指定了监听器类为 org.springframework.web.context.ContextLoaderListener。

第八步：修改 Struts 的配置文件：struts.xml

最后还需要对 Struts 的配置文件 struts.xml 进行修改，指定 reg 对应的 class 为 regAction，与 applicationContext.xml 文件中的该 Action 对应，配置信息如下：

```
……
<action name="reg"   class="regAction">
<result name="input">/reg.jsp</result>
    <result name="success">/success.jsp</result>
    <result name="error">/error.jsp</result>
</action>
……
```

第九步：运行结果

工程部署完成后，在浏览器中输入地址：http://localhost:8899/ssh/reg.jsp
填写如下注册信息后，单击 Submit 按钮提交表单信息，注册界面如图 19-7 所示。

图 19-7　注册界面

单击 Submit 按钮提交表单，并将数据插入到 tbl_user 表中，显示注册成功的界面。

小结

Struts 2 作为 MVC2 的 Web 框架，自推出以来不断受到开发者的喜爱，得到广泛的应用。Spring 在某些方面方便了 Struts 的开发。Hibernate 作为对象持久化的框架，能显著地提高在数据库操作层软件开发的效率与生产力。这 3 种流行框架的整合应用，可以发挥各自的优势，高效率地开发出 Web 系统。

在 Web 项目中加入 Struts 2 的支持，首先需要将 Struts 2 的 jar 包载入，需要加入的 jar 包如下所示：

- commons-logging-1.0.4.jar
- freemarker-2.3.8.jar

- log4j-1.2.9.jar
- ognl-2.6.11.jar
- struts2-core-2.0.8.jar
- xwork-2.0.3.jar

接着还需要在 web.xml 中加入 Struts 2 的 FilterDispatcher，添加完毕后的 web.xml 文件如下所示：

```xml
<?xml version="1.0" encoding="UTF-8"?>
<web-app version="2.4"
    xmlns="http://java.sun.com/xml/ns/j2ee"
    xmlns:xsi="http://www.w3.org/2001/XMLSchema-instance"
    xsi:schemaLocation="http://java.sun.com/xml/ns/j2ee
    http://java.sun.com/xml/ns/j2ee/web-app_2_4.xsd">
    <filter>
        <filter-name>struts2</filter-name>
        <filter-class>org.apache.struts2.dispatcher.FilterDispatcher</filter-class>
    </filter>

    <filter-mapping>
        <filter-name>struts2</filter-name>
        <url-pattern>/*</url-pattern>
    </filter-mapping>

    <welcome-file-list>
        <welcome-file>index.jsp</welcome-file>
    </welcome-file-list>
</web-app>
```

在加入了 Struts 2 的 WEB 项目中加入 Hibernate 3 的支持，首先也需要将对应的 jar 包导入，加入 Hibernate 后，jar 包列表如下所示：

- antlr-2.7.5H3.jar
- asm.jar
- cglib-2.1.3.jar
- commons-beanutils.jar
- commons-collections-2.1.1.jar
- commons-lang.jar
- commons-logging-1.0.4.jar
- dom4j-1.6.1.jar
- freemarker-2.3.8.jar
- hibernate3.jar
- jta.jar
- log4j-1.2.11.jar
- log4j-1.2.9.jar
- mysql-connector-java-5.0.4-bin.jar
- ognl-2.6.11.jar
- struts2-core-2.0.8.jar
- xwork-2.0.3.jar

另外还需要提供一个 Hibernate 的配置文件：hibernate.cfg.xml，该配置文件的格式如下所示：

```xml
……
<hibernate-configuration>
    <session-factory>
        <!-- 在后台打印 sql 语句 -->
        <property name="show_sql">true</property>
        <!-- 指定 sql 的本地方言，根据连接的数据库确定-->
        <property name="dialect">org.hibernate.dialect.MySQLDialect</property>
```

```xml
        <!-- 指定 jdbc url -->
        <property name="connection.url">jdbc:mysql://localhost:3306/ssh</property>
        <!-- 数据库的用户名 -->
        <property name="connection.username">root</property>
        <!-- 数据库的密码 -->
        <property name="connection.password">root</property>
        <!-- 设定数据库的驱动类，MySql 的驱动 jar 包为 mysql-connector-java-5.0.4-bin.jar，驱动类为 com.mysql.jdbc.Driver -->
        <property name="connection.driver_class">com.mysql.jdbc.Driver</property>

        <!--指定 0 到多个 hbm.xml 映射文件-->
        <mapping resource="amigo/ssh/dao/User.hbm.xml" />
    </session-factory>
</hibernate-configuration>
```

加入 Hibernate 3 持久层技术后，有关数据库操作的部分调用 Hibernate 来实现。

在 Struts 2 + Hibernate 3 的项目中加入 Spring 的好处是：事务管理和业务逻辑类的管理都被交给 Spring 2。首先也需要将 jar 包拷贝到 lib 目录下。

接下来还需要编写 Spring 的配置文件（例如 applicationContext.xml）。最后要想在启动时加载 Spring 的配置文件，需要在 web.xml 中配置对应的监听器（listener），并指定 Spring 的配置文件。配置信息如下所示：

```xml
......
<context-param>
    <param-name>contextConfigLocation</param-name>
    <param-value>classpath*:applicationContext*.xml</param-value>
</context-param>

<listener>
    <listener-class>org.springframework.web.context.ContextLoaderListener</listener-class>
</listener>
......
```

Spring 的配置文件中配置数据源和进行事务管理的配置信息如下所示：

```xml
<bean id="dataSource" class="com.mchange.v2.c3p0.ComboPooledDataSource" destroy-method="close">
    <property name="driverClass">
        <value>com.mysql.jdbc.Driver</value>
    </property>
    ......
</bean>

<!--定义了 Hibernate 的 SessionFactory -->
<bean id="sessionFactory"
    class="org.springframework.orm.hibernate3.LocalSessionFactoryBean">
    <property name="dataSource">
        <ref local="dataSource" />
    </property>
    <property name="mappingResources">
        <list>
            <value>amigo/ssh/dao/User.hbm.xml</value>
        </list>
    </property>
    <property name="hibernateProperties">
```

```xml
            <props>
                ......
            </props>
        </property>
</bean>

<bean id="transactionManager"
    class="org.springframework.orm.hibernate3.HibernateTransactionManager">
    <property name="sessionFactory" ref="sessionFactory" />
</bean>

<bean id="transactionInterceptor"
     class="org.springframework.transaction.interceptor. TransactionInterceptor">
    <property name="transactionManager" ref="transactionManager" />
    <property name="transactionAttributes">
        <props>
            ......
        </props>
    </property>
</bean>

<!-- 定义 BeanNameAutoProxyCreator-->
<bean class="org.springframework.aop.framework.autoproxy.BeanNameAutoProxyCreator">
    <property name="beanNames">
        <list>
            <!-- 需要自动创建事务代理的 bean-->
        </list>
            <!-- 此处可增加其他需要自动创建事务代理的 bean-->
    </property>
    <!-- 下面定义 BeanNameAutoProxyCreator 所需的事务拦截器-->
    <property name="interceptorNames">
        <list>
            <value>transactionInterceptor</value>
        </list>
    </property>
</bean>
```

加入 Spring 2 后，事务管理被交给 Spring，Hibernate 的数据库配置也被加入到 Spring 中，因此 Hibernate 的配置文件 hibernate.cfg.xml 此时可以删除。

第20章 SSH 实例——个人备忘录系统

【本章导读语】

在学习了 Struts 2、Hibernate 3 框架技术后，为了使读者对所学的知识有一个较全面的认识并能综合性地运用，本章将采用这 3 种框架技术进行整合开发个人备忘录系统。

个人备忘录系统的功能虽然不复杂，但是能使读者对所学的知识进行巩固和提高，还能使读者对系统开发时进行的需求分析、架构设计、数据库设计、详细设计和编码实现的过程有一个清晰的理解。

本章实现采用了如下技术：
- Struts 2 框架：用于实现表现层和控制层，它提供了丰富的表现层标签，方便开发人员进行 JSP 页面的开发。
- Hibernate 3 框架：用于实现持久层。
- Spring 2 框架：用于实现对业务逻辑类和 Action 的管理，并负责统一管理事务。
- extreme components：开源的分页技术。
- EL：表达式语言，用在 JSP 页面中。

20.1 系统需求分析

个人备忘录系统主要完成备忘信息的录入、编辑、删除和查看功能，以及到规定的时间进行提醒的功能。另外，因为不同的用户在个人备忘录系统中都有不同的备忘录信息，所以必须提供用户注册的功能。系统管理员可管理注册用户的信息，以及系统所有的备忘信息。

20.1.1 系统用户

个人备忘录系统包括三类用户，分别为：系统管理员、注册用户和非注册用户。

其中注册用户可以进行登录、录入、编辑、删除和查看自身的备忘信息的操作。

非注册用户不能浏览备忘信息，但是可以进行注册的操作，注册后即成为注册用户。

在本系统中，系统管理员只有一个，其用户名为 admin，他可对所有用户信息进行管理，进行用户信息的查看、修改和删除操作。

20.1.2 系统功能需求

个人备忘录系统主要包括两大功能模块：前台模块和后台管理模块。其中前台模块的功能包括：
- 用户注册。
- 用户登录。
- 查看备忘类型列表。
- 添加备忘类型。

- 修改备忘类型。
- 删除备忘类型。
- 根据用户名获得该用户的备忘列表信息。
- 添加备忘信息。
- 修改备忘信息。
- 删除备忘信息。
- 备忘提醒。
- 更新备忘信息状态。

后台管理模块的功能包括：
- 用户登录。
- 查看所有用户信息列表。
- 修改用户。
- 删除用户。

20.2 系统架构设计

本系统整合了 Struts 2、Hibernate 和 Spring 技术，分页采用 extremecomponents 组件，系统的核心架构图如图 20-1 所示。

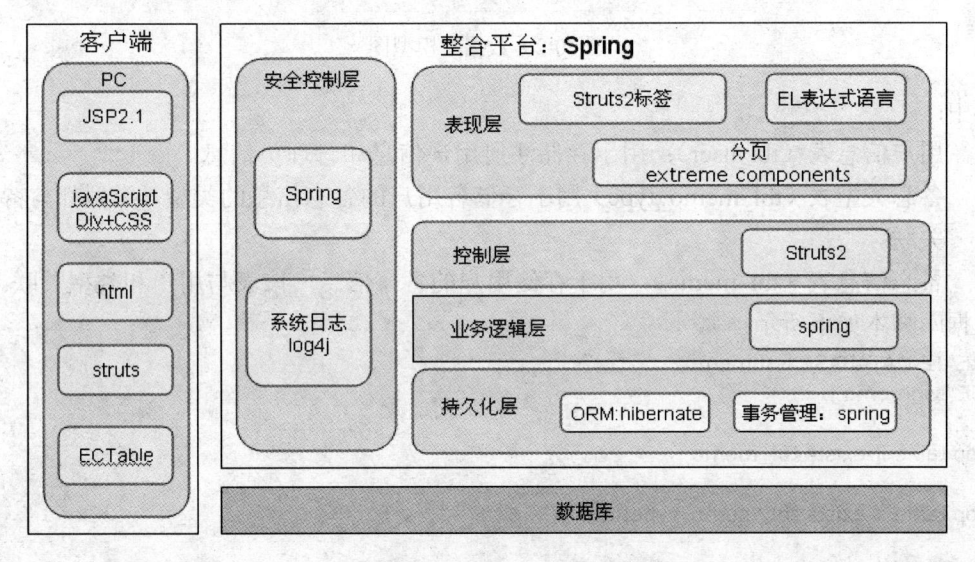

图 20-1 系统的核心架构图

本系统采用 MVC 模式，主要包括表现层、控制层、业务逻辑层和持久化层，其中：
- 表现层：主要为 JSP 页面，采用了 Struts 2 标签、EL 表达式语言，分页采用了 extremecomponents 组件。
- 控制层：采用 Struts2 的 Action 进行控制。
- 业务逻辑层：业务逻辑层各业务逻辑类的管理采用 Spring 技术进行统一管理。
- 持久化层：该层采用的 OR Mapping 工具为 Hibernate，而对事务的控制统一采用 Spring 进行管理。

20.3 数据库设计

本系统包括三张表，分别为用户信息表、备忘类型表和备忘信息表，数据库的模型如图 20-2 所示。

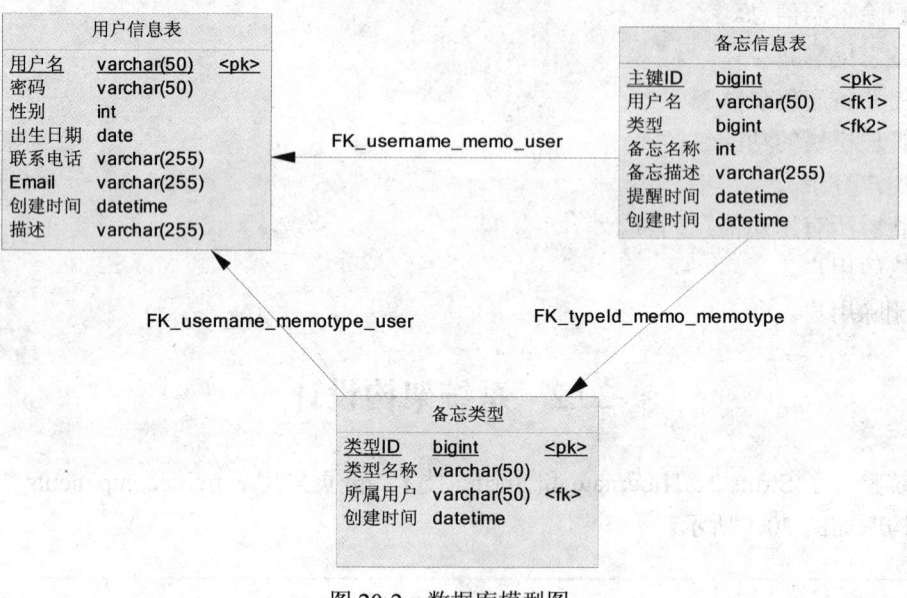

图 20-2 数据库模型图

其中：
- 用户信息表（tbl_user）：用于存储注册用户信息和管理员信息。
- 备忘类型表（tbl_memo_type）用于存储各用户的备忘信息的类型，类型都与特定用户关联。
- 备忘信息表（tbl_memo）：用于存储用户的备忘信息，该表与用户和类型关联。

数据库脚本如下所示：

```sql
CREATE DATABASE 'sshmemo';
USE 'sshmemo';

drop table if exists tbl_memo;

drop table if exists tbl_memo_type;

drop table if exists tbl_user;

/*==============================================================*/
/* Table: tbl_memo                                              */
/*==============================================================*/
create table tbl_memo
(
   memoId               bigint not null auto_increment comment '主键ID',
   username             varchar(50) not null comment '用户名',
   typeId               bigint not null comment '类型',
   name                 int not null comment '备忘名称',
   description          varchar(255) comment '备忘描述',
```

```sql
    remindTime              datetime comment '提醒时间',
    createTime              datetime not null comment '创建时间',
    status                  int(2) not null comment '状态，0：初始态，1：已查看',
    primary key (memoId)
)
comment = "备忘信息表";

/*==============================================================*/
/* Table: tbl_memo_type                                         */
/*==============================================================*/
create table tbl_memo_type
(
    type                    bigint not null auto_increment comment '类型ID',
    name                    varchar(50) not null comment '类型名称',
    username                varchar(50) not null comment '所属用户',
    createTime              datetime not null comment '创建时间',
    primary key (type)
)
comment = "备忘类型";


/*==============================================================*/
/* Table: tbl_user                                              */
/*==============================================================*/
create table tbl_user
(
    username                varchar(50) not null comment '用户名',
    password                varchar(50) not null comment '密码',
    gender                  int comment '性别',
    birthDate               date comment '出生日期',
    tel                     varchar(255) comment '联系电话',
    email                   varchar(255) comment 'Email',
    createTime              datetime not null comment '创建时间',
    description             varchar(255) comment '帐户简述',
    primary key (username)
)
comment = "用户信息表";

alter table tbl_memo add constraint FK_typeId_memo_memotype foreign key (typeId)
    references tbl_memo_type (type) on delete restrict on update restrict;

alter table tbl_memo add constraint FK_username_memo_user foreign key (username)
    references tbl_user (username) on delete restrict on update restrict;

alter table tbl_memo_type add constraint FK_username_memotype_user foreign key (username)
    references tbl_user (username) on delete restrict on update restrict;

INSERT INTO 'tbl_user' ('username', 'password', 'gender', 'birthDate', 'tel', 'email', 'createTime',
'description') VALUES ('admin','admin',0,'2008-11-21','13555556666', 'xiexingxing1121@126.com','2008-
08-16 14:40:00',NULL);

    INSERT INTO 'tbl_user' ('username', 'password', 'gender', 'birthDate', 'tel', 'email', 'createTime',
'description') VALUES ('amigo','amigo',0,'1982-11-21','13444444444', 'xiexingxing1121@126.com','2008-
09-20 20:00:00',NULL);
```

在 MySQL 中运行该脚本，可创建一个 sshmemo 数据库，在其中建立 tbl_user、tbl_memo_type 和 tbl_memo 三张表，并在数据库中建立这三者之间的外键关联关系。最后在用户信息表（tbl_user）中建立用户名为 admin 的用户记录。

20.4 系统详细设计

20.4.1 注册用户管理

（1）模块功能与结构。

该模块包括显示用户列表、用户注册、修改用户信息和删除用户信息的功能。该模块的模块结构如图 20-3 所示。

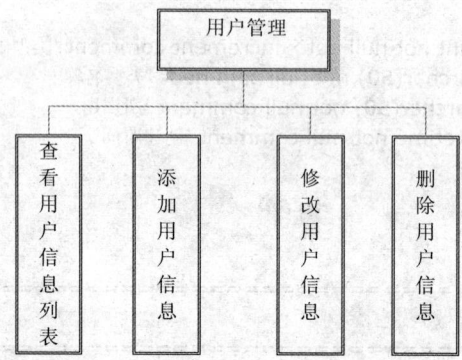

图 20-3 用户信息管理的模块结构

（2）类图。

该模块的类图如图 20-4 所示。

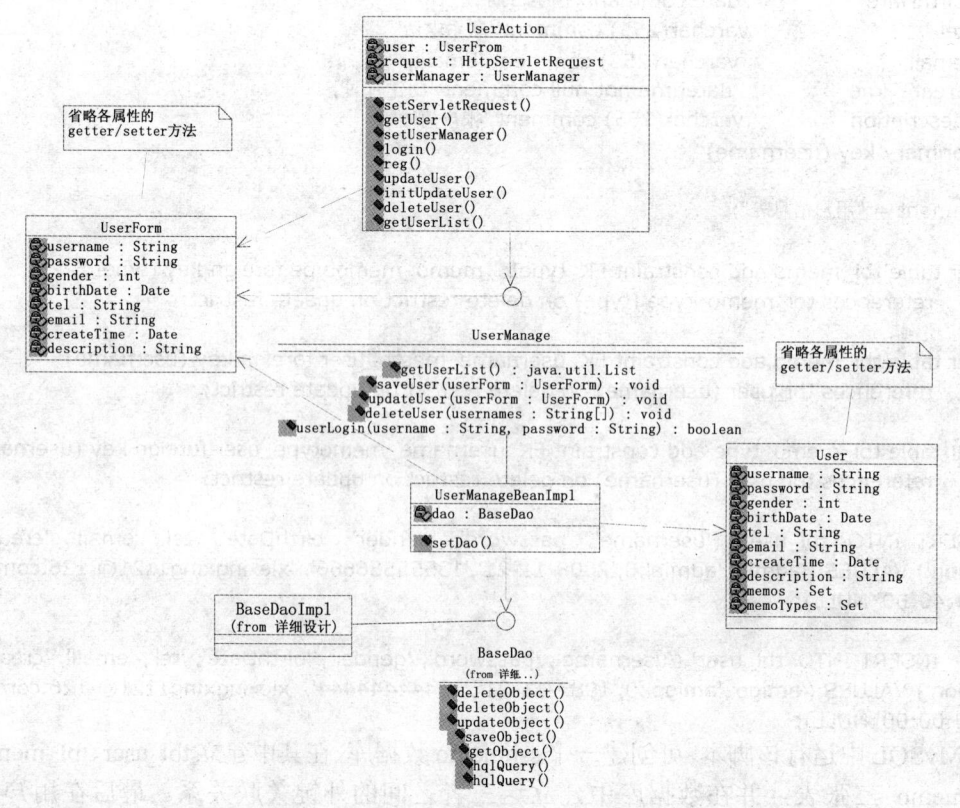

图 20-4 用户管理模块的类图

- UserManager 和 UserMangerImpl 类。

业务逻辑接口 UserManager 及其实现类 UserManagerImpl 的方法如下所示：

public void saveUser(UserForm userForm)：用户注册。

public void updateUser(UserForm userForm)：修改用户信息。

public void deleteUser(String[] usernames)：根据传入的用户名数组删除多个用户的信息。

public List<User> getUserList()：获取用户信息列表。

public boolean userLogin(String username, String password)：验证登录信息是否正确，正确返回 true，否则，返回 false。

public void setDao(BaseDao dao)：实现类的方法，用于注入 BaseDao 来进行数据库的操作。

- UserAction 类。

UserAction 类为用户管理的 Action 类，为用户管理的控制器，所包括的方法如下所示：

public void setServletRequest(HttpServletRequest request)：该类需要对 request 进行操作，因此需要实现 ServletRequestAware 接口，而该 setter 方法是 ServletRequestAware 接口要求实现的。

public UserForm getUser()：获取用户表单信息。

public void setUserManager(UserManager userManager)：通过Spring注入业务逻辑对象。

public String login()：用户登录。

public String reg()：用户注册。

public String updateUser()：修改用户信息。

public String initUpdateUser()：获得初始化用户信息页面所需的信息。

public String deleteUser()：删除用户信息。

public String getUserList()：获取用户信息列表。

- User 类。

tbl_user表的POJO对象，因为与tbl_memo_type和tbl_memo表存在一对多关联，所以具有MemoType和Memo的集合对象。

- UserForm 类。

用户信息表单对象，该类的属性与 User 类类似。

20.4.2 备忘类型管理

（1）模块功能与结构。

该模块包括显示备忘类型列表、添加、修改和删除备忘类型的功能。该模块的模块结构如图 20-5 所示。

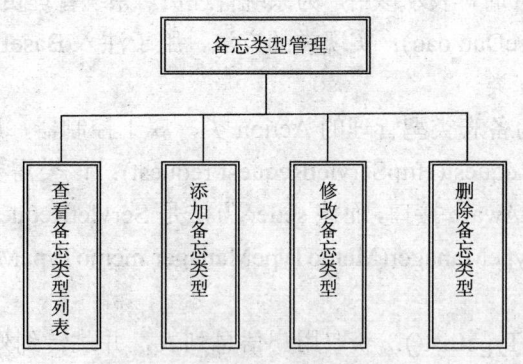

图 20-5　备忘类型管理的模块结构

（2）类图。

该模块的类图如图 20-6 所示。

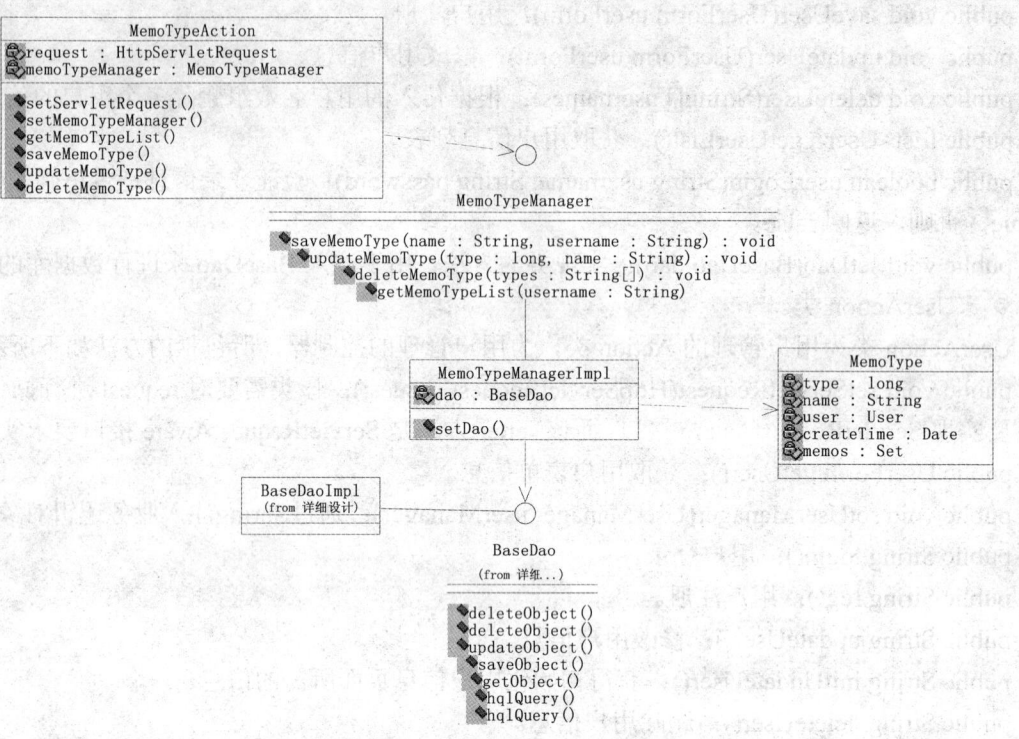

图 20-6　备忘类型管理模块的类图

- MemoTypeManager 和 MemoTypeMangerImpl 类。

备忘类型管理的业务逻辑接口 MemoTypeManager 及其实现类 MemoTypeManagerImpl 的方法如下所示：

public void saveMemoType(String name, String username)：保存备忘类型，其中 name 为类型名称，username 为所属用户的名称。

Public void updateMemoType(long type, String name)：更新备忘类型，其中 type 为需要修改的备忘类型的名称，name 为类型的新名称。

Public void deleteMemoType(String[] types)：根据类型数组删除多个备忘类型的信息。

Public List<MemoType> getMemoTypeList(String username)：根据用户名查询该用户的类型列表，若 username 为 admin 时，表示该用户为系统管理员，系统管理员能够查看所有的类型信息。

Public void setDao(BaseDao dao)：实现类的方法，用于注入 BaseDao 来进行数据库的操作。

- MemoTypeAction 类。

MemoTypeAction 类为备忘类型管理的 Action 类，属于控制器，所包括的方法如下所示：

public void setServletRequest(HttpServletRequest request)：该类需要对 request 进行操作，因此需要实现 ServletRequestAware 接口，而该 setter 方法是 ServletRequestAware 接口要求实现的。

public void setMemoTypeManager(MemoTypeManager memoTypeManager)：通过 Spring 注入业务逻辑对象。

public String getMemoTypeList()：获取用户信息列表，并跳转到列表页面进行显示。

public String saveMemoType()：保存备忘类型信息。

public String updateMemoType()：修改备忘类型信息。

public String deleteMemoType()：删除备忘那个类型。

- MemoType 类。

Tbl_memo_type 表的 POJO 对象，因为 tbl_memo 表存在一对多关联，所以具有 Memo 的集合对象。

- BaseDao 接口及其实现类 BaseDaoImpl。

该类为系统的 Dao 类，它包括对数据进行操作的方法，它所包括的方法如下所示：

public void deleteObject(Object obj)：删除传入的对象。

public void deleteObject(Class class1, Serializable serializable)：根据主键和类信息删除某 POJO 对象。

public void updateObject(Object obj)：更新传入的对象。

public void saveObject(Object obj)：保存对象。

public Object getObject(Class class1, Serializable serializable)：获得某个对象。

public List hqlQuery(String hsql)：根据查询语句获得满足该查询条件的对象列表。

public List hqlQuery(String hsql, Object obj)：根据查询语句获得满足该查询条件的对象列表。

20.4.3 备忘信息管理

（1）模块功能与结构。

该模块包括显示备忘信息列表、显示即时提醒信息、添加、修改和删除备忘信息的功能。该模块的模块结构如图 20-7 所示。

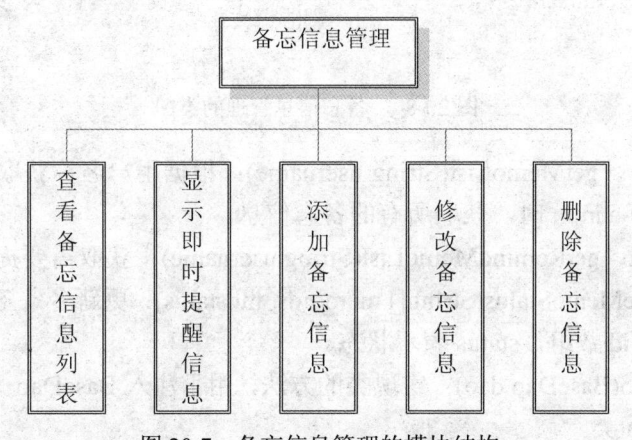

图 20-7　备忘信息管理的模块结构

（2）类图。

该模块的类图如图 20-8 所示。

- MemoManager 和 MemoMangerImpl 类。

备忘信息管理的业务逻辑接口类 MemoManager 及其实现类 MemoManagerImpl 的方法如下所示：

public void saveMemo(MemoForm memoForm)：保存备忘信息。

Public void updateMemo(MemoForm memoForm)：修改备忘信息。

Public void deleteMemos(String[] memoIds)：根据传入的备忘信息 id 数组删除多个备忘信息。

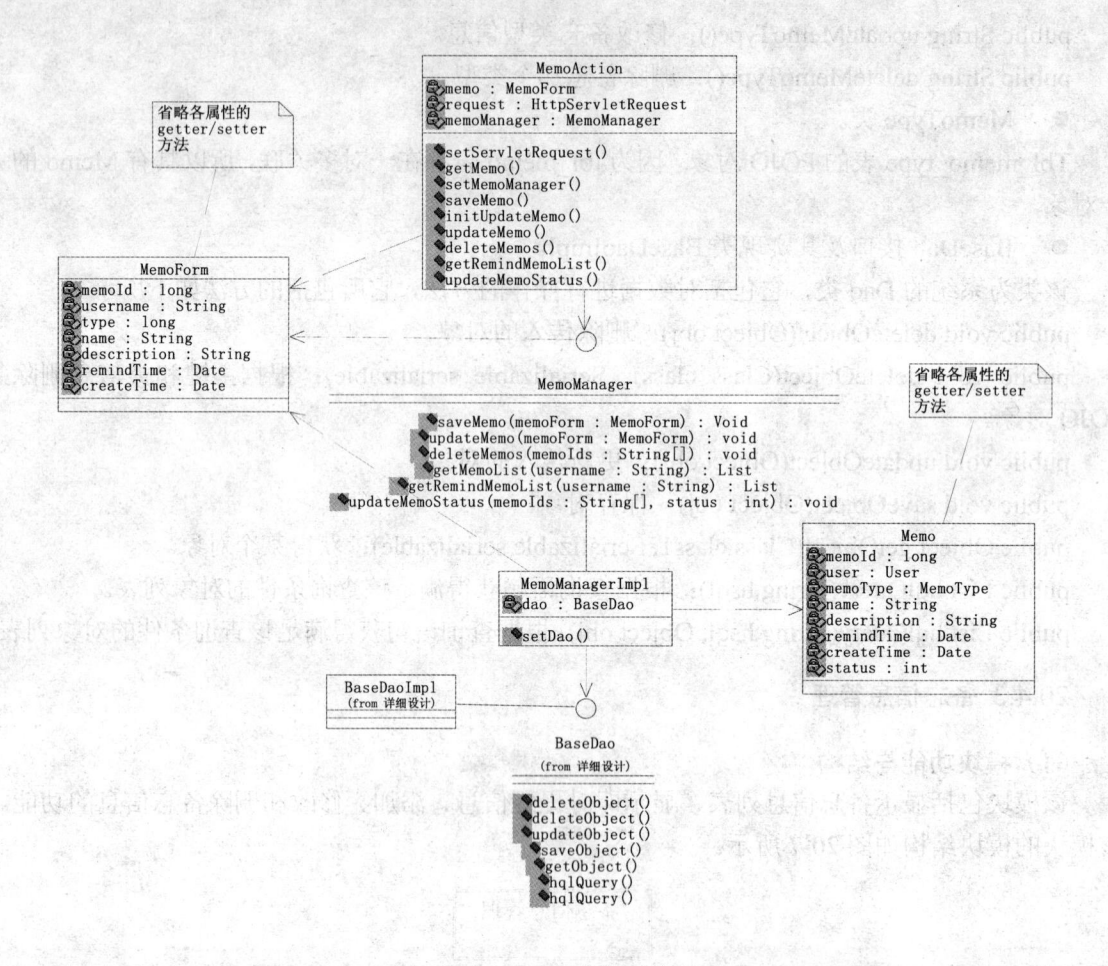

图 20-8　备忘信息管理的类图

public List<Memo> getMemoList(String username)：根据用户名称获取其能查看的备忘信息列表，当 username 为 admin 时，获取所有的备忘信息。

Public List<Memo> getRemindMemoList(String username)：获取需要提醒的备忘信息列表。

Public void updateMemoStatus(String[] memoIds, int status)：更新多条备忘信息的状态，其中 memoIds 为备忘信息 id 数组，status 表示状态。

Public void setDao(BaseDao dao)：实现类的方法，用于注入 BaseDao 来进行数据库的操作。

● MemoAction 类。

MemoAction 类为备忘信息管理的 Action 类，为备忘信息管理的控制器，所包括的方法如下所示：

public void setServletRequest(HttpServletRequest request)：该类需要对 request 进行操作，因此需要实现 ServletRequestAware 接口，而该 setter 方法是 ServletRequestAware 接口要求实现的。

public MemoForm getMemo()：获取备忘信息表单。

public void setMemoManager(MemoManager momoManager)：通过 Spring 注入业务逻辑对象。

public String saveMemo()：保存备忘信息。

public String initUpdateMemo()：初始化更新备忘信息的界面。

public String updateMemo()：更新备忘信息。

public String deleteMemos()：根据传入的备忘 id 数组删除对应的备忘信息。
public String getRemindMemoList()：获取需要提醒的备忘信息列表。
public String updateMemoStatus()：更新备忘信息状态。

- Memo 类。

tbl_memo 表的 POJO 对象，因为与 tbl_memo_type 和 tbl_user 表存在多对一的关联，所以具有 MemoType 和 User 两个对象，属性分别为 memoType 和 user。

- MemoForm 类。

备忘信息表单对象，该类的属性与 Memo 类类似。

20.5 系统实现设计

20.5.1 系统搭建

读者可以参考前一章建立 Web 工程的方法在 Eclipse 中新建一个名为 sshmemo 的动态 Web 工程，并按照前一章的整合方式将需要的 jar 包放入 WEB-INF/lib 目录中，并配置 web.xml 等文件的信息。

操作完成后工程的结构如图 20-9 所示。

图 20-9　系统的目录结构

其中：

- amigo.sshmemo.dao：包括系统的 DAO 文件以及各表的 Hibernate 映射文件。
- amigo.sshmemo.service：包括系统的业务逻辑类。
- amigo.sshmemo.action：包括系统的 Action。
- WebRoot 目录中的 user、memotype 和 memo 目录：存放 3 个模块的 JSP 文件。

WEB-INF/lib 目录中的 jar 包列表如图 20-10 所示。

antlr-2.7.2.jar	hibernate-annotations.jar
antlr.jar	itext-1.1.4.jar
asm.jar	jaas.jar
asm-attrs.jar	jacc-1_0-fr.jar
burlap-2.1.12.jar	jakarta-oro-2.0.8.jar
c3p0-0.9.0.jar	JAMon.jar
cglib-2.1.jar	jaxen-1.1-beta-4.jar
cglib-nodep-2.1_2.jar	jcommon-1.0.6.jar
cleanimports.jar	jcotel.jar
commons-attributes-api.jar	jdbc2_0-stdext.jar
commons-attributes-compiler.jar	jdo2.jar
commons-beanutils-1.6.jar	jta.jar
commons-chain-1.1.jar	log4j-1.2.9.jar
commons-codec-1.3.jar	mysql-connector-java-5.0.4-bin.jar
commons-collections-3.0.jar	ognl-2.6.11.jar
commons-dbcp.jar	oro-2.0.8.jar
commons-digester.jar	oscache-2.1.jar
commons-fileupload.jar	poi-2.5.1.jar
commons-httpclient.jar	proxool-0.8.3.jar
commons-lang-2.0.jar	quartz.jar
commons-logging-1.0.4.jar	servlet.jar
commons-logging-api-1.1.jar	spring.jar
commons-pool-1.2.jar	spring-hibernate3.jar
commons-validator.jar	standard-1.0.2.jar
concurrent-1.3.2.jar	struts2-core-2.0.8.jar
connector.jar	struts2-spring-plugin-2.0.8.jar
cos.jar	struts-core-1.3.5.jar
db-ojb-1.0.3.jar	swarmcache-1.0rc2.jar
dom4j-1.6.jar	xapool.jar
easymock.jar	xerces-2.6.2.jar
easymockclassextension.jar	xml-apis.jar
ehcache-1.1.jar	xwork-2.0.3.jar
extremecomponents-1.0.1.jar	
fillBean.jar	
freemarker-2.3.8.jar	
hessian-2.1.12.jar	
hibernate3.jar	

图 20-10 系统的 jar 包

web.xml 需要添加 Struts 2 的 FilterDispatcher，并需要配置 Spring 的监听器，使得在工程启动时能自动加载 Spring 的默认配置文件（WEB-INF 下的 applicationContext.xml）。web.xml 文件的内容如下所示：

```xml
<?xml version="1.0" encoding="UTF-8"?>
<web-app version="2.4"
    xmlns="http://java.sun.com/xml/ns/j2ee"
    xmlns:xsi="http://www.w3.org/2001/XMLSchema-instance"
    xsi:schemaLocation="http://java.sun.com/xml/ns/j2ee
    http://java.sun.com/xml/ns/j2ee/web-app_2_4.xsd">
  <filter>
     <filter-name>struts2</filter-name>
     <filter-class>org.apache.struts2.dispatcher.FilterDispatcher</filter-class>
  </filter>
```

```xml
    <filter-mapping>
        <filter-name>struts2</filter-name>
        <url-pattern>/*</url-pattern>
    </filter-mapping>

    <!-- 中文编码 -->
    <filter>
        <filter-name>struts-cleanup</filter-name>
        <filter-class>org.apache.struts2.dispatcher.ActionContextCleanUp
        </filter-class>
    </filter>

    <filter-mapping>
        <filter-name>struts-cleanup</filter-name>
        <url-pattern>/*</url-pattern>
    </filter-mapping>

    <listener>
        <listener-class>
            org.springframework.web.context.ContextLoaderListener
        </listener-class>
    </listener>
</web-app>
```

struts.xml 文件的内容如下所示：

```xml
<!DOCTYPE struts PUBLIC
    "-//Apache Software Foundation//DTD Struts Configuration 2.0//EN"
    "http://struts.apache.org/dtds/struts-2.0.dtd">

<struts>
    <!-- 指定国际化配置文件 -->
    <constant name="struts.custom.i18n.resources" value="validationMessages"/>
    <constant name="struts.locale" value="zh_CN"/>
    <constant name="struts.i18n.encoding" value="UTF-8"/>

    <include file="struts-default.xml"/>
    <package name="amigo" extends="struts-default">
    </package>
</struts>
```

20.5.2 实现 DAO 组件层

（1）BaseDao 接口及其实现类 BaseDaoImpl。

在 amigo.sshmemo.dao 包下建立 BaseDao 接口以及其实现类 BaseDaoImpl，这两个类与前一章【例 19-3】中的内容相同，在此不再赘述。

（2）tbl_user 表的映射文件：User.java 和 User.hbm.xml。

在 amigo.sshmemo.dao 包中建立 tbl_user 表的 Hibernate 映射文件：User.java 和 User.hbm.xml。其中 User.java 类的代码如下所示：

```java
package amigo.sshmemo.dao;

import java.io.Serializable;
```

```java
import java.util.Date;
import java.util.HashSet;
import java.util.Set;

/**
 * 用户信息表对应的 POJO 对象.
 */
public class User implements Serializable {
    private static final long serialVersionUID = 1L;

    /** 用户名. */
    private String username;

    /** 密码. */
    private String password;

    /** 性别*/
    private int gender;

    /** 出生日期. */
    private Date birthDate;

    /** 联系电话.*/
    private String tel;

    /** Email. */
    private String email;

    /** 创建时间*/
    private Date createTime;

    /** 描述.*/
    private String description;

    /** 关联的备忘信息. */
    private Set<Memo> memos = new HashSet<Memo>(0);

    /** 关联的备忘类型. */
    private Set<MemoType> memoTypes = new HashSet<MemoType>(0);

    // 省略各属性的 getter/setter 方法
}
```

Hibernate 映射文件 User.hbm.xml 的内容如下所示:

```xml
<?xml version="1.0" encoding='UTF-8'?>
<!DOCTYPE hibernate-mapping PUBLIC
                    "-//Hibernate/Hibernate Mapping DTD 3.0//EN"
                    "http://hibernate.sourceforge.net/hibernate-mapping-3.0.dtd" >

<hibernate-mapping package="amigo.sshmemo.dao">
    <class name="User" table="tbl_user">
        <id name="username" column="username" type="java.lang.String" length="50">
            <generator class="assigned"/>
        </id>
```

```xml
        <property name="password" column="password" type="java.lang.String" not-null="true" length="50"/>
        <property name="gender" column="gender" length="2" />
        <property name="birthDate" column="birthDate" type="java.util.Date" />
        <property name="tel" column="tel" type="java.lang.String" length="255"/>
        <property name="email" column="email" type="java.lang.String" length="255"/>
        <property name="createTime" column="createTime" type="java.util.Date" not-null="true" />
        <property name="description" column="description" type="java.lang.String" length="255"/>
        <set name="memos" inverse="false" cascade="save-update">
            <key column="username"/>
            <one-to-many class="Memo"/>
        </set>

        <set name="memoTypes" inverse="false" cascade="save-update">
            <key column="username"/>
            <one-to-many class="MemoType"/>
        </set>
    </class>
</hibernate-mapping>
```

（3）tbl_memo 表的映射文件：Memo.java 和 Memo.hbm.xml。

在 amigo.sshmemo.dao 包中建立备忘信息表（tbl_memo）的 Hibernate 映射文件：Memo.java 和 Memo.hbm.xml。其中 Memo.java 类的代码如下所示：

```java
package amigo.sshmemo.dao;

import java.io.Serializable;
import java.util.Date;

/**
 * 备忘信息表（tbl_memo）对应的 POJO 对象.
 */
public class Memo implements Serializable {
    private static final long serialVersionUID = 1L;

    /** 主键 ID. */
    private long memoId;

    /** 所属用户. */
    private User user;

    /** 备忘信息类型. */
    private MemoType memoType;

    /** 备忘名称. */
    private String name;

    /** 备忘描述. */
    private String description;

    /** 提醒时间. */
    private Date remindTime;

    /** 创建时间. */
```

```
        private Date createTime;
        // 省略各属性的 getter/setter 方法
    }
```
Hibernate 映射文件 Memo.hbm.xml 的内容如下所示:
```xml
<?xml version="1.0" encoding='UTF-8'?>
<!DOCTYPE hibernate-mapping PUBLIC
                        "-//Hibernate/Hibernate Mapping DTD 3.0//EN"
                        "http://hibernate.sourceforge.net/hibernate-mapping-3.0.dtd" >

<hibernate-mapping package="amigo.sshmemo.dao">
    <class name="Memo" table="tbl_memo">
        <id name="memoId" column="memoId">
            <generator class="native"/>
        </id>
        <property name="name" column="name" type="java.lang.String" not-null="true" length="50"/>
        <property name="description" column="description" type="java.lang.String" length="255"/>
        <property name="remindTime" column="remindTime" type="java.util.Date" not-null="true" />
        <property name="createTime" column="createTime" type="java.util.Date" not-null="true" />
        <property name="status" column="status" type="java.lang.Integer" not-null="true" />

        <many-to-one name="user" column="username" class="User" not-null="true" lazy="false" />
        <many-to-one name="memoType" column="typeId" class="MemoType" not-null="true" lazy="false" />
    </class>
</hibernate-mapping>
```
其中 username 和 type 字段分别与 tbl_user 和 tbl_memo_type 表的主键建立关联，与它们存在多对一的关联关系。

(4) tbl_memo_type 表的映射文件：MemoType.java 和 MemoType.hbm.xml。

在 amigo.sshmemo.dao 包中建立备忘类型表（tbl_memo_type）的 Hibernate 映射文件：MemoType.java 和 MemoType.hbm.xml。其中 MemoType.java 类的代码如下所示：

```java
package amigo.sshmemo.dao;

import java.io.Serializable;
import java.util.Date;

/**
 * 备忘类型表（tbl_memo_type）对应的 POJO 对象.
 */
public class MemoType implements Serializable {
    private static final long serialVersionUID = 1L;

    /** 类型 id，自增主键. */
    private long type;

    /** 类型名称. */
    private String name;

    /** 所属用户. */
    private User user;
```

```
        /** 创建时间. */
        private Date createTime;

        /** 关联的备忘信息. */
        private Set<Memo> memos = new HashSet<Memo>(0);

        // 省略各属性的 getter/setter 方法
}
```

Hibernate 映射文件 MemoType.hbm.xml 的内容如下所示：

```xml
<?xml version="1.0" encoding='UTF-8'?>
<!DOCTYPE hibernate-mapping PUBLIC
                    "-//Hibernate/Hibernate Mapping DTD 3.0//EN"
                    "http://hibernate.sourceforge.net/hibernate-mapping-3.0.dtd" >

<hibernate-mapping package="amigo.sshmemo.dao">
    <class name="MemoType" table="tbl_memo_type">
        <id name="type" column="type">
            <generator class="native"/>
        </id>
        <property name="name" column="name" type="java.lang.String"  not-null="true" length="50"/>
        <property name="createTime" column="createTime" type="java.util.Date" not-null="true" />

        <many-to-one name="user" column="username" class="User"  not-null="true" />

        <set name="memos" inverse="false" cascade="save-update">
            <key column="typeId"/>
            <one-to-many class="Memo"/>
        </set>
    </class>
</hibernate-mapping>
```

该表的 usernmae 对象与 tbl_user 表存在外键关联，因此它与 User 对象是多对一关系。tbl_memo 表的 typeId 又与该表存在外键关联，因此 MemoType 与 Memo 之间是一对多关系。

（5）配置 applicationContext.xml。

在 WebRoot/WEB-INF/applicationContext.xml 需要配置 Hibernate 的连接信息，以及映射文件信息，并且需要在该文件中统一进行事务管理，该文件的内容如下所示：

```xml
<?xml version="1.0" encoding="UTF-8"?>
<!DOCTYPE beans PUBLIC "-//SPRING//DTD BEAN//EN"
    "http://www.springframework.org/dtd/spring-beans.dtd">

<beans>
    <bean id="dataSource" class="com.mchange.v2.c3p0.ComboPooledDataSource" destroy-method="close">
        <property name="driverClass">
            <value>com.mysql.jdbc.Driver</value>
        </property>
        <property name="jdbcUrl">
            <value>jdbc:mysql://localhost/sshmemo</value>
        </property>
        <property name="user">
            <value>root</value>
```

```xml
        </property>
        <property name="password">
            <value>root</value>
        </property>
        <property name="maxPoolSize">
            <value>80</value>
        </property>
        <property name="minPoolSize">
            <value>1</value>
        </property>
        <property name="initialPoolSize">
            <value>1</value>
        </property>
        <property name="maxIdleTime">
            <value>20</value>
        </property>
    </bean>

    <!--定义了 Hibernate 的 SessionFactory -->
    <bean id="sessionFactory" class="org.springframework.orm.hibernate3.LocalSessionFactoryBean">
        <property name="dataSource">
            <ref local="dataSource" />
        </property>
        <property name="mappingResources">
            <list>
                <value>amigo/sshmemo/dao/User.hbm.xml</value>
                <value>amigo/sshmemo/dao/Memo.hbm.xml</value>
                <value>amigo/sshmemo/dao/MemoType.hbm.xml</value>
            </list>
        </property>
        <property name="hibernateProperties">
            <props>
                <prop key="hibernate.dialect">org.hibernate.dialect.MySQLDialect</prop>
                <prop key="show_sql">true</prop>
                <prop key="hibernate.jdbc.batch_size">20</prop>
            </props>
        </property>
    </bean>

    <bean id="transactionManager"
        class="org.springframework.orm.hibernate3.HibernateTransactionManager">
        <property name="sessionFactory" ref="sessionFactory" />
    </bean>

    <bean id="transactionInterceptor"
        class="org.springframework.transaction.interceptor.TransactionInterceptor">
        <!-- 事务拦截器 bean 需要依赖注入一个事务管理器 -->
        <property name="transactionManager" ref="transactionManager" />
        <property name="transactionAttributes">
            <!-- 下面定义事务传播属性-->
            <props>
                <prop key="save*">PROPAGATION_REQUIRED</prop>
                <prop key="update*">PROPAGATION_REQUIRED</prop>
```

```xml
            <prop key="delete*">PROPAGATION_REQUIRED</prop>
            <prop key="login*">PROPAGATION_REQUIRED</prop>
            <prop key="*">PROPAGATION_REQUIRED,readOnly</prop>
        </props>
    </property>
</bean>

<!-- 定义 BeanNameAutoProxyCreator-->
<bean class="org.springframework.aop.framework.autoproxy.BeanNameAutoProxyCreator">
    <!-- 指定对满足哪些 bean name 的 bean 自动生成业务代理 -->
    <property name="beanNames">
        <list>
            <!-- 需要自动创建事务代理的 bean-->
        </list>
        <!-- 此处可增加其他需要自动创建事务代理的 bean-->
    </property>
    <!-- 下面定义 BeanNameAutoProxyCreator 所需的事务拦截器-->
    <property name="interceptorNames">
        <list>
            <value>transactionInterceptor</value>
        </list>
    </property>
</bean>

<bean id="baseDao" class="amigo.sshmemo.dao.BaseDaoImpl">
    <property name="sessionFactory">
        <ref bean="sessionFactory" />
    </property>
</bean>
</beans>
```

20.5.3 注册用户管理

（1）实现业务逻辑层。

在 amigo.sshmemo.service.user 包中建立备忘类型的业务逻辑接口 UsereManager.java 以及其实现类 UserManagerImpl.java，业务逻辑类包括获取用户信息列表、新增、修改和删除用户信息的方法。

接口类 UserManager.java 的代码如下所示：

```java
package amigo.sshmemo.service.user;

import java.util.List;

import amigo.sshmemo.action.user.UserForm;
import amigo.sshmemo.dao.User;

/**
 * 用户信息管理的业务逻辑接口类.
 */
public interface UserManager {
    public void saveUser(
            UserForm userForm) throws Exception;
```

```java
    public void updateUser(
            UserForm userForm) throws Exception;

    public void deleteUser(
            String[] usernames) throws Exception;

    public List<User> getUserList() throws Exception;

    public boolean userLogin(
            String username,
            String password) throws Exception;

    public User getUser(
            String username) throws Exception;
}
```

其实现类 UserManagerImpl.java 的代码如下所示：

```java
package amigo.sshmemo.service.user;

import java.util.ArrayList;
import java.util.Date;
import java.util.List;

import org.apache.commons.beanutils.BeanUtils;

import amigo.sshmemo.action.user.UserForm;
import amigo.sshmemo.dao.BaseDao;
import amigo.sshmemo.dao.User;

/**
 * 用户信息管理的业务逻辑实现类.
 */
public class UserManagerImpl implements UserManager {
    private BaseDao dao;

    public void setDao(BaseDao dao) {
        this.dao = dao;
    }

    /**
     * 用户注册.
     * @param userForm 用户表单
     */
    public void saveUser(UserForm userForm) throws Exception {
        User user = new User();
        BeanUtils.copyProperties(user, userForm);
        user.setCreateTime(new Date());

        // 保存用户信息对象
        dao.saveObject(user);
    }

    /**
     * 修改用户信息
```

```java
 * @param userForm 用户表单
 */
public void updateUser(UserForm userForm) throws Exception {
    // 获取用户信息对象
    User user = (User) dao.getObject(User.class,
            userForm.getUsername());

    // 更新用户信息
    user.setGender(userForm.getGender());
    user.setEmail(userForm.getEmail());
    user.setDescription(userForm.getDescription());
    user.setBirthDate(userForm.getBirthDate());
    dao.updateObject(user);
}

/**
 * 删除多个用户的信息
 * @param usernames 用户名称数组
 */
public void deleteUser(String[] usernames) throws Exception {
    for (int i = 0; i < usernames.length; i++) {
        // 获取用户信息对象
        User user = (User) dao.getObject(User.class,
                usernames[i]);
        // 删除用户信息对象
        dao.deleteObject(user);
    }
}

/**
 * 获取用户信息列表
 * @return 返回用户信息列表
 */
public List<User> getUserList() throws Exception {
    List<User> userList = dao.hqlQuery(
            "from User");
    return userList;
}

/**
 * 用户登录.
 * @param username 用户名
 * @param password 密码
 * @return 当用户登录信息正确时，返回 true，否则，返回 false
 */
public boolean userLogin(String username, String password) throws Exception {
    String hql = "select count(*) from User as obj where obj.username=? and obj.password=?";
    List paramList = new ArrayList();
    paramList.add(username);
    paramList.add(password);

    int count = Integer.parseInt(
```

```
                    dao.hqlQuery(hql, paramList.toArray()).get(0).toString());
            if (count > 0) {
                // 用户名或密码输入正确
                return true;
            } else {
                return false;
            }
        }

        /**
         * 获取用户信息.
         * @param username 用户名
         * @return 返回 username 的用户信息
         */
        public User getUser(
                    String username) throws Exception {
            User user = (User) dao.getObject(User.class, username);
            return user;
        }
    }
```

接下来还需要在 Spring 的配置文件 applicationContext 中配置该业务逻辑类，配置信息如下所示：

```xml
<!--用户信息管理业务逻辑类 -->
<bean id="userManager" class="amigo.sshmemo.service.user.UserManagerImpl">
    <property name="dao">
        <ref bean="baseDao" />
    </property>
</bean>
```

（2）实现控制层。

接着在 amigo.sshmemo.action.user 包下创建用户管理的 Action 类 UserAction.java，该类的代码如下所示：

```java
package amigo.sshmemo.action.user;

import java.util.List;

import javax.servlet.http.HttpServletRequest;

import org.apache.commons.beanutils.BeanUtils;
import org.apache.struts2.interceptor.ServletRequestAware;

import amigo.sshmemo.dao.User;
import amigo.sshmemo.service.user.UserManager;

import com.opensymphony.xwork2.ActionSupport;
/**
 * 用户管理的 Action.
 */
public class UserAction extends ActionSupport implements ServletRequestAware {
    private static final long serialVersionUID = 1L;

    /** 用户表单对象. */
```

```java
public UserForm user;

private HttpServletRequest request;

/** 用户管理的业务逻辑类. */
private UserManager userManager;

public void setServletRequest(HttpServletRequest request) {
    this.request = request;
}

public UserForm getUser() {
    return user;
}

public void setUserManager(UserManager userManager) {
    this.userManager = userManager;
}

/**
 * 用户登录.
 */
public String login() throws Exception {
    boolean flagSuccess = userManager.userLogin(user.getUsername(),
            user.getPassword());
    if (flagSuccess) {

        return "main"; // 登录成功
    } else {
        request.setAttribute("message", "登录失败!");
        return "login"; // 登录失败
    }
}

/**
 * 用户注册.
 */
public String reg() throws Exception {
    userManager.saveUser(user);
    return "main";
}

/**
 * 初始化修改用户信息界面.
 * @return 跳转到修改用户信息界面
 */
public String initUpdate() throws Exception {
    String username = request.getParameter("username");
    User userObj = userManager.getUser(username);
    BeanUtils.copyProperties(user, userObj);
    return "update";
}
```

```java
/**
 * 修改用户信息.
 * @return 跳转到用户列表显示的 Action 路径
 */
public String update() throws Exception {
    userManager.updateUser(user);
    return this.list();
}

/**
 * 删除用户信息.
 * @return 跳转到用户列表显示的 Action 路径
 */
public String delete() throws Exception {
    String[] usernames = request.getParameterValues("username");
    this.userManager.deleteUser(usernames);
    return this.list();
}

/**
 * 跳转到用户列表显示页面.
 * @return 跳转到用户显示的 Action.
 */
public String list() throws Exception {
    List<User> userList = this.userManager.getUserList();
    request.setAttribute("userList", userList);
    return "list";
}
}
```

Action 类创建后，需要在 struts.xml 文件中进行相应配置，配置信息如下：

```xml
<!-- 配置用户管理的 Action -->
<action name="*UserAction"  class="userAction" method="{1}">
    <result name="list">/user/userList.jsp</result>
    <result name="update">/user/updateUser.jsp</result>
    <result name="main">/user/main.jsp</result>
    <result name="login">/user/login.jsp</result>
    <result name="success">/success.jsp</result>
    <result name="error">/error.jsp</result>
</action>
```

Action 类在 Spring 中统一管理，添加的配置信息如下所示：

```xml
<!-- 用户信息管理的 Action-->
<bean id="userAction" class="amigo.sshmemo.action.user.UserAction">
    <property name="userManager">
        <ref bean="userManager" />
    </property>
</bean>
```

（3）实现表现层。

在 WebRoot/user 目录中创建本模块的 JSP 页面，其中用户列表页 userList.jsp 代码如下：

```jsp
<%@ page language="java" pageEncoding="UTF-8"%>
<%@ taglib prefix="s" uri="/struts-tags" %>
<%@ taglib uri="/WEB-INF/extremecomponents.tld" prefix="ec" %>
<html>
```

```html
<head>
    <title>用户列表</title>
    <link href="${pageContext.request.contextPath}/css/extremecomponents.css" rel="stylesheet" type="text/css">
    <script src="${pageContext.request.contextPath}/js/select.js"></script>
    <script language="javascript">
        function doSubmit() {
            if(!hasChecked(subForm.username)) {
                alert("请选择需要删除的用户!");
                return false;
            } else {
                if(!confirm("您确定要删除吗?")) {
                    return false;
                } else {
                    subForm.submit();
                }
            }
        }
    </script>
</head>
<body>
    <form name="subForm"
          method="post" action="${pageContext.request.contextPath}/deleteUserAction.action">
        <table width="98%" align="center" border="0" cellpadding="4" cellspacing="1">
            <tr>
                <td>
                    <input type="checkbox" name="checkbox2"
                        onclick="checkboxselect(document.subForm.username, document.subForm.checkbox2.checked)" style="border:0px"/>
                    全选
                    <input type="button" name="delall" value="删除所选" onclick="return doSubmit();"/>
                </td>
            </tr>
            <tr>
                <td height="74">
                    <table width="100%" border="0">
                        <tr>
                            <td>
                                <ec:table items="userList" action="?"
                                    imagePath = "${pageContext.request.contextPath}/images/ec/*.gif"
                                    cellpadding = "1" width = "100%" locale = "zh_CN"
                                    sortable="false" var = "user" filterable = "false" form="subForm">
                                    <ec:row highlightRow="true">
                                        <ec:column property="checkbox" title="选择" width="30" sortable="false">
                                            <input type="checkbox" name="username" value="${user.username}" style="border:0px"/>
                                        </ec:column>
                                        <ec:column property="username" title="用户名" width="60"/>
                                        <ec:column property="gender" title="性别" width="60">
                                            <script>
                                            <!--
```

```
                var gender = '${user.gender}';
                if(gender=='0') {
                    document.write('女');
                } else {
                    document.write('男');
                }
                //-->
            </script>
        </ec:column>
        <ec:column property="birthDate" title="出生日期" width="120" cell="date" format="yyyy-MM-dd"/>
        <ec:column property="tel" title="电话" width="70"/>
        <ec:column property="email" title="Email" width="120"/>
        <ec:column property="createTime" title="创建时间" width="150" cell="date" format="yyyy-MM-dd HH:mm:ss"/>
        <ec:column property="description" title="描述" width="200"/>
        <ec:column property="操作" style="text-align:center" filterable="false" width="*">
            <a href="${pageContext.request.contextPath}/initUpdateUserAction.action?username=${user.username}">
                <img src="${pageContext.request.contextPath}/images/ec/edit.gif" border="0" alt="修改">
            </a>
        </ec:column>
                                        </ec:row>
                                    </ec:table>
                                </td>
                            </tr>
                        </table>
                    </td>
                </tr>
            </table>
        </form>
    </body>
</html>
```

用户注册页面 reg.jsp 的代码如下所示：

```
<%@ page contentType="text/html; charset=UTF-8" %>
<%@ taglib prefix="s" uri="/struts-tags" %>

<html>
    <head>
        <title>注册用户</title>
        <meta http-equiv="Content-Type" content="text/html; charset=UTF-8"/>
    </head>
    <body>
        <s:form action="regUserAction">
            <s:textfield name="user.username" label="用户名"></s:textfield>
            <s:password name="user.password" label="密码"></s:password>
            <s:select label="性别" name="user.gender"
                list="#{'1' : '男', '0' : '女'}"
                listKey="key"
                listValue="value" value="0"/>
            <s:textfield name="user.birthDate" label="出生日期"></s:textfield>
            <s:textfield name="user.tel" label="联系电话"></s:textfield>
```

```jsp
            <s:textfield name="user.email" label="Email"></s:textfield>
            <s:textfield name="user.description" label="描述"></s:textfield>
            <s:submit></s:submit>
        </s:form>
    </body>
</html>
```

修改用户信息页面 updateUser.jsp 的代码如下所示：

```jsp
<%@ page contentType="text/html; charset=UTF-8" %>
<%@ taglib prefix="s" uri="/struts-tags" %>

<html>
    <head>
        <title>更新用户信息</title>
        <meta http-equiv="Content-Type" content="text/html; charset=UTF-8"/>
    </head>
    <body>
        <s:form action="updateUserAction">
            <s:textfield name="user.username" label="用户名" readonly="true" ></s:textfield>
            <s:select label="性别" name="user.gender"
                list="#{'1' : '男', '0' : '女'}"
                listKey="key"
                listValue="value" value="0"/>
            <s:textfield name="user.birthDate" label="出生日期"></s:textfield>
            <s:textfield name="user.tel" label="联系电话"></s:textfield>
            <s:textfield name="user.email" label="Email"></s:textfield>
            <s:textfield name="user.description" label="描述"></s:textfield>
            <s:submit></s:submit>
        </s:form>
    </body>
</html>
```

用户登录界面 login.jsp 的代码如下所示：

```jsp
<%@ page contentType="text/html; charset=UTF-8" %>
<%@ taglib prefix="s" uri="/struts-tags" %>

<html>
    <head>
        <title>用户登录</title>
        <meta http-equiv="Content-Type" content="text/html; charset=UTF-8"/>
    </head>
    <body>
        <font color="Red">${message}</font>
        <s:form action="loginUserAction">
            <s:textfield name="user.username" label="用户名"></s:textfield>
            <s:password name="user.password" label="密码"></s:password>
            <s:submit></s:submit>
        </s:form>
    </body>
</html>
```

（4）运行效果。

在浏览器中输入登录界面 login.jsp，输入系统管理员的用户名（admin）和密码（admin），如图 20-11 所示。

图 20-11 用户登录界面

在图 20-11 中，输入完毕后，单击 Submit 按钮进行提交，界面如图 20-12 所示。

图 20-12 用户列表界面

在图 20-12 中单击修改按钮，进入修改用户信息界面，如图 20-13 所示。

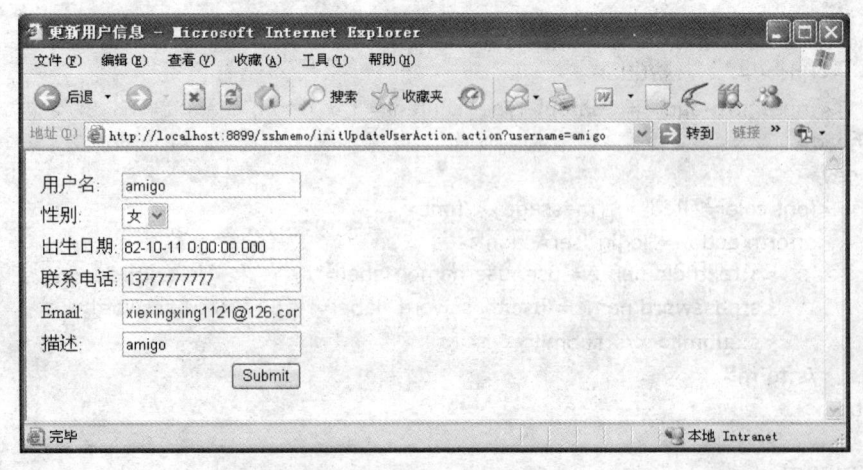

图 20-13 修改用户信息界面

在图 20-13 中修改完用户信息后，单击 Sumbit 按钮提交修改。

在图 20-12 的用户列表界面中，勾选需要删除的用户后，单击"删除所选"按钮，弹出删除确认对话框，如图 20-14 所示。

图 20-14 删除用户信息确认对话框

在图 20-14 中单击"确定"按钮，删除所选中的用户信息。

在浏览器中输入注册界面 reg.jsp 页面的地址，在注册界面中填写用户信息，界面如图 20-15 所示。

图 20-15 用户注册界面

在图 20-15 中单击 Submit 按钮，完成用户信息的注册。

20.5.4 备忘类型管理

（1）实现业务逻辑层。

在 amigo.sshmemo.service.memotype 包下建立备忘类型的业务逻辑接口 MemoTypeManager.java 以及其实现类 MemoTypeManagerImpl.java，业务逻辑类包括获取备忘类型列表、新增、修改和删除备忘类型的方法。

接口 MemoTypeManager.java 的代码如下所示：

```java
package amigo.sshmemo.service.memotype;

import java.util.List;

import amigo.sshmemo.dao.MemoType;

/**
 * 备忘类型的业务逻辑接口类.
```

```java
 */
public interface MemoTypeManager {
    public void saveMemoType(
            String name,
            String username) throws Exception;

    public void updateMemoType(
            long type,
            String name) throws Exception;

    public void deleteMemoType(
            String[] types) throws Exception;

    public List<MemoType> getMemoTypeList(
            String username) throws Exception;

    public MemoType getMemoType(
            long type) throws Exception;
}
```

其实现类 MemoTypeManagerImpl.java 的代码如下所示:

```java
package amigo.sshmemo.service.memotype;

import java.util.List;

import amigo.sshmemo.dao.MemoType;

/**
 * 备忘类型的业务逻辑接口类.
 */
public interface MemoTypeManager {
    /**
     * 保存备忘类型.
     * @param name 备忘名称
     * @param usernmae 所属用户
     */
    public void saveMemoType(
            String name,
            String username) throws Exception;

    /**
     * 修改备忘类型.
     * @param type 类型 id
     * @param name 备忘名称
     */
    public void updateMemoType(
            long type,
            String name) throws Exception;

    /**
     * 删除备忘类型.
     * @param types 类型 id 数组
     */
    public void deleteMemoType(
```

```java
        String[] types) throws Exception;

    /**
     * 根据用户名称获取其能查看的备忘类型列表.
     * 说明：当 username 为 admin 时，获取所有的备忘类型
     * @param username 用户名称
     * @return 返回备忘类型列表
     */
    public List<MemoType> getMemoTypeList(
            String username) throws Exception;

    /**
     * 根据主键查询备忘类型.
     * @param type 备忘类型 id
     * @return 返回主键为 type 的备忘类型对象
     */
    public MemoType getMemoType(
            long type) throws Exception;
}
```

接下来还需要在 Spring 的配置文件 applicationContext 中配置该业务逻辑类，配置信息如下所示：

```xml
<!--备忘类型管理业务逻辑类 -->
<bean id="memoTypeManager"
    class="amigo.sshmemo.service.memotype.MemoTypeManagerImpl">
    <property name="dao">
        <ref bean="baseDao" />
    </property>
</bean>
```

（2）实现控制层。

接着在 amigo.sshmemo.action.memotype 包中创建备忘类型管理的 Action 类 MemoTypeAction.java，该类的代码如下所示：

```java
package amigo.sshmemo.action.memotype;

import java.util.List;
import java.util.Map;

import javax.servlet.http.HttpServletRequest;
import org.apache.struts2.interceptor.ServletRequestAware;
import org.apache.struts2.interceptor.SessionAware;

import amigo.sshmemo.dao.MemoType;
import amigo.sshmemo.service.memotype.MemoTypeManager;
import com.opensymphony.xwork2.ActionSupport;

/**
 * 备忘类型管理的 Action.
 */
public class MemoTypeAction extends ActionSupport
        implements ServletRequestAware, SessionAware {
    private static final long serialVersionUID = 1L;

    /** 类型名称.*/
    private String name;
```

```java
/** 类型 id. */
private long typeId;

private HttpServletRequest request;

private Map<String,String> session;

/** 备忘类型管理的业务逻辑类. */
private MemoTypeManager memoTypeManager;

// 省略 request、session 和 memoTypeManager 的 setter 方法
// 省略 name、typeId 的 getter/setter 方法


/**
 * 保存备忘类型.
 * @return 跳转到备忘类型列表显示的 Action 路径
 */
public String save() throws Exception {
    String username = session.get("username");
    if (username == null) {
        request.setAttribute("message", "对不起，您未登录，请先登录!");
        return "login";
    }

    this.memoTypeManager.saveMemoType(name, username);
    return this.list();
}


/**
 * 初始化修改备忘类型界面.
 * @return 跳转到修改用户信息界面
 */
public String initUpdate() throws Exception {
    String type = request.getParameter("type");
    MemoType memoType = this.memoTypeManager.getMemoType(
            Long.parseLong(type));
    typeId = Long.parseLong(type);
    name = memoType.getName();
    return "update";
}


/**
 * 修改备忘类型.
 * @return 跳转到备忘类型列表显示的 Action 路径
 */
public String update() throws Exception {
    String type = request.getParameter("type");
    this.memoTypeManager.updateMemoType(
            Long.parseLong(type),
            name);
    return this.list();
```

```java
    }

    /**
     * 删除用户信息.
     * @return  跳转到用户列表显示的 Action 路径
     */
    public String delete() throws Exception {
        String[] types = request.getParameterValues("type");
        this.memoTypeManager.deleteMemoType(types);
        return this.list();
    }

    /**
     * 跳转到用户列表显示页面.
     * @return  跳转到用户显示的 Action.
     */
    public String list() throws Exception {
        String username = session.get("username");
        if (username == null) {
            request.setAttribute("message", "对不起,您未登录,请先登录!");
            return "login";
        }

        List<MemoType> memoTypeList = memoTypeManager.getMemoTypeList(
                username);
        request.setAttribute("memoTypeList", memoTypeList);
        return "list";
    }
}
```

Action 类创建后,需要在 struts.xml 文件中进行相应配置,配置信息如下:

```xml
<!-- 备忘类型管理的 Action -->
<action name="*MemoTypeAction"  class="memoTypeAction" method="{1}">
    <result name="list">/memotype/memoTypeList.jsp</result>
    <result name="update">/memotype/updateMemoType.jsp</result>
    <result name="login">/user/login.jsp</result>
</action>
```

Action 类在 Spring 中统一管理,添加的配置信息如下所示:

```xml
<!-- 备忘类型管理的 Action-->
<bean id="memoTypeAction"
        class="amigo.sshmemo.action.memotype.MemoTypeAction">
    <property name="memoTypeManager">
        <ref bean="memoTypeManager" />
    </property>
</bean>
```

(3)实现表现层。

在 WebRoot/memotype 目录中创建本模块的 JSP 页面,其中备忘类型列表页 memoTypeList.jsp 代码如下所示:

```jsp
<%@ page language="java" pageEncoding="UTF-8"%>
<%@ taglib prefix="s" uri="/struts-tags" %>
<%@ taglib uri="/WEB-INF/extremecomponents.tld" prefix="ec" %>
<html>
```

```html
<head>
    <title>备忘类型列表</title>
    <link href="${pageContext.request.contextPath}/css/extremecomponents.css" rel="stylesheet" type="text/css">
    <script src="${pageContext.request.contextPath}/js/select.js"></script>
    <script language="javascript">
        function doSubmit() {
            if(!hasChecked(subForm.type)) {
                alert("请选择需要删除的备忘类型!");
                return false;
            } else {
                if(!confirm("您确定要删除吗?")) {
                    return false;
                } else {
                    subForm.submit();
                }
            }
        }
    </script>
</head>
<body>
    <form name="subForm" method="post" action="${pageContext.request.contextPath}/deleteMemoTypeAction.action">
        <table width="98%" align="center" border="0" cellpadding="4" cellspacing="1">
            <tr>
                <td>
<input type="button" name="addUser" value="添加" onclick="window.location.href='${pageContext.request.contextPath}/memotype/addMemoType.jsp'" />  
<input type="checkbox" name="checkbox2" onclick="checkboxselect(document.subForm.type, document.subForm.checkbox2.checked)" style="border:0px"/>
全选
<input type="button" name="delall" value="删除所选" onclick="return doSubmit();"/>
                </td>
            </tr>
            <tr>
                <td height="74">
                    <table width="100%" border="0">
                        <tr>
                            <td>
<ec:table items="memoTypeList"
action="?"
imagePath = "${pageContext.request.contextPath}/images/ec/*.gif"
cellpadding = "1" width = "100%"
locale = "zh_CN" sortable="false"
var = "memoType" filterable = "false" form="subForm">
    <ec:row highlightRow="true">
    <ec:column property="checkbox" title="选择" width="30" sortable="false">
        <input type="checkbox" name="type" value="${memoType.type}" style="border:0px"/>
    </ec:column>
    <ec:column property="type" title="类型 ID" width="100"/>
        <ec:column property="name" title="类型名称" width="100"/>
```

```
            <ec:column property="user.username" title="创建人" width="120"/>
            <ec:column property="createTime" title="创建时间" width="150" cell="date" format="yyyy-MM-dd HH:mm:ss"/>
            <ec:column property="操作" style="text-align:center" filterable="false" width="*">
                <a href="${pageContext.request.contextPath}/initUpdateMemoTypeAction.action?type=${memoType.type}">
                    <img src="${pageContext.request.contextPath}/images/ec/edit.gif" border="0" alt="修改">
                </a>
            </ec:column>
        </ec:row>
    </ec:table>
                            </td>
                        </tr>
                    </table>
                </td>
            </tr>
        </table>
    </form>
</body>
</html>
```

添加备忘类型页面 addMemoType.jsp 的代码如下所示:

```
<%@ page contentType="text/html; charset=UTF-8" %>
<%@ taglib prefix="s" uri="/struts-tags" %>

<html>
    <head>
        <title>新增备忘类型</title>
        <meta http-equiv="Content-Type" content="text/html; charset=UTF-8"/>
    </head>
    <body>
        <s:form action="saveMemoTypeAction">
            <s:textfield name="name" label="类型名称"></s:textfield>
            <s:submit></s:submit>
        </s:form>
    </body>
</html>
```

修改备忘类型页面 updateMemoType.jsp 的代码如下所示:

```
<%@ page contentType="text/html; charset=UTF-8" %>
<%@ taglib prefix="s" uri="/struts-tags" %>

<html>
    <head>
        <title>更新备忘类型</title>
        <meta http-equiv="Content-Type" content="text/html; charset=UTF-8"/>
    </head>
    <body>
        <s:form action="updateMemoTypeAction">
            <input type="hidden" name="type" value="<s:property value='typeId' />" />
            <s:textfield name="name" label="类型名称"></s:textfield>
            <s:submit></s:submit>
        </s:form>
```

```
        </body>
</html>
```

（4）运行效果。

在图 20-11 所示的登录界面中输入普通用户的用户名（如 amigo）和密码（如 amigo），然后单击 Submit 按钮，进入普通用户的主界面，在该界面中点击"备忘类型管理"，呈现备忘类型列表界面，如图 20-16 所示。

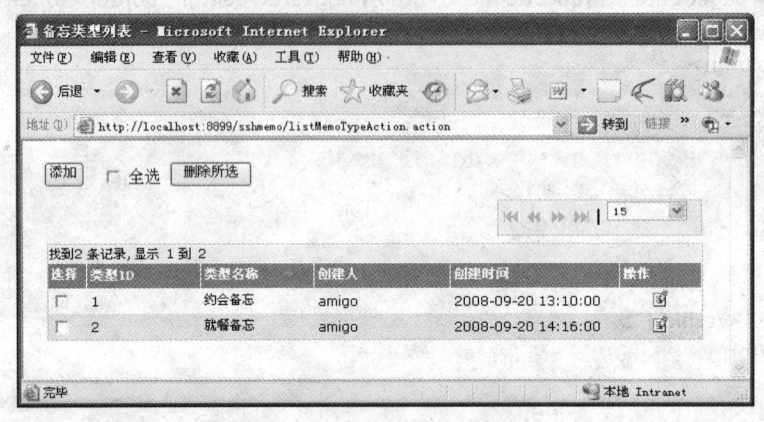

图 20-16　备忘类型列表界面

在图 20-16 中单击"添加"按钮，呈现添加备忘类型界面，如图 20-17 所示。

图 20-17　添加备忘类型界面

在图 20-17 中添加"类型名称"后，单击 Submit 按钮提交备忘类型信息。

在图 20-16 的列表页中单击修改按钮　进入备忘类型修改界面，如图 20-18 所示。

图 20-18　备忘类型修改界面

在图 20-18 中修改"类型名称"后，单击 Submit 按钮提交修改。

在图 20-16 的列表页中选择需要删除一个或多个备忘类型后单击"删除所选"按钮，将会出现如图 20-19 所示的删除确认对话框。

图 20-19　备忘类型删除确认对话框

在图 20-19 中单击"确定"按钮完成备忘类型的删除操作。

20.5.5　备忘信息管理

（1）实现业务逻辑层。

在 amigo.sshmemo.service.memo 包下建立备忘信息的业务逻辑接口 MemoManager.java 以及其实现类 MemoManagerImpl.java，业务逻辑类包括获取备忘信息列表、新增、修改和删除备忘信息的方法。

接口类 MemoManager.java 的代码如下所示：

```java
package amigo.sshmemo.service.memo;

import java.util.List;

import amigo.sshmemo.action.memo.MemoForm;
import amigo.sshmemo.dao.Memo;

/**
 * 备忘类型的业务逻辑接口类.
 */
public interface MemoManager {
    public void saveMemo(
            MemoForm memoForm) throws Exception;

    public void updateMemo(
            MemoForm memoForm) throws Exception;

    public void deleteMemos(
            String[] memoIds) throws Exception;

    public List<Memo> getMemoList(
            String username) throws Exception;

    public List<Memo> getRemindMemoList(
            String username) throws Exception;

    public void updateMemoStatus(
            String memoId,
            int status) throws Exception;
```

```java
    public Memo getMemoById(
            long memoId) throws Exception;
}
```

其实现类 MemoManagerImpl.java 的代码如下所示:

```java
package amigo.sshmemo.service.memo;

import java.util.ArrayList;
import java.util.Date;
import java.util.List;

import org.apache.commons.beanutils.BeanUtils;

import amigo.sshmemo.action.memo.MemoForm;
import amigo.sshmemo.dao.BaseDao;
import amigo.sshmemo.dao.Memo;
import amigo.sshmemo.dao.MemoType;
import amigo.sshmemo.dao.User;

/**
 * 备忘信息的业务逻辑实现类.
 */
public class MemoManagerImpl implements MemoManager {
    private BaseDao dao;

    public void setDao(BaseDao dao) {
        this.dao = dao;
    }

    /**
     * 保存备忘信息.
     * @param memoForm 备忘信息表单对象
     */
    public void saveMemo(
            MemoForm memoForm) throws Exception {
        // 获取用户对象
        User user = (User) dao.getObject(
                User.class,
                memoForm.getUsername());

        // 获取备忘类型对象
        MemoType memoType = (MemoType) dao.getObject(
                MemoType.class,
                memoForm.getType());

        // 设置备忘信息对象
        Memo memo = new Memo();
        BeanUtils.copyProperties(memo, memoForm);
        memo.setCreateTime(new Date());
        memo.setUser(user);
        memo.setMemoType(memoType);
        memo.setStatus(0); // 初始态

        // 保存备忘信息
```

```java
        dao.saveObject(memo);
}

/**
 * 修改备忘信息.
 * @param memoForm 备忘信息表单对象
 */
public void updateMemo(
            MemoForm memoForm) throws Exception {
    // 获取备忘信息对象
    Memo memo = (Memo) dao.getObject(
            Memo.class,
            memoForm.getMemoId());

    // 获取备忘类型对象
    MemoType memoType = (MemoType) dao.getObject(
            MemoType.class,
            memoForm.getType());

    // 更新备忘信息对象
    memo.setDescription(memoForm.getDescription());
    memo.setMemoType(memoType);
    memo.setName(memoForm.getName());
    memo.setRemindTime(memoForm.getRemindTime());
    dao.updateObject(memo);
}

/**
 * 删除备忘信息.
 * @param memoIds 备忘信息 id 数组
 */
public void deleteMemos(
            String[] memoIds) throws Exception {
    for (int i = 0; i < memoIds.length; i++) {
        long memoId = Long.parseLong(memoIds[i]);
        // 获得备忘信息对象
        Memo memo = (Memo) dao.getObject(Memo.class,
                memoId);
        // 删除备忘信息对象
        dao.deleteObject(memo);
    }
}

/**
 * 根据用户名称获取其能查看的备忘信息列表.
 * 说明：当 username 为 admin 时，获取所有的备忘信息
 * @param username 用户名称
 * @return 返回备忘信息列表
 */
public List<Memo> getMemoList(
            String username) throws Exception {
    List paramList = new ArrayList();
```

```java
        String hql = "from Memo as obj where obj.user.username=?";
        paramList.add(username);
        List<Memo> memoList = dao.hqlQuery(hql,
                paramList.toArray());
        return memoList;
    }

    /**
     * 获取需要提醒的备忘信息列表.
     * @param username 用户名称
     * @return 返回需要提醒的备忘信息列表
     */
    public List<Memo> getRemindMemoList(
            String username) throws Exception {
        List paramList = new ArrayList();
        String hql = "from Memo where username = ? " +
                "and status = 0 and remindTime is not null and remindTime < ?";
        paramList.add(username);
        paramList.add(new Date());

        // 查询需要提醒的备忘信息列表
        List<Memo> memoList = dao.hqlQuery(hql,
                paramList.toArray());
        return memoList;
    }

    /**
     * 更新备忘信息的状态.
     * @param memoId 备忘信息 id
     * @param status 状态
     */
    public void updateMemoStatus(
            String memoId, int status) throws Exception {
        // 获得备忘信息对象
        Memo memo = (Memo) dao.getObject(Memo.class,
                Long.parseLong(memoId));

        // 更新状态
        memo.setStatus(status);
        dao.updateObject(memo);
    }

    /**
     * 根据主键查询备忘信息对象.
     * @param memoId 备忘信息 id
     * @return 返回备忘信息对象
     */
    public Memo getMemoById(long memoId) throws Exception {
        Memo memo = (Memo) dao.getObject(
                Memo.class,
                memoId);
        return memo;
    }
```

}

接下来还需要在 Spring 的配置文件 applicationContext 中配置该业务逻辑类，配置信息如下所示：

```xml
<!--备忘信息管理业务逻辑类 -->
<bean id="memoManager" class="amigo.sshmemo.service.memo.MemoManagerImpl">
    <property name="dao">
        <ref bean="baseDao" />
    </property>
</bean>
```

（2）实现控制层。

接着在 amigo.sshmemo.action.memo 包中创建备忘信息管理的 Action 类 MemoAction.java，该类的代码如下所示：

```java
package amigo.sshmemo.action.memo;

import java.util.List;
import java.util.Map;

import javax.servlet.http.HttpServletRequest;

import org.apache.commons.beanutils.BeanUtils;
import org.apache.struts2.interceptor.ServletRequestAware;
import org.apache.struts2.interceptor.SessionAware;

import amigo.sshmemo.dao.Memo;
import amigo.sshmemo.dao.MemoType;
import amigo.sshmemo.service.memo.MemoManager;
import amigo.sshmemo.service.memotype.MemoTypeManager;

import com.opensymphony.xwork2.ActionSupport;

/**
 * 备忘信息管理的 Action.
 */
public class MemoAction extends ActionSupport
        implements ServletRequestAware, SessionAware {
    private static final long serialVersionUID = 1L;

    /** 备忘信息表单对象. */
    private MemoForm memo;

    private List memoTypes;

    private HttpServletRequest request;

    private Map<String,String> session;

    /** 备忘信息管理的业务逻辑类. */
    private MemoManager memoManager;

    private MemoTypeManager memoTypeManager;
```

```java
// 省略 request、session 和 memoManager 的 setter 方法
// 省略 memo、memoTypes 的 getter/setter 方法

/**
 * 初始化添加备忘信息页面.
 * @return 跳转到添加备忘信息页面
 */
public String initSave() throws Exception {
    String username = session.get("username");
    if (username == null) {
        request.setAttribute("message", "对不起，您未登录，请先登录!");
        return "login";
    }

    List<MemoType> memoTypeList = memoTypeManager.getMemoTypeList(
            username);
    this.setMemoTypes(memoTypeList);
    memo = new MemoForm();
    return "save";
}

/**
 * 保存备忘信息.
 * @return 跳转到备忘信息列表显示的 Action 路径
 */
public String save() throws Exception {
    String username = session.get("username");
    if (username == null) {
        request.setAttribute("message", "对不起，您未登录，请先登录!");
        return "login";
    }

    memo.setUsername(username);
    this.memoManager.saveMemo(memo);
    return this.list();
}

/**
 * 初始化修改备忘信息界面.
 * @return 跳转到修改备忘信息界面
 */
public String initUpdate() throws Exception {
    String username = session.get("username");
    if (username == null) {
        request.setAttribute("message", "对不起，您未登录，请先登录!");
        return "login";
    }

    List<MemoType> memoTypeList = memoTypeManager.getMemoTypeList(
            username);
    this.setMemoTypes(memoTypeList);
    String memoId = request.getParameter("memoId");
```

```java
            Memo memoObj = memoManager.getMemoById(
                    Long.parseLong(memoId));
            BeanUtils.copyProperties(memo, memoObj);
            return "update";
    }

    /**
     * 修改备忘信息.
     * @return 跳转到备忘信息列表显示的 Action 路径
     */
    public String update() throws Exception {
        this.memoManager.updateMemo(memo);
        return this.list();
    }

    /**
     * 删除备忘信息.
     * @return 跳转到备忘信息列表显示的 Action 路径
     */
    public String delete() throws Exception {
        String[] memoIds = request.getParameterValues("memoId");
        this.memoManager.deleteMemos(memoIds);
        return this.list();
    }

    /**
     * 获得用户所有的备忘跳转到备忘信息列表显示页面.
     * @return 跳转到备忘信息列表显示页面.
     */
    public String list() throws Exception {
        String username = session.get("username");
        if (username == null) {
            request.setAttribute("message", "对不起，您未登录，请先登录!");
            return "login";
        }

        List<Memo> memoList = memoManager.getMemoList(
                username);
        request.setAttribute("memoList", memoList);
        return "list";
    }

    /**
     * 跳转到备忘信息列表显示页面.
     * @return 跳转到备忘信息列表显示页面.
     */
    public String listRemind() throws Exception {
        String username = session.get("username");
        if (username == null) {
            request.setAttribute("message", "对不起，您未登录，请先登录!");
            return "login";
        }
```

```java
            List<Memo> memoList = memoManager.getRemindMemoList(
                    username);
            request.setAttribute("memoList", memoList);
            return "listRemind";
        }

        /**
         * 跳转到备忘信息列表显示页面.
         * @return 跳转到备忘信息列表显示页面.
         */
        public String updateStatus() throws Exception {
            String memoId = request.getParameter("memoId");
            // 将状态修改为1（0：0：初始态，1：已查看）
            this.memoManager.updateMemoStatus(
                    memoId, 1);
            return this.listRemind();
        }
}
```

Action 类创建后，需要在 struts.xml 文件中进行相应配置，配置信息如下：

```xml
<!-- 备忘信息管理的 Action -->
<action name="*MemoAction"  class="memoAction" method="{1}">
    <result name="listRemind">/memo/remindMemoList.jsp</result>
    <result name="list">/memo/memoList.jsp</result>
    <result name="update">/memo/updateMemo.jsp</result>
    <result name="save">/memo/addMemo.jsp</result>
    <result name="login">/user/login.jsp</result>
</action>
```

Action 类在 Spring 中统一管理，添加的配置信息如下所示：

```xml
<!-- 备忘信息管理的 Action-->
<bean id="memoAction" class="amigo.sshmemo.action.memo.MemoAction">
    <property name="memoManager">
        <ref bean="memoManager" />
    </property>
    <property name="memoTypeManager">
        <ref bean="memoTypeManager" />
    </property>
</bean>
```

（3）实现表现层。

在 WebRoot/memo 目录下创建本模块的 JSP 页面，其中备忘信息列表页 memoList.jsp 代码如下所示：

```jsp
<%@ page language="java" pageEncoding="UTF-8"%>
<%@ taglib prefix="s" uri="/struts-tags" %>
<%@ taglib uri="/WEB-INF/extremecomponents.tld" prefix="ec" %>
<html>
    <head>
        <title>备忘信息列表</title>
        <link href="${pageContext.request.contextPath}/css/extremecomponents.css" rel="stylesheet" type="text/css">
        <script src="${pageContext.request.contextPath}/js/select.js"></script>
        <script language="javascript">
            function doSubmit() {
```

```
                    if(!hasChecked(subForm.memoId)) {
                        alert("请选择需要删除的备忘信息!");
                        return false;
                    } else {
                        if(!confirm("您确定要删除吗?")) {
                            return false;
                        } else {
                            subForm.submit();
                        }
                    }
                }
            </script>
        </head>
        <body>
            <form name="subForm" method="post" action="${pageContext.request.contextPath}/deleteMemoAction.action">
                <table width="98%" align="center" border="0" cellpadding="4" cellspacing="1">
                    <tr>
                        <td>
                            <input type="button" name="addUser" value="添加"
                                onclick="window.location.href='${pageContext.request.contextPath}/initSaveMemoAction.action'"/>
                              
                            <input type="checkbox" name="checkbox2"
                                onclick="checkboxselect(document.subForm.memoId, document.subForm.checkbox2.checked)" style="border:0px"/>
                            全选
                            <input type="button" name="delall" value="删除所选" onclick="return doSubmit();"/>
                        </td>
                    </tr>
                    <tr>
                        <td height="74">
                            <table width="100%" border="0">
                                <tr>
                                    <td>
<ec:table items="memoList" action="?"
imagePath = "${pageContext.request.contextPath}/images/ec/*.gif"
cellpadding = "1"   width = "100%" locale = "zh_CN"
sortable="false" var = "memo" filterable = "false"
form="subForm">
<ec:row highlightRow="true">
<ec:column property="checkbox" title="选择" width="30" sortable="false">
<input type="checkbox" name="memoId" value="${memo.memoId}" style="border:0px"/>
</ec:column>
<ec:column property="memoId" title="ID" width="40"/>
<ec:column property="name" title="备忘名称" width="100"/>
<ec:column property="memoType.name" title="类型名称" width="100"/>
<ec:column property="user.username" title="所属用户" width="120"/>
<ec:column property="description" title="描述" width="120"/>
<ec:column property="remindTime" title="提醒时间" width="150" cell="date" format="yyyy-MM-dd HH:mm:ss"/>
<ec:column property="createTime" title="创建时间" width="150" cell="date" format="yyyy-MM-dd
```

```
HH:mm:ss"/>
    <ec:column property="操作" style="text-align:center" filterable="false" width="*">
    <a
    href="${pageContext.request.contextPath}/initUpdateMemoAction.action?memoId=${memo.memoId}">
    <img src="${pageContext.request.contextPath}/images/ec/edit.gif" border="0" alt="修改">
    </a>
    </ec:column>
    </ec:row>
    </ec:table>
                                </td>
                            </tr>
                        </table>
                    </td>
                </tr>
            </table>
        </form>
    </body>
</html>
```

查看提醒信息的列表页面 remindMemoList.jsp 的代码如下所示:

```
<%@ page language="java" pageEncoding="UTF-8"%>
<%@ taglib prefix="s" uri="/struts-tags" %>
<%@ taglib uri="/WEB-INF/extremecomponents.tld" prefix="ec" %>
<html>
    <head>
        <title>备忘提醒信息列表</title>
        <link href="${pageContext.request.contextPath}/css/extremecomponents.css" rel="stylesheet" type="text/css">
    </head>
    <body>
        <form name="subForm" method="post" action="${pageContext.request.contextPath}/deleteMemoAction.action">
            <table width="98%" align="center" border="0" cellpadding="4" cellspacing="1">
                <tr>
                    <td>
<ec:table items="memoList" action="?"
imagePath = "${pageContext.request.contextPath}/images/ec/*.gif"
cellpadding = "1" width = "100%" locale = "zh_CN"
sortable="false" var = "memo" filterable = "false"
form="subForm">
<ec:row highlightRow="true">
<ec:column property="memoId" title="ID" width="40"/>
<ec:column property="name" title="备忘名称" width="100"/>
<ec:column property="memoType.name" title="类型名称" width="100"/>
<ec:column property="user.username" title="所属用户" width="120"/>
<ec:column property="description" title="描述" width="120"/>
<ec:column property="remindTime" title="提醒时间" width="150" cell="date" format="yyyy-MM-dd HH:mm:ss"/>
<ec:column property="createTime" title="创建时间" width="150" cell="date" format="yyyy-MM-dd HH:mm:ss"/>
<ec:column property="操作" style="text-align:center" filterable="false" width="*">
    <a
    href="${pageContext.request.contextPath}/updateStatusMemoAction.action?memoId=${memo.me
```

```
moId}">
    <img src="${pageContext.request.contextPath}/images/ec/edit.gif" border="0" alt="不再提醒">
    </a>
    </ec:column>
    </ec:row>
    </ec:table>
                </td>
            </tr>
        </table>
    </form>
</body>
</html>
```

新增备忘信息页 addMemo.jsp 的代码如下所示:

```
<%@ page contentType="text/html; charset=UTF-8" %>
<%@ taglib prefix="s" uri="/struts-tags" %>

<html>
    <head>
        <title>新增备忘信息</title>
        <meta http-equiv="Content-Type" content="text/html; charset=UTF-8"/>
    </head>
    <body>
        <s:form action="saveMemoAction">
            <s:textfield name="memo.name" label="备忘名称"></s:textfield>
            <s:select label="备忘类型" name="memo.type"
                list="memoTypes"
                listKey="type"
                listValue="name"/>
            <s:textfield name="memo.description" label="描述"></s:textfield>
            <s:textfield name="memo.remindTime" label="提醒时间"></s:textfield>
            <s:submit></s:submit>
        </s:form>
    </body>
</html>
```

修改备忘信息页 updateMemo.jsp 的代码如下所示:

```
<%@ page contentType="text/html; charset=UTF-8" %>
<%@ taglib prefix="s" uri="/struts-tags" %>

<html>
    <head>
        <title>更新备忘信息</title>
        <meta http-equiv="Content-Type" content="text/html; charset=UTF-8"/>
    </head>
    <body>
        <s:form action="updateMemoAction">
            // ...内容同 addMemo.jsp
        </s:form>
    </body>
</html>
```

（4）运行效果。

在图 20-11 所示的登录界面中输入普通用户的用户名（如 amigo）和密码（如 amigo），然后单击 Submit 按钮，进入普通用户的主界面，在该界面中点击"备忘信息管理"，呈现备忘信息列表界面，如图 20-20 所示。

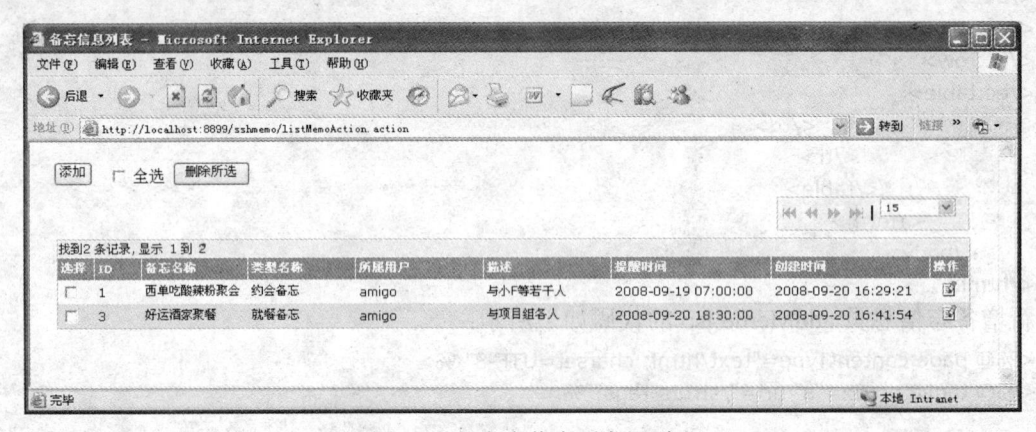

图 20-20　备忘信息列表界面

在图 20-20 中单击"添加"按钮，进入新增备忘信息页面，如图 20-21 所示。

图 20-21　新增备忘信息页面

在图 20-21 中填写备忘信息后，单击 Submit 按钮提交备忘信息。

在图 20-20 中单击修改按钮，进入修改备忘信息界面，如图 20-22 所示。

图 20-22　修改备忘信息界面

第 20 章　SSH 实例——个人备忘录系统　　495

在图 20-20 所示的备忘信息列表界面中选择需要删除的备忘信息后，单击"删除所选"按钮，弹出备忘信息删除确认对话框，如图 20-23 所示。

图 20-23　备忘信息删除确认对话框

在图 20-23 中单击"确定"按钮，删除所选中的记录。
查看提醒信息列表界面如图 20-24 所示。

图 20-24　查看提醒信息列表界面

在图 20-24 中单击不再提醒的按钮，该条备忘信息的状态将被改变，而从"备忘信息"列表中消失。

小结

本章以一个个人备忘录系统的实例，实现了用户管理、备忘类型管理和备忘信息管理模块，本实例详细介绍了如何开发一个 Struts 2 + Hibernate 3 + Spring 2 的 Web 应用。

在本实例中，采用 Spring 框架统一管理事务，因此不需要在业务逻辑代码中加入对事物的控制，对代码进行了优化。本系统采用 C3P0 连接池技术提高了系统的运行效率。

为了解决输入信息引起乱码的问题，需要在 web.xml 中添加如下 Filter：

```xml
<!-- 中文编码 -->
<filter>
    <filter-name>struts-cleanup</filter-name>
    <filter-class>org.apache.struts2.dispatcher.ActionContextCleanUp</filter-class>
</filter>

<filter-mapping>
    <filter-name>struts-cleanup</filter-name>
    <url-pattern>/*</url-pattern>
</filter-mapping>
```

另外还需要在 Struts 2 的配置文件中添加如下配置信息：

```xml
<constant name="struts.locale" value="zh_CN"/>
<constant name="struts.i18n.encoding" value="UTF-8"/>
```

当然，本实例还有不少需要进行改进的地方，例如对 session 中用户名是否存在的验证可以使用 Struts 2 的拦截器来实现，从而不必出现那么多重复的代码。

对输入文本的验证可采用 Struts 2 提供的验证框架进行验证，使用验证配置文件进行统一管理。另外若需要对本实例进行国际化，可采用 Struts 2 提供的国际化的方法对输入界面的文本信息，以及各界面的提示信息进行国际化，另外对输入验证的提示信息也可采用 Struts 2 提供的国际化方法实现国际化。

在本实例中，并未对异常进行管理，对异常的管理可采用 Spring 的 AOP 进行拦截后统一管理，这样对异常的处理不会被分散在各个类中。

第 21 章　SSH 实例——个人收支管理系统

【本章导读语】

本章以个人收支管理系统为例，讲述如何使用 Struts 2 + Hibernate3 + Spring 2 开发 Java EE 应用系统。本系统采用 MVC 模式，并将系统分成 DAO 层、业务逻辑层、控制层和表现层，这种划分能使系统具有良好的扩展性和可维护性。

本章实例在使用 Struts 2 框架时，使用到 Struts 2 的如下内容：
- 作为 MVC 框架使用，Action 类负责拦截系统中的用户请求，并调用相应的业务逻辑类进行处理。
- 使用 Struts 2 提供的验证框架，方便地采用可配置的方式对系统的各输入进行验证。
- 采用 Struts 2 提供的国际化方法，对系统的信息进行国际化。
- 采用 Struts 2 提供的自定义标签，简化页面的开发。

在使用 Hibernate 3 框架时，主要使用它来进行数据库的操作，Hibernate 提供了使用面向对象编程的方式操作数据库，而要做的操作只是将表按照 Hibernate 提供的映射方法映射成 POJO 类和映射文件，为了减少重复代码，本实例提供了 BaseDao 类及其实现类来进行数据库的操作，它提供了数据库常见操作的方法，可以满足系统的需要，一般情况下不需要进行扩展。

本章实例还使用了 Spring 2 框架，并利用 Spring 2 框架提供的 IoC 容器来管理系统中的所有组件（例如业务逻辑组件和控制器组件），并管理各组件之间的依赖关系。

在进行统计报表的开发时，本系统使用的是完全基于 Java 的开源图形报表工具 JFreeChart，JFreeChart 能生成各种各样的统计图表，例如饼图、柱状图、时序图和甘特图等，本实例主要使用它生成饼图和时序图来展现个人收/支情况。

21.1　系统需求分析

个人收支管理系统主要包括个人收支类型信息、收支信息和统计分析 3 个功能模块。

个人收支类型模块的功能包括：
- 查看收支类型列表。
- 添加收支类型。
- 编辑收支类型。
- 删除收支类型。

收支信息管理模块的功能包括：
- 查看收支信息列表。
- 添加收支信息。
- 编辑收支信息。
- 删除收支信息。

统计分析模块的功能包括：

- 收/支月统计报表。
- 收/支年统计报表。

21.2 系统架构设计

本系统整合了 Struts 2、Hibernate 和 Spring 技术，图形报表工具采用的是开源工具 JFreeChart，分页采用 extremecomponents 组件，系统的核心架构图如图 21-1 所示。

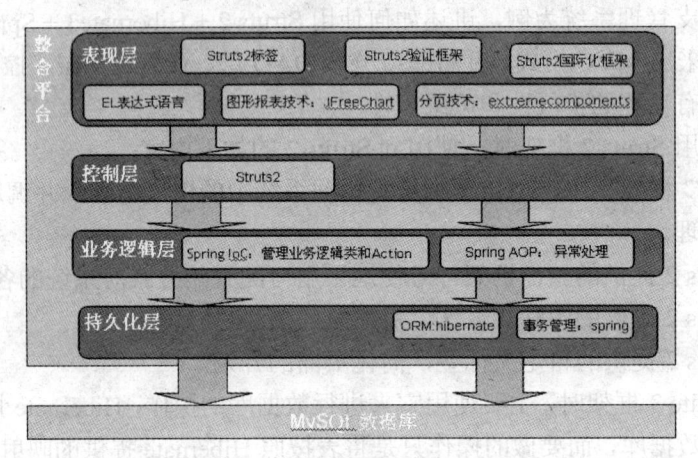

图 21-1 系统的核心架构图

本系统采用 MVC 模式，主要包括表现层、控制层、业务逻辑层和持久化层，其中：

- 表现层：主要为 JSP 页面，采用了 Struts 2 标签、EL 表达式语言，分页采用了 extremecomponents 组件，图形报表采用开源图形报表 JFreeChart。本实例还使用了 Struts 2 提供的强大的验证框架来进行输入验证。
- 控制层：采用 Struts 2 的 Action 进行控制。
- 业务逻辑层：业务逻辑层各业务逻辑类的管理采用 Spring 技术进行统一管理，对异常的处理也使用 Spring AOP 来进行异常拦截。
- 持久化层：该层采用的 OR Mapping 工具为 Hibernate，而对事务的控制统一采用 Spring 进行管理。
- 数据库：本系统的数据库采用 MySQL 5.0，数据库建模的工具采用 PowerDesigner。

21.3 数据库设计

本系统包括两张表，分别为收支类型表和收支信息表，数据库的模型如图 21-2 所示。

图 21-2 数据库模型图

其中：
- 收支类型表（tbl_type）：存储收支类型信息。
- 收支信息表（tbl_income_expense）：表示收入与开支的信息的详细记录。

数据库脚本如下所示：

```sql
CREATE DATABASE `sshincomeexpense`;
USE `sshincomeexpense`;

drop table if exists tbl_income_expense;

drop table if exists tbl_type;

/*==============================================================*/
/* Table: tbl_income_expense                                    */
/*==============================================================*/
create table tbl_income_expense
(
   id                   bigint not null auto_increment comment '主键 ID',
   typeId               bigint not null comment '类型',
   name                 varchar(50) not null comment '名称',
   description          varchar(255) comment '描述',
   money                double not null comment '收入/开销',
   flag                 int not null comment '标志（0:收入,1:开支)',
   startDate            datetime not null comment '开始日期',
   endDate              datetime not null comment '结束日期',
   createTime           datetime not null comment '创建时间',
   primary key (id)
)
comment = "收支信息表";

/*==============================================================*/
/* Table: tbl_type                                              */
/*==============================================================*/
create table tbl_type
(
   ID                   bigint not null auto_increment comment '主键 ID',
   typeName             varchar(50) not null comment '类型名称',
   createTime           datetime not null comment '创建时间',
   description          varchar(255) comment '帐户简述',
   primary key (ID)
)
comment = "收支类型表";

alter table tbl_income_expense add constraint FK_typeId_type_incomeexpense foreign key (typeId)
      references tbl_type (ID) on delete restrict on update restrict;
```

在 MySQL 中运行该脚本，可创建一个 sshincomeexpense 数据库，在其中建立 tbl_type 和 tbl_income_expense 两张表，并建立两者的外键关联关系。

21.4 系统详细设计

21.4.1 收支类型管理

（1）模块功能与结构。

该模块包括显示收支类型列表、添加、修改和删除收支类型信息的功能。该模块的模块结构如图 21-3 所示。

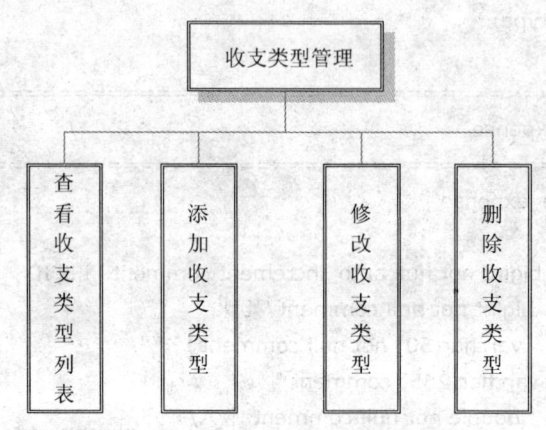

图 21-3 收支类型管理的模块结构

（2）类图。

该模块的类图如图 21-4 所示。

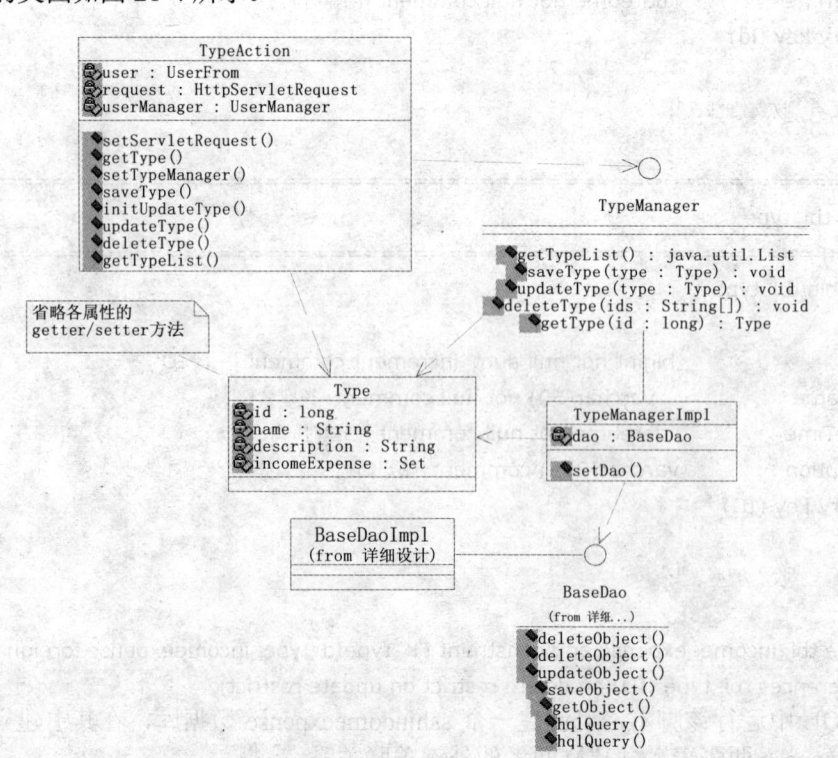

图 21-4 收支类型管理模块的类图

- TypeManager 和 TypeManagerImpl 类。

业务逻辑接口 TypeManager 及其实现类 TypeManagerImpl 的方法如下所示：

public void saveType (Type type)：保存收支类型。

public void updateType (Type type)：更新收支类型。

public void deleteType (String[] ids)：根据传入的 id 数组删除多个收支类型。

public List getTypeList()：获取收支类型列表。

public Type getType (long id)：根据 id 获取收支类型对象。

public void setDao(BaseDao dao)：实现类的方法，用于注入 BaseDao 来进行数据库的操作。

- TypeAction 类。

TypeAction 类为收支类型管理的 Action 类，为收支类型管理的控制器，所包括的方法如下所示：

public void setServletRequest(HttpServletRequest request)：该类需要对 request 进行操作，因此需要实现 ServletRequestAware 接口，而该 setter 方法是 ServletRequestAware 接口要求实现的。

public Type getType ()：获取收支类型对象。

public void setTypeManager(TypeManager typeManager)：通过 Spring 注入业务逻辑对象。

public String saveType()：保存收支类型。

public String initUpdateType()：获得初始化修改收支类型页面所需的信息。

public String updateType ()：修改收支类型。

public String deleteType()：删除收支类型。

public String getTypeList()：获取收支类型列表。

- Type 类。

tbl_type 表的 POJO 对象，因为与 tbl_type 表存在一对多关联，所以具有 IncomeExpense 对象集合。

21.4.2 收支管理

（1）模块功能与结构。

该模块包括显示收支信息列表、添加、修改和删除收支信息的功能。该模块的模块结构如图 21-5 所示。

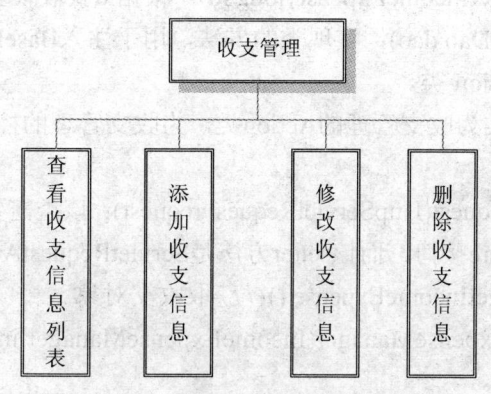

图 21-5 收支管理的模块结构

(2) 类图。

该模块的类图如图 21-6 所示。

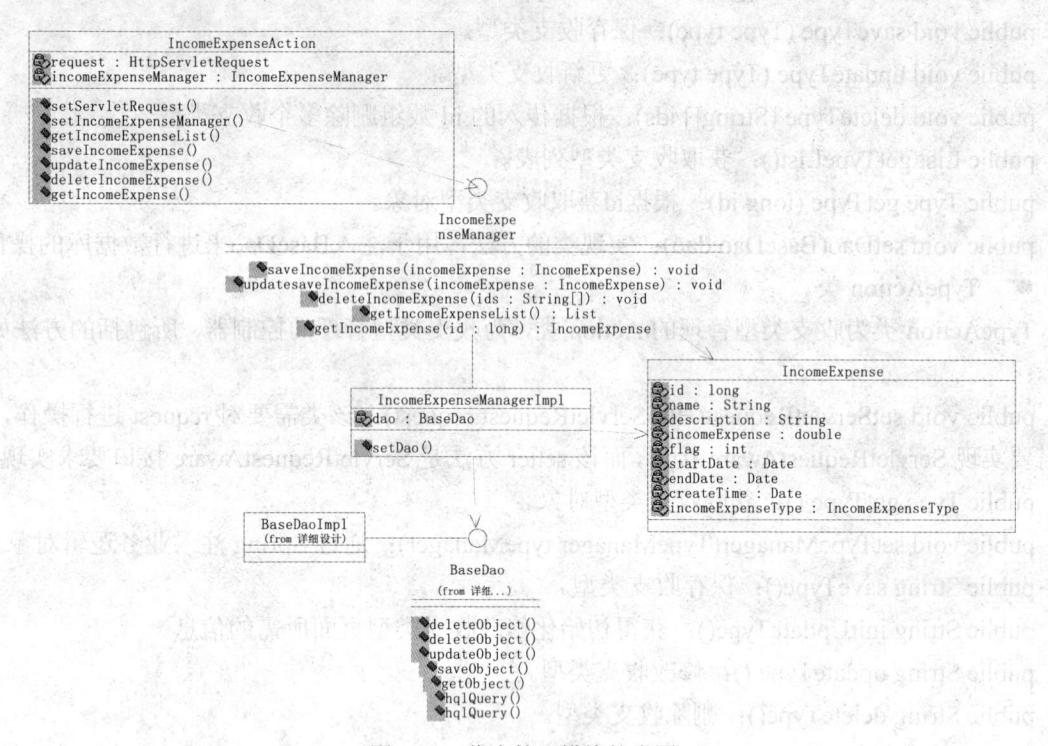

图 21-6 收支管理模块的类图

- IncomeExpenseManager 和 IncomeExpenseManagerImpl 类。

业务逻辑接口 IncomeExpenseManager 及其实现类 IncomeExpenseManagerImpl 的方法如下所示：

public void saveIncomeExpense (IncomeExpense incomeExpense)：保存收支信息。

public void updateIncomeExpense (IncomeExpense incomeExpense)：修改收支信息。

public void deleteIncomeExpense (String[] ids)：根据传入的 id 数组删除多个收支信息。

public List getIncomeExpenseList()：获取收支信息列表。

public IncomeExpense getIncomeExpense(long id)：根据id获取收支信息对象。

public void setDao(BaseDao dao)：实现类的方法，用于注入BaseDao来进行数据库的操作。

- IncomeExpenseAction 类。

IncomeExpenseAction类为收支管理的Action类，为收支管理的控制器，所包括的方法如下所示：

public void setServletRequest(HttpServletRequest request)：该类需要对request进行操作，因此需要实现ServletRequestAware接口，而该setter方法是ServletRequestAware接口要求实现的。

public IncomeExpense getIncomeExpense ()：获取收支对象。

public void setIncomeExpenseManager(IncomeExpenseManager incomeExpenseManager)：通过Spring注入业务逻辑对象。

public String initSaveIncomeExpense()：获得添加收支信息页面所需要的信息（类型列表信息）。

public String saveIncomeExpense()：保存收支信息。
public String updateIncomeExpense()：修改收支信息。
public String initUpdateIncomeExpense()：获得初始化修改收支信息页面所需的信息。
public String deleteIncomeExpense ()：删除收支信息。
public String getIncomeExpenseList()：获取收支信息列表。

- IncomeExpense 类。

tbl_income_expense表的POJO对象，因为与tbl_type表存在多对一关联，所以具有Type对象。

21.4.3 统计报表

（1）模块功能与结构。

该模块包括月收入报表、月开销报表、年收入报表、年开销报表、月收支统计报表、年收支统计报表的功能。该模块的模块结构如图21-7所示。

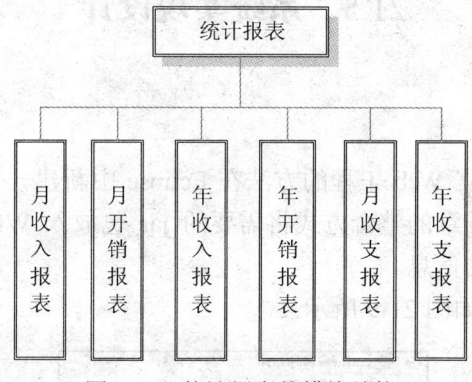

图 21-7 统计报表的模块结构

（2）类图。

该模块的类图如图21-8所示。

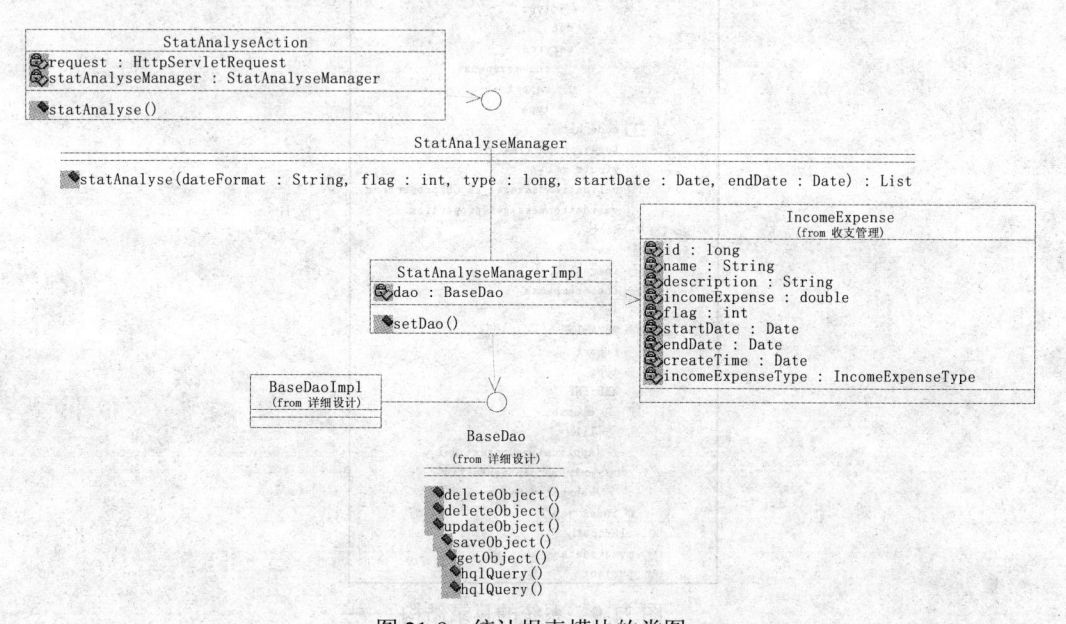

图 21-8 统计报表模块的类图

- StatAnalyseManager 和 StatAnalyseManagerImpl 类。

业务逻辑接口类 StatAnalyseManager 及其实现类 StatAnalyseManagerImpl 的方法如下所示：

public List statAnalyse(StatAnalyseForm form)：获得统计分析信息列表，其中form为统计分析的查询表单。

- StatAnalyseAction 类。

StatAnalyseAction类为统计报表的Action类，为统计报表的控制器，所包括的方法如下所示：

public void setServletRequest(HttpServletRequest request)：该类需要对request进行操作，因此需要实现ServletRequestAware接口，而该setter方法是ServletRequestAware接口要求实现的。

public String statAnalyse()：获得统计分析信息，并跳转到统计分析报表显示页。

- IncomeExpense 类。

tbl_income_expense表的POJO对象，因为与tbl_type表存在多对一关联，所以具有Type对象。

21.5 系统实现设计

21.5.1 系统搭建

读者可以参考前一章建立 Web 工程的方法在 Eclipse 中新建一个名为 sshincomeexpense 的动态 Web 工程，并按照前一章的整合方式将需要的 jar 包放入 WEB-INF/lib 目录下，并配置 web.xml、struts.xml 等文件的信息。

操作完成后工程的结构如图 21-9 所示。

图 21-9 系统的目录结构

其中：
- amigo.sshincomeexpense.dao：包括系统的 DAO 文件以及各表的 Hibernate 映射文件。
- amigo.sshincomeexpense.service：包括系统的业务逻辑类。
- amigo.sshincomeexpense.action：包括系统的 Action。
- WebRoot 目录下的 incomeexpense、type 和 report 目录：分别用来存放收支信息管理、收支类型管理和统计报表 3 个模块的 JSP 文件。

WEB-INF/lib 目录中的 jar 包列表、web.xml 的配置，以及 strtus.xml 文件的初始配置与前一章一样，在此不再赘述。

21.5.2 实现 DAO 组件层

（1）BaseDao 接口及其实现类 BaseDaoImpl。

在 amigo.sshmemo.dao 包下建立 BaseDao 接口，以及其实现类 BaseDaoImpl，这两个类与【例 19-3】中的内容相同，再此不再赘述。

（2）tbl_type 表的映射文件：Type.java 和 Type.hbm.xml。

tbl_type 表（收支类型表）对应的 POJO 文件为 Type.java，该类的代码如下所示：

```java
package amigo.sshincomeexpense.dao;

import java.io.Serializable;
import java.util.Date;
import java.util.HashSet;
import java.util.Set;

/**
 * 收支类型表（tbl_type）对应的 POJO 对象.
 */
public class Type implements Serializable {
    private static final long serialVersionUID = 1L;

    /** 类型 id，自增主键. */
    private long id;

    /** 类型名称. */
    private String typeName;

    /** 创建时间. */
    private Date createTime;

    /** 描述. */
    private String description;

    /** 关联的备忘收支信息. */
    private Set<IncomeExpense> incomeExpenses = new HashSet<IncomeExpense>(0);

    // 省略各属性的 getter/setter 方法
}
```

tbl_type 表对应的 Hibernate 映射文件 Type.hbm.xml 的内容如下所示：

```xml
<?xml version="1.0" encoding='UTF-8'?>
<!DOCTYPE hibernate-mapping PUBLIC
        "-//Hibernate/Hibernate Mapping DTD 3.0//EN"
        "http://hibernate.sourceforge.net/hibernate-mapping-3.0.dtd" >

<hibernate-mapping package="amigo.sshincomeexpense.dao">
    <class name="Type" table="tbl_type">
        <id name="id" column="id">
            <generator class="native"/>
        </id>
        <property name="typeName" column="typeName" type="java.lang.String" not-null="true" length= "50"/>
        <property name="createTime" column="createTime" type="java.util.Date" not-null="true" />
        <property name="description" column="description" type="java.lang.String" length="255"/>

        <set name="incomeExpenses" inverse="false" cascade="save-update">
            <key column="id"/>
            <one-to-many class="IncomeExpense"/>
        </set>
    </class>
</hibernate-mapping>
```

（3）tbl_income_expense 表的映射文件：IncomeExpense.java 和 IncomeExpense.hbm.xml。

tbl_income_expense 表（收支信息表）对应的 POJO 文件为 IncomeExpense.java，该类的代码如下所示：

```java
package amigo.sshincomeexpense.dao;

import java.io.Serializable;
import java.util.Date;

/**
 * 表 tbl_income_expense（收支信息表）表的 POJO 对象
 */
public class IncomeExpense implements Serializable {
    private static final long serialVersionUID = 1L;

    /** 收支信息 id，自增主键. */
    private long id;

    /** 收支类型. */
    private Type type;

    /** 名称. */
    private String name;

    /** 金额. */
    private double money;

    /** 描述. */
    private String description;
```

```java
        /** 标志（0:收入,1:开支). */
        private int flag;

        /** 开始日期. */
        private Date startDate;

        /** 结束日期. */
        private Date endDate;

        /** 创建时间. */
        private Date createTime;

        // 省略各属性的 getter/setter 方法
    }
```

tbl_income_expense 表对应的 Hibernate 映射文件 IncomeExpense.hbm.xml 的内容如下所示：

```xml
<?xml version="1.0" encoding='UTF-8'?>
<!DOCTYPE hibernate-mapping PUBLIC
                "-//Hibernate/Hibernate Mapping DTD 3.0//EN"
                "http://hibernate.sourceforge.net/hibernate-mapping-3.0.dtd" >

<hibernate-mapping package="amigo.sshincomeexpense.dao">
    <class name="IncomeExpense" table="tbl_income_expense">
        <id name="id" column="id">
            <generator class="native"/>
        </id>
        <property name="name" column="name" type="java.lang.String"  not-null="true" length="50"/>
        <property name="money" column="money" type="java.lang.Double"  not-null="true"/>
        <property name="description" column="description" type="java.lang.String" length="255"/>

        <property name="flag" column="flag" type="java.lang.Integer" not-null="true"/>
        <property name="startDate" column="startDate" type="java.util.Date" not-null="true" />
        <property name="endDate" column="endDate" type="java.util.Date" not-null="true" />
        <property name="createTime" column="createTime" type="java.util.Date" not-null="true" />

        <many-to-one name="type" column="typeId" class="Type"   not-null="true" lazy="false" />
    </class>
</hibernate-mapping>
```

（4）配置 applicationContext.xml。

在 WebRoot/WEB-INF/applicationContext.xml 中需要配置 Hibernate 的连接信息，以及映射文件信息，并且需要在该文件中统一进行事务管理，该文件的内容如下所示：

```xml
<?xml version="1.0" encoding="UTF-8"?>
<beans xmlns="http://www.springframework.org/schema/beans"
        xmlns:xsi="http://www.w3.org/2001/XMLSchema-instance"
        xsi:schemaLocation="http://www.springframework.org/schema/beans
http://www.springframework.org/schema/beans/spring-beans-2.0.xsd">
    <bean id="dataSource"
        class="com.mchange.v2.c3p0.ComboPooledDataSource" destroy-method="close">
        <property name="driverClass">
```

```xml
            <value>com.mysql.jdbc.Driver</value>
        </property>
        <property name="jdbcUrl">
            <value>jdbc:mysql://localhost/sshincomeexpense</value>
        </property>
        // ...同上一章
    </bean>

    <!--定义了 Hibernate 的 SessionFactory -->
    <bean id="sessionFactory"
class="org.springframework.orm.hibernate3.LocalSessionFactoryBean">
        <property name="dataSource">
            <ref local="dataSource" />
        </property>
        <property name="mappingResources">
            <list>
                <value>amigo/sshincomeexpense/dao/Type.hbm.xml</value>
                <value>amigo/sshincomeexpense/dao/IncomeExpense.hbm.xml</value>
            </list>
        </property>
        // ...同上一章的该文件对应内容
    </bean>

    // ...
    <bean id="baseDao" class="amigo.sshincomeexpense.dao.BaseDaoImpl">
        <property name="sessionFactory">
            <ref bean="sessionFactory" />
        </property>
    </bean>
</beans>
```

21.5.3 收支类型管理

（1）实现业务逻辑层。

在 amigo.sshincomeexpense.service.type 包中建立收支类型管理的业务逻辑接口 TypeManager.java 和实现类 TypeManagerImpl.java。其中接口类的代码如下所示：

```java
package amigo.sshincomeexpense.service.type;

import java.util.List;

import amigo.sshincomeexpense.action.type.TypeForm;
import amigo.sshincomeexpense.dao.Type;

/**
 * 收支类型的业务逻辑接口类.
 */
public interface TypeManager {
    public List<Type> getTypeList() throws Exception;

    public void saveType(TypeForm form) throws Exception;
```

```java
    public void updateType(TypeForm form) throws Exception;

    public void deleteMemoType(
            String[] types) throws Exception;

    public Type getType(long id) throws Exception;
}
```

该类对应的实现类 TypeManagerImpl.java 的代码如下所示：

```java
package amigo.sshincomeexpense.service.type;

import java.util.Date;
import java.util.List;

import amigo.sshincomeexpense.action.type.TypeForm;
import amigo.sshincomeexpense.dao.BaseDao;
import amigo.sshincomeexpense.dao.Type;

/**
 * 备忘类型的业务逻辑实现类.
 */
public class TypeManagerImpl implements TypeManager {
    private BaseDao dao;

    public void setDao(BaseDao dao) {
        this.dao = dao;
    }

    /**
     * 查询收支类型列表.
     * @return 返回收支类型列表
     */
    public List<Type> getTypeList() throws Exception {
        List<Type> typeList = dao.hqlQuery("from Type");
        return typeList;
    }

    /**
     * 保存收支类型.
     * @param form 收支类型表单对象
     */
    public void saveType(TypeForm form) throws Exception {
        Type type = new Type();
        type.setCreateTime(new Date());
        type.setDescription(form.getDescription());
        type.setTypeName(form.getTypeName());
        // 保存收支类型对象
        dao.saveObject(type);
    }
```

```java
/**
 * 修改收支类型.
 * @param form 收支类型表单对象
 */
public void updateType(TypeForm form) throws Exception {
    // 获得类型对象
    Type type = (Type) dao.getObject(Type.class,
            form.getId());
    type.setTypeName(form.getTypeName());
    type.setDescription(form.getDescription());
    // 更新收支类型对象
    dao.updateObject(type);
}

/**
 * 删除收支类型.
 * @param ids 类型 id 数组
 */
public void deleteType(String[] ids) throws Exception {
    for (int i = 0; i < ids.length; i++) {
        // 获得收支类型对象
        Type type = (Type) dao.getObject(Type.class,
                Long.parseLong(ids[i]));
        // 删除备忘类型对象
        dao.deleteObject(type);
    }
}

/**
 * 根据主键查询收支类型.
 * @param id 收支类型 id
 * @return 返回主键为 id 的收支类型对象
 */
public Type getType(long id) throws Exception {
    Type type = (Type) dao.getObject(Type.class, id);
    return type;
}
}
```

业务逻辑类需要在 Spring 中进行注册，添加的配置信息如下所示：

```xml
<!--收支类型管理业务逻辑类 -->
<bean id="typeManager" class="amigo.sshincomeexpense.service.type.TypeManagerImpl">
    <property name="dao">
        <ref bean="baseDao" />
    </property>
</bean>
```

（2）实现控制层。

接着在 amigo.sshincomeexpense.action.type 包中创建收支类型管理的 Action 类 TypeAction.java，该类的代码如下所示：

```java
package amigo.sshincomeexpense.action.type;
```

```java
import java.util.List;

import javax.servlet.http.HttpServletRequest;

import org.apache.commons.beanutils.BeanUtils;
import org.apache.struts2.interceptor.ServletRequestAware;

import amigo.sshincomeexpense.dao.Type;
import amigo.sshincomeexpense.service.type.TypeManager;

import com.opensymphony.xwork2.ActionSupport;

/**
 * 收支类型管理的 Action.
 */
public class TypeAction extends ActionSupport implements ServletRequestAware {
    private static final long serialVersionUID = 1L;

    /** 收支类型表单.*/
    private TypeForm type;

    private HttpServletRequest request;

    /** 收支类型管理的业务逻辑类. */
    private TypeManager typeManager;

    // 删除各属性的 getter/setter 方法

    /**
     * 获得收支类型列表信息.
     * @return 跳转到收支类型列表显示页面.
     */
    public String list() throws Exception {
        List<Type> typeList = typeManager.getTypeList();
        request.setAttribute("typeList", typeList);
        return "list";
    }

    /**
     * 保存收支类型.
     * @return 跳转到收支类型列表显示的 Action 路径
     */
    public String add() throws Exception {
        typeManager.saveType(type);
        return this.list();
    }

    /**
     * 初始化修改收支类型界面.
     * @return 跳转到修改收支类型界面
     */
```

```java
public String initUpdate() throws Exception {
    String id = request.getParameter("id");
    Type typeObj = typeManager.getType(Long.parseLong(id));
    // 将收支类型对象的属性置入表单对象中
    BeanUtils.copyProperties(type, typeObj);
    return "update";
}

/**
 * 修改收支类型.
 * @return 跳转到收支类型列表显示的 Action 路径
 */
public String update() throws Exception {
    String id = request.getParameter("id");
    typeManager.updateType(type);
    return this.list();
}

/**
 * 删除收支类型.
 * @return 跳转到收支类型列表显示的 Action 路径
 */
public String delete() throws Exception {
    String[] ids = request.getParameterValues("id");
    typeManager.deleteType(ids);
    return this.list();
}
}
```

收支类型表单对象 TypeForm.java 的代码如下所示：

```java
package amigo.sshincomeexpense.action.type;

import java.io.Serializable;

/**
 * 收支类型表表单对象.
 */
public class TypeForm implements Serializable {
    private static final long serialVersionUID = 1L;

    /** 类型 id */
    private long id;

    /** 类型名称. */
    private String typeName;

    /** 描述. */
    private String description;
    // 省略各属性的 getter/setter 方法
}
```

Action 类需要在 struts.xml 文件中进行配置，添加的配置信息如下所示：

```xml
<!-- 收支类型管理的 Action -->
<action name="*TypeAction"   class="typeAction" method="{1}">
    <result name="list">/type/typeList.jsp</result>
    <result name="update">/type/updateType.jsp</result>
</action>
```

因为 Action 类被统一交给 Spring 去管理，所以还需要在 Spring 的配置文件中进行相应配置，添加的配置信息如下所示：

```xml
<!-- 收支类型管理的 Action-->
<bean id="typeAction"
    class="amigo.sshincomeexpense.action.type.TypeAction" scope="prototype">
    <property name="typeManager">
        <ref bean="typeManager" />
    </property>
</bean>
```

（3）实现表现层。

在 WebRoot/type 目录中建立收支类型列表页 typeList.jsp，该页的信息如下所示：

```jsp
……
<body>
<form name="subForm" method="post"
 action="${pageContext.request.contextPath}/deleteTypeAction.action">
<table width="98%" align="center" border="0" cellpadding="4" cellspacing="1">
    <tr>
        <td>
            <input type="button" name="addType" value="添加"
onclick="window.location.href='${pageContext.request.contextPath}/type/addType.jsp'"/>
  
            <input type="checkbox" name="checkbox2"
onclick="checkboxselect(document.subForm.id,       document.subForm.checkbox2.checked)" style="border:0px"/>
全选<input type="button" name="delall" value="删除所选" onclick="return doSubmit();"/>
        </td>
    </tr>
    <tr>
        <td>
        <ec:table items="typeList" action="?"
        imagePath = "${pageContext.request.contextPath}/images/ec/*.gif"
        cellpadding = "1" width = "100%" locale = "zh_CN"
        sortable="false"   var = "type" filterable = "false" form="subForm">
        <ec:row highlightRow="true">
         <ec:column property="checkbox" title="选择" width="30">
            <input type="checkbox" name="id" value="${type.id}" style="border:0px"/>
         </ec:column>
         <ec:column property="id" title="类型 ID" width="60"/>
         <ec:column property="typeName" title="类型名称" width="100"/>
         <ec:column  property="createTime"  title="创建时间"  width="150"  cell="date"
format="yyyy-MM-dd HH:mm:ss"/>
         <ec:column property="description" title="描述" width="200"/>
```

```html
            <ec:column property="操作" style="text-align:center" filterable="false" width="*">
                <a href="${pageContext.request.contextPath}/initUpdateTypeAction.action?id=${type.id}">
                    <img src="${pageContext.request.contextPath}/images/ec/edit.gif" border="0" alt="修改">
                </a>
            </ec:column>
        </ec:row>
    </ec:table>
                </td>
            </tr>
        </table>
    </form>
</body>
</html>
```

添加收支类型的 JSP 页面 addType.jsp 的代码如下所示：

```jsp
<%@ page contentType="text/html; charset=UTF-8" %>
<%@ taglib prefix="s" uri="/struts-tags" %>
<html>
    <head>
        <title>新增收支类型</title>
        <meta http-equiv="Content-Type" content="text/html; charset=UTF-8"/>
    </head>
    <body>
        <s:form action="addTypeAction">
            <s:textfield name="type.typeName" label="类型名称"></s:textfield>
            <s:textfield name="type.description" label="描述"></s:textfield>
            <s:submit></s:submit>
        </s:form>
    </body>
</html>
```

修改收支类型的 JSP 页面 updateType.jsp 的代码如下所示：

```jsp
……
<title>更新收支类型</title>
……
<body>
    <s:form action="updateTypeAction">
        <input type="hidden" name="type.id" value="<s:property value='type.id' />" />
        <s:textfield name="type.typeName" label="类型名称"></s:textfield>
        <s:textfield name="type.description" label="描述"></s:textfield>
        <s:submit></s:submit>
    </s:form>
</body>
</html>
```

（4）运行效果。

在浏览器中输入首页 index.jsp 页面的地址，选择"收支类型管理"，显示收支类型管理列表界面，如图 21-10 所示。

第 21 章 SSH 实例——个人收支管理系统

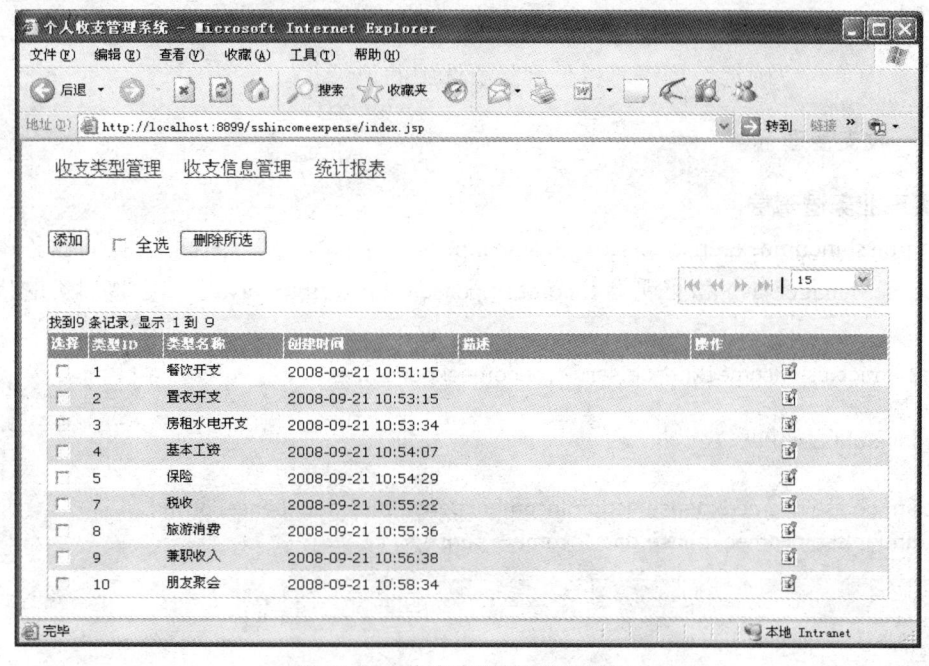

图 21-10 收支类型管理列表界面

在图 21-10 中单击"添加"按钮，呈现添加收支类型界面，如图 21-11 所示。

图 21-11 添加收支类型界面

在图 21-11 中填写收支类型信息后，单击 Submit 按钮，提交类型信息。

在收支类型管理列表界面中单击修改按钮，进入修改收支类型界面，如图 21-12 所示。

图 21-12 修改收支类型界面

在收支类型管理列表界面中选择需要删除的收支类型后，单击"删除所选"按钮，在弹出的删除确认框中单击"确定"按钮，将会删除所选中的记录。

21.5.4 收支管理

（1）实现业务逻辑层。

在 amigo.sshincomeexpense.service.incomeexpense 包中建立收支信息管理的业务逻辑接口 IncomeExpenseManager.java 和实现类 IncomeExpenseManagerImpl.java。其中接口类的代码如下所示：

```java
package amigo.sshincomeexpense.service.incomeexpense;

import java.util.List;

import amigo.sshincomeexpense.action.incomeexpense.IncomeExpenseForm;
import amigo.sshincomeexpense.dao.IncomeExpense;

/**
 * 收支信息管理的业务逻辑接口类.
 */
public interface IncomeExpenseManager {
    public List<IncomeExpense> getIncomeExpenseList(
            String startDate, String endDate, String flag) throws Exception;

    public void saveIncomeExpense(IncomeExpenseForm form) throws Exception;

    public void updateIncomeExpense(IncomeExpenseForm form) throws Exception;

    public void deleteIncomeExpense(String[] ids) throws Exception;

    public IncomeExpense getIncomeExpense(long id) throws Exception;

    public double getTotalIncome(
            String startDate, String endDate) throws Exception;

    public double getTotalExpense(
            String startDate, String endDate) throws Exception;
}
```

该类对应的实现类 IncomeExpenseManagerImpl.java 的代码如下所示：

```java
package amigo.sshincomeexpense.service.incomeexpense;

import java.text.SimpleDateFormat;
import java.util.ArrayList;
import java.util.Date;
import java.util.HashMap;
import java.util.List;
import java.util.Map;

import org.apache.commons.beanutils.BeanUtils;
```

```java
import amigo.sshincomeexpense.action.incomeexpense.IncomeExpenseForm;
import amigo.sshincomeexpense.dao.BaseDao;
import amigo.sshincomeexpense.dao.IncomeExpense;
import amigo.sshincomeexpense.dao.Type;

/**
 * 备忘类型的业务逻辑实现类.
 *
 * @author <a href="mailto:xiexingxing1121@126.com">AmigoXie</a>
 */
public class IncomeExpenseManagerImpl implements IncomeExpenseManager {
    private BaseDao dao;

    public void setDao(BaseDao dao) {
        this.dao = dao;
    }

    /**
     * 查询某段时间之内的收支信息列表.
     * @param startDate 开始时间
     * @param endDate 截止时间
     * @param flag 标志（0:收入,1:开支）
     * @return 返回在开始时间和截止时间（包括）之间的收支信息列表
     */
    public List<IncomeExpense> getIncomeExpenseList(
            String startDate, String endDate, String flag) throws Exception {
        String hql = "from IncomeExpense as obj where 1=1 ";
        Map paramMap = new HashMap();

        if (flag != null && !"".equals(flag.trim())) {
            hql += " and obj.flag=" + flag;
        }

        SimpleDateFormat sdf = new SimpleDateFormat("yyyy-MM-dd");
        if (startDate != null && !"".equals(startDate.trim())) {
            hql += " and obj.startDate >= :startDate ";
            paramMap.put("startDate", sdf.parse(startDate));
        }

        if (endDate != null && !"".equals(endDate.trim())) {
            hql += " and obj.endDate <= :endDate";
            paramMap.put("endDate", sdf.parse(endDate));
        }

        List<IncomeExpense> list = dao.hqlQuery(hql, paramMap);
        return list;
    }

    /**
     * 保存收支信息.
     * @param form 收支类型表单对象
```

```java
 */
public void saveIncomeExpense(IncomeExpenseForm form) throws Exception {
    IncomeExpense incomeExpense = new IncomeExpense();
    BeanUtils.copyProperties(incomeExpense, form);
    // 获得收支对象
    Type type = (Type) dao.getObject(Type.class,
            form.getTypeId());

    incomeExpense.setCreateTime(new Date());
    incomeExpense.setType(type);
    // 保存收支对象
    dao.saveObject(incomeExpense);
}

/**
 * 修改收支信息.
 * @param form 收支信息表单对象
 */
public void updateIncomeExpense(IncomeExpenseForm form) throws Exception {
    IncomeExpense incomeExpense = (IncomeExpense) dao.getObject(
            IncomeExpense.class, form.getId());
    // 获得收支对象
    Type type = (Type) dao.getObject(Type.class,
            form.getTypeId());
    incomeExpense.setType(type);
    BeanUtils.copyProperties(incomeExpense, form);
    // 更新收支对象
    dao.updateObject(incomeExpense);
}

/**
 * 删除收支信息.
 * @param ids 收支信息 id 数组
 */
public void deleteIncomeExpense(String[] ids) throws Exception {
    for (int i = 0; i < ids.length; i++) {
        // 获得收支信息对象
        IncomeExpense IncomeExpense = (IncomeExpense) dao.getObject(
                IncomeExpense.class,
                Long.parseLong(ids[i]));
        // 删除收支信息对象
        if (IncomeExpense != null) {
            dao.deleteObject(IncomeExpense);
        }
    }
}

/**
 * 根据主键查询收支信息.
 * @param id 收支信息 id
 * @return 返回主键为 id 的收支信息对象
```

```java
 */
public IncomeExpense getIncomeExpense(long id) throws Exception {
    IncomeExpense incomeExpense = (IncomeExpense) dao.getObject(
            IncomeExpense.class, id);
    return incomeExpense;
}

/**
 * 获取某段时间内的总收入.
 * @param startDate 开始时间
 * @param endDate 截止时间
 * @return 返回在开始时间和截止时间之间的总收入
 */
public double getTotalIncome(String startDate, String endDate)
        throws Exception {
    // flag 标志（0:收入,1:开支）
    String hql = "from IncomeExpense as obj where obj.flag=0 ";
    Map paramMap = new HashMap();

    SimpleDateFormat sdf = new SimpleDateFormat("yyyy-MM-dd");
    if (startDate != null && !"".equals(startDate.trim())) {
        hql += " and obj.startDate >= :startDate";
        paramMap.put("startDate", sdf.parse(startDate));
    }

    if (endDate != null && !"".equals(endDate.trim())) {
        hql += " and obj.endDate <= :endDate";
        paramMap.put("endDate", sdf.parse(endDate));
    }

    Double totalIncome = 0.0;
    if (dao.hqlQuery(hql, paramMap).size() > 0) {
        totalIncome = (Double) (dao.hqlQuery("select sum(obj.money) " + hql,
                paramMap).get(0));
    }
    return totalIncome.doubleValue();
}

/**
 * 获取某段时间内的总开销.
 * @param startDate 开始时间
 * @param endDate 截止时间
 * @return 返回在开始时间和截止时间之间的总开销
 */
public double getTotalExpense(String startDate, String endDate)
        throws Exception {
    // 与getTotalIncome(...)方法类似，略
}
}
```

业务逻辑类需要在 Spring 中进行注册，添加的配置信息如下所示：

```xml
<!--收支信息管理业务逻辑类 -->
<bean id="incomeExpenseManager"
    class="amigo.sshincomeexpense.service.incomeexpense.IncomeExpenseManagerImpl">
    <property name="dao">
        <ref bean="baseDao" />
    </property>
</bean>
```

(2) 实现控制层。

接着在 amigo.sshincomeexpense.action.incomeexpense 包中创建收支信息管理的 Action 类 IncomeExpenseAction.java，该类的代码如下所示：

```java
package amigo.sshincomeexpense.action.incomeexpense;

import java.util.List;

import javax.servlet.http.HttpServletRequest;

import org.apache.commons.beanutils.BeanUtils;
import org.apache.struts2.interceptor.ServletRequestAware;

import amigo.sshincomeexpense.dao.IncomeExpense;
import amigo.sshincomeexpense.dao.Type;
import amigo.sshincomeexpense.service.incomeexpense.IncomeExpenseManager;
import amigo.sshincomeexpense.service.type.TypeManager;

import com.opensymphony.xwork2.ActionSupport;

/**
 * 收支信息管理的 Action.
 */
public class IncomeExpenseAction extends ActionSupport implements ServletRequestAware {
    private static final long serialVersionUID = 1L;

    /** 收支信息表单.*/
    private IncomeExpenseForm incomeExpense;

    private HttpServletRequest request;

    /** 收支信息管理的业务逻辑类. */
    private IncomeExpenseManager incomeExpenseManager;

    /** 收支类型管理的业务逻辑类. */
    private TypeManager typeManager;

    private List types;

    private String startDate;

    private String endDate;

    private String flag;
```

// 省略各属性的 getter/setter 方法

```java
/**
 * 获得收支信息列表信息.
 * @return 跳转到收支信息列表显示页面.
 */
public String list() throws Exception {
    startDate = request.getParameter("startDate");
    endDate = request.getParameter("endDate");
    flag = request.getParameter("flag");

    List<IncomeExpense> incomeExpenseList = incomeExpenseManager.getIncomeExpenseList(
            startDate, endDate, flag);
    double totalIncome = incomeExpenseManager.getTotalIncome(startDate, endDate);
    double totalExpense = incomeExpenseManager.getTotalExpense(startDate, endDate);

    request.setAttribute("incomeExpenseList", incomeExpenseList);
    request.setAttribute("totalIncome", totalIncome);
    request.setAttribute("totalExpense", totalExpense);
    return "list";
}

/**
 * 初始化新增收支信息界面.
 * @return 跳转到添加收支信息界面
 */
public String initAdd() throws Exception {
    List<Type> typeList = typeManager.getTypeList();
    this.setTypes(typeList);
    incomeExpense = new IncomeExpenseForm();
    return "add";
}

/**
 * 保存收支信息.
 * @return 跳转到收支信息列表显示的 Action 路径
 */
public String add() throws Exception {
    incomeExpenseManager.saveIncomeExpense(incomeExpense);
    return this.list();
}

/**
 * 初始化修改收支信息界面.
 * @return 跳转到修改收支信息界面
 */
public String initUpdate() throws Exception {
    String id = request.getParameter("id");
    IncomeExpense incomeExpenseObj = incomeExpenseManager.getIncomeExpense(
            Long.parseLong(id));
```

```java
            // 将收支信息对象的属性置入表单对象中
            incomeExpense = new IncomeExpenseForm();
            BeanUtils.copyProperties(incomeExpense, incomeExpenseObj);
            // 获得类型的下拉列表
            List<Type> typeList = typeManager.getTypeList();
            this.setTypes(typeList);
            return "update";
        }

        /**
         * 修改收支信息.
         * @return 跳转到收支信息列表显示的 Action 路径
         */
        public String update() throws Exception {
            incomeExpenseManager.updateIncomeExpense(incomeExpense);
            return this.list();
        }

        /**
         * 删除收支信息.
         * @return 跳转到收支信息列表显示的 Action 路径
         */
        public String delete() throws Exception {
            String[] ids = request.getParameterValues("id");
            incomeExpenseManager.deleteIncomeExpense(ids);
            return this.list();
        }
    }
```

收支信息的表单类 IncomeExpenseForm.java 的代码如下所示:

```java
package amigo.sshincomeexpense.action.incomeexpense;
import java.io.Serializable;
import java.util.Date;
/**
 * 收支信息表单对象
 */
public class IncomeExpenseForm implements Serializable {
    private static final long serialVersionUID = 1L;
    /** 收支信息 id. */
    private long id;

    /** 收支类型. */
    private long typeId;

    /** 名称. */
    private String name;

    /** 金额. */
    private double money;

    /** 描述. */
```

```java
    private String description;

    /** 标志（0:收入,1:开支). */
    private int flag;

    /** 开始日期. */
    private Date startDate;

    /** 结束日期. */
    private Date endDate;
    // 省略各属性的 getter/setter 方法
}
```

Action 类需要在 struts.xml 文件中进行配置，添加的配置信息如下所示：

```xml
<!-- 收支信息管理的 Action -->
<action name="*IncomeExpenseAction" class="incomeExpenseAction" method="{1}">
    <result name="list">/incomeexpense/incomeexpenseList.jsp</result>
    <result name="update">/incomeexpense/updateIncomeExpense.jsp</result>
    <result name="add">/incomeexpense/addIncomeExpense.jsp</result>
</action>
```

因为 Action 类被统一交给 Spring 去管理，所以还需要在 Spring 的配置文件中进行相应配置，添加的配置信息如下所示：

```xml
<!-- 收支信息管理的 Action-->
<bean id="incomeExpenseAction"
        class="amigo.sshincomeexpense.action.incomeexpense.IncomeExpenseAction"
        scope="prototype">
    <property name="incomeExpenseManager">
        <ref bean="incomeExpenseManager" />
    </property>
    <property name="typeManager">
        <ref bean="typeManager" />
    </property>
</bean>
```

（3）实现表现层。

在 WebRoot/type 目录中建立收支信息列表页 incomeexpenseList.jsp，该页的代码如下所示：

```jsp
<%@ page language="java" pageEncoding="UTF-8"%>
<%@ taglib prefix="s" uri="/struts-tags" %>
<%@ taglib uri="/WEB-INF/extremecomponents.tld" prefix="ec" %>
<html>
    <head>
        <title>收支信息列表</title>
        <link href="${pageContext.request.contextPath}/css/extremecomponents.css" rel="stylesheet" type="text/css">
        <script src="${pageContext.request.contextPath}/js/select.js"></script>
        <script language="javascript">
            function doSubmit() {
                if(!hasChecked(subForm.id)) {
                    alert("请选择需要删除的收支信息!");
                    return false;
                } else {
```

```
                    if(!confirm("您确定要删除吗?")) {
                        return false;
                    } else {
                        subForm.submit();
                    }
                }
            }

            // 提交查询
            function submitQuery() {
                var form = document.subForm;
                form.action = "${pageContext.request.contextPath}/listIncomeExpenseAction.action";
                form.submit();
            }
        </script>
    </head>
    <body>
        <form name="subForm" method="post"
              action="${pageContext.request.contextPath}/deleteIncome ExpenseAction.action">
            <table width="98%" align="center" border="0" cellpadding="4" cellspacing="1">
                <tr>
                    <td colspan="3">
                        <font color="Red">总收入:${requestScope.totalIncome}</font>
                          
                        <font color="Red">总开支:${requestScope.totalExpense}</font>
                          
                        <font color="Red">总结余:${requestScope.totalIncome - requestScope.totalExpense}</font>
                    </td>
                </tr>
                <tr>
                    <td>
                        开始时间:<input type="text" name="startDate" value="<s:property value='startDate' />"/>
                            
                        截止时间:<input type="text" name="endDate" value="<s:property value='endDate' />" />
                    </td>
                    <td width="120">
                        <table>
                            <s:select label="标志" name="flag"
                                list="#{'' : '--全部--', '1' : '开支', '0' : '收入'}"
                                listKey="key"
                                listValue="value" />
                        </table>
                    </td>
                    <td width="450">
                        <input type="button" value="查询" onclick="javascript:submitQuery();"/>
                    </td>
                </tr>
                <tr>
```

```html
                        <td colspan="3">
                            <input type="button" name="addIncomeExpense" value="添加"
        onclick="window.location.href='${pageContext.request.contextPath}/initAddIncomeExpenseAction.action'"/>
                              
                            <input type="checkbox" name="checkbox2"
                                onclick="checkboxselect(document.subForm.id,
document.subForm.checkbox2.checked)" style="border:0px"/>
                            全选
                            <input type="button" name="delall" value="删除所选" onclick="return
doSubmit();"/>
                        </td>
                    </tr>
                    <tr>
                        <td colspan="3">
<ec:table items="incomeExpenseList" action="?"
imagePath = "${pageContext.request.contextPath}/images/ec/*.gif"
cellpadding = "1" width = "100%" locale = "zh_CN"
sortable="false" var = "incomeExpense" filterable = "false"
form="subForm">
<ec:row highlightRow="true">
<ec:column property="checkbox" title="选择" width="30">
<input type="checkbox" name="id" value="${incomeExpense.id}" style="border:0px"/>
</ec:column>
<ec:column property="id" title="ID" width="60"/>
<ec:column property="name" title="名称" width="100"/>
<ec:column property="type.typeName" title="收支类型" width="100"/>
<ec:column property="flag" title="种类" width="60">
    <script>
    <!--
    var flag = '${incomeExpense.flag}';
    if (flag=='0') {
        document.write('收入');
    } else {
        document.write('开支');
    }
    //-->
    </script>
</ec:column>
<ec:column property="money" title="金额" width="100"/>
<ec:column property="startDate" title="开始日期" width="100" cell="date" format="yyyy-MM-dd"/>
<ec:column property="endDate" title="截止日期" width="100" cell="date" format="yyyy-MM-dd"/>
<ec:column property="createTime" title="创建时间" width="150" cell="date" format="yyyy-MM-dd HH:mm:ss"/>
<ec:column property="description" title="描述" width="200"/>
<ec:column property="操作" style="text-align:center" filterable="false" width="*">
    <a
href="${pageContext.request.contextPath}/initUpdateIncomeExpenseAction.action?id=${incomeExpense.id}">
```

```
            <img src="${pageContext.request.contextPath}/images/ec/edit.gif" border="0" alt="修改">
        </a>
    </ec:column>
  </ec:row>
</ec:table>
                </td>
              </tr>
            </table>
        </form>
    </body>
</html>
```

添加收支信息的 JSP 页面 addIncomeExpense.jsp 的代码如下所示：

```
<%@ page contentType="text/html; charset=UTF-8" %>
<%@ taglib prefix="s" uri="/struts-tags" %>
<html>
    <head>
        <title>新增收支信息</title>
        <meta http-equiv="Content-Type" content="text/html; charset=UTF-8"/>
    </head>
    <body>
        <s:form action="addIncomeExpenseAction">
            <s:select label="收支类型" name="incomeExpense.typeId"
                list="types"
                listKey="id"
                listValue="typeName"/>
            <s:textfield name="incomeExpense.name" label="名称"></s:textfield>
            <s:textfield name="incomeExpense.money" label="金额"></s:textfield>
            <s:select label="标志" name="incomeExpense.flag"
                list="#{'1' : '开支', '0' : '收入'}"
                listKey="key"
                listValue="value" value="0"/>
            <s:textfield name="incomeExpense.startDate" label="开始日期"></s:textfield>
            <s:textfield name="incomeExpense.endDate" label="截止日期"></s:textfield>
            <s:textfield name="incomeExpense.description" label="描述"></s:textfield>
            <s:submit></s:submit>
        </s:form>
    </body>
</html>
```

修改收支信息的页面 updateIncomeExpense.jsp 的代码如下所示：

```
……
<title>更新收支信息</title>
……
<s:form action="updateIncomeExpenseAction">
<input type="hidden" name=" incomeExpense.id"
    value="<s:property value='incomeExpense.id' />" />
// 同 addIncomeExpense.jsp 页面，略
```

（4）运行效果。

在浏览器中输入首页 index.jsp 页面的地址，选择"收支信息管理"，显示收支信息管理列表界面，如图 21-13 所示。

第 21 章　SSH 实例——个人收支管理系统

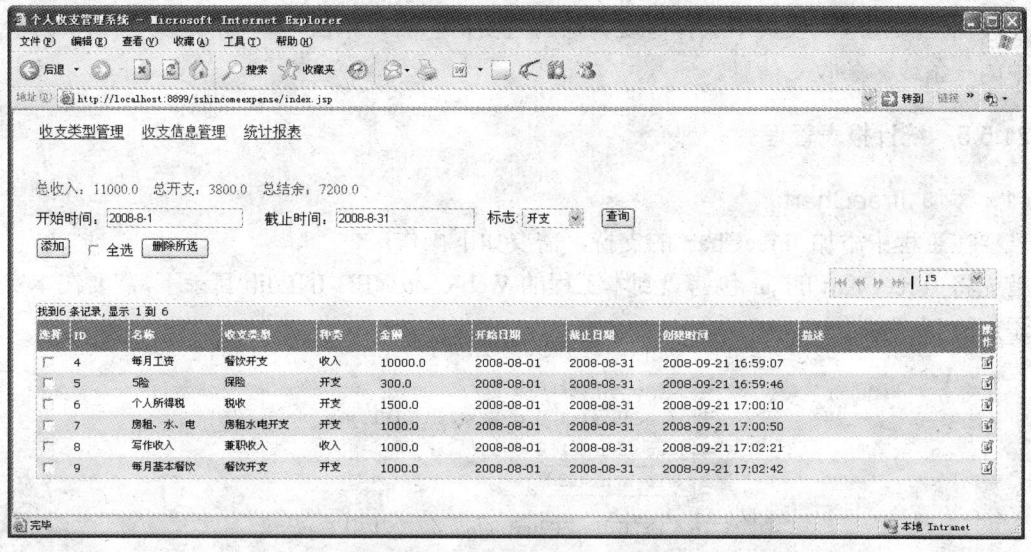

图 21-13　收支信息管理列表界面

在图 21-13 中单击"添加"按钮，呈现添加收支信息界面，如图 21-14 所示。

图 21-14　添加收支信息界面

在收支信息管理列表页中单击修改按钮，进入修改收支信息界面，如图 21-15 所示。

图 21-15　修改收支信息界面

在收支信息管理列表页中选择需要删除的收支信息后,单击"删除所选"按钮,将会删除所选中的一条或多条收支信息。

21.5.5 统计报表管理

(1) 添加 JfreeChart。

若要在工程中添加 JFreeChart 的支持,需要如下操作:

首先将 JFreeChart 的 jar 包拷贝到本工程的 WebRoot/WEB-INF/lib 目录下,需要在本实例基础上添加的 jar 包如图 21-16 所示。

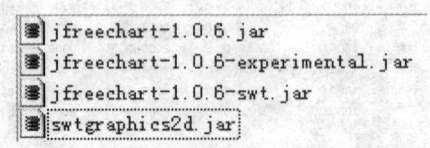

```
jfreechart-1.0.6.jar
jfreechart-1.0.6-experimental.jar
jfreechart-1.0.6-swt.jar
swtgraphics2d.jar
```

图 21-16 添加 JFreeChart 的 jar 包及其相关 jar 包

接下来还需要在 web.xml 文件中添加 JFreeChart 的 Servlet,添加的配置内容如下所示:

```xml
<!-- JFreeChart 的 Servlet,用于图片显示 -->
<servlet>
    <servlet-name>DisplayChart</servlet-name>
    <servlet-class>org.jfree.chart.servlet.DisplayChart</servlet-class>
</servlet>

<servlet-mapping>
    <servlet-name>DisplayChart</servlet-name>
    <url-pattern>/DisplayChart</url-pattern>
</servlet-mapping>
```

(2) 实现业务逻辑层。

在 amigo.sshincomeexpense.service.report 包中建立统计分析的业务逻辑接口 StatAnalyseManager.java 和实现类 StatAnalyseManagerImpl.java。其中接口类代码如下所示:

```java
package amigo.sshincomeexpense.service.report;

import java.util.List;
import amigo.sshincomeexpense.action.report.StatAnalyseForm;

/**
 * 统计分析业务逻辑接口类.
 */
public interface StatAnalyseManager {
    /**
     * 获得统计分析信息列表.
     * @param form 统计分析查询表单
     * @return
     * @throws Exception
     */
    public List statAnalyse(StatAnalyseForm form) throws Exception;

    /**
     * 获得时序图信息.
```

```
     * @param form 查询信息表单
     * @return 返回满足查询条件的时序图信息列表
     */
    public List getTimeSeriesList(StatAnalyseForm form) throws Exception;
}
```

该类对应的实现类 StatAnalyseManagerImpl.java 的代码如下所示：

```java
package amigo.sshincomeexpense.service.report;

import java.util.*;

import amigo.sshincomeexpense.action.report.StatAnalyseForm;
import amigo.sshincomeexpense.dao.BaseDao;

/**
 * 统计分析业务逻辑接口类.
 */
public class StatAnalyseManagerImpl implements StatAnalyseManager {
    private BaseDao dao;

    public void setDao(BaseDao dao) {
        this.dao = dao;
    }

    /**
     * 获得统计分析饼图信息列表.
     * @param form 统计分析查询表单
     * @return 返回满足查询条件的统计分析信息列表
     */
    public List statAnalyse(StatAnalyseForm form) throws Exception {
        List returnList = new ArrayList();
        StringBuffer where = new StringBuffer();
        Map paramMap = new HashMap();

        if (form.getFlag() != null && !"".equals(form.getFlag())) {
            where.append(" and obj.flag = :flag");
            paramMap.put("flag", form.getFlag());
        }

        if (!"-1".equals(form.getTypeId())) {
            where.append(" and obj.type.id=" + form.getTypeId());
        }

        if (form.getStartDate() != null) {
            where.append(" and obj.startDate >= :startDate ");
            paramMap.put("startDate", form.getStartDate());
        }

        if (form.getEndDate() != null) {
            where.append(" and obj.endDate <= :endDate");
            paramMap.put("endDate", form.getEndDate());
```

```java
                }

                String groupBy = " group by obj.type.typeName";

                // 获得满足条件的收支记录的类型列表
                List typeList = dao.hqlQuery(
                        "select obj.type.typeName from IncomeExpense as obj where 1=1 " + where.toString() +
                        groupBy, paramMap);

                //装载返回列表
            if (typeList != null && typeList.size() > 0) {
                for (int i = 0; i < typeList.size(); i++) {
                    String typeName = (String) typeList.get(i);
                    Map<String, String> map = new HashMap<String, String>();
                    // 类型名称
                    map.put("typeName", typeName);
                    // 获得某类型的总金额
                    paramMap.put("typeName", typeName);
                    List moneyList = dao.hqlQuery(
                        "select sum(obj.money) from IncomeExpense as obj where 1=1 "
                        + where.toString() + " and obj.type.typeName=:typeName",
                            paramMap);
                    Double totalMoney = (Double) moneyList.get(0);
                    if (totalMoney != null) {
                    map.put("totalMoney", totalMoney.toString());
                    } else {
                    map.put("totalMoney", new String("0.0"));
                    }
                    // 将装载好的 map 放入返回列表中
                    returnList.add(map);
                }
            }
        return returnList;
}

/**
 * 获得时序图信息.
 * @param form 查询信息表单
 * @return 返回满足查询条件的时序图信息列表
 */
public List getTimeSeriesList(StatAnalyseForm form) throws Exception {
    List returnList = new ArrayList();
    StringBuffer where = new StringBuffer();
    Map paramMap = new HashMap();

    if (form.getFlag() != null && !"".equals(form.getFlag())) {
        where.append(" and obj.flag = :flag");
        paramMap.put("flag", form.getFlag());
    }

    if (!"-1".equals(form.getTypeId())) {
```

```java
            where.append(" and obj.type.id=" + form.getTypeId());
        }

        if (form.getStartDate() != null) {
            where.append(" and obj.startDate >= :startDate ");
            paramMap.put("startDate", form.getStartDate());
        }

        if (form.getEndDate() != null) {
            where.append(" and obj.endDate <= :endDate");
            paramMap.put("endDate", form.getEndDate());
        }

        String hql = this.getReportHql(form.getDataFormat(),
                where.toString());
        List list = dao.hqlQuery(hql, paramMap);
        //装载返回列表
    if (list != null && list.size() > 0) {
        for (int i = 0; i < list.size(); i++) {
            Object[] values = (Object[]) list.get(i);
            Map<String, String> map = new HashMap<String, String>();
            // 总金额
            map.put("totalMoney", values[0].toString());
            // 日期
            if ("yyyy".equals(form.getDataFormat())) {
            map.put("time", values[1].toString());
            } else {
            map.put("time", values[1].toString() + "-" + values[2].toString());
            }

            // 将装载好的 map 放入返回列表中
            returnList.add(map);
        }
    }
        return returnList;
}

/**
 * 构造 hql 语句.
 * @param timeUnit 可为 yyyy 和 yyyy-MM-dd,
 *                 其中 yyyy 表示按年份统计，yyyy-MM 表示按月统计
 * @param where 现有的 where 条件
 * @return 返回构造好的 hql 语句
 */
private String getReportHql(
            final String timeUnit, final String where) {
    StringBuffer sb = new StringBuffer();
    sb.append("select sum(obj.money), ");
    if ("yyyy".equals(timeUnit)) {
        sb.append("year(obj.startDate) ");
    } else {
```

```
            sb.append("year(obj.startDate), month(obj.startDate) ");
        }
        sb.append(" from IncomeExpense as obj where 1=1 ");
        sb.append(where);

        if ("yyyy".equals(timeUnit)) {
            sb.append(" group by year(obj.startDate)");
        } else {
            sb.append(" group by CONCAT(year(obj.startDate), '-', month(obj.startDate))");
        }
        return sb.toString();
    }
}
```

业务逻辑类需要在 Spring 中进行注册,添加的配置信息如下所示:

```xml
<!-- 统计报表业务逻辑类 -->
<bean id="statAnalyseManager"
        class="amigo.sshincomeexpense.service.report.StatAnalyseManagerImpl">
    <property name="dao">
        <ref bean="baseDao" />
    </property>
</bean>
```

(3) 实现控制层。

接着在 amigo.sshincomeexpense.action.report 包中创建统计报表的 Action 类 StatAnalyseAction.java, 该类的代码如下所示:

```java
package amigo.sshincomeexpense.action.report;

import java.util.List;

import javax.servlet.http.HttpServletRequest;
import org.apache.struts2.interceptor.ServletRequestAware;

import amigo.sshincomeexpense.dao.Type;
import amigo.sshincomeexpense.service.report.StatAnalyseManager;
import amigo.sshincomeexpense.service.type.TypeManager;

import com.opensymphony.xwork2.ActionSupport;

/**
 * 统计分析的 Action.
 */
public class StatAnalyseAction extends ActionSupport implements ServletRequestAware {
    private static final long serialVersionUID = 1L;

    private HttpServletRequest request;

    private StatAnalyseForm form;

    /** 统计报表的业务逻辑类. */
    private StatAnalyseManager statAnalyseManager;
```

```java
        /** 收支类型管理的业务逻辑类. */
        private TypeManager typeManager;

        /** 收支类型. */
        private List types;

        // 省略各属性的 getter/setter 方法

        /**
         * 获得初始化统计报表查询输入界面
         * @return 跳转到统计报表查询输入界面
         */
        public String initQuery() throws Exception {
            List typeList = typeManager.getTypeList();
            Type type = new Type();
            type.setTypeName("--请选择--");
            type.setId(-1);
            typeList.add(0, type);
            this.setTypes(typeList);
            return "statAnalyseQuery";
        }

        /**
         * 获得统计报表的信息，跳转到报表显示页.
         * @return 跳转到报表显示页
         */
        public String chart() throws Exception {
            List pieInfoList = statAnalyseManager.statAnalyse(form);
            List timeSeriesList = statAnalyseManager.getTimeSeriesList(form);

            request.setAttribute("pieInfoList", pieInfoList);
            request.setAttribute("timeSeriesList", timeSeriesList);
            request.setAttribute("timeUnit", form.getDataFormat());
            return "statAnalyse";
        }
}
```

统计分析查询的表单类 StatAnalyseForm.java 类的代码如下所示：

```java
package amigo.sshincomeexpense.action.report;

import java.io.Serializable;
import java.util.Date;

/**
 * 统计分析查询表单.
 */
public class StatAnalyseForm implements Serializable {
    private static final long serialVersionUID = 1L;

    /** 日期格式，可为 yyyy 和 yyyy-MM，其中 yyyy 表示按年统计，yyyy-MM 表示按月统计. */
    private String dataFormat;
```

```java
/** 标志（0:收入,1:开支). */
private String flag;

/** 类型 id. */
private String typeId;

/** 开始时间. */
private Date startDate;

/** 截止时间. */
private Date endDate;

// 省略各属性的 getter/setter 方法
}
```

Action 类需要在 struts.xml 文件中进行配置，添加的配置信息如下所示：

```xml
<!-- 统计报表的 Action -->
<action name="*StatAnalyseAction" class="statAnalyseAction" method="{1}">
    <result name="statAnalyseQuery">/report/reportSearch.jsp</result>
    <result name="statAnalyse">/report/report.jsp</result>
</action>
```

因为 Action 类被统一交给 Spring 去管理，所以还需要在 Spring 的配置文件中进行相应配置，添加的配置信息如下所示：

```xml
<!-- 统计报表的 Action-->
<bean id="statAnalyseAction"
        class="amigo.sshincomeexpense.action.report.StatAnalyseAction"
        scope="prototype">
    <property name="typeManager">
        <ref bean="typeManager" />
    </property>
    <property name="statAnalyseManager">
        <ref bean="statAnalyseManager" />
    </property>
</bean>
```

（4）实现表现层。

在 WebRoot/report 目录中建立报表查询页面 reportSearch.jsp，该页的代码如下所示：

```jsp
<%@ page contentType="text/html;charset=UTF-8"%>
<%@ taglib prefix="s" uri="/struts-tags" %>

<html>
    <head>
        <title>统计报表查询</title>
        <meta http-equiv="Content-Type" content="text/html; charset=UTF-8"/>
    </head>
    <body>
        <s:form action="chartStatAnalyseAction" name="reportForm" target="myFrame">
            <table>
                <tr>
                    <td>
```

```html
				<table>
					<s:select label="收支类型" name="form.typeId"
		list="types" listKey="id" listValue="typeName" value="-1"/>
				</table>
			</td>
			<td>
				<table>
					<s:select label="标志" name="form.flag"
		list="#{'1' : '开支', '0' : '收入'}" listKey="key" listValue="value" value="0"/>
				</table>
			</td>
			<td>
				<table>
					<s:select label="统计步长" name="form.dataFormat"
						list="#{'yyyy' : '年', 'yyyy-MM' : '月'}"
						listKey="key"
						listValue="value" value="yyyy"/>
				</table>
			</td>
		</tr>
		<tr>
			<td>
				<table>
		<s:textfield name="form.startDate" label="开始日期"></s:textfield>
				</table>
			</td>
			<td>
				<table>
		<s:textfield name="form.endDate" label="截止日期"></s:textfield>
				</table>
			</td>
			<td>
				<table>
					<s:submit></s:submit>
				</table>
			</td>
		</tr>
	</table>
</s:form>

<table width="95%" border="0" align="center"
	cellpadding="4" cellspacing="0" class="border_tabel" id="print">
	<tr>
		<td align="center" height="450" valign="top" width="100%">
			<iframe height="450" id="myFrame" name="myFrame" frameborder="0"
			width="100%"
				scrolling="yes" marginheight="0" src="about:blank">
			</iframe>
		</td>
	</tr>
</table>
```

```jsp
    </body>
</html>
```

报表页面 report.jsp 显示统计的饼图信息以及时序图信息，该页面的代码如下所示：

```jsp
<%@ page contentType="text/html;charset=UTF-8"%>
<%@ taglib prefix="s" uri="/struts-tags" %>
<%@ page import="org.jfree.data.general.DefaultPieDataset,
            org.jfree.chart.servlet.ServletUtilities,
            org.jfree.chart.labels.StandardPieSectionLabelGenerator,
            java.text.NumberFormat,
            java.util.*,
            org.jfree.chart.plot.PiePlot3D,
            org.jfree.util.Rotation,
            org.jfree.chart.ChartFactory,
                org.jfree.chart.JFreeChart,
                org.jfree.data.time.TimeSeries,
                org.jfree.data.time.Month,
                org.jfree.data.time.TimeSeriesCollection,
                org.jfree.data.time.*"%>
<%
//==================饼图==============
//设置数据集
DefaultPieDataset dataset = new DefaultPieDataset();
List pieInfoList = (List) request.getAttribute("pieInfoList");
for (int i = 0; i < pieInfoList.size(); i++) {
    Map map = (Map) pieInfoList.get(i);
    String typeName = (String) map.get("typeName");
    double totalMoney = Double.parseDouble((String) map.get("totalMoney"));
    dataset.setValue(typeName, totalMoney);
}

JFreeChart chart = ChartFactory.createPieChart3D(
        null, dataset, true, true, false);

//获得 3D 的水晶饼图对象
PiePlot3D pieplot3d = (PiePlot3D) chart.getPlot();
//设置开始角度
pieplot3d.setStartAngle(150D);
//设置方向为"顺时针方向"
pieplot3d.setDirection(Rotation.CLOCKWISE);
//设置透明度，0.5F 为半透明，1 为不透明，0 为全透明
pieplot3d.setForegroundAlpha(0.7F);
pieplot3d.setNoDataMessage("无数据显示");

//显示各项所占的百分比
pieplot3d.setCircular(true);
pieplot3d.setLabelGenerator(new StandardPieSectionLabelGenerator("{0} = {2}({1})",
        NumberFormat.getNumberInstance(),
        NumberFormat.getPercentInstance()));

String filename = ServletUtilities.saveChartAsPNG(chart, 550, 400, null, session);
```

```jsp
String graphURL = request.getContextPath() + "/DisplayChart?filename=" + filename;

//===============时序图===============
String timeUnit = (String) request.getAttribute("timeUnit");
List timeSeriesList = (List) request.getAttribute("timeSeriesList");
//流量统计时间线
TimeSeries timeSeries = null;
if ("yyyy".equals(timeUnit)) { //年
    timeSeries = new TimeSeries("查询统计时序图", Year.class);
} else if ("yyyy-MM".equals(timeUnit)) { //月
    timeSeries = new TimeSeries("查询统计时序图", Month.class);
}
//时间曲线数据集合
TimeSeriesCollection lineDataset = new TimeSeriesCollection();
String title = "年份";
//构造数据集合
if (timeSeriesList != null) {
    for (int i = 0; i < timeSeriesList.size(); i++) {
        Map map = (Map) timeSeriesList.get(i);
        double totalMoney = Double.parseDouble((String) map.get("totalMoney"));
        String time = (String) map.get("time");
        int year = Integer.valueOf(time.substring(0,4)).intValue();
        if ("yyyy".equals(timeUnit)) { //年
            timeSeries.add(new Year(year), totalMoney);
        } else if ("yyyy-MM".equals(timeUnit)) { //月
            title = "月份";
            int month = Integer.valueOf(time.substring(5, time.length())).intValue();
            timeSeries.add(new Month(month, year), totalMoney);
        }
    }
}
lineDataset.addSeries(timeSeries);
JFreeChart timeSeriesChart = ChartFactory.createTimeSeriesChart("查询统计时序图",
        title, "查询次数", lineDataset,
        true, true, true);

String timeSeriesFilename = ServletUtilities.saveChartAsPNG(timeSeriesChart, 550, 400, null, session);
String timeSeriesGraphURL = request.getContextPath() + "/DisplayChart?filename=" + timeSeriesFilename;
%>
<html>
    <head>
        <title>统计图显示</title>
        <meta http-equiv=Content-Type content="text/html; charset=UTF-8">
    </head>
    <body>
        <table>
            <tr>
                <td align="center">
                    <img id="reportPic" src="<%= graphURL %>" width="550" height="400" border="0" usemap="#<%= filename %>">
```

```
                </td>
                <td align="center">
                    <img id="reportPic" src="<%= timeSeriesGraphURL %>" width="550" height="400" border="0" usemap="#<%= timeSeriesFilename %>">
                </td>
            </tr>
        </table>
    </body>
</html>
```

（5）运行效果。

在浏览器中输入首页 index.jsp 页面的地址，选择"统计报表"，显示统计报表的查询界面，如图 21-17 所示。

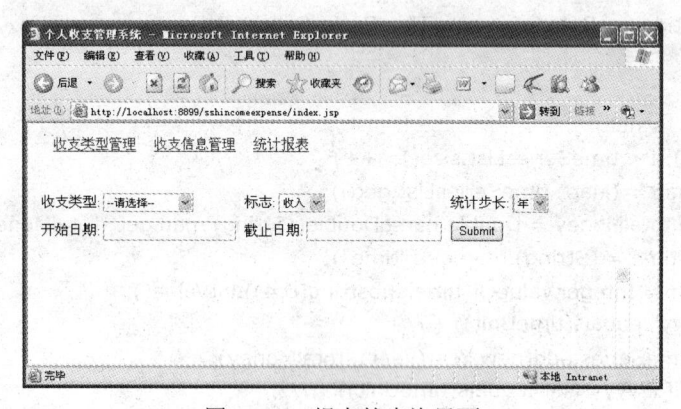

图 21-17　报表的查询界面

在图 21-17 中输入查询信息后，单击 Submit 按钮提交表单，将显示报表界面，如图 21-18 所示。

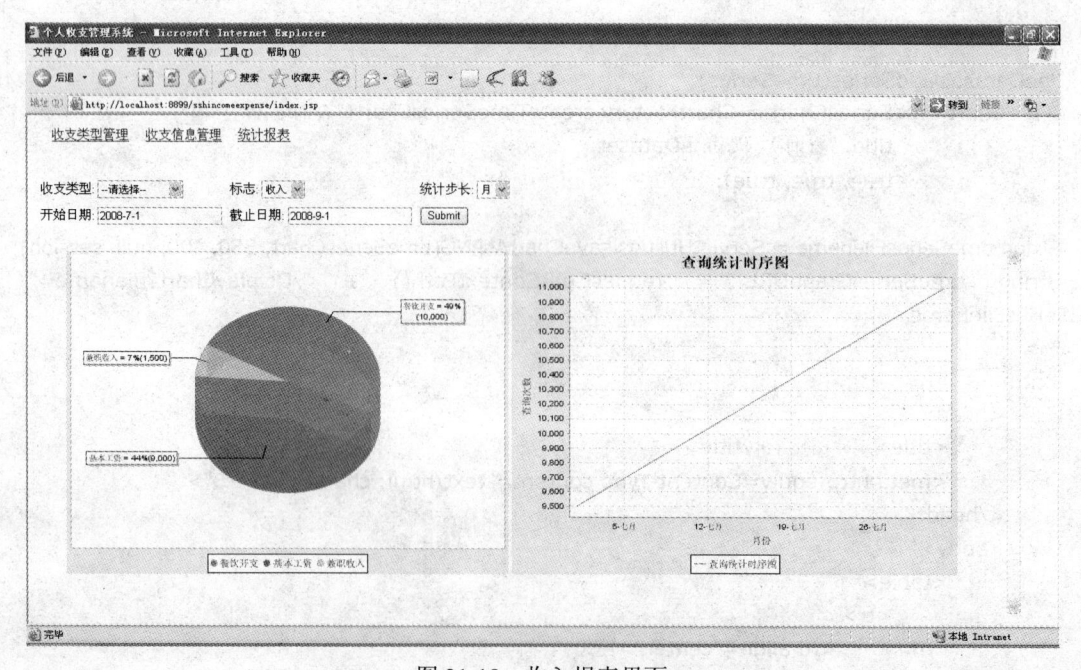

图 21-18　收入报表界面

图 21-18 查询的是对收入进行按月统计，其中左侧显示的是按月时收入的安排情况，右侧的时序图显示的是收入随月的变化曲线。若要进行开支的按年查询，可在"标志"中选择"开支"，在"统计步长"中选择"年"，显示的图形如图 21-19 所示。

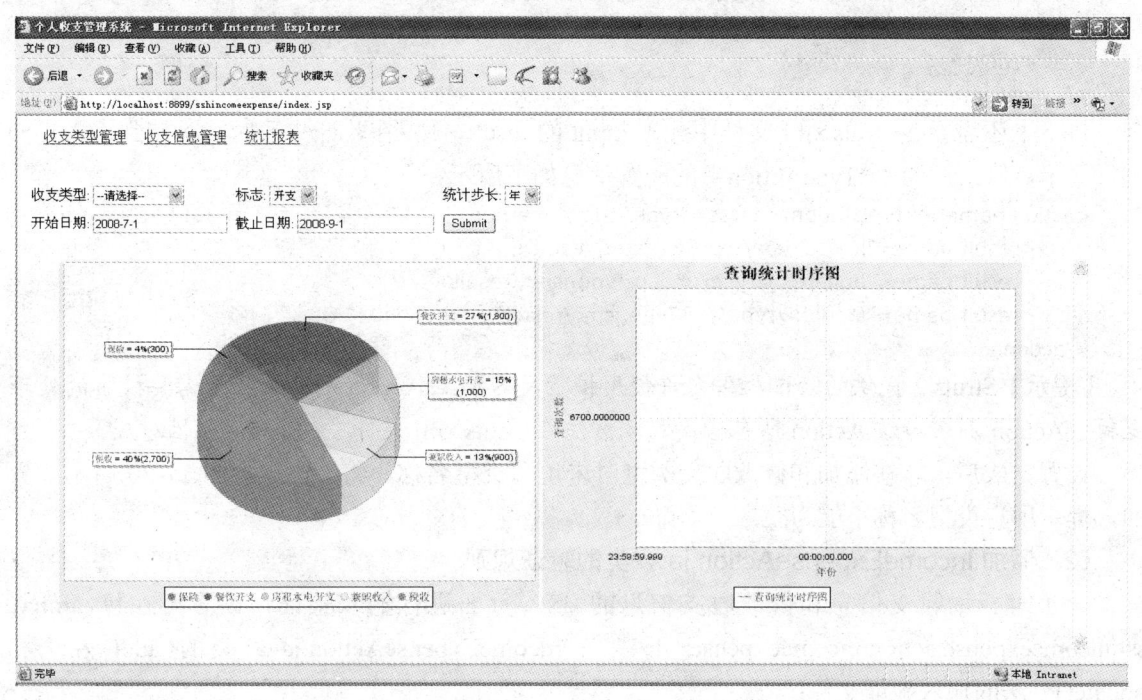

图 21-19 开支按年查询界面

21.5.6 添加输入验证

本实例使用 Struts 2 提供的强大的验证框架对新增收支类型、修改收支类型、添加收支信息和修改收支信息的 JSP 页面进行输入验证。

（1）添加 TypeAction.java 类的验证规则。

为了对新增收支类型和修改收支类型的 JSP 页面进行输入验证，读者可在包 amigo.sshincomeexpense.action.type 下建立 TypeAction.java 类的 add()方法和 update()方法的输入验证文件：

TypeAction-addTypeAction-validation.xml 和 TypeAction-upateTypeAction-validation.xml

在该验证配置文件中需要为 type 对象的 typeName 进行必填验证和正则表达式验证（必须为长度为 1~50 之间的字母或汉字），验证文件采用的是字段验证风格，这两个验证文件的内容如下所示：

```xml
<?xml version="1.0" encoding="GBK"?>
<!DOCTYPE validators PUBLIC "-//OpenSymphony Group//XWork Validator 1.0.2//EN"
    "http://www.opensymphony.com/xwork/xwork-validator-1.0.2.dtd">

<validators>
    <field name="type.typeName">
        <field-validator type="requiredstring">
            <param name="trim">true</param>
            <message>类型名称不能为空</message>
```

```xml
            </field-validator>
            <field-validator type="regex">
                <param name="expression"><![CDATA[(\w{1,50})]]></param>
                <message>类型名称输入不合法，必须为长度为 1~50 之间的字母或汉字</message>
            </field-validator>
        </field>
</validators>
```

接下来还需要在 struts.xml 文件中配置 input 的 result，使得在验证失败时能跳转到输入界面进行显示，修改后的"*TypeAction"的配置信息如下所示：

```xml
<action name="*TypeAction"   class="typeAction" method="{1}">
    <result name="list">/type/typeList.jsp</result>
    <result name="update">/type/updateType.jsp</result>
    <result name="input">/type/{1}Type.jsp</result>
</action>
```

【提示】Struts 2 提供的验证框架允许使用校验类名加上 Action 别名来指定需要校验的处理逻辑，Action 别名与该 Action 所包含的处理方法在 struts.xml 文件中的 name 属性对应。

设置完成后，若在添加和修改收支类型时未填写类型名称，将会出现如图 21-20 所示的界面，提示用户类型名称不能为空。

（2）添加 IncomeExpenseAction.java 类的验证规则。

为了对新增收支信息和修改收支信息的 JSP 页面进行输入验证，读者可在包 amigo.sshincomeexpense.action.incomeexpense 下建立 IncomeExpenseAction.java 类的 add()方法和 update()方法的输入验证文件：

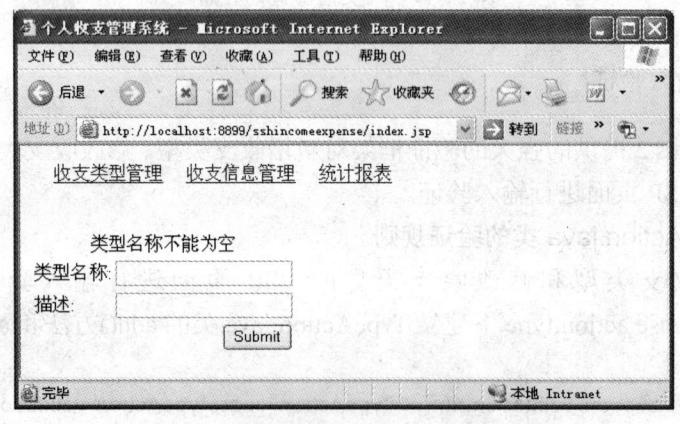

图 21-20　输入验证界面

```
IncomeExpenseAction-addTypeAction-addIncomeExpenseAction.xml
IncomeExpenseAction-upateIncomeExpenseAction-validation.xml
```

在该验证配置文件中需要为 incomeExpense 对象的 name、money、startDate 和 endDate 进行必填验证，并对 name 进行正则表达式验证，对 startDate 和 endDate 进行日期验证，验证文件采用的是字段验证风格。这两个验证文件的内容如下所示：

```xml
<?xml version="1.0" encoding="GBK"?>
<!DOCTYPE validators PUBLIC "-//OpenSymphony Group//XWork Validator 1.0.2//EN"
    "http://www.opensymphony.com/xwork/xwork-validator-1.0.2.dtd">
<validators>
    <field name="incomeExpense.name">
```

```xml
        <field-validator type="requiredstring">
            <param name="trim">true</param>
            <message>收支信息名称不能为空</message>
        </field-validator>
        <field-validator type="regex">
            <param name="expression"><![CDATA[(\w{1,50})]]></param>
            <message>收支信息名称输入不合法，必须为长度为 1~50 之间的字母或汉字</message>
        </field-validator>
    </field>

    <field name="incomeExpense.money">
        <field-validator type="required">
            <message>金额不能为空</message>
        </field-validator>
    </field>

    <field name="incomeExpense.startDate">
        <field-validator type="required">
            <message>开始日期不能为空</message>
        </field-validator>
        <field-validator type="date">
            <param name="min">1900-01-01</param>
            <param name="max">2100-01-01</param>
            <message>开始日期输入不合法</message>
        </field-validator>
    </field>

    <field name="incomeExpense.endDate">
        <field-validator type="required">
            <message>截止日期不能为空</message>
        </field-validator>
        <field-validator type="date">
            <param name="min">1900-01-01</param>
            <param name="max">2100-01-01</param>
            <message>截止日期输入不合法</message>
        </field-validator>
    </field>
</validators>
```

接下来还需要在 struts.xml 文件中配置添加和修改收支信息失败的 input 的 result，使得在验证失败时能跳转到输入界面进行显示，将"*IncomeExpenseAction"这个 action 修改如下：

```xml
<action name="*IncomeExpenseAction" class="incomeExpenseAction" method="{1}">
    <result name="list">/incomeexpense/incomeexpenseList.jsp</result>
    <result name="update">/incomeexpense/updateIncomeExpense.jsp</result>
    <result name="add">/incomeexpense/addIncomeExpense.jsp</result>
    <result name="input">/incomeexpense/{1}IncomeExpense.jsp</result>
</action>
```

在这里因为 input 的转向是 JSP 页面，而又需要获得收支类型的信息，所以还需要在 Action 中添加如下两个 validate 方法：

```
/**
 * 在添加收支信息页面验证失败时，因为跳转的是添加页面，
```

```
 * 会导致丢失下拉列表信息，可采用此方法获取信息
 */
public void validateAdd() throws Exception {
    // 判断是否有错误信息
    if (hasFieldErrors()) {
        // 获取收支类型下拉列表信息
        //只要先判断存在与否，再确定是否查询
        if (this.types == null) {
            List<Type> typeList = typeManager.getTypeList();
            this.setTypes(typeList);
        }
    }
}

public void validateUpdate() throws Exception {
    // 与 validateAdd 获取的信息一致
    this.validateAdd();
}
```

【提示】有些读者可能会有疑问，为什么不在 struts.xml 中使用如下语句将 input 的指向跳转到初始化添加和修改界面的 action 呢？

```
<result name="input" type="redirect">/initAddIncomeExpenseAction.action</result>
```
原因在于使用该种方式时，将会丢失验证的错误信息。

设置完成后，若在添加和修改收支信息时未填写任何信息，将会出现如图 21-21 所示的界面，提示各项必填输入不能为空。

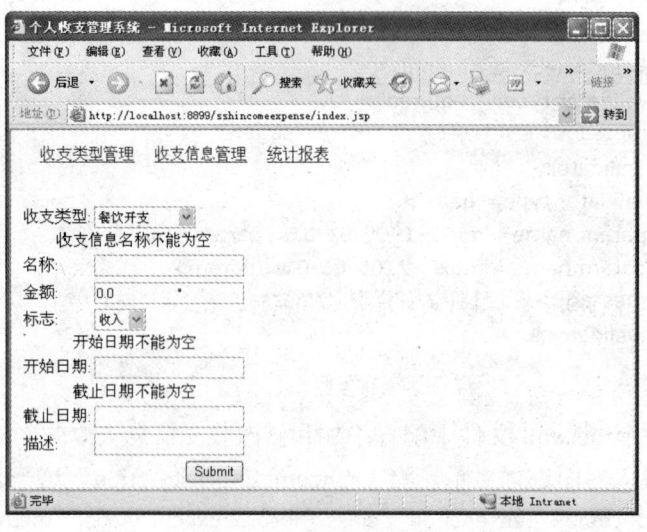

图 21-21　添加或修改收支信息验证失败界面

小结

本章通过个人收支管理系统的设计和编码实现，来学习如何在 Java EE 项目中使用 Struts 2、Hibernate 3 和 Spring 2 框架，以及如何在 Java EE 项目中集成报表的功能，另外还向读者展示了如何在设计和编写代码时，保持良好的分层思想，构造可扩展性和可维护性好的系统。

若要在 Java EE 项目中集成 JFreeChart 开源图形报表工具，除了需要在 CLASSPATH 中添加 JFreeChart 的 jar 包及其相关的 jar 包外，还需要在 web.xml 中添加 JFreeChart 的 Servlet，配置信息如下所示：

```xml
<!-- JFreeChart 的 Servlet，用于图片显示 -->
<servlet>
    <servlet-name>DisplayChart</servlet-name>
    <servlet-class>org.jfree.chart.servlet.DisplayChart</servlet-class>
</servlet>

<servlet-mapping>
    <servlet-name>DisplayChart</servlet-name>
    <url-pattern>/DisplayChart</url-pattern>
</servlet-mapping>
```

构造三维水晶饼图的参考代码如下所示：

```java
//设置数据集
DefaultPieDataset dataset = new DefaultPieDataset();
List pieInfoList = (List) request.getAttribute("pieInfoList");
dataset.setValue("初级程序员", 5000);
dataset.setValue("中级程序员", 4000);
dataset.setValue("高级程序员", 1000);
JFreeChart chart = ChartFactory.createPieChart3D(
        null, dataset, true, true, false);
//获得 3D 的水晶饼图对象
PiePlot3D pieplot3d = (PiePlot3D) chart.getPlot();
//设置开始角度
pieplot3d.setStartAngle(150D);
//设置方向为"顺时针方向"
pieplot3d.setDirection(Rotation.CLOCKWISE);
//设置透明度，0.5F 为半透明，1 为不透明，0 为全透明
pieplot3d.setForegroundAlpha(0.7F);
//显示各项所占的百分比
pieplot3d.setCircular(true);
pieplot3d.setLabelGenerator(new StandardPieSectionLabelGenerator("{0} = {2}({1})",
        NumberFormat.getNumberInstance(),
        NumberFormat.getPercentInstance()));
```

在获得图形报表的数据时，需要在 HQL 中使用聚合函数，例如 count(…)和 sum(…)等，另外还需要使用 group by 子句对数据进行分组。例如，若需要按年查询收入的变化情况，可使用如下 HQL 语句：

```
select sum(obj.money), year(obj.startDate) from IncomeExpense as obj where obj.flag=0 group by year(obj.startDate);
```

上面的 HQL 语句查询的是每条记录为 Object 数组，可使用如下 Java 代码得到所需的信息：

```java
for (int i = 0; i < list.size(); i++) {
    Object[] values = (Object[]) list.get(i);
    System.out.println("totalMoney=" + values[0].toString());
    System.out.println("time =" + values[0].toString());
}
```